E. CECIL

WHO DID WHAT

The Book of Kells
The unknown monks who illuminated the Book of Kells – an account of the Gospels and local records – in the 6th century were members of an Irish community which helped keep alight the flame of Christianity at a time when the survival of the religion was in doubt. They left for posterity not merely a priceless artifact, but a beacon of hope for humanity and a lasting testimony to individual achievement

WHO DID WHAT

The Mitchell Beazley

Illustrated Biographical Dictionary

First published 1974
Revised edition 1979
This edition 1985

ISBN 0 85533 572 6

Filmsetting by Hourds Typographica

Printed and bound in Portugal by Printer Portuguesa LDA

Edited and designed by
Mitchell Beazley
International Limited
14–15 Manette Street
London W1V 5LB

Consultant Editors
Don E. Fehrenbacher, M.A., Ph.D., D.H.L., Coe Professor of American History, University of Stanford, Calif.;
Douglas Harvey, M.Sc., Financial Director, Texaco Ltd.;
D. W. Lomax, M.A., D.Phil., Professor of Spanish, University of Birmingham;
M. J. MacLeod, M.A., Ph.D., Professor of Latin American History, University of Pittsburgh;
Patrick Moore, O.B.E., F.R.A.S., author, astronomer and broadcaster;
L. G. R. Naylor, M.A., author and historian;
J. R. L. Southam, M.A., Barrister-at-Law, Legal Adviser, Gas Council.

Principal Advisers
Bronwyn C. Bennett; Michael J. Bennett, B.Sc., Ph.D., D.I.C., A.R.C.S., A.E.A.; Nicolas Bentley, F.S.I.A., author and artist; J. D. Boreham, D.L.C., A.S.I.A.; Ronald Burrow, B.A., F.R.C.O.; Hugh D. B. Clarke, B.A.; D. B. Clegg, M.A.; Richard Cooper, M.A.; Diana de Deney, LL.B.; Rev. P. Doble, M.A.; J. T. Enticott, B.A.; W. G. Fuge, M.A.; P. M. Gardner, M.A.; M. R. Heafford, M.A., B.Litt.; P. E. Heafford, M.A., B.Sc.; Anne McG. Howat, M.B., Ch.B.; D. B. Howat, B.Sc.; H. Frank Humphris; M. P. James, M.A., Dip. Arch.; Francis King; Graham Marchant, M.A.; J. N. Mattock, M.A., Ph.D.; P. Mitter, M.A., Ph.D.; R. G. Newey, M.A.; Rawhide C. Papritz; A. P. Paterson, N.D.H., M.Ed.; D. E. Pollard, M.A., Ph.D.; H. M. Radford, B.A., M.Litt.; G. B. Rattray, B.Sc., A.I.C.T.A.; David Robinson; R. T. Rowley, B.A., B.Litt., F.S.A.; T. T. B. Ryder, M.A., Ph.D.; James Shepherd, B.A.; M. H. Shotton, M.A.; John Skorupski, M.A., Ph.D.; A. Wyn Lloyd, M.A., A.B.Ps.S.

A

Aalto, Alvar (1898-1976) Finnish architect who was already developing the international modernist style during the late 1920s. Major works by him include the early Library at Viipuri and convalescent home at Paimio, and, later, a Hall of Residence at Massachusetts Institute of Technology, Cambridge, Mass.

Abdul-Hamid II (1842-1918) Sultan of Turkey (1876-1909), who was largely responsible for the Armenian Atrocities (1895-6) (the massacre of Armenian subjects by Kurdish irregulars). Brought to power by a liberal movement which had deposed his brother Murad V, Abdul-Hamid suspended the constitution in 1878 and ruled as a dictator. In 1908 he was forced to call a parliament by the Young Turk Movement, which at that time was supported by Mustapha KEMAL. Abdul-Hamid attempted an unsuccessful counter-revolution (1909) and was deposed and then exiled.

Abd-er-Rahman I (731-88) Arab Emir of Cordoba (756-88), founder of the Omayyad dynasty that ruled Spain for three centuries. He escaped the slaughter accompanying the overthrow of the Omayyad dynasty in Syria (750) and made his way to Spain, where he defeated the deposed Amir Yusuf (756). Making Cordoba his capital, he ended near-anarchy and instituted governmental and other reforms. He enriched it with hospitals, schools and a mosque.

Abel, Niels Henrik (1802-29) Norwegian mathematician, who made fundamental contributions to the study of functional equations, elliptic functions and integrals of algebraic functions. His work shows the influence of the new and rigorous analytic work that began in the 19th century.

Abel, Rudolph (1902-72) Russian master-spy in the US, who sent top secret information to the Soviet Union from his Brooklyn photography shop. Apprehended and sentenced to a long gaol term, Abel was exchanged with the American pilot Gary POWERS in 1962.

Abraham (c. 2000 BC) Traditionally the first Hebrew Patriarch, the 'father of a multitude of nations'. He left his native Ur to settle in what is now southern Israel, where he founded the line that was to produce the twelve tribes of Israel.

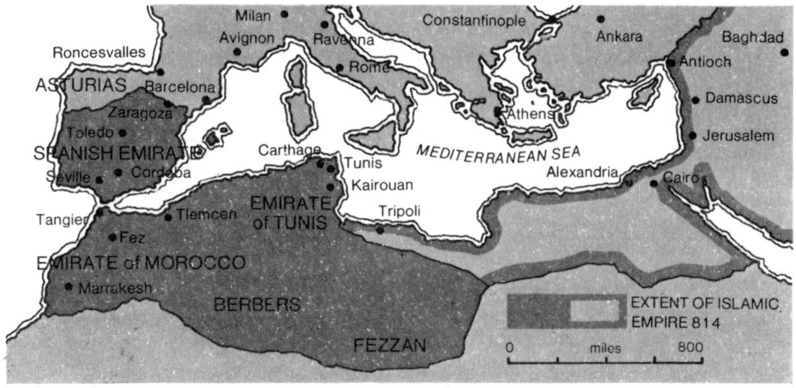

The map above shows the range of Arab domains at the time of their dominance of the Iberian peninsula. Abd-er-Rahman I founded one of Islam's great dynasties of western Europe, and many traces of it remain in Spain

abu-Bakr (573-634) First Muslim caliph and founder of the Arab Empire. An early convert to the teachings of MOHAMMED, he succeeded him as Arab leader and by means of brilliant desert strikes subdued the Arab tribes which, united for the first time under Mohammed, had begun to revolt. Later expansionist moves into Syria and Iraq founded the empire that reached its peak under Muawiyah I.

Acheson, Dean Gooderham (1893-1971) American lawyer and statesman who, as Secretary of State under President TRUMAN, was a principal architect of US foreign policy after the Second World War.

Acheson, Edward Goodrich (1856-1931) American industrial chemist, who in 1891 discovered silicon carbide ('Carborundum'). In 1899 Acheson used the electric furnace to manufacture synthetic graphite, which has important applications in the electronics industry.

Acton, John Emerich Edward Dalberg, 1st Baron (1834-1902) English historian who was one of the most influential of his time. Although he never completed a book, he planned the *Cambridge Modern History* while teaching at Cambridge University (1895-1902), and his essays and lectures were published after his death. A Roman Catholic and a Liberal, he was a strong supporter of GLADSTONE. Acton was a Member of Parliament (1859-65), and received a peerage through Gladstone in 1869.

Adam, Robert (1728-92) Scottish architect and interior designer who led the Classical Revival in English domestic architecture. Not only the designs of his buildings, but every detail of their furnishings and decoration influenced 18th-century architecture throughout the world. His father, William Adam, and his brothers James and John were also architects. Robert lived in Rome for three years where his intensive study of Roman architecture proved a lasting inspiration to the development of his own elegant and restrained Neo-Classicism. He designed many country houses, and in London, the screen and gateway of the Admiralty in Whitehall.

Much of Robert Adam's outstanding 18th-century architecture is still to be seen. Above, Kenwood, London

Adamov, Arthur (1908-70) Russo-French dramatist and pioneer of the Theatre of the Absurd. He began his literary career as a Surrealist poet, but went on to write *The Confession* (1938-43), an autobiographical work in which he reveals the profound sense of alienation to be seen in his early plays, of which *The Parody* (1945) and *The Invasion* (1950) are two of the best known.

Adams, Brooks (1848-1927) American historian, who, in *America's Economic Supremacy* (1900), predicted that within 50 years the US would become supreme in world economics and that the world would be dominated by Russia and the US.

Adams, John (1735-1826) Second President of the United States (1797-1801) and one of the authors of the Declaration of Independence. Vice-President under WASHINGTON, he was elected President in 1796. His distrust of younger politicians and an authoritarian manner made him hard to work with. Adams stood for a second term, but was defeated by JEFFERSON and devoted the rest of his life to writing. Adams, a barrister, was the first American ambassador to Britain (1785).

Adams, John Couch (1819-92) English astronomer, joint discoverer with LE VERRIER of the planet Neptune. In 1841 he investigated variations in the observed positions of the planet Uranus, and deduced from them the presence of an undiscovered planet. By 1845, he had completed his investigations. Meanwhile Le Verrier had reached the same conclusion and his predictions led to the discovery of Neptune from the Berlin Observatory in 1846.

Adams, John Quincy (1767-1848) Sixth President of the United States (1825-9), son of John ADAMS, the second President. He drafted the Monroe Doctrine and was a leading campaigner for the abolition of slavery. In 1817, President MONROE appointed Adams Secretary of State, in which office he formulated the isolationist Monroe Doctrine in an attempt to prevent any further colonial encroachment of the European nations upon the American continent.

Adams, Samuel (1722-1803) American revolutionary politician and one of the most formative influences on American opinion in the years before the War of Independence (1775-83). He was leader of the radicals in the Masschusetts legislature (1765-74), and author of many revolutionary documents, including *Massachusetts Resolves*. Adams was also a leader of the agitation which led to the Boston Massacre (1770) and the Boston Tea Party (1773), and called and managed the first Continental Congress (1774), which marked the start of united colonial opposition to Britain. He was a signatory of the Declaration of Independence (1776).

Adams, William (1564-1620) The first English navigator to visit Japan. After serving the Barbary Company for about 11 years, Adams joined the Dutch marine and in 1600 reached Kyushu in the *Charity*. His knowledge of shipbuilding and nautical mathematics commended him to IYEYASU, who gave him an estate. Adams spent the rest of his life in Japan, helping the English East India Company to establish a factory there.

Addington, Henry (1757-1844) British Prime Minister, who succeeded his close friend PITT the Younger. His ministry negotiated the short-lived Treaty of Amiens with France (March 1802-May 1803) but Addington lacked incisiveness when war was resumed and he resigned in 1804. From 1812 to 1821 he was Home Secretary in the ministries of Lord LIVERPOOL. During a period of industrial and social unrest his policies were severe, though not unduly repressive by the standards of the time.

Addison, Joseph (1672-1719) English poet and essayist and co-founder with Sir Richard STEELE, of the *Spectator* (1711-12). Addison found a growing number of readers eager for periodicals and set out, in his magazine, to give them a genteel review of art, philosophy, manners and morals.

Adenauer, Konrad (1876-1967) German statesman, Chancellor of the German Federal Republic (West Germany) from 1949 to 1963. A Catholic Rhinelander and Lord Mayor of Cologne (1917-33), Adenauer supported the French plan for an autonomous Rhineland in 1919. A member of the Centre Party during the Weimar Republic (1918-33), he was a consistent anti-Nazi. When HITLER visited Cologne (1933) Adenauer had the Nazi flag taken down and consequently was removed from office. During the Nazi régime he was twice arrested. In 1945, he became Mayor of Cologne again and founded the

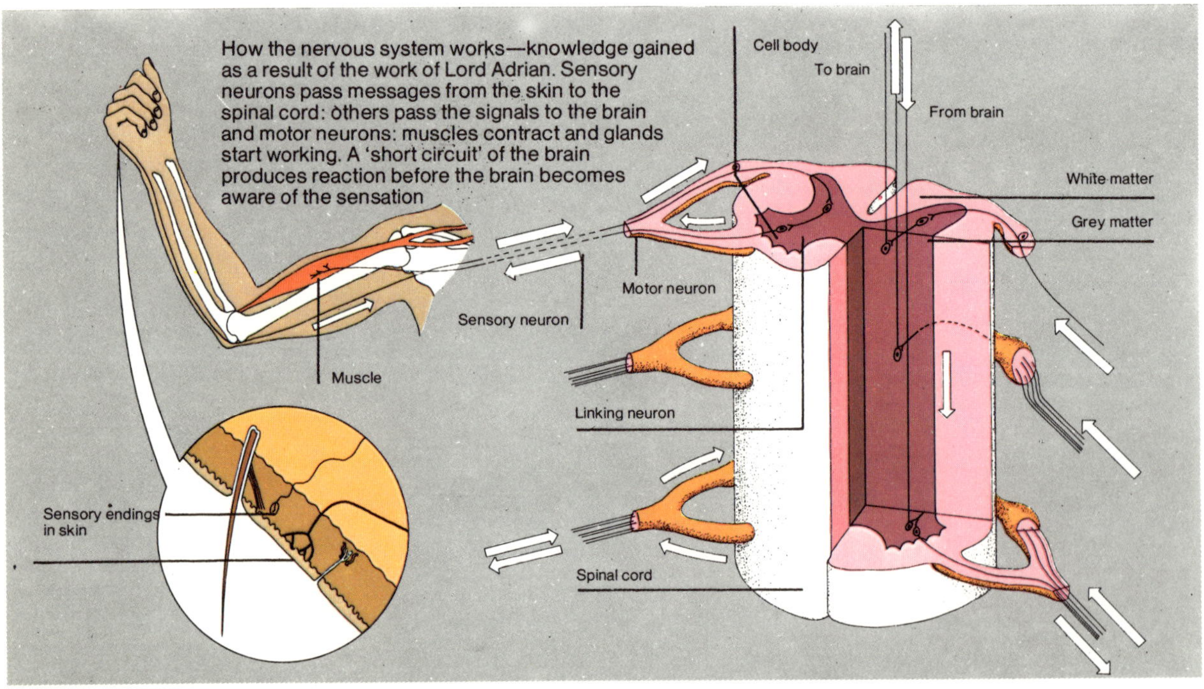

How the nervous system works—knowledge gained as a result of the work of Lord Adrian. Sensory neurons pass messages from the skin to the spinal cord: others pass the signals to the brain and motor neurons: muscles contract and glands start working. A 'short circuit' of the brain produces reaction before the brain becomes aware of the sensation

Christian Democrat Party. He was elected to the Bundestag in 1949 and became Federal Chancellor.

Adler, Alfred (1870-1937) Austrian psychiatrist and psychologist, originator of the concept of the inferiority complex. Each child, he thought, becomes conscious of smallness, dependence and possible weakness of some organ. To compensate for this the child strives either consciously or unconsciously for specific goals that will offset his feelings of inadequacy. An excessive sense of inferiority or the failure to achieve his self-imposed objectives may cause anxiety and aggression.

Adler, Larry (born 1914) American harmonica player whose virtuosity has given the 'mouth organ' new status. VAUGHAN WILLIAMS and MILHAUD have written for him. He has composed film scores.

Adrian, or **Hadrian, IV (c. 1100-59)** The only English pope (1154-9), who crowned Frederick Barbarossa Holy Roman Emperor, an act so unpopular that Adrian had to leave Rome for several months. His insistence on Church overlordship over all monarchs and their realms led to increasing conflict with Barbarossa and to the refusal (1156) to grant Ireland to HENRY II.

Adrian, Lord (1889-1977) English physiologist who, with Sir Charles Sherrington, unravelled the mechanism by which nerves carry messages to and from the brain. Until this mechanism was known, it was impossible for anyone to understand disorders of the nervous system. In 1932 the two men were jointly awarded a Nobel Prize for their work.

Aelfric (c. 995-c. 1020) English abbot and writer, author of *Homilies,* the first Christian texts in the English vernacular. He is considered to be the greatest prose writer of Anglo-Saxon times.

Aeschylus (525-456 BC) Greek dramatist, who wrote the *Oresteia* trilogy – *The Agamemnon, Choephori* and *Eumenides.* Aeschylus transformed the essentially choric works of the Athenian tragic drama festival – then characterized by a single actor and a chorus responding to each other in lyrical alternation – into drama, by introducing a second actor and reducing the chorus. He also introduced the trilogy into the tragic festival, which took the form of a competition. Of his 90 or so plays, only seven survive. The *Oresteia* trilogy is concerned with offences against the Gods by Agamemnon's family, and the Gods' revenge. *The Suppliant Women* is the first play of a trilogy, the other two being lost, as is *Prometheus Bound* (460 BC). *Seven Against Thebes* is the surviving third play of a trilogy. *The Persians* (427 BC) is a play on its own about contemporary events and inspired by the author's experience in the Greek army against the Persians at Marathon.

Aeschylus's drama is recreated more than two thousand years after his death

Aesop (6th cent. BC) Greek author of the oldest and most famous collection of animal fables, whose aim was to point a moral or highlight human foibles. Originally used as references by orators and writers, they were not read widely until medieval times.

Aga Khan I see HASAN, Ali Shah

Agasias of Ephesus (2nd cent. BC) Greek sculptor of the late Hellenistic period, creator of the marble *Borghese Warrior,* now in the Louvre. The warrior appears to be a close copy of the earlier work of the school of LYSIPPUS. Agasias's warrior is important since it has for many centuries served as a standard for exact anatomy.

Agassiz, Jean Louis (1807-73) American naturalist and geologist of Swiss origin, who pioneered the study of geology and zoology in America and founded the Museum of Comparative Anatomy at Harvard. One of the ablest biologists of his day, he published prolifically on both living and fossil fish and his epoch-making *Researches on Fossil Fishes* (1833-44), which classifies nearly 1000 extinct species, became the springboard for the scientific study of extinct life in general. In 1836 Agassiz made an important contribution to geological knowledge by revealing that Switzerland was once covered by sheet ice. He then went to America, where he taught geology to both lay and specialist audiences.

Agesander (1st cent. BC) Rhodian sculptor who was mentioned in PLINY's *Natural History* as being the co-creator, with Athenodoros and Polydoros, of *Two Sons of Agesander,* the Hellenistic statue, in marble, depicting the death of the Trojan priest Laocoön and his two sons. This work, found in Rome (1506), greatly impressed MICHELANGELO, and was an important influence on the sculpting of the human form from the 16th century onwards.

Agostino di Duccio (1418-81) Florentine sculptor, architect, and possibly goldsmith, who carved the marble altar in Modena Cathedral. His best-known work consists of tombs and low-relief panels of great linear beauty which form the decoration for the interior of the Tempio Malatestiano in Rimini.

Agricola, Georgius (1494-1555) German scholar and physician, known as the father of mineralogy. His work, the first to be based on practical knowledge and direct observation, initiated the development of modern geology and the study of metals. In *De Re Metallica* (1555), he summarized all that was then known of mining and smelting.

Agricola, Gnaeus Julius (c. 37-93) Roman general who pacified Britain. As its governor (78-84) he continued the invasion begun by Julius CAESAR and CLAUDIUS, using force and conciliation to extend Rome's frontiers. He conquered North Wales, northern England and lowland Scotland, achieving his northernmost victory at Mons Graupius (probably near Aberdeen) over the Caledonians. Agricola was the father-in-law of the historian TACITUS and the subject of his informative, if flattering, study *Agricola.*

Agrippa, Cornelius (c. 1486-1535) German scholar, magician and cabalist, author of *Three Books on Occult Philosophy,* first published in 1531 (written *c.* 1510). This compendium of astrology, music, geometry and necromancy attempted to provide a rationale for all the occult sciences and became a handbook for students of the occult.

Agrippa, Marcus (c. 63-12 BC) Roman general and statesman, and close friend of AUGUSTUS, who has been called the 'architect of the Roman empire'. Agrippa planned the campaigns of 44-30 BC, which brought Augustus to supreme power and ended the old republic. After suppressing disorders in Gaul and Germany (38 BC), he fought against Pompeius Sextus (36 BC) and helped to defeat MARK ANTHONY's forces at Actium (31 BC). From 27-15 BC Agrippa was virtually Augustus's deputy, alternating with the Emperor between Rome and the provinces. A brilliant engineer, he built aqueducts, the Pantheon, and prepared a map of the known world.

Airy, Sir George Biddell (1801-92) English astronomer, who determined the mass of the Earth. During his long tenure as Astronomer Royal (1835-81), he modernized the equipment of Greenwich Observatory, and brought order to the quantities of astronomical data that had accumulated since the mid-18th century. He instituted the regular recording of sunspots in 1874 and observed the transit of Venus. Airy was a disciplinarian, whose stubborness occasionally hampered the work of his colleagues, who included John Couch ADAMS and FARADAY.

Akbar the Great (1542-1605) Mogul emperor of India. At the age of 13 he inherited the territories conquered by his grandfather, BABER, and within 50 years, through his military genius and personal energy, had established a powerful empire covering the whole of northern India. The unification of this vast area was supported by his deliberate policy of toleration towards conquered subjects, allowing freedom of worship to non-Muslims. As a patron of the arts, Akbar introduced a new epoch, the greatest achievements of which were the architectural masterpiece of Fathepur Sikri, and a splendid series of manuscripts.

Akhmatova, Anna (1888-1966) Russian poet and one of the founders of the Acmeist group, whose members sought to replace the vagueness and affectations of Symbolism with compactness, simplicity and clarity of style. Among her many volumes of love poetry are *Beads* (1914) and *The White Flock* (1917). In 1946, her poetry was banned, having been declared socially nonconstructive, but in 1959 she was 'rehabilitated' and later proclaimed the greatest woman poet in Russian literature.

Alaric (c. 370-410) Visigothic king (395-410) who conquered Rome (410). At first a general of Gothic auxiliaries for the Emperor Theodosius I, Alaric was elected king of the Visigoths and ravaged southern Greece until halted by the pro-Roman Vandal Stilicho. After Stilicho's death in 408, his army joined Alaric who, after three sieges of Rome, became the first foreigner for 800 years to capture the city.

Alba, Duke of see ALVA, Duke of

Alban, St (4th cent.) The first English martyr, converted to Christianity by a persecuted priest whom he sheltered in his Verulamium (St Albans) home. Alban was later arrested and executed at a site which subsequently attracted veneration, and in 429 became the location for St Alban's Abbey.

Albee, Edward (born 1928) American dramatist who wrote *Who's Afraid of Virginia Woolf?*, a success on both stage and screen. He began his career with contributions to the Theatre of the Absurd in *The Zoo Story* (1958) and *The American Dream* (1961). A later success was his adaptation of Carson MCCULLERS's novel, *The Ballad of the Sad Café* (1963). His subsequent work includes *Tiny Alice* (1964), *A Delicate Balance* (1966), for which he was awarded the Pulitzer Prize, *Seascape* (1975) and *The Lady from Dubuque* (1980).

Albemarle, 1st Duke of see MONCK, George

Albéniz, Isaac (1860-1909) Spanish composer who was among the first to use traditional Spanish idioms. As a pianist he was a child prodigy. He stowed away on a ship bound for Puerto Rico at the age of nine, working his passage by giving recitals, and for years continued touring until he was about 30, when he went to Paris to study composition with D'INDY and Dukas. He wrote operas and much keyboard music, and is probably best remembered for his suite for piano, *Iberia* (1906-9), the movements of which represent the musical traditions of various Spanish provinces.

Albers, Joseph (1888-1976) German pioneer of abstract painting and one of the most influential artists in the Bauhaus group. While at the Bauhaus, Albers worked chiefly in the field of design in glass and ceramics. In 1933 he emigrated to the US and taught in Black Mountain College, North Carolina, then at Yale and Harvard, influencing a whole generation by his teaching. His best known work is *Homage to the Square*.

Albert I (1875-1934) King of the Belgians (1909-34), whose military efforts hampered the German invasion and contributed to the Allied offensive of 1918. An energetic leader, who patronized the arts and initiated legal and social reforms, Albert was killed while rock climbing near Namur.

Albert, Prince Consort (1819-61) German-born husband and adviser to Queen VICTORIA who, despite his political competence, never managed to overcome popular disapproval. Marrying Victoria in 1840, Albert quickly became an informal but powerful member of government. He was insistent on developing the Crown's influence as an impartial force in domestic affairs and he repeatedly clashed with Lord PALMERSTON over foreign policy. In addition to his lasting influence on Victoria's reign, Albert was a devoted patron of the arts and a prime organizer of the Great Exhibition of 1851.

Alberti, Leone (1404-72) Early Renaissance Italian architect, playwright, musician and painter. Alberti designed the Tempio Malatestiano at Rimini and also worked in Florence and knew BRUNELLESCHI. There he completed the façade of the church of Sta Maria Novella (1470) with a design excecuted in polychrome marble and based upon the system of 'harmonic proportions'. His 10-volume treatise *De Re Aedificatoria* dealt with painting, sculpture and education as well as architecture.

Albuquerque, Affonso d' (1453-1515) Portuguese governor of India (1509-15) who extended Portugal's influence far to the east. His first achievement was the capture (briefly) of Ormuz in the Persian Gulf (1507), a principal trading centre of the East. As Governor of India, he captured Goa (1510) and made it the capital of Portugal's eastern empire, seized Malacca (1511), reconquered Ormuz (1515), sent expeditions as far east as the Spice Islands (Moluccas), and extended Portuguese tradeship routes to China and Siam.

Alcibiades (c. 450-404 BC) Athenian politician and general who persuaded the Athenians to join an alliance against Sparta (421 BC), which provoked the last of the Peloponnesian Wars and led to the collapse of the Athenian Empire (404 BC). While leading an unsuccessful attack on Sicily (415 BC), Alcibiades was recalled to stand trial for mutilating statues of Hermes.

He escaped and joined the Spartans, giving them advice ruinous to Athens and persuading the Ionian allies of Athens to revolt. He soon lost the confidence of the Spartans and conspired with the opposition in Athens. He finally regained short-lived favour in Athens when he attached himself to the fleet, and helped to defeat the Spartan navy and recover Chalcedon and Byzantium (411-409 BC). His defeat at Notium (407 BC) brought his dismissal from command. After the collapse of Athens, he fled to Phrygia where he was murdered at the instigation of the Spartans.

Alcock, Sir John (1892-1919) English aviator, who, with Sir Arthur Whitten Brown (1886-1948), completed the first non-stop transatlantic flight (1919). Their twin-engined bi-plane aircraft took 16 hours 27 minutes to fly 1936 miles from Newfoundland to Ireland. Alcock's flight was complicated by instrument failure, fog and turbulence. Brown repeatedly had to climb on the wings to hack off thickening ice.

Alcuin (735-804) English scholar, adviser on education to CHARLEMAGNE and defender of orthodoxy against the Adoptionist heresy (the view that JESUS was not born divine but became the Son of God at His Baptism). He contributed a detailed refutation of the heresy to the Council of Frankfurt in 793 and in 800 took up the dispute with the heretic Bishop Felix of Urgel. Abbot at Tours from 796, his school became an influential educational centre.

Aldington, Richard (1892-1962) English poet, one of the founders of the 20th-century school of poetry known as 'imagism'. Following the lead of the philosopher T. E. Hulme, Aldington and his American wife, Hilda Doolittle, aimed to write 'cheerful, dry and sophisticated' poetry which would render particulars exactly and not deal in vague generalities. His *Collected Poems* appeared in 1928 and he wrote one of the outstanding novels of the First World War, *Death of a Hero* (1929).

Alexander (1888-1934) King of Yugoslavia (1921-34), who succeeded his father, Peter Karadjordjevic, as ruler of the united kingdom of Serbs, Croats and Slovenes set up in 1918. Animosity between Serbs and Croats led Alexander to proclaim a royal dictatorship in 1929, and in the same year the triune state was renamed Yugoslavia. His policies favoured the Serbs at home, and a Balkan peace based on a treaty between Yugoslavia, Rumania and Czechoslovakia abroad. In October 1934, on a state visit to France, he was murdered by an assassin hired by the Ustase, a Croatian nationalist secret society.

Alexander I (1777-1825) Tsar of Russia (1801-25) who entered the War of the Third Coalition against France in 1805. After the defeat of the Russians at Friedland (1807), Alexander made peace with NAPOLEON at Tilsit, but the latter's economic, German and Polish policies and his Hapsburg marriage prejudiced the Treaty and led to the French invasion of Russia (1812). Alexander joined the War of the Fourth Coalition and took part in the invasion of France by the allies in 1814 and the overthrow of Napoleon. At the Congress of Vienna (1815) he obtained a kingdom of Poland under his own protection, and at home initiated a domestic policy of reform based on the partial alleviation of serfdom and the reorganization of the central administration of the Empire. In European affairs Alexander sought to provide for the collective security of the major powers (Austria, Prussia and Russia) by sponsoring the Holy Alliance, which ultimately became identified with the doctrine of coercive intervention against actual or threatened revolution.

Alexander II (1818-81) Tsar of Russia (1855-81). After succeeding his father, NICHOLAS I, during the Crimean war (which exposed the inadequacies of the Tsarist régime), he sanctioned a policy of modernizing reform. Polish unrest in 1863 and an attempt to assassinte him (1866) caused him to resume despotic rule at home, and to initiate an aggressive policy abroad, leading to war with Turkey (1877-8) and imperial conquest in Central Asia. He refused to call a Constituent Assembly to prepare for parliamentary government, and was condemned to death by a secret revolutionary society, The People's Will and was assassinated.

Alexander III 'The Great' (356-323 BC) King of Macedon (336-323 BC) whose conquests culturally cross-fertilized Europe and Asia. He acquired Greek culture from his tutor ARISTOTLE and political power from his murdered father, PHILIP II. The youthful king first proved his military genius in lightning strikes on Thessaly, Thrace, Illyria and Thebes and by 335 he had gained ascendancy over all Greece. He then struck at the gigantic Persian empire founded by CYRUS THE GREAT and ruled by DARIUS III and his troops crushed the Persian armies at Granicus and Issus before overrunning Tyre and Gaza, occupying Egypt and turning east to Persia and India. In less than ten years, weaving 21,000 miles through southwest Asia from the Bosporus to the Indus Valley, Alexander seized intact an empire as big as the US and quadrupled the size of the world known to the Greeks. Alexander conserved the civilization he conquered, linking two great cultures of Greece and Persia in one Greek-speaking civilization that ran from India to Spain. On his death his generals, PTOLEMY, Seleucus and others divided up his empire. Culturally, Alexander's Hellenistic world endured – helping Greek art and architecture to enter India, and the Asian faiths founded by ZOROASTER and JESUS to penetrate Europe.

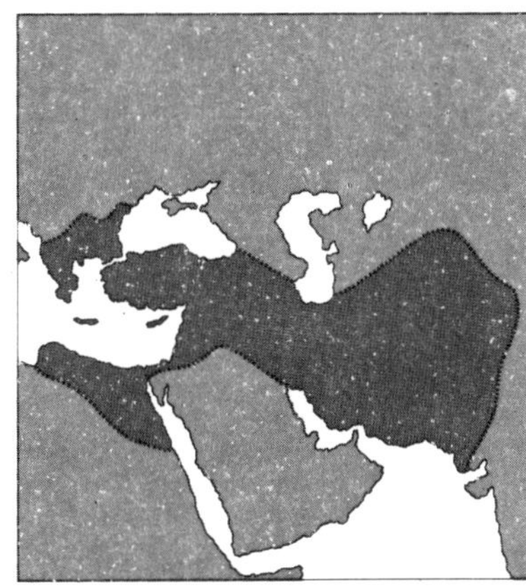

Napoleon's 'model hero', Alexander the Great was a military genius. His empire ranged from Greece to the Indus

Alexander III (1845-94) Tsar of Russia (1881-94). His reign was marked by the persecution of the Jews and the repression of liberal ideas, as a result of which the first Russian Marxist group was formed (1883). To counter the expansion of Germany, Alexander concluded the secret Franco-Russian Alliance (sometimes referred to as the Dual Alliance) of 1894, which played an important part in the balance of power before the First World War. During the last years of his reign Russian's Far Eastern territories were developed under the guidance of the Minister of Finance and Communications, WITTE.

Alexander Nevski (c. 1220-63) Russian national hero, who kept the nucleus of what is now Russia intact against Mongol, Swedish and German pressures. Recognizing the futility of opposing the all-powerful Mongols, he held them off with tribute payments. Alexander earned the name Nevski by defeating Swedish troops near the river Neva (1240). Two years later he crushed the Teutonic Knights in a battle on frozen Lake Peipus.

Alfonsín, Raúl (born 1927) President of Argentina since 1983, when he defeated the long dominant Peronist Party and ended almost eight years of military rule. Elected leader of the Unión Cívica Radical in 1982, since becoming President he has undertaken measures to purge the military and prosecute members for human rights abuses.

Alfred the Great (849-99) West Saxon king (871-99), who halted the Danish conquest of England. During the whole of his brother ETHELRED's reign and much of his own, he fought off successive invasions of Wessex, ending in his victory at Ethandune (878) when he forced the Danes to sue for peace. The Danes were cleared from Wessex and the western half of Mercia but were granted north and eastern England. In 885-6 Alfred fought off the East Anglian Danes and took London, and later repelled another invasion attempt in a series of land and naval engagements. During periods of peace he built a strong defensive system and set up a permanent national militia. As a civil administrator, Alfred drew up a code of laws, reorganized finance and promoted learning, attracting scholars from western Europe to his court. A scholar himself, he translated BEDE'S *History*, BOETHIUS'S *Consolations*, and Pope GREGORY'S *Pastoral Care*. He also inspired the *Anglo-Saxon Chronicle*.

Algardi, Alessandro (1602-54) Italian sculptor with a special gift for portraiture. His principal works were the marble tomb of Pope Leo XI (1645) and a relief of Leo driving ATTILA from Rome.

Ali, Muhammad (born 1942) US boxer, born Cassius Clay, who in 1964 defeated Sonny Liston for the world heavyweight championship. In 1967 he was deprived of his title for refusing to serve in the US army on religious grounds. In 1971 he returned to the ring after his appeal was upheld, but lost to Joe Frazier. He regained his title in 1974, lost it in 1978 to Leon Spinks but regained it the same year to become the first man to win the title three times.

Allen, Woody (born 1935) American film actor, writer, producer and director, best known in his typical comic role as a flustered, New York Jewish neurotic. His films include *Bananas* (1971), *Everything You Always Wanted to Know About Sex* (1972), *Play It Again Sam* (1972), *Annie Hall* (1977), which won four academy awards, *Manhattan* (1979) and *Zelig* (1983).

Allenby, Edmund, Viscount (1861-1936) British cavalry general who, in the First World War, conquered Palestine by defeating the Turks. He took Jerusalem in 1917.

Almagro, Diego de (c. 1475-1538) Spanish soldier, prominent among the conquistadors who served with PIZARRO in Peru. Almagro later led an expedition to conquer Chile and became the first European to travel overland far to the south as he made his way through the Andes from Cuzco to near Concepción (1535-7), and reached the Pacific coast by crossing the Atacama Desert. Immediately after this expedition, Almagro led a revolt against Pizarro and was captured and executed.

Almeida-Garrett, João Baptista da Silva Leitão de (1799-1854) Portuguese statesman and writer. While exiled in England and France (1823) (having been involved in the uprising of 1820), he assimilated the new Romanticism, and on returning to Portugal with the victorious Liberals (1833), he introduced Romantic styles and attitudes into Portuguese literature. He founded an academy of dramatic art and began to write nationalist plays, such as *Frie Luiz de Sousa* (1843) and the traditional *Ballads* (1843), he also wrote a semi-autobiographical work entitled *Journeys in My Own Land* (1846).

Almoravides see IBN-TASHFIN

Altdorfer, Albrecht (c. 1480-1538) Bavarian artist, who produced many religious woodcuts, but is best known for his small landscapes. His paintings are mostly of the Danubian region and the Austrian Alps, and the human figures in them are usually only incidental (e.g. *St George in the Forest*). His imaginative studies of pine forests and mountains anticipate modern 'pure' landscape. Altdorfer was also one of the first artists to produce landscape etchings.

Alva, Duke of (1508-82) Spanish general whose skill at arms was matched only by his brutality. Alva was sent by PHILIP II of Spain to the Spanish Netherlands (1567) to suppress growing nationalism and the Protestant heresy. Alva executed the Flemish ringleaders Egmont and Horn, ruthlessly punished, by the new Council of Blood, thousands of dissidents, permitted atrocities by Spanish troops, and announced unpopular tax demands. Protestants and Catholics united under WILLIAM OF ORANGE and seized four provinces. Alva retook all except the provinces of Holland and Zeeland before returning to Spain (1573).

Amenhotep III (14th cent. BC) Ancient Egyptian king of the 18th Dynasty (reigned 1417-1379 BC). The 18th Dynasty reached its peak during Amenhotep III's reign, and despite raids by the Hittites and Bedouin, peace was maintained. He built the Temple of Luxor and completed the great Temple of Amon.

Amici, Giovanni (1786-1863) Italian astronomer who invented the first direct-vision spectroscope (a device for splitting up white light into a spectrum) and improved the optical microscope. He was the first man to examine the pollen tube in flowering plants and to recognize its role in plant reproduction.

Amin, Idi (born c. 1925) President of Uganda (1971-9). Amin joined the British army in the colony of Uganda, became commander of independent Uganda's army in 1966, and in 1971 overthrew the President, Milton OBOTE. In 1972 he expelled 80,000 Asian Ugandans, and withstood a pro-Obote attack from Tanzania. He was elected President of the Organization of African Unity in 1975. His erratic behaviour inspired several attempted coups, and in 1979 his government was overthrown. Amin fled the country and still lives in exile.

Amis, Kingsley (born 1922) English novelist, associated with the literary aggression aimed at life in Britain in the 1950s. Among many other works, he wrote *Lucky Jim* (1954), and *Jake's Thing* (1979).

Ammianus Marcellinus (c. 330-400) The last great Roman historian, author of *Rerum gestarum libri*. This continuation of the *Histories* of TACITUS covered the period 96-378, but only the part covering the years 353-378 survives.

Amos (8th cent. BC) Hebrew prophet, whose picturesque and gloomy predictions were compiled, probably long after him, to form the Old Testament Book of Amos. A semi-nomadic shepherd from the pastoral area near Bethlehem, Amos was the first Hebrew prophet to declare that there is only one God.

Ampère, André Marie (1775-1836) French physicist. Within a week of OERSTED's announcement in 1820 of his discovery that an electric current affects a nearby magnet, Ampère reported major extensions of Oersted's results, and by 1824 had established a full physical and mathematical description of the static interaction of currents with magnets and with each other.

Amundsen, Roald (1872-1928) Norwegian polar explorer, first man to reach the South Pole and to navigate the North West Passage. Sailing in the small sloop *Gjöa* with six companions, Amundsen succeeded where FROBISHER and many others had failed, in forcing a complete northwest sea passage from Europe to the Pacific through the Davis Strait and the Victoria Strait (1903-6). On this expedition, Amundsen also fixed the position of the magnetic North Pole. He was beaten to the geographical North Pole by PEARY, but successfully raced SCOTT to the South Pole. Starting 60 miles nearer than Scott, Amundsen's party reached the South Pole in 53 days, on 14 Dec. 1911. With ELLSWORTH and Nobile, Amundsen made the first air crossing of the Arctic over the North Pole in the airship *Norge* (1926). Amundsen died in a North Sea flying accident while searching for Nobile's lost balloon expedition to the North Pole.

An earlier start, a shorter route and the use of husky dogs enabled Amundsen to reach the South Pole before his rival, the ill-fated Scott. Scott had chosen ponies as pack animals and was forced to kill them when their unsuitability was proved.

Anaxagoras (c. 500-428 BC) Greek philosopher who taught that all matter contains elemental particles; an entity is defined by the predominance of one element.

Anaximander (6th cent. BC) Greek philosopher who taught that the universe evolved from the interaction of mutually repulsive and mutually attractive elements.

Andersen, Hans Christian (1805-75) Danish writer, celebrated for his *Fairy Tales* (1835). After various crises in his career he was befriended by Jonas Collin, the Director of the Royal Theatre in Copenhagen who sent him to school and then to Copenhagen University. Under the personal patronage of King Frederick VI, he went to Italy. Soon afterwards, his first novel *The Improvisatore* (1835) appeared and was immediately successful. In the same year the first of the fairy tales appeared. Though they sold slowly at first, they brought him international fame.

Anderson, Carl David (born 1905) American physicist who discovered the positron and the first meson. Observing tracks of cosmic rays in a cloud chamber, Anderson found some identical to those of electrons but oppositely curved in a magnetic field. These positrons (positive electrons) had been suggested by the theories of DIRAC. In 1935 Anderson observed a mu-meson, a particle whose mass lay between those of the electron and the proton. Such a particle had been predicted by YUKAWA, but the predicted particle (the pi-meson) was different and not found until 1947.

Anderson, Elizabeth Garrett (1836-1917) English physician who was the first woman to qualify in medicine in Britain. In 1883 she became Dean of the London School of Medicine for Women.

Anderson, Maxwell (1888-1959) American dramatist, who restored verse drama to the American repertoire, but is best known for *What Price Glory?* (1924). His verse dramas on modern subjects include *Winterset* (1935), *Knickerbocker Holiday* (1938) and *Key Largo* (1939). His *Lost in the Stars* (1950), with music by Kurt WEILL, was based on Alan Paton's novel *Cry the Beloved Country*.

Anderson, Sherwood (1876-1941) American short story writer and novelist, best known for naturalistic books depicting the American as a disorientated man, as in the successful *Winesburg, Ohio* (1919), sketches of puzzled people in a small mid-western town.

Andrade, Antonio de (c. 1580-1634) Portuguese Jesuit missionary who, in 1624, set out from India for Lhasa to ascertain the truth of a report that Christians were living in Tibet. He did not reach Lhasa, but was the first European to discover one of the principal sources of the Ganges in the Himalayas.

Andrea del Sarto (1486-1531) Florentine painter, whose works are characterized by a subtle modelling of forms similar to LEONARDO's and a compositional balance like that of RAPHAEL. Some of his most important paintings are frescoes, as in the churches of the Scalzi and the Annunziata, Florence. He also painted a number of panels which include holy families and portraits. The beauty of his work lies mainly in his development of a colouristic technique, as distinct from the more traditional linear approach of Florentine painters.

Andropov, Yuri Vladimirovich (1914-84) Soviet political leader and first secretary of the Communist Party from 1982 to 1984. In 1951 he was assigned to the staff of the Central Committee in Moscow, and served as Soviet ambassador in Hungary (1953-6). His role in the suppression of the Hungarian uprising in 1956 earned him a decoration. In 1967 he became an alternate member of the Politburo and head of the KGB. In 1973 he became a voting member, and in 1982, after the death of BREZHNEV, he was elected first secretary of the Communist Party and President of the Soviet Union.

Andros, Sir Edmund (1637-1714) English colonial governor who, in 1686, became James II's governor of the newly created union of colonies, Dominion of New England. He enraged the hitherto largely self-governing and Nonconformist colonists by trying to enforce Anglican religious uniformity and English government taxes. Hearing that James II had been deposed, the New Englanders arrested Andros (on a charge of trying to seize the Connecticut charter) and dissolved the union. Andros was sent to England for trial but was immediately released. He later became Governor of Virginia (1692-8), Maryland (1693-4) and Guernsey (1704-6).

Angelico, Fra (c. 1387-1455) Italian Dominican friar, who is best known for a series of frescoes in the cells of the Florentine monastery of San Marco (*c.* 1440). Intended as aids to contemplation, they reveal a narrative directness and spatial order similar to MASACCIO's work.

Anne of Cleves see HENRY VIII

Anne (1665-1714) Queen of Great Britain and Ireland (1702-14), the last Stuart to rule Britain, during whose reign Britain became a great power. The era was dominated by the War of the Spanish Succession (1702-13), but at home England and Scotland were united (1707), political parties became more clearly differentiated, and writers like ADDISON, DEFOE and SWIFT made the age important in literature.

Anouilh, Jean (born 1910) French dramatist whose work dominated the theatre in the 1940s and 1950s. Particularly noteworthy were his plays on classical themes, rewritten in modern terms, *Eurydice* (1942) and *Antigone* (1944).

Anselm (1033-1109) Italian-born Benedictine monk and philosopher, who developed the 'ontological argument' for the existence of God in his treatise *Proslogian.* Anselm became Archbishop of Canterbury in 1093, and was canonized in 1494.

Anson, Admiral George (1697-1762) English naval commander and administrator, nicknamed 'father of the navy', for his reforms which improved naval efficiency. His heavy loss of men through scurvy on a voyage round the world (1740-4) led to James Lind's discovery that lime juice cures the complaint.

Antelami, Benedetto (mid-12th cent.) Sculptor, architect, and a key figure in early Italian sculpture whose work is best seen in *The Deposition* (1178), and in the reliefs of the doors of the Baptistry of Parma Cathedral. Little is known about his origins, although stylistically his sculpture appears to be linked with Provence.

Anthemius of Thralles (6th cent.) Greek mathematician who advised on the mathematical bases for the design of the masterpiece of Byzantine architecture, the domed church of Sta Sophia, Constantinople.

Antonius, Marcus (c. 82-30 BC) Roman leader, whose defeat by OCTAVIAN established rule by emperors. Under the patronage of Julis CAESAR, whom he supported in the civil war, Antonius became a leading soldier and politician. In 44 BC he was consul with Caesar and his oratory drove out Caesar's republican assassins. He enraged Octavian, Caesar's heir, by his affair with CLEOPATRA and by apparent plans to appropriate the Eastern Empire. In the ensuing civil war, Antonius and Cleopatra were defeated by Octavian at Actium (31 BC) and fled to Egypt, where Antonius committed suicide.

Antonius Pius (86-161) Roman emperor (138-161) whose patronage of learning, protection of Christians, legal and tax reforms, new aqueducts and baths, and 'welfare state' provisions marked a period of peace and prosperity throughout the Roman Empire. His name was given to the Antonine Wall built between the firths of Forth and Clyde (142) to protect Roman Britain from the warlike Picts and Scots.

Antony, Mark see ANTONIUS, Marcus

Ape (1839-89) Pseudonym of Carlo Pellegrini, British caricaturist of Victorian high society. His work, which appeared mainly in the journal *Vanity Fair* (1862-80), represented 'not only what he saw but what he knew' (Sir David Low) and later influenced Max BEERBOHM.

Apollinaire, Guillaume (1880-1918) French poet and art critic who participated in various *avant-garde* movements that flourished in France at the turn of the century. Friend of painters such as PICASSO, BRAQUE and others, Apollinaire was influenced by their art and himself experimented in his later poetry with verse forms in an attempt to bring Cubism, with its new vision of the world, to poetry. His best known poems appeared in the collections *Alcools* (1913) and *Calligrammes* (1918). He also wrote the play *Les Mamelles de Tirésias* (1918), for which it is said he coined the term 'drame surréaliste'.

Apollonius (3rd cent. BC) Greek mathematician, known as 'The Great Geometer', whose treatise, *Conic Sections,* deals with fundamental geometrical concepts. Apollonius's work formed the basis for further studies of conic sections, which are the geometrical figures (such as the ellipse, parabola and hyperbola) obtained when a plane cuts a cone at various angles.

Apollonius Rhodius (c. 295-c. 240 BC) Alexandrian scholar and epic poet who had a fiery quarrel with Callimachus, his teacher, on the nature of poetry. Claiming that epic poetry was not obsolete, Apollonius attempted to prove his point with a vast epic, the *Argonautica.* Its four books contain many passages of high poetic quality, notably in their portrayals of romantic love as expressed by Medea in her passion for Jason.

Appert, Nicholas (1752-1841) French pastrycook who in 1809 won 12,000 francs offered by NAPOLEON in 1795 for a practical process for preserving food. The method was to

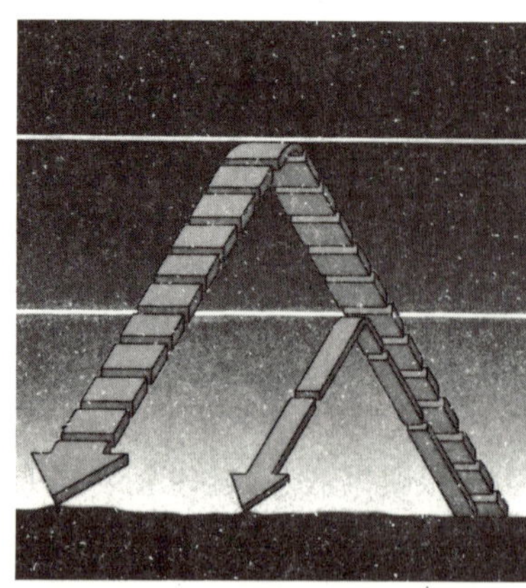

Appleton and Heaviside layers in the Earth's atmosphere. Long waves bounce off lower, Heaviside, layer and short-wave signals from the upper, Appleton, layer

heat the food in glass bottles and then seal it from the air with corks while it was still hot.

Appleton, Sir Edward Victor (1892-1965) English physicist who revealed the presence of layers of charged particles in the atmosphere. In 1923, he suggested that some radio signals bounce off layers of ions at a height of about 65 miles (HEAVISIDE-KENNELLY layer) and 150 miles (Appleton layer). His investigations were of the greatest importance to broadcasting, and the techniques he originated paved the way for the development of radar.

Apuleius (2nd cent.) Roman writer, author of *The Golden Ass*, the only Latin novel surviving in its entirety. An imaginative and witty work, it tells the story of Lucius who, too curious about the black arts, is turned into an ass.

Aquinas, Thomas (1225-74) Catholic philosopher and theologian. Aquinas joined the newly founded Dominicans, immersed himself in academic life, and eventually became a professor, although much of his life was spent in wandering around Europe's universities. He adapted ARISTOTLE's philosophy to Christian dogma, carefully distinguishing faith from reason, and arrived at his 'Five Ways', which argue from man's experience of the world to the existence of God. His greatest works are the *Summa Theologica* and the *Summa contra Gentiles*. He was canonized in 1323 and declared a Doctor of the Church in 1567.

Arafat, Yasir (born 1929) Leader of the Palestine Liberation Organization (PLO) and one of the first Palestinians to advocate guerrilla war against Israel. In 1974 he was recognized by Arab leaders as the 'sole legitimate representative of the Palestinian people'. Arafat's status and that of the PLO were enhanced by UN recognition of the PLO and his membership (1981) of the Islamic peace commission.

Arany, Janos (1817-82) Hungarian poet, author of the epic trilogy *Toldi, Toldi's Love* and *Toldi's Evening* (1847-54), whose hero, a violent, self-defeating man, symbolizes Hungary itself. One of Hungary's major poets, he began as a teacher and itinerant actor and fought in the War of Independence of 1848. He became a professor of Hungarian language and literature at Nagykörös Gymnasium and translated SHAKESPEARE and ARISTOPHANES into Hungarian.

Arbuthnot, John (1667-1735) Scottish doctor, essayist and satirist, best known as the creator of John Bull, the archetypal Englishman.

Archer, Frederick Scott (1813-57) English inventor, in 1850, of the wet collodion photographic process. Though a cumbersome portable laboratory was necessary for outdoor photography, Archer's process superseded both daguerrotype (invented by DAGUERRE) and calotype (invented by TALBOT), being more sensitive to light and producing good quality glass negatives. For 30 years it continued to be widely used until replaced by gelatine-based emulsion.

Archer, Fred (1857-86) English jockey who won 147 out of the 530 races which he entered in his most successful year (1874).

Archimedes (c. 287-212 BC) Greek mathematician and inventor, and the most important scientist of antiquity. He invented various mechanical devices and engines of war, but his chief fame rests on mathematical and physical inventions. In geometry, Archimedes greatly extended the method of exhaustion invented by EUDOXUS for calculating areas. His method of finding the area of a parabolic segment resembles the much later technique of integration. He gave a systematic account of the determination of centres of gravity, and laid the foundations of the science of hydrostatics. The Archimedes principle was his discovery that submerged bodies displace their own volume of liquid and have their weight diminished by an amount equal to the weight of liquid displaced. Using this principle he was able to determine whether the gold in a crown belonging to the King of Syracuse in Sicily had been alloyed with baser metals. Archimedes was killed by a Roman soldier when Syracuse fell to the Romans.

Archimedes's screw is said to have been invented to remove water from the hold of a ship for the King of Syracuse

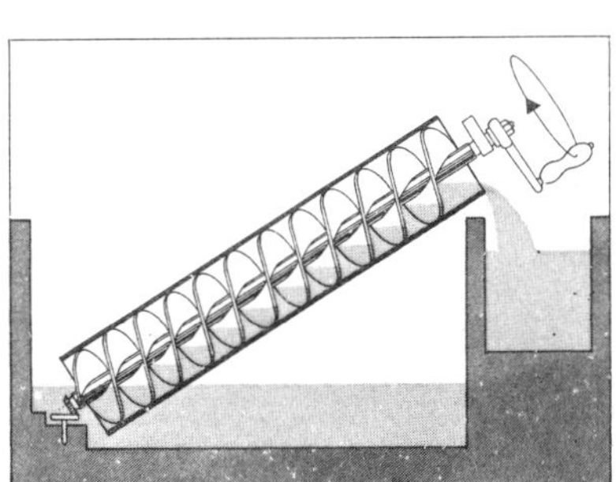

Archipenko, Alexander (1887-1964) Russian sculptor who worked chiefly in wood, stone and bronze (from plaster originals). He went to Paris in 1908, where he was closely associated with the Cubist movement and is important for the explorations he made into the relationship of concave and convex areas, and his use of holes to open up the plastic form, creating a new idiom in modern sculpture.

Ardashir I (3rd cent.) King of Persia (*c.* 224-40), who revived Persian nationalism and built a new Persian empire extending from the Euphrates to Seistan and Herat. Ardashir established a unified state from a loose confederation of vassal kingdoms, founded or rebuilt many cities, and made Zoroastrianism the state religion.

Arden, John (born 1930) English dramatist, author of *Sergeant Musgrave's Dance* (1959). His prize-winning radio play *The Life of Man* made his name.

Aretino, Pietro (1492-1556) Italian humanist and satirist, whose castigation of his contemporaries earned him the name 'The Scourge of Princes'.

Argand, Jean Robert (1768-1822) French mathematician, who, in 1806, reintroduced a geometrical method of representing complex numbers. The numbers are formal solutions of algebraical equations involving the square roots of negative numbers. Argand diagrams are now widely used in mathematics, theoretical mechanics and electricity.

Argyll, 1st Duke of see CAMPBELL, Archibald, 1st Duke of Argyll

Ariosto, Lodovico (1474-1533) Italian poet second only to DANTE and author of satires, lyrics and comedies as well as the masterpiece, *Orlando Furioso*. This recounted the wars between CHARLEMAGNE and the Saracens, the adventures and loves of the Christian knights, Orlando and Ruggiero and the mock-heroic deeds of the English knight, Astolfo. The language is elegant and harmonious, the result of frequent polishing and revision before the definitive edition of 1532. His seven letters, the *Satire*, contain a subtle, vivid portrayal of the times, whilst his five comedies, especially the *Cassaria* (1531), mark the birth of Renaissance theatre.

Aristarchus of Samos (3rd cent. BC) Greek astronomer, the first to suggest that the Earth revolves about the Sun, His treatise, *On the Sizes and Distances of the Sun and Moon,* though inaccurate, was an important step forward in mathematical astronomy.

Aristides (c. 530-c. 468 BC) Athenian general and statesman, chief organizer of the Delian League, from which the Athenian Empire grew. He was instrumental in persuading some Spartan-dominated Ionian city-states to transfer their allegiance to Athens (478 BC), resulting in the Delian League. In earlier years he was ostracized for opposing the naval policy of THEMISTOCLES, but when Athens was attacked by the Persians (480 BC) he returned and was a successful commander at Salamis, Plataea, and off the coast of Byzantium.

Aristophanes (c. 448-c. 380 BC) Greek dramatist pre-eminent in the Old Comedy genre. Eleven of his 40 or so comedies survive. In the early group (425-410 BC) – *The Acharnians, The Knights, The Clouds, The Wasps, The Birds, Lysistrata* and *Thesmophoriazusae* – he retained the traditional chorus as an important element whose nature often gives the play its title. In the later group (405-388 BC) – *The Frogs, The Parliament of Women, Ecclesiazusae* and *Plutus* – the chorus is less in evidence and the play more liberated from traditional formalism. Aristophanes was a brilliantly intelligent conservative with the greatest contempt for democracy and the solemnities of such establishment dramatists as AESCHYLUS, EURIPIDES and SOPHOCLES, of whom he made savage fun in *The Frogs*.

Aristotle (c. 384-322 BC) Greek philosopher who was a student at PLATO's Academy and later a teacher there. Aristotle covered an enormous range in his work and was the inventor of logic (he called it *analytics*) as a separate systematic discipline. His best-known work in this field is his theory of the syllogism – for example, All men are mortal. Socrates is a man; therefore Socrates is mortal. Aristotle's influential theory of causality (in *Physics*) states that every event has four causes: *material,* the matter involved; *formal,* the way this is placed; *efficient,* what triggers off the change; and *final,* what the event tends towards. His theory of categories sets out the 10 different elements that Aristotle recognizes in any situation such as place, time, quality, quantity and the like. His works include *De Anima, Metaphysics* and *Nicomachean Ethics*.

Arius (4th cent. AD) Alexandrian priest who held that Christ was a created, not a divine being. The controversy initiated by the Arian heresy raged until his death (*c.* 335).

Arkwright, Sir Richard (1732-92) English inventor and industrialist, who, possibly with the help of others, developed the first practical way of mechanical spinning using rollers, which he patented in 1769. At first these machines were powered by animals, then at Cromford, Derbyshire, by water (1771) and, finally, by steam (1790). Arkwright invented, or introduced, machinery to carry out the remaining preparatory processes. His mill at Cromford was one of the wonders of the age, resulting in his being one of the first 'capitalists' of the Industrial Revolution.

Arminius, Jacobus (1560-1609) Dutch Protestant theologian. He opposed the Calvinist doctrine that God had predestined everyone to salvation or damnation, putting forward the less harsh view that salvation was open to all believers and penitents. His ideas, set out in *Remonstrance* (1610), had a liberalizing effect on Protestant theology.

Armstrong, Daniel Louis (1900-71) American negro trumpet virtuoso, bandleader and vocalist, whose influence on the stature of jazz internationally was, perhaps, greater than that of any other musician. Armstrong's roots, in every sense, were in New Orleans, his home town. He sang for money as a child and, committed to an orphan's home at 13, where he learned to play the cornet. His first and only mentor, Joe 'King' OLIVER, took him to Chicago where, in a few years, he was being billed as 'The world's greatest trumpet player'. He made his first of many trips to Europe in 1932, toured Japan, Ghana and the West Indies during the 1950s. In his later years he ceased the innovation on which his early fame rested, but he remained the complete entertainer.

As a child, Louis Armstrong sang for money in the streets of New Orleans

Armstrong, Neil (born 1930) 'That's one small step for a man, one giant leap for mankind' were the words spoken by Armstrong, an American astronaut, who commanded the Apollo 11 spacecraft and was the first man to walk on the Moon, at 2.56 pm on 21 July 1969.

Arnauld, Antoine (1612-94) French Jansenist theologian who led an anti-Jesuit reform movement. His *L'Art de penser* known as the 'Port Royal Logic', remained a textbook on elementary logic until the 19th century.

Arne, Thomas Augustine (1710-78) English composer whose most famous work *Rule Britannia* formed part of the music he wrote for the masque *Alfred.* He is remembered also for his settings of Shakespeare in songs such as *Where the bee sucks* and *Blow, blow, thou winter wind.* Arne's reputation was greatest for his music for the contemporary theatre, which included plays, operas and masques.

Arnold, Benedict (1741-1801) American army officer, who deserted to the British during the War of Independence (1775-83). He acquitted himself with honour in the early Revolutionary battles, but later joined the British as a spy, for which he was scorned by the British public when he visited England at the war's end.

Arnold of Brescia (c. 1100-55) Italian ascetic priest who opposed the holding of temporal powers and possessions by the papacy and clergy, and led a Roman revolt against the Pope. Driven in turn from Brescia, France and Zurich for his religious unorthodoxy and protests against Church corruption, he went to Rome (1145) and became leader of the revolt that had already ousted the Pope (1143) and established republican rule in Rome. ADRIAN IV quelled the rebellion with the aid of Barbarossa and Arnold was hanged.

Arnold, Matthew (1822-88) English poet, critic and educationalist. Son of Thomas ARNOLD, he accepted an Inspectorship of Schools in 1851 and strove to introduce true national education and foster the spread of culture. He studied European education, reporting to the Newcastle and Taunton Royal Commissions (1861, 1868). In *Culture and Anarchy* (1869) and *Essays in Criticism* (1865, 1888) he attacked British complacency and materialism. Poetry played a central role in his life – 'The Scholar

Gypsy' and 'Thyris' exemplify his romantic, nostalgic poems, while 'Sohrab and Rustum' is in restrained epic style.

Arnold, Thomas (1795-1842) English educationalist who, as headmaster of Rugby School (1828-42), established the ideal of the English public school concept of education. His use of the prefect-system, encouragement of personal responsibility and emphasis upon a religious basis all became associated with the public school system. He introduced modern history into the curriculum and was concerned to educate boys who would serve Church and State in the context of the 19th-century British Empire.

Arnolfo di Cambio (c. 1245-c. 1302) Italian architect and sculptor who, it is generally agreed, was architect of the first cathedral of Florence (begun 1294). Little of his decorative work remains there now. A pupil of Nicola PISANO, Arnolfo worked with him on the Pulpit at Siena (1265-8). He struck a new note of innovation in his wall-tomb for Cardinal de Braye in S Domenico, Orvieto (*c.* 1282).

Arp, Jean (1887-1966) French sculptor and abstract painter, who, in 1912, exhibited with the *Blaue Reiter* group with KANDINSKY and others and later was one of the leading exponents of Dadaism.

Arrabal, Fernando (born 1932) Spanish dramatist and novelist, pioneer of the Abstract Theatre and exponent of the Theatre of the Absurd, after the manner of BECKETT. His plays and novels portray the grotesque aspects of life; in *Picnic in the Country* (1952) the countryside is a battlefield where the picnickers have all been shot and *The Car Cemetery* (1962) is a derisive satire in which life is lived in a used-car dump. Arrabal's work has never been accepted in Spain. He writes in French and lives and works in France.

Arrhenius, Svante August (1859-1927) Swedish chemist who developed the ionic theory of electrolytes. In 1887 he proposed that electrolytes (substances whose solutions conduct electricity) split up in solution into electrically charged particles, called ions, which conduct current. After years of controversy, his theory was accepted and in 1903 he was awarded the Nobel Prize for Chemistry.

Artaud, Antonin (1896-1948) French director, dramatist and theorist, who was the first to produce (1925) Surrealist plays. With Roger VITRAC he founded the Theatre Alfred Jarry. Their Surrealist productions included Vitrac's plays and one act of Claudel's *Partage du Midi* as a farce.

Arthur (c. 6th cent.) British king, perhaps legendary, the hero of an enormous cycle of mythological romances. In the fanciful 12th-century chronicle of Geoffrey of Monmouth, Arthur is said to have defeated the invading Saxons at Mt Badon and died at the Battle of Camlan (537). In Arthurian legend Arthur founded the Knights of the Round Table, but took little part in their exploits. The legend-cycle, which emerged principally in medieval French verse and prose romances, especially the verse of CHRETIEN DE TROYES, was later retold by MALORY and TENNYSON.

Ashkenazy, Vladimir (born 1937) Soviet pianist who won first prize in the Queen Elizabeth Piano Competition in Brussels in 1956, and in 1962 shared first prize with John Ogdon in the prestigious Moscow Tchaikovsky Piano Competition.

Jean Arp used simple motifs, like this marble torso, to capture the essence of the female form

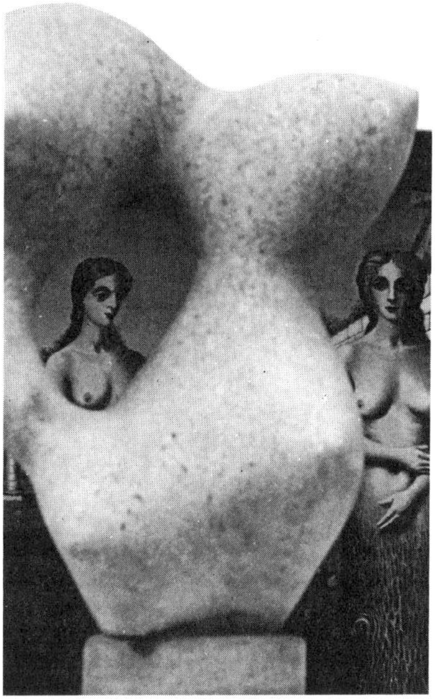

Ashton, Sir Frederick (born 1906) English choreographer who joined the Sadler's Wells Ballet in London (1935), now the Royal Ballet, and was its chief choreographer until 1963 and director (1963-70). His classics include *Cinderella* (1948), *Ondine* (1958), *La Fille Mal Gardee* (1960) and *A Month in the Country* (1976).

Ashurbanipal (ruled 669-26 BC) Assyrian king, whose library helped modern scholars to reconstruct Mesopotamia's ancient history. He was a grandson of SENNACHERIB, and ruled Babylonia, Persia, Egypt and Syria, the most powerful and cultured monarch of his time. His library at Nineveh (rediscovered by LAYARD, 1845-7) held 22,000 clay tablets inscribed in cuneiform with Assyrian, Babylonian and Sumerian historical, literary, religious and scientific texts. Bilinguals and syllabaries in the hitherto unknown Sumerian tongue helped De Sarzec and Woolley to rediscover sites of Mesopotamia's (and the world's) first civilization. Ashurbanipal's Assyrian Empire died with him and was supplanted by the Chaldean Empire, the greatest king of which was NEBUCHADNEZZAR II.

Asoka (3rd-2nd cents. BC) Indian emperor of the Mauryan Dynasty, whose empire embraced two-thirds of the Indian subcontinent. Revolted by the bloodshed of his expansionist wars and converted to Buddhism, Asoka proclaimed the Buddhist code of toleration, truthfulness and abstention from killing in edicts inscribed throughout his empire on pillars and rocks. Asoka put his edicts into practice with reforms that enriched the empire, sent Buddhist monks overseas, and embarked on 'morality tours' through his domains. But though he gave his brahmanical subjects freedom to worship, within 50 years of his death Brahman opposition to his Buddhist tenets had helped to crush the Mauryan Dynasty – India's last great ruling house till BABER founded the Mogul Dynasty, 17 centuries later.

Aspdin, Joseph (1779-1855) English bricklayer who in 1824 invented 'Portland' cement, a pre-burnt mixture of powdered limestone and clay, which after the addition of water achieves rock-like hardness. Portland cement is one of the principal modern building materials as a constituent of mortar and concrete.

Asquith Herbert Henry (1858-1928) British Liberal statesman and Prime Minister (1908-16). From 1905 to 1908 he was Chancellor of the Exchequer in the government of CAMPBELL-BANNERMAN, whom he succeeded as Prime Minister, and in office had to deal with the Suffragette movement, industrial unrest and Irish Home Rule. He was in power at the outbreak of the First World War and from May 1915 headed a coalition government until ousted in December 1916 by a combination of LLOYD GEORGE and the Conservatives, after disputes over the war leadership. The subsequent feud between the Asquithian Liberals and the supporters of Lloyd George seriously weakened the Liberal Party.

Astaire, Fred (born 1899) American dancer whose career has spanned musical comedy, vaudeville and the cinema, in which his partners have included Ginger Rogers, Judy Garland and Rita Hayworth. Astaire took the tap dance (born of clattering British clog dances and syncopated negro dance rhythms) and spiced it with ballet movements and Yankee humour. He created a new form of musical film in the 1930s, perfected by 'shooting' each dance sequence up to 30 times, then drastically editing, itself a new cinema technique. His many films include *Top Hat, Funny Face,* and *Broadway Melody*.

Astor, John Jacob (1763-1848) German-born American multimillionaire whose fortune was based on the fur trade and, later, New York real estate. Astor found and endowed the Astor Library, New York. At his death his personal estate was $20 million, but increases in land values in New York had raised it to about $250 million by the end of the century.

Lady Astor was a tireless champion of women's rights and an influential political hostess between the wars

Astor, Nancy Witcher, Viscountess (1879-1964) American-born British MP who succeeded her husband as the Unionist member for Plymouth in 1919 and was the first woman to take her seat in the House of Commons. She was an active political hostess between the wars and it was said that much government policy in the 1930s was decided at her house parties at Cliveden in Buckinghamshire.

Athanasias the Great (c. 293-373) Alexandria-born saint who was one of the four great Greek Doctors of the Church and helped to frame the basis of present-day Christianity at the Council of Nicaea in 325. Athanasias's unswerving idealism and lifelong opposition to the Arian heresy inspired both fierce loyalty and violent hatred, and his life swung between the extremes of public veneration and rejection. Although he became Primate of Egypt and was Bishop of Alexandria for 46 years, Athanasias spent 17 of those years in enforced exile in the Arabian desert, owing to the Arianism of Emperor Constantius and his successors. He wrote many polemical pieces against Arianism, and commentaries on the Scriptures. The Creed named after him is thought to have been written by St AMBROSE.

Attenborough, Sir Richard Samuel (born 1923) English actor, producer and director, famous for his fine character performances in many war and adventure films. Among his best-known films are *In Which We Serve* (1942), *Brighton Rock* (1947), *The Great Escape* (1963), *Seance on a Wet Afternoon* (1946) and *10 Rillington Place* (1971). His first venture as a director was *Oh! What a Lovely War* (1969); he went on to direct *Young Winston* (1972), *A Bridge Too Far* (1977) and *Ghandi* (1982), a project which had obsessed him for nearly 20 years, and which won eight Academy Awards.

Attila (c. 406-53) King of the Huns (433-53), called the 'Scourge of God', who overran Europe from the North Sea to the Caspian and terrorized the crumbling Roman Empire. After consolidating his loosely organized Hun kingdom, he crossed the Danube with his multinational cavalry, ravaged the Eastern Roman Empire (447-50) as far as Constantinople, and forced Theodosius II to make huge protection payments. Next he thrust west through Gaul (451), demanding half the Western Roman Empire and reaching Orleans before suffering his only defeat, by Roman and Visigothic troops at Châlons-sur-Marne. Attila next devastated northern Itay (452), but quickly left, probably forced out by famine. He died suddenly just before a second invasion of Italy, and his empire, lacking stability, fell apart.

Attlee, Clement Richard, Earl (1883-1967) British Prime Minister (1945-51) during whose period of office the Welfare State was implemented. From 1922 to 1924 he was Parliamentary Private Secretary to the Labour leader Ramsay MACDONALD, and held office in the Labour administrations of 1924 and 1930, becoming party leader in 1935. From 1943 to 1945 Attlee was deputy Prime Minister to CHURCHILL in the Second World War coalition government and Prime Minister after Labour was returned to power in 1945. His ministry put through a programme of nationalization (railways, coal mines, road transport) and social reform (National Health Service and an extension of National Insurance). Though quiet and modest, Attlee was a shrewd politician, holding together and in balance the mutually hostile left and right wings of the Labour Party. During his premiership India was granted independence (1947).

Attwood, Thomas (1783-1856) British radical politician, currency reformer and Chartist leader. He was MP for Birmingham from 1832 to 1840 and one of the founders of the Birmingham Political Union (1829) whose agitation helped to secure the Parliamentary Reform Act of 1832. As a Chartist organizer Attwood represented the more moderate and constitutional section of the movement.

Auden, Wystan Hugh (1907-73) English-born poet, who was one of the most versatile and technically accomplished of all modern poets, and the most important of a group of English poets who were influenced by Marxism in the 1930s. His first published works were *Poems* (1930) and *The Orators* (1932). After teaching and making documentaruy films, he left England for Spain and drove an ambulance for the Republicans in the Spanish Civil War. Auden emigrated to America in 1939, and became more meditative and lyrical. In *The Age of Anxiety* (1947), *Nones* (1952) and *The Shield of Achilles* (1955) he began to write on moral and religious themes from a Christian viewpoint. He also wrote verse plays and critical essays.

Audubon, John James (1785-1851) American ornithologist and artist who painted all the species of birds in the United States known in the early 19th century. He met with little success in America, so in 1826 he sent his work to Europe, where it was published as *The Birds of America* in four volumes (1827-38). Audubon became a great success, and published *Ornithological Biography* (1831-9) and *A Synopsis of the Birds of North America* (1839).

Auenbrugger, Leopold (1722-1809) Austrian physician who pioneered the use of percussion (tapping with the finger) to diagnose diseases of the heart and lungs. His simple discovery, that the chest of a patient, when it is tapped, sometimes sounds different when healthy than when diseased, is one of the cornerstones of modern medicine.

Augustine of Canterbury (6th-7th cent.) Saint, evangelizer of Saxon England, first Archbishop of Canterbury and the founder of the bishoprics of London and Rochester. In 596 he led a band of 40 missionary monks sent by GREGORY THE GREAT to convert the pagan Saxons and come to terms with the Christian Britons. In the first assignment he had considerable success, beginning with King Ethelbert of Kent: in the second he failed, the British bishops in Wales, Devon and Cornwall refusing to recognize him as Archbishop.

Augustine of Hippo, St (354-430) The most outstanding theologian in Christian antiquity, who successfully welded New Testament thought with Neoplatonism.

Augustus (63 BC-AD 14) First Roman Emperor (27 BC-AD 14), born Gaius Octavian, great nephew and heir of Julius CAESAR. After Caesar's death, Augustus sought to be dictator but compromised with his rival (ANTONIUS Marcus), and with Lepidus, they became joint rulers of the empire (Triumvirs), defeating the republicans at Philippi (42 BC). Enraged by the conduct of Antonius with CLEOPATRA and believing them to be about to take the Eastern Roman Empire, Augustus fought and defeated them at Actium (31 BC) to become sole ruler of the Empire. He restored all the constitutional forms of the republic but was invested by the senate with the power of *imperium* and designated Augustus, 'Exalted' (27 BC). Augustus's reign was marked by constitutional reforms, a growth in wealth, economic stability and able administration of the provinces.

Augustus II (1670-1733) Elector of Saxony and King of Poland (1697-1704 and 1709-33) whose attempts at territorial gain led to Polish subservience to Russia. Encouraged by success in his war in Turkey, Augustus joined Russia's PETER I in attacking Swedish-held Livonia (1700). This provoked CHARLES XII of Sweden to begin a devastating war on Polish soil, and Augustus was deposed (1704) by his nobles. When Peter I defeated Charles XII at Poltava in the Ukraine (1709), Augustus regained his throne, but his attempts to make the elective crown hereditary caused a civil war, which further weakened war-torn Poland and enabled Russia to interfere at will with his successors.

Aurangzeb (1618-1707) Last great Mogul emperor of India (1658-1707), during whose reign the Muslim Hindustan empire attained its greatest extent and wealth. Aurangzeb grasped power by imprisoning his father and murdering his three brothers, and by conquest extended his rule over all of northern and central India. Aurangzeb's religious bigotry undermined the empire he had built and provoked revolts and unsuccessful wars with the Hindu Marathas led by SHIVAJI (1689-1705). The founding of the Maratha kingdom started the erosion of Mogul power and, ultimately, Britain's seizure of India.

Aurelius, Marcus (121-180) Roman emperor (161-80) and Stoic philosopher. Aurelius held equanimity to be the supreme goal in life, achieved by living in tune with nature, and requiring the virtues of wisdom, justice, fortitude and temperance, dictated by reason. His philosophy is outlined in *Meditations,* which also indirectly reflect his practical concern with his position as a statesman and general.

Aurelius Prudentius Clemens see PRUDENTIUS

Austen, Jane (1775-1817) English novelist, who wrote on the life and manners of comfortable country society with delicate wit and subtle characterization. With her quiet, ironic style Austen illuminates common hopes, desires and frictions. Her books, the best known being *Pride and Prejudice, Sense and Sensibility* and *Emma,* were published between 1811 and 1818. She spent an easy, uneventful life of security in the south of England and in her books there is no violence, little outward passion and few incidents, but she perfected the art of the novel of ordinary life.

Austin, John (1790-1859) English jurist who has had a lasting influence on English jurisprudence and legal education. Suspecting BLACKSTONE of confusion, and (in his *The Province of Jurisprudence Determined* 1832) incorporating the utilitarian principles of his friends BENTHAM and MILL he clarified the distinction between law and morality. In later lectures, published in 1863, he analysed the fundamental ideas underlying all mature legal systems and demonstrated the need for the constant critical analysis of legal concepts.

Avicenna (980-1037) Persian philosopher and physician, who absorbed and developed Greek philosophy, science and medicine. He was chief physician to the hospital at Baghdad and court physician to the caliphs. His influence on medical practice was considerable.

Avogadro, Amadeo (1776-1856) Italian physicist who, in 1811, advanced the hypothesis, now named after him, that at standard pressure and temperature equal volumes of all gases contain the same number of molecules. When the quantity of gas involved is the molecular weight in grams this number is Avogadro's constant ($6{\cdot}025 \times 10^{23}$). He was one of the first scientists to distinguish between molecules and atoms, and his ideas play a fundamental role in the theory of gases and in physical chemistry. Avogadro's hypothesis was only accepted after his death.

Ayer, Sir Alfred Jules (born 1910) English philosopher whose best known work is the antimetaphysical *Language, Truth and Logic* (1936), a concise, lucid exposition of the doctrines of the Vienna Circle – a logical positivist school of philosophers. Later works include *Thinking and Meaning* (1947), *The Problem of Knowledge* (1956), *Metaphysics and Common Sense* (1969) and *Philosophy in the 20th century* (1982). He was Wykeham Professor of Logic at Oxford (1959-78).

Aylward, Gladys (1903-70) English missionary, who travelled overland through Russia to China, where she took Chinese nationality and was known as Ai-weh-deh, 'the virtuous one'. In 1938, during the Sino-Japanese war, she led almost 100 refugee children away from the advancing Japanese, travelling for a month by foot, over the mountains from Yangcheng to Sian. She returned to England in 1949, but later settled in Taiwan, where she ran an orphanage.

B

Babbage, Charles (1792-1871) English originator of the modern computer, who spent most of his life trying to eliminate errors in mathematical and astronomical tables by having them automatically calculated and printed by machines. He used much of his own fortune on this work and received financial help from the British Government. Babbage's first computer or 'difference engine' (1827) compiled and printed tables of logarithms from 1 to 108,000. His more complex 'analytical machine' was to be capable of undertaking any type of calculation. It would have been steam-driven and programmed by means of machined cards, but was never completed.

Babel, Isaak (1894-c. 1941) Russian author whose major work, *Red Cavalry* (1926), was based on his experiences in Poland during the Cossacks' campaign. His short stories are powerful works of pathos and irony, outstanding for their descriptive comments on war. Babel fought with the Tsarist army in the First World War, and during STALIN's purges he was sent to a concentration camp, where presumably he died. His reputation was officially restored in 1957.

Baber (1483-1530) Muslim Turkish conqueror of northern India and founder of its last major ruling family, the Mogul (i.e. Mongol) dynasty, which reached its peak under his grandson AKBAR. Having lost Ferghana, his inherited kingdom, and Samarkand, which he had conquered, Baber crossed the Hindu Kush and captured Kabul. Defeat by the Uzbegs (1514) ended his attempts to regain his kingdom and he turned to northern India, which he mastered after victories at Panipat (1526) and Kanwaha (1527). An effective administrator, he improved the road taxation and land measurement systems.

Babeuf, François Emile (1760-97) French egalitarian socialist and conspirator against the Directory who organized a left-wing movement of former Jacobins into the 'Society of Equals'. Babeuf propagated egalitarian socialism in the belief, that, in the words of his manifesto, 'Nature has given each man the right to enjoy an equal share in all property'. In 1796 he was arrested but committed suicide.

Bach, Carl Philipp Emanuel (1714-88) Influential German composer, third son of J. S. BACH, who contributed to the early evolution of the symphony. HAYDN said of him, 'Everything I know I have learnt from Emanuel Bach'; and MOZART: 'He is the father, we the children.'

Bach, Johann Christian (1735-82) German composer, the eleventh of J. S. BACH's sons. He came to be known as 'the English Bach' after settling in London in 1762. Bach's ability as melodist and orchestrator is shown in his operas, symphonies, concertos and songs. He was music master to GEORGE III's family, a friend of GAINSBOROUGH and an influence on the young MOZART.

Bach, Johann Sebastian (1685-1750) German composer who brought European music to one of its highest peaks of achievement. During his lifetime Bach was known mainly as a fine organist who composed music as part of his duties as town organist, court musician and (from 1723) as Cantor (musical director) at St Thomas's Church, Leipzig. It was only when his work came to light again in the 19th century (largely through the efforts of MENDELSSOHN) that he was recognized as being among music's towering geniuses. Early in his career Bach declared his intention to write 'A properly regulated church music dedicated to the glory of God', and composed chorale preludes and fugues for organ and cantatas to Lutheran texts for use in church services. The expression of his strong Protestant faith was to culminate in his choral masterpieces, the *St Matthew Passion* (1729) and the *Mass in B Minor*. Some of his secular works were written to specific commissions; the set of six *Brandenburg Concertos* (1721) for the Margrave of Brandenburg; the 30 *Goldberg Variations* for harpsichord for the patron of one of Bach's pupils; the *Musical Offering* (1747) for, and based on a theme provided by, FREDERICK THE GREAT. Another work dating from Bach's last years, and uncompleted at his death, is *The Art of Fugue*, a set of studies in counterpoint probably intended for harpsichord. Bach married twice and fathered 20 children. Several of his sons continued the family's musical tradition and themselves became distinguished figures. The most notable among them were C. P. E. BACH and J. C. BACH.

Bacon, Francis (1561-1626) English philosopher, lawyer, statesman and author who was the first important writer of essays in English. Bacon rose to high legal office: he was Attorney-General (1613), Lord Keeper (1617) and Lord Chancellor (1618). He was made Viscount St Albans in 1621, but was convicted of bribery, and banished from Parliament. It was Bacon's ambition to reinterpret phenomena on rational rather than Aristotelian principles, and his philosophical works are an exposition of the state of knowledge at the time.

Bacon, Francis (born 1909) British painter, whose work is characterized by the individuality of his style and by amorphous malformations of the human figures, portrayed invariably in isolation, to a sinister, somewhat repulsive effect.

Baden-Powell, Robert, 1st Baron (1857-1941) English founder of the Boy Scout movement. Drawing on his experiences as a professional soldier and scout in India and Africa, he stressed the need for character development rather than military discipline. British youth hero-worshipped Baden-Powell after his 215-day defence of Mafeking (1899-1900) during the Boer War, and after 1908, scout troops sprang up throughout the country, and the movement gradually became international. In 1910 Baden-Powell left the army to devote his life to scouting and, with his sister, founded the Girl Guides.

Badoglio, Pietro (1871-1956) Italian soldier who formed a government and declared war on his former allies, the Germans, when MUSSOLINI resigned and Italy collapsed (1943) during the Second World War. Badoglio, who commanded the victorious Italian Army in its Ethiopian campaign (1935-6), resigned following defeats inflicted by the Greeks in the Albanian theatre (1940).

Baedeker, Karl (1801-59) German publisher, bookseller and writer of travel guides. In 1829 he issued a guide book to Coblenz and followed it with a series of books which would enable travellers to dispense with paid guides. The first was a guide to the Rhine from Mainz to Cologne.

Baer, Karl von (1792-1876) Estonian embryologist whose work, showing the fundamental similarities between all vertebrate embryos, made an important contribution to evolutionary theory. He showed that in all vertebrates there are potential or 'germ' layers that give rise to the various organs and tissues. These and other similarities between foetuses of different species led him to postulate that individuals of different species diverge during their embryonic development from a primary or archetypal form. He also discovered the mammalian ovum.

Baffin, William (1584-1622) British explorer who was among the first to study magnetic variation, which had long troubled mariners dependent on the magnetic compass. He piloted several expeditions seeking a northwest passage around America, reaching Greenland (1612) and Spitsbergen (1613), the east of North America and the west of Greenland (1615-16), and discovered Baffin Bay. On the voyage during which he discovered Baffin Bay (1615-16), he went as far north as 77°45′, which remained for 236 years the record northerly latitude reached. His careful magnetic observations led to the making of the first magnetic chart.

Baird, John Logie (1888-1946) Scottish-born pioneer of television. In 1922, he began research into a system which depended on scanning the scene with a rapidly moving spot of light (the flying spot system). Four years later he gave the first demonstration of a television picture. The British Broadcasting Corporaton adopted Baird's system for their first television programme in 1929, but in 1937 it was abandoned in favour of an electronic scanning system.

Bakr, abu- see ABU-BAKER

Bakst, Leon Nikolayevich (1866-1924) Russian painter-designer who worked with DIAGHILEV and whose ballet decors set new trends in theatre design.

Bakunin, Mikhail (1814-76) Russian anarchist aristocrat and guards officer who resigned his commission over Russia's maltreatment of the Polish nationalist rebels. His pamphlet *Reaction in Germany* (1842) and his revolutionary ideas led to his permanent exile. He was involved in the February Revolution (Paris 1848) and helped to inspire the Czech rising (Prague 1948) and the Saxony revolt (1849). In 1849 he was arrested in Dresden, but though condemned to death by the authorities in both Berlin and Vienna, he was not executed but imprisoned in Austria, then handed over to the Russians and sent to Siberia (1855). After six years he escaped and devoted the rest of his life to West European revolutionary movements.

Balakirev, Mily Alexeyvich (1837-1910) Russian composer who founded and led the important group of Russian nationalist composers known as 'The Five' or 'The Mighty Handful', including RIMSKY-KORSAKOV, MUSSORGSKY, BORODIN and Cui. 'The Five' aimed to establish a musical standpoint in Russian music that looked to Russia's history, folk-music and literature rather than to the West. Balakirev wrote two symphonies and a symphonic poem, *Tamara* (dedicated to LISZT), though he composed little after a nervous breakdown in the 1870s.

Balanchine, George (born 1904) Russian-born choreographer and pioneer of the American 'classic' ballet. DIAGHILEV'S last main choreographer, he founded the School of American Ballet, later the New York City Ballet, in 1934. Balanchine helped form a new American style of ballet which combined exuberant athletic movements with classical Russian dance. Balanchine collaborated for many years with STRAVINSKY on works such as *Agon* and *Orpheus*.

Balboa, Vasco Nuñez de (1475-1517) Spanish explorer, the first European to see the Pacific. He was a Spanish settler in Hispaniola (now Haiti and the Dominican Republic), where he joined a fleet taking provisions to San Sebastian settlement in Panama (1510). Findng the settlement deserted, Balboa continued to Darien where he later became Governor. He conquered the surrounding areas and, hearing of an ocean and rich lands over the mountains, led an expedition (1513) that reached the Pacific, which Balboa claimed for Spain. Pedrarias Davila, a bitter rival of Balboa, was sent out to replace him as Governor of Darien and had him tried for treason and beheaded.

Baldwin, Stanley, 1st Earl of Bewdley (1867-1947) English statesman, three times Prime Minister (1923-4, 1924-9 and 1935-7). In 1926 Baldwin's government out-manoeuvred the General Strike, but subsequently had to contend with the beginning (1929) of the depression and mass unemployment. Baldwin served in RAMSAY MACDONALD'S National Government of 1931 as Lord President of the Council and became PM again in 1935. He failed to appreciate the dangers of Nazi resurgence and his ministry was tainted by appeasement of the dictators MUSSOLINI and HITLER. He was instrumental in the abdication of EDWARD VIII (1936).

Balfour, Arthur James, 1st Earl of (1848-1930) English statesman who, as Foreign Secretary in 1917, was responsible for the declaration committing Britain to support the establishment of a Jewish national home in Palestine on condition that the rights of 'existing non-Jewish communities' in Palestine were guaranteed. The Balfour Declaration was ratified by the other Allied governments and resulted in Britain being given the League of Nations Mandate in Palestine (1920).

Balmer, Johann Jakob (1825-98) Swiss physicist who found the first mathematical formula describing the wavelengths of spectral lines. Balmer's simple formula fitted part of the hydrogen spectrum, but could not be explained without quantum theory.

Balsamo, Giuseppe see CAGLIOSTRO, Count Alessandro di

Baltimore, David (born 1938) American microbiologist who in 1975 shared the Nobel Prize for Physiology or Medicine with Howard Temin for his work on the 'interaction between tumor viruses and the genetic material of the cell'. Working independently of Temin, he proved the existence of reverse transcriptase, the enzyme necessary for viral genetic information to be incorporated into an animal cell.

Baltimore, George Calvert, 1st Baron, see CALVERT, George

Balzac, Honoré de (1799-1850) French novelist of world stature and architect of the massive *Comédie Humaine*, which comprises over 50 volumes depicting every aspect of contemporary society, and an enormous range of human types. Despite obvious imperfections in style and technique, Balzac's exceptional powers of observation enabled him to transpose the raw material from notebooks and memory into lasting fictional works. The portraits of his main protagonists are etched brilliantly and boldly – the miser Grandet, the naïve Birotteau, Gobseck, cousin Pons, Vautrin and the student Rastignac. Balzac's lifelong struggle to keep his creditors at bay is reflected in his novels, whose themes are dominated by financial intrigue and the corrupting power of money, which he recognized as one of the dynamic forces in society. The principal titles of the *Comédie Humaine* include: *La Peau de Chagrin* (1831); *Le Curé de Tours* (1832); *Eugénie Grandet* (1833); *Le Père Goriot* (1834); *César Birotteau* (1837); *La Cousine Bette* (1846) and *Le Cousin Pons* (1847). Balzac was also the author of some memorable short stories (e.g. *Facino Cane*) and of the *Contes drôlatiques* and *Un Episode sous la Terreur* (1832-7).

Banda, Hastings Kamuzu (born 1905) First Prime Minister of Malawi. While practising medicine in London, Banda organized opposition to the Federation of the Rhodesias and to Nyasaland, where he took up politics (1958). In 1959 he was arrested for belonging to the illegal Malawi Congress Party, but was released in 1960 and appointed Prime Minister of Nyasaland in 1963. When independence was conceded by Britain in the following year he became the first Prime Minister of Malawi, and President in 1966.

Bandaranaike, Solomon (1899-1959) Prime Minister of Ceylon, now Sri Lanka, from 1956 until 1959, when he was assassinated by a Buddhist monk. His policies were continued by his wife, Sirimavo, who entered politics on her husband's death and became Prime Minister (1960-5), the first woman in the world to hold such an office.

Bannister, Sir Roger Gilbert (born 1929) British athlete. The first person to run a mile in under four minutes, at Oxford in 1954, he ran the distance in 3 min. 59.4 secs.

Banting, Sir Frederick (1891-1941) Canadian doctor, who with Charles BEST discovered a treatment for diabetes. With the help of J. J. R. Macleod they discovered that small clumps or islands of cells in the pancreas secrete a hormone known as insulin and went on to show the key role of insulin in regulating the level of sugar in the blood. Insulin therapy is now a standard treatment for diabetes. In 1923 Banting and Macleod were awarded a Nobel Prize.

Barber, Samuel (1910-81) American composer best known for his *Adagio for Strings* (1936). He has written two symphonies, the first of which, cast in a condensed, single-movement form, is among the best by any American composer. He has also completed a series of song cycles in which his gifts have probably found their most effective expression.

Bardot, Brigitte (born 1934) French actress who gained worldwide fame as the 'sex kitten' in such films as *And God Created Woman* and *Heaven Fell That Night* (1957), directed by her then husband, Roger Vadim.

Barents, Willem (16th cent.) Dutch navigator who explored the waters north and northeast of Norway, later called the Barents Sea, in an attempt to find a North East Passage to eastern Asia. On his third voyage, he sighted Bear Island and West Spitsbergen, which he mistook for Greenland. His team rounded Novaya Zemlya but was trapped by ice and wintered ashore – the first Europeans to do so that far north. Barents died on the return journey.

Baring, Sir Francis (1740-1810) English founder of Baring Brothers and Company (1806), one of the world's strongest financial houses. He combined opportunism, expertise and integrity, qualities which successive Baring generations cultivated and maintained. Directly engaged in overseas developments, especially in America, he was a key figure in government finance, notable during the Napoleonic Wars, when he was a negotiator in the Louisiana Purchase (1802).

Barnard, Christian (born 1922) South African surgeon, the first man to transplant the human heart (1967).

Barnard, Edward Emerson (1857-1923) American astronomer who discovered 16 comets. Barnard was a pioneer of astronomical photography, and at the Lick Observatory, California, made an important series of photographs of the Milky Way. He discovered Jupiter's fifth satellite by direct observation, and photographed a nebulous ring of matter ejected from Nova Auriga. In 1895, while at Yerkes Observatory, he showed that the dark 'lanes' in the Milky Way are caused by dust obstructing starlight.

Barnardo, Thomas (1845-1905) English physician and philanthropist, founder of the Dr Barnardo Homes for destitute children. While a medical student at the London Hospital, Barnardo determined to devote himself to the care of homeless orphans he had seen abandoned in the streets of London's East End. By 1870 he had raised enough money to found the first home for boys in Stepney. The number of homes grew rapidly, and they still flourish today, providing shelter and education for orphans.

Barnum, Phineas T. (1810-91) American showman who, in the 1880s, with James Bailey, staged the world-famous circus known as 'The Greatest Show on Earth'.

Baroja, Pio (1872-1956) Leading 20th-century Spanish novelist, who belonged to the 'Generation of 1898', a group of ex-anarchist and ex-Marxist writers who attacked Spanish traditions and tried to arouse Spain from its alleged decadence. Baroja was its most sceptical member and all his novels (he wrote over 100) show a total hostility to

any values other than that of vigorous action. Some deal with Basque and Spanish history, notably the Carlist wars; others, such as the *Struggle for Life* (1904), portray anarchist plots, long debates about Spanish regeneration or are simple adventure stories, such as *The Restlessness of Sandy Andia* (1911).

Barrie, Sir James Matthew (1860-1937) Scottish dramatist, who wrote *Peter Pan* (1904), *Dear Brutus* (1917) and *Mary Rose* (1920), sentimental fantasies for children. Among his other plays were *The Professor's Love Story* (1895), *Quality Street* (1903), *The Admirable Crichton* (1903) and *What Every Woman Knows* (1908).

Barry, Sir Charles (1795-1860) English architect of the Houses of Parliament, London (1839-52). His designs for the Travellers' Club and the Reform Club, London, draw their inspiraton from Italian Renaissance palatial architecture. His small Gothic churches, designs for castles and his conception of the Palace of Westminster are characterized by a controlled medievalism.

Barry, Comtesse du see DU BARRY, Comtesse

Barrymore, John (1882-1942) American actor and film-star, famous for his interpretation of Hamlet (1922 and 1925) and his 'great profile'. He was the brother of Ethel and Lionel Barrymore, who both performed in films and plays.

Barth, Heinrich (1821-65) German explorer and geographer of North Africa. With his compatriot Adolf Overweg, Barth joined James Richardson's British expedition to the Western Sudan, organized by the government to open up trade with the Sudan. The expedition left Tripoli (1850) and travelled south across the Sahara to Kano. Barth took control of it when Richardson died at Bornu, and – dogged by sickness – reached the Benue River from Lake Chad. The expedition then swung west and travelled more than 1000 miles to Timbuktu (previously reached by CAILLIÉ). Barth returned to Europe in 1855. His published account of the five-year marathon, *Travels and Discoveries in North and Central Africa* (1857-8), described the 10,000-mile journey and included the first description of the Middle Niger from Timbuktu to Say.

Barth, Karl (1886-1968) Swiss Protestant theologian who revolutionized 20th-century religious thought by breaking with rational theological systems and putting the humanity of JESUS and the concrete reality of God back into the centre of religious belief. His *Commentary on the Romans* (1922) marked the beginning of what is called dialectical or crisis theology. His violent opposition to the HITLER régime cost him his professorship at Bonn University.

Bartók, Béla (1881-1945) Hungary's foremost 20th-century composer. The main influences on Bartók as a young composer were LISZT, BRAHMS and Richard STRAUSS. From 1905, in collaboration with KODALY, he began to collect Balkan folk music. His discoveries influenced his composition and much of the 'modernism' in his own work which so attracted hostility during his lifetime was a result of his synthesizing the melodic and rhythmic elements of folk music. Bartók's most important compositions are the opera *Bluebeard's Castle* (1911) and the balletic mime play *The Miraculous Mandarin* (1919); his three piano concertos and his second violin concerto; *Mikrokosmos,* the set of 153 piano studies; the *Music for Strings, Percussion and Celesta* and the *Sonata for Two Pianos and Percussion.*

Baryshnikov, Mikhail (born 1948) International ballet dancer who was a member of the Kirov Ballet in Leningrad from 1967 until he defected from the USSR in 1974. He performed with the American Ballet Theatre (1974-8), the New York City Ballet (1978-9) and returned to the American Ballet Theatre as artistic director in 1980. He appeared in the film *The Turning Point* in 1977.

Bashoh see MATSUO BASHOH

Basie, William 'Count' (1904-84) American negro pianist and composer and leader of one of the few 'big bands' to survive the impact of small group jazz music.

Basil the Great (c. 330-79) One of the four great Greek Doctors of the Church. After visiting monastic centres all over the Eastern Empire, he settled at Annesi in Cappadocia and formed a monastic community of his own. Here he formulated a rule which is still the basis of monastic life in the Greek Orthodox Church, which enjoins both manual work and hours of liturgy.

Baskerville, John (1706-75) English printer and a major innovator in typography. In 1750 he began experiments in type-founding and set up his own printing house. In 1758 he published his edition of MILTON's works and was appointed printer to Cambridge University, where he printed the Bible, The Book of Common Prayer and the works of many Latin authors. The Baskerville typeface is commonly used today.

Bassano, Jacopo (c. 1510-92) Italian painter, of the Venetian school, whose work was at first much influenced by that of TITIAN. Later he developed a more individual style. He painted night scenes, rustic subjects and religious works, all of which tend to contain a large number of figures and animals. Genuine paintings by Bassano are rare.

Bateman, Henry (1887-1970) British humorous artist, who specialized in caricaturing the habits and manners of the upper and middle classes. His work, usually in sequence form, dealt largely with social gaffes or with trivial events that led to disaster; they were often depicted in colour, e.g. *The Man who Lit his Cigar before the Royal Toast*. Bateman's work, frequently represented in *Punch*, was popular in the 1920s and 1930s.

Bates, Henry Walter (1825-92) British naturalist who explored the Amazon Basin studying South American fauna. Bates travelled 1400 miles up the Amazon and collected 8000 previously unknown insect species. He published his discoveries in *The Naturalist on the Amazon* (1863). Bates's other principal contribution to biology was to perceive and explain the phenomenon of mimicry among separate insect species.

Bateson, William (1861-1926) English biologist who coined the term 'genetics'. His work on plant inheritance, based upon that of Gregor MENDEL, led him to conclude that certain characteristics are not inherited independently but invariably go together. This was later explained as gene linkage.

Batista y Zaldivar, Fulgencio (1901-73) Cuban dictator overthrown by Fidel CASTRO. He participated in the army revolt against President Machada in 1931-3, then led the coup that deposed Cespedes, the provisional President. He was elected President of Cuba (1940-4) and became provisional President again in 1952 after deposing President Prio. He was re-elected in 1954 and assumed dictatorial powers. His régime, noted for its harshness and brutality, was overthrown in 1959 and he fled to the Dominican Republic.

Baudelaire, Charles (1821-67) French poet and art critic, prosecuted for obscenity on the appearance of his volume of poems, *Les Fleurs du Mal* (1857). The subtle power of his language and his use of striking associations (*correspondances*) paved the way for the Symbolist movement and established Baudelaire among the greatest of French poets. He was an admirer of the works of Edgar Allan POE, and translated many of the American's works into French.

Bayer, Adolf von (1835-1917) German chemist and industrialist noted for his synthesis of organic chemicals, especially indigos and arsenical compounds. He was awarded a Nobel Prize for Chemistry in 1905.

Bayle, Pierre (1647-1706) French philosopher and lexicographer, who is regarded as the founder of 18th-century rationalism. His major work, the *Dictionnaire historique et critique* (1697), a collection of essays on topics ranging from philosophy and history to religion, is particularly important for its undermining of traditional beliefs, by the use of critical footnotes which occupy far more space than the main text. In this work, Bayle foreshadows the ironical style of the French *encyclopédistes*.

Baylis, Dame Lilian (1874-1937) British theatre manager, who founded the Old Vic and Sadler's Wells companies. As manager of the Victoria Theatre, later known as the Old Vic, she planned and presented opera, ballet and drama at popular prices, but her range of Shakespearian productions established the Old Vic's tradition of pure drama.

A graceful decadence and morbid atmosphere characterize Beardsley's work

Beardsley, Aubrey (1872-98) English illustrator, who was influential in the evolution of Art Nouveau, the international decorative style of the 1890s. His output was extensive and he had achieved an international reputation before his early death. His use of a flowing line with strongly contrasting blacks and whites was combined with a sensitive gift for decorative motifs. Among his best-known illustrations are those for WILDE's *Salomé,* POPE's *The Rape of the Lock,* and JONSON's *Volpone.*

Beatrix, Queen of the Netherlands (born 1938) Beatrix was the first child of the then Crown Princess Juliana and Prince Bernhard. She became heir presumptive in 1948 at the time of her mother's accession. Her marriage to West German diplomat Claus von Amsberg in 1966 was controversial, but her right was preserved. She became queen in 1980 when her mother abdicated in her favour.

Beaumarchais, Pierre de (1732-99) French dramatist, two of whose plays were the bases of operas by MOZART and ROSSINI. His first success, *The Barber of Seville* (Mozart), was presented at the Comédie Française in 1775. *The Marriage of Figaro,* a social satire, appeared in 1784.

Beaumont, Francis (c. 1584-1616) English dramatist, who, in collaboration with John FLETCHER, wrote ten plays. On his own, Beaumont wrote two comedies, *The Woman Hater* and *The Knight of the Burning Pestle.* Although contemporaries of SHAKESPEARE, Beaumont and Fletcher were more influenced by Ben JONSON.

Beaumont, William (1785-1853) American army surgeon whose *Experiments and Observations on the Gastric Juice and the Physiology of Digestion* (1833) is often called the greatest single contribution to the history of gastric physiology. Beaumont's approach was practical to a degree; he made his classic observations directly through a large unhealed fistula, or opening, in the stomach of a wounded patient. He was thus able to give an accurate and complete description of the gastric juice, including the identification of hycrochloric acid present.

Beauvoir, Simone de (born 1908) French novelist and essayist, concerned mainly with the Existentialist concept of the importance of freedom in a life subject to laws and controls. Together with SARTRE, she founded the literary review *Les Temps Modernes* (1946) and is the author of the treatise *Le Deuxième Sexe* (1949) and *Les Mandarins* (1954). Perhaps her most interesting works are the volumes of reminiscences – *Mémoires d'une Jeune Fille rangée* (1958) and *La Force de l'Age.*

Beaverbrook, William, 1st Baron (1879-1964) Canadian-born British politician and proprietor of mass-circulation newspapers. He became a financier (1900) and in 1910 moved to England to become first an MP and then Minister of Information in 1918. He gained control of the *Daily Express* (1916), the *Sunday Express* (1918) and the *Evening Standard* (1923), and set new standards in popular journalism, using the papers for his Empire Crusade (1930). In 1936 he tried to prevent EDWARD VIII'S abdication. A member of CHURCHILL'S government throughout the Second World War, be became Minister of Aircraft Production (1940-1), Minister of Supply (1941-2) and Minister of War Production (1942). As a supporter of the British Empire, he backed the Suez campaign in 1956 and opposed Britain's entry into the EEC.

Beccaria, Cesare (1738-94) Italian jurist and economist, who wrote the influential work on criminal law reform, *Crimes and Punishments* (1764). He denounced the savagery of contemporary trials and punishments, condemned torture, criticized the death penalty, urged that punishment should be commensurate with crime and stressed that it should aim to prevent it. In economics Beccaria pioneered the application of mathematics to economic analysis.

Becket, Thomas à (c. 1118-70) English saint, Archbishop of Canterbury, whose murder at Canterbury Cathedral after quarrelling with the king dramatized England's medieval Church-versus-State conflict. When HENRY II, whose friend he had been, made him Archbishop (1162), Becket angered Henry by zealously upholding the rights of the church against secular authority. In particular he refused to approve the Constitutions of Clarendon because they allotted to secular authorities the punishment of clerics convicted by ecclesiastical courts. Becket went into exile in France (1164-70), returning after a reconciliation with Henry, but within a month the quarrel was renewed. An unguarded expression of rage by Henry was acted on by four of his knights, who murdered Becket on the steps of the altar at Canterbury.

Beckett, Samuel (born 1906) Irish dramatist, novelist and poet who was awarded the Nobel Prize for Literature in 1969. He received international recognition with his play *Waiting for Godot* (1953), which is concerned with the absurdity of mankind's situation and has become a key work in the Theatre of the Absurd. Beckett's themes are characterized by a preoccupation with the Misery of man even in sophisticated societies. Death, decay and a vision of society bent on helpless self-destruction are themes which are found in *Endgame* (1957), *Krapp's Last Tape* (1960), *Happy Days* (1961), *Play* (1963), *Come and Go* (1965). Beckett ignores conventional dramatic structure and development and creates a static form made up of a loose series of images. Apart from his first novel, *Murphy* (1938), written in English, he mainly writes in French (he has lived in Paris since 1937). His other novels include *Malone Dies* (1951) and *The Unnamable* (1953).

Beckmann, Max (1884-1950) German Expressionist artist, influenced by Fauvism and Cubism, whose work usually embodied a social message.

Becquerel, Antoine Henri (1852-1908) French physicist who discovered radioactivity. In 1896, following Roentgen's discovery of X-rays, Becquerel investigated whether fluorescent substances give off X-rays as well as visible light and in 1901, after painstaking research, found an entirely new kind of radiation coming from within the uranium atoms in the fluorescent uranium salts. His colleague, Marie CURIE, named the phenomenon radioactivity.

Bede 'The Venerable' (673-735) English historian, theologian and scholar, whose *Ecclesiastical History of the English People* is the main source of knowledge of early English history. Bede, a Northumbrian priest, wrote more than 30 books, including a prose and a verse life of Cuthbert, and works on grammar and physical science.

Beerbohm, Sir Max (1872-1956) British caricaturist and satirist of intellectual and political society, who was at his most active during the 1890s. His best-known work is in *The Poet's Corner* (1904) and *Rossetti and his Circle* (1922). Although Max (as he signed himself) was only moderately talented as a draughtsman, his ability to catch a likeness and his sense of the ridiculous compensated for his technical limitations. He usually worked in line and wash, with or without colour. He was also a skilful literary parodist.

Beethoven, Ludwig van (1770-1827) German composer who brought the symphony to its peak as a form of musical expression. Beethoven first made his mark as a piano virtuoso, but in 1800 the opening performance of his First Symphony began the cycle that was to culminate in the great Ninth ('Choral') Symphony in 1824. Despite the handicap of growing deafness he sustained a remarkable output until 1812, the main works of the period including the Third ('Eroica', dedicated to NAPOLEON), Sixth ('Pastoral'), Seventh and Eighth Symphonies and the Fourth and Fifth ('Emperor') Piano Concertos. The opera *Fidelio* also belongs to this period (1804), its theme of the individual triumphing over despotism expressing Beethoven's political ideals. From 1812-17, the composer wrote little, but later he began work on the Mass in D (1824) and the Ninth Symphony. Beethoven, brought up as a Roman Catholic, abandoned this religion for an individual, pantheistic 'deism' of the kind expressed in Schiller's 'Ode to Joy', and a setting of this poem constituted the last choral movement of the Ninth.

Begin, Menachem (born 1913) Prime Minister of Israel (1977-83). He worked with Egyptian President Anwar SADAT to reach an agreement between their two countries. Begin and Sadat shared the Nobel Peace Prize in 1978. Winning re-election by a narrow margin in the 1981 parliamentary elections, Begin continued to maintain a hard line on Israel's security interests and on Israeli-occupied Judea, Samaria and Gaza, but his popularity fell during Israel's invasion of Lebanon (1982). He resigned office in 1983.

Behan, Brendan (1923-64) Irish dramatist, who wrote *The Quare Fellow* (1954), based on his experiences of Borstal, prison and the IRA. His next play, *The Hostage* (1958), was originally written in Gaelic. He started, but did not finish, a third, *Richard's Cork Leg*.

Behrens, Peter (1868-1938) German architect and pioneer of industrial design, the most influential and renowned of whose buildings is the Turbine Factory, Berlin (1909), which is completely lacking in ornament and has side walls of glass and steel. He first worked as an Art Nouveau painter-designer in Germany but his later involvement in industrial design led him to favour a severely functional approach. This he applied at all levels, from the design of miners' lamps to his vigorous and bold industrial buildings for the German AEG Electrical Company. His non-industrial work, exemplified by the German Embassy, St Petersburg (Leningrad), demonstrates his strong and forceful Neo-Classicism.

Behring, Emil von (1854-1917) German immunologist and winner of a Nobel Prize for Medicine in 1901, who with his Japanese colleague Shibasaburo Kitasato, demonstrated immunity to diphtheria and tetanus in animals. They showed that blood serum from animals that had been challenged by the toxins of either disease contained antitoxins which could confer a short-lived resistance when injected into man. In 1913 he found that a mixture of toxins and antitoxins gave more lasting immunity – a discovery that is the basis of modern immunization therapy.

Beiderbecke, Leon 'Bix' (1903-31) American jazz cornetist, pianist and composer. Self-taught, Beiderbecke was one of the first white musicians to achieve a status in jazz accorded normally to negro artistes, but wide recognition of his talent did not come until after his death.

Bekr, abu- see ABU-BAKR

Belínsky, Vissarión Grigórievich (1811-48) Russian critic and journalist, whose writings formed the basis of Russian literary criticism. He was largely responsible for the Russian conviction that literature should express ideas, and his anti-imaginative opinions still persist in Russia.

Belisarius (c. 505-65) Commander of the Byzantine army, who recovered much of the Western Roman Empire for the Eastern Emperor JUSTINIAN. He saved Justinian's throne by suppressing a revolt in Constantinople (532); crushed the Vandal kingdom in North Africa (534); drove THEODORIC's Ostrogoths from Italy (535-40); and fought Persia's Khosrau I in the east (541-2).

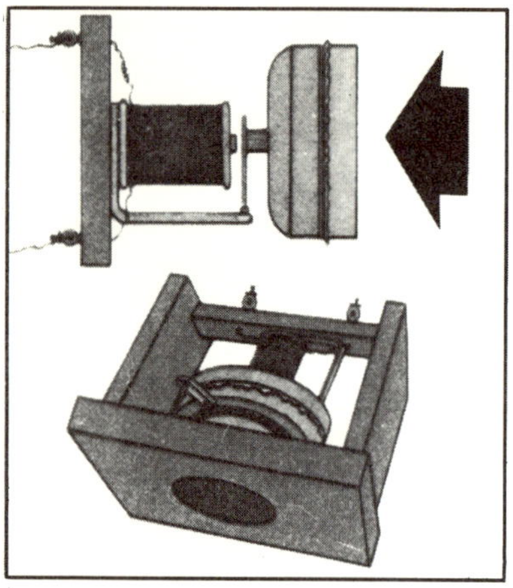

The prototype Bell telephone: the same diaphragm was used both for sending and receiving speech

Bell, Alexander Graham (1847-1922) Scottish-born American physicist and inventor who, in 1876, developed the first telephone. Bell's invention grew out of research in speech mechanics he had conducted while training teachers for the deaf. Among his other inventions were an electric probe for detecting bullets in the human body and the grooved wax cylinder with spiral sound track for Thomas EDISON's phonograph.

Bell, Sir Charles (1774-1842) British anatomist and surgeon, the first man to describe paralysis of the facial nerve, or Bell's palsy. He was also the first to show the difference between sensory and motor nerves and to prove that they sprang from different roots in the spinal column.

Bellini, Giovanni (c. 1430-1516) One of the leading artists of the Venetian school of painting, and an outstanding influence on classical painting in general. He maintained a large workshop and had many pupils, among them TITIAN, GIORGIONE and, briefly, TINTORETTO. Much of Bellini's work consists of altar-pieces and paintings of the Madonna and child, in both of which he evolved compositional formulae that were adopted by many later Venetian painters. His mature work is remarkable for its colour harmonies, which were of marked originality in their day. At the end of his life Bellini undertook a large-scale mythological picture (*The Feast of the Gods,* 1514), which was the starting point for Titian's later works in this grandiose and colourful genre.

Belloc, Hilaire (1870-1953) Naturalized English writer, born in France, who with CHESTERTON represented a view of the world which admired tradition and opposed the social ideas of SHAW and WELLS. Belloc was a poet, historian, social commentator and novelist; he handled serious subjects in a sprightly, paradoxical way.

Bellow, Saul (born 1915) American novelist, who has a particular sympathy for lonely, intelligent men, usually Jews, at grips with the problems of the contemporary world. In his early novels, *Dangling Man* (1944) and *The Victim* (1947), Bellow showed an awareness of psychology and a subtle understanding of relations between Jew and Gentile. *The Adventures of Augie March* (1953) and *Henderson the Rain King* (1959) are picaresque novels employing rich, colloquial language. Subsequent novels include *Herzog* (1964), *Humboldt's Gift* (1975) and *The Dean's December* (1982). He was awarded the Nobel Prize in Literature (1976).

Bembo, Pietro (1470-1547) Italian cardinal and scholar whose works were influential in establishing Italian as a literary language. A typeface bearing his name was cut to print one of his works.

Ben Bella, Mohammed (born 1919) Algerian politician who led resistance to the French, was twice arrested by them, escaped and directed the Algeria National Movement from exile (1952-6). Following independence, Ben Bella became Premier of Algeria, and President, by national referendum, in 1963. After overcoming a revolt in 1964, he was deposed in a coup led by BOUMEDIENNE in 1965 and detained in custody until 1980.

Benchley, Robert Charles (1889-1945) American journalist and humorist who wrote for various New York publications and acted in successful Hollywood film shorts. His humour was urbane, wry, and frequently self-directed.

Benedict of Nursia (c. 480-c.547) Italian saint, founder of the monastic order known by his name. Early in life, Benedict became disgusted by Roman dissipation and lived as a hermit. Although he had never been ordained, a community of monks asked him to become their abbot. This he accepted but was driven back to his hermitage, when, angered by his strict rule, the monks tried to poison him. He went on to organize a number of other small monastic communities and finally, in about 529, a monastery at Monte Cassino, where he founded his Benedictine Order.

Beneš, Eduard (1884-1948) Czech statesman and co-founder of Czech independence. Of peasant birth, he was educated at the universitites of Prague, Dijon, Paris, Berlin and London, and in 1915 joined MASARYK in Paris to work for Czechoslovakian independence. Success at the Paris Peace Conference resulted in his becoming Foreign Minister of the new State (1918-35). Beneš was President of his country when, in 1938, by the Munich Agreement between HITLER and CHAMBERLAIN, Britain and France abandoned it to the Nazis. As a result, Beneš resigned. He became President of the Czechoslovak government-in-exile in London (1941-5), after which he returned to Prague. He had, however, lost the confidence of STALIN, and consequently lost control of the government to the communists, who were protected by Russia, and was forced to resign. He died soon afterwards.

Benet, Stephen Vincent (1898-1943) American poet, who wrote 'John Brown's Body' (1928), a long narrative poem about the American Civil War. Most of his major works in poetry and prose explored American National character, history and legend. Benet's historical short stories achieved more popularity than his novels.

Ben Gurion, David (1886-1973) Israeli statesman and politician and architect of the independent state of Israel. Polish-born, he settled in Palestine in 1906 and was exiled by the Turks in 1915. As a Zionist and an Allied sympathizer, he helped to organize the Jewish Legion in America and fought in it under ALLENBY. In 1930 he became leader of the Mapai (Labour) Party, and Chairman of the Jewish Agency for Palestine (1935-48), proclaiming independence of Israel in 1948. He was Prime Minister and Minister of Defence of the new state, 1949-53 and 1955-63, when he resigned, though remaining in the Knesset.

Bennett, Arnold (1867-1931) English novelist whose reputation rests mainly on his regional novels, depicting the life of his native area, the Potteries, an area of Staffordshire, England. His best-known work is *The Old Wives' Tale* (1908), a finely detailed, naturalistic novel depicting the lives of the daughters of a draper. *Anna of the Five Towns* (1902) offers a picture of life in a provincial Wesleyan community; Bennett also depicted Potteries life in short stories. Bennett also wrote a mass of prose for magazines.

Bentham, Jeremy (1748-1832) English philosopher, legal and economic theorist and reformer, and one of the chief proponents of Utilitarianism, whose central doctrine states that all human action must be aimed at producing the greatest happiness for the greatest number. It is by this criterion, Bentham said, that a man must judge the law and all other social institutions and practices that he might wish to reform.

Benz, Karl (1844-1929) German pioneer of the internal combustion engine designed specifically for the propulsion of vehicles, and, hence, of the modern automobile. After some success with an earlier two-stroke in 1885 which, first applied to a tricycle, achieved great success when installed in a four-wheel vehicle in 1893. Benz was the first man to make and sell light, self-propelled vehicles built to a standardized pattern. Hundreds had been built by the turn of the century.

Berg, Alban (1885-1935) Austrian composer and one of SCHOENBERG's leading disciples. He met Schoenberg in 1904 and won recognition with his opera *Wozzeck,* first performed in 1925, which vindicated the new atonal methods of his teacher. The progression of his style may be traced from the opera through the *Chamber Concerto* (1925) and the *Lyric Suite* (1925-6), to the unfinished but powerful 12-note opera *Lulu* (1937), taken from WEDEKIND's play *Pandora's Box.*

Bergius, Friedrich (1884-1949) German chemist, who developed a method of treating coal or heavy oil with hydrogen to produce petrol. The Bergius process was introduced in 1912 and allowed German industry to produce gasoline independently of imported crude oil.

Bergman, Ingmar (born 1918) Swedish director of the theatre and cinema whose international reputation rests mainly on his work for the latter. Bergman is singular among film makers for his use of 'repertory' actors, giving his work a rare homogeneity. Stylistically he is best known for his mystical, expressionist, heavily symbolic films, including *The Seventh Seal* (1956), a medieval allegory with its famous personification of a chess-playing Death, which first established him internationally. More recent films by Bergman include *Cries and Whispers* (1972), *Scenes from a Marriage* (1974), *Autumn Sonata* (1978) and *Fanny and Alexander* (1980).

Bergson, Henri (1859-1941) French philosopher and author of many works, including *Creative Evolution* (1906). A revolutionary and influential study of experience, it stressed intuition as the source of experience and saw the evolution of matter as affected by the *élan vital,* a disorderly, constantly diverging life-force, producing new from old. An important influence on Marcel PROUST, Bergson too was concerned with the nature of time, which he saw as an inner 'duration' – the true reality. He was awarded the Nobel Prize in Literature (1927).

Beria, Lavrenti Pavlovich (1899-1953) Soviet politician and police chief, notorious for his harsh methods as STALIN's deputy. A Georgian of peasant stock, he was made Commissar for Internal Affairs (1938), and engineered the execution of his predecessor Yezhov, who had organized Stalin's 'purge' trials. He became deputy Prime Minister in 1941, and Stalin's principal Minister during the Second World War. Following Stalin's death (1953) he ruled briefly with MALENKOV and MOLOTOV and tried to use his secret police to make himself dictator, but was arrested, tried and executed.

Bering, Vitus Jonassen (1680-1741) Danish navigator who showed that Asia and America are separated by sea and discovered Alaska. He served in the Russian Navy and was commissioned by PETER THE GREAT to determine whether Siberia and North America were linked by land. Sailing from Eastern Siberia's Kamchatka River (1728), Bering pushed north through the sea and strait (later named after him) to latitude 67°18′, and concluded that the strait separated Asia from America.

Berio, Luciano (born 1925) Italian composer who, with STOCKHAUSEN, pioneered spatial effects in modern music. The pieces in an orchestral or vocal cycle may be switched round to create new relationships, or the order of certain groups of notes may be varied. Much of his music, including his simpler *Folk Songs,* has been written for Cathy Berberian, the American soprano who was for a time his wife.

Berkeley, George (1685-1753) Irish idealist philosopher who held that material phenomena exist only in so far as we perceive them; the universe is a constant perception in the mind of God. *Treatise concerning the principles of Human Knowledge* (1710) and *Three dialogues between Hylas and Philonous* (1713) expound his doctrine.

Berlin, Irving (born 1888) American of Russian birth and self-taught composer of some of the most popular songs ever written. Berlin, whose real name is Izzy Baline, began as a singing waiter in bars in New York's Bowery. 'Alexander's Ragtime Band' (1911) was his first big hit. His many other songs include 'I'm Dreaming of a White Christmas', 'Cheek to Cheek' and 'How Deep is the Ocean?' He wrote the Broadway musical *Call Me Madam* (1950).

Berlioz, Hector (1803-69) Leading French composer of the Romantic era. Berlioz was intended by his father, a provincial doctor, to study medicine, but soon switched to music. One of the most likeable personalities in the history of Romantic music, Berlioz composed almost always on a large scale, often demanding massive forces. His structural weaknesses were more than offset by his vitality, subtlety of orchestral tone colour and originality. Berlioz's choral works include *The Childhood of Christ, The Damnation of Faust* and a fine setting of the *Requiem.* He wrote overtures, including *Les Francs Juges* and *Roman Carnival.* His symphonies were the *Symphonie Fantastique, Harold in Italy* (after BYRON) and *Romeo and Juliet* (after SHAKESPEARE). His operas include *Benvenuto Cellini, Beatrice and Benedict* as well as his masterpiece, *The Trojans,* of which complete performances are rare owing to its scale and production demands.

Bernadette (1844-79) French saint whose visions of the Virgin Mary resulted in the establishment of Lourdes as a healing shrine and one of the greatest places of pilgrimage in Christendom. She was born in Lourdes, and her 18 visions of the Virgin Mary (who appeared to Bernadette as a beautiful lady) in 1858 occurred in a cave on the River Gave. Admitted to the Convent of the Sisters of Charity at Nevers, she died in 1879 and was canonized in 1933.

Bernard of Clairvaux (1091-1153) French religious reformer, who rallied his fellow countrymen to the Second Crusade (which began in 1147). Under his influence the Cistercian Order of monks grew so rapidly that by the time Bernard died, there were 388 Cistercian monasteries in existence, 68 of them direct foundations from his own abbey at Clairvaux. As his reputation as an orator grew, Bernard was invited to intervene in important Church matters of administration and policy. In theology, he advocated the worship of the Virgin Mary and is said to have originated Christocentrism. He was canonized in 1174.

Bernard, Claude (1813-78) French physiologist, who was the first to show that the pancreas had a function in the digestion of sugar and protein, and that the liver could take the sugars that were broken down in digestion and build them up into a more complex sugar known as glycogen. This was the first time that anyone had shown that the body could actually build up substances on its own. He also discovered the existence of vasomotor nerves (the nerves that control the diameter and tension of the blood vessls and so direct the blood supply to various parts of the body).

Bernhardt, Sarah (1844-1923) French actress, often considered the outstanding tragedienne of the late 19th century. She first became known through her Cordelia in *King Lear* (1872). Her most famous role was Phèdre; among her other outstanding roles were Marguérite in *The Lady of the Camelias* and the Queen in *Ruy Blas*. She also played Hamlet and other male roles, such as NAPOLEON's son in Rostand's *L'Aiglon*.

Bernini, Gianlorenzo (1598-1680) Italian sculptor, mostly in marble, who influenced the Italian Baroque style. In the Vatican, Bernini worked as an architect as well as a sculptor and designed the Piazza of St Peter's. The intensity of Bernini's religious feelings made him a suitable interpreter of the upsurge of religious emotion during the Counter-Reformation, as can be seen in the *Ecstasy of St Teresa*.

Bernoulli, Daniel (1700-82) Swiss doctor and mathematician, whose most important work. *Hydrodynamica* (1738), deals with the theory of statics and the motion of fluids. He found practical uses for his theories; for example, their relation to the propulsion of ships.

Bernoulli, Jakob (1654-1705) Swiss mathematician, who worked on the theory of infinite series, studied various special curves and laid the foundations of the calculus of variations. This he developed after LIEBNIZ had discovered infinitesimal calculus and about which they corresponded.

Bernoulli, Johann (1667-1748) Swiss mathematician and the first to use 'g' to denote acceleration due to gravity. He worked on various problems of calculus, particularly the properties of curves, his work overlapping with that of his brother Jakob BERNOULLI, whom he succeeded at Basel University in 1705.

Bernstein, Leonard (born 1918) American composer and conductor whose best-known work is his score for the musical *West Side Story* (1957), with its choreography by Jerome ROBBINS. Bernstein's compositions show widely ranging influences, from atonality and the Jewish liturgy to jazz and various forms of popular music. His other works include a symphony *The Age of Anxiety* (1944), the operetta *Candide,* based on VOLTAIRE's story, and another musical *On the Town* (1944). As a conductor, Bernstein has shown himself to be an outstanding interpreter of the music of IVES and COPLAND, and MAHLER.

Berruguete, Alonso (c. 1489-1561) Spanish architect and artist who, as court painter to CHARLES V, undertook a number of altars which incorporated painting, carved reliefs and statues in architectural settings. An outstanding sculptor, Berruguete was the founder of the Mannerist style in Spain.

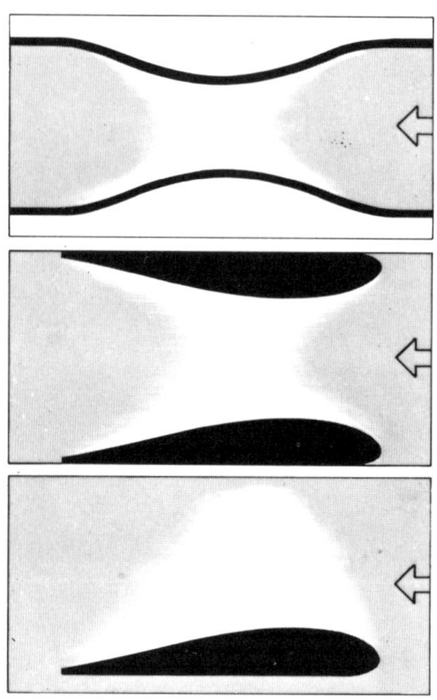

Daniel Bernoulli's *Hydrodynamica* of the 18th century propounded principles which hold good today in explaining the theory of flight. Top, constricted air is speeded up. Centre, pressure drops on the upper surfaces of aerofoils when placed in the stream. Bottom, the same applies to one aerofoil, causing the lift conditions that give rise to a plane's flight

Berry, Chuck (born 1926) American singer and composer of rock and roll music. He plays the guitar, saxophone and piano, has been on many concert tours and made numerous television appearances since 1955, and has had a great influence on the development of rock and roll music. His most famous records include *Johnny B. Goode, Rock and Roll Music, Roll Over Beethoven* and *Louis Louis*.

Berthollet, Claude Louis (1748-1822) French chemist, who established the 'Law of Mass Action', the basis to the control and understanding of chemical reactions. In 1803, he suggested that the readiness with which two substances react together depends on their masses. But it was not until 1863 that another chemist, Guldberg, showed that concentrations (not masses) determine the rate at which substances react.

Berzelius, Jöns (1779-1848) Swedish chemist who prepared the first accurate lists of atomic weights by analysing compounds. He used oxygen as the standard to which all other weights were referred. His other contributions to chemistry included work on electrolysis, organic radicals, catalysts and chemical nomenclature and notation.

Bessel, Friedrich (1784-1846) German astronomer and mathematician, who was the founder of modern precision work in observational astronomy. His important work on HALLEY's comet in 1804 led within six years to his appointment as Director of Königsberg Observatory. In 1838, he was the first man to calculate accurately the distance of a star from Earth.

Bessemer, Sir Henry (1813-98) English metallurgist, who pioneered the large-scale manufacture of steel by decarbonizing iron. The underlying principle of his invention, announced in 1856, was that carbon could be removed by blowing air through the molten metal. Bessemer's process, and subsequent improvements by SIEMENS, began the era of cheap steel.

Best, Charles (1899-1978) Canadian physiologist who, with F. G. BANTING, discovered insulin treatment for diabetes.

Betjeman, Sir John (1906-84) English poet who wrote with affection of out-of-the-way places, odd views, old Victorian buildings and the little formalities and pretensions of suburban living. His poems show neat observation expressed in clear, witty language, and often have a pleasantly nostalgic tone. In 1972 he was appointed Poet Laureate.

Betti, Ugo (1892-1953) Italian dramatist, who wrote *The Burnt Flowerbed* (1953). His other plays, *Corruption in the Palace of Justice* (1949), *Crime on Goat Island* (1950) and *The Joker* (1951), although performed in Italy, were unknown in Britain and America until his death.

Bevan, Aneurin (1897-1960) Welsh Labour politician of mining stock and architect of the National Health Service, introduced in 1948 when he was Minister of Health (1945-51). After a brief period as Minister of Labour in 1951, he resigned because of the Health Service charges introduced by GAITSKELL, and thereafter, throughout the early 1950s, the rivalry between the two was tense and often bitter. In 1956, however, he reached agreement with Gaitskell and after supporting him in opposition to unilateral nuclear disarmament in 1957, they grew closer together. Bevan was a brilliant, and often colourful and irreverant orator. He became deputy leader of the Labour Party after the election of 1959.

Beveridge, William Henry, 1st Baron Tuggal (1879-1963) English economist and founder of the British 'Welfare State'. An authority on unemployment insurance, he was responsible for much of the thinking behind the social legislation introduced by LLOYD GEORGE. Under his directorship (1909-16) labour exchanges were established. In 1941 Beveridge was appointed Chairman of the Committee on Social Insurance and Allied Services. Practically all the major recommendations embodied in the Committee's report, called the 'Beveridge Report' (1942), were adopted by the 1945 administration.

Bevin, Ernest (1881-1951) English Labour politician and former trade union organizer who rose to be his country's Foreign Secretary. A farm labourer at first, he became a docker and, in 1911, assistant general secretary of the dockers' union. By 1921 he had combined about 50 unions into the world's largest, the Transport and General Workers' Union. He became a member of the Trades Union Congress General Council in 1925 and its Chairman in 1937, playing a considerable part in organizing the General Strike of 1926 and in the negotiations which concluded it. An outspoken opponent of Fascism, Bevin was appointed Minister of Labour in CHURCHILL's 1940 Second World War government and Foreign Secretary in ATTLEE's government (1945-51).

Beyle, Henri see STENDHAL

Bhave, Acharya Vinoba (1895-1982) Indian philosopher. An ardent disciple and pupil of GANDHI, he founded the *Bhoodan* ('land-gift') and *Sarvadoya* ('welfare for all') movements in 1951 as his answer to the problem of malnutrition and hunger riots. What started as a barefoot mission throughout India to persuade the wealthy to give up their land resulted in the donation to the poor of over five million acres. Bhave is regarded in India as the most notable ascetic and 'saint' since Gandhi.

Bichat, Marie François (1771-1802) French anatomist, pathologist and physiologist, who founded the science of histology (the study of tissues).

Biddle, John (c. 1615-62) English schoolmaster and theologian, called the 'Father of English Unitarianism'. He refuted the deity of the Holy Ghost in a tract known as *Twelve Arguments* (1647), for which he was imprisoned, issued two further tracts on the subject, but was released under surveillance after CHARLES I's death. After the Act of Oblivion (1652) gave him complete freedom, he held Sunday meetings of his followers, who were called Biddellians or Unitarians. Biddle's later attacks on the doctrines of the established Church resulted in more spells in prison, where he ultimately died.

Bierce, Ambrose (1842-c. 1914) American satirist and short story writer who wrote with a sardonic, cynical wit, mixing the graphic descriptive powers of the newspapermen with the gloom of his own nature. His stories from the Civil War, *Tales of Soldiers and Civilians* (1891), are authentic records of the grimness of the conflict. He disappeared on a visit to Mexico, which was in the grip of civil war.

Billy the Kid (1859-81) American outlaw whose full name was William H. Bonney, and who became one of the most infamous gunmen of the American southwest – ranking in Wild West history with figures like Jesse JAMES and Sam Bass. Caught in 1880, and sentenced to be hanged for three murders, he escaped from gaol in 1881 after killing two deputies, but was tracked down and shot by Lincoln County sheriff, Pat Garrett.

Binet, Alfred (1857-1911) French psychologist who produced an early set of scales for measuring intelligence and educational attainment and who pioneered the use of pictures and inkblots to detect emotions and prejudices. Rejecting the emphasis which his German contemporaries were placing on the study of elementary reactions and sensations, he devised ingenious experiments to test the higher mental processes.

Bingham, Hiram (1875-1956) American explorer-archaeologist whose discovery, in 1911, of the Inca mountain city of Machu Picchu in the Peruvian Andes, helped historians to retell the story of Peru before PIZARRO.

Birdseye, Clarence (1886-1956) American industrialist and inventor who developed a technique for deep-freezing foods. The first Birds Eye commercial pack was placed on the market in 1929. With most foods, the thawed-out items prove to be more palatable, and often more nutritious, than canned foods.

Birkenhead, F. E. Smith, 1st Earl of (1872-1930) English barrister, politician and law reformer, a brilliant orator and wit. In the House of Commons he supported CARSON in opposing Home Rule for Northern Ireland, but as Lord Chancellor (1919-22) negotiated the Irish Treaty (1921). He initiated a major reform and simplification of England land law, which achieved lasting form in the Law of Property Acts of 1922 and 1925 and other statutes.

Bismarck, Prince Otto von (1815-98) German statesman and creator of a united, imperial Germany. Bismarck came from a Junker family, an ultra-royalist who favoured a powerful army, a strong Protestant church and the suppression of democracy. He believed in German unity, but only if it could be achieved under Prussian leadership. He served as ambassador to Russia and France (1859-62) and on his return to Prussia was appointed Chancellor. Bismarck concentrated on strengthening the Prussian army, despite parliamentary opposition, and turned his attention to making Prussia the dominant force in Europe. His ambitions were realized in the successful war against Denmark (1864) and in the Austro-Prussian and Franco-Prussian wars

(1866 and 1870). He became Chancellor of Germany when the Empire was proclaimed in 1871, was created a prince and for the next nineteen years dominated European diplomacy. In domestic policy the codification of the law, nationalization of the railways and a continuing emphasis on military efficiency were means by which Bismarck reinforced the German state. After the accession of the youthful WILLIAM II (1888), Bismarck's régime was challenged by the new expansionist Pan-German movement and he was dismissed by the Kaiser in 1890.

Bizet, Georges (1838-75) French composer who wrote the opera *Carmen* (1875), based on a story of romantic passion and death in Spain by MERIMÉE. All his life he strove for recognition as a composer of opera, and in addition to *Carmen* wrote *The Pearl Fishers* (1863) and *The Fair Maid of Perth* (1866). But apart from *Carmen*, almost his only works remembered today are the two orchestral suites based on incidental music to DAUDET's *L'Arlésienne* and the early *Symphony in C.*

Bjerknes, Vilhelm (1862-1951) Norwegian physicist and meteorologist who, with his son Jakob (born 1897), developed weather forecasting based on the concepts of air masses and polar fronts. In 1897, he discovered the circulation theorems which led to the development of physical hydrodynamics. This, in turn, made possible the scientific study of wind and water movements on a global scale. After the First World War they showed that cyclonic depressions (which largely determine weather in middle latitudes) are made up of two air masses: one warm and moist (from the tropics), and the other cold and dry (from the polar regions). The two are separated by a sloping interface which they called a polar front – a zone of fast-changing weather conditions.

Black, Joseph (1728-99) Scottish chemist and physicist who originated the ideas of specific and latent heat. In the 1760s, he found that as ice is heated, it melts with no immediate temperature rise. He explained this by introducing the concept of latent heat, the heat absorbed by a substance changing state, such as from solid to liquid, without a temperature rise.

Blackbeard (17th-18th cent.) English pirate called Edward Teach, notorious for his depredations along the Virginia and North Carolina coast and in the Caribbean Sea, where he blockaded ports and plundered ships. In 1718, the Governor of Virginia sent two sloops against him, and after a fierce battle he was killed, his head being taken to Virginia as a trophy.

Blackstone, Sir William (1723-80) English jurist whose *Commentaries on the Laws of England* (1765-9) is the most influential work in the later development of the common law in England and America. The four volumes concern the rights of persons, the rights of things, public wrongs and private wrongs. Although oversimplified and antiquarian, his work was a law book both comprehensible to the layman and of exceptional authority to the lawyer. He was the first professor of law at Oxford (1758), a Member of Parliament and a Judge of the Court of Common Pleas (1770).

Blackwell, Elizabeth (1821-1910) American physician, the first woman to qualify as a doctor of medicine. In the face of tremendous opposition, she finally gained admission to Geneva Medical School, New York, where she was ostracized by her fellow students and the public. She graduated in 1849 at the head of her class, but the loss of an eye forced her to abandon her ambition of becoming a surgeon, and she established a hospital run entirely by women in New York in 1857.

Blair, Eric see ORWELL, George

Blake, Robert (1599-1657) English admiral and general outstandingly successful against four separate enemies. In the English Civil War, Blake destroyed RUPERT's Royalist squadron off Spain (1650) and captured 17 treasure ships of the Portuguese, who had sheltered Rupert. During the Dutch War (1652-3) he repeatedly clashed with Dutch fleets and ended their naval supremacy. In 1654 he scoured the Mediterranean exacting from North African pirate states reparations for damage done to British merchants and severely damaged Tunis for resisting. During the Spanish War he sank a Spanish treasure fleet in the strongly defended harbour of Santa Cruz (Tenerife). Meanwhile he did much to improve English naval tactics and discipline.

Blake, William (1757-1827) English artist, engraver and poet of the Romantic movement who, using his own process of engraving from etched copper plates, which he called 'illuminated printing', produced volumes of his own verse, illustrated and coloured by hand. In 1789 he published *Songs of Innocence* and in 1794 *Songs of Experience,* among the best known of his lyrical poems. In 1793 he wrote *The Marriage of Heaven and Hell,* a prose work, heavy with mysticism and etched with symbolic and mythological designs. He is most famous for his brilliant series of original illustrations of the Book of Job (1825), and, at the time of his death, was working on a set of engravings to illustrate DANTE. Almost unrecognized in his own day, Blake's poetry later influenced RUSKIN and the Pre-Raphaelites. As an artist, he achieved recognition only late in his life, though he is now remembered for his engravings rather than for his poetry.

Blanc, Jean Charles Louis (1811-82) French socialist, writer and politician, and publisher of *L'Organisation du Travail* (1840), in which he denounced the capitalist principle of competitive industry and proposed both a theory of equal wages and a system of state-subsidized workshops. His *L'Histoire de Dix Ans,* was a criticism of the régime of LOUIS PHILLIPE and contributed to the unrest which led to the Revolution of 1848. In that year he became a member of the Provisional Government and headed an industrial commission to consider the problem of unemployment. His idea of 'National Workshops' was unpractical in the turmoil of the revolutionary situation, and he was forced to flee to England after the left wing of the Revolution was suppressed in June 1848. He did not return to France until 1871.

Blanchard, Jean Pierre (1753-1809) French pioneer balloonist who in 1784, with the American aeronaut John Jeffries, became the first to measure air temperatures from a manned balloon. In this way, he extended the meteorological experiments of Alexander WILSON and anticipated those of Hermite. In 1785 Blanchard and Jeffries made the first air crossing of the English Channel (Dover–Calais) and delivered the first international airmail consignment. Blanchard's other aeronautical 'firsts' included the first parachute drop (of a cat or a dog) from a balloon in 1785, and the first balloon ascents in England (1784) and America (1793).

Blanqui, Louis August (1805-81) French socialist who took part in the French Revolution of 1830. After attempting insurrection (1839) Blanqui suffered numerous terms of imprisonment. Having served a ten-year sentence imposed by the Provisional Government after the Revolution of 1848 on a fabricated charge of treason, he led the working class and socialist Central Republican Party and formulated his ideas about socialism and the dictatorship of the proletariat as the only means of achieving Communism. Blanqui was active in the downfall of NAPOLEON III and inspired the Paris Commune (1871), though he was in custody.

Blasco Ibañez, Vicente (1867-1928) Spanish naturalist writer and republican politician, author of *Blood and Sand* (1908) and *The Four Horsemen of the Apocalypse* (1916).

Blavatsky, Helena (1831-91) Russian spiritualist, founder of Theosophy (a mystical philosophy loosely based on Indian religious thought) and co-founder, with Colonel Henry Olcott, of the Theosophical Society, in 1875. Madame Blavatsky claimed direct access to 'divine truth' by psychic communication with invisible Indian 'masters' and outlined her revelations in two popular textbooks of the occult: *Isis Unveiled* (1877) and *The Secret Doctrine* (1888).

Blaxland, Gregory (1778-1853) English-born pioneer in Australia who (with William Lawson and William Wentworth) first crossed the Blue Mountains of New South Wales. In 1810 he explored up the Warragamba River and in 1813 crossed the gorges of the Blue Mountains, discovering Mount Blaxland and the Bathurst Plains.

Blériot, Louis (1872-1936) French aircraft designer and aviator who, in 1909, became the first man to fly across the English Channel. The flight from Calais to Dover took 37 minutes. As a designer Blériot was responsible for a number of design innovations, including a system by which the pilot could operate elevators and ailerons by remote control.

Bligh, William (1754-1817) British naval officer, captain of the mutinous crew of the 220-ton *Bounty*. As Captain COOK's master, Bligh discovered breadfruit on Tahiti and his voyage in the *Bounty* was to introduce breadfruit trees to the West Indies. His crew, led by the mate, Fletcher CHRISTIAN, were disenchanted with his leadership and sought to end the voyage and settle on a Pacific island with their Tahitian mistresses. They seized the ship near the Friendly Islands and cast Bligh adrift with 18 sailors in the open longboat. After a 45-day voyage of 4000 miles, Bligh reached Timor in Indonesia. A master seaman and navigator, Bligh later distinguished himself at the Battles of Camperdown and Copenhagen.

Bliss, Sir Arthur (1891-1975) English composer, once regarded as an *enfant terrible,* who reached the peak of the English musical establishment by becoming Master of the Queen's Musick (1953). Bliss developed an early reputation for unorthodox combinations of instruments, but a strong sense of pageantry revealed itself in his *Colour Symphony* (1922). His choral symphony *Morning Heroes* was performed in 1930, and in 1935 he wrote the score for the film *Things to Come*. His ballet scores include *Checkmate* and *Miracle in the Gorbals*.

Bloch, Ernst (1880-1959) Swiss-born American composer. His finest compositions *Piano Quintet* (1923) and the second two of his four string quartets rank among the most distinguished 20th-century chamber works. Bloch's Jewish ancestry was acknowledged in his best-known works, which include a rhapsody for cello and orchestra, *Schelomo* (1916), and the *Sacred Service* (1933) for baritone, chorus and orchestra for the Jewish Sabbath morning service.

Blok, Aleksandr Aleksandrovich (1880-1921) Russian poet whose poem 'The Twelve' (1918) is a mystical, Symbolist story of twelve Red Guardsmen, analogous to the Apostles, and an apologia for the Bolshevik Revolution. Blok was the outstanding poet of the Symbolist school who felt that his poetry could be understood only by those who were in sympathy with his mystical experience. His best work was written between 1908 and 1916 and is contained in the third volume of his poems *Verses about Russia*.

Blériot (right) with another intrepid French birdman, Pegoud

Blondin, Charles (1824-97) French equilibrist, who became the world's most famous tightrope walker for his crossing of Niagara Falls in 1859. He repeated this feat many times, with startling variations: crossing blindfolded, on stilts, in a sack, pushing a wheelbarrow carrying a man, and even stopping to cook and eat an omelette.

Blood, Col. Thomas (c. 1618-80) Irish adventurer who, in 1671, planned and carried out the theft of the Crown Jewels from the Tower of London. Arrested while trying to escape, he was imprisoned in the Tower, though later pardoned by King CHARLES II.

Bloomer, Amelia (1818-94) American women's rights campaigner. She founded and edited the *Lily,* the first American magazine for women, and wrote articles on education, unjust marriage laws and female suffrage. As part of her campaign for the emancipation of women she popularized the full trousers, then known as 'bloomers'.

Bloomfield, Leonard (1887-1949) American linguistics scholar and author of *Language* (1933), which has exercised an important influence on the American approach to linguistics. Bloomfield was one of the Structuralist school of linguistic theorists, using the strictly scientific approach which is now considered his main contribution to linguistics.

Blücher, Gebhard von (1742-1819) Prussian field-marshal who acted as commander-in-chief in the final stages of the Napoleonic wars. He commanded the army of the Lower Rhine and after NAPOLEON's return from Elba, was wounded and defeated at Ligny two days before Waterloo (1815). Nevertheless, he succeeded in joining forces with WELLINGTON, and ensured the defeat of the French.

Blum, Léon (1872-1950) French politician and socialist leader in the inter-war years. The DREYFUS affair (1898-9) helped to form his socialist convictions and brought him into contact with JAURÈS, whose disciple he became. He became Prime Minister when, in 1936, the Popular Front government of Left and Centre parties, opposed to Fascism, took office. His economic policy was based on the

Keynesian idea of invigorating the economy by stimulating purchasing power, but inflation and financial crises prevented its application. His government was sabotaged by pro-Fascist industrial and financial interests, and his resignation was forced, but he was again Prime Minister for a short time in 1938. In 1942 he was tried at Riom by the Vichy government of PÉTAIN, charged with being responsible for France's military unpreparedness, but defended himself so ably that he fixed the responsibility for that failure on his accusers. Blum was interned in Germany until 1945, but on his release became head of France's caretaker government of 1946-7.

Blunden, Edmund (1896-1974) English poet whose best work has been his sad, pitying reflections on his experiences in the First World War, yet drawing strength from a love of nature. *Poems 1914-30* and the prose work *Undertones of War* (1928) are moving recollections of that time. He was Professor of Poetry at Oxford (1966-8).

Blunt, Anthony Frederick (1907-83) English art historian and spy for the Soviet Union. He met PHILBY, Burgess and MACLEAN at Cambridge, from where he started spying. He worked in British Intelligence during the war and passed information to the Russians. In 1951 he helped Burgess and Maclean to defect. After Philby's defection in 1964, Blunt confessed and was given immunity in return. His spying activities were only made public in 1979, when Andrew Boyle's book exposing Blunt, *A Climate of Treason,* was published. His knighthood was annulled in that year. A distinguished art historian, he was Director of the Courtauld Institute of Art (1947-74) and Surveyor of the Queen's Pictures (1945-72).

Blyth, Chay (born 1940) Scottish yachtsman who circumnavigated the world solo (1970-1), held the record for sailing the Atlantic, from Cape Verde to Antigua (1977), won the Round Britain race (1978) and the Observer/Europe I double-handed transatlantic race with Robert James in record time (1981).

Boadicea (1st cent. AD) British Queen of the Iceni tribe who rebelled against the Romans after they had seized the lands of her late husband, Prasutagus, King of the Iceni. All East Anglia, and south-eastern Britain rose under Boadicea while the Roman governor Paulinus was in Wales. TACITUS said that Boadicea burnt Roman Colchester and St Albans, killing 70,000 Romans and British collaborators before Paulinus annihilated her army near Fenny Stratford. Boadicea either died of shock or poisoned herself, but her revolt supposedly persuaded NERO to ease conditions for the British. Her statue at the reins of her chariot, looks across Westminster Bridge towards the Houses of Parliament in London.

Queen Boadicea led the Iceni of eastern England in revolt against the Romans

Boas, Franz (1858-1942) American anthropologist and pioneer of American-Indian studies, whose *Changes in Bodily Form in Descendants of Immigrants* (1911) demonstrates that cranial proportions, previously considered as a racial characteristic, adapt according to environment. His *Handbook of American-Indian Languages* (1911) marks the start of structuralist linguistics, by proposing that a specific language should be studied according to its own structure, rather than as part of the Indo-European language system.

Bobadilla, Francisco de (15th-16th cent.) Spanish soldier, who succeeded COLUMBUS as Viceroy of the Indies in 1499. He imprisoned Columbus in 1500, but exceeded his instructions in sending the explorer to Spain in irons. Bobadilla had earlier acquired a military reputation when fighting against the Moors of Spain and in the siege of Granada (1492). Recalled under arrest to Spain, he perished on the voyage from the Indies.

Boccaccio, Giovanni (1313-75) Italian writer and poet, whose *Il Decameron* is one of the world's acknowledged masterpieces. Its episodes, which are short and dynamic, range from bawdy farce to tragedy. Boccaccio studied commerce and law at Naples, where he mixed with courtiers and poets and perhaps met Fiammetta, a woman whom he immortalized in his writings. He met PETRARCH in 1350, while he was working on the *Decameron*, and the two remained friends until Petrarch's death in 1374. Other works of Boccaccio include a study of DANTE and the Latin treatises which established his reputation.

Boccherini, Luigi (1743-1805) Italian cellist and composer who holds an important place in the development of chamber music. A relatively lightweight talent beside his contemporaries HAYDN and MOZART, Boccherini concentrated mainly on the 102 string quartets and the 125 string quintets, a form he virtually invented and which makes up the major part of his considerable output of chamber works. He also wrote 20 symphonies, and a *Stabat Mater*.

Boccioni, Umberto (1882-1916) Italian sculptor and co-founder (1910) of the Italian Futurist movement, the aims of which were a break with the past and the embodiment in art of the speed and dynamism of the 20th century. In his sculpture, wire, glass, cardboard and wood express the energy beneath the surface of volume and the actual motion of an object in its environment.

Böcklin, Arnold (1827-1901) Swiss portrait and landscape artist whose paintings reflect the preoccupation with death of the late Romantics and Symbolists.

Bode, Johann (1747-1826) German astronomer, who published a mathematical relation to express the distances of the planets from the Sun (Bode's Law), a formula first suggested in 1772 by J. D. Titius.

Bodley, Sir Thomas (1545-1613) English diplomat in Denmark, France and the United Provinces (1585-96), who refounded the library (begun by Cobham and Humphrey, Duke of Gloucester) at Oxford University, now world famous as the Bodleian Library.

Bodoni, Giambattista (1740-1813) Italian printer and outstanding typographer. The son of a printer, he became a compositor and later the head of the Duke of Parma's printing house. He issued editions of the Greek, Latin, French and Italian classics, which became famous for their typography.

Boehm, Theobald (1794-1881) German jeweller, inventor and flautist who developed the 'Boehm system' of finger control for the flute. This was a radical innovation which extended the flute's range and remains in use today. The principle was applied, less successfully, to clarinet, oboe and bassoon.

Boehme, Jakob (1575-1624) German mystic who contended that insight is obtained by direct divine revelation. His speculations had considerable influence on non-conformist sects and on later existentialist thinkers like KIERKEGAARD.

Boerhaave, Hermann (1668-1738) Dutch physician who introduced bedside teaching in medical schools.

Boethius (480-524) Roman philosopher and statesman who held high office under THEODORIC but was imprisoned for conspiracy in 522. Awaiting his execution, he wrote *On the Consolations of Philosophy*, a poetic work extolling stoicism, Neoplatonism and self-knowledge.

Bogart, Humphrey (1899-1957) American stage and screen actor who established himself in hoodlum roles in gangster movies of the 1930s, beginning with *The Petrified Forest* (1936). He later matured into a fine dramatic actor in some of the best films of the period, including *The Maltese Falcon* (1941), *Casablanca* (1942) and *To Have and Have Not* (1944), in which he first starred with Lauren Bacall, whom he subsequently married. Bogart's talent for comedy was rewarded by an Oscar for Best Actor for his role in *The African Queen* (1954).

Bogart made his name in the gangster movies of the 1930s. Later, he starred in some of Hollywood's greatest films

Böhm-Bawerk, Eugen von (1851-1914) Austrian economist, Minister of Finance, and critic of MARX. In his *Capital and Interest* (1884-9) and *Positive Theory of Capital* (1891) he used the marginal utility theory of value, the satisfaction yielded by the last increment of consumption, to develop his theory of interest as the measure of individual preference for goods at the present as against at some future time. He stressed also that the employment of capital increases the 'roundaboutness' of production, and although this process is eventually subject to diminishing returns with respect to time, the end product is of better quality.

Bohr, Niels (1885-1962) Danish physicist who devised a new model of the atom which effectively combined the RUTHERFORD model of the atom with PLANCK's quantum theory of radiation. The model was able to account for the known patterns of atomic radiation as seen in spectra. The theory led to later systems of quantum mechanics which start from more general principles and correct certain limitations of Bohr's model. Bohr was awarded the 1922 Nobel Prize for Physics.

Boiardo, Matteo Maria (1441-94) Italian lyric poet, who, in the *Orlando Innamorato* created the Italian Romantic epic. The first poem to combine the Arthurian and Carolingian traditions of romance, it was the point of departure for ARIOSTO's *Orlando Furioso*. Early in life, Boiardo became a favourite at the court of Ferrara, acting as diplomat and administrator. In 1469 he went to Reggio, where he fell in love with Antonia Caprera, who inspired his *Canzoniere*.

Boileau-Despréaux, Nicolas (1636-1711) French poet, satirist and critic whose work *L'Art poétique* (1674) laid down the principles of classical French literature. Regarded as one of the doyens of French literary criticism. Boileau was the author of a number of satires on contemporary literature (1666-8) and also published a translation of LONGINUS, as well as other works of criticism and a mock epic, *Le Lutrin*. In 1669, he received a pension from LOUIS XIV and eventually became, with RACINE, a royal historian. It is perhaps for his biting epigrams and sayings that Boileau is best remembered.

Bokassa I (born 1921) President of the Central African Republic (1966-77) and Emperor of the Central African Empire (1977-9), Jean-Bedel Bokassa came to power in a military coup in 1966, and in 1977 crowned himself emperor in an elaborate ceremony and changed the name of the country. A 1979 coup, with military aid provided by the French government, removed Bokassa, who went into exile, and replaced him with his cousin David Dacko.

Bohr's atom resembles a miniature solar system with a central nucleus and planetary electrons. Right, Bohr's model of the hydrogen atom. It has one electron (A), the fundamental unit of negative electricity circling the nucleus, which bears one unit of positive electricity. It must move in one of several well-defined orbits or energy-levels, known, in order of distance from the nucleus, as the K-shell, L-shell and so on. When the electron moves from one energy level to another, it emits or absorbs radiation. If the jump is inward, energy is emitted; if the jump is outward, energy is absorbed.

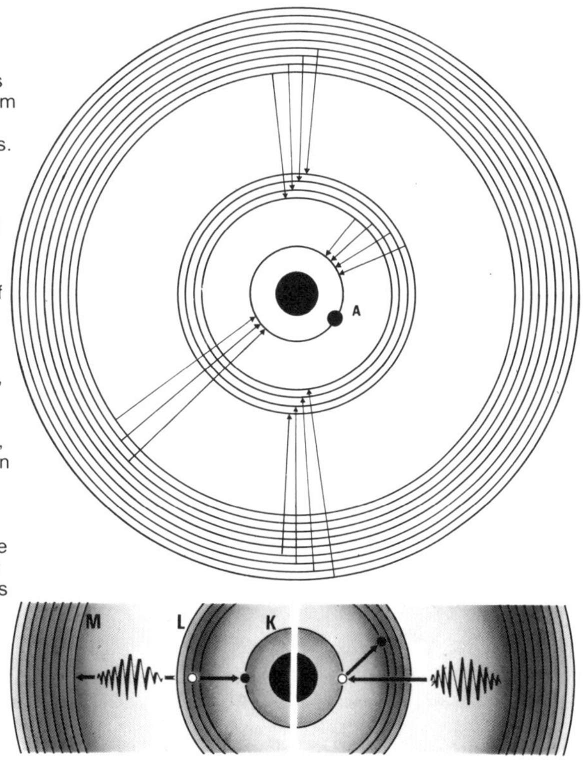

Boldrewood, Rolf (1826-1915) Pen name of T. A. Browne, Australian novelist, born in London, who was one of the first writers to give an authentic picture of pioneering life in Australia. *Robbery Under Arms* (1888) is the story of a bushranger, Captain Starlight. Boldrewood's appreciation of life in the wilds, and his intimate knowledge of squatters and miners (he was magistrate and commissioner of goldfields), also appeared in *The Squatter's Dream* and *The Miner's Right* (both 1890).

Boleslav I (11th cent.) First King of Poland (effectively 992-1025), called 'Chrobry' (the Mighty), who built his principality into a great power reaching from the Bug to the Elbe and from the Baltic to the Carpathians. Boleslav founded a national administrative system, established an independent Polish Church and built a strong army. He was able to expand his territories at the expense of the Holy Roman Emperor Otto III, seizing eastern Pomerania, by which he gained a seaboard along the Baltic; taking Cracow, Moravia, and Silesia and gaining Lusatia and Bohemia. Three wars against Otto's successor, Henry II, during which Poland lost some large western gains, ended with the peace of Bautzen (1018), by which Poland kept Lusatia. In the same year Boleslav took Kiev (1018) and won overlordship of Russia. He was officially crowned king only in the year of his death.

Boleyn, Anne see HENRY VIII

Bolívar, Simón (1783-1830) Venezuelan revolutionary leader, who liberated much of South America from Spanish rule. Bolívar travelled in Europe, where he became influenced by the ideas of John LOCKE and the philosophers of the 18th-century French Enlightenment. His early attempts at revolt ended when, after hard fighting, he was driven out of Venezuela and Colombia (1815) by the royalist forces, and fled to exile in Jamaica. He returned in 1818 with British volunteers, raised an army, crossed the Andes and established the independence of Colombia and later Venezuela. In 1822 he liberated Ecuador and took over command of the Peruvian army from San Martín. With his army, Bolívar conquered and liberated the territory now called Bolivia (1825). His overall plan for his country was that of a republican confederation, but he came up against the narrow-minded regionalism of his countrymen. Betrayed by the separatism of his own men he died disappointed.

Böll, Heinrich (born 1917) German novelist and story writer, author of *Group Portrait with Lady* (1971) in which an imaginary author builds up a portrait of a woman through interviews with people who knew her. The novel is remarkable for its often satirical mini-biographies of Böll's contemporaries from the inter-war years to the 1970s. Böll's early writings were concerned with the problems of those involved in war and its aftermath, among which *Acquainted with the Night* (1953) is outstanding as an exposé of Germany's post-war 'economic miracle'. *Traveller, if you come to Spa* (1950), a collection of stories, is one of his major achievements. Böll was awarded the Nobel Prize for Literature in 1972.

Bologna, Giovanni (c. 1529-1608) Flemish-born sculptor who worked in Florence, and was the prime exponent of the Mannerist style. His works were designed to be seen from a variety of viewpoints. Among the best known are his *Rape of a Sabine* (completed 1583), and, in Florence, *Venus of the Groticella* (*c.* 1575-6), the bronze *Flying Mercury* (1564) and the equestrian statue of Cosimo I (1587), set on a low plinth in the new style inaugurated by MICHELANGELO. His *Apennine* (1580-2) in Pratrolino, a giant representing the River Nile, is regarded as the eighth wonder of the world.

Bolyai, János (1802-60) Hungarian mathematician, who was one of the pioneers of non-Euclidian geometry. He showed that a consistent system (that is, one not leading to internal contradictions) could be set up without EUCLID's postulate of parallels, which states that only one parallel to a given line can be drawn through a point. His work was published in 1831, and duplicated ideas of GAUSS and LOBACHEVSKY.

Bondfield, Margaret Grace (1873-1953) First woman cabinet minister in Britain. She became a trade union official and Chairman of the General Council of the Trades Union Congress in 1923, and the first woman to hold cabinet office when appointed Minister of Labour (1929-31), by Ramsay MACDONALD. She was attacked by the left wing of the Labour Party as she had opposed the General Strike, and supported the lowering of unemployment insurance benefits.

Bonhoeffer, Dietrich (1906-45) German Protestant theologian who saw his own role as that of uniting Christians and non-Christians and establishing a 'church of the world', for which traditional theology and the established church are superfluous. Bonhoeffer's non-religious interpretation of the Gospels, and his attempts to free Christianity of metaphysics and the supernatural, have guided the churches in the Communist bloc and provoked much radical thinking. His critics claim, however, that what he is advocating is not Christianity at all, but simply social involvement. An active member of the anti-Nazi resistance movement in Germany, he was killed by the Gestapo in a concentration camp.

Boniface (c. 680-755) English saint, and evangelizer of the Germans. Author of the first Latin grammar written in English, he lived as a monk in England until he was 40 and was created first Bishop of Mainz and then Archbishop of Western Germany. After reorganizing the West German and Frankish Churches he set out to evangelize the Frieslanders, but was killed by them near Dokkum in Holland.

Bonington, Richard P. (c. 1802-28) British watercolour painter, whose technique and use of colour derived from a study of the Venetians and was much influenced by DELACROIX.

Bonnard, Pierre (1867-1947) French painter in the *intimisme* manner, a recorder of quiet interiors and bourgeois domesticity, expressed in muted tones. He also worked as designer for the state, as an illustrator and a poster artist. After 1900 his palette brightened, though in landscape he did not seek an Impressionist's truth to natural effects, but truth to a poetic 'idea' in accordance with which the painter might modify nature.

Bonner, Neville (born 1918) The first Australian aboriginal MP.

Bonney, William H. see BILLY THE KID

Bonnie Prince Charlie see STUART, Charles Edward

Boole, George (1815-64) English mathematician and logician who developed an algebra of logic which allowed a variety of logical problems to be dealt with as algebraic operations. Of humble origin, Boole was Professor of Mathematics at Cork University at the age of 34.

Boone, Daniel (1734-1820) American frontiersman and folk hero. As a hunter and trapper, he gained unique knowledge of the largely unexplored Kentucky region after crossing the Appalachians from the settled seaboard colonies. In 1769 he was engaged to explore the country beyond the mountains, carve a road through the Cumberland Gap, and escort settlers to three projected settlements. He did this, showing great enterprise and courage in his struggles with the Indians. He established fortified border-posts (one of which is now Boonesboro), and effectively began the colonization of Kentucky.

Booth, Charles (1840-1916) English social reformer, who introduced new and improved standards of statistical measurement in *Life and Labour of the People in London* (1891-1903). This book, which contains a series of coloured maps showing income levels street by street, demonstrates the relationship between poverty and depravity on the one hand, and between economic security and decent standards of living on the other. He was a member of the Royal Commission on the Poor Law (1905-9), and published his ideas on poverty among the old in *Poor Law Reform* (1910).

Booth, Edwin (1833-93) American actor and founder of the New York Players Club. His actor brother, John Wilkes BOOTH, assassinated LINCOLN.

Booth, John Wilkes (1838-65) American actor and assassin of Abraham LINCOLN. Booth was a Confederate sympathizer with an insatiable thirst for notoriety and shot President Lincoln at Ford's Theatre, Washington, during a performance on 14 Apr. 1865. He escaped to Virginia but was pursued and died, possibly by his own hand, while resisting arrest. The theory that Booth was involved in a wider conspiracy has not been proved.

Booth, William (1829-1912) British religious leader, founder of the Salvation Army. His early contact with poverty as a pawnbroker's assistant aroused a passion for social justice, which he allied to a strong evangelical faith. As a Methodist preacher in London, he attracted a large following, which he organized into a Christian Mission for saving souls and relieving distress. In 1878 the movement was reorganized on military lines as the Salvation Army. Recognition and support for General Booth's crusade came with the publication of *In Darkest England and the Way Out* (1890).

Bopp, Franz (1791-1867) German philologist, the first to attempt the scientific comparison of the grammars of the Indo-European languages.

Borchert, Wolfgang (1921-47) German short story writer, dramatist and poet whose work is a condemnation of war. He used his experiences in the Second World War to produce plays of intense realism, one of which was *The Man Outside* (1947).

Bordet, Jules (1870-1961) Belgian bacteriologist who discovered that the serum of an animal immunized against a disease could be used to ascertain its presence in other animals. He was awarded a Nobel Prize for Medicine in 1919.

Borelli, Giovanni (1608-79) Italian mathematician, astronomer and biologist who first explained the action of muscles in mechanical terms. His theories of muscles and bones acting as systems of levers and pulleys were basically correct.

Borg, Bjorn (born 1956) Swedish tennis player who was the dominant figure in men's tennis in the mid and late 1970s. He is particularly noted for winning five consecutive men's singles titles at Wimbledon (1976-80). He announced his retirement in 1983.

Borges, Jorge Luis (born 1899) Argentinian poet, essayist and novelist, who invented the *ficción* (fiction), an extended analogy of a metaphysical theme which, when applied to everyday experience, can lead to nightmarish conclusions, as in the works of POE and KAFKA. A selection of his works was published in English in 1962 under the title *Labyrinths*.

Borgia, Cesare (c. 1475-1507) Son of Pope Alexander VI and his clever, unscrupulous chief tool for building BORGIA fortunes in Italy. Cesare, a cardinal at 17, enlarged his personal power by reputedly murdering his elder brother; seizing and terrorizing central Italy; attempting to loosen the Spanish hold on Naples by contriving the murder of the King of Aragon's nephew (Cesare's own brother-in-law); and murdering members of Italy's powerful, rebellious ORSINI family. Imprisoned by his enemies after Alexander's death, Cesare escaped, but died fighting in Navarre. His deeds won the admiration of MACHIAVELLI, who falsely portrayed Cesare's selfish schemes as far-sighted plans for uniting Italy.

Borgia, Lucrezia (1480-1519) Italian aristocrat, popularly renowned as a scheming poisoner, but in reality the victim of her father, Pope Alexander VI, and brother, Cesare BORGIA, who had her make four political marriages: first by proxy to the Spanish Count of Aversa (annulled by her father); secondly to Giovanni SFORZA (also annulled by her father); thirdly to Alfonso of Aragon, Duke of Bisceglie (ended by Alfonso's murder, arranged by Cesare); and finally, when she was 22, to Alfonso of Este, later Duke of Ferrara. After Alexander's death, Lucrezia helped to make Ferrara a centre for Renaissance artists and writers.

Boris I (10th cent.) King of Bulgaria, who established his country's national language and religion. He became a Christian probably from political motives and made Eastern Orthodoxy Bulgaria's state faith, using force where necessary. By favouring a Slavonic Church Liturgy (pioneered by CYRIL and Methodius), he helped to establish Slavonic as Bulgaria's official tongue. Boris retired to a monastery in 889 but emerged to blind and depose his incompetent successor – his eldest son, Vladimir.

Borodin, Aleksandr (1833-87) Distinguished Russian professor of chemistry who, in his spare time, became one of the influential group of Russian composers known as 'The Five'. His work ranged from the attractive symphonic poem, *In the Steppes of Central Asia* (1880), to one of the finest of Russian operas, *Prince Igor* (1890, completed posthumously by RIMSKY-KORSAKOV and Glazunov). His important *Second Symphony*, with its atmosphere of medieval pageantry, was made up of material prepared for the opera.

Borromini, Francesco (1599-1667) The chief exponent of the Baroque in Italian architecture. His first Roman work, S Carlo alle Quattro Fontane (1634-44), has an elliptical rather than a circular ground plan and a honeycomb dome. Borromini achieved an illusion of movement by a clever placing of concave and convex curves. His architectural style was too personal to be immediately popular with his own contemporaries, and he was dismissed in the middle of his work on Sta Agnese in the Piazza Navona, although his designs were used in the construction of the façade. His final work, the Collegio di Propaganda Fide, is uncompromisingly austere.

Boru, Brian see BRIAN BORU

Bosch, Hieronymus (c. 1450-1516) Netherlandish painter, whose inventive fantasies, although no longer fully understood, are still regarded with deep interest. Many of his paintings are religious allegories on the theme of man's sinfulness, the best known often depicting nightmarish hell scenes or landscapes with fantastic creatures, as in the *Garden of Delights* (*c.* 1510). Bosch's work, which may be said to anticipate that of BRUEGEL, was immensely popular in the 16th century and often copied.

Bossuet, Jacques-Bénigne (1627-1704) French theologian and moralist, renowned for his pulpit oratory, particularly his *Oraisons funèbres*. His *Discours sur l'histoire universelle* (1681), an educational work written for the Dauphin (whose tutor he was at the time) is regarded as the first attempt at a philosophy of history.

Boswell, James (1740-95) Scottish lawyer, biographer and man of letters, who wrote *The Life of Samuel Johnson* (1791), one of the world's outstanding biographies. Boswell first met JOHNSON in 1763 and saw him at intervals for the next 20 years. At Johnson's death (1784) he began to work on the *Life* with indefatigable energy, and keen, minute observations of the character of his subject. Boswell was also a highly individual diarist and memoir writer; some of his indiscreet, amusing papers, such as his *London Journal*, and his travels in Europe, have been rescued from obscurity by 20th-century scholarship.

Botha, Louis (1862-1919) South African soldier and statesman and first Premier of the Union of South Africa (1910-19). An opponent of both KRUGER and of war with Britain, he nevertheless joined his countrymen on the outbreak of the Boer War and eventually became commander-in-chief of the Boer force at Ladysmith (1900) and defeated the British at Colenso. During his premiership Botha followed a policy of economic expansion and racial harmony. His support of Britain and the Allies in the First World War alienated HERTZOG, and he had to crush a rebellion against this policy before beginning the campaign which ended in the conquest of German South West Africa (1915).

Botha, Pieter Willem (born 1916) South African Prime Minister from 1978, who formed the multiracial advisory council on constitutional change in 1980, the first institution of its kind in South Africa. He also established the Southwest Africa Territorial Force in 1980 to defend the disputed territory of Namibia.

Bottger, Johann Friedrich (1682-1719) German alchemist to AUGUSTUS II, and the first European to rediscover (1710) the method of making true hard porcelain, then only known from oriental samples. In 1710, Augustus established the famous porcelain works at Meissen, near Dresden. The manufacturing processes, involving the fusion of kaolin (china clay) with calcareous (and later felspathic) flux at 1300-1400°C, were closely guarded secrets. Dresden-ware remained supreme until 1768, when kaolin was also used to produce hard porcelain at Sèvres.

Botticelli, Sandro (c. 1445-1510) Florentine painter, who was a favourite artist of the MEDICI circle. His celebrated mythological pictures painted for a member of the Medici family (e.g. *The Birth of Venus*, *c.* 1478-86) are characterized by delicate colouring, shallow modelling of the human form, and an emphasis, derived from the work of POLLAIUOLO, on outline. *The Birth of Venus*, which reveals Botticelli's preoccupation with antiquity, includes the first

Two examples of allegories: above, the nightmarish work of Bosch; below, the gentle grace of Botticelli

monumental image of a naked goddess that had been seen since Roman times. The picture has, nevertheless, a quasi-religious meaning. In his later years Botticelli became a follower of the religious reformer SAVONAROLA, and his religious paintings reverted to an archaic style which is often intensely emotional. Botticelli produced a complete set of drawings illustrating DANTE's *Divine Comedy* which are remarkable for their sensitivity of line and gentle grace.

Bottomley, Horatio (1860-1933) English financier, MP and promoter of fraudulent companies. He was also the founder of the weekly journal *John Bull* and printer of *Hansard*. For 20 years, he managed to frustrate numerous attempts to convict him of fraud, but in 1922, he was prosecuted for fraudulently advertising in his magazine, and was sentenced to seven years' penal servitude. He died in poverty.

Boucher de Crêvecoeur de Perthes, Jacques (1788-1868) French pioneer of Palaeolithic archaeology, who was largely responsible for establishing the existence of prehistoric man. After finding chipped-flint hand-axes beside the bones of prehistoric animals in the Somme valley (1837), he claimed that the men who made the tools were contemporary with the animals, and that, therefore, man's origins were 'antediluvial'. French scientists rejected his arguments, which were upheld by British scientists in 1859.

Boucher, François (1703-70) French Rococo artist and protégé of Madame de POMPADOUR. Boucher became Director of the Academy and chief painter at the court of LOUIS XV, and in addition designed tapestries, stage sets and vignettes for the Sèvres porcelain factory. His subject matter ranges from the sensual delights seen in his interpretations of mythology, to pastoral and landscape scenes, portraits and genre paintings. Boucher's versatility, together with his technical virtuosity, were qualities much admired in his day, appealing to the senses rather than the mind with whimsical, light-hearted and often witty subjects.

Boudicca see BOADICEA

Boulanger, Georges (1837-91) French soldier-politician, who plotted to overthrow the Third Republic. As War Minister (1886) his introduction of military reforms, his patriotism and handsome appearance made him widely popular, and when a change of government (1887) relegated him to a provincial command, right wing dissidents and royalists persuaded him to mount a *coup d'état* to seize power for the so-called 'League of Patriots'. At the critical moment when all was prepared (March 1889), he lost his nerve and failed to act, fled to Brussels, then to Jersey, and was convicted *in absentia* of high treason. He committed suicide.

Boulanger, Nadia (1887-1979) French composer and one of the most influential teachers in 20th-century music. Taking her inspiration from STRAVINSKY, she has included among her pupils Lennox BERKELEY as well as the important American composers HARRIS and COPLAND. Her sister was Lili Boulanger (1893-1918), who was, in 1914, the first woman to win the Prix de Rome, for which Nadia had been runner-up in 1908.

Boulez, Pierre (born 1925) French composer and conductor who made his reputation with *Le Marteau sans Maître*, a song cycle for contralto and chamber orchestra and a key-work in post-war European music. He has had considerable influence on contemporary music through his interpretations of the most important 20th-century composers, and through his own works. Boulez was a pupil of MESSIAEN, and BARRAULT's musical director (1948).

Boulton, Matthew (1728-1809) English engineer, a pioneer of engineering technology at the outset of the Industrial Revolution. In 1775 he went into partnership with James WATT to manufacture steam engines. Boulton had the engineering skills which, after 18 uncertain years, made Watt's invention a commercial and financial success and one of the cornerstones of the Industrial Revolution. Boulton was the centre of an influential group of scientists and industrialists, the Lunar Society of Birmingham, which included among its members Joseph PRIESTLEY, Josiah WEDGWOOD and James KEIR.

Boumédienne, Houari (1927-78) Algerian soldier-revolutionary, who established a socialist state in Algeria. Boumédienne worked with BEN BELLA to drive the French out of Algeria and to establish its independence. By 1956 Boumédienne was in command of the militant rebellion in Algeria, and in 1960 went to Tunis to train and command the 60,000 strong National Liberation Army assembled their ready to invade Algeria. Following the independence granted by DE GAULLE, and finding the government of President Ben Khedda insufficiently socialist, he used his army to march on Algiers, depose Ben Khedda and install Ben Bella as Prime Minister and President. Boumédienne himself retained the position of Minister of Defence and used the army to crush all opposition to socialization of the country. In 1963 he became the First Deputy Premier, and in 1965 ousted Ben Bella to become virtual dictator.

Bournonville, August (1805-1879) Founder of Danish Ballet, who studied in Paris with the great teacher Vestris, then returned to Denmark in 1829 and was appointed ballet master. The most famous of his 36 ballets is *La Sylphide*.

Bouts, Dieric (c. 1410-85) Dutch painter, who was influenced by Rogier van der WEYDEN, but whose homely religious scenes have much less intensity of feeling.

Bowen, Elizabeth Dorothea Cole (1899-1973) Irish novelist, who has been described as a 'poet working in prose'. Her sensitive, quiet books, the best known of which is *Death of the Heart* (1938), analyse states of mind and conflicts of emotion.

Bowen, Norman (1887-1956) Canadian-born American geologist, a pioneer of petrography (the science of rock composition). His research was on the structure and chemical composition of igneous

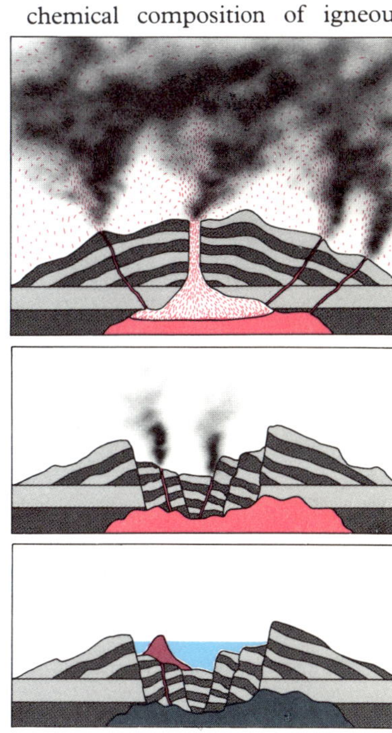

Cross-section of an explosive volcano. Bowen helped unravel its mysteries

rocks (those cooled from a molten state) and metamorphic rocks (those altered by heat and pressure).

Bowie, David Robert Jones (born 1947) English popular musician who became a cult figure with his distinctive melodies and lyrics and flamboyant stage performances. His first hit was *Space Oddity* in 1969. Other well-known records include *The Man Who Sold the World* (1971), *The Rise and Fall of Ziggy Stardust and the Spiders from Mars* (1972), *Aladdin Sane* (1973) and *Let's Dance* (1983). He has turned to acting in recent years, appearing in the films *The Man Who Fell to Earth* (1976) and *Merry Christmas Mr Lawrence* (1983).

Bowman, Isaiah (1878-1950) American geographer who prompted major geographic studies of large areas. His *Forest Physiography* (1911) was the first detailed study of the physical geography of the United States. As director of the American Geographic Society of New York (1915-35), he made it an immensely useful tool for international geographic studies – mapping all of Central and South America, and exploring polar and other aspects of world geography. His grasp of international affairs, revealed in *The New World: Problems in the Political Geography* earned him the post of adviser to presidents WILSON and ROOSEVELT.

Boyce, William (1710-79) English composer and organist who, after deafness wrecked his career, edited the famous collection known as *Cathedral Music* (1760-78), a landmark in musicology. Boyce's own compositions included music for church and stage, but he was also a gifted instrumental composer, and his eight one-movement symphonies continue to receive deserved hearings in the concert hall.

Boyle, Robert (1627-91) Irish-born physicist and chemist, who formulated a law governing the behaviour of gases. In 1660, he put forward his gas law which stated that, at a given temperature, the pressure of a gas is proportional to its volume. In chemistry, Boyle introduced the idea of elements, and distinguished between mixtures of elements and chemical compounds, in which the elements are combined together.

Bracton, Henry de (13th cent.) English jurist who wrote the first systematic treatise on English law, *The Laws and Customs of England* (unfinished; first published 1569). In it, he stressed the recorded practice and procedure of the English royal courts and cited decided cases as precedents. This work and the cases collected in his *Note Book* indicate the increasing importance of precedent in the development of common law. He was an ecclesiastic and sat as a judge.

Bradford, William (1590-1657) English Puritan and Pilgrim Father. An early Congregationalist, Bradford went to Leyden (1607) with the first English separatists. He helped to draw up the Mayflower Compact, was elected governor of Plymouth (1621), and re-elected 30 times at annual elections. Bradford was a strong administrator, coping with famine, Indian troubles and internal quarrels, and maintaining the independence of Plymouth against Massachusetts. He co-operated with other Puritans in the Pequot War (1637) and in the New England Confederation (1643).

Bradlaugh, Charles (1833-91) British politician, who, as a free-thinker, was refused permission by the House of Commons to take his seat, because he declined to take the oath. In 1876, Bradlaugh was convicted of advocating birth control, and sentenced to imprisonment. The sentence was quashed on appeal. Elected as a Radical MP for Northampton (1880), he refused to take the oath, but offered to 'affirm'. A Select Committee ruled that he had no right to do so, and when Bradlaugh then offered to take the oath, this was objected to on the grounds that it would not be binding on a free-thinker. Though re-elected three times, he was excluded on each occasion. When he insisted on taking his seat, he was removed by the police (1881). A new Speaker decided (1886) that he had the right to take the oath and he was allowed to take his seat. In 1888 he promoted the Oath Act, which secured the right of affirmation in the Commons and the law courts.

Bradley, Francis Herbert (1846-1924) British philosopher. His *Appearance and Reality* (1893) is a critical survey of the general categories of thought (space, time, causality, quality, relation and the like). He found them to be inconsistent with one another and representative only of the world of appearance. He concluded that there is a real world, which lies beyound thought, which is indivisibly One and Absolute.

Bradley, James (1693-1762) English astronomer who, in 1727, discovered the aberration of light (the apparent displacement of a star's position due to the movement of the Earth during the time it takes the light to travel from the star). In 1742 he succeeded HALLEY as Astronomer Royal. Bradley discovered the nutation (oscillation) of the Earth's axis, after observations lasting 20 years.

Bradman, Sir Donald (born 1908) Australian cricketer who was the most prolific scorer in the game. He played in 52 test matches and in his career made 117 centuries with a first class average of 99.94 runs. His score of 452 not out against Queensland in 1929-30 was a record for 29 years.

Bradstreet, Anne (c. 1612-72) American poet, whose *Tenth Muse* (1650) was one of the first works of poetry to be published by a woman in English. Born in Northampton, England, she settled in New England, and her introspective meditations on family life reflect the theological and moral preoccupations of the Puritan community.

Brady, Mathew (c. 1823-96) American photographer known principally for his Civil War battle pictures, but who was also a pioneer of the daguerreotype technique. Brady photographed 18 United States presidents, before dying penniless in a New York hospital.

Bragg, Sir William Henry (1862-1942) English physicist who with his son, William Lawrence, worked, using X-rays, on the determination of the structures of crystals. In 1915 the Braggs became intrigued by the distinctive patterns Max von Laue had produced on photographic plates by passing X-rays through crystals. Their work showed how the structure of crystals could be deduced from the patterns they produced. Father and son were awarded the 1915 Nobel Prize for Physics.

Brahe, Tycho (1546-1601) Danish astronomer and mathematician, the most accomplished and systematic observer of the skies before the use of telescopes. His suggestion that comets are heavenly bodies, not exhalations of the Earth's atmosphere, was a refutation of the doctrine that planets were fixed to solid crystalline spheres, and struck a blow at the Aristotelian theory. However, he could not bring himself to accept a fully heliocentric Solar System, maintaining that the Earth remained still at the centre, with the Moon and Sun revolving around it, while the other planets revolved around the Sun. Brahe was assisted by his pupil KEPLER, who later used Brahe's observations of Mars to determine his three laws of planetary motion. In 1576 Frederick II gave Brahe the island of Hven, where he built the observatory of Uraniborg ('Castle of the Heavens'), equipped with the best instruments then available. He perfected the art of astronomical observation before the advent of the telescope, obtaining many remarkably accurate results, and calculating the length of the year to within one second and thus laid the basis of the Gregorian calendar.

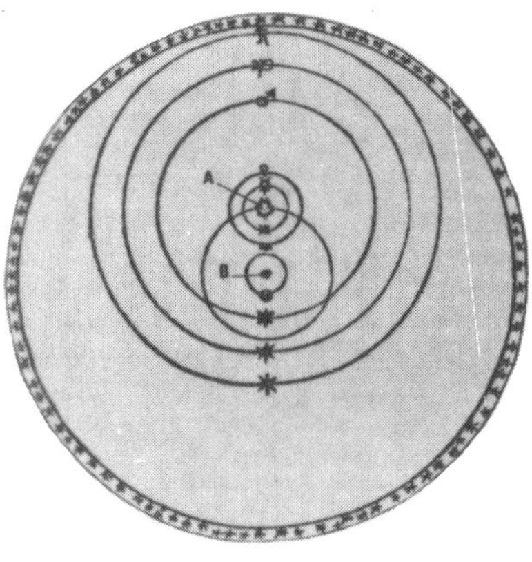

Brahe believed that while the planets moved around the Sun A, the Sun in turn orbited the Earth B

Brahms, Johannes (1833-97) German composer, who, following in the tradition of BEETHOVEN, became the leading symphonist of the Romantic-Classical school, and was said to have destroyed many works which failed to satisfy his exacting standards. His four symphonies were composed between 1876 and 1885. His other most important compositions were the two piano concertos (1861 and 1882); the Violin Concerto (1879), written for JOACHIM; the Double Concerto for Violin and Cello (1888); the great *German Requiem* (1868), to a Lutheran text; and a large body of chamber music. As a lyric composer, Brahms represented an antithesis to WAGNER's dramatic Romanticism. LISZT and Joachim recognized his importance, and SCHUMANN's help and friendship firmly established his career.

Braille, Louis (1809-52) French inventor of the Braille system of reading for the sightless, who was himself blinded at the age of three. While a scholar and later a teacher, at the Institute of Blind Youth in Paris, Braille developed a system of embossed dots to enable the blind to reach by touch. This was published first in 1829 – and in a more complete form in 1837. In 1932, a form known as Standard English Braille became accepted for worldwide use.

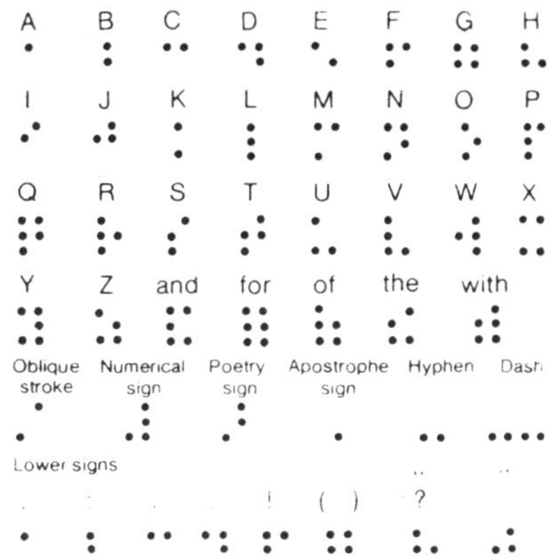

Braille's alphabet and numerals gave the blind a fingertip sight

Bramah, Joseph (1748-1814) Prolific English inventor of the ball-valve and syphon system water closet (patented 1778), which is the basis of the flushing system still in use. This was the first of many inventions that brought him fame and wealth. His factory in Pimlico was an important training ground for engineers and inventors of machine tools.

Bramante, Donato (1444-1514) Influential Italian architect of the High Renaissance, who was influenced by ALBERTI and LEONARDO. He first worked in Milan where he evolved an individual classical style, using central plans for churches and chapels, and reintroducing coffering on domes, a popular feature in Roman architecture. In 1499 he went to Rome, where he built the cloisters for Sta Maria della Pace (1500), whose perfect detailing and use of the classical architrave are reminiscent of Roman buildings. His Tempietto di S Pietro in Montorio is a circular building, the form and details of which closely resemble those of a classical temple.

Brancusi, Constantin (1876-1957) Rumanian sculptor who arrived in Paris in 1904, having walked across Europe. Brancusi's original style was classical and academic, but from 1907, influenced by RODIN, his forms became simplified. Brancusi's considerable importance for the development of 20th-century sculpture is in the sense of the freedom which emanates from the simplicity and monumental grandeur of his work; e.g. *Bird in Space* (1925), his rare pierced work in wood, *King of Kings* (1937) or his *Colonne sans Fin* in steel (also 1937).

Brando, Marlon (born 1924) American film actor whose first big success in the cinema was as the incoherent Kowalski in *A Streetcar Named Desire* (1952). He has since starred in many different roles, including that of Mark Antony in *Julius Caesar* (1953), the Englishman Fletcher CHRISTIAN in *Mutiny on the Bounty* (1962), the title role in *The Godfather* (1972) and the American in Bertolucci's controversial *Last Tango in Paris* (1972).

Brandt, Willy (born 1913) West German politician, born Karl Frahm, the first socialist Chancellor of the Federal Republic. His socialist writings forced him to seek refuge in Norway when the Nazis came to power (1933). He worked as a journalist in Sweden and after returning to Berlin in 1945, was elected to the Berlin Chamber of Deputies in 1950. He became its President (1955-7) and, in 1957, Burgomaster of West Berlin. He became West German Minister of Foreign Affairs and Vice-Chancellor (1966-9) in Kiesinger's coalition government, and was elected Chancellor in 1969. The Ostpolitik policy of non-aggression and friendship pacts with USSR and countries of eastern Europe which he pursued earned him the Nobel Peace Prize in 1971. He resigned (1974) when a close aide was exposed as a spy. He headed the Independent Commission on International Development (1977).

Braque, Georges (1882-1963) French painter, one of the founders of the Cubist movement. In 1907 he met PICASSO and soon afterwards began to study CÉZANNE's paintings, two events of fundamental importance to the development of Cubism, with its concern with the nature of pictorial space. Braque's work at this time was cool and somewhat detached. Its characteristic subject-matter was the still-life. Later, he reintroduced more sensuous and formal elements into his paintings, but retained the sense of discipline. Examples of his best known work are *Large Nude*, one of his early paintings, *Violin and Palette*, from his transitional period, and *The Echo*, which shows the brighter colours of his later work.

Braun, Eva (1912-45) Mistress of Adolf HITLER. She worked as a photographer's assistant, and lived with Hitler after she met him in 1936. So far as is known, she never exercised any political influence. She and Hitler were married in Berlin the day before they committed suicide together.

Braun, Wernher von (1912-77) German-born rocket engineer who pioneered the V2 rocket used to bombard Britain in the Second World War. The first missile was launched from the rocket research site at Peenemunde on the Baltic in 1942. Von Braun's rockets came too late to influence the course of the Second World War, but their political and military significance has been considerable. Von Braun and many of his associates later went to the US, where he led the group which put America's first satellite into orbit on 31 Jan. 1958. Von Braun was later responsible for the Saturn rocket developments for the Apollo lunar programme. His books include the *History of Rocketry and Space Travel* (1966).

Brecht, Bertolt (1898-1956) German dramatist, director and the most widely influential theorist in the modern theatre. His Expressionist work, represented by *Baal* (1923) and *A Man's a Man* (1926), create imaginary, romantic worlds. His Marxist and didactic period began with *The Threepenny Opera* (1928) and includes *Saint Joan of the Stockyards*. *Mother Courage* and *The Caucasian Chalk Circle* belong to his third period, which is more concerned with character and the complexity of human relationships. From 1949, he ran his own company, the Berliner Ensemble, and developed his dramatic theories in writings.

Breton, André (1896-1966) French essayist, novelist, critic and one of the founders of the Surrealist movement, the basis of which he established in his *Manifeste du surréalisme* (1924) and *Second manifeste du surréalisme* (1930). His novel *Nadja* (1928) is regarded as a masterpiece of Surrealist writing.

Breuil, Henri (1877-1961) French priest and archaeologist whose studies shed new light on the Old Stone Age cave paintings of Europe and Africa. During the early 1900s he published a number of books to prove the antiquity of the prehistoric cave paintings in western Europe, notably the Palaeolithic animal paintings at Altamira in Spain and Lascaux in France, many of them 20,000 and some possibly 60,000 years old. Equally important was his influence on the rejection of the old system in which one 'epoch' followed another, to the more accurate and complex sequence of 'cultures', showing how some had flourished simultaneously. He also copied and publicized the strange rock painting of southern Africa.

Brezhnev, Leonid Ilyich (1906-82) Soviet politician who succeeded KHRUSCHEV as First Secretary of the Central Committee of the Communist Party of the Soviet Union in 1964. A Ukrainian, he trained as a metallurgist and engineer, and became prominent in 1952, the year before STALIN's death, when he was appointed to the Central Committee of the Communist Party. Brezhnev was effectively head of state from 1960, when he succeeded Voroshilov as Chairman of the Praesidium of the Supreme Soviet, and in 1964 took over Russia's top political office when he replaced Khruschev as First Secretary (title altered to 'Secretary General' in 1966) of the Party. It was Brezhnev, the strongest member of the collective three-man leadership (with KOSYGIN and Podgorny), who ordered the invasion of Czechoslovakia in 1968 and who formulated the doctrine of limited sovereignty, by which the USSR claims the right to intervene whenever it considers that socialism in the 'satellite' countries is threatened from within. He adopted a rapprochement policy with the United States and the West, while pursuing an aggressive policy furthering Soviet interests in Africa and the Middle East. In 1979 he sent Soviet troops into Afghanistan, and in 1981 threatened intervention in Poland's internal affairs. Soviet relations with China continued to deteriorate under his leadership.

Brian Boru (926-1014) King of Ireland (1002-14), whose victory in the Battle of Clontarf (1014) crushed Viking attempts to conquer all Ireland. Succeeding to the kingdom of Munster (978), he conquered the provincial kings and was recognized by them as King of all Ireland. Some of the resentful, displaced rulers allied with leaders of the Danish and Norse invaders, and although Brian defeated them at Clontarf, his death in the battle reduced Ireland to political anarchy, the cause of later invasions.

Briand, Aristide (1862-1932) French statesman notable for his efforts on behalf of international peace and Franco-German reconciliation, for which he was awarded the Nobel Peace Prize in 1926. He was 11 times Prime Minister of France, between 1909 (when he succeeded CLEMENCEAU) and 1929, though he held office for a total period of less than 5 years. As Foreign Minister from 1925 to 1932, his influence on French foreign policy was supreme. With STRESEMANN Briand formulated the Locarno Treaties of 1925, which confirmed Germany's frontiers with France and Belgium and the demilitarized Rhineland zone. In 1928 he concluded the Kellogg-Briand pact with Frank Kellogg, COOLIDGE's Secretary of State, renouncing the use of war as an instrument of national policy.

Bridges, Robert (1844-1930) English scholarly poet who made some interesting metrical experiments. He was an intelligent, retiring man who was not well known, even when he became Poet Laureate in 1913. He was the friend and encourager of Manley HOPKINS, though a stern critic of Hopkins's more daring work. Bridges's long 'Testament of Beauty' (1929) is a major poem.

Bridgewater, Francis, 3rd Duke of (1736-1803) The founder of Britain's canal system. In 1759 Parliament authorized the Duke to build a canal to link the collieries on his estates at Worsley with Salford and Manchester. He employed the engineer James BRINDLEY, who in two years built the 10-mile long canal, including the famous aqueduct across the Irwell. The efficiency of the canal as a means of transporting coal lowered its price and started a canal-building boom in Britain.

Bright, John (1811-89) British orator and Liberal statesman whose political career began in the campaign of the anti-Corn Law League, which he led in collaboration with COBDEN. He was an MP almost continuously from 1843 until his death, representing Durham, Manchester and Birmingham. In the 1850s Bright opposed the Crimean War and pressed for the transfer of Indian administration from the East India Company to the Crown (India Act, 1858). He supported the admission of Jews to the House of Commons and was influential in the campaign, which led to the Parliamentary Reform Act of 1867. Bright was President of the Board of Trade (1868-70) in GLADSTONE's first Liberal ministry, but opposed the Liberal government's intervention in Egypt in 1882 and Gladstone's crusade for Irish Home Rule. His independent provincialism and serious mind were representative of the mid-19th-century reformer.

Bright, Richard (1789-1858) English physician and medical researcher who discovered that kidney disease could be diagnosed from the presence of albumin in the

Arms . . .

Germany's V2 rocket marked the zenith of military technology before the advent of nuclear weapons in the Second World War. It was nearly 47 feet long, burned oxygen and alcohol at a rate of 300 lb a second and carried a one-ton warhead with which it hit London from a range of 200 miles. Braun's V2 rocket founded a new generation of once-unimaginable weaponry, the intercontinental ballistic missiles with nuclear warheads—but was itself the latest in a long line of military hardware stemming back to the ballista and catapult, and beyond (right). The V2 had more in common with the Big Bertha long range gun of the First World War than with the other aspects of arms, being designed to terrorize the defenceless into submission, rather than to defeat the enemy in the field

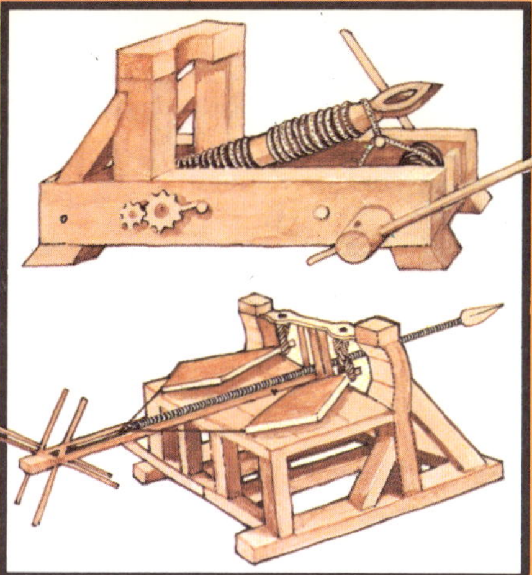

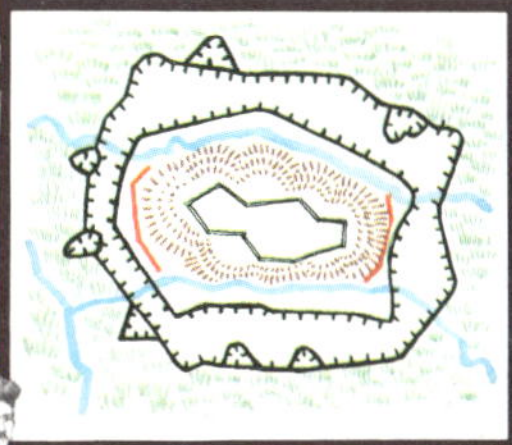

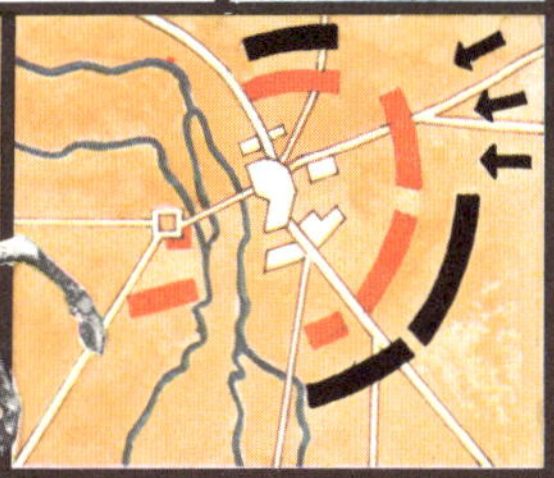

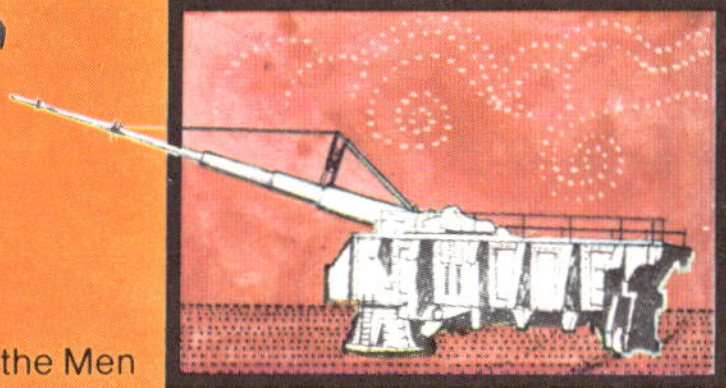

. . . and the Men

The strategy of all-out war is decided by the leaders of nations. Below, Stalin, Roosevelt and Churchill meet to discuss the overthrow of the Third Reich

urine. The condition, formally known as Bright's disease, is now known to be a number of separate diseases, including acute and chronic nephritis.

Brindley, James (1716-72) Pioneer English canal builder. Although illiterate and without any kind of formal education, he was an inventor of genius. In 1752 he devised a water-driven pump for draining a mine, and later designed a silk mill. These works led the Duke of BRIDGEWATER in 1759 to engage Brindley to build the Bridgewater canal. The success of the canal (part of which went by aqueduct over the River Irwell) led to a career in canal building which included the Grand Trunk, Birmingham, and Chesterfield canals – 365 miles in all.

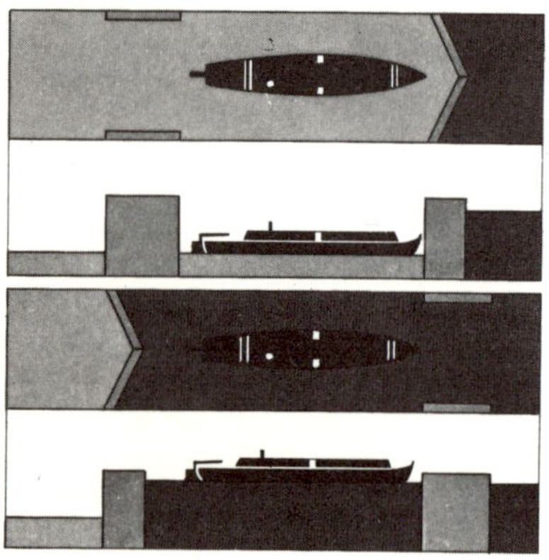

Pioneered by men like Bridgewater and Brindley, a canal depends on its locks. The pressure of the river race holds the angled gate shut, while the water level rises, bearing the craft upward

Britten, Sir Benjamin (1913-76) English composer, the foremost of his generation. In 1945 he wrote the score that became the *Variations and Fugue on a Theme of Purcell (Young Person's Guide to the Orchestra)* for an educational film. The same year, his opera *Peter Grimes* (based on CRABBE's poem 'The Borough') was produced at Covent Garden, and its success was directly responsible for the revival of opera in post-war England. Britten's gift for subtle empathy between words and music has made him one of the finest song writers of his day and is seen equally well in his HARDY settings, *Winter Words* (1953), the opera *Billy Budd* (1951), and *War Requiem* (1962), which intersperses the Latin text with poems by Wilfred OWEN. He wrote works for many distinguished soloists, particularly the tenor, Peter Pears. He composed most effectively for children, as in the church opera, *Noye's Fludde* (1959). With Pears, Britten founded the annual music festival at Aldeburgh, Suffolk, where his most recent opera, *Death in Venice,* was first performed in 1973.

Brongniart, Alexandre (1770-1847) French geologist who established the sequence of the rocks of the Tertiary period in France on the basis of their fossils. Brongniart also made his mark on theoretical palaeontology; his broad classification of living and fossil reptiles is still basically used today. With a group of colleagues, he also laid the foundations of the chemistry of ceramics.

Bronstein, Lev Davidovitch see TROTSKY, Lev Davidovitch

Brontë, Anne (1820-49) English novelist, who wrote *Agnes Grey* (1847) and *The Tenant of Wildfell Hall* (1848), novels of less dramatic qualities than those of her sisters, Charlotte and Emily.

Brontë, Charlotte (1816-55) English novelist, author of *Jane Eyre* (1847), the eldest of three precocious sisters, all novelists. Brought up by their eccentric father at Haworth, his bleak Yorkshire parsonage, all three fashioned their own world of the imagination. Charlotte wrote, with her sisters, the *Poems of Currer, Ellis and Acton Bell* (1846), which were the pseudonyms under which the sisters wrote. She then wrote *Jane Eyre,* which, despite some faults, was a new departure in the novel, mixing romantic love with grim realism and, for the first time, analysing the world of emotion from the woman's point of view. Charlotte, the longest lived of the sisters, spent some time in Brussels and wrote of her life in Yorkshire and Belgium in the novels *Shirley* (1849) and *Villette* (1852).

Brontë, Emily (1818-48) English novelist, who wrote *Wuthering Heights* (1847), one of the most powerful 19th-century novels. Writing in an elemental world far from the daily life of Victorian England, Emily presented evil as a disinterested force of nature; her characters are buffeted by passions they can no more control than they can the storms of the Yorkshire moors. She was the second of the Brontë sisters.

Bronzino, Agnolo (1503-72) Florentine painter, well known for his family of the MEDICI portraits (e.g. *Eleanora of Toledo and her son, c.* 1550). These are elegant but cold works in which more attention is paid to textures than to the sitter's personality.

Brook, Peter (born 1925) Considered by some to be the most original and dynamic British producer and director of his generation. While in his twenties, he directed at the Shakespeare Memorial Theatre, Stratford, and made his name in London with *Doctor Faustus* (1943). Since 1956 he has worked in France as much as in Britain. Since 1962, he has directed the Royal Shakespeare Company productions, including *Marat/Sade* (1964) and his widely acclaimed *A Midsummer Night's Dream* (1970). In the 1970s he worked principally with the Centre for Theatre Research, which he helped to found, and is based in Paris. He toured extensively with the centre, then returned to Stratford in 1978 to direct *Antony and Cleopatra.* His films include *The Beggar's Opera* (1952), *Lord of the Flies* (1962), *King Lear* (1969) and *Meetings with Remarkable Men* (1979).

Brooke, Rupert (1887-1915) English poet, who was one of a number of young, talented writers who died during the First World War. He had grown up in the prosperous idyllic years of the first decade of the century, and his early poems, like 'Grantchester', spoke nostalgically of stability and enduring values. He welcomed the war with a patriotic flourish, but seemed to foresee his own death in 'The Soldier', an impressive sonnet. The *Letters from America,* introduced by Henry JAMES, containing fresh reports from a journey there, appeared in 1916.

Brosse, Salomon de (c. 1565-1626) French architect who designed a number of French châteaux, notably Coulommiers and Blérancourt. He also worked as an architect in Paris, where he built the Palais de Luxembourg and probably the façade of the church of St Gervais.

Brougham and Vaux, Henry, 1st Baron (1778-1868) English jurist who played a significant part in governmental reforms. In 1828 his speech in Parliament on law reform led to far-reaching changes in civil procedure, through him slave-trading became a felony, and as Lord Chancellor (1830-4) he helped the great Reform Bill through the House of Lords (1832). He was also responsible for the reform of the privy Council's judicial committee and for the establishment of London's Old Bailey.

Brouwer, Adriaen (c. 1605-38) Flemish artist, who specialized in pictures of drinking or brawling peasants in tavern settings, which are in the tradition of BRUEGEL and have a similar ironical humour. He spent the first half of his working life in Holland, where he may have been a pupil of Frans HALS.

Brown, Sir Arthur Whitten see ALCOCK, Sir John

Brown, Ford Madox (1821-93) British painter, a follower, though not actually a member, of the Pre-Raphaelites. He shared the social ideals of RUSKIN and MORRIS.

Brown, John (1735-88) Scottish physician who advanced the then-revolutionary proposition that diseases can be caused by weakness in the system rather than by a positive predisposition to contract disease. Brown strenuously opposed such treatment as bloodletting, but used instead doses of stimulating drugs.

Brown, John (1800-59) American anti-slavery crusader, who led a raid in Kansas in which five alleged slave-owners were killed. In an attempt to provoke a slave rebellion in Virginia he raided a government arsenal at Harper's Ferry, Virginia (18 Oct. 1859), but was captured by a company of marines commanded by Robert E. LEE. After being tried for insurrection, treason and murder, he was convicted and hanged at Charleston, Virginia (2 Dec. 1859). He is commemorated in 'John Brown's Body', one of the most popular marching songs of the American Civil War.

Brown, Lancelot (1715-83) British landscape gardener and architect, known as 'Capability Brown', who developed the natural style of landscape gardening, transforming tens of thousands of acres into landscape 'pictures'. Born in Northumberland, he went south to work under William KENT, from whose basic ideas his own style evolved. Believing that house and grounds should be a unity, he became an architect, and built several houses in the Palladian style. The chief elements of Brown's landscapes were winding drives, serpentine rivers, large lakes, broad sweeps of undulating lawn or pasture stretching up to the house, and groups of mainly deciduous trees, of which he planted hundreds of thousands. Vestiges of his work survive in 25 English counties and more complete examples are to be seen at Kew Gardens, Harewood House and Blenheim Palace. Brown was called 'Capability' because of his habit of referring to the potential of the estates on which he was working as 'capabilities'.

Browne, Sir Thomas (1605-82) English doctor and author, whose ornate and solemn style is typified by the *Religio Medici* (1643), a work of personal reflection on religious and philosophic themes, showing delight in the paradoxes and mysteries of Christianity.

Browne, Robert (c. 1550-c. 1633) English separatist clergyman, the pioneer of Congregationalism, which holds that congregations should govern themselves. In the US, Congregationalism is honoured for its connection with the Pilgrim Fathers.

Browning, Elizabeth Barrett (1806-61) English poet, who married Robert BROWNING against her father's wishes.

Browning, Robert (1812-89) English poet, who analysed character and states of mind, particularly in his unique dramatic monologues. His verse displays a fund of invention and a love of unusual incidents, words and rhymes, and he devised the dramatic monologue for his needs.

Broz, Josip See TITO, Marshal

Bruce, James (1730-94) British explorer who rediscovered the source of the Blue Nile and was the first European to trace it to its confluence with the White Nile. His five-volume *Travels to Discover the Source of the Nile in the Years 1768-73* (1790) recorded his journey down the Red Sea and though Ethiopia to its capital, Gondar, and Lake Tana, the beginning of the Blue Nile, and from there down the Blue Nile to the confluence at Khartoum, and on to Aswan.

Bruckner, Anton (1824-96) Major Austrian symphonist whose works are characterized by broad, slowly expanding themes drawn across an often enormous canvas; the slow movement of his *Seventh Symphony* (1883) is an outstanding example. Shortly before he was 40, he heard *Tannhäuser*, and thenceforth WAGNER became a dominant influence on him. Between 1865 and 1896 he composed nine symphonies which became progressively more powerful in their expression. Bruckner's church music, including a *Te Deum* (1884), conveys a deep sense of unity with a God-created world.

Bruegel, Pieter (c. 1525-69) The most important Flemish painter of the 16th century. His best-known works are genre scenes depicting the life and customs of peasant communities – pictures which earned him the nickname 'Peasant Bruegel'. He was, however, an educated man and his interest in such subjects was detached and frequently satirical. Paintings like *The Peasant Wedding* (*c.* 1565) are not so much descriptions of specific events as thinly veiled comments on the coarse appetites of mankind in general. Others, which satirize mankind's follies, are based on popular proverbs, as in *The Blind Leading the Blind* (1568). On his return from a journey to Italy, Bruegel made a series of drawings of alpine scenery which he used in several landscape compositions, some of which contain unobtrusive religious incidents. The motifs of these alpine scenes also recur in some of the five landscapes which illustrate the seasonal cycle (1565).

Brugmann, Friedrich (1849-1919) German philologist whose *Foundations of the Comparative Grammar of Indo-Germanic Languages* (1886-93) surveyed the whole field of Indo-European linguistics and organized the material clearly. He stressed the fact that phonetic laws are fixed and apply without exceptions.

Brulé, Etienne (c. 1592-1633) French explorer of much of the Great Lakes system of North America. He first went to Quebec with Samuel de CHAMPLAIN (1608) and became the first European to travel in the Michigan and Ontario areas, and explored Lakes Huron (1611), Ontario (1615), and Superior (1621). Brulé learned to speak the Algonquin language and lived with the Huron Indians, who eventually boiled and ate him.

Brummell, George Bryan ('Beau') (1778-1840) English dandy renowned for his wit and elegant style of dress. He was a close friend of the Prince Regent, later GEORGE IV, and enjoyed a great social success. Gambling debts caused him to flee to France, where he lived in poverty and died in an insane asylum at Caen.

Brunel, Isambard Kingdom (1806-59) Great English engineer of the 19th century. Son of Marc Isambard Brunel (1769-1849), who designed and built the Thames tunnel from Wapping to Rotherhithe (1825-43), Brunel first designed the Clifton suspension

For years a wreck in the Falkland Is., the *Great Britain* has returned to Bristol, where it was built by Isambard Brunel

bridge in 1829 (it was completed in 1864). In 1833 he became chief engineer of the Great Western Railway and constructed all its viaducts, bridges and tunnels, including the Royal Albert Bridge across the River Tamar into Cornwall. In 1838 he designed the *Great Western*, the first wooden steam ship built to cross the Atlantic, followed in 1845 by the *Great Britain*, the first large iron-hulled screw-driven steam ship. Then in 1853 he began the construction of the *Great Eastern*, the largest ship of its day. Though a failure as a passenger ship it was used in 1866 to lay the first transatlantic telegraph cable.

Brunelleschi, Filippo (1377-1446) Italian architect and pioneer of the early Florentine Renaissance. His first work in Florence was to design a dome to span the enormous crossing of its cathedral, an unprecedented feat of engineering. His characteristic use of grey and white surfaces was first evident in the miniature Pazzi chapel in Florence. Later, he built the two important and finely proportioned Florentine basilicas of S Lorenzo and S Spirito, and, in 1421, designed the elegant arcade of the Foundling Hospital, Florence. His most famous secular work is the Pitti Palace, Florence.

Bruno (c. 1030-1101) German saint and founder of the Carthusian Order of monks. In 1084, some eight years after being dismissed from his university teaching post in France, he and six companions formed a community with a very harsh Rule of Worship, penitence and work at the Grande Chartreuse, a remote and wild spot in the Massif Central. Later, they founded two further houses, La Torre in Calabria and the Charterhouse at San Stefano-in-Basco. Bruno was never formally canonized.

Bruno, Giordano (1548-1600) Italian Dominican who posited that the universe was made up from single indivisible particles, or 'monads'. This theory greatly influenced LIEBNIZ. Bruno opposed Aristotelian logic and was burnt at the stake for heresy in 1600.

Brunton, Sir Lander (1844-1916) Scottish physician and one of the founders of modern pharmacology, whose classic textbook, *The Action of Medicines* (1887), focused students' minds on the biochemical effects of medicines at the level of cells and tissues.

Brutus, Marcus Junius (c. 85-42 BC) Roman leader of the republican conspirators against Julius CAESAR. He sided with POMPEY against Caesar, but after defeat at Pharsalus (46 BC), was pardoned by Caesar and given the governorship of Cisalpine Gaul. He was praetor in Rome (44 BC) and was to have been Caesar's governor in Macedonia but joined the conspirators who stabbed Caesar to death (44 BC). Lacking any effective plan to re-establish republican rule, Brutus fled to Macedonia where his army was defeated at Philippi (42 BC) by Octavian (later AUGUSTUS) and Marcus ANTONIUS. After the defeat Brutus committed suicide.

Buber, Martin (1878-1965) Austrian philosopher. He was born in Vienna where he studied, but later moved to Frankfurt to lecture in Jewish theology. His most influential work was *I and Thou* (1923), which expounded in mystical terms the differing relations between man and things (I – it) and interpersonal or man to God relations (I – Thou). HITLER's rise led to Buber's moving to Jerusalem.

Buchan, John (1875-1940) Scottish historian and novelist, author of dashing popular adventures such as *Prester John* (1910), *The 39 Steps* (1915) and *Greenmantle* (1916). He was created 1st Baron Tweedsmuir.

Buchanan, George (1506-82) Scottish humanist, poet and political philosopher. Educated at the Universities of Paris and St Andrews, Buchanan divided his time during the years 1520-60 between Scotland and France, according to the existing political climate, teaching (one of his pupils was MONTAIGNE), translating Greek literature and writing poetry. A definite Calvinist by 1560, he turned against MARY STUART in 1567 and became tutor to JAMES VI. His most important political work *De Jure regni spud scotos* (1579) is a plea for limited monarchy.

Büchner, Georg (1813-37) German dramatist, who wrote *Woyzec*, the basis of Alban BERG's opera *Wozzeck*. This melancholy study of the life and death of an illiterate soldier was written in reaction to Romanticism and foreshadows the work of such playwrights as TOLLER and BRECHT. His only other important play, *Danton's Death* (1835), is about the French Revolution.

Buck, Pearl (1892-1973) American novelist, many of whose books are about life in China, where she was brought up and to which she returned as a missionary teacher. In her trilogy *The Good Earth* (1931), *Sons* (1932) and *A House Divided* (1935) she showed a sympathetic understanding of the Chinese. *The Good Earth* gained her a Pulitzer Prize, and in 1938 she became the first American woman to receive the Nobel Prize for Literature.

Buddha see GAUTAMA BUDDHA

Buhari, Major-General Muhammadu (born 1942) President of Nigeria since 1983, when he overthrew the government of Shehu Shagari. He was a member of the Supreme Military Council (1976-7) and Military Secretary of the Nigerian Army (1978).

Bukharin, Nikolai Ivanovich (1888-1938) Russian journalist and politician who, after escaping from exile in Siberia in 1910, joined LENIN in Austria. As a member of the Politburo (1918-29) and president of the Third International (1926-9), he was one of the major ideologists of the Communist Party. After Lenin's death in 1924, Bukharin supported STALIN against TROTSKY in the belief that Stalin was Lenin's political heir, but in 1929 he was expelled from the Communist party as a Trotskyite. He was readmitted and appointed editor of *Izvestia* in 1934, but in 1937 he was tried for anti-Soviet activities and betraying the cause of Communism. He was executed in March 1938.

Bulganin, Nikolai Alexandrovich (1895-1975) Soviet politician and soldier, one of the leaders of the USSR after STALIN's death in 1953. He joined the Communist Party in 1917 and served in the secret police (Cheka) from 1918 until 1922, when he became involved in economic affairs and in industry. During the Second World War he became a general and was promoted to Marshal of the USSR in 1947, and held the post of Defence Minister from 1947 to 1949 and again from 1953 to 1955. He became Deputy Chairman of the Council of Ministers in 1949 and Chairman following Stalin's death, from 1955 until 1958, when he was expelled from the Presidium for opposing KHRUSCHEV.

Bull, John (1563-1628) English composer and organist, one of whose virginal pieces may have been the basis for the British national anthem, 'God Save the Queen' (known in America as 'My Country, 'tis of Thee'). By his compositions for the virginal Bull became a pioneer of keyboard repertory and contrapuntal keyboard style, an ingenious professional rather than an inspired composer. He spent the last 11 years of his life as organist at Antwerp Cathedral.

Bülow, Hans Guido von (1830-94) German conductor and pianist who promoted the music of WAGNER and BRAHMS and who was the first international celebrity of the baton. Bülow's wife (LISZT's daugher Cosima) left him for Wagner.

Bunch, Ralph Johnson (1904-71) United Nations diplomat; one of several American negroes appointed to senior administrative posts by President Franklin ROOSEVELT. He was awarded the Nobel Peace Prize (1950). He began his career as an academic specializing in philosophy and social anthropology at various American, British and South American universities. He was appointed adviser to the US Government on colonial and international affairs and conferences 1941-5; US Commissioner, Caribbean Community 1945-7; Principal Director, United Nations Trusteeship Department (1947-54), and UN Mediator in Palestine 1948-9. In the civil war following independence of the Belgian Congo (now Zaïre) in 1960, he was the UN representative on the spot.

Bunsen, Robert (1811-99) German chemist and pioneer of modern spectroscopy. He is best remembered for inventing the Bunsen burner, which allowed him, with Gustave KIRCHHOFF, to make a careful study of the light emitted by compounds heated to incandescence. They found that compounds emit light with wavelengths characteristic of the elements they contain.

Buñuel, Luis (1900-84) Spanish writer and film director whose first films were the Surrealist fantasies *Un Chien Andalou* (1928, made with DALI) and *L'Age d'Or* (1930), which at first shocked the public. Buñuel continued to provide shocks in later films such as *Viridiana* (1961), outraging religious feeling with a parody of The Last Supper, and in *Belle de Jour* (his first film in English), an effective study of sexual fantasy. Throughout his career, working in Europe and Mexico. Buñuel followed his obsession with satirizing the fantasies and hypocrisies of sex and religion in middle class society, in such films as *Tristana* (1970) and *The Discreet Charm of the Bourgeoisie* (1972).

Bunyan, John (1628-88) English non-conformist preacher and author of *Pilgrim's Progress*. Besides its religious interest as a moral allegory, *Pilgrim's Progress* is a model of narrative and descriptive skill. Bunyan was a man of little education and his art sprang from the Bible and folk-tales. Among his other notable works, always on religion or morality, are *Grace Abounding* (1666), a spiritual autobiography, and *The Life and Death of Mr Badman* (1680), a vivid picture of a misspent life.

Burckhardt, Jakob (1818-97) Swiss cultural historian, who, in his masterpiece *The Civilisation of the Renaissance in Italy* (1861), took the Italian Renaissance as the birthdate of modern man.

Burghley, 1st Baron see CECIL, Sir William

Burke, Edmund (1729-97) Irish-born Whig politician and political theorist, who attacked American governments, criticized the power of George III and the Indian administration of HASTINGS. He opposed the French Revolution in *Reflections on the French Revolution* (1790) and was a leading supporter of WILBERFORCE's fight against slavery.

Burke, Robert O'Hara (1820-61) Irish-born Australian explorer who led the first south-north crossing of Australia. He left Melbourne (1860) with 17 men, and provisions on 26 camels and 28 horses. With a small advance party he laid food dumps at Cooper's Creek, Queensland, then pushed north with W. J. Wills, Charles Gray and John King. They reached the Gulf of Carpentaria (1861), but were weakened by hunger, and on the return journey Gray died. The others regained Cooper's Creek, but found it to be deserted. Burke and Wills died of starvation, but King was saved by aborigines.

Burne-Jones, Sir Edward (1833-98) English painter of medieval, romantic and chivalrous themes, reflecting the interests he shared with his friends and fellow Pre-Raphaelites William MORRIS and Dante Gabriel ROSSETTI. His style was strongly influenced by BOTTICELLI.

Burney, Fanny (1752-1840) English novelist and diarist, who first made popular the social novel of domestic life, enlivened with comedy. Her early novels, *Evelina* (1778) and *Cecilia* (1782), catch the tone of the everyday events of her own social world. She wrote a memoir of her father, a historian of music, and under her married name, D'Arblay, published a diary which contained lively sketches of Dr JOHNSON and GARRICK.

Burns, Robert (1759-96) Scottish poet, who broke through the formal artificiality of 18th century verse with a lyricism which grew from the ballad poetry of the border. He was an unsuccessful farmer, but after the publication of this dialect *Poems* (1786) he prospered and lived an amorous, dissipated life. The pungent diction of his dialect, his unusual metres, and his humanity and passion helped to revivify English poetry. The range of his satiric and humorous lyrics was wide, from the acid scorn of 'Holy Willie's Prayer' to the wild energy of 'Tam o'Shanter' and 'The Jolly Beggars'.

Burroughs, William (born 1914) American writer noted for his experiments in fictional form. Among his innovations is the 'cut-up', a mosaic of phrases drawn from widely disparate sources, then recombined in novel patterns. His most widely known works are *The Naked Lunch* (1959), *The Soft Machine* (1968), *The Wild Boys* (1971) and *Cities of the Red Night* (1981).

Burroughs, William Seward (1855-98) American inventor, who in 1892 patented the first commercially successful adding machine. Numbers, selected by a typewriter-type keyboard, were stored and added by means of sets of toothed gears, similar to the modern mechanical adding machine.

Burt, Sir Cyril (1883-1971) English psychologist who pioneered the use of psychology as a means of solving social problems. The intelligence tests and methods of statistical analysis which he devised are significant in their own right, but also have led to important contributions to the study of juvenile delinquency.

Burton, Richard (1925-84) Welsh actor noted for his distinctive speaking voice, whose real name was Richard Jenkins. By the 1950s he had a reputation as a leading Shakespearian actor. He made his film debut in *The Last Days of Dolwyn* (1948). From the early 1950s he concentrated on cinema, appearing in such films as *The Robe* (1953), *Cleopatra* (1962), *Who's Afraid of Virginia Woolf* (1966), *Wild Geese* (1978) and *1984* (1984), which appeared posthumously. He was married five times, twice to the actress Elizabeth Taylor.

Burton, Sir Richard Francis (1821-90) British explorer and writer, translator of the 'Arabian Nights' tales. He travelled in India; made a pilgrimage to Mecca disguised as a Pathan; exlored Somaliland, the lakes of central Africa (discovering Lake Tanganyika with SPEKE while trying to trace the sources of the Nile) and the Gold Coast. He recounted his travels in a number of vividly informative books, including *Pilgrimage to Al-Medinah and Meccah* (1855) and *First Footsteps in East Africa* (1856).

Busch, Wilhelm (1832-1908) German artist, whose unconventional calligraphic techniques and characters, often created as if from the realms of fantasy, introduced into cartoon drawing a style that was comic in itself. His verse-and-picture story *Max und Moritz* (1865) was one of the first examples of the comic strip. It inspired W. R. HEARST to commission the American artist, Rudolf Dirks, to produce *The Katzenjammer Kids* for Hearst's King Features Syndicate in the American newspapers.

Bush, George Herbert Walker (born 1924) American Vice President whose career in politics began in 1966, when he was elected to the House of Representatives from Texas. Losing a campaign for the Senate in 1970, he was appointed United States ambassador to the United Nations by President NIXON. Bush was United States liaison officer to the People's Republic of China under President FORD (1974) and head of the CIA (1976-7). In 1980, after campaigning unsuccessfully against Ronald REAGAN for the Republican nomination, he was selected by Reagan as his running mate and elected Vice President.

Busoni, Ferrucio (1866-1924) Italian composer of *Dr Faustus* (1925). The opera, based on a pre-GOETHE version of the Faust legend, was completed by one of his students after his death. Through his anti-romantic temperament, he pioneered the return to classicism in 20th-century music. He was also the first composer to conceive a choral piano concerto (1903-4). Busoni's importance lies in the intellectual integrity which is reflected in all his work. As a pianist, he ranked with the greatest virtuosi of the last 100 years.

Butler, Josephine (1828-1906) English social reformer, a dedicated campaigner for the rehabilitation of prostitutes. In Britain, as in other countries, prostitution was tacitly tolerated although restricted by law. To Mrs Butler, this implied acceptance of prostitution, and her unremitting concern and agitation led to the eventual repeal of the Contagious Diseases Acts of 1864-9, which permitted the arrest and medical treatment of prostitutes in garrison towns.

Butler, Richard Austen, Baron Butler of Saffron Walden (1902-82) English politician who was Conservative Minister of Education (1941-5). During this time he was responsible for the Education Act (1944) which provided free primary and secondary education for all. He held major cabinet posts (1951-64), before being named Master of Trinity College, Cambridge, and made a life peer in 1965.

Butler, Samuel (1835-1902) English satirist and novelist, who attacked most of the Victorian attitudes towards life. He refused to enter the Church and went instead to farm sheep in New Zealand; he drew on this experience in *Erewhon* (1872), an inventive satire on progress, with some touches worthy of SWIFT. On his return to London in 1865 Butler was a persistently mocking critic of scientists, music critics and teachers. He liked odd attitudes and insisted that HOMER was a woman. In *The Way of All Flesh* (1903) he attacked the Victorian family.

Butterick, Ebeneezer (1826-1903) American tailor and shirt-maker who, in the 1840s, devised a technique for printing and cutting paper dress-making patterns. They could be used by anyone with one of the new sewing machines, such as that of SINGER.

Buxtehude, Diderik (1637-1707) Danish organist and composer who helped to found the public concert with a series of musical evenings in Lübeck from 1673. Although Buxtehude was among the founding fathers of organ playing and composition, much of his music is now lost. The surviving church cantatas and organ compositions prove him to have been a major composer.

Buys Ballot, Christoph (1817-90) Dutch meteorologist who stated the law named after him. In 1857, while Director of the Royal Netherlands Meteorological Institute, he announced the law, which states that, if you stand with your back to the wind in the northern hemisphere (outside the equatorial zone), there is low atmospheric pressure to your left and high to your right; the opposite is true in the southern hemisphere. Unknown to Buys Ballot, the American William Ferrel had already independently deduced this law months before.

Byng, John (1704-57) British admiral, shot for neglect of duty. Just before the Seven Years' War he was sent to protect Britain's base on the Mediterranean island of Minorca, but failed to drive off an attacking French fleet. Believing himself seriously outgunned and outmanned, he withdrew to Gibraltar, where he was court-martialled, found guilty and given the mandatory death sentence. Despite a recommendation for mercy Byng was shot to appease the enraged public. This provoked VOLTAIRE's celebrated remark that the English sometimes shot an admiral *pour encourager les autres* (to encourage the others).

Byrd, William (c. 1542-1623) English musician who became the greatest composer of the Elizabethan period. A lifelong Roman Catholic, Byrd was appointed by ELIZABETH I to be joint organist of the Chapel Royal with TALLIS, who may have been his teacher. With Tallis, he was granted a monopoly to print music, though the first printing of his *Gradualia* (1605) was suppressed under JAMES I as politically subversive. Byrd was master of all the musical forms of his day, important for his madrigals, the body of distinguished church music that he wrote for both Catholic and Anglican services, and for helping to lay the foundations of a future keyboard style.

Byron, Lord George Gordon, (1788-1824) English poet, whose scandalous, colourful conduct and popular poetry made him, especially on the Continent, one of the leading figures of the Romantic movement. Byron's 'Childe Harold' (1812-18) and his many verse-tales gave poetry the movement, historical stories and foreign landscapes that SCOTT had introduced to the novel. In *Don Juan* (1819-24), satire, cheerful cynicism, colloquial diction, imagery and descriptive writing cover a sure understanding of psychology and a bleak, sometimes despairing, view of human nature. Byron died of fever at Missolonghi, Greece, in the fight for Greek independence.

C

Cabot, John (1425-c. 1500) Venetian immigrant to England (*c.* 1484), the first of England's ocean explorers. Seeking a sea route to Asia he sailed from Bristol (1497) and reached Cape Breton Island, Canada, which he mistook for northeastern Asia. The following year, backed by HENRY VII, he reached south Greenland (the first European known to do so since Viking times), then crossed to North America and followed its coast southward to the Delaware.

Cabot, Sebastian (c. 1476-1557) English explorer who accompanied his father, John CABOT, on one or both of his voyages and, while seeking the North West Passage, reached Hudson Bay (1509). He was in HENRY VIII's army sent to aid FERDINAND V of Castile and was appointed Pilot Major of the Spanish Navy. While leading an expedition to find the Spice islands, Ophir, and Cathay, he entered and explored far up the River Plate, in South America. He returned to England, where he founded and became Governor of the Merchant Adventurers.

Cabral, Pedro Alvares (c. 1460-c. 1526) Portuguese discoverer of Brazil. At the head of 13 trading vessels which set out for India (1500), Cabral's route took too westerly a course and he sighted the Brazilian coast of South America, which he claimed for Portugal. After four of his fleet (including the ship carrying Bartholomeu DIAS) sank in a storm, the rest continued to India, traded successfully, and returned laden with spices, porcelain, aromatic woods and pearls.

Cadamosto, Alvise da (c. 1432-c. 1511) Venetian navigator who explored the West African coast for HENRY THE NAVIGATOR of Portugal. On his first voyage (1455), Cadamosto went to the Madeiras and Canaries, and down the Sahara coast to Senegal and Gambia. During his second voyage down the African coast (1456) he was blown out to sea and claimed to have discovered the Cape Verde Islands. His long account of his voyages describes Portuguese settlements, trading and tribal customs in Africa.

Cadillac, Antoine de la Mothe (1658-1730) French founder of Detroit. He went to America as a soldier (1683) and became commander of the post at Mackinac (1694). Eager to build personal wealth and further the French fur trade in North America, he gained a land grant, and in 1701, with 100 French settlers and soldiers, founded a colony consisting of a civil settlement called Ville d'Etroit (Detroit) enclosed by Fort Pontchartrain.

Caesar, Gaius Julius (100-44 BC) Roman general and dictator of the Roman empire. After gaining popularity by public displays of democratic feeling and by vast expenditure on public entertainments, Caesar arranged and joined the First Triumvirate (60 BC) with POMPEY and Crassus. This ruled in place of the discredited but constitutional oligarchic party. Caesar was elected consul the following year. He built his military reputation on campaigns in northwest Europe (58-51 BC), during which he isolated and crushed Gaul, and made brief forays into Britain (55 and 54 BC). These victories, recounted in his *On the Gallic War*, brought northwest Europe into the orbit of Rome's Mediterranean civilization, so shaping the future of Europe. After these victories, the Senate, prompted by Pompey, demanded that Caesar disband his armies or be declared an enemy. Caesar crossed the river Rubicon into Italy with his army and defeated Pompey at Pharsalus (48 BC). Now dictator of Rome, Caesar unified the empire by equitable reforms and extended citizenship to subject peoples. He refused the offer of the crown (44 BC), but his rule became more absolute. He was killed by Republican conspirators led by BRUTUS.

Cage, John (born 1912) American composer who pioneered the concepts of chance and indeterminacy in modern music. In this he has had a considerable influence over such European composers as STOCKHAUSEN and BERIO. Cage studied with SCHOENBERG and COWELL. In the 1930s he invented the 'prepared piano', an instrument modified to produce an unfamiliar range. His 10-hour composition *Empty Voices* was first performed in 1979.

Calamity Jane (1852-1903) American frontierswoman whose real name was Martha Jane Canary, and who became a flamboyant legend in her own lifetime. She usually dressed in men's clothes, and worked heroically nursing the sick during the 1878 smallpox epidemic at Deadwood, South Dakota.

Calder, Alexander (1898-1973) American sculptor who invented the mobile and became a leading figure in the school of sculptors who work in metal. His *Mobile* (1934) consists of a variety of objects suspended in a black frame; *Red Petals* (1942) is made of metal and wire, transformed into boughs and leaves.

Callaghan, Leonard James (born 1912) British Labour politician. He entered Parliament as member for Cardiff South in 1945 and sat for Cardiff South-East from 1950. He was elected leader of the Labour Party and became Prime Minister in April 1976. He is the only Prime Minister in British history to have held all of the major offices of state: Chancellor of the Exchequer (1964-7), Home Secretary (1967-70) and Foreign Secretary (1974-6). He was defeated by the Conservatives in the General Election of 1979, and resigned as leader of the Opposition in 1980.

Callas, Maria (1923-77) American soprano of Greek parentage who combined personality and musical skill to become the leading operatic soprano of her day.

Calne, Roy (born 1930) English surgeon who, in 1968, after several years of successfully transplanting human kidneys, became the first surgeon to transplant the human liver.

Calvert, George, 1st Baron Baltimore (c. 1580-1632) English colonizer associated, with his son Cecilius (1605-75), with the founding of Maryland (named after CHARLES I's queen, Henrietta Maria). Calvert was granted a charter to colonize Newfoundland (1623), but found the land too cold and was granted another (1632) to colonize and govern between the Potomac and the 40th parallel. He died before the charter was issued but his son sent the first colonists to found St Mary's City at the mouth of the Potomac.

Calvin, John (1509-64) French theologian and religious reformer, founder of the Calvinist branch of the Protestant church. The *Institutes of Christian Religion* was the most systematic Protestant theological treatise of the Reformation. Although few Protestants now believe in predestination, Calvin's somewhat austere doctrine has greatly influenced the reformed religions, especially the state Protestantism of northern Europe and the Puritan movement in both Britain and North America, although some of the harsher features have softened with time.

Cambyses II (6th cent. BC) Achaemenid King of Persia (530-522 BC), who continued the conquests of his father, CYRUS THE GREAT, by adding Egypt to his empire. In 525 BC he invaded Egypt, and after defeating the Egyptians at Pelusium, captured Thebes and Memphis. The submission of the Greeks of Libya and Cyrene which followed gave him control of their wealth. Cambyses planned expeditions against Ethiopia and Carthage; but although he occupied North Ethiopia, he was forced to withdraw for lack of supplies. He died mysteriously, perhaps by his own hand.

Camões, Luís Vaz de (c. 1524-80) Portugal's outstanding literary figure and lyric poet. His masterpiece, *The Lusiads* (1572), is an epic poem exalting Portuguese history and the voyages of Vasco da GAMA. Camões's collection of lyric poems *Rhymes* was published posthumously in 1595. A master of every verse form, his sufferings and philosophical meditations in these anguished and deeply felt works express the uniquely Portuguese *saudade-soledade* (a yearning, with overtones of loneliness) as no other Portuguese poet has ever done.

Campbell, Archibald, 1st Duke of Argyll (c. 1651-1703) Scottish soldier responsible (with John Campbell, 1st Earl of Breadalbane, and Sir John Dalrymple) for the Massacre of Glencoe. He supported William of Orange in the Revolution of 1688 and was deputed to offer him the Scottish crown (1689). In February 1692, Campbell clan troops quartered with the Macdonalds in the Argyllshire pass of Glencoe, and butchered some 40 of their hosts, including the Macdonald Chieftain MacIan. The pretext was the Macdonalds' suspected disloyalty to WILLIAM III, but massacre also struck a blow at the Campbells' traditional clan enemies.

Campbell, Colen (1673-1729) Scottish architect who introduced the Palladian style into England. Mereworth Castle, Kent, modelled on PALLADIO's Villa Rotunda, is the most correct example of this style. In 1715, he published *Vitruvius Britannicus,* a collection of designs of buildings mainly by contemporary British architects which first aroused Lord Burlington's interest in architecture. Burlington House, London, which he remodelled in 1718-19, and Compton Place, Eastbourne, are other examples of Campbell's works still in existence.

Campbell, Sir Malcolm (1885-1948) English racing driver who became one of the most successful speed record-breakers on both land and water. Between 1924 and 1935 he broke the land speed record nine times raising it to 301·13 mph. When he turned to boats, he broke the water speed record three times, raising it to 141·75 mph. His son, Donald Campbell (1921-67), continued Sir Malcolm's record-breaking attempts and reached 328 mph in a last, fatal attempt on the water speed record.

Campbell-Bannerman, Henry (1836-1908) English Prime Minister and head of the Liberal government which came to power in 1905 after ten years of Conservative and Unionist rule. As Liberal leader in the Commons (1899) he advocated conciliation of the Boers during the South African War of 1899-1902 and criticized the more extreme tactics (concentration camps) used by Britain during the campaign. He became Prime Minister on the resignation of BALFOUR, and his party gained a sweeping victory in the election of 1906. His government began the policy of reconciliation in South Africa which led to the grant of self-government (1909).

Campen, Jacop van (1595-1657) Dutch 17th-century architect who was influenced by PALLADIO. Probably his best building is the Mauritshuis (1633-5), in the Hague, a mellow brick building in which the giant pilasters and pediment are combined with the Dutch type of hipped roof. His other works are the Amsterdam Town Hall, now the Royal Palace, and the Nieuwe Kerk in Haarlem.

Campion, Edmund (1540-81) English Jesuit martyr who was tortured, convicted of treason and hanged at Tyburn for encouraging the Catholic community outlawed by ELIZABETH I after her excommunication in 1570. Unable to accept Anglicanism, Campion, a brilliant scholar and orator, left England for Rome in 1573, when he became a Jesuit priest, returning to his country as head of the first Jesuit mission to England in 1580. He was canonized in 1970.

Campion, Thomas (1567-1619) English lyric poet and musician, who amongst a series of books of songs, published *Observations in the Art of English Poesie* (1602), which questioned formalized conventional notions on the art of writing verse.

Camus, Albert (1913-60) Algerian-born French novelist, dramatist and essayist, winner of the Nobel Prize for Literature in 1957. His early sympathy with Existentialist ideas is reflected in philosophical essays like *Le mythe de Sisyphe* (1942) and symbolic novels such as *L'Etranger, La Peste* (1947) and *La Chute* (1956). They explore the nature of action in an absurd world, the problem of suffering, and the reconciliation of the claims of art with those of political responsibility. In the postwar years, the rift with SARTRE's Existentialist views became more marked as Camus argued against cynicism and nihilism, revealing his compassion and humanitarian outlook. Among his other notable publications were his treatise *L'Homme revolté* (1951) and a number of plays – *Le Malentendu* (1944), *Caligula* (written 1938, produced 1946), *Les Justes* (1949) and *L'Etat de siège* (1948). He died in a motor accident.

Canaletto, Antonio (1697-1768) Italian artist and etcher, who is celebrated for his views of Venice and Rome. His early style was impressionistic, but Canaletto's colours sharpened and his technique became crisp, with an emphasis on detail facilitated by the use of the *camera obscura*. In *Ascension Day at Venice,* which depicts the city during one of its most important festivals, Canaletto captures the essential vitality of the scene and contrasts it with the timelessness of the buildings, which are particularly Venetian.

Canary, Martha Jane see CALAMITY JANE

Canning, George (1770-1827) English statesman who supported the revolt of the Spanish American colonies (1823). A Foreign Secretary in 1807, Canning initiated the Peninsular War policy. A quarrel and duel with CASTLEREAGH in 1809 restricted him to a series of minor offices until 1822 when, as a result of Castlereagh's suicide, he was reinstated as Foreign Secretary and appointed Leader of the House of Commons. He continued the later policy of Castlereagh in abandoning the Congress system and the policy of non-intervention, and his support of independence movements in Europe anticipated the extension of British trade. Canning became Prime Minister and Chancellor of the Exchequer in 1827, for the last five months of his life.

Cano, Sebastian del (16th cent.) Spanish navigator who completed the first circumnavigation of the globe. He sailed on one of MAGELLAN's five ships (1519) and, after Magellan's death and heavy casualties among senior officers, rose to command the *Vittoria*, the only one of the five ships fit for the long journey home from the Spice islands. The homeward voyage, by the route already known through the Indian Ocean and round the Cape of Good Hope, took nine months. Few of the crew survived.

Canova, Antonio (1757-1822) Italian Neo-classic sculptor, chiefly in marble, who was often inspired by the erotic myths of Greece, as in *Cupid and Psyche* (1793). His *Tomb of Maria Christina* (1798), which treated the figures in the round, was revolutionary for tomb sculpture.

Cantor, Georg (1845-1918) German mathematician, whose most famous work deals with the theory of infinity and the theory of sets. He extended the numerical series introduced by FOURIER. His set theory was a new departure in maths, and forms the basis of much modern mathematical analysis.

Canute II (c. 994-1035) Danish king of England (1016-35), who ruled a short-lived northern empire. Successfully finishing his father SWEYN's fight with Ethelred II, he was elected King of all England by the Witan (the English Saxon Parliament) in 1016 and married Ethelred's widow. Canute pursued a policy of reconciliation, respecting local customs, sending back to Denmark his Danish fleet and soldiers except for a bodyguard of house carls and a fleet of 40 ships. In 1026 he inflicted a major defeat on a Norwegian-Swedish attack on Denmark and was able to take over Norway and became its king (1028). There are many stories about Canute, including the one that he tried in vain to stop the incoming tide to show his sycophantic followers the limitations of his powers.

Cão, Diogo (15th cent.) Portuguese mariner who first pushed the exploration of Africa's west coast far south of the Equator. On his first voyage (1482-4), he discovered the mouth of the Congo and sailed on to Cape St Mary (13°26'S). On his last known voyage (1485-6), he reached Monte Negro (15°41'S) and beyond that Cape Cross, within 150 miles of the Tropic of Capricorn. At each of the four points he set up commemorative pillars.

Capet, Hugh see HUGH CAPET

Capone, Alphonso, 'Al' (1895-1947) Italian-born American gangster, who built up a criminal organization during the Prohibition era (1919-33). Running the illicit liquor trade, gambling saloons and brothels in Chicago, Capone maintained his position by wholesale elimination of his rivals and is said to have been responsible for over 500 murders. In 1930, the FBI attempted to convict him, but lacked sufficient evidence to obtain his impeachment. He was eventually sentenced to 11 years' imprisonment in 1931 for tax evasion.

Capote, Truman (1924-84) American novelist, whose work centres frequently on lonely people fighting against society in the Southern States of American. His book *In Cold Blood* (1966), a detailed reconstruction of a particularly mindless and brutal murder, was hailed as a new type of prose narrative. His earlier work, e.g. *Other Voices, Other Rooms* (1948) about the painful development of a homosexual boy, is more Gothic in style.

Capp, Al (born 1909) Creator of the American comic strip *Li'l Abner* (1934). His work, which deals with the tribulations of an eccentric mountain community, satirizes American national institutions.

Caravaggio, Michelangelo Merisi da (1573-1610) Italian artist, with whom the development of *chiaroscuro* (contrasts between light and shade) is chiefly associated. it is apparent even in his earliest important commission: a series of large pictures of the life of ST MATTHEW for a chapel in S Luigi dei Francesi in Rome. In one of these, *The Calling of St Matthew*, the darkness of the scene is dramatically relieved by a shaft of light which falls directly on the saint. The original altar-piece of *St Matthew and the Angel* in the same chapel was rejected. Exception was also taken to another radical innovation by Caravaggio: an uncompromisingly realistic interpretation of religious scenes conceived as contemporary events, biblical characters being depicted as peasants with dirty feet and sweating faces. Caravaggio's aim was to bring his religious scenes closer to ordinary experience and this he attempted to do partly by eschewing reverential poses and by bringing sharply-lit figures close to the picture plane, where his realistic treatment of his characters could not be ignored. Caravaggio's influence was greatest outside Italy, where it spread both to France, in the painting of LA TOUR, and the Netherlands (Utrecht school).

Cardano, Geronimo (1501-76) Italian physician and mathematician, who produced the first accurate account of typhus fever, and was the first to publish solutions to cubic and quartic equations, and calculations on the theory of probability. Among his many publications were an attack on the medical practices of his day, a work on the treatment of syphilis, and some notes on the teaching of deaf, dumb and blind people. His most important mathematical publication was The Great Art, or The Rules of Algebra (1545), a fundamental text in the study of algebra. It contained his solutions of cubic equations and work done by his former servant, Lodovico Ferrari, on quartic equations. Cardano's other principal mathematical work was *The Book of the Game of Chance,* which sets out a theory of probability not fully formalized until the work of PASCAL a century later.

Carducci, Giosuè (1835-1907) Italian critic, poet and Nobel Prize winner who advocated a return to classicism in fiction and attempted to introduce classical metrical schemes into contemporary Italian poetry. The patriotic evocation of Italy's past and the visions of her future which permeate his poetry, notably *Primitive Odes* (1877-89) and *Rhymes and Rhythms* (1899), have caused him to be hailed as the national poet of Modern Italy.

Carey, Joyce (1888-1957) English novelist, whose many books have a buoyant optimism rare in 20th-century writing. His first novels, *Aissa Saved* (1932) and *The African Witch* (1936), showed remarkable sympathy for African character and problems. His chief works are contained in two trilogies. The first, including *The Horse's Mouth* (1944), is a study of closely interrelated lives, full of skilful characterization. The second, starting with *A Prisoner of Grace* (1952), links English politics, social history and religion. He also wrote poetry, stories and political studies, such as *The Case for African Freedom* (1941).

Carlson, Chester (1906-68) American inventor of the dry copying process called xerography (1937). The process uses electrostatic charges to form a copy of an original in fine carbon powder.

Carlyle, Thomas (1795-1881) British historian and journalist whose work offers a powerful social and political commentary on his times. He was concerned with the role of the 'hero' in history and most of his writing depicts events through the lives of men and women. He also examined the drabness and bitterness occasioned by social structures. His works included *The French Revolution* (1837), *Frederick the Great* (1865) and *Chartism* (1839), all distinguished by a dramatic use of dialogue and imagery.

Carnegie, Andrew (1835-1919) Scottish industrialist who expounded a 'Gospel of Wealth' theory (1889) in which half a man's duty was to get wealth and the other half to redistribute the surplus for the general welfare. Carnegie emigrated to America in 1848 and worked for the Pennsylvania Railroad before concentrating (from 1873) on steel manufacture and founding the US Steel Corporation (1901). Notable beneficiaries of his philanthropy were educational institutes in Pittsburgh and Washington and American and Scottish universities.

Carothers, Wallace (1896-1937) American chemist who led the research team at the Du Pont Company, which, in 1935, developed nylon, the first completely man-made fibre.

Carpaccio, Vittore (c. 1460-c. 1523) Venetian painter, whose work often depicts the ceremonial pageantry of his native city. His most famous work is the early narrative cycle, *The Legend of St Ursula* (1490-8).

Carpenter, Nathanael (17th cent.) English geographer who published the first geographical study to be written in English. It was ahead of its time in stressing the spatial relationships between geographical phenomena, and in the scientific spirit in which he described them.

Carracci, Annibale (1560-1609) Italian artist, who was one of the first eclectic painters, absorbing elements from a number of sources, notably MICHELANGELO, RAPHAEL, TITIAN and antique art. His most famous work, the ceiling fresco in the gallery of the Farnese Palace, Rome (1597-1604), combines narrative mythological scenes with a scheme of simulated architecture and sculpture evolving from Michelangelo's Sistine Chapel ceiling. The work was influential in the development of 17th-century illusionistic decorative schemes.

Carroll, Lewis (1832-98) English mathematician and writer, whose imaginative fantasies are among the most original prose works of the 19th century. The famous 'nonsense' books, *Alice in Wonderland* (1865), *Through the Looking-Glass* (1871), and the poem, 'Hunting of the Snark' (1876), do not lack sense, but are parodies of sense which, following an idiosyncratic logic, point out the absurdities in apparently normal behaviour.

Carson, Edward (1854-1935) Anglo-Irish barrister and politician who, in 1912, was instrumental in raising a force of 80,000 men (Ulster Volunteers) to resist Home Rule for Ireland. From 1905 he led the Protestant movement against Home Rule and established (1911) the Ulster Unionist Council and a draft Constitution for Ulster. In 1915-16 he helped LLOYD GEORGE and the Tories to remove ASQUITH from office as PM, and became a member of Loyd George's war cabinet. He was created a life peer in 1921 and sat as Lord of Appeal from 1921 to 1929. After the war, in contrast to his earlier intransigence, he tried to find a compromise solution to the Irish problem.

Carson, Kit (1809-68) American frontiersman famous for pioneering west of the Mississippi (as Daniel BOONE was famous east of it). He became successively teamster, trapper, Indian fighter, hunter, and army scout and ranged from Texas to Oregon during a hectic career.

Carter, Howard (1873-1939) English Egyptologist who discovered the tomb of Tutankhamun (14th century BC), the first royal tomb to be found almost intact.

Carter, James Earl (born 1924) Thirty-ninth President of the US. After graduating from the US Naval Academy he served in the navy until 1953. He was a senator for Georgia (1962-6) and governor of that state (1971-4) before being nominated Democratic presidential candidate to run against Gerald FORD in 1976. In defeating Ford he became the first president from the 'South' since the Civil War. As president, he was admired for his courage and integrity, but was found wanting in leadership. He was defeated overwhelmingly by Ronald Reagan in the election of 1980.

Caruso, Enrico (1873-1921) Italian operatic tenor who was the first singer to owe world-wide fame to the gramophone. By the time of his death he had made 154 recordings. His most popular roles were Carnio in *Pagliacci*, Rodolpho in *La Bohème* and the duke in *Rigoletto*.

Carver, John (c. 1576-1621) English merchant and first governor of Plymouth Colony, in what is now Massachusetts. After joining the Pilgrim Fathers in Holland (1609), Carver obtained a charter to settle in the New World, raised money for the *Mayflower* and collected the London pilgrims. He sailed with some 100 colonists, including English Puritans seeking religious freedom. When they reached Cape Cod (1620), Carver became governor of new-born Plymouth Colony in accordance with the Mayflower Compact, an improvised agreement for democratic self-government. He and half the colony died in the first severe winter.

Casals, Pablo (1876-1973) Spanish virtuoso cellist whose interpretations, particularly of the unaccompanied cello suites of J. S. BACH, combined great technical skill with philosophical and humanitarian depths. In 1905 he formed a legendary trio consisting of himself, the violinist Jacques Thibaud and the pianist Alfred Cortot. From 1940 Casals remained in exile to show his dislike for the Spanish régime.

Casanova, Giovanni Jacopo (1725-98) Italian adventurer whose exploits and guises dazzled European high society. After expulsion from a seminary for scandalous conduct, Casanova was variously a preacher, alchemist, and violin player. In 1755, he was jailed for sorcery, but quickly engineered a daring escape. Casanova fled to Paris, where he introduced a lottery, accumulated a fortune, and mixed with the Empress CATHERINE II, VOLTAIRE, Madame de POMPADOUR and Cagliostro. After a brief career in espionage, Casanova settled down as a librarian and wrote his bawdy memoirs. They were not published in unexpurgated form until 1960.

Casement, Roger (1864-1916) Irish nationalist and British consular offical. Casement joined the British Consular Service in 1892 and won fame and a knighthood (1911) through his reports on the exploitation and maltreatment of rubber-tapping workers in the Congo (1903) and in Brazil (1910). During his consular career he canvassed the cause of Irish nationalism, and on retiring from the Service became an active Irish Nationalist. When war broke out in 1914 he went to Germany and tried – unsuccessfully – to raise a brigade of Irish prisoners of war to fight against Britain. He landed in Ireland from a German submarine in 1916, just before the Easter Rising, but was caught, taken to London, tried for high treason and hanged. His remains were subsequently disinterred from Pentonville gaol and taken to Ireland, where he is regarded as a patriot and martyr by Irish republicans.

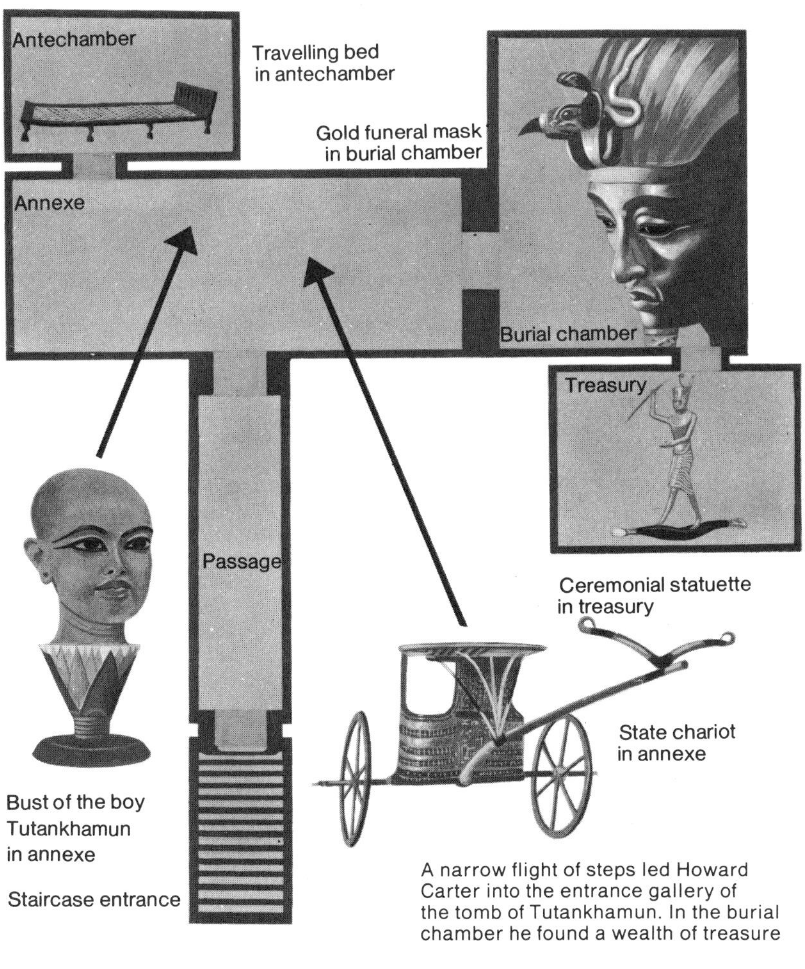

A narrow flight of steps led Howard Carter into the entrance gallery of the tomb of Tutankhamun. In the burial chamber he found a wealth of treasure

Casey, Richard Gardiner (1890-1976) Governor-General of Australia (1965-9) who was Australia's minister to the United States from 1940 to 1942 and, from 1942 to 1943, a member of the War Cabinet in Britain. In 1944 he was appointed Governor of Bengal.

Casimir III (1310-70) King of Poland (1333-70), called 'the Great'. Succeeding his father LADISLAS I, Casimir made peace with the Teutonic Knights and Bohemia, and formed an alliance with Hungary which helped him to acquire Galicia (1340) and, with it, much trade. Casimir's domestic measures checked aristocratic oppression of the peasants, founded towns, reformed administration and currency, built national defence and supported industry and commerce. He founded Cracow University (1364), later to become Eastern Europe's intellectual capital.

Casimir IV (1427-92) King of Poland (1447-92), who made his country a great Central European power. Inheriting both Poland and Lithuania, he worked to preserve the union and to restore Polish lands lost to the Teutonic Knights. Helped by Prussian towns, he regained the lost western and northern territories (1454-66), restoring Poland's Baltic outlet, absorbing western Prussia, and gaining overlordship of Eastern Prussia. To preserve the Polish-Lithuanian union he adopted an anti-German policy which he maintained only by granting to his nobles wide privileges and the right to elect the monarch. As a result of his enlightened approach to the freedom of opinion, Poland became a refuge of scholars and a centre of culture.

Caslon, William (1692-1766) English printer, noted for the distinction and legibility of his type. He established a type foundry and his work became known throughout Europe. The Caslon type-face is still used in book printing.

Cassidy, Butch (1866-1910) American cowboy and rustler, who became a leader of the Wild Bunch, a group of outlaws operating mainly from 'Hole in the Wall' in the wilds of Wyoming. In 1902, Cassidy and his companion Harry Longabough, the Sundance Kid, fled the West and sailed for South America accompanied by Etta Place, who had joined the outlaws. The trio committed several robberies before Cassidy and Longabough were killed by soldiers in Bolivia.

Cassini, Giovanni (1625-1712) Italian-born French astronomer, who greatly extended knowledge of the Solar System. While Professor of Astronomy at Bologna (1650-69), Cassini calculated the rotation periods of Venus, Mars and Jupiter. In 1669 he was appointed Director of LOUIS XIV's new Paris Observatory. In the following years he discovered the division that separated the rings of Saturn (the 'Cassini Division') and calculated the eccentricity of the Earth's orbit. He began the work, carried on by his son Jacques, which confirmed that the Earth was not a perfect sphere. Between 1671 and 1684 he discovered four satellites of Saturn and estimated the distance from Mars to the Sun.

Castagno, Andrea del (c. 1423-57) Florentine painter, whose early work (e.g. *Last Supper*, c. 1445-50) was influenced by MASACCIO's and later by that of DONATELLO.

Castiglione, Baldassarre (1478-1529) Italian courtier and author of one of the 16th century's most popular books, *The Courtier* (1528) – an illuminating but idealized picture of Italian Renaissance court society. Born of an aristocratic family, he served the Duke of Urbino as a diplomat, eventually becoming Papal Nuncio in Spain.

Castlereagh, Robert Stewart, Viscount (1769-1822) Anglo-Irish statesman, who was responsible for the Fourth Coalition, consisting of Britain, Russia, Austria and Prussia, which defeated NAPOLEON. Among the the causes he espoused were the union of Britain and Ireland, and Catholic emancipation, the rejection of which (1801) by George III caused his resignation and that of PITT. He also served at the India Office (1802) and was War Secretary (1805-6; 1807-9). His duel with CANNING (1809) led to his enforced retirement for some years. After becoming Foreign Secretary in 1812, he sought to establish the balance of power and diplomatic order in Europe which became known as the 'Congress System', though Castlereagh became progressively disillusioned with its reactionary pretensions. He committed suicide in 1822.

Castro, Fidel (born 1927) Cuban revolutionary politician who overthrew BATISTA's dictatorship (1959) and made Cuba a socialist state. Son of an immigrant from Spain, he became a militant socialist, and was captured in 1953 while leading an attack on the Moncada Barracks with the purpose of seizing arms and ammunition. He was sentenced to 15 years' imprisonment by the Batista régime, but was released under an amnesty in 1955. He went to Mexico where he organized a Cuban revolutionary movement, and returned secretly to the island with a small force, including 'Che' GUEVARA. He took to the Sierra Maestra mountains and recruited more men (1956). After inflicting a series of defeats on government forces, he took Havana on 1 Jan. 1959 and seized political power. In 1961 he declared himself Marxist-Leninist and requested Russian aid. Missile sites were installed and missiles and other equipment shipped to Cuba by Russia, which provoked the United States and resulted in the major international 'Cuba crisis' of October 1962. He remained firmly in power, however, and in the 1970s sent troops to African nations to expand Cuban influence. The CARTER administration saw a slight improvement in relations between Cuba and the United States.

Cather, Willa (1873-1947) American novelist, who wrote affectionately about immigrant and pioneer life in the agricultural West. *O Pioneers!* (1913) and *My Antonia* (1918) are set in the frontier world of the Nebraska prairies where she spent her childhood. Her work is imbued with a sense of history coloured by Roman Catholicism.

Catherine of Aragon, see HENRY VIII

Catherine II 'the Great' (1729-96) German-born Empress of Russia (1762-96) who continued PETER I's work of westernization and expansion. After forcing her unpopular husband Peter III to abdicate, she made St Petersburg rival Paris as a cultural showplace, by patronizing Italian opera, painting, sculpture and architecture, and popularizing French etiquette, literature, and liberal philosophy. Catherine corresponded with VOLTAIRE and the French *encyclopédistes* and favoured social reforms proposed by MONTESQUIEU and BECCARIA, but she also extended serfdom (forced by the powerful Russian nobles) and suppressed liberalism. Under Catherine's brilliant generals (who included Suvorov and one of her numerous lovers, Potemkin) Russian troops seized Byelorussia from Poland (in and after 1772) and the Crimea from Turkey.

Cato, Marcus Porcius (234-149) BC) Roman statesman and writer, author of the first important Latin prose works, including a history of Rome and a treatise on agriculture.

Catullus, Gaius Valerius (c. 84-c. 54 BC) The first Roman personal poet whose works survive. His many short poems, in lyric, iambic and elegaic metres, though written with great care and an attention to Greek models which delighted his sophisticated circle, convey a deep sincerity, rising to passion, especially when he writes of his love for Lesbia. His four longer poems, and especially No. 64 on the Marriage of Pelius and Thetis, more clearly show his learning and the influence on him of Alexandrian poetry.

Cauchy, Augustin Louis (1789-1857) French mathematician, who wrote three main treatises on analysis and calculus between 1821 and 1828. At the same time, he developed the theory of functions of a complex variable, which is fundamental to many fields of applied mathematics.

Cavallini, Pietro (c. 1250-c. 1330) Roman painter and mosaicist. His works (e.g. mosaics in the church of Sta Maria in Trastevere, in Rome; frescoes in St Cecilia, also in Rome), although dependent on the stylized forms of Byzantine art, echo the classical spirit of antique painting.

Cavell, Edith Louisa (1865-1915) British nurse, shot by the Germans for aiding the escape of Allied soliders from Belgium. Matron at the Berkendael Medical Institute, Brussels, she helped some 200 English, French and Belgian soldiers to escape to the Dutch frontier. For this she was shot in 1915.

Cavendish, Henry (1731-1810) English chemist and physicist who calculated the Earth's mass. Isaac NEWTON had stated his famous law of gravitation in an equation involving the Earth's mass and an undetermined constant called the gravitational constant. Cavendish performed a delicate experiment to measure the gravitational force of attraction between two metal balls and from this calculated the constant. He used the constant in Newton's equation to calculate the Earth's mass. His result, nearly 7000 trillion tons, was about 10 per cent higher than modern estimates.

Cavour, Count Camillo (1810-61) Italian statesman who, with GARIBALDI, accomplished the union of Italy. With Count Cesare Balbo, he started the nationalist newspaper *Il Risorgimento* (The Resurrection) in 1847, advocating a representative system of government for Piedmont, which in 1848 was granted a constitution by Charles Albert (King of Savoy and ruler of Piedmont-Sardinia). Cavour entered politics in 1848 and, after holding several portfolios, he became Premier in 1852, and developed and modernized his native Piedmont's agriculture, industry, communications and army. Believing that he could unite Italy by bringing her onto the international stage, he took Piedmont into the Crimean War, and in 1858 signed a secret treaty with NAPOLEON III (Plombières) whereby France and Piedmont were to make war on Austria. He resigned (1859) then Napoleon III made a premature peace with Austria without consulting him, but returned to office in 1860 to accomplish the union of Tuscany, Parma, Romagna and Modena with Piedmont. Garibaldi, meanwhile, recruited and led a patriot army to victory in Sicily and Naples. He advanced on Rome and met Cavour, at the head of the Piedmontese army, at the River Volturno. The two leaders proclaimed a united Kingdom of Italy on 17 Mar. 1861, with VICTOR EMMANUEL II as king.

Caxton, William (c. 1422-91) England's first printer, who produced the works of MALORY, GOWER and CHAUCER as well as translations of VIRGIL's *Aeneid* and French romances. In 1476, he set up his press at Westminster, after a successful career as a merchant and printer in Bruges, where his first press was established.

Cayley, Sir George (1773-1857) English engineer and inventor who was the founder of the science of aerodynamics and a pioneer in aerial navigation. His paper *On Aerial Navigation* (1809) defined the problem of heavier-than-air flight. The culmination of his aeronautical career came in 1853, when a large glider he had constructed carried his coachman on a flight of about 500 yards across a valley. This was the first successful manned heavier-than-air flight.

Cecil, Sir Robert, Earl of Salisbury (c. 1563-1612) English statesman, who was the vital link between the Tudor government of ELIZABETH I and the Stuart government of JAMES I. Trained by his father, Sir William CECIL, in statecraft, he became Secretary of State in 1596 and was mainly responsible for the smooth accession in England (1603) of James VI of Scotland, who made him an earl (1605). An able administrator, he negotiated peace with Spain (1604), dealt with the Gunpowder Plot and endeavoured to improve the royal finances. His last act was to arrange the marriage of James's daughter Elizabeth to Frederick, Elector Palatine; their descendant, George of Hanover, became King of Britain in 1714.

Cecil, William, 1st Baron Burghley (1520-98) English statesman who steered his country through its golden Elizabethan age. A courtier by birth, he took a prudent middle course in politics and religion which enabled him to gain influence, survive MARY I's anti-Protestant purge, and become ELIZABETH I's most trusted minister. As administrative head of government he increased economic and cultural growth by keeping England at peace until 1585 and supported the establishment of the Church of England. Cecil possessed Elizabeth's confidence to a remarkable degree but opposed her dynastically undesirable wish to marry LEICESTER. He hired spies to foil Catholic plots and executed those who threatened the throne, including MARY, Queen of Scots.

Cellini, Benvenuto (1500-71) Florentine sculptor and goldsmith, whose fame rests largely on his semi-scandalous autobiography, *The Life of Benvenuto, the son of Giovanni Cellini written by himself in Florence*. Dictated as he worked to a young scribe (1558-66), this work presents him as an archetypal Renaissance figure. The best-known piece of Cellini's few remaining works is a salt-cellar (1540-3) made for King Francis I, now in Vienna. Most of his sculptures are in Florence; the largest, the *Nymph of Fontainebleau* (1543-4), an elegant and sophisticated relief, is in the Louvre.

Celsius, Anders (1701-44) Swedish astronomer who devised the centigrade temperature scale, now used by scientists throughout the world. In 1742 he proposed a temperature scale that divided the difference between the freezing and boiling points of water into 100 equal intervals.

Celsus (2nd cent. AD) Platonist philosopher and opponent of the emergent Christianity which, he argued, cut across the traditional values of humanity. There was, he said, little evidence to support the miracles of JESUS.

Cervantes Saavedra, Miguel de (1547-1616) Spanish novelist and dramatist, who, elderly, disgraced and in debt after a lifetime of adventure, wrote *Don Quixote* (Part I, 1605, Part II, 1615), one of the most widely translated works of all time. The story may be said to have paved the way for the novels of FIELDING, SMOLLETT and DICKENS, and in its treatment of madness and illusion, directly influenced DOSTOEVSKY. Cervantes followed Part I of Don Quixote with the short romantic adventure works *Exemplary Novels* (1613) and some one-act farces and plays. His final work, *Persiles and Sigismunda* (published posthumously, 1616) is a long, heroic romance whose prologue contains Cervantes's farewell to life.

Ceulen, Ludolph van (1540-1610) German mathematician, who devoted almost his whole life to finding a numerical approximation for the value of π, and eventually obtained it, correct to 35 places of decimals. Some German textbooks of the 16th century refer to π as 'Ludolphische Zahl' (Ludolph's number).

Cézanne, Paul (1839-1906) French artist, who was a leading influence on the Impressionists. His early work betrayed strong passions: romantic, indeed erotic, in subject, the paint rich and sensuous in both colour and texture. Contact with

Impressionism not only brightened his palette, but above all focused his attention on nature and away from romantic visions. From then on he attempted to realize a comprehensive vision of nature through the media of still-life, landscape and portrait. This change in his outlook is exemplified by the painting of *Bathers* made towards the end of his life, in which the female nude is no longer erotic, but an architectonic element. Unlike the Impressionists, Cézanne did not seek to render nature's surface and her fluctuations, but to discover her permanent qualities. To this end he developed a technique of modelling forms, defining space, and indicating tones, all in terms of coloured strokes placed on the canvas with infinite care. His revolutionary use of colour, which emphasized the structure and volume of objects, slight distortions in the interests of higher truth, and his demonstration that the technique of painting could still evolve, made him highly influential on innumerable later painters, notably the Cubists.

Chadwick, Sir James (1891-1974) English physicist who in 1932 discovered the neutron, a particle similar in mass to a proton but without an electric charge. Being neutral it penetrates atoms easily and is therefore an efficient means of splitting nuclei. The greater splitting ability of neutrons was important in developing the technical processes required for making atomic power, for bombs and nuclear reactors. He was awarded a Nobel Prize in 1935.

Chagall, Marc (1887-1985) Russian-born painter, whose colourful fantasies and strange juxtapositions of objects strongly influenced Surrealist painters. He studied in St Petersburg under BAKST, the stage designer, and in 1910 went to Paris where he met APOLLINAIRE, LÉGER, DELAUNAY and MODIGLIANI. He returned to Russia in 1971, but found the authorities' preoccupation with social realism incompatible with his own ideas. The rest of his life had been spent largely between Paris and New York, illustrating books, designing stage sets, painting pictures and working in glass, as well as designing tapestries and mosaics. Chagall's designs decorate several other buildings, including the Knesset (the Israeli parliament building), and the Paris Opéra.

Chain, Ernst (1906-79) British biochemist of German origin who shared a Nobel Prize with Sir Alexander FLEMING and Lord Florey in 1945. His systematic investigation of antibacterial substances produced by fungi and other microorganisms led to a reinvestigation of penicillin and proved to be the foundation of the antibiotics industry.

Chaka (c. 1773-1828) Zulu chieftain and founder of the Zulu empire. He became chief of his own tribe in 1816 and, by the incorporaton of other tribes, united the Zulus into a powerful nation by the mid-1820s, when he is thought to have ruled 50,000 people. At the time of his assassination in September 1828 he dominated an area as large as France. Those of the surrounding tribes who would not swear allegiance to Chaka were obliged to flee, and it is estimated that approximately one million people were killed during his chieftainship. He developed a new battle formation for his *impis,* or regiments, and equipped them with new weapons, the short stabbing assegai, which compelled his warriors to fight at close quarters.

Chamberlain, Houston Stewart (1855-1927) English philosopher, who refined the theory of the superiority of the so-called Aryan race, which became the Nazi creed. His theory of 'Germanism', which embodied all that he conceived as being the best in European history, appeared in his *The Foundations of the 19th Century* (originally written in German, 1911). The book was not simply a glorification of the Germanic, but a broad survey of European culture. Nazi anti-Semitism can also be traced to Chamberlain, whose writings were, however, largely derived from those of Gobineau. He supported Germany against England in the First World War, and became a naturalized German in 1916.

Chamberlain, Joseph (1836-1914) English statesman who laid the economic foundations of the British Commonwealth. He was made President of the Board of Trade by GLADSTONE in 1880, and was responsible for the Bankruptcy Act of 1883 and other financial and economic reforms. He resigned from the Government in 1886 over his opposition to Gladstone's Irish Home Rule policy, and his defection split the Liberal Party and toppled the Government. From 1891 he was leader of the Liberal Unionists. In 1895 he joined SALISBURY'S Conservative-Unionist coalition as Colonial Secretary. As part of his imperialist theories he supported the idea of Imperial preference, by which the British Dominions and Colonies were to become a self-contained economic unit. He resigned from the Government in 1903, in order to campaign for an extension of Tariff Reform, which was intended as a form of moderate protection for British industry. His campaign embarrassed and divided the Conservative-Unionist government of BALFOUR and was largely responsible for the defeat of the Party in the 1906 election.

Chamberlain, Neville (1869-1940) Son of Joseph CHAMBERLAIN, and Prime Minister whose term was noted for its policy of appeasement of MUSSOLINI and HITLER, culminating in the infamous Munich Agreement (1938). Chamberlain became Prime Minister in 1937 in succession to BALDWIN. Ill-informed about foreign affairs, he believed he could negotiate personally with the dictators, while realizing that Britain was ill-prepared for war. His apparent political myopia caused the resigntion (1938) of his Foreign Minister, EDEN, who was replaced by HALIFAX. Chamberlain persisted in appeasement until the Germans occupied Prague, when he belatedly guaranteed the integrity of Poland. He was forced to declare war on Germany (3 Sept. 1939) when the Nazis invaded Poland, and upon their occupation of Norway, criticism of his lack of war leadership by a hostile House of Commons compelled him to make way for CHURCHILL.

Chambers, Ephraim (c. 1680-1740) English pioneer of modern encyclopaedias with his *Cyclopaedia* (1728). Chambers covered the arts and the sciences so comprehensively that he was elected a member of the Royal Society. It clearly influenced DIDEROT'S *Encyclopédie* (1751-77) and the first *Encyclopaedia Britannica* (1771).

Chambers, Sir William (1723-96) English architect whose work is a combination of English Palladianism and the Neo-Classicism of SOUFFLOT. His best-known work, Somerset House (1776-86) in the Strand, has an impressive river front and a portico facing the Strand. He also built the Casino at Marino, a villa at Roehampton and Duddingston House, Edinburgh, and wrote *A Treatise on Civil Architecture* (1759). The only testimony of his early voyages to India and China is the Pagoda in Kew Gardens, but Chambers retained links with France, begun when he trained under BLONDEL.

Champlain, Samuel de (c. 1567-1635) French explorer and colonizer in Canada who founded the city of Quebec (1608), the first permanent European settlement in America north of Florida. From there he explored south to Lake Champlain (1609), making allies of the Huron Indians. He explored the Ottawa River (1613) and probed Lakes Huron and Ontario with BRULÉ (1615).

Champollion, Jean François (1790-1832) French Egyptologist whose deciphering of Egyptian hieroglyphics helped historians to read scripts up to 5000 years old. He spent years studying the Rosetta Stone – a black basalt slab found in Egypt by French troops in 1799 – which bore three seemingly identical inscriptions: one in (readable) Greek, and two in undecipherable Egyptian scripts – demotic (cursive writing) and hieroglyphic ('picture' writing). It was Champollion who, in 1822, made the first full translations after discovering that hieroglyphic script consisted of both phonograms (sound-signs) and ideograms (sense-signs).

Chancellor, Richard (16th cent.) English navigator who inaugurated trade between England and Russia. He commanded a ship in Sir Hugh Willoughby's fleet to find a north-east passage to India (1553), was separated from the others by bad weather, rounded North Cape and the Kola Peninsula, and crossed the White Sea, before travelling overland to Moscow, where he negotiated a trade treaty. Chancellor died in a shipwreck while returning from a second Moscow visit.

Chandler, Raymond Thornton (1888-1959) American author whose detective novels feature the tough private eye Philip Marlowe, and include *The Big Sleep* (1939), *Farewell, My Lovely* (1940) and *The Long Goodbye* (1953), all of which were made into films.

Chandragupta I (4th cent.) Indian Rajah of Magadha who founded the Gupta dynasty (320-480), the golden age of Hinduism. By conquest and marriage he dominated the Ganges valley and began a period of peace and prosperity during which Hindu culture embraced most of the Indus and Ganges valleys, with art, literature, music, sculpture, painting and scientific studies all flourishing.

Chanel, Gabrielle (Coco) (c. 1883-1971 French fashion designer who revolutionized women's fashion, beginning in the 1920s with a straight, simple, uncorseted line and with many elements of her designs borrowed from men's clothing. She is associated with short hair, costume jewellery, the Chanel suit, jersey dresses, bell-bottom trousers, trench coats and Chanel No. 5 perfume.

Chao K'uang-yin (10th cent.) Chinese emperor (960-76) who, as T'ai Tsu (Grand Progenitor), founded the Sung dynasty (960-1280), during which Chinese culture enjoyed one of its most creative periods, especially in painting and pottery, but also in literature and philosophy. An ambitious general, Chao K'uang-yin used military power to seize the throne. China had been deeply divided among war lords since the decline of LI YUAN'S T'ang dynasty in the 9th century, but Chao built a strong, centralized government with a reformed civil service structure in northern China. When he died, he had mastered most of the south.

Chao Meng-fu (1254-1322) Chinese poet, scholar, calligrapher and painter, who rose to high office under the Mongol rule of the Yüan dynasty, and eventually became Secretary of State for War to KUBLAI KHAN. His famous equestrian and figurative paintings were suited to official tastes, but his landscapes and bamboos, painted in a lucid, calligraphic manner, are in the style practised by the literati. The technique of creating solid form with a single brush movement, at which Chao excelled, was later adopted by other artists.

Chaplin, Sir Charles (1889-1977) English director-writer who has become probably the best-known actor in the history of the cinema. He first went to America in 1910 with Fred Karno's company and on a second tour, in 1913, was persuaded to join Mack Sennett at Keystone, where he began in one-reelers. The tramp character – the 'little man' who somehow always won through – made him world famous. Chaplin's early films contain some of his best work, demonstrating his gift for mime. Later, he not only starred in films, but also directed them, including classics such as *The Gold Rush* (1924), *City Lights* (1931) and *Modern Times*.

Chardin, Jean Baptiste (1699-1779) French painter, of still-life and everyday scenes (genre paintings), whose appeal lay in their honesty and simplicity, pervaded as they are by a reflective calm devoid of sentiment or didactic moral purpose. The objects in his pictures, however commonplace, are subjected to intense scrutiny, and forms, surfaces and textures are realized with great fidelity. His distinctive greys, creams and rusts thickly but delicately applied, show that Chardin possessed the virtuosity, characteristic of his age, in the handling of his materials.

Chardonnet, Hilaire Comte de (1839-1924) French founder of the artificial silk industry. In the 1880s, after studying silk worms as an assistant to PASTEUR, he discovered a method of making a silk-like thread from nitrocellulose which he called rayon. Developments of this process by British chemists led, in 1892, to viscose rayon, on which most modern artificial silk is based.

Charlemagne (742-814) King of the Franks (768-814), and Western (Holy Roman) Emperor, who built the biggest empire in western Europe since that of Rome. Inheriting the Frankish kingdom, Charlemagne fought to unify all Germanic peoples in one Christian empire by seizing Saxony, Bavaria and Lombard Italy and fighting Avars, Moors and Slavs in border battles which pushed his empire's boundaries east to the Elbe and Danube and south into Spain. He gained Pope Leo III's support for refounding the Western Roman Empire, but on Christian, Germanic lines, with centralized government on a feudal basis. Charlemagne revived Latin learning, established reading schools and cathedral and monastic schools throughout the empire, and was a patron of the arts and sciences.

Charles I (1288-1342) King of Hungary and the first of the Anjou line, which gave the nation power and prosperity. He ruled as an absolute monarch, discarding dissident feudal lords as his councillors and using men from the middle classes. He granted privileges to towns to encourage their growth and reformed the fiscal system.

Charles I (1600-49) King of Great Britain and Ireland (1625-49), son of JAMES I, who was beheaded as a 'tyrant, traitor, murderer and public enemy' when his claims to absolute rule brought to a head the power struggle between Crown and Parliament. Dominated at first by his minister, BUCKINGHAM, he waged costly and inconclusive foreign wars with Spain and France, for which he kept demanding money from

Parliament. This, and his High Church leanings, caused clashes with the predominantly Puritan Parliament; for 11 years (1629-40) Charles, invoking the doctrine of the divine right of kings, tried to rule without Parliament, raising money by forced loans, and other means. Eventually his need of money with which to go to war with Presbyterian Scotland (1639) led him to seek help from Parliament, which demanded increased powers in return. The long struggle, marked by the Petition of Right of 1628 (which attempted formally to curb the king's powers) and the Grand Remonstrance of 1641 (which listed the grievances against Charles), ended in deadlock and outbreak of the English Civil Wars (1642-6, 1648). CROMWELL's Parliamentarians defeated the Royalists and the Rump Parliament instigated Charles's trial.

Charles II (1630-85) King of Great Britain and Ireland (1660-85), nicknamed the 'merry monarch'. Exiled under the Commonwealth, Charles was invited by Parliament to return to the throne 18 months after Oliver CROMWELL's death. Determined 'Not to go on his travels again', Charles sought to strengthen the monarchy by an alliance with LOUIS XIV of France which might destroy England's chief commercial rivals, the Dutch, and free the king from financial dependence on Parliament, but the Dutch wars of the reign (1664-7 and 1672-4) were not successful. The reign saw a reaction against Puritan austerities. Restoration drama enlived the theatre, experimental science was encouraged through the Royal Society (1662), art and architecture flourished, WREN producing his masterpiece of St Paul's after the fire of 1666, which largely destroyed London. Although tolerant Charles failed to help Catholics and dissenters because of the opposition of his strongly Anglican parliament.

Charles II (1661-1700) King of Spain (1665-1700), during whose reign the problem of the Spanish Succession emerged. Charles's wish was to keep the last Spanish empire intact for his successor, and, resenting the two partition treaties of 1698 and 1700 agreed between LOUIS XIV and WILLIAM III, Charles willed the entire empire to Louis's grandson, Philip, and so helped to precipitate the War of the Spanish Succession.

Charles IV 'The Fair' (1294-1328) King of France (1322-8), whose renewal of hostilities with England anticipated the Hundred Years' War (1337-1453). He occupied most of Guienne and Gascony, but restored them to England, except for Agenais and Bazadais in 1327. He intervened also in Flanders to protect French interests. The last Capetian King, Charles was succeeded by the House of Valois.

Charles V (1337-80) King of France (1364-80), who saved the nation from the English in the first phase of the 100 Years' War. Becoming Regent (1356), Charles agreed to the Peace of Bretigny (1360), which granted a third of France to Edward III of England. After gaining support from the factious States-General and the provincial assemblies, and raising money to buttress the army and navy, Charles was ready to fight. Under Bertrand du GUESCLIN, his troops struck back at the English, forcing them into a few pockets, principally round Bayonne, Brest, Calais and Cherbourg.

Charles V (1500-58) Hapsburg King of Spain (1516-50) and Holy Roman Emperor (1519) who ruled an immense empire that far outstripped the traditional Germanic limits of the Holy Roman Empire by including the Low Countries, Franche-Comté, Spain, Naples, and soon vast New World possessions, won by conquistadores such as CORTES and PIZARRO. Charles had no real policy for dealing with the disparate elements of his Empire and was content to deal piecemeal with problems as and when they occurred. He altered little in Spain, using it mainly as a source of taxation revenue, and in the Netherlands welded all the loosely connected provinces into a whole by applying a common system of law, taxation and parliamentary assembly. His eventual domination of Italy was a by-product of a long rivalry with FRANCIS I of France. Hostilities between the two ended with the Treaty of Crécy (1544), which favoured the Empire. In Germany, Charles fought and defeated the Lutheran states, but gave Lutherans equal rights with Catholics in the Peace of Augsburg (1555).

Charles VII (1403-61) King of France during whose reign the 100 Years' War ended. When he came to the throne, England, under HENRY V, held all northern and some of south-western France. As the Dauphin, Charles was a mere figurehead; it was JOAN OF ARC who led the French armies in their victories over the English (1428-31).

Charles VIII (1470-98) King of France (1483-98), who added Brittany to his kingdom when he married Anne of Brittany (1491). He bought neutrality from England, Spain and the Holy Roman Empire (which had all wanted to keep Brittany independent of France) with gifts of land and treaties, while he pursued his ambition to reclaim the kingdom of Naples for the house of Anjou. He invaded Italy in 1495, but was repulsed.

Charles X (1757-1836) King of France (1824-30) who with his minister Polignac provoked the French revolution of 1830 by the Ordinances of St Cloud, a series of repressive decrees. In 1789, as Comte d'Artois, he had fled to Scotland, from which he returned in 1814.

Charles XII (1682-1718) King of Sweden (1697-1718), whose daring military exploits ended in national disaster. In 1700-2, he brilliantly wrecked a Danish-Polish-Russian alliance aimed at despoiling Sweden, by crushing Denmark, driving Russian troops out of Swedish-held Livonia, and ravaging Poland (deposing AUGUSTUS II). He then invaded Saxony (1706), which became his springboard for an attack on Moscow (1707). Charles underestimated the Russian winter and Russian scorched-earth tactics. He lost the decisive battle of Poltava (1709), which left him, with MAZEPA, a temporary fugitive and finished Swedish supremacy. Charles was killed invading Norway.

Charles (Philip Arthur George), Prince of Wales (born 1948) The eldest son of Queen Elizabeth II and Prince Philip, Duke of Edinburgh, and heir to the British throne. He was given the title Prince of Wales in 1958, and invested at Caenarvon Castle in 1968. He was educated at Gordonstoun and Trinity College, Cambridge. He served in the Royal Navy (1971-6), and in 1981 married Lady Diana Spencer, youngest daughter of the eighth Earl Spencer. The have two sons, Prince William, born in 1982, and Prince Harry, born in 1984.

Chasles, Michel (1793-1880) French mathematician, who was one of the founders of modern projective geometry. His works have become standard textbooks on the origins and development of geometry.

Chateaubriand, François René de (1768-1848) French novelist, poet and politician whose short novels, *Atala* and *René* (1801 and 1805), are sometimes said to mark the birth of the Romantic hero in French fiction. He was renowned for the exotic settings of his tales, some of which were inspired by his travels in the New World. Chateaubriand was in America when the Revolution began and returned to Paris to fight with the emigrés, but later fled to England in 1793, where he lived in great poverty until 1800, translating novels and teaching French in order to live. He was recalled to serve under NAPOLEON, but soon resigned and went abroad once more. After Waterloo, he became ambassador in Berlin and later in London and Rome, and in 1823 became Foreign Minister to LOUIS XVIII. Other notable works by Chateaubriand include his *Essai sur les révolutions* (1797); *Le Génie du Christianisme* (1802; of which *Atala* and *René* originally formed part), a rambling, historico-cultural work intended as an apologia for the Church; *Les Martyrs* (1809); *Les Mémoires d'outre-tombe* and autobiographies published posthumously.

Chaucer, Geoffrey (c. 1340-1400) English poet, 'Father of English literature' who wrote *The Canterbury Tales,* a collection of medieval stories, planned as part of a larger design of which only the Prologue and 22 tales were completed. Chaucer's pilgrims are drawn from many different spheres of medieval life and in the prologue each pilgrim is described in a series of vivid portraits which are by turn satirical, hostile, ironic or amused. In the main body of the work each character tells a tale, ranging from courtly romance to rumbustious ribaldry, comic anecdote to philosophical or religious fable. Between 1359 and 1372 Chaucer translated *Le Roman de la Rose* from the French, and in 1369 composed his earliest datable work, *The Book of the Duchess,* on the occasion of the death of Blanche, wife of John of Gaunt. After 1372, he was called upon to make several ambassadorial journeys abroad, to Flanders, France, Lombardy and Italy, where he gained an almost unique knowledge of DANTE and BOCCACCIO, and is thought to have met PETRARCH. *The House of Fame* and *The Parlement of Foules* were probably composed at this time, rich in descriptive passages and light in mood, on the favourite medieval theme of love; and 'Troilus and Criseyde', a long, narrative poem modelled on Boccaccio's 'Il Filostrato', in which Chaucer used rime royal, a stanza of seven lines. In the 1380s Chaucer began *The Canterbury Tales,* in which foreign influences give way to Englishness.

Chekhov, Anton (1860-1904) Russian dramatist and master of theatrical tragi-comedy, whose work foreshadowed important trends in modern drama. It was, however, as an author of short stories that he first attracted attention. His early plays were one-act farces and tragedies. His first full-length plays, *Ivanov* (1887), *The Wood Demon* (1889) and *The Seagull* (1896), were all failures. He had decided to give up play-writing when he met Nemirovich-Danchenko, who wanted to revive *The Seagull* at the Moscow Art Theatre, then run by him and Stanlislavsky. This production, which interpreted with proper feeling Chekhov's delicate poise between the tragic and the absurd, was the beginning of his success in the theatre. In 1898, he rewrote *The Wood Demon* as *Uncle Vanya*; then came *The Three Sisters* (1901) and *The Cherry Orchard* (1904). He lived the last years of his life in Yalta, where his house is maintained as his memorial.

Cheng Ho (15th cent.) Chinese admiral who made his country mistress of the Indian Ocean and of Indonesia. A Muslim eunuch at the court of Emperor Yung Ho, of the Ming dynasty, he was sent on seven expeditions (1405-34), which visited Indonesia, Ceylon, India, Arabia and East Africa. Cheng Ho's armadas (the first consisting of 63 junks carrying 28,000 men) traded with and cowed the states they visited. In 1415, 16 states made tribute payments to the Chinese emperor. Cheng Ho brought back foreign curiosities including zebras and giraffes, but with his last voyage (1430-34) China's unprecedented show of interest in the outside world came to an end.

Chénier, André Marie de (1762-94) French poet whose *Bucoliques* and *Iambes,* poignant and sometimes withering satires, written during imprisonment under the Terror, show him to be classical in spirit, though in lyrical fervour a precursor of the Romantics. Purged as a rebel, his execution robbed France of one of her greatest poets.

Chernenko, Konstantin Ustinovich (born 1911) Soviet Head of State since 1984 of Siberian peasant origin. He joined the Communist party (1931), was an aide of BREZHNEV's, and became a member of the Politburo (1978). A conservative, he opposed ANDROPOV in the leadership contest of 1982.

Chesterton, Gilbert Keith (1874-1936) English writer, who set his hand to all types of literature – poetry, novels, stories, essays and controversial pamphlets. Chesterton's attitudes were Catholic, Romantic and traditional; together with BELLOC, he opposed the socialist ideas of SHAW. In his exuberant, fanciful novels, including

Conversation piece: Shaw, Belloc and Chesterton in the 1930s

The Napoleon of Notting Hill (1904), *The Man who was Thursday* (1908), *The Flying Inn* (1914), there is an element of social preaching behind the fancy.

Chiang Kai-Shek (1887-1975) Chinese soldier-politician. A professional officer, he was training with the Japanese army at the outbreak of the Chinese Revolution of 1911. He returned to China and became chief of staff to SUN YAT-SEN. In 1923 he went to Moscow to study Red Army methods, but despite Sun Yat-Sen's broadening of the *Kuomintang* (Chinese Nationalist Party) to admit Communists, he remained an anti-Communist. In 1928, three years after Sun's death, he set up a Kuomintang government in Nanking, and thereafter fought local war-lords, Japanese invading armies and Communists led by MAO TSE-TUNG. He was captured by the Communists in 1936, but was released on the intervention of CHOU EN-LAI to continue fighting the Japanese. Chiang was head of the Chinese government and Commander-in-Chief of the armed forces throughout the Second World War and during the subsequent civil war with the Communists (1946-8). He was defeated in 1948 and forced to withdraw to Taiwan where, with US support, he established the anti-Communist Republic of China.

Chichester, Sir Francis (1901-72) English sailor and airman, who set a record for the single-handed passage of the Atlantic in 1962. In 1966-7 he circumnavigated the world in his yacht *Gipsy Moth,* sailing 29,000 miles in 226 days.

Chikamatsu, Monzaemon (1653-c. 1725) One of Japan's outstanding dramatists, who wrote about 160 Joruri and Kabuki plays. These plays, based on popular myths and legends or historical themes, involve the use of elaborate scenery, a revolving stage and stylized make-up. While retaining their traditions, Chikamatsu broke through their rigid formalism by using original characters and situations.

Childe, Vere Gordon (1892-1957) Australian archaeologist and prehistorian who is famous for his comprehensive writings in such books as *Man Makes Himself* (1936) and *What Happened in History* (1942). He explained both cogently and with authority how the Old World civilizations began, and initiated, by his stress on the links between primitive cultures, a new international approach to archaeology. Childe saw prehistory in terms of social and technological development, and he showed how the stages of Palaeolithic (Old Stone Age) savagery and Neolithic (New Stone Age) barbarianism led to the Bronze Age 'urban' revolution in Mesopotamia in 3000 BC.

Chirico, Giorgio de (1888-1978) Founder of the Italian school of metaphysical painting, who came to adopt an imitative, academic style.

Chomsky, Noam (born 1928) American linguistics theorist. In his *Syntactic Structures* (1957) he proposed that the sentence is the basic component of language and that, from a few basic sentence types, an infinity of actual sentences can be produced by a series of rules codified as transformational grammar. The computer, with its potential for translation and information storage, inspired this attempt to establish how sentences are generated. Chomsky has also published *Aspects of the Theory of Syntax, Language and Mind,* and political works.

Chopin, Frédéric François (1810-49) Polish Romantic composer and pianist who embodied his country's national aspirations, although he lived outside Poland from the age of 18, mostly in Paris; his father was French. Apart from his two piano concertos, he wrote almost entirely for solo piano. In his valses, nocturnes (invented by FIELD), preludes, studies, mazurkas and polonaises, he often achieved a small-scale perfection. For some time he lived with novelist George SAND, who took him to Majorca in an attempt to relieve his tuberculosis. The 1848 Revolution in France drove Chopin to Britain, and in the following year he returned to Paris, where he died.

Chou En-Lai (1898-1976) Premier of the State Council of the Chinese People's Republic. Of Mandarin rank, he was educated at Nankai University and in Germany and Paris, where he became a Communist. Chou helped to found the Red Army in 1931 with MAO TSE-TUNG, whom he accompanied on the Long March (1934-5). As one of the Chinese Communist leaders in 1936 he was responsible for co-operation between the Communist forces and CHIANG KAI-SHEK's Nationalist Party in fighting the Japanese invaders. In 1949 Chou became Premier and Foreign Minister in the new Communist government. He played a major role in leading China into close co-operation with the Third World, and while remaining committed to Mao, helped to restrain some of the excesses of the Cultural Revolution in 1966. An experienced diplomat, Chou handled the negotiations which led to a *détente* with the West and culminated in China's re-admission to the UN as a member of the Security Council (1971).

Chrétien de Troyes (12th cent.) French poet and author of extravagant tales of courtly love, some of the earliest extant Arthurian romances, including *Erec et Enide* (*c.* 1170), *Lancelot, ou le chevalier de la Charette,* and *Percival.*

Christ see JESUS CHRIST

Christian, Fletcher (18th cent.) English leader of the *Bounty* mutiny (1789), in protest against the alleged brutality of Captain William BLIGH. Arms were seized and the ship's officers cast adrift. While Bligh succeeded in making his way back to England, the 25 mutineers sailed on to Tahiti. Christian is believed to have sailed to Pitcairn Island and there set up a colony. Whether Christian died there or made his way back to England is not known.

Christie, Dame Agatha (1891-1976) English author who was a prolific and popular writer of detective stories. Her novels include *The Mysterious Affair at Styles* (1920), which introduced her famous character Hercule Poirot, a cunning but eccentric Belgian detective, *The Murder of Roger Ackroyd* (1926), considered a classic of the detective genre, *Murder at the Vicarage* (1930), which introduced Miss Marple, an elderly English spinster sleuth, *Murder on the Orient Express* (1934), *And Then There Were None* (1940) and *Curtain* (1975). She also wrote plays, including *The Mousetrap* (1952), which holds a world record for the longest continuous run at one theatre.

Churchill, John, 1st Duke of Marlborough (1650-1722) One of England's greatest generals. He helped to stamp out MONMOUTH's rebellion (1685), backed WILLIAM III's accession, and survived ill-documented charges of treason. His career reached its climax when he was commander-in-chief of the Anglo-Dutch armies in the War of the Spanish Succession (1702-14). He drove the French out of Spanish Gelderland (1702) with victories at Kaiserwerth, Venlo and Liège. With Prince Eugène of Savoy, he defeated a Franco-Bavarian force at Blenheim, Bavaria (1704). He later routed the French at Ramillies

(1706), so winning Brabant and Flanders and then, with Eugène, defeated the French at Oudenarde (1708). Victory was won also at Malplaquet (1709), but with greater losses than the French.

Churchill, Lord Randolph (1849-95) English Conservative statesman, and a son of the Duke of Marlborough, who advocated Tory democracy whilst leading the 'fourth party', a group of progressive Conservative MPs, from 1880 to 1885. As Chairman of the Central Union of Conservative Associations (1884) he demanded more power for constituency associations. He was Secretary for India (1885-6), and the youngest politician for over a century to become Chancellor of the Exchequer (1886). By resigning in protest against increased military expenditure he ended his political career.

Churchill, Sir Winston Leonard Spencer (1874-1965) British statesman, Prime Minister during Britain's 'finest hour' (Battle of Britain, 1940), historian and painter. The son of Lord Randolph CHURCHILL, he began his career as a soldier, serving with a lancer regiment at the battle of Omdurman (1898). As a war correspondent in South Africa (1899-1900) he was captured by Boers, but escaped. First elected to Parliament in 1900 as a Conservative, he joined the Liberals in 1904, largely on account of his Free Trade principles. As First Lord of the Admiralty (1911-15), when he thought war likely he laid on a 'practice mobilization' and then kept the Fleet at war stations. He was held responsible for the disaster of the Dardanelles expedition against the Turks in 1915, and resigned to serve on the Western Front. Later he became Secretary for War (1918-21), the Colonial Secretary (1921-2). He joined the Conservatives in 1922 and, though Chancellor of the Exchequer from 1924 to 1929, was thereafter kept out of office by his insistence in warning the country – against his party's beliefs – that Nazi Germany was a menace, and by his rejection of concessions his Party were making in India. On the outbreak of the Second World War public opinion forced Neville CHAMBERLAIN to make him First Lord of the Admiralty. After Chamberlain resigned he became Prime Minister (10 May 1940), and Minister of Defence. He was leader of the Opposition during ATTLEE's Labour administration (1945-51) and Prime Minister again (1951-55).

Cicero, Marcus (106-43 BC) Roman lawyer, politician and philosopher whose Latin treatises, based on PLATO, ARISTOTLE and their schools, and on the Stoics, introduced Greek philosophy to ancient Rome. A celebrated orator and advocate, he also wrote on rhetoric, and many of his speeches survive, as do many of his letters.

'Cicero' see BAZNA, Elysea

Cid, El (c. 1040-99) Popular name (from the Arabic, Sayyid, 'Lord') for the Spanish warrior hero Rodrigo Diaz de Vivar. He fought brilliantly for Sancho II of Castile, then for Sancho's successor Alfonso VI. Exiled (1081) for suspected treachery, he became a soldier of fortune and fought for the Moorish kings of Saragossa. Later (1089-94), El Cid used war and intrigue for personal gain, taking Valencia and Murcia, until defeated by the Moors.

Cimabue, Giovanni (c. 1240-1302) Florentine artist whom DANTE called the most famous painter before GIOTTO, whose teacher he may have been. His outstanding work, the huge *Madonna Enthroned* (*c.* 1285), departs from the tradition of Byzantine icons and mosaics in its size, architectural severity of design and tendency towards a more naturalistic description of the human form.

Clare, John (1793-1864) English poet, who wrote of rural life, experience as a farm worker, and was known as the 'Northamptonshire Peasant Poet'. *The Shepherd's Calendar* (1827) and *The Rural Muse* (1835) show his genuine lyrical talent. His most moving verse is that written later in his life, describing his solitude and desolation when confined to an asylum.

Clark, Lord Kenneth McKenzie (1903-83) English art historian, who was a professor at Oxford, director of the National Gallery in London (1934-45) and Chairman of the Arts Council of Great Britain (1955-60). His writings include *Leonardo da Vinci* (1939), *Rembrandt and the Italian Renaissance* (1966), *The Romantic Rebellion* (1974), *Another Part of the Wood* (1975) and *Animals and Men* (1977). His television lecture series *Civilisation,* a cultural survey, was very popular.

Clark, William (1770-1838) American explorer and soldier who, with Meriwether LEWIS, commanded the expedition which in 1804-6 first crossed North America from St Louis to the Pacific, exploring and mapping much of what is now the north-western US. On the return journey Clark independently explored the Yellowstone River while Lewis explored Maria's River, and the two men rejoined each other near the Yellowstone-Missouri confluence. During the expedition Clark mapped the land, sketched its wildlife, and wrote the records which provided the material for *History of the Expedition under the Commands of Captains Lewis and Clark* (1814).

Clarke, Arthur Charles (born 1917) English science-fiction writer noted for the scientific background in his works, which include *Childhood's End* (1953), *A Fall of Moondust* (1961), *Voices from the Sky* (1965), *Imperial Earth* (1976) and *2010; Odyssey Two* (1982). Stanley Kubrick's film *2001: A Space Odyssey* (1969) was based on his short story 'The Sentinel'.

Claude Gellée see CLAUDE LORRAIN

Claude, Georges (1870-1960) French engineer who is best known for perfecting a process for liquefying air (1902) and the separation of its constituent gases by distillation of the liquid. The process enabled oxygen and nitrogen to be prepared on an industrial scale.

Claude Lorrain (1600-82) French landscape painter, who evolved a technique of dividing his landscapes, which usually embodied some mythological or historical incident, into receding planes, with features such as trees or classical ruins judiciously placed to help draw the eye into the distance. Although he made a number of drawings in the Roman *campagna,* his landscapes are not always topographically exact, but rather ideal, attempting by means of hazy lighting and a suggestion of infinite distance, more to evoke a golden age than portray specific places.

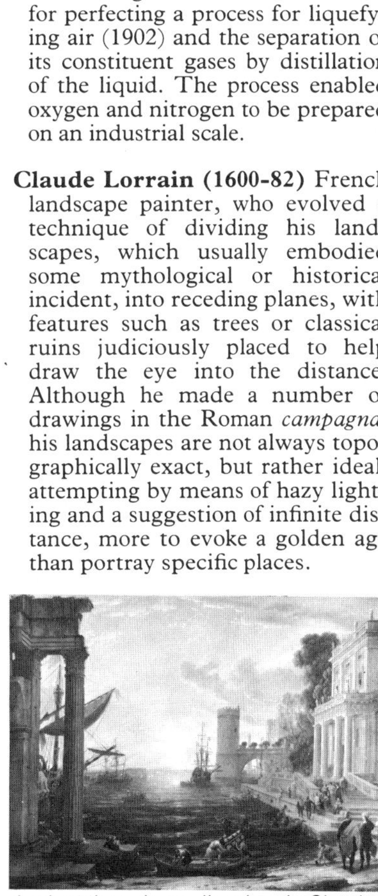

Ancient times in medieval garb: Claude Lorrain's *Departure of the Queen of Sheba*

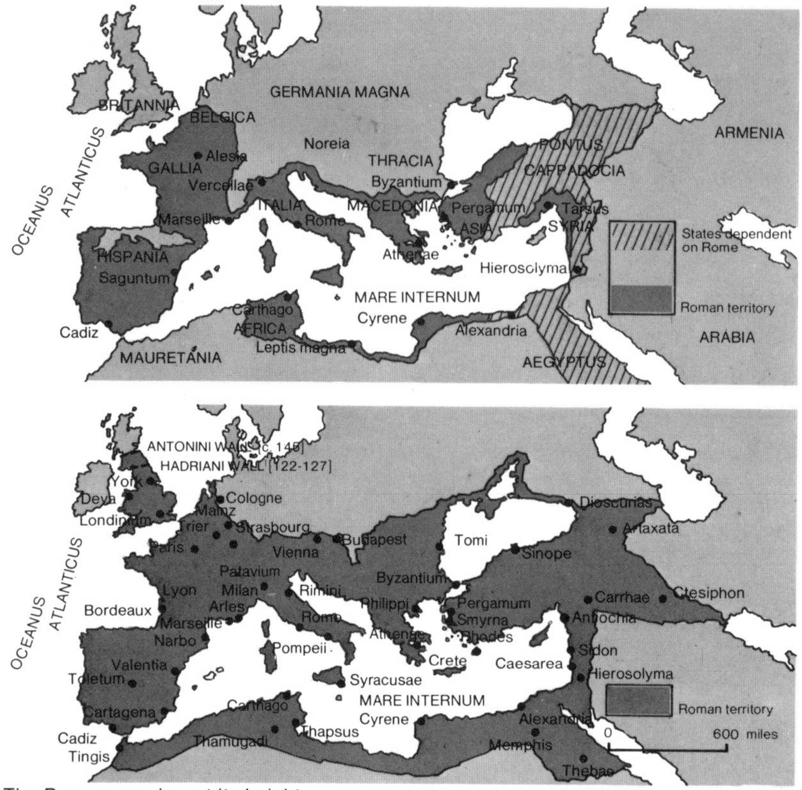

The Roman empire, at its height, encompassed nearly all of Europe. It stretched north to Scotland, south into Africa. Claudius helped extend its boundaries

Claudian (4th cent.) Greek-speaking Alexandrian and the last important classical Latin poet. His writings range from eulogies of his patron the emperor Honorius and his adviser Stilicho to unrestrained satirical attacks on common enemies. He wrote vigorously and eloquently in the classical tradition and revealed himself as a master of description, notably in the unfinished epic, *De rapto Proserpinae*.

Claudianus, Claudius see CLAUDIAN

Claudius I (10 BC-AD 54) Roman emperor (41-54), who, following Julius CAESAR's attacks, began the long-lasting Roman occupation of Britain (43). A coarse and deformed man, he was present at the triumphant crossing of the Thamesis (Thames) and at the capture of Camulodunum (now Colchester), where he founded a Roman colony. Claudius adopted a literal policy in Rome's provinces, and advanced the organization of an imperial bureaucracy. Before his death, allegedly by poison, he made his adopted son, NERO, emperor.

Clay, Cassius see ALI, Muhammad

Clausius, Rudolph (1822-88) German physicist who in 1850 enunciated the second law of thermodynamics and introduced the concept of entropy. He gave the first systematic treatment to kinetic gas theory, and suggested a new theory of electrolysis, later taken up by ARRHENIUS.

Cleese, John Marwood (born 1939) English writer and actor who was a prominent member of the team which created and starred in the zany, satirical BBC television comedy series *Monty Python's Flying Circus*. He began his career in revue with the Cambridge Footlights, and in the late 1960s worked as a writer and performer with *The Frost Report*. After *Monty Python,* he wrote and co-starred with his first wife, Connie Booth, in another BBC comedy series *Fawlty Towers*. His film successes include *And Now for Something Completely Different* (1971), *Monty Python and the Holy Grail* (1974), *The Life of Brian* (1979) and *The Meaning of Life* (1983).

Clemenceau, Georges (1841-1929) French statesman who led France to victory in the First World War. He began political life as Mayor of Montmartre. As a Radical deputy (1876-93) he earned his nickname 'The Tiger' by the ferocious wit of his speeches. Fiercely republican, anticlerical and anti-socialist, Clemenceau was among the most ardent defenders of DREYFUS during his trial. His denunciation of France's military incompetence during the first three years of the First World War led to his becoming Prime Minister when, in 1917, defeat seemed imminent. His courage and determination held France together through the defeats early in 1918 and made possible her recovery and the attack which led to victory in November 1918. His authoritarianism and the results of the Paris Peace Conference of 1919, for which he was held responsible, led to his downfall in 1920. During his retirement he repeatedly warned of German military resurgence in 1940.

Clement I (c. 30-c. 100) Italian pope, recognized as the first of the Apostolic Fathers (early Christian writers who were the associates of the apostles) and writer of the *Epistle to the Corinthians*. Written (*c*. 96) to the church at Corinth to calm a dispute there which had caused several presbyters to be dismissed, the epistle is chiefly important for stating the basis of the Christian ministry.

Cleopatra VII or **VI (69-30 BC)** Graeco-Macedonian Queen of Egypt, mistress of Julius CAESAR and Marcus ANTONIUS. Caesar met her when he pursued his rival POMPEY into Egypt, and restored her to her throne. She became Caesar's mistress and lived with him in Rome. After his assassination (41 BC), she returned to Egypt and bewitched Marcus Antonius, commander of the eastern Roman empire. Dreams of mastering the entire Mediterranean as a kingdom for Cleopatra and himself led Antonius to divorce Octavia for Cleopatra, provoking the disastrous war with Octavia's brother, Octavian (later the emperor AUGUSTUS), in which Antonius and Cleopatra were defeated at Actium (31 BC). Antonius committed suicide and Cleopatra, failing to charm Octavian, also killed herself.

Cleveland, Stephen Grover (1837-1908) American President who forced Britain to accept arbitration of the British Guiana-Venezuela frontier dispute (1897). His first term as President (1885-9) was marked by excessive use of the Presidential veto and his second (1893-7) by a Wall Street panic in 1893, which led to unpopular deflationary measures and the use of troops in strike-breaking. After winning the Presidential election in 1884 he became the first Democratic President of the United States for 28 years.

Clive, Robert (1725-74) English soldier and statesman who founded British India. Fighting for the British East India Company against its French counterpart for supremacy in India, he checked French power by seizing Arcot with a tiny force (1751), then ended it by taking Calcutta (1757). In defeating 50,000 enemy troops with 3200 soldiers and artillery at Plassey (1757), Clive mastered India's richest province, Bengal, and became virtually its ruler. He returned to Britain in 1760, but was sent out again, as Governor of Bengal (1764-7), to end disorder there. He obtained the document granting the East India Company full sovereignty over all Bengal, making it the secure nucleus for a British empire in India. Clive reorganized the civil and military service of the Company and raised salaries to end corrupt private trading and acceptance of gifts. He returned to Britain again (1767) addicted to opium (perhaps to ease chronic illness) and committed suicide.

Clouet, Jean the Younger (c. 1485-c. 1545) French court painter, whose son, François, succeeded him. Both father and son made a number of precisely drawn portrait drawings in black, red and white chalk, of which Jean's are thought to be more psychologically expressive.

Clovis I (c. 466-511) King of the Salian Franks (481-511), who became ruler of all the Frankish tribes, founded the first powerful state in France with Paris as its capital, and drew up the Salic Law. Using murder, intrigue and war, he extended his Merovingian kingdom (centred at first on Tournai in western Belgium) into an empire comprising most of present-day France, Belgium, western Germany and the Netherlands. Clovis became a Christian and built a church at Paris, but his empire, divided between his four sons, did not survive his death.

Cnut see CANUTE II

Cobbett, William (1762-1835) English politician, journalist and historian of rural life, His *Rural Rides* (1830) is an honest and vivid account of early 19th-century life. Cobbett was a soldier (1784-91) and spent many years in the US. In 1800 he returned to England and began *Cobbett's Weekly Political Register,* in which he set forth his radical political views.

Cobden, Richard (1804-65) British radical publicist, who, with BRIGHT, secured the repeal of the Corn Laws (1846). The plight of cotton mill operatives in Manchester caused him to devote his time to campaigning for Free Trade. He was active in the Anti-Corn Law League (1839-46), and was elected MP for Stockport. He lost his seat (1857) largely as a result of his opposition to the Crimean War. Although re-elected in 1859, he refused Cabinet office under PALMERSTON in order to remain independent. In 1860 he secured a reduction of tariffs in trade between Britain and France. During the American Civil War (1861-5) he played a valuable role in easing the tense relations between LINCOLN's administration and the government of Palmerston.

Cockcroft, Sir John Douglas (1897-1967) English physicist who, with Ernest Walton, was the first to split the atom, using artificially accelerated sub-atomic particles. In the 1920s Cockcroft and Walton built a voltage multiplier which could accelerate charged sub-atomic particles to extremely high velocities. In 1932, using protons as bullets for their 'atomic gun', they bombarded lithium. The alpha particles (helium nuclei) produced showed that the protons had reacted with the lithium nuclei to produce helium. Cockcroft and Walton were awarded the Nobel Prize for Physics in 1951.

Cockerell, Charles Robert (1788-1863) English architect who developed a highly original and forceful Neo-classical style based on studies of classical architecture in Greece and Italy, and also upon his study of WREN and the English baroque. His major works are the Ashmolean Building, Oxford, St George's Hall, Liverpool, and various branch offices of the Bank of England.

Cockerell, Sir Christopher Sydney (born 1910) English engineer who invented the hovercraft. In 1953 he began experimenting with ways of reducing the friction around the hulls of boats, in order to increase their performance. Cockerell discovered that a cushion of air was the best method of achieving this and, with the British government's backing, the pioneer SRN-1 hovercraft was built, and demonstrated its capability by crossing the English Channel in 1959. By 1965, the hovercraft industry was well established. The main uses for these transporters are for fast ferry and patrol duties.

Cocteau, Jean (1889-1963) French dramatist, poet, novelist, film director and designer. In 1912, he met DIAGHILEV, for whom he created ballets and mimes. like many writers of the period (e.g. GUIDE, GIRAUDOUX, ANOUILH, SARTRE), he showed a predilection for refashioning ancient myths. His rewriting of classical themes in *Orphée* (1927) and *Antigone* (1928) was followed by melodramas such as *La Machine infernale* (1934), a revival of the Oedipus legend, and the heroic-romantic play *L'Aigle à deux têtes* (1946). One of his most outstanding films was *La Belle et la bête* (1945) and he was also author of two novels, *Thomas l'Imposteur* (1923) and *Les Enfants terribles.* Cocteau's remarkable versatility and talents enabled him to play a significant role in artistic and literary experiments between the wars.

Cody, Samuel Franklin (1862-1913) Texas-born pioneer aviator who became a British citizen and played an important part in the development of flight. He experimented with man-lifting kites, helped to build the first British dirigible (steerable airship) and constructed an aeroplane of his own in 1908. The tree to which he used to tether his aircraft remains a memorial to him at the Royal Aircraft Establishment at Farnborough. He died when his aircraft crashed.

Cody, William Frederick (1846-1917) American frontiersman and showman who helped to create the popular image of the Wild West. He gained his nickname 'Buffalo Bill' as a bison hunter who reputedly shot 4280 bison in 17 months to feed men building a railroad through Kansas. In 1872, by then an experienced messenger, teamster, hunter and army scout, he starred with HICKOK and others in Wild West shows. In 1883, Cody formed the most famous of all, Buffalo Bill's Wild West Show, a spectacular circus that toured the United States and Europe, featuring, among others, Annie Oakley and the Sioux chieftain SITTING BULL.

Coe, Sebastian Newbold (born 1956) English athlete who won gold medals in the 1500 metre race and silver medals in the 800 metres at the Moscow Olympics in 1980 and at the Los Angeles Olympics in

1984. He is the only athlete to hold world records at 800 metres, 1000 metres, 1500 metres and a mile simultaneously.

Coke, Sir Edward (1552-1634) English, the champion of common law against the royal prerogative and a great Chief Justice. As Attorney-General to ELIZABETH I (from 1594) he supported the authority of government and displayed a violent hatred for its enemies in his prosecutions of RALEIGH, ESSEX and the Earl of Southampton. But under JAMES I as Chief Justice, first of the Court of Common Pleas (1603-13) then of the Court of King's Bench (1613-16), he changed his attitude, denied the King's right to make law by proclamation and urged the supremacy of the common law over both King and Church. Finally he led the Parliamentary opposition to CHARLES I, especially by blocking his demands for subsidies. The Petition of Right (1628) was based on Coke's ideas.

Colbert, Jean Baptiste (1619-83) French statesman, Chief Minister of LOUIS XIV in succession to MAZARIN, whose agent he had been. Appointed officially Controller General of Finance (1665), he reformed the corrupt financial administration and widened direct and indirect taxation. He built up a major export trade based on state-sponsored industries employing foreign craftsmen, founded trading companies and colonies (notably in Canada) to encourage overseas trade and supported new communications projects, including a major road and canal system, and a substantial merchant navy. As Secretary of State for the Marine (from 1668), he created the French navy.

Coleridge, Samuel Taylor (1772-1834) English philosopher, critic and poet of fantasy and the supernatural. In the *Lyrical Ballads* (1798), written in collaboration with WORDSWORTH, Coleridge agreed to write of the supernatural, and his great success is in the strange haunting realms of 'The Ancient Mariner', 'Kubla Khan' and 'Christabel'. The ode on 'France' (1798) and 'Dejection' (1802) are the best of his other poems. He was the main philosopher of the Romantic movement, though his criticism is interesting for its insights rather than its ordered system.

Coleridge-Taylor, Samuel (1875-1912) English composer who wrote the cantata *Hiawatha's Wedding Feast* (1898). This was later extended to form part of a trilogy, including *The Death of Minnehaha* (1899) and *Hiawatha's Departure* (1900), all based on LONGFELLOW's poem. He studied with Stanford, and his talents were recognized and praised by SULLIVAN and ELGAR, though his death occurred before he had attained full development.

Colet, John (c. 1467-1519) English scholar and theologian, promoter of the New Learning and founder of St Paul's School, London. Educated and ordained at Oxford, Colet's critical and original interpretation of the Bible profoundly influenced ERASMUS. Like MORE, Colet pressed for ecclesiastical reform, constantly deploring the ignorance and corruption of the clergy. He became Dean of St Paul's in 1505, founding the school with the fortune inherited from his father.

Colette, Sidonie Gabrielle (1873-1954) French novelist and foremost woman writer of her age, whose sensitive studies of a youth's love for an older woman in *Chéri* (1920) and *La Din de Chéri* (1926) established her as a major writer. In the early sketches of the 'Claudine' series (e.g. *Claudine à l'Ecole,* 1900; *Claudine à Paris,* 1901) she collaborated with her first husband, the novelist and music critic Henri Gauthier Villars ('Willy'). But it was in the post-war years that she produced her best works, including *Le Blé en herbe* (1923), *La Chatte* (1933) and the famous *Gigi* (1943).

Collins, Wilkie (1824-89) English novelist and pioneer of detective fiction in England. His first mystery story, *The Dead Secret,* appeared in 1857. The best of its successors, all very popular, are *The Woman in White* (1860) and *The Moonstone*

The Burgundian girl who was a legend in her own lifetime – Sidonie Colette

(1868). Collins was a friend of DICKENS, and his descriptive writing has affinities with Dickens's style.

Columba (521-97) Irish missionary saint. The evangelizer of Scotland, he preached the gospel to the heathen Picts and founded a monastery on the island of Iona.

Columbus, Christopher (1451-1506) Genoese-born explorer for Spain, whose voyage to the Americas in 1492 achieved for him the credit for their discovery (although the Vikings had reached America centuries before). Columbus, who believed the Earth to be round, and that only the Atlantic separated Europe from eastern Asia, offered to find John II of Portugal a sea route to the Orient by sailing westward, but finally took his offer to FERDINAND and Isabella of Spain (1484), who agreed to back him. On 3 August 1492, Columbus sailed from Palos with the *Santa Maria,* the *Pinta* and the *Niña,* and on 12 Oct. reached San Salvador Island in the Bahamas. He went on to explore the north coast of Cuba, which he thought to be part of mainland Asia, and an island which he imagined was Cipango (Japan), and named it Hispaniola. Columbus received unprecendented honours on his return to Spain, and in 1493 led 17 shiploads of colonists to Hispaniola and discovered Dominica, Puerto Rico and Jamaica. On his third voyage (1498), he discovered Trinidad, and on a last journey (1502-4), explored the east coast of Central America from Honduras to Panama, believing throughout that all his discoveries were in the Orient.

Comenius, Johann Amos (1592-1670) Moravian theologian, politician and educationalist who originated a scheme requiring universal education, a pooling of knowledge and reformed teaching methods. His own textbooks were revolutionary in their grading and use of pictures. *Gate of Language Unlocked* (1631), a Latin textbook, was translated into 16 languages, while *The Visible World in Pictures* was in use for 200 years. A visit by Comenius to England (1641-2) led to the founding of the Royal Society. LEIBNIZ and others were influenced by his ideas.

Comte, Auguste (1798-1857) French philosopher, inventor of the term 'sociology', who put forward a system of positivist philosophy based on the methods of science. Comte stated that human thought

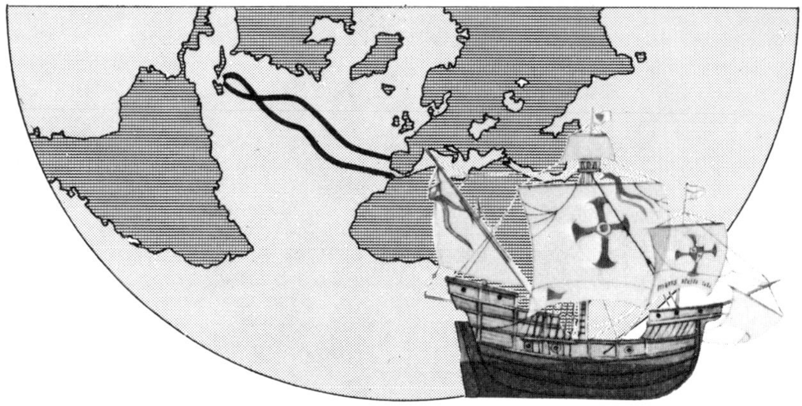

Columbus's route across the North Atlantic, and his tubby little carrack, the *Santa Maria.* The carrack never made the return journey—it was wrecked in the West Indies

passes through a theological and metaphysical stage before becoming scientific, whence it evolves from the simple and general to the complex and special. For instance, in the sequence of mathematics, astronomy, physics, chemisty, biology and sociology, each branch of knowledge draws on the preceding one. Sociology, the scientific study of society, completes the series. He also advocated a positive social organization with a rational religion in the style of the Enlightenment and the French Revolution.

Compton-Burnett, Ivy (1892-1969) English novelist, who constructed her books almost entirely from dialogue. Her 19 novels achieve their effect by the calm way in which cruelty and violence in eccentric families are revealed through the conversations of her characters.

Condé, Prince de see LOUIS II de Bourbon

Confucius (c. 551-479 BC) Chinese philosopher (K'ung Fu-tzu), who exercised more influence on Chinese culture than any other thinker. His *Analects* (collected sayings) do not constitute a religion or carry a profound intellectual message, but simply stress man's duty to man within social units from the family to the state. Confucius saw keeping to one's station as the surest way of curbing political anarchy, but also stressed the hereditary lord's obligation to set an ethical example by practising inner integrity, loyalty, altruism and love for his fellow men. While Confucian doctrines helped autocrats such as SHIH HUANG TI and WU TI to retain power, they also gave China's rulers a philosophy which put ambition in a social perspective.

Congreve, William (1670-1729) English dramatist, pre-eminent among Restoration comedy writers. His first play, *The Old Bachelor* (1693), was followed by *The Double Dealer* (1694) and *Love for Love* (1695), which took him to the height of his popularity. While his *The Mourning Bride,* in verse, was a success, *The Way of the World* (1700) was a failure. This so annoyed Congreve that he retired to live as a country gentleman. Now it is generally considered his best play and is often revived. It provides actresses with a fine comedy role in the part of the heroine, Millament.

Conn (2nd cent.) Irish king of Connaught who reputedly founded a northern Irish kingdom and a line of 'high kings', including the Cormac and Niall of the Nine Hostages.

Conrad II the Salian (c. 990-1039) King of Germany and Holy Roman Emperor (1024-39), who founded the Salian or Franconian dynasty and began Germany's great imperial phase. He crushed rebel factions in Germany (1025-30), added Lusatia (1031) and Burgundy (1033-4) to his empire, and did much to overcome northern Italy (1036-7).

Conrad III (1093-1152) King of Germany who founded the Hohenstaufen dynasty of Holy Roman Emperors (1138-1268). Lacking the statesmanship to keep Germany united, Conrad, a member of the Waiblinger family, was forced to cede Saxony (1142) to Henry the Lion, leader of the Welf (Guelph) family, which had formerly ruled the empire. Conrad's reign thus tortured Germany with struggles between Welfs and Waiblingers (Guelphs and Ghibellines), and saw German expansion against the Slavs and Scandinavians.

Conrad, Joseph (1857-1924) Polish-born English writer of short stories and novels that combine stirring adventure with profound analyses of human psychology. Conrad went to sea and became an English master mariner. His first novel, in English, was published in 1895. *Lord Jim* (1900), *Heart of Darkness* (1902) and *Nostromo* (1904) show a fluent and effective English prose style. In his works he often studied men put to the test in lonely places, using his novels to expound his view of human nature.

Conscience, Hendrik (1812-83) Belgian writer, whose outstanding historical novel *The Lion of Flanders* (1838) is an epic story of the revolt of the Flemish municipalities against France and their victory at the Battle of the Golden Spurs (1302). It was the first novel written in the Flemish tongue, giving the movement for the revival of the language its symbol of the lion.

Constable, John (1776-1837) One of the outstanding English landscape painters of the 19th century. His love for the mills and waterways of his native Suffolk and his acquaintance with Dutch Realist landscapes were at odds with his admiration for the order and clarity of the tradition of the 'ideal' landscapes of CLAUDE LORRAIN. He attempted to maintain the spontaneity of his oil sketches done in the open, while presenting an organized and digested experience of landscape. At the Paris Salon in 1824, Constable received the recognition he lacked in England. His influence on DELACROIX was profound and also important in the development of the Impressionist painters.

Constantine I 'The Great' (c. 280-337) Emperor of Rome (306-37), the first to embrace Christianity, who moved the imperial centre of gravity east from Rome to Constantinople, and made Christianity the religion of the Empire. He fought his way (306-14) to become undisputed western Emperor and reversed DIOCLETIAN's policies by reuniting the partitioned Empire. The position of the Emperor was henceforth to be absolute and hereditary. Constantine made Byzantium on the Bosporus his new capital, renaming it Constantinople. It was modelled on Rome but was more strategically placed at the crossroads of Europe and Asia, in the empire's richer and more secure eastern zone (later the Byzantine empire). Constantine presided over the first general Council of Nicaea (325), when the Nicene Creed was adopted.

Cook, James (1728-79) English sea captain whose voyages of exploration were among the greatest of 18th-century achievements. Cook accurately charted New Zealand and the east coast of Australia (1768-71). He correctly surmised the existence of Antarctica and discovered and mapped many tropical islands. He was murdered by natives in Hawaii on his third voyage in search of a northwest passage.

Coolidge, Calvin (1872-1933) Thirtieth President of the United States. He first gained public attention when, as Governor of Massachusetts in 1919, he broke a strike of the Boston city police. As HARDING's Vice-President, he succeeded to the office on Harding's death in 1923, and in 1924 was elected to serve a second term (1925-9). His irresolution in the face of business excesses and commercial profiteering led to the Wall Street crash and the world-wide depression of 1929.

Cooper, James Fenimore (1789-1851) American novelist, who was the first to portray, in his Leatherstocking stories, a distinctively American way of life and thought. His best-known work is *The Last of the Mohicans* (1826).

Copernicus, Nicolaus (1473-1543) Polish astronomer, who revolutionized theories of the motion of the planets and laid the foundations of modern astronomical studies. In his principal work, *The Revolutions of the Heavenly Bodies,* Copernicus refuted the theory propounded by PTOLEMY and went back to original Greek writers to discover that a heliocentric theory of the Solar System had been proposed, but not generally accepted. He adopted the assumption that the Earth was moving, and discovered that a simpler and more consistent theory of the Solar System arose from it. Copernicus's conclusions gained wide acceptance through the work and teachings of KEPLAR and GALILEO, and are the basis for all later studies of the planets' motions.

Less than twice the length of Chichester's single-handed yacht, Cook's *Endeavour* carried more than a hundred men – officers, crew and scientists – on its epoch-making journey around the Pacific Ocean

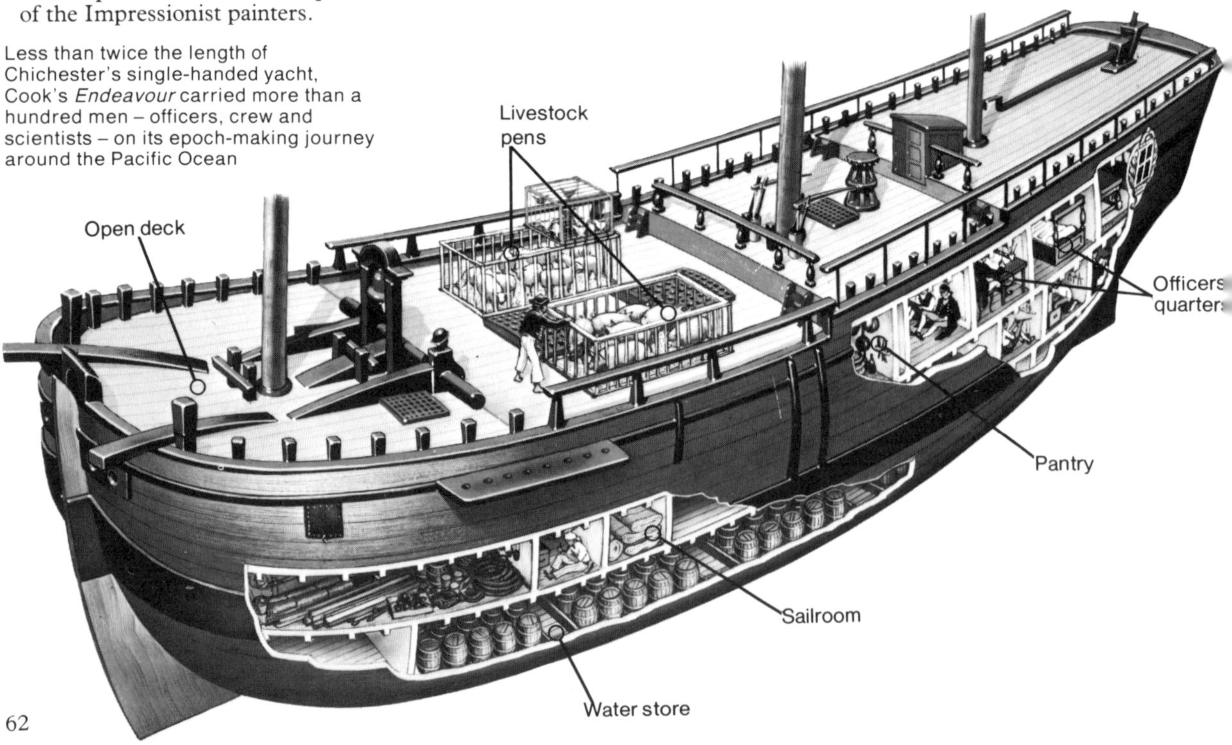

Copland, Aaron (born 1900) American composer and writer whose early work *Piano Variations* (1930) was marked by intellectual austerity and expressed the alienation of urban life. In humanizing his style, Copland turned increasingly to more 'pastoral' subjects, such as the cowboy tunes he used in the ballet *Billy the Kid* (1938) and the charming Shaker hymn-tune incorporated into *Appalachian Spring* (1944). Copland has also written film scores, notably for the film versions of WILDER's *Our Town* and STEINBECK's *Of Mice and Men.*

Corday, Charlotte (1768-93) French patriot and noblewoman who stabbed the Jacobin Jean-Paul MARAT to death in his bath on 13 July 1793 and was guillotined on 17 July. She was a Girondin who supported the principles of the French Revolution but not the Reign of Terror, and disagreed with the radical policies espoused by Marat.

Corelli, Arcangelo (1653-1713) Italian violinist and composer who established the *concerto grosso,* a musical form in which a small group of instruments is contrasted with a larger orchestral group. A pioneer in playing and writing for the violin, Corelli spent most of his musical life at the court of Cardinal Ottoboni in Rome.

Cori, Charles (born 1896) American biochemist of Czech origin who shared a Nobel Prize in 1947 with his wife, Gerty Cori, and Bernardo Houssay for their investigation of the process by which glycogen (animal starch) is converted into glucose, the main energy-yielding molecule in living tissues.

Cori, Gerty see CORI, Charles

Cornelius, Peter von (1783-1867) German painter, who was an influential member of the Nazarenes, a group of German artists working in Rome. Emulating the primitive Italian and northern artists, they worked together on frescoes in the Casa Batholdy and Casino Massimo. Cornelius himself was much influenced by the sophisticated composition and detailed technique of RAPHAEL. After returning to Munich in 1819, Cornelius embarked on a systematic programme for the revival of art in Germany, through his teaching and complex fresco cycles.

Coriolis, Gaspard Gustave de (1792-1843) French mathematician and engineer who formulated laws to describe moving bodies. He showed that the ordinary equations of motion can be applied to a rotating system by including a special inertial force at right angles to the motion of the body and to the axis of rotation. This 'Coriolis' force is important in all problems of rotational dynamics.

Corneille, Pierre (1604-84) French dramatist and the first great writer of classical tragedy in France. He was inspired to write a comedy, *Mélite,* after seeing farces staged by a touring company that visited his birthplace, Rouen. Its success in Paris encouraged him to continue writing plays. His first tragedy, *Médée* (1635), led to his appointment as salaried playwright by RICHELIEU, with whom he later quarrelled. After returning to Rouen, he wrote *Le Cid* (1637), a new kind of romantic heroic comedy and his most frequently revived play. Although it fitted awkwardly into the classical style which was then *de rigueur,* it established Corneille as France's leading dramatist, until he was superseded by RACINE. His principal tragedies are on classical themes – *Horace* (1640), *Cinna* (1641), *Polyeucte* (1642), *La Mort de Pompée* (1643). His only comedy after his early period was *Le Menteur* (1643).

Cornwallis, Charles, 1st Marquess (1738-1805) British major-general whose defeat virtually ended the American War of Independence. During the War he seized New York, and forced WASHINGTON's retreat through New Jersey. Later, disobeying orders to avoid major risks, he entered Virginia, where Washington's troops, backed by a French fleet offshore, trapped Cornwallis and his lesser troops at Yorktown, forcing their surrender. Later, as Governor-General of India (1786-93; 1805), he pioneered major administrative reforms. Viceroy of Ireland (1798-1801) at the time of the Union, he resigned when Catholic emancipation was not granted. Cornwallis negotiated the 1802 Treaty of Amiens, which brought a brief pause during the Napoleonic wars with the French.

Corot, Jean Baptiste (1796-1875) French classical landscape artist. His work falls into two main categories: firstly, the large synthetic landscapes painted for exhibition at the Salon, which are in the tradition of CLAUDE LORRAIN (e.g. *Souvenir de Montfortaine,* 1864); and secondly, the smaller, informal paintings which reflect his love of working out of doors, and influenced the Impressionists, notably PISSARRO, who was Corot's pupil. Corot's mature style is marked by a subtlety of tonal modulation which led BAUDELAIRE to describe him as a 'harmonist' rather than a colourist.

Correggio, Antonio (c. 1494-1534) Italian artist, who was an important forerunner of the 17th-century ceiling painters. His two greatest works are in Parma: the cupolas of S Giovanni Evangelista (1520-3) and the Cathedral (1526-30). In both of these are the formal types exemplified in the work of RAPHAEL and MICHELANGELO, but the main effect is of a mass of figures soaring into an illusionary space that denies the architectural solidity of the cupola itself. Correggio also painted a number of pictures illustrating the loves of the gods, which are characterized by a delicacy of modelling of human forms that derives ultimately from LEONARDO.

Cortés, Hernando (1485-1547) Spanish conqueror of Mexico. Cortés emigrated to the West Indies

George Washington accepts the surrender of Cornwallis at Yorktown

(1504) and was appointed by Diego VELASQUEZ, Cuba's governor, to lead an expedition to Mexico, where he landed (1519) with 500 men. MONTEZUMA, the Aztec monarch, believing Cortés to be the god Quetzalcoatl, sent him conciliatory gifts, but Cortés, surrounded by hostile Aztecs, took Montezuma hostage. The Aztecs revolted but, after heavy losses and a long siege, Cortés took Tenochtitlan, the capital, ended Aztec power (1521), and became Governor of Mexico. The King of Spain, alarmed by Cortés's ambition, ousted him.

Cortona, Pietro da (1596-1669) Italian Baroque architect, whose work is characterized by a verve and theatricality achieved by amassing shapes and using unusual surface details such as giant pilasters. His first church in Rome, SS Luca e Martina (1635-50), is a wildly exuberant building and the façade of his church Sta Maria della Pace (1656-7) provides a theatrical backdrop to the Piazza he designed in front of it.

Cosa, Juan de la (c. 1460-1510) Spanish navigator whose first-hand knowledge helped him to make the earliest surviving world map, which shows the New World discoveries of the 1490s. As Captain of the *Santa Maria,* he accompanied COLUMBUS on his first transatlantic voyage (1492-3), and later (between 1499 and 1508) piloted expeditions to explore northern South America, where he was killed by American Indians. His large, hand-drawn world map (1500), which took account of the discoveries of Columbus, CABOT and others, can be seen in the Naval Museum, Madrid.

Cotton, John (1584-1652) English-born American clergyman, whose influence in the civil and ecclesiastical affairs of New England was greater than that of any other minister. Educated at Cambridge, where the Puritan ethic flourished, Cotton fled from his vicarage at Boston, England, to Boston, Massachusetts, in 1633. Speedily establishing himself as a religious and political leader, he successfully opposed 'liberals' like Roger WILLIAMS. A man of great learning, with a prolific pen, he wrote catechisms, commentaries on prayer and works on Congregationalism. His best-known book was *The Way of the Churches of Christ in New England* (1645).

Coulomb, Charles Augustin de (1736-1806) French physicist who discovered the inverse square law for the force between electric charges. The practical unit of charge is called after him. This law states that the force between two charges is proportional to their product and inversely proportional to the square of the distance between them. He found a similar law for magnetic poles.

Couperin, François (1668-1733) French harpsichordist and composer, among the first to use picturesque, or programmatic, titles for pieces of music and who wrote a classic on harpsichord technique, *L'Art de toucher le clavecin* (1717). Couperin was the most outstanding of a family of five generations of musicians. RAVEL paid him tribute in his set of six piano movements, *Le Tombeau de Couperin* (1917), four of which he later orchestrated.

Courbet, Gustave (1819-77) French realist painter, who believed resolutely that painting should be a democratic depiction of the life of the workers and the peasantry. He fulfilled this ambition in such famous works as *The Stonebreakers* (1849) and *The Burial of Ornans* (1850), the latter portraying a peasant funeral. His political convictions led him to identify himself with the Paris Commune of 1871, and he was forced to flee to Switzerland after his part in the demolition of NAPOLEON's memorial column in the Place Vendôme. Courbet was largely self-taught, and tried to free his landscapes from the compositional clichés of contemporary French art, thereby anticipating Impressionism. Although friendly with BAUDELAIRE and PROUDHON, the philosopher of socialism, Courbet remained wholly independent in spirit, and countered official neglect by mounting separate exhibitions of his work during the international exhibitions of 1855 and 1867.

Cournand, André (born 1895) American physician of French origin who, with Werner Forssman and Dickinson Richards, developed the technique of cardiac catheterization, for which they were awarded a Nobel Prize in 1956. The cardiac catheter is a fine tube that is inserted into a blood vessel in the arm or leg; guided by X-ray-assisted visual display, it is then worked upstream or downstream to the heart. It can be used to take direct pressure readings, withdraw blood samples for analysis, or inject dyes opaque to X-rays, and so assist in the diagnosis of cardiac conditions.

Cousteau, Jacques-Yves (born 1910) French pioneer of underwater exploration and its techniques. Cousteau developed skin-diving gear, in particular the aqualung, to carry out free-diving exploration of shallow seas, and in the Mediterranean found enough sunken Greek and Roman wrecks to reconstruct ancient trade routes. He has also made a number of discoveries about underwater life in the Red Sea, Caribbean and Indian Ocean.

Coward, Sir Noël (1899-1973) All-round man of the English theatre, whose plays include *Bitter Sweet, Cavalcade, Private Lives* and *Blithe Spirit.* He also wrote and acted in revues and films and often appeared in cabaret.

Cowell, Henry (1897-1966) American composer and a leading experimentalist in US music. He introduced the tone-cluster in which whole blocks of piano keys are struck with fist or forearm. Cowell, self-taught, was a true original, exploring acoustic and percussive techniques, indeterminacy and random selection. He was an influential teacher, and CAGE was among his pupils.

Cowper, William (1731-1800) English poet, who wrote the ballad 'John Gilpin' (1785). Cowper was a barrister, but his career was hin-

Noël Coward in an early production of his great success *Private Lives.*

dered by recurrent bouts of mania. He retired to the country and wrote the *Olney Hymns* (1779) and *The Task* (1785), in which he shows his delight in rural scenes.

Crabbe, George (1754-1832) 'Though nature's sternest painter, yet the best', wrote BYRON of Crabbe, whose principal narrative poems are grimly realistic pictures of the hardships of country life. In such typical works as 'The Parish Register' (1807) and 'The Borough' (1810), the harshness of the lives of the poor is set against the flat, grey countryside of the Suffolk fens. Crabbe was aided and encouraged by Edmund BURKE and Dr JOHNSON. 'The Borough' was the source of BRITTEN's opera 'Peter Grimes'.

Crane, Hart (1899-1932) American poet, who tried to assert the positive 'myth of America' against the disillusionment he saw in modern poetry, particlarly in ELIOT's *Waste Land*. He wrote a long poem of the old and new America called *The Bridge* (1930), which takes Brooklyn Bridge as a symbol and WHITMAN as one of the heroes. After a turbulent, drunken life, Crane committed suicide by leaping from a ship.

Cranmer, Thomas (1489-1556) English archbishop who compiled the liturgies of the Church of England. Cranmer was appointed Archbishop of Canterbury by HENRY VIII for his assistance in the struggle with Pope CLEMENT VII for a divorce from Catherine of Aragon. In 1533 Cranmer annulled the marriage and accepted Henry as Supreme Head of the Church of England (1534). Cranmer extended the English Reformation by having English Bibles placed in all churches. He compiled Edward VI's prayer books (1549 and 1552), and evolved a church whose doctrines compromised between those of Rome and Geneva. Before it took root under ELIZABETH I, the Catholic Queen MARY condemned him as a heretic (1555), despite his admission of papal supremacy. He later retracted, and was burnt at the stake.

Crashaw, Richard (c. 1612-49) English poet, whose ornate, religious verse is the closest in English literature to the traditions of the continental Baroque style. His sacred poetry is exotic, sometimes, as in 'The Flaming Heart,' a hymn to ST TERESA, showing mystical passion and a confident command of elaborate imagery. His main work, *Steps to the Temple* (1646), combines ecstatic devotional verse with graceful secular lyrics.

Crazy Horse (c. 1842-77) American Indian chief of the Oglala Sioux tribe, whose Indian name was Jashunca-Uitco. He defeated General George Crook at the Rosebud River (17 June 1876), and assisted SITTING BULL in the massacre of General George CUSTER's force at Little Big Horn (25 June 1876). He was shot while resisting imprisonment for allegedly planning a revolt.

Crick, Francis (born 1916) British geneticist who, with James WATSON, proposed the first model of a deoxyribonucleic acid (DNA) molecule. The DNA molecule has the basic structure of a double helix, and it is now known to carry inheritable genetic material. Crick and Watson showed how this material is replicated during cell division and how the DNA molecule has series of bases which serve as patterns for ordering the genetic material so that it can be reproduced accurately. With a colleague, Maurice Wilkins, they won a Nobel Prize in 1962.

Crippen, Dr Hawley (1862-1910) American doctor, who killed his wife with poison, Crippen, a US citizen, settled in London in 1900. Soon after, he began an extra-marital affair, and in January 1910 his wife disappeared. A search of Crippen's house revealed her remains. Crippen, who was traced aboard an ocean liner by wireless telegraphy (the first time it was used in criminal detection), was convicted of the murder and then hanged.

Cripps, Stafford (1889-1952) English lawyer and politician, Chancellor of the Exchequer in

Crippen is arrested, with his girl companion dressed as a boy

Le Petit Journal

ADMINISTRATION
61, RUE LAFAYETTE, 61
Les manuscrits ne sont pas rendus
On s'abonne sans frais dans tous les bureaux de poste

5 CENT. SUPPLÉMENT ILLUSTRÉ 5 CENT.

21me Année — Numéro 1.030

DIMANCHE 14 AOUT 1910

ABONNEMENTS

ARRESTATION DU DOCTEUR CRIPPEN ET DE MISS LE NEVE SUR LE PONT DU « MONTROSE »

ATTLEE's Labour government. In 1939 he was expelled from the Labour Party for advocating a Popular Front against Neville CHAMBERLAIN's policy of appeasement. As Ambassador to Moscow in 1940 he improved Anglo-Soviet relations considerably and, as Special Envoy to India in 1942, he offered the country dominion status, which was rejected by both GHANDI and JINNAH. He became President of the Board of Trade in 1945, and as Chancellor of the Exchequer (1947-50) introduced the policy of austerity for which his chancellorship is remembered. His were the first geniune attempts at economic planning, however, and his policy of income restraint was a pioneering one.

Crispus, Gaius see SALLUST

Cristofori, Bartolommeo (1655-1731) Italian craftsman who in the early 18th century developed the first pianoforte (piano). His principal contribution was replacing harpsichord jacks with hammers.

Croce, Benedetto (1866-1952) Italian philosopher who believed in the central role of history and aesthetics. Anti-positivist, he regarded the world as living spirit, manifesting itself through history and working at four levels – aesthetic, logical, economic and ethical. Art, he thought, manifests itself not in the objects produced, but in the prior intuition of the artist and the later one of the beholder.

Crockett, Davy (1786-1836) American frontiersman. In 1813, he scouted for Andrew Jackson against the Creek Indians, but as a Congressman subsequently opposed Jackson's Indian and land policies. Crockett died helping defend San Antonio's Alamo fort against 4000 Mexican troops trying to crush Texan independence.

Croesus (6th cent. BC) last king of Lydia (560-546 BC), who by conquest dominated what is now the western half of Turkey and built a legendary personal fortune through trade. His kingdom was conquered and absorbed by CYRUS of Persia.

Crome, John (1768-1821) Leading artist of the Norwich school of English landscape painters. His work, which was much influenced by HOBBEMA, is characterized by a freshness of observation and a sensitivity to effects of light, noticeable especially in his delicate depiction of trees.

Crompton, Samuel (1753-1827) English inventor of the spinning mule, so called because it was developed from a hybrid of HARGREAVES's jenny and ARKWRIGHT's water frame spinning machine, both of which had serious limitations. He developed the mule secretly in 1779, after five years of work, and attempted to pass off the machine's product as his own. However, the superior quality and fineness of this yarn gave him away and he was tricked into revealing the mechanism of his (unpatented) spinner to the manufacturers of Bolton. Eventually he received a government grant of £5000, but this was insignificant compared to the financial benefits derived from his invention.

Cromwell, Oliver (1599-1658) Lord Protector of England and head of the republican Commonwealth that came to rule England, Scotland and Ireland between the execution of CHARLES I (1649) and the Restoration of CHARLES II (1660). During the Civil War, Cromwell's highly trained Puritan troops held together the Parliamentary supporters in eastern England and turned the Battle of Marston Moor (1644) against the Royalists. After the war, he supported the execution of Charles and became a member of the ruling Council of State. He re-conquered Ireland, massacring dissident citizens, and crushed Scotland, returning to London eventually to take the position of Lord Protector. Ruling as virtual dictator under the Instrument of Government (1653), Cromwell reorganized the Church along tolerant lines, made peace with Holland and Denmark, and successfully fought Spain in the West Indies and Spanish Netherlands (1655-8). Cromwell's protectorate did not long survive after his death.

Cromwell, Thomas (c. 1485-1540) English statesman who carried out HENRY VIII's Reformation to increase royal power at the expense of the Church. After trading successfully abroad, Cromwell became a financial adviser to nobles, an agent and favourite of WOLSEY and, by the early 1530s, a leading member of the House of Commons. He became the king's secretary (1534), drafted and engineered through Parliament most of Henry's Reformation Acts (1532-9), and ruthlessly carried out the dissolution of the monasteries and the confiscation of their property for the crown. His reward was a barony and the positions of Lord Privy Seal, Vicar General, and Deputy Head of the English Church. He lost the king's favour by negotiating his marriage with the unprepossessing Anne of Cleves (the 'Flanders mare') to win the support of Protestant German princes. Although Cromwell became Earl of Essex (1540), he was beheaded for heresy and treason.

Cruikshank, George (1792-1878) British caricaturist and illustrator, who was famous for his satires against the Prince Regent, later George IV, in *The Scourge,* a satirical journal. His very large output included the illustrations for DICKENS's *Sketches by Boz* and *Oliver Twist,* as well as for many other books. Later he became a teetotaller and produced a celebrated series of drawings (*The Bottle,* 1847) advocating temperance.

Culpeper, Nicholas (1616-54) English physician and botanist whose herbal remedies described in *London Pharmocopeia* (1654) were widely used in the treatment of disease for many generations. He was a strong opponent of secrecy in medical matters and translated many learned works.

Cummings, Edward Estlin (1894-1962) American lyric poet, who in his verse experimented with layout, typography and punctuation to suggest movement in time and space.

Curie, Marie (1867-1934) Polish-born French chemist who, with her husband Pierre, pioneered the earliest research into radioactivity. This remarkable husband and wife team worked for years in the late 1890s to establish that the uranium ore, pitchblende, owed much of its radioactivity to tiny quantities of highly active impurities. In 1898, the Curies discovered a new element which they named polonium (in honour of Marie's homeland). But Marie believed there was another still more active element in the ore. After four more years of painstaking work, they isolated a tenth of a gram of another new element from the several tons of ore with which they had started. They called it radium. Its tremendous radioactivity was a first glimpse of the huge energies obtainable from atomic processes. Marie eventually died of leukaemia, brought on by constant exposure to radiation.

Curie, Pierre (1859-1906) French physicist who studied the relationship between magnetism and heat. He showed that above a certain critical temperature (now called the Curie point) ferromagnetic substances lose their magnetism. He also established that the ease with which a substance becomes magnetized is proportional to its temperature, a principle now called Curie's law. With his wife Marie, he pioneered research on radioactivity.

Currie, James (1756-1805) Scottish doctor who pioneered the use of cold water in the treatment of fever. Until Currie's time, it was widely thought that fevers were beneficial and it was the practice to let the fever burn itself out, the patient often being killed in the process. Currie saw that it was important to keep the patient's temperature as near normal as possible. His success promoted water cures (hydrotherapy) for many diseases, and the use of clinical thermometers.

Curtis, Cyrus (1850-1933) American publisher and journalist who founded the *Ladies' Home Journal* (1879) and the Curtis Publishing Company. In 1897 he bought the *Saturday Evening Post*, and the *New York Evening Post*.

Curzon, George Nathanial (1859-1925) British statesman and proponent of Britain's Imperial aspirations. He became Under-Secretary for India at the age of 32, for Foreign Affairs at 37, and Viceroy of India at 39. There he pursued a policy so independent that it was said of the government of India during his rule that it often behaved to Britain like that of a 'foreign and far from friendly power.' He held various offices under LLOYD GEORGE in the War Cabinet (1916-19), and as Foreign Secretary from 1919 to 1924 he arranged the British settlement with Turkey at the Lausanne Conference (1923). It was Curzon's ambtion to be Prime Minister and a bitter disappointment to him when, in 1923, BALDWIN achieved the premiership, but a dedicated aristocrat and 'a most superior person', Curzon was hampered by his own personality throughout his political career.

Marie Curie, joint discoverer of radium, received her early scientific training from her father at their home in Warsaw

Custer, Colonel George Armstrong (1839-76) American soldier who distinguished himself during the Civil War (1861-5) and was promoted to brevet Major General. His subsequent controversial career reached its climax in 1876, when, in command of the 7th Cavalry at Little Big Horn, Custer and the 108 troopers were annihilated by the combined Sioux and Cheyenne tribes. It was the most spectacular victory achieved by the Indians against the US troops.

Cuvier, Baron Georges (1769-1832) French naturalist, who in *The Animal Kingdom Arranged in Conformity with its Organization,* classified the animal kingdom on the basis of comparative anatomy. He is sometimes said to have founded the science of palaeontology (the study of fossils), as his research covered animals, both living and fossil.

Cyrus II, 'The Great' (c. 600-529 BC) King of Persia (550-529 BC) who founded the Achaemenid dynasty (named after his ancestor Achaemenes), and built the biggest empire the world had then known. Cyrus united the Medes and Persians, defeating a coalition of neighbouring powers and extending Persian power to the Mediterranean. His army of mobile bowmen proved invincible, and in less than 20 years took much of Greece, Asia Minor, Mesopotamia and northern and eastern Iran, building a state that reached from India to the Aegean and the Egyptian border. A statesman as well as a soldier, Cyrus spurned the scorched-earth tactics of Assyrian war-lords such as SENNACHERIB, and treated the defeated peoples humanely, respecting their cultural traditions and taking them into the army and administration on an equal footing with the Persians. He was killed fighting the Massagetae east of the Caspian.

Czerny, Carl (1791-1857) Austrian composer and pianist remembered for his piano studies familiar to generations of keyboard students as practice pieces. A pupil of BEETHOVEN and a teacher of LISZT, Czerny also wrote many other kinds of piano music.

Cuyp, Aelbert (1620-91) Dutch painter, who is best known for his landscapes, which usually contain horses and riders, or cows, and sometimes both. He was one of the few Dutch exponents of the tranquil 'ideal' landscape, but his work has more of a pastoral character than that of CLAUDE LORRAIN, from whom he derived his poetic effects of golden evening sunlight.

Cyrano de Bergerac, Savinien de (1619-55) French dramatist (*Le Pédant joué*; *La Mort d'Agrippine*), author of satirical romances and model for ROSTAND's play, *Cyrano de Bergerac*.

D

Daguerre, Louis Jacques Mandé (1789-1851) French artist and inventor, who, in 1837, after a partnership with NIEPCE, perfected the process of heliography. The result of the 'daguerrotype' process was a single direct positive photograph, with the disadvantage that no copies could be made.

Daimler, Gottlieb (1834-1900) German engineer who, together with BENZ, was one of the most important contributors to the development of the petrol engine automobile. After working for various engineering firms, in 1872 Daimler joined OTTO's firm where, during the next decade, in conjunction with MAYBACK and others, he improved the four-cycle gas engine. In 1882, he and Maybach resigned to set up a factory to develop a light, internal combustion engine, which ran at higher speeds than those of Benz's. In 1885 Daimler placed an engine on a wooden bicycle, creating the world's first motorcycle. Two years later he used the engine to power a four-wheeled vehicle, one of the first true automobiles. He founded the Daimler motor company in 1890.

Daladier, Edouard (1884-1970) Co-signatory with Neville CHAMBERLAIN of the Munich Agreement with HITLER. Having twice been briefly Premier of France (1933 and 1934), he became Prime Minister for the third time in 1938. He was a Socialist, a pacifist and a supporter of the policy of appeasement towards Hitler. Like Neville Chamberlain he believed that the Munich Pact, signed in September 1938, would ensure European peace, or at least buy time for re-armament. When war was declared DALADIER formed a war cabinet, but resigned in March 1940. After the collapse of France he was put under house arrest by the Vichy régime, where he remained until the end of the war. He played a prominent part in radical politics from 1945 until 1959, when he retired after DE GAULLE became President – an outcome which he had tried to prevent.

Dalai Lama, 14th (born 1935) Tibetan Buddhist leader and ruler *in absentia* of the world's last theocracy. After being named the reincarnation of the Buddha Chenrezi when only four years old, the Dalai became involved in a power struggle with the rival Panchen Lama. Although the Chinese conquest brought a temporary *détente,* the Dalai Lama fled to India in 1959, claiming China had failed to respect Tibetan autonomy.

Dali, Salvador (born 1904) Spanish Surrealist painter, who credits himself with having invented 'paranoic-critical activity', described by him as 'a spontaneous method of irrational understanding based on the interpretative critical association of delirious phenomena'. After trying his hand at Cubism, Futurism and metaphysical painting, Dali joined the Surrealists in 1929. His painting is meticulously accurate, highly finished, and sometimes appears to be deliberately sensational.

Expelled from the Academy of Fine Arts in Madrid, Dali was the enfant terrible of the Surrealist School of Painting

Dalton, John (1766-1844) English chemist who defined an atom as the smallest particle of a substance that can take part in a chemical reaction. He also stated that, because elements are in the form of atoms, they must combine together in definite proportions. He made the first tentative calculations of atomic weights, on a scale based on the atomic weight of hydrogen as one. Dalton also contributed to meteorology and physics, in which he formulated the law of partial pressures, which states that, in a vessel containing a mixture of gases, the total pressure is equal to the sum of the pressures that each gas would exert if it alone occupied the vessel.

Damocles (4th cent. BC) Greek courtier in Sicily remembered in the phrase 'the sword of Damocles'. According to CICERO, the sycophantic Damocles extravagantly acclaimed the happiness of his master, DIONYSIUS, who responded by inviting Damocles to a sumptuous feast, and seating him beneath a sword hung by a single hair, to symbolize the ever-present threat of peril, even amid good fortune.

Daniell, John Frederic (1790-1845) English chemist who developed the first electric cell with a long working life. Alessandro VOLTA's earlier battery was a great innovation, but its current ran down quickly. In 1836, Daniell designed a cell that could produce a steady current for some time.

D'Annunzio, Gabriele (1863-1938) Italian poet, dramatist, novelist and adventurer. After his early sensual poems and short stories he became a prolific writer of novels, of which the best known are *The Child of Pleasure* (1889), *The Intruder* (1892) and *The Flame of Life* (1900). The d'Annunzian hero, an egoist verging on the superman, immersed in sensuality and aesthetics, recurs throughout his works.

Dante, Alighieri (1265-1321) Italy's most famous poet and author of *The Divine Comedy,* one of the greatest European epic poems and a comprehensive survey of medieval theology, thought and literature. In this and other works he created a new, non-dialect poetic language which was to become the basis of modern Italian.

Danti, Vincenzo (1530-76) Italian sculptor whose art is best seen in the group depicting the execution of the Baptist, Baptistery, Florence (1571). Influenced by MICHELANGELO, Danti was asked to supply sculpture and painting for Michelangelo's funeral ceremonies in 1564, and the proximity of his style to that of Michelangelo is seen in the bronze figure of *Julius II* (1555), the *Venus Anadyomene,* and *Honour Overcoming Falsehood.* Danti's importance lies chiefly in his appointment as one of the first teachers in the newly founded Academia del Disegno, Perugia (1573). His treatise on proportion, published in 1567, was dedicated to the Grand Duke Cosimo de MEDICI.

Danton, George Jacques (1759-94) One of the principal leaders and greatest orators of the French Revolution. A lawyer by profession, he rose to become Administrator of Paris in 1791 and Minister of Justice in 1792. As Leader of the right wing of the Jacobins, he was not among the most dedicated of the Terrorists, and as a member of the Committee of Public Safety his speeches were more patriotic than revolutionary, notably in his use of the power of oratory to rally the nation's courage following the Austrian invasion (1792). His carelessness in financial matters enabled ROBESPIERRE to indict him before the Revolutionary Tribunal, and he was guillotined in 1794.

Darby, Abraham (1678-1717) English ironfounder who played a notable part in the Industrial Revolution. At Coalbrookdale, Shropshire, in 1709, he manufactured high-grade iron, ideal for casting, in a coke-fuel furnace. This was a major discovery, for the use of charcoal in blast furnaces had until that time imposed economic and technical limitations on the industry's growth. The Coalbrookdale works produced iron boilers for Newcomen's steam engines, the world's first iron bridge over the nearby River Severn (1779), iron rails, an iron canal aqueduct, an iron boat (1788) and the first railway locomotive with a high pressure boiler (1802).

Darby, John (1800-82) English clergyman and theological writer who established the Plymouth Brethren in England. The Brethren originated in Dublin as a non-denominational group dedicated to Christian fellowship. Puritanical and fundamentalist, Darby's Plymouth Brethren recognized no official ministry but centred their worship on a commemorative 'breaking of bread'. In 1845 the movement began to split into the Open and the Exclusive Brethren, a more rigid wing led by Darby. There have been more divisions since, but most modern Brethren, widely scattered over England, Ireland, the US and Europe, belong to open assemblies.

Darius I (c. 558-486 BC) King of Persia, who ruled the Achaemenid Empire at its height, and pushed Persia's boundaries east beyond the Indus and west into Europe. His conquests were not principally to extend the empire but to reach natural frontiers which could be held against the enemies beyond. Like all rulers of the Persian Empire, he treated the conquered peoples humanely and on an equal footing with the Persians. Darius's only major failure was his defeat by Athens, when he attempted to punish the Greek states for aiding Persia's rebellious Ionian cities. His two expeditions against Greece failed, the second ending in defeat by Athens at Marathon (490 BC). He died preparing a third expedition.

Darling, Grace (1815-42) English heroine, the daughter of a lighthouse-keeper at Longstone off the northeast coast of England, who, with her father, took out a small boat in a stormy sea to rescue the survivors of the wrecked steamship *Forfarshire* (1838).

Darwin, Charles Robert (1809-82) British naturalist and the main proponent of the modern theory of evolution in biology. *On the Origin of Species by Means of Natural Selection* (1859), based on the evaluation of his observations on a five-year scientific expedition to South America and the Pacific, outlined a theory according to which species develop by natural selection through survival of the fittest, and a gradual differentiation through adaptation. Darwin's other great work, *The Descent of Man* (1871), uses evolutionary principles to trace the development of man from a more primitive animal that gave rise also to the anthropoid apes.

Daudet, Alphonse (1840-97) French author of picturesque tales and burlesque novels. Today, his best-known works are *Lettres de mon moulin,* tales of Provençal life (1866), and his novel *Tartarin de Tarascon* (1872) and its sequels, *Tartarin sur les Alpes* and *Port-Tarascon.* He also wrote *L'Arlésienne* (1872), a play for which BIZET composed the incidental music.

Daumier, Honoré (1808-79) French caricaturist, whose thousands of lithographs, made for the journals *La Caricature* and *Charivari,* are of both artistic and social interest. His earlier works were politically inspired, and he was imprisoned in 1832 for caricaturing LOUIS PHILIPPE. He was also a gifted painter and sculptor, achieving lively and suggestive *chiaroscuro* (light and shade) effects, and was drawn particularly to the theme of Don Quixote. He was much admired by the young CÉZANNE, and by VAN GOGH.

David, St (6th cent.) Patron saint of Wales. Traditionally of royal descent and the founder of numerous churches in South Wales, his shrine at St David's, Pembrokeshire, was a place of pilgrimage in medieval times. Very little else is known about his life or work.

David (10th cent. BC) Founder of a dynasty that ruled Judah for 400 years, until NEBUCHADNEZZAR conquered it. David, a Bethlehem shepherd, was summoned (either for his skilful harp-playing or for his slaying of the giant Philistine, Goliath) to the court of SAUL, King of Israel (north Palestine). On the death of Saul's son, David was accepted by the Israelites as their king, captured Jerusalem and made it his capital, beat off the Philistines from Israel, and conquered other hostile groups.

David, Gerrard (c. 1450-1523) Netherlandish painter of religious scenes which are notable for their craftsmanship and simple piety. His style, based on that of the 15th-century Dutch painters, became dated once Italian painting achieved an influence in northern Europe.

David, Jacques (1748-1825) French artist, of the Neo-classical school. His painting, *The Oath of the Horatii* (1784), which proclaims the Roman civic virtues, is now recognized as the foundation stone of French Neo-classicism. Later, *The Death of Socrates* and *Brutus Condemning his Sons to Death* enhanced the esteem in which David was held by the public. David engaged in political activities during the 1789 Revolution, and his *The Dead Marat* was a powerful piece of revolutionary propaganda.

Davis, Dwight (1879-1945) American lawn tennis enthusiast (later a politician) who established the Davis Cup competition. In 1900, he donated a silver cup to be presented annually to the nation winning an international men's tennis championship. By 1914, the Davis Cup competition was established on a world-wide basis.

Davis, John (c. 1550-1605) One of ELIZABETH I'S chief navigators, remarkable for the extent of his explorations, from Baffin Island to the Falklands. Davis made three voyages, from 1586, in a fruitless search for the elusive North West Passage, but his journeys drew attention to the abundance of fish and fur-bearing animals in the northeast section of America.

Davy, Sir Humphry (1778-1829) English chemist who studied the effects of electric currents on compounds. Davy became interested in William Nicholson's discovery that electricity passing through water splits it up into its component elements hydrogen and oxygen. In 1807, Davy built a huge battery and by passing current through molten potash he isolated a metal he called potassium. From soda he produced another metal which he named sodium. At the same time, he worked on an electro-chemical theory in which he discussed the relationship between electrical and chemical actions on compounds. Much of his work was developed further by his brilliant young protégé, Michael FARADAY. In 1815, Davy invented the miner's safety lamp, in which a metal gauze surrounding the flame prevents it from igniting any inflammable gas.

Day Lewis, Cecil (1904-72) English poet and critic, born in Ireland, contemporary at Oxford with AUDEN and SPENDER, with whom he formed the core of the left-wing poetic movement of the 1930s. He showed his individual lyrical talent in works like 'Transitional Poem' (1929) and 'Overtures to Death' (1938). He translated VIRGIL and VALÉRY and was appointed Poet Laureate in 1968. He wrote fine criticism in *The Poetic Image* (1947), an autobiography, *The Buried* (1960), and many detective stories under the pseudonym Nicholas Blake.

Dayan, Moshe (1915-81) Israeli general and Minister of Defence in Golda MEIR's government, who headed the Israeli army forces during the Sinai campaign, the Six-Day War (1967), and again during the war of late 1973. He served as foreign minister under Menachem BEGIN (1977-9).

Debussy, Claude-Achille (1862-1918) The Leading Impressionist composer in French music, whose style has direct parallels with the techniques of Impressionism, in painting. Debussy was influenced by the work of the Symbolist poets, BAUDELAIRE and VERLAINE, but most of all by WAGNER, even though Debussy's own music was a profound reaction against the senior composer. *L'Après-midi d'un faune* (1894), a tone poem based on a poem by MALLARMÉ was his first major work. His later compositions include the opera *Pelléas et Mélisande* (1902) and the three symphonic sketches, *La Mer* (1905). Debussy also wrote an early string quartet of distinction. His last chamber works – the sonatas for cello, flute, viola, harp and for violin – showed him exploring ever more deeply into harmonic originality.

Defoe, Daniel (c. 1660-1731) English author of *Robinson Crusoe* (1719), one of the earliest English novels. He was a prolific and versatile writer whose political pamphlets, often attacking religious intolerance or the Jacobites, twice caused his imprisonment. He founded and largely wrote a well-known periodical, the *Review* (1704-13), Defoe wrote his outstanding full-length works, including *Robinson Crusoe, Moll Flanders, A Journal of the Plague Year* (1722) and *Roxana* (1724), quite late in life; their energy and crowded detail reflect his varied life as a merchant, traveller, soldier under WILLIAM III and secret agent in Scotland.

Degas, Edgar (1834-1917) Leading French Impressionist painter possessing the characteristic feeling for the instantaneous, for nature caught at a specific moment. Unlike MONET, PISSARRO and SISLEY, he cared little for landscape, preferring to concentrate on the human figure. He extended the traditional compositional disciplines beyond academic conventions, achieving seemingly arbitrary, but in fact carefully contrived, effects. He did not hesitate, for instance, to bisect a figure by the frame or to place major figures off-centre. He often used pastels, through which he achieved remarkable colouristic effects. Late in life, he made many wax models (later cast in bronze) of ballet dancers in motion which have an affinity with the work of RODIN.

De Gaulle, Charles André Joseph Marie (1890-1970) French soldier-statesman who rallied the 'Free French', persuading them to continue to fight after France's defeat by Germany in the Second World War. A general in 1940, he was appointed Under-Secretary of Defence in Reynaud's government, but, seeing French surrender as inevitable, he decided that England must become the base for continued French resistance. He commanded the 'Free French' forces until 1944 and was virtual head of a French government in exile, becoming recognized head of the Provisional French Government following liberation. In 1946 he chose to resign rather than meet opposition demands to reduce military expenditure. In 1958 De Gaulle was recalled to power by President Coty to deal with French Algerian opposition to the proposals for Algerian independence, and was elected President in December of that year. In 1960 he gave France an independent nuclear military force and tried to restore her status as a great power. During the 1960s he succeeded in stabilizing the economy, industry and social life of France, but at the expense of democratic liberties. In January 1966 he was re-elected President for another seven-year term, during which he took France out of the North Atlantic Treaty Organization (1966), formally rejected Britain's entry into the European Economic Community (1967) and openly supported French Canadian separatism in his Quebec speech of 1967. After a year of industrial unrest and student riots (1968) he appealed to the country for a fresh mandate, but was defeated in a constitutional referendum and retired in 1969.

Delacroix, Eugène (1798-1863) French painter, who is usually considered as the great exponent of Romanticism, in opposition to the classical INGRES. His first Salon picture, *Dante and Virgil Crossing the Styx* (1822), depicts a morbid scene derived from GÉRICAULT's *Raft of the Medusa*. Delacroix was an eclectic artist who drew inspiration from such diverse sources as RUBENS, CONSTABLE, BONINGTON and Lawrence. These influences combined to produce the brilliant colour and free handling of *Death of Sardanapalus* (1829), a subject drawn from BYRON, who, with SHAKESPEARE and SCOTT, became Delacroix's principal source of inspiration. In 1832 he visited Morocco, where, for him, antiquity lived on in the Arabs he encountered in the streets, as depicted in *Femmes d'Algers* (1834). His water-colour sketchbooks reveal a proto-Impressionistic observation of the brilliance of light and the existence of complementary colours in shadows.

De la Mare, Walter (1873-1956) English author whose poetry and other work concentrates on the themes of childhood, innocence and the magical. His language is often lyrical and haunting. De la Mare published some 50 volumes and was awarded the Order of Merit at 80.

Delius, Frederick (1862-1934) Self-taught English composer of German descent whose famous works are *Appalachia* (1904), variations on a slave song, *Brigg Fair* (1908), based on an English folk song and the tone poem *On Hearing the First Cuckoo in Spring* (1913). Delius possessed a highly personal, impressionistic style, unique in English music. Influenced by GRIEG and DEBUSSY, he nevertheless worked in isolation at a time when music was not highly regarded in his homeland. After 1889, Delius lived in France.

De Mille, Cecil Blount (1881-1959) American Hollywood producer-director and writer, famous for his Biblical spectaculars. His career centred around epic films, with 'a cast of thousands', including *The Ten Commandments* and *Samson and Delilah*.

Deng Xiaoping (born 1904) Chinese Communist Party leader who rose to be Secretary General of the party in the early 1960s, but was purged during the Cultural Revolution of the late 1960s. He reappeared on the political scene (1973-6), but was purged again following the death of his supporter CHOU EN-LAI in early 1976. After MAO TSE-TUNG's death later in 1976, Deng Xiaoping re-emerged as a principal leader of the party.

Derain, André (1880-1954) French painter, a leading member of the *Fauves,* whose pure colour, bold brushwork and joyful response to landscape are all to be seen in the Thames views painted while on two visits to London. He flirted briefly with Cubism before reverting to a less daring, more elegant style.

Descartes, René (1596-1650) French philosopher, inventor of analytical geometry. His philosophic aim was to unify all science by means of the appropriate single method – namely that of geometry, which possessed the required properties of clarity and simplicity. His influence has spread throughout modern philosophy, to both rationalist and empiricist. In *Discourse on Method* (1637) he set out his basic theory – that the method for the proper guidance of reason is the systematic doubt of everything until one arrives at clear and simple ideas that are beyond doubt. In this, the one fundamental certainty is reached, in his famous words *Cogito ergo sum* (I think therefore I am).

Des Prés Josquin (c. 1440-1521) Flemish musician who became the leading composer of the High Renaissance and who was the first important modern composer. Apart from some secular songs, he wrote church music exclusively, including masses, motets and a *Stabat Mater*. He was among the first to develop a style which attempted to express in music the value and meaning of the words being set.

De Valera, Eamon (1882-1975) American-born Irish Republican statesman. During the Easter Rising of 1916 he commanded a body of Irish Volunteers and was captured and sentenced to death by the British, but was later reprieved. De Valera became Prime Minister when his party *Fianna Fáil* (founded in 1926) was able to form a government in 1932, and in 1937 the constitution of the Free State was revised naming it Eire. De Valera held the premiership until 1948. From 1951-4 and again 1957-9 he was Prime Minister of the Republic of Ireland (recognized by Britain in 1949). He was President of the Republic (1957-73), when he was succeeded by Erskine Childers.

Devine, George (1910-66) British actor, theatre manager and director, who founded and directed the English Stage Company at London's Royal Court Theatre (1956-65). He began his career as an actor and in 1938 became director and manager of the London Theatre Studio. He made his West End debut as a director with Daphne du Maurier's *Rebecca* (1940). After the war, Devine directed the Young Vic company.

De Witt, Jan (1625-72) Dutch Republican statesman who backed the States Party against the autocratic power of the House of Orange and was murdered by its supporters. De Witt became the Dutch leader during WILLIAM III's minority and made large concessions to end the first Anglo-Dutch war (1654); in the second (1665-7), helped by the admirals de RUYTER and TROMP, and his own brother, Cornelius, he secured the favourable Treaty of Breda. With peace restored he improved the nation's finances and strengthened the Dutch trading hold on the East Indies. He passed the Permanent Edict to ensure Republican administration (1667) and made the Triple Alliance with England and Sweden against LOUIS XIV (1668), but when Louis invaded Holland (1672), de Witt was forced to resign and was killed by Orangists.

Diaghilev, Sergei Pavlovich (1872-1929) Russian impresario whose ability to recognize talent led to a renaissance of Western ballet. After introducing shows of Russian painting and music to Paris, Diaghilev established his newly founded French- and Russian-backed Ballets Russes in 1908. His company deeply influenced Western ballet, using male dancers, striking costumes, vividly imaginative décor and new and startling music, in ballets such as *Scheherazade* and *L'Après-midi d'un faune*. The qualities of drama, vitality, colour and imaginative fantasy in works like *Petrouchka* and *The Firebird* were due entirely to Diaghilev's ability to exploit the talents of his artistes.

Dias, Bartholomeu (c. 1450-1500) Portuguese navigator who first rounded the southern tip of Africa as part of his country's search for a sea route to the Orient. Dias rounded the Cape of Good Hope, touching in at Mossel Bay, and continued round to the Great Fish River before turning back along the coast, discovering Table Mountain on the way home.

Diaz de Vivar, Rodrigo see CID, El

Dickens, Charles (1812-70) English novelist who wrote many of the outstanding social novels of the 19th century. He began as a journalist and his novels make extensive use of detailed documentary writing. Many of his works were written in monthly instalments, the first being *The Pickwick Papers* (1836-7), which showed his powers as a humorist. Dickens concentrated on the exposure of contemporary social evils: *Oliver Twist* (1837-8) depicted life in workhouses and in the violent criminal underworld; *Nicholas Nickleby* (1838-9) satirized tyrannical educational establishments. Such later works as *Hard Times* (1852), *Little Dorrit* (1855-7), *Our Mutual Friend* (1864-5) and *Great Expectations* (1880-1) deal with the social effects of money and the evil it can generate. Dickens was adept at creating grotesque fantastic figures, like Quilp, the dwarf in *The Old Curiosity Shop* (1840-1). Two others, Mrs Gamp and Pecksniff, appear in *Martin Chuzzlewit* (1843-4), in which Dickens criticizes American life after a visit to the United States. Much autobiographical material appears in *David Copperfield* (1849-50). Dickens liked dramatics and undertook tours of personal readings, delivered to enthusiastic audiences.

Dickinson, Emily (1830-86) American poet who wrote short, ecstatic lyrics, often about death and life after death. Her poems are notable for their simple, startling language, fresh imagery and occasional, whimsical humour.

Diderot, Denis (1713-84) French *encyclopédiste,* philosopher and writer. In 1745, he embarked with d'Alembert on the 20-year task of editing the *Encyclopédie,* whose aim was to demonstrate the essential principles and application of every art and science. The first volume was published in 1751. Diderot was also the author of plays, novels as well as literary and art criticism.

Diesel, Rudolf (1858-1913) German engineer and inventor of the internal combustion engine that bears his name. In 1890 he conceived the idea of compressing a fuel-air mixture so highly that it ignited spontaneously. Between then and 1897 (with KRUPP of

Esson and Maschinenfabrik of Augsburg) he perfected the engine which, having no electrical ignition system, is simpler and more trouble-free than the petrol engine. It also uses a lower grade and, therefore, cheaper fuel. Diesels came into their own as the motive power for heavy transport vehicles, rail cars, boats and locomotives.

Dietrich, Marlene (born 1904) German actress and singer who first achieved fame as the night-club singer in Josef van Sternberg's *The Blue Angel* (1930), becoming a symbol both for destructiveness and for the decadence of Europe. Since the early 1950s, she has made an equally successful career in international cabaret.

Diocletian (245-313) Roman emperor (284-305) who reorganized the administration of the Empire, ending all outward form of republicanism and local self-government, ruling as absolute monarch.

Diogenes, Apolloniates (5th cent. BC) Greek philosopher and physician who held that air was the fundamental basis of all things. His belief that human intelligence emanated from air influenced HIPPOCRATES, who came to believe that diseases such as epilepsy occurred when the supply of air to the brain was hindered.

Dionysius the Elder (c. 430-367 BC) Greek tyrant (unconstitutional ruler) of Syracuse in Sicily 405-367 BC) whose successes made Syracuse the biggest and most powerful Greek city. Dionysius rose by demagogy from being a clerk to a dictator, crushing opposition, helped by secret police and troops, often mercenaries from Gaul and Spain.

Dionysius Exiguus (c. 500-560) Scythian scholar who made his calculation of CHRIST's birth date the basis of modern chronology.

Dionysius Traz (2nd-1st cent. BC) Greek grammarian, author of *Techné Grammatiké,* the first Greek grammar, the basis of all European grammars.

Diophantus (c. 3rd cent. AD) Greek Mathematician, who wrote *Arithmetica,* a famous treatise on algebra. His name is particularly associated with problems requiring the solution of an equation containing up to four variables.

Dior, Christian (1905-57) French fashion designer whose New Look, launched in the spring of 1947, swept the fashion world. His was considered the leading fashion design house between 1945 and the mid-1960s.

Dioscorides, Pedanios (1st cent. AD) Greek physician who wrote the first pharmacopoeia (a catalogue of drugs and their preparation) detailing the uses of plants as drugs. His five-volume work *De Materia Medica* was used for over 1500 years.

Disney, Walt (1901-66) American cartoon film producer. Although credited with the creation of Mickey Mouse, Donald Duck, etc, Disney was in fact a film entrepreneur and established an organization that produced some 340 short animated films and many full length cartoon features. He made his mark in 1928 with the first animated sound film *Steamboat Willie*. The style typified in the cartoons produced by his studios at Burbank, California, influenced all branches of the industry until the early 1950s when he began to produce nature films, and later, drama and comedy films.

Disraeli, Benjamin (1804-81) British statesman, Prime Minister and author, who identified the Conservative Party with social reform and the promotion of Empire. He was Chancellor of the Exchequer (1852, 1858-9 and 1867) and as Leader of the Commons introduced the Reform Bill of 1867. He was Prime Minister for a brief period in 1868 and from 1874 to 1880. During his second premiership he advocated a forward foreign policy and gave imperialism a popular appeal by sponsoring the Royal Titles Bill of 1876 by which VICTORIA became Empress of India. At home the government codified and extended social legislation (slum clearance, public health and merchant seamen's conditions of service) but there was no move towards incisive government intervention. Defeats in the Afghan and Zulu wars (1878-9), GLADSTONE's moral condemnation of 'Beaconsfieldism', the recession in British commercial and industrial prosperity at the end of the decade and his own ill health, all contributed to Disraeli's defeat (1880).

Dixon, Jeremiah see MASON, Charles

Doenitz, Karl (1891-1980) German U-boat commander and HITLER'S successor as Führer. As submarine commander in the First World War, he became a fervent believer in the efficacy of submarine warfare, and as Hitler's U-boat flag officer during the Second World War he was responsible for the wolf-pack system of U-boat operations and for sinking many millions of tons of Allied shipping. He succeeded Raeder as Grand Admiral in 1943, and on Hitler's death in 1945 surrendered to the Allies in May. He was sentenced at Nuremberg to ten years' imprisonment.

Domagk, Gerhard (1895-1964) German biochemist, who in 1932 established that a dye, prontosil red, could control streptococcus infections. Subsequently, the antibacterial action was found elsewhere to be due to only part of the molecule, the sulphonamide group. This outstanding discovery led to the development of a range of drugs effective in the treatment of several highly pathogenic infections, including some varieties of pneumonia. Among those whose lives were saved was Domagk's daughter, who had been infected accidentally in the laboratory. Domagk was awarded a Nobel Prize for Physiology and Medicine.

Domenichino, II (1581-1641) Italian decorative painter who studied under the CARRACCI family and worked with Annibale in the Palazzo Farnese, in Rome. The frescoes in S Andrea della Valle, Rome (1624-8), are his principal religious works, but he is best remembered for his landscapes.

Domingo, Placido (born 1941) Spanish tenor who made his operatic debut at Monterrey, Mexico, in 1961. He made his Metropolitan debut in 1968, and his Covent Garden debut in 1971 in *Tosca*. His controlled vocal technique and his acting ability have made him one of the world's leading tenors.

Dominic (1170-1221) Spanish saint who founded the Order of Preaching Friars of Dominicans, a group of highly trained priests skilled in the arts of debate. In 1203, he was chosen to accompany Bishop Diego on a mission to convert the Albigensians of Languedoc. Dominic deprecated the use of threats or force, employing carefully prepared and persuasive public discussion. In 1207, the Albigenses murdered the papal legate, so Innocent III organized and launched a military campaign against their overlord, Count Raymund of Toulouse. During the consequent five years of massacre, Dominic continued his campaign of persuasion, and in 1216, based in Toulouse, he founded the Order of Preaching Friars to continue his work.

Domitian (51-96) Roman emperor (81-96), who built a 300-mile line of forts and blockhouses called the *Limes Germanicus* from the upper Rhine (near Bonn) to the upper Danube (near Regensburg), the rivers themselves forming a natural defence between the North Sea and the Black Sea.

Donatello, Donato Di Niccolo (c. 1386-1466) Florentine sculptor. His early Gothic style reflects the influences of GHIBERTI, MICHELOZZO and BRUNELLESCHI (with whom he worked for a while), but Donatello soon developed an individual style of revolutionary boldness. The quality of Donatello's art was first seen in his two marble figures of *St Mark*, which showed a recognition of the individual human's worth, and *St George* (or *San Michele*), demonstrating the new development of perspective, creating with mathematical precision a definite space for the figures. His later style, examples of which are *St John the Baptist* in Venice, and the *Magdalen* in Florence, is more dramatically expressive than his earlier work.

Donders, Franz (1818-89) Dutch oculist, who discovered the process by which the eye focuses on different objects, and, with Von Graefe, was a pioneer in the science of ophthalmology. The scientific formulation of glasses to correct short and long sight and astigmatism owes a great deal to the work of the two men.

Donizetti, Gaetano (1797-1848) Italian composer who wrote over 60 operas in a light, melodic style that also often shows a strong individual vein of comedy. The best known of his operas are *The Elixir of Love* (1832), the more dramatic *Lucia di Lammermoor* (1835), based on a novel by Sir Walter SCOTT, and *Don Pasquale* (1843).

Donne, John (c. 1572-1631) English poet and clergyman whose passionate, sharply-reasoned verse made him the outstanding poet of early 17th-century English literature. The principal figure of the metaphysical poets, his genius appeared in the *Songs and Sonnets* in which he made the love lyric conversational and dramatic, laced with obscure knowledge and strange metaphor.

Doppler, Christian Johann (1803-53) Austrian physicist who discovered a wave effect now named after him. In connection with the colour of double stars, he suggested that there is a change in colour depending on whether the star is moving towards or away from the observer. He drew upon the analogous effect of the pitch of sounds whose source is moving.

Dostoevsky, Fyodor Mikhailovich (1821-81) Russian writer, whose major works tackle the great metaphysical, religious and philosophical themes. His last novel, *The Brothers Karamazov* (1879-80), was the crown of his literary achievement, a story of parricide and jealousy between brothers which deals with the problems of atheism and belief in the existence of God. Dostoevsky's first novel *Poor Folk* (1845) was an instant success, acclaimed by BELÍNSKY as a masterpiece. In 1849, however, he was arrested for subversive activities and condemned to death, only to be reprieved in the execution yard. The experience affected him deeply and aggravated the epilepsy from which he had begun to suffer. He was subsequently sentenced to four years' hard labour, and later wrote *The House of the Dead* (1860-2), based on his prison experiences. Dostoevsky was continually burdened by heavy debts and two of his major works, *Crime and Punishment* (1866) and *The Idiot* (1868) were written in an effort to stave off his creditors. With these novels and with *The Demons* (1871-2) he became well-known and more prosperous.

Douglas, David (1798-1834) Scottish explorer and plant collector, who introduced numerous species of trees and shrubs into Britain from North America where he had been sent by the Horticultural Society after training in the Glasgow Botanic Garden. From British Columbia and California he sent home nearly all their indigenous conifers and maples now familiar in Britain, as well as common mahonia, snowberry, red flowering currant, and many other species. The Douglas Fir is a tree of major importance to forestry.

Douglas-Home, Sir Alec (born 1903) Scottish peer and politician who created a precedent by renouncing his hereditary peerage in order to become Prime Minister. He was Foreign Secretary when the Prime Minister, MACMILLAN, retired in 1963, and in order to succeed him Douglas-Home renounced his peerage and was later elected MP for Kinross and West Perthshire. As Foreign Secretary (1960-3) he signed the nuclear test-ban treaty in Moscow (1963). In July 1964, he presided at the Commonwealth Prime Ministers' Conference, but his short-lived premiership (1963-4) was overshadowed by the impending election and an economic crisis. He resigned after a narrow defeat in the 1964 General Election, but was later appointed Foreign Secretary by Edward HEATH when the Conservatives won the 1970 election. He was created a life peer (Baron Home of the Hirsel) in 1974.

Doyle, Sir Arthur Conan (1859-1930) Scots-born author and doctor and creator of Sherlock Holmes, one of the most famous detectives in fiction. *A Study in Scarlet* (1887) was the first Holmes story. Over the next 40 years Doyle wrote a series of Holmes adventures and also historical and romantic novels, including *The White Company* (1891) and *The Lost World* (1912).

Doyle, Richard (1824-83) British humorous artist, who, designed the original cover of *Punch*, where he was on the staff (1843-50). He produced several albums of linear sketches, depicting mainly middle-class society, with a fanciful wit and a marked sense of the absurd. He also contributed illustrations to three of DICKENS's *Christmas Books*.

D'Oyly Carte, Richard (1844-1901) British impresario and theatre manager, famous for his presentation of GILBERT and SULLIVAN's operas.

Draco (late 7th cent. BC) Athenian lawmaker who produced Athens' first known written code of law. It made trivial offences punishable by death, and so gave rise to the adjective 'draconian' to describe any savage edict or system. It aroused such hatred that SOLON repealed all but its laws on murder.

Drake, Francis (c. 1540-96) English explorer, adventurer, and naval captain who circumnavigated the world and served the Crown by harassing the treasure ships of Spain. Throughout the early 1570s, Drake was a celebrated privateer on the Spanish Main, his most legendary exploit being the attack on Nombre de Dios in 1572. After decimating a Spanish naval unit at Porto Bello, Drake sailed on to the Isthmus of Panama, where he saw the Pacific, and prayed for 'life and leave to sail once in an English ship in that sea'. During his next major voyage (1577-80), he not only crossed the Pacific but became the first Englishman to sail around the world. Drake lost two ships while attempting passage of the hazardous Strait of Magellan, but managed to steer his vessel, the *Pelican*, through safely, renaming her *Golden Hind*. Continuing up the west coast of the New World, Drake headed west to Java, rounded the Cape of Good Hope, and reached England in September 1580. He was subsequently knighted by the queen, despite Spanish protest. In 1587, Drake sailed into Cadiz and attacked PHILIP II of Spain's Armada, a feat popularly known as 'singeing his Catholic majesty's beard'.

Draper, John William (1811-82) English-American chemist and physiologist, who founded photochemistry by recognizing that chemical reactions could be brought about by molecules absorbing light energy. Draper also showed that all substances glow a dull red at about 525°C (called the Draper point), above which, in increasing the temperature, more of the visible light region is added until the glow becomes white.

Drebbel, Cornelius van (1572-1633) Dutch inventor who built the first 'submarine', which, in about 1620, was rowed successfully 12-15 feet under the Thames. The outer hull consisted of greased leather over a wooden framework and it was propelled either on or beneath the surface by eight oars sealed through the sides with leather flaps. The next significant stage in submarine development was over 250 years later. Drebbel also discovered a bright scarlet dye which was used with effect in the manufacture of Gobelin tapestries.

Dreyfus, Alfred (1859-1935) French army officer of Jewish blood who was the focus and victim of the 'Dreyfus Case' which split France into two hostile factions at the turn of the century. Dreyfus was a staff captain in the army in 1894 when, on flimsy evidence, he was unjustly convicted of giving military information to Germany and imprisoned on Devil's Island. After years of public agitation, in 1899 a new trial was finally forced, at which Count Marie Charles Esterhazy confessed that he had forged the documents that constituted the only real evidence against Dreyfus. Dreyfus was found guilty with extenuating circumstances and pardoned, which did not satisfy the Dreyfusards including ZOLA, who continued their agitation until the case went to the Appeal Court. There the sentence was quashed and the innocent Dreyfus reinstated and promoted. He went on to distinguish himself in the First World War and received the Legion of Honour (1919).

Drinker, Cecil (1887-1956) American inventor (1929) of the iron lung.

Dryden, John (1631-1700) English poet, dramatist and essayist who was the driving force of a literary movement that began with the Restoration in 1660. He followed the ideal of the Royal Society towards clarity and elegance, but retained the imaginative fire of the Elizabethans. In verse, he fashioned the heroic couplet into the perfect metre for the irony and bite of his satires, *Absalom and Achitophel* (1681), *The Medal* and *Mac-Flecknoe* (1682). His best-known plays are *Marriage à la Mode* (1673), a comedy, and *All for Love* (1678), the story of ANTONY and CLEOPATRA. His criticism, unsystematic but clearsighted, appeared in various essays and prefaces. The most famous is the *Essay of Dramatic Poesy* (1668), a model of the new lucid prose style, containing a vindication of English drama.

Duarte, José Napoléon (born 1926) President of El Salvador (1980-82) and again since 1984. He was Mayor of San Salvador three times, and a founder and the first General Secretary of the centre right Christian Democratic Party. Since the late 1970s the Republic of El Salvador has been embroiled in civil war. Duarte was elected President (1972), but was not allowed to serve his term; he was imprisoned, then exiled (1972-9). He returned to El Salvador after a coup (1979) and was a member of the ruling junta (1980-82). Elections for the Constituent Assembly were held (1982), a coalition government was formed and a political independent, Dr Alvaro Magaña, appointed President. However, Duarte was re-elected in 1984.

Du Barry, Comtesse (c. 1746-93) French mistress of LOUIS XV, who dominated both the king and his court. Successor to the Marquise de POMPADOUR as the king's mistress (1768), Madame Du Barry became a patroness of artists and writers.

Du Bellay, Joachim (1522-60) France's first poet to use the sonnet form. In 1549, he published *L'Olive*, 115 Petrarchan sonnets to an imaginary mistress. A visit to Rome inspired another sequence, *Les Antiquités de Rome* (1558), and, in the same year, his disenchantment with the city and homesickness for France resulted in *Les Regrets*, satirical elegies of melancholic beauty, which analysed his emotions. With RONSARD, he formed the Pléiade a group of poets who advocated a rejection of medieval traditions and a return to the major 'genres'. Du Bellay's *Déffense et illustration de la langue française* (1549), setting out many of their precepts, became a landmark in the history of French literature.

Dubček, Alexander (born 1921) Czechoslovak Communist politician who attempted to moderate the repressive orthodox Communism of his country, He was elected First Secretary of the Czechoslovak Communist Party in 1968, but his attempt to liberalize and democratize the country's Communist government provoked the USSR to invade Czechoslovakia, using tanks to suppress popular support for Dubček, and to bring about his resignation. His popularity made it dangerous to remove him from public life immediately, but the importance of his office was reduced gradually until, in 1970, he was dismissed from public life, expelled from the Communists and forced to work outside Prague.

Duccio di Buoninsegna (c. 1255-c. 1318) Italian artist, who founded the Sienese school of painters and was one of the first artists to infuse the stylized forms of Byzantine art with a new naturalism and humanity. His masterpiece is the *Maestà*, painted for the high altar of Siena Cathedral (1308-11). The scenes originally on the reverse, depicting the life of Christ and the Passion, reveal a new narrative power, while the Madonna and Child on the front are figures of unprecedented substance. The tenderness and grace of these figures were to become characteristic of the Sienese school.

Duchamp, Marcel (1887-1968) French artist and aesthetic philosopher, who was one of the most influential figures in modern art. Developing from Post-Impressionism to Cubism, he painted *Nude Descending a Staircase* (1911), a landmark in the evolution of Cubism and Futurism. In 1914 he invented the 'ready-made', an object of normal daily use presented as a work of art, and thus challenging the accepted values and critical criteria of such works. Most famous of his 'ready-mades' are the *Bicycle Wheel*, mounted on a stool, and the *Fountain*, a urinal. From 1915 to 1923 he worked on another celebrated work *The Bride Stripped bare by her Bachelors, Even*, a sexual allegory painted on glass. During the late 1920s Duchamp's interest in art was superseded by a preoccupation with chess, to which he devoted the latter part of his life.

Dudley, Robert, 1st Earl of Leicester (c. 1532-88) English courtier and favourite suitor of ELIZABETH I, whom he influenced for some 30 years. He became a privy councillor in 1559, and after the death in suspicious circumstances of his wife Amy Robsart (1560) became the suitor of Elizabeth, who finally refused him. She nevertheless made him Earl of Leicester and enjoyed his lavish hospitality at Kenilworth Castle. Forgiving his court intrigues and secret marriage to the widow of the Earl of Essex, she gave him command of English troops fighting Spain in the Low Countries (1585), and of the English forces gathered to resist the expected Spanish Armada invasion.

Dulles, John Foster (1888-1959) American Secretary of State (1953-9) who conceived the theory of 'brinkmanship' in international relations: the idea that a statesman should, when necessary, take his country to the edge of war, but not beyond. Dulles negotiated and concluded the Japanese peace treaty (1950-1) in the TRUMAN administration and in 1953, as Secretary of State under EISENHOWER, adopted strongly anti-Communist policies which earned him a reputation for inflexibility in matters concerning the USSR and Communist China. An internationalist, Dulles became senior United States adviser at the United Nations founding conference in 1945 and was three times US delegate to the UN.

Dumas, Alexandre (Dumas père) (1802-70) French dramatist and novelist, best known for his swashbuckling historical romances such as *The Three Musketeers* and *The Count of Monte Cristo* (1844). He also wrote travel books, stories for children and memoirs. His son, Alexandre Dumas fils (1824-95), devoted most of his career to the stage. He wrote *The Lady of the Camélias* (1848), a popular romantic novel later transformed into his first play (1852). He enjoyed considerable success as a playwright during the Second Empire.

Dunant, Jean Henri (1828-1910) Swiss founder of the International Red Cross. Having witnessed appalling suffering for want of medical attention on the battlefield of Solferino in 1859, he advocated the establishment of a permanent organization and an international convention for the aid of the wounded. The first international meeting was held at Geneva in October 1863, when the fundamental principles of the organization were laid down, and in August 1864 the Geneva Convention was adopted by a diplomatic conference of 26 nations. In 1901 Dunant shared the first Nobel Peace Prize with Frédéric Passy, a founder of the International Peace League.

Duncan, Isadora (1878-1927) American-born English dancer, who disliked the distortions and artificiality of ballet and tried to restore simplicity, spontaneity and true emotion to dancing. Together with Edward Gordon CRAIG, she devised productions based on architectural forms, drapery and lighting effects with dancers dressed in simple Greek tunics. Her influence on modern choreographers from Michel Fokine to Martha GRAHAM is incalculable. A pioneer of Women's Liberation she campaigned against corsets and in favour of a less male-dominated view of marriage.

Dunlop, John Boyd (1840-1921) Scottish veterinary surgeon, who in 1888 patented his pneumatic bicycle tyre, which revived Thompson's earlier concept. He began experiments with an air-filled tyre to cushion his son's bicycle against the bumpy cobbles of the day, after the family's doctor had prescribed cycling to improve the boy's health. Together with W. H. Du Cros, Dunlop formed a company to exploit the tyre, but later sold his patent rights to Du Cros and derived only a small profit from his invention. The firm developed into the Dunlop Rubber Company.

Duns Scotus, John (c. 1265-c. 1308) Scottish theological philosopher who, opposing the doctrine of AQUINAS, held that faith was divorced from reason. He emphasized the individuality of things and believed that will, rather than reason, was the ruling principle. Known as the 'Subtle Doctor', Duns Scotus was one of a line of Franciscan scholars whose views precipitated a schism in Catholic theology.

Dunstable, John (c. 1370-1453) English mathematician, astrologer and composer, who exercised a considerable influence on both English and continental music in the early 15th century. Dunstable's importance is that, working at a time when traditional counterpoint was a serious restriction, he introduced a new sense of flexibility and melodic invention.

Dürer, Albrecht (1471-1528) The outstanding German artist of the Renaissance in northern Europe. While in Italy Dürer was influenced by the colours of BELLINI and became interested in the writings of LEONARDO. Not content with the traditional role of the northern European artist as little more than an artisan (unlike the artist in Italy), he tried to achieve a status for painters equal to that of scholars and humanists. One aspect of this preoccupation was his study of the theoretical basis of art, which resulted in an influential treatise on proportion (1528). Although he regarded himself primarily as a painter, his paintings are relatively few, his fame depending largely on his graphic work. This consisted of wood-cuts and copperplate en-

Dürer's fame rests largely on engravings but he was an outstanding watercolourist, a technique little used in his day

gravings, some being single prints, such as the famous *Knight, Death and the Devil* (1513), but most of them forming a series illustrating religious themes such as the Passion, the Apocalypse or the life of the Virgin. These prints set new standards of technical perfection and during the 16th century their compositions and expressive qualities were imitated by artists throughout Europe. Dürer was among the first to produce water colours painted directly from the landscape.

Durrell, Lawrence (born 1912) English poet and novelist, whose best-known work, the four novels of the *Alexandria Quartet* (1957-60), are typical of his recurrent theme of the meeting of eastern and western cultures in the lands of the eastern Mediterranean.

Duse, Eleonora (1859-1924) Italian actress, who rivalled BERNHARDT as the greatest tragedienne of their era. Though less spectacular than Bernhardt, Duse was more academic in her creation of great roles. She made her name in *Les Fourchambault* (1878) and in D'ANNUNZIO's plays. She was at her zenith in IBSEN's *Rosmersholm*.

Duvalier, François (1907-71) Dictator of Haiti, known as 'Papa Doc', who was regarded by his people as the incarnation of the Voodoo god, Baron Samedi. A physican by training, he was elected President in 1957, obtained dictatorial powers from the national assembly and maintained them by means of a private army of thugs, the *Tontons Macoutes* (bogeymen), by voodoo, and by deliberately keeping the population poor, primitive and illiterate. His régime was condemned by the International Commission of Jurists (1966) for its 'innumerable excesses'. He repulsed several attempts by Haitian exiles to invade Haiti and overthrow his government.

Dvořák, Antonin (1841-1904) Czechoslovakia's leading symphonic composer, who began his career as a butcher's boy. Dvořák joined the orchestra formed under SMETANA at the Prague National Theatre as a viola player, and meanwhile practised composition. BRAHMS saw some of his scores and became his friend and adviser. Czech folk music had always been an underlying if indirect influence in Dvořák's work and after he became head of the National Conservatory in New York (1892) the negro spiritual came to play a similar role. The theme of the famous slow movement of his Symphpony No. 9 (*From the New World*) is an original tune by Dvořák, but clearly shows where its influences lay. Besides his nine symphonies, Dvořák composed prolifically. His other orchestral works include the sets of *Slavonic Rhapsodies* and *Slavonic Dances*; and several concert overtures, including *Carnival*. He also wrote operas, songs, a *Te Deum* and *Requiem* as well as a good deal of chamber music.

Dyck, Sir Anthony van (1599-1641) Flemish artist, who was Court Painter to CHARLES I of England. At a very early age he was RUBENS's most gifted assistant in Antwerp. He travelled widely in Italy, where he produced some of the portraits for which he is now best known. The greatest period of his career began in 1632, when he was appointed as a painter to the court of Charles I in London. Among his pictures for Charles was the 'dismounted' equestrian portrait now in the Louvre.

Dylan, Bob (born 1941) American popular singer and composer who was one of the originators of the folk-rock style of music. He taught himself to play the guitar, piano and harmonica, and became popular on concert tours and in recordings in the 1960s. He has composed many songs, including *Blowin' in the Wind, The Times They Are A-Changin'* and *Lay, Lady, Lay*.

E

Eastman, George (1854-1932) American inventor of the flexible roll film system of photography. In 1884, Eastman patented a photographic film, consisting of paper smeared with gel emulsion. Four years later, he produced the famous Kodak (a meaningless, but, as Eastman hoped, a catchy trademark) camera, which was quite light and used the new roll film. The camera was shrewdly marketed, with the slogan, 'You press the button – we do the rest'. The paper of the film was replaced by celluloid (1889) and then (1924) by cellulose acetate.

Eckert, John Presper (born 1919) American electrical engineer, who, in 1946, with John William Mauchly, made the first electronic computer, called ENIAC. This massive device used 18,000 radio valves and thus considerable electrical power. Removal of the resulting heat presented a major problem. The valves were also unreliable and the machine functioned only for short periods.

Eddington, Sir Arthur (1882-1944) English astronomer who discovered the relationship between mass and luminosity of stars. He was appointed Plumian Professor of Astronomy at Cambridge University in 1913, and three years later began investigating the interiors of stars, and showed how energy is transmitted through the body of a star, which he recognized to be made up of gas. Eddington was one of the first scientists to appreciate the importance of EINSTEIN's theory of relativity.

Eddy, Mary Baker (1821-1910) American religious leader and founder of the Christian Science movement. Setting out her views in *Science and Health with Key to the Scriptures* (1875) Mrs Eddy taught that disease and pain are evidence of mental error and can be cured by spiritual healing, that everything material is an illusion. She believed that God is the only reality and that as men learn the truth, so they will cease to sin. She founded the First Church of Christ, Scientist, in Boston in 1879 and also organized the publication of an international newspaper, the *Christian Science Monitor*.

Eden, Anthony, 1st Earl of Avon (1897-1977) British statesman who as Prime Minister authorized military intervention in Egypt (November 1956) to recover control of the Suez Canal, which had been nationalized by the government of NASSER. As Foreign Secretary during the 1930s, he worked for League of Nations action against HITLER and MUSSOLINI, and opposed the policy of appeasement, over which he resigned in 1938. When CHURCHILL became Prime Minister in the Second World War coalition government, Eden was appointed Foreign Secretary and after the war led the British delegation to the San Francisco Conference (1945) which established the United Nations. When the Conservatives were returned to power he was again appointed Foreign Secretary (1951), and in 1955 he succeeded Churchill as Prime Minister. His health had been failing, however, and United Nations, United States and USSR condemnation of the Anglo-French intervention in Egypt led to his resignation in 1957.

Edison, Thomas Alva (1847-1931) American inventor, with more than a thousand patents to his credit. His professional life began at 12 when, as a railway newsboy, he printed and published his own paper (the first ever to be printed on a train). Later he became a telegraph operator and developed his interest in electrical technology through the acquisition of FARADAY's writings. With the proceeds from his development of an improved stock market ticker in 1870, he set up the world's first industrial research laboratory in Newark, New Jersey. He made major contributions to telegraphy (1874), the development of telephones (1877), incandescent light (1879), the phonograph (1877), electric generating equipment, motion photography and storage batteries (1900-10). His major contribution to cinematography (1891) was the introduction of 35 mm celluloid film with perforations along each edge, allowing sprocketed gear-wheels inside both the camera and projector to transport the film forward a defined distance and in precise alignment.

Edward the Confessor (c. 1002-66) King of England (1042-66) whose alleged promises to Duke William of Normandy provoked the Norman invasion. Recalled from France, where he was brought up, by Hardecanute to be his heir, Edward became more monk than king (hence the name 'the Confessor'), allowing first Norman favourites and later his father-in-law Earl Godwin of Wessex to run the government. Lacking direct heirs, he reputedly named first his cousin William of Normandy, then Harold, Godwin's son, as his successor – so giving both a claim to the throne. He built the first Westminster Abbey, in which he was buried.

Edward I (1239-1307) King of England (1272-1307) whose reformist measures place him, with HENRY II, as one of the two greatest plantagenet kings. Leaning heavily on the new, monied middle class for financial support, he used Parliament to endorse plans to extend royal authority and promulgate reforms such as the weakening of feudalism, and this began a new age in English government. England gained mastery of Great Britain under his rule, by the crushing of Wales and Scotland. He died, leaving Edward II to deal with ROBERT THE BRUCE's Scottish revolt.

Edward III (1312-77) King of England (1327-77) who defeated the French at Crécy (1346). His long reign is notable for martial exploits against the Scots and the beginning of the 100 Years' War against the French. At home, his reign was remarkably peaceful, his court being regarded as Europe's most magnificent. Economic problems resulting from the Black Death and Edward's subjugation to his son, John of Gaunt, caused civil strife which marred the reign of Richard II.

Edward, 'The Black Prince' (1330-76) English leader of campaigns against the French in the 100 Years' War. At the battle of Crécy (1346) Edward, who was Prince of Wales, won the insignia still borne by his successors – ostrich plumes and the mottoes *homout; ich dene* (courage; I serve). He led the English troops who won the major battle of Poitiers (1356) and captured France's John II, whom England traded for a ransom payment of a large area of France. Prince Edward ruled from Bordeaux as Prince of Aquitaine (1362-72) but lost control in a revolt, and resigned Aquitaine to his father, EDWARD III. His nickname, supposedly from his wearing black armour, was not used until the 16th century.

Edward IV (1442-83) King of England (1461-70 and 1471-83), the first of the House of York (1461-85). As a great-great-grandson of EDWARD III he succeeded (where his father, Richard of York, had failed) in pressing his claim to the throne. Backed by Parliament, he unseated Henry VI and crushed his Lancastrian backers. In the relative peace that followed, Edward patronized trade and culture (befriending the pioneer printer William CAXTON) and left to his son Edward V a throne solvent for the first time since HENRY II.

Edward VII (1841-1910) King of Great Britain (1901-10). He was the eldest son of Queen VICTORIA and Prince ALBERT. The queen, jealous of her own position and distrustful of Edward's abilities, denied him experience of state business or access to Cabinet papers until 1892, and he became the leader of fashionable society, enjoying racing, yachting, sport and continental travel. The personal influence and power of the monarchy declined during his reign.

Edward VIII (1894-1972) King of Great Britain (20 Jan.-11 Dec. 1936), whose abdication caused great consternation and public controversy. As Prince of Wales, his personal charm and preference for informality had made him widely popular. He became king on the death of his father, GEORGE V. The abdication crisis occurred because he wished to marry Mrs Wallis Simpson, an American, whose second divorce was pending and who was therefore unlikely to be acceptable as queen. The proposal of a morganatic marriage (one between a person of exalted status and a partner of inferior rank who does not share the dignities accorded to the partner, nor inherit his or her possessions) was rejected and after one of the shortest reigns in British history, the King renounced the throne, without having been crowned. He was created Duke of Windsor by his brother, GEORGE VI, who succeeded him. He lived for the rest of his life in Paris with Mrs Simpson, whom he married in 1937.

Ehrlich, Paul (1854-1915) German bacteriologist, who founded chemotherapy, the science of the chemical treatment of disease. Previous chemical cures had been accidental. His most important discoveries, the compounds trypan red and salvarsan, were effective in the treatment of trypanosomiasis and syphilis respectively. Although it was hoped then that all infectious diseases could be so cured, the more common smaller bacteria remained resistant to chemical treatments until DOMAGK's discoveries 25 years later.

Eichendorff, Joseph von (1788-1857) German poet and novelist who epitomized the German Romantic movement. In his poems and in his story *Memoirs of a Good-for-Nothing,* he conveys the moods and longing of the individual, often contrasting the pettiness of day-to-day existence with the beauty and unfathomability of love, religion and nature. Many composers, including MENDELSSOHN and SCHUMANN, set his poems to music.

Eichmann, Karl Adolf (1906-62) German administrator of HITLER's Jewish extermination policy. As a Gestapo agent during the *Anschluss* (annexation) of Czechoslovakia in 1939, he was responsible for the deportation of 35,000 Jews. His sinister skills as an administrator were given free rein in 1941, when GOERING ordered the 'final solution of the Jewish question' to be carried out. Eichmann organized special extermination squads and was personally responsible for the logistics of the deportation and extermination of millions of Jews. He escaped to Argentina after the war, but was captured clandestinely by Israeli agents in 1960, tried in Israel in 1961, and executed the following year.

Eiffel, Alexandre Gustave (1832-1923) French engineer best known for his design of the tower built for the Paris Exhibition of 1889 and which bears his name. Eiffel's greatest interest was in bridges, and he also designed the framework for the Statue of Liberty in New York Harbour (1885), and the locks on the Panama Canal (1893). Eiffel founded the world's first aerodynamics laboratory at Auteuil, France, in 1912.

Einstein, Albert (1879-1955) German-American physicist who proposed the theory of relativity. In 1905 he announced four new and fundamental ideas in physics: the special theory of relativity (which seeks to account for the constant speed of light); the equation relating mass and energy; the theory of Brownian movement; and the photon theory of light. In 1916 he first presented his general theory of relativity, and spent much of his later life applying the theory to cosmological problems. At the other extreme of the scale of size, he never accepted as satisfactory the usual interpretations of the new quantum mechanics in terms of probabilities and conducted a long and lively (if unsuccessful) open debate in favour of determinism. These diverse but fundamental interests led Einstein to turn his attention to the problem of formulating a single theory to cover both gravitation and electrodynamics. Just as general relativity, based on the general geometry of RIEMANN, sought to explain gravitation as a property of space (whose geometry was a function of the matter contained in it), so this unified field theory sought to explain electrodynamics in addition to gravitation. This remains an unfinished line of investigation. In 1933, when the Nazis gained power in Germany, Einstein emigrated to

The atom bomb, sinister fruit of the researches of Einstein

the United States. Just before the Second World War, after uranium had been split (by HAHN in Germany), Einstein was prompted to contact President F. D. ROOSEVELT. This approach led to the establishment of the Manhatten Project to develop the atomic bomb. Einstein's contributions to science were vast. His general theory of relativity led to a new era in cosmological research and speculation. The equivalence of mass and energy, stated in his famous equation $e=mc^2$, was demonstrated with devastating effect in the atomic bombs. Element 99 (einsteinium) is named after him.

Like earlier military heroes – Washington and Grant – Eisenhower became US President

Einthoven, Willem (1860-1927) Dutch physiologist, who developed electrocardiography. In 1903 Einthoven invented the string galvanometer, with which he was able to measure the varying electrical potentials of the heart. Subsequently, he improved the device and by 1906 was correlating variations in the patterns of the electrocardiograms with types of heart disorder. He was awarded the 1924 Nobel Prize for Physiology and Medicine.

Einsenstein chose as his subjects some of the great moments of Russian history

Eisenhower, Dwight David (1890-1969) American general and United States President (1953-61). During the early part of the Second World War, he was Chief-of-Staff, Operations Division, Washington, becoming Commander-in-Chief of the Allied Forces in North Africa in 1942. As Supreme Commander, Western Europe (1944-5) his ability to co-ordinate the activities of Allied staff was perhaps his most valuable contribution to the war. He was Supreme Commander of NATO forces in Europe (1950-2) when he resigned his commission to run for President as Republican candidate, and defeated the Democratic candidate, Adlai STEVENSON. He was elected for a second term, again defeating Stevenson, in 1956 by a margin of nearly 10 million votes. During Eisenhower's first presidential term, the US was occupied with a campaign against 'Communist subversion', and domestic legislation included an extension of the social security programme, with some support for civil rights. His popularity waned during his second term as a result of economic recession, the US spy plane incident on the eve of summit talks with Russian leaders (1960) and doubts about his health.

Eisenstein, Sergei (1898-1948) Soviet film director and theorist chiefly notable for his development of 'montage' (the cinematic art of editing and assembling pieces of film to give a new expressive force to the elements). A famous example was the Odessa Steps sequence in *The Battleship Potemkin* (1925), in which he cuts from the apparently mechanical advance of the soldiers to the disorganized panic of the citizens and specific images – a runaway pram, shattered spectacles.

More than any other landmark, the Eiffel Tower symbolizes Paris. Built for the Paris exhibition of 1889, it was the outstanding achievement of engineer and bridge-builder Alexandre Eiffel. During his last years, Eiffel made use of the tower for experiments in aerodynamics

His films, *Strike* (1924), *October* (1927), *Alexander Nevski* (1938) and *Ivan the Terrible* (1942-6) are regarded as classics.

Eleanor of Aquitaine (c. 1122-1204) Queen of France (1137-52, when her marriage to Louis VII was annulled), and of England (1154-1204), who played a dominant role in French and English politics for many years. Her importance lay in her possession of the vast duchy if Aquitaine, which she brought to HENRY II of England. In 1173 she supported her sons in unsuccessful rebellion against HENRY II, after he had been continually unfaithful to her. After Henry's death she took RICHARD I's part against an attempt by her other son, JOHN, to displace him from the throne. She was a patroness of poets and troubadours, introduced chivalric courts of law into England and took part in the Second Crusade (1147-9).

Elgar, Sir Edward (1857-1934) English composer in the British musical renaissance of the early 20th century. He was self-taught, and worked as a local violinist and teacher until, in 1899, a performance of his orchestral set, the *Enigma Variations,* brought him overnight fame. This, and his oratorio *The Dream of Gerontius* (1900, to a text by NEWMAN), established him as a major figure at home and on the Continent. He went on to write two symphonies, a violin concerto and the *Introduction and Allegro* for strings, as well as the set of five *Pomp and Circumstance* marches (No. 1 containing the tune for 'Land of Hope and Glory'). His best works such as his cello concerto or the symphonic study *Falstaff,* display a remarkable introspective sensitivity. After the death of his wife in 1920, Elgar's creative drive seemed to break down during the last 14 years of his life.

Born into a musical household. Elgar was 42 before his *Enigma Variations* made him famous

Elgin, Thomas Bruce, 7th Earl of (1766-1841) British diplomat famous for acquiring the so-called 'Elgin Marbles'. Between 1803-12, while envoy to Turkey, he shipped portions of the Parthenon's sculptured frieze to England from Athens, then controlled by the Turks.

Elijah (9th cent. BC) Hebrew prophet of Yahweh (Jehovah), who ranks with MOSES as a founder of Judaism and hence of Christian belief. Coming from Judah (southern Palestine), he opposed worship of the old fertility god Baal, enforced as a state religion in Israel (northern Palestine) by King Ahab's Phoenician queen Jezebel. Elijah insisted on unswerving obedience to the moral dictates of his 'God of Righteousness' even at the cost of the interests of the state.

Eliot, George (1819-80) Pen-name of Mary Ann Evans, English novelist, whose books are a realistic portrait of provincial, Victorian life. Her principal works, *The Mill on the Floss* (1860), *Middlemarch* (1871-2) and *Daniel Deronda* (1876), revolve around the theme of the value of human suffering in the creation of a contented, philosophical existence. She was commercially successful and gained a reputation for unconventionality. George Eliot began her literary career as a reviewer, translater and then assistant editor of the *Westminster Review.* The early *Scenes from Clerical Life* (1858) impressed the literary world, including DICKENS and THACKERAY.

Eliot, Thomas Stearns (1888-1965) American-born English poet, critic and playwright, who was the central figure in the modern English poetic tradition. The tone and rhythm of his language has influcenced most of the poetry written in English since the Second World War. His early poetry, in *Prufrock* (1917) and *The Waste Land* (1922), was stern and anti-romantic, a picture of contemporary sickness built from myth, anthropology and older English poetry. He used an imagery drawn from popular songs, pub conversations and oriental mysticism. Later in life, Eliot described himself as royalist in politics, Anglo-Catholic in religion and classical in literature. In his poetry, especially in *Ash Wednesday* (1930) and *The Four Quartets* (1943), he writes of the great themes of the Christian tradition in a dry, ironic style, with dignity and great depth of emotion. Eliot was an influential critic, relating the poetic tradition to the new circumstances of the modern world. In his plays, he revived verse drama in the English theatre. His four modern tragi-comedies with religious overtones, especially *Murder in the Cathedral* (1935), reached a wider audience than even his crowning poetic achievement, 'Little Gidding', in *The Four Quartets.*

Elizabeth I (1533-1603) Queen of England and Ireland (1558-1603), and last of the Tudor monarchs, who gave her name to an age of outstanding national achievement. She succeeded MARY I and, with the help of her minister William CECIL, disposed of a potential rival to the throne (1587), MARY, QUEEN OF SCOTS. She established a middle-of-the-road National Church aimed at preventing extremist revolts and, though at odds with Catholic France and Spain, kept clear of costly wars until 1585. In 1588 her navy scattered PHILIP II's great Armada, and her privateer-explorers, headed by Sir Francis DRAKE and Sir Walter RALEIGH, ravaged Spanish America. Under Elizabeth, new chartered companies (notably the East India Company) carried English trade and colonists overseas. The growing national prosperity helped to finance the first English theatres, for which SHAKESPEARE, MARLOWE and JOHNSON wrote their most famous plays. Elizabeth died a childless spinster.

Elizabeth II (born 1926) Queen of Great Britain. She succeeded her father, GEORGE VI, in 1952, and has continued to reign while most other monarchies have fallen out of favour. While retaining much of the tradition and ceremony associated with the British crown, she has, with the aid of her family, reinforced the institution of the monarchy and achieved world-wide popularity by international visits, informality, and the acceptance of media coverage of her activities.

Ellington, Edward Kennedy 'Duke' (1899-1974) American composer, band-leader and pianist, and one of the most important influences on popular music in the 20th century. As the organizer and leader of a jazz orchestra, his reputation internationally is as great as that of Louis ARMSTRONG's as a soloist. To mark United Nations Day in 1973, Ellington and his orchestra performed a 'Sacred Concert', written by him, in Westminster Abbey, London.

Ellis, Henry Havelock (1859-1939) English psychologist and author whose seven-volume *Studies in the*

Psychology of Sex (1897-1928) promoted the scientific study of sex. He was also a pioneer in the study of dreams and hallucinogenic drugs.

Ellison, Ralph Waldo (born 1914) American short story writer and essayist who won a National Book Award (1953) for his first novel, *Invisible Man* (1952). The book deals with the prejudice and hostility faced by a young black man in the United States.

Ellsworth, Lincoln (1880-1951) American polar explorer and civil engineer who made the first air crossing of Antarctica. With AMUNDSEN and Nobile, he made the first trans-Arctic flight over the North Pole in the airship *Norge* (1926) and, with pilot Herbert Hollick Kenyon, made the first aeroplane crossing of Antarctica (1935).

Elsheimer, Adam (1578-1610) German artist, who was much praised for his small, highly finished landscapes painted on copper, particularly by REMBRANDT.

Eluard, Paul (1895-1952) French poet and leading member of the Surrealists (and one of the movement's founders, along with André BRETON and Louis Aragon) from 1919 to 1938. His poems of the time are striking for their mysterious images and sensuous language. In 1936, as a result of the Spanish Civil War, he proclaimed the need for greater commitment by poets to their fellow men. During the Second World War, he became known as the poet of the Resistance through war poems such as 'Poésie et vérité' (1942) and 'Au rendezvous allemand' (1944).

Emerson, Ralph Waldo (1803-82) 'Nature is the incarnation of thought', wrote Emerson, American philosopher and poet, who met COLERIDGE, WORDSWORTH and CARLYLE whilst on a tour of Europe. He blended the humanitarian nature-worship of Romantic Europe with a belief that America had unrivalled opportunities to create a new social and moral order. His ideas were set out in *Nature* (1836).

Empedocles (5th cent. BC) Greek philosopher, physician and democrat who originated the theory of four elements – fire, air, water, earth – as the basic substances from which all else is made. They are combined in varying proportions, according to the unifying and separating agency of the principles of Love and Strife, which in turn explains all change.

Empson, William (1906-84) English poet and critic whose work aims at a subtle, complex and rigorous analysis of experience. His principal critical work, *Seven Types of Ambiguity* (1930), is a linguistic study of shades of meaning.

Enders, John (born 1897) American microbiologist whose discovery, with Frederick Robbins and Thomas Weller, that the poliomyelitis virus could be grown in tissue other than nerve tissue was an essential step in the development of polio vaccines. In 1962 he produced the first successful measles vaccine. The three men were awarded a joint Nobel Prize for Medicine (1954).

Engels, Friedrich (1820-95) German political writer and disciple of Karl MARX, with whom he collaborated in formulating the theory of dialectical materialism. As agent in England of his father's textile business (1842-4) he took an interest in the workers' conditions and, under the influence of the Chartist movement, wrote *The Condition of the Working Classes in England* (1844). This brought him into touch with Marx, then an exile in England, and together they wrote the *Communist Manifesto* (1848). While Marx was doing research and writing in London, Engles supported him, and from 1870 until Marx's death (1883) he helped Marx with his writings. He completed the latter's *Das Kapital* (1894), which Marx left unfinished.

Ennius, Quintus (239-c. 169 BC) Roman poet, known as the father of Roman poetry. His works, which survive only in fragments, range from tragedy and comedy to satire and didactic poetry, and reveal him as a poet who approached his Greek models in his originality. His preeminence at Rome was achieved by the rugged grandeur of his (probably) unfinished hexameter epic of Roman History, the 18-volume *Annales*.

Epicurus (c. 342-270 BC) Greek philosopher whose name has mistakenly become synonymous with luxury and an excessive love of pleasure. In fact. he taught that the supreme goal is the happiness which comes from peace of mind, achieved by banishing fear of the gods and fear of death, and by avoiding immediate pleasures that are outweighed by greater consequent pains.

Epstein, Sir Jacob (1880-1959) American-born British sculptor whose style and technique were highly original, and it became customary for any new work of his to be greeted with uproar. Among Epstein's more important busts are those of Somerset MAUGHAM, Albert EINSTEIN and George Bernard SHAW. Epstein's sculpture possessed a nervous tension, shown in one of his last works. *Christ in Majesty* (1957), cast in unpolished aluminium.

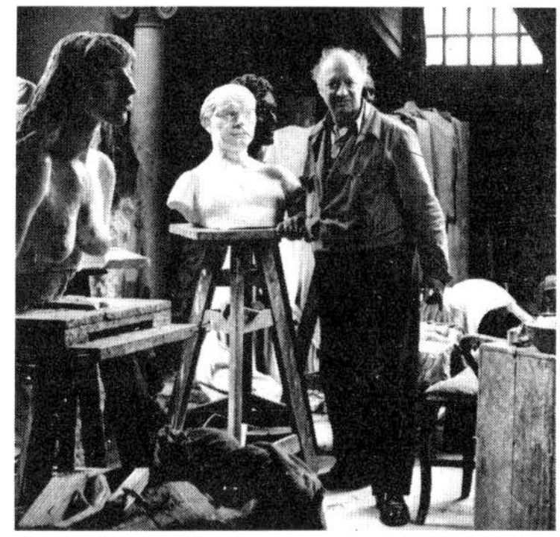

The work of Sir Jacob Epstein often caused a sensation. In 1907 it was declared by some to be obscene

Erasmus, Desiderius (c. 1466-1536) Dutch Renaissance theologian and scholar whose Greek versions of the New Testament showed for the first time that contemporary Latin translations were defective. As editor and commentator, he did much to publish the writings of the Christian Fathers, and generally promoted classical scholarship. His satire, *In Praise of Folly*, written for his friend Sir Thomas MORE, is the best remembered of his works. Although sympathetic to sources implicit in the Reformation movement, he had the scholar's dislike for violent political and religious upheaval and never openly joined the reformers.

Eratosthenes (3rd cent. BC) Greek astronomer and geographer who calculated the circumference of the Earth.

Erhard, Ludwig (1897-1977) Architect of the West German 'Economic Miracle'. He was appointed Minister of Economic Affairs by ADENAUER in 1949, and retained the post until be became Chancellor of the Federal Republic in 1963. After 1965 his coalition government of Christian Democrats and Free Democrats proved increasingly difficult to control and he resigned in November 1966 to be succeeded as Chancellor by Kiesinger. Erhard's policies as Economics Minister, and later as Chancellor, were fundamental, with other factors, such as Marshall Aid, to the growth of the German economy to a position of almost unrivalled prosperity in Europe.

Eric the Red (10th cent.) Norwegian mariner and discoverer of Greenland (*c.* 982). Eric sailed west from Iceland and the landfall he made was so visually appealing compared to Iceland that he named it Greenland. In the following year, a number of Icelandic Vikings settled there.

Ericsson, Leif (10th-11th cents.) Norse mariner, son of ERIC THE RED, who, according to the Icelandic sagas, made a westward expedition on which he discovered Helluland ('Land of the Flat Stone'), Markland ('Woodland') and Vinland. These discoveries are thought to relate specifically to Labrador, Nova Scotia and New England, though the 1965 evidence of the Vinland map is now known to have been a post-1920s forgery. Impressed by the moderate weather and natural maritime resources, Ericsson's party set up a colony for the winter, and recent archaeological finds suggest that the site was on the Newfoundland Coast.

Ernst, Max (1891-1976) German-born Surrealist painter whose technical innovations have had a considerable influence. Most notably, these were collage (compositions embodying scraps of paper, cloth or other material stuck onto the canvas), frottage (an impression of substances achieved by rubbing paper over a grainy surface), and automatic writing, a fundamental Surrealist technique (allowing the unconscious to rule the creative process). Ernst was one of the few Surrealist painters to gain fame in other media.

Eshkol, Levi (1895-1969) Israeli politician and the young state of Israel's third Prime Minister. Born at Kiev, he migrated to Palestine in 1913 and served in the First World War with the Jewish battalion of the Royal Fusiliers. He founded a number of kibbutzim, became Secretary of the Jewish Federation of Labour, and of the Jewish Labour Party. He was Minister of Agriculture and Development (1951) in BEN GURION's government and later Prime Minister (1963-9). During his Ministry Israel defeated the Egyptian Alliance in the Six-Day War (1967).

Essex, Robert Devereux, 2nd Earl of (1566-1601) English courtier, soldier, statesman and poet, successor to RALEIGH and the Earl of LEICESTER as favourite of the ageing ELIZABETH I. He led flamboyant military expeditions to Cadiz and the Azores, and gained political power as Earl Marshal of England (1597) and Lord Lieutenant of Ireland (1599). By his absences from court, his marriage, his feud with the Cecils, and his disobedience in making a truce with Tyrone in Ireland, he fell into Elizabeth's disfavour and was imprisoned (1599-1600). His plot to seize government control ended in failure and his ultimate execution.

Estaing, Valéry Giscard d' (born 1926) French politician who in 1956 was first elected as a *deputé*. He was Minister of Finance in 1962-6 and 1969-74. In May 1974, as the candidate of the Right, he defeated François MITTERAND to become the third President of the Fifth Republic and the youngest for 75 years. He was defeated by Mitterand in 1981.

Ethelbert (c. 522-616) English King of Kent, promulgator of the first Anglo-Saxon law code, the earliest known document in any Germanic language. He was baptized a Christian by St AUGUSTINE.

Euclid (3rd-2nd cent. BC) 'There is no royal road to geometry', said Euclid, Greek mathematician, to PTOLEMY I, who sought an easy way to learn the science. Euclid created the *Elements,* a fundamental geometric treatise, building up a number of theorems deduced from axioms and definitions and including the work of HIPPOCRATES and EUDOXUS. The *Elements,* in 13 books, was translated into Arabic in the 8th century and into Latin in the 11th. The first English version was published in the 18th century. Euclid was widely known as a teacher, and founded a school of mathematics in Alexandria.

Eudoxus (408-347 BC) Greek mathematician, astronomer and geographer, known for his theory of proportions, later expounded by EUCLID. He also devised a method for calculating areas, a precursor of the integral calculus method of solving such problems. His star map was long in use, and his method of explaining planetary motion in terms of spheres foreshadowed the epicycles of PTOLEMY. He estimated the Earth's circumference, prepared a world map and wrote a treatise on geography.

Eugene of Savoy (1663-1736) French-born soldier, statesman and diplomat who raised Austria to the rank of a European power. A far-sighted statesman, he advocated consolidation of the Hapsburg lands as a basis for imperial power in Germany. He was patron of Baroque artists and an art collector.

Euler, Leonhard (1707-83) Swiss mathematician, who was the first great systematic expounder of the methods of mathematical analysis. His *Introduction to the Analysis of Infinite Numbers* (1748) was as fundamental to mathematical analysis as was EUCLID's *Elements* to geometry, and he wrote two other major textbooks on infinitesimal calculus. Euler's application of calculus to geometrical problems in a study of curves (1760) was the first successful attempt to combine these two aspects of mathematics. He first treated trigonometrical functions mathematically, and formulated and devised the notation for many other commonly used theorems.

Euripides (484-406 BC) Greek dramatist, one of the three outstanding tragic poets of the ancient Greek theatre. Euripides was more interested than AESCHYLUS and SOPHOCLES in character and the personal predicament, and less bound than they by the archaic rules of the ancient drama. He wrote about 90 plays, of which 17 tragedies and one satyr-play remain. His subjects were tragedies of passion, politics and war. *The Bacchae,* produced after his death, is generally considered his finest play. It shows Euripides at his most mature and depicts irrational emotion taking over from the newer, more precarious human attribute of reason and self-control.

Evans, Sir Arthur (1851-1941) English archaeologist, who discovered Europe's oldest civilization. Evans began digging at Knossos in 1899, and excavated a magnificent, labyrinthine palace – arguably that of the legendary King Minos. Evans's finds showed that Crete's hitherto unknown civilization, which he named Minoan, flourished between 2500 and 1400 BC, and was transmitted to Europe by the Cretans.

Evans, Dame Edith (1888-1976) British actress, who took the female leads in SHAW's *Heartbreak House* and *The Millionairess* and played most of the leading women's roles in SHAKESPEARE during several seasons at the Old Vic. Her genius for comedy, first praised by critics in DRYDEN's *All for Love* (1922), showed itself to perfection in Restoration comedies.

Evans, Mary Ann see ELIOT, George

Evelyn, John (1620-1706) English gentleman and diarist who left a vivid record of the cultivated life of his time. The *Diary* is remarkable for its extent and its individual portraits. Evelyn became Secretary to the Royal Society, and his writings on engraving, architecture, navigation and gardening were popular and influential.

Evren, Kenan (born 1918) President of Turkey since 1980, when, as Chief of Staff of the armed forces, he led the military in a bloodless coup. He sought to restore peace to Turkey after years of unrest, by restricting political activity, strengthening the powers of the state and restoring limited democracy through a new constitution approved by referendum (1982). The election in 1983 returned a civil government to power.

Eworth, Hans (16th cent.) Dutch painter, whose portraits, which follow HOLBEIN in their precision of detail, are allegorical, e.g. *Juno, Minerva and Venus eclipsed by the Majesty and Beauty of Queen Elizabeth* (1569).

Eyck, Jan van (c. 1390-1441) Influential painter of the early Netherlandish school. In 1425 he was recorded as Court Painter to Philip the Good, the Duke of Burgundy, for whom he also acted as a diplomat, travelling to Spain and Portugal. His most famous work (part of which has been attributed to his brother Hubert) is the *Adoration of the Lamb,* an altarpiece in St Bavon, Ghent, completed in 1432. It is remarkable for the realism with which van Eyck represented the various elements, the portraits of the donors, the nude Adam and Eve, and the central panel in which the adoration is seen against a detailed landscape, which appears to recede into the distance through its atmospheric perspective. The faithful detail, brilliance of colour and subtle effects of light found in this work and in private commissions, such as the *Arnolfini Marriage* (1434), were made possible by van Eyck's perfection of a fluid oil medium and varnish. A number of small portraits mark the emergence in his work of easel painting as an activity as important as manuscript illustration.

Eyre, Edward John (1815-1901) British colonial Governor in Australia who explored much of southern Australia. He travelled widely in New South Wales, South Australia and Western Australia, and led an expedition (1840-1) to establish a land route along the barren coast of the Great Australian Bight.

Eysenck, Hans (born 1916) German-born British psychologist known for his insistence on a rigorously scientific approach to psychology and for his study of the human personality. His main concern in personality research has been to submit psychological data to experimental and quantitative assessment.

Ezekial (c. 6th cent. BC) One of the major Hebrew prophets of the Old Testament. He believed that God ruled the destinies of all nations. While stressing individual moral responsibility, like JEREMIAH, he also described the worship of an ideal religious state centred on the reconstructed Temple. This vision of divine glory became the basis of a branch of Jewish mysticism. Scholars are divided about the date of the Book of Ezekiel, which is divided into two main parts, dealing first with the fall of Jerusalem and then with the return of the exiles from Babylon.

F

Fabius Maximus (3rd cent. BC) Roman general and consul, whose military delaying tactics and avoidance of decisive battles earned him the name 'Cunctator' (the Delayer) and inspired the adjective Fabian to describe any strategy based on attrition. Made dictator (217 BC) during the Second Punic War, he avoided pitched battles and instead harassed Italy's Carthaginian invaders by attacks on their supplies.

Fahrenheit, Gabriel Daniel (1686-1736) German-Dutch physicist who was the first to use mercury in a thermometer. Fahrenheit's thermometer measured a wider range of temperatures more accurately than hitherto, encouraging him to devise the scale that took his name. The Fahrenheit scale places the freezing point of water at 32° and boiling point at 212°.

Fairfax, Thomas, 3rd Baron Fairfax of Cameron (1612-71) Scottish peer, Commander-in-Chief of the victorious Parliamentarian army in the English Civil War. He turned defeat into victory as a cavalry officer at Marston Moor (1644) then, as Captain-General of the New Model Army, welded it into the tool that won for the Parliamentarians the decisive Battle of Naseby (1645). Fairfax commanded CROMWELL's Commonwealth army until 1650 when he resigned because he opposed the invasion of Scotland. He opposed CHARLES I's execution and eased the way for the return of CHARLES II.

Faisal I (1885-1933) Comrade-in-arms of T. E. LAWRENCE and first King of Iraq. Accompanied by Lawrence, he advanced to Akaba in 1917 with his forces, which eventually formed the right wing of ALLENBY's army. Later that year he led his troops into Jerusalem and Damascus. He was acclaimed King of Syria by a national congress (1920), but was deposed by the French. After a plebiscite, he was placed on the throne of Iraq by Britain, who held the League of Nations mandate for that country. By steering a diplomatic course in a difficult period, he guided Iraq to independence and membership of the League of Nations (1932).

Faisal II (1935-58) King of Iraq, who was murdered in a military *coup d'état.* He succeeded to the throne at the age of four on the death of his father, Ghazi, and gained full power in 1953. He supported NASSER in the Suez crisis of 1956. Sharing the aims of his cousin, HUSSEIN of Jordan, in February 1958, he agreed to a federation of Iraq and Jordan in opposition to the United Arab Republic of Egypt and Syria. In July 1958, however, General Abdul Karim al-Kassem led a military revolt and Faisal and his household were assassinated.

Falconnet, Etienne-Maurice (1716-91) French sculptor and director (1757-66) of the Sèvres porcelain factory; at the height of his middle period, when he created works such as *Bathing Nymph* (1757), which embody in marble the essence of French Rococo. Invited to Russia by CATHERINE II, Falconnet worked there from 1766-9 on a Baroque-style equestrian statue of PETER THE GREAT. The statue is notable for its vigour and the technical brilliance of the rearing horse, and appears to have developed from an idea by BERNINI in a terracotta sketch of LOUIS XIV on horseback. It was later borrowed by DAVID for his portrait of NAPOLEON.

Falla, Manuel de (1876-1946) Spanish composer who gave his country's music its international status. He spent some time in Paris, where he was a friend of DEBUSSY and worked for DIAGHILEV. Andalusian folk song was Falla's main influence, but he incorporated it into a personal style full of rhythm and colour in such works as the ballets *The Three-Cornered Hat* and *Love, the Magician,* and, for piano and orchestra, *Nights in the Gardens of Spain.*

Fangio, Juan-Manuel (born 1911) Argentinian racing driver, five times World Champion (1951, 1954-7). After winning 24 Grand Prix races, he retired in 1958.

Fantin-Latour, Henri (1836-1904) French painter, best known for his flower pieces and his portrait of the Impressionists, *Homage to Manet* (1870).

Faraday, Michael (1791-1867) English physicist, whose discovery of electro-magnetic induction revealed the principle of the electric motor and dynamo, the transformer and the telephone. He was the first to demonstrate continuous motion of a current-carrying wire in a magnetic field (a primitive motor) and the continuous production of current from a conductor moving in a field (a primitive dynamo). He developed the laws of electrolysis. His work on dielectric constants was independent of, though later than, the then unpublished work of CAVENDISH. He found that magnetic fields cause a rotation of the plane of polarized light, and was the first to investigate the behaviour of dia-magnetic substances. Faraday knew little mathematics and therefore conceived the theoretical explanations of his discoveries in terms of graphic notions of lines of force. MAXWELL later developed a full mathematical treatment of electrodynamic theory.

With a battery, iron ring and galvanometer, Faraday made the first electrical transformer

Fargo, William George (1818-81) American co-founder of the West's most famous stagecoach company. Carrying gold, silver, mail, freight and passengers, the Wells Fargo stagecoaches became the quickest means of travel across the newly settled heartlands of the continent.

Farnese, Alexander, Duke of Parma (1545-92) Spanish soldier who recovered the southern provinces of the Netherlands for his uncle PHILIP II. Alexander was the most distinguished member of a family which ruled the Parma duchies from 1545 to 1731. As a young man he joined Philip's half-brother, Don JOHN OF AUSTRIA, serving with him in Italy and Belgium (1571-8). As Regent of the Netherlands (1578), by military skill and astute diplomacy Farnese regained Ypres, Bruges, Ghent and Antwerp and their hinterlands by 1585. His later operations in the Netherlands were hindered by Spanish preparations for the Armada and intervention in France against HENRY IV.

Farr, William (1807-83) English doctor who was a pioneer of preventive social medicine. He was one of the first men to realize that statistics, properly applied, could be an important weapon in the fight against disease, and a leader in the 19th-century fight to improve public health and sanitary conditions.

Fassbinder, Rainer Werner (1946-82) German film director whose many productions were made in Munich on a small budget with a regular group of actors. He became known internationally for *The Bitter Tears of Petra von Kant* (1972), *Fear Eats the Soul* (1974) and *The Marriage of Maria von Braun* (1978).

Faulkner, William (1897-1962) American novelist who produced a series of impressionistic, sometimes violent and brutal stories of life in the southern states of America. His later novels constituted a saga of the degeneration of family and community in the Deep South, called by the author Yoknapatawpha County. His main works were *The Sound and the Fury* (1929), *As I Lay Dying* (1930), *Sanctuary* (1931) and *Light in August* (1932).

Fauré, Gabriel (1845-1924) French composer, organist and the most influential teacher of French music of his generation. RAVEL was among his pupils. Fauré's own style was one of delicate elegance. His best-known works are his *Requiem,* his *Pavane* for chorus ad lib. and orchestra, and the children's *Dolly Suite* for piano duet.

Fawkes, Guy (1570-1606) English Roman Catholic conspirator in the unsuccessful Gunpowder Plot to blow up the House of Lords (1605) as a protest against the treatment of Catholics. This event is commemorated in England by the burning of effigies called 'guys' on November 5.

Fechner, Gustav (1801-87) German pioneer in psychophysics, who in 1860 formulated the law (first postulated by WEBER) that the intensity of a sensation is proportional to the logarithm of the stimulus. However, he thought more of his philosophic system, which attributed souls to all aspects of nature, including the plants and stars.

Félix, Elisa see RACHEL

Fellini, Federico (born 1920) Italian film director whose works often reflect his personal obsessions, either the fantasy world of the individual, as in *8½* (1963) or the degeneration of society as in *La Dolce Vita* (1959) and *Fellini Satyricon* (1969). His early films, sad comedies like *La Strada* (starring his wife Giulietta Masina), showed Fellini's concern with the values of modern society and his fascination with clowns and circuses which was to run through all his films, notably *I Clowns* (1970). Other well-known films include *Roma* (1972), *Amarcord* (1974), *Orchestra Rehearsal* (1979), *City of Women* (1981) and *The Ship Sails On* (1983).

Fénelon, François de Salignac de la Mothe (1651-1715) French novelist and theologian. A priest, he became tutor to LOUIS XIV's grandson the Duc de Bourgogne, for whose instruction he wrote *Télémaque,* a tale of adventure which adds a chapter to HOMER's *Odyssey.* In 1695 he was appointed Archbishop of Cambrai, but had become attracted to Quietism, a doctrine which holds that the way to Christian perfection is the way of inner contemplation. Fénelon was relegated to his diocese when Quietism was declared a heresy by the Pope. His other important publications included the *Traité de l'éducation des filles* (1687) and *Dialogues des morts* (1712).

Ferdinand I (1503-64) Austrian Holy Roman Emperor (1556-64) of the Hapsburg dynasty who succeeded his brother CHARLES V. Ferdinand claimed Bohemia and Hungary when his brother-in-law Louis II of Bohemia and Hungary was killed by the Turks at the battle of Mohács (1526). Ferdinand was elected King and established hereditary Austrian-Hapsburg rule in Bohemia and Hungary.

Ferdinand II (1578-1637) Holy Roman Emperor (1619-37), defender of Catholic and Hapsburg interests during the 30 Years' War, who was the true founder of the Austrian empire centred in Vienna. An ardent Catholic, with absolutist political ideas, Ferdinand's attempt as King to enforce his views in Bohemia (1617-18) led to rebellion and the temporary loss of the Bohemian crown. After his election as Emperor, Ferdinand recovered Bohemia (1620), which henceforth was a hereditary Hapsburg dominion. By the Edict of Restitution (1629), he tried to restore to the Catholic Church all lands lost since 1552, but was forced to abandon the Edict in 1635. Ferdinand finally crushed Protestantism in Austria, but was more tolerant in Hungary, where the Turkish threat impelled preferential treatment for the people. He was the last Emperor to attempt to unify central Europe.

Ferdinand V of Castile (II of Aragon, III of Naples) **(1452-1516)** King whose marriage (1469) to Isabella of Castile united Spain. Together, the 'Catholic Kings' warred against Granada, expelling the Moors, restored order to the country and encouraged COLUMBUS's voyage of discovery.

Ferdinand of Brunswick (1721-92) German soldier, whose masterful strategy in the Seven Years' War (1756-63) tied down large French forces in Germany, thus aiding Britain in her colonial conquests in North America and India. Brother-in-law and close friend of FREDERICK II, Ferdinand made his military reputation between 1757 and 1759, when he restored the shattered allied forces and defeated the French at Crefeld (1758) and Minden (1759), thus relieving the pressure on Frederick in the East.

Fermi, Enrico (1901-54) Italian-American physicist who built the first nuclear reactor. In the early 1930s he established the theory of beta decay and discovered the statistical laws obeyed by such elementary particles as the electron. In 1938, during the rise of Fascism, he left Italy for the United States, where he began to search for a way of producing a controlled, self-sustaining nuclear fission reaction – the key to a new and virtually inexhaustible source of energy. Eventually, in 1942, in a squash court at Chicago University, Fermi's nuclear reactor was built and tested. Its success heralded the beginning of the age of nuclear power. A year later Fermi was in Los Alamos, New Mexico, helping to develop the atomic bomb.

Feydeau, Georges (1862-1921) French dramatist and past-master of the bedroom farce. His two best known plays are *Le Dindon* (1889) and *Occupe-toi d'Amélie* (1908). His economy of style and theatrical expertise have led to some of his plays being included in the *Comédie Française* repertoire.

Feynman, Richard Phillips (born 1918) American physicist who developed the quantum approach to electromagnetic theory. In 1948, working with Julian Schweinger, he developed a means of avoiding the mathematical ambiguities in the original quantum electrodynamics of HEISENBERG and Dirac, and produced a far more powerful theory than theirs.

Fibonacci, Leonardo (c. 1170-1230) Italian mathematician who introduced Arabic numerals into Europe where they soon replaced the Roman system, particularly among merchants and traders. Fibonacci, who was among the foremost mathematical scholars of Medieval Europe, was a champion in the mathematical tournaments which were popular at that time. He was the author of a number of books on arithmetic and geometry.

Field, John (1782-1837) Irish composer and virtuoso pianist who invented the 'nocturne', a one-movement piece, usually for piano, evoking a night reverie. Field, a former pupil of Clementi's, also wrote seven piano concertos. He settled in Russia in 1803 and died there, having toured Europe from his base, St Petersburg.

Field, Marshall (1834-1906) American merchant whose Chicago-based establishment, Marshall Field & Co., was the first department store and, for 25 years, the world's largest. High-volume sales were the key to Field's low prices and varied selection.

Fielding, Henry (1707-54) English author and magistrate who helped to establish the novel as a literary form in England. His main work, *Tom Jones* (1749), is a human comedy, influenced in its form by CERVANTES, in which energy, spirit and honesty are celebrated as the finest human virtues. It breaks from the tradition of the novel of conventional morals, particularly from the work of RICHARDSON, which Fielding satirized in *Joseph Andrews* (1742). In the 1730s Fielding supported himself and his wife by writing burlesques and comedies for the stage. He became a barrister in 1740, and was made Justice of the Peace for Westminster in 1748. He vigorously suppressed hooligans and petty criminals, whose world he depicted in his satire *Jonathan Wild the Great* (1743).

Fields, W. C. (1879-1946) American screen comedian whose career began as a juggler in vaudeville. His screen character was lazy, dishonest and drunken, given to cheating and kicking children and lovable pets, an hilarious antidote to the contemporary sentimentality. Among his best known films are (with Mae WEST) *My Little Chickadee* (1940) and *Never Give a Sucker an Even Break* (1941).

'My little passion fruit, my little flower of the desert': comedian W. C. Fields and sultry comedienne Mae West

Figgins, Jesse Dade (1867-1944) American palaeontologist whose discovery of flint tools near Folsom, New Mexico, established that man lived in America as far back as 10,000 years ago. Until the discovery of the so-called Folsom points, it was believed that man had lived in America for only a few thousand years before the birth of CHRIST.

Fillmore, Millard (1800-74) Thirteenth President of the United States (1850-3), and supporter of the slavery compromise of 1850. As a congressman, Fillmore gained something of an anti-slavery reputation by supporting the prohibition of the domestic slave trade and opposing the annexation of Texas as a slave state. But on becoming President after TAYLOR's death (July 1850), his signing of the Compromise of 1850, particularly the Fugitive Slave Law, made him unpopular in the North.

Firdausi (c. 930-c.1020) Persian poet, author of the great epic masterpiece *The Book of the Kings,* which tells the history of the heroes of Iran from the early legends to the fall of the Sassanids, with long accounts of famous battles and warriors. Its stories included that of Sohrab and Rustam, later retold by Matthew ARNOLD.

Fischer, Bobby (born 1943) American chess player who captured the world championship in 1972 by defeating Boris Spassky of the Soviet Union. Fischer won his first US championship at the age of 14. In 1975 he refused to defend his world title.

Fischer Von Erlach, Johann (1656-1723) Austrian architect, who with HILDEBRANDT was a leader of the Austrian Baroque. The Karlskirche in Vienna (begun in 1716), with its mighty dome, is his masterpiece. He studied in Rome before settling in Vienna, where he was appointed Court Architect. His Italian experiences, together with his training as a stucco-worker and sculptor, led to his developing a vigorously plastic style.

Fisher, John Arbuthnot, 1st Baron Fisher of Kilverstone (1841-1920) British admiral who was largely responsible for preparing the Royal Navy for efficient action in the First World War. He promoted the use of torpedoes, revolutionized training and tactics, and insisted on outbuilding the Germans in 'Dreadnought' class battleships. His forthright views made him many enemies, and in 1910 he retired after a dispute with the Commander-in-Chief, Channel Fleet. CHURCHILL, as First Lord of the Admiralty (1914), recalled him as his First Sea Lord, but Fisher would not tolerate Churchill's interference with his dispositions and resigned in 1915.

FitzGerald, Edward (1809-83) English translator and poet whose famous version of the *Rubáiyát of Omar Khayyám* is a recreation of the Persian original. The combination of melancholy and sensuality, and the rhythms of an original four-line stanza, have given the poem an enduring popularity.

Fitzgerald, Ella (born 1918) American jazz singer who won world acclaim for her smooth effortless style. Her first hit was *A-Tisket A-Tasket* in 1938. After 1942 she soloed in nightclubs, theatres and concerts, and established an international reputation. She also appeared in films.

Fitzgerald, F. Scott (1896-1940) American novelist and story writer whose work portrays 'the Jazz Age', the time of social and economic change after the First World War. His early works, including *This Side of Paradise* (1920) and *The Beautiful and the Damned* (1922), are reflections of his generation's yearning for a sophisticated, hedonistic life. *The Great Gatsby* (1925) examines the division between wealth and youth, between possessions and ideals, written in meticulous prose.

Fitzgerald, Garret (born 1926) Irish Prime Minister who was elected Fine Gael member of the Irish Parliament for Dublin South East in 1969. He was Minister for Foreign Affairs (1973-7), became leader of the Fine Gael Party (1977), and was elected Prime Minister (1981-2) and again (1983).

Fitzgerald, Sir Anthony (1470-1538) English judge who helped to establish the importance of case law. His *Great Abridgement* (1516) summarized the most important medieval legal judgments suitable as precedents for future decisions.

Fizeau, Armand Hippolyte (1819-96) French physicist, who devised the first terrestrial method of measuring the velocity of light. In 1849 he set up a powerful lamp on a hilltop and a large mirror on another, five miles away, measuring the time it took a flash of light to make the round trip from lamp to mirror and back, by means of a toothed wheel which interrupted the beam.

Flaherty, Robert (1884-1951) American pioneer of documentary film whose early career as an explorer led him to his first film, the famous study of the Eskimo, *Nanook of the North* (1920). His later film, *Man of Aran* (1937), a study of the fishing community on the tiny island off the Irish coast, influenced the British documentary makers of the 1930s. Other films by Flaherty include *Elephant Boy* (1937) and *Louisiana Story* (1948).

Flamsteed, John (1646-1719) English astronomer, the first Astronomer Royal, and compiler of a star catalogue. Flamsteed's early observations were published in the Philosophical Transactions of the Royal Society, and gained him the attention of the scientific community. The influence of his colleague, Sir Jonas Moore, with CHARLES II, secured for Flamsteed the appointment of Astronomer Royal in 1675, and he was put in charge of the newly established observatory at Greenwich. Working alone, and paying for much of the vital equipment himself, he recorded over 20,000 stellar observations.

Flaubert, Gustave (1821-80) French novelist, whose works have become masterpieces of world literature. His first novel, *Madame Bovary* (1857), for which he and his publisher were tried (for offences against public morals) and acquitted, is the story of a bored provincial woman's unfulfilled dreams of romantic love, her degradation and ultimate self-destruction. His painstaking documentation, shrewd observation and realist style put Flaubert in the front rank of European novelists. His other important novels were *Salammbô* (1862), an exotic and barbaric tale of ancient Carthage, and *A Sentimental Education* (1869), which explored a young romantic's disillusionment with contemporary Paris, partially reflecting the author's own life. However, it is in the *Trois Contes* (1877) that Flaubert's art is revealed in its purest form.

Flecker, James Elroy (1884-1915) English poet and dramatist who tried to combine classical lucidity with a strain of exoticism. His famous poem, 'The Golden Journey to Samarkand' (1913), is sensuously evocative of the romantic east, as is his best-known play *Hassan,* first staged in 1922 with music by DELIUS.

Flémalle, Master of (c. 1378-1444) The most important Flemish artist before van EYCK. His chief work is probably the *Mérode Altar* (c. 1425), an example of the early use of oil paint instead of tempera. The various domestic objects in the central panel of this altarpiece, the Annunciation, have a specific religious symbolism and are painted with realistic detail.

Fleming, Sir Alexander (1881-1955) Scottish bacteriologist, who, in 1928, discovered the bacteria-killing properties of the fungus *Penicillium notatum*. His discovery was quite accidental. Some *Penicillium* fungus had fallen by chance into a preparation of bacteria that Fleming was about to throw away; he noticed that no bacteria had grown in the vicinity of the fungus. He recognized the importance of this but did not isolate the antibiotic substance. In 1945 Fleming shared a Nobel Prize with Florey and CHAIN who, during the Second World War, isolated the antibiotic and called it penicillin.

Fleming, Ian Lancaster (1908-64) English writer, the creator of James Bond. After service as a Naval Intelligence Officer, he began his series of novels in 1953 with *Casino Royale*, the debut of his super-spy hero who featured in a number of works, several of which have been made into highly successful films.

Fleming, Sir John Ambrose (1849-1945) English electrical engineer who developed the first electronic valve after EDISON's discovery (1883) that electricity will flow between a heated filament and a metal wire sealed in an evacuated glass bulb. Fleming investigated the phenomenon and quickly discovered that the heated filament was giving off electrons, an effect soon to be known as thermionic emission. By 1904 he had utilized it to produce a simple diode or rectifying valve, to convert alternating current to direct current.

Fletcher, John (1579-1625) English dramatist, famous for his collaboration with Francis BEAUMONT. Of the 50 plays attributed to their partnership, about 40 are believed to have been written entirely by Fletcher. The three most important products of their collaboration were *Philaster* (1610), *A Maid's Tragedy* and *A King and No King* (1611). These were written in the new romantic tragi-comedy form perfected by SHAKESPEARE, with whom Fletcher is thought to have collaborated in the writing of *Henry VIII* and *The Two Noble Kinsmen*. Fletcher's best-known plays were a pastoral, *The Faithful Shepherdess,* and a farcical comedy, *The Wild Goose Chase*.

Foch, Ferdinand (1851-1929) Marshal of France, under whose leadership the Allies achieved victory in the First World War. Foch joined the army in 1870 and became the General Staff's artillery specialist. He proved to be a considerable military tactician in the early battles of the war (Marne, 1914). In May 1917, he became Chief of Staff to the French commander, PÉTAIN, but it was soon clear that he was abler than his chief, and as a result, in April 1918, he was appointed Supreme Commander on the Western Front. The Allied armies took the offensive in July and by November he had driven the Germans to seek an armistice. Foch retired after participating in the Paris Peace Conference (1919).

Greatest of France's First World War generals, Marshal Foch led the Allied Armies to victory in 1918

Fokker, Anthony Herman (1890-1939) Pioneer Dutch, later naturalised American, aircraft designer and industrialist. After building his first aeroplane in 1911, and receiving little support, he left Holland for Germany, where he received financial backing. Many fighter planes of his design took part in the First World War. Fokker perfected an interrupter mechanism that allowed a machine gun to fire through whirling propeller blades without damaging them. After 1918, he established factories first in Amsterdam and then in the United States, concentrating on making commercial aircraft.

Fontenelle, Bernard Le Bovier de (1657-1757) French philosopher and writer, who was the first to present scientific knowledge in literary form. His *Entretiens sur la pluralité des monds* (1686), an elegant, religiously sceptical 'conversation' on astronomy, the possibility of life on other planets, and the relative smallness of man and his world, did more to awaken popular interest in astronomy and to secure fashionable acceptance of COPERNICUS's theories than any other work.

Fonteyn, Dame Margot (born 1919) English ballerina whose performance as *The Sleeping Beauty,* when the Royal Ballet first performed in New York in 1948, established the pre-eminence of the company and her own international standing. Dame Margot helped to popularize ballet in Britain by her dancing with Robert Helpmann during the 1940s, and in the 1960s established a famous partnership with Rudolf NUREYEV. Her talent for controlled, expressive dancing won her recognition as prima ballerina of the Royal Ballet, and her tours confirmed the quality of British ballet to international audiences.

Ford, Ford Madox (1873-1939) English critic, novelist and editor, an influential figure in the London literary world, and an acute observer of his contemporaries. He founded *The English Review* and *The Transatlantic Review*. As a novelist he is famous for a tetralogy, *Parade's End* (1924-8), about Western civilization approaching the First World War.

Ford, Gerald Rudolf (born 1913) Thirty-eighth President of the US, inaugurated 9 August 1974 following Richard NIXON's resignation in the wake of the Watergate scandal. He declined the vice-presidential nomination in 1968, but following the resignation of Spiro Agnew he became Vice-President in December 1973. Ford graduated from Yale Law School in 1941, saw wartime service in the US Navy and won nomination to the House of Representatives in 1949, becoming Republican minority leader in 1965. A 'moderate Republican', he strove hard for the establishment of better relations between the US and the People's Republic of China. He was defeated by Democrat Jimmy Carter in the presidential election of 1976.

Ford, Henry (1863-1947) American industrialist and automobile manufacturer who invested and developed mass-production assembly-line techniques to provide cheap and reliable 'motoring for the millions', and pioneered high-wage, high-output labour utilization. The vehicle on which the fortunes of the Ford Motor company were built was the 'Model T', introduced in 1909 and produced continuously until 1927, by which time more than 15 million had been made. With his son, Edsel, he engaged in tractor manufacture (from 1915) and from 1924 steadily expanded the manufacture overseas of his vehicles. In 1940, he set up the Willow Run bomber aircraft plant which became vital to the Allies.

Ford, John (c. 1586-1639) English dramatist, who wrote *'Tis Pity She's a Whore,* the only play by which he is widely known. This tragedy of a brother's incestuous passion for his sister was staged by Visconti in a spectacular revival in Paris (1961). Ford also wrote another violent tragedy, *The Broken Heart,* and an historical drama, *Perkin Warbeck.*

Ford, John (1895-1973) American film director, noted chiefly for his Westerns which are marked by his involvement with the legend of the pioneering West. His films include the classic *Stagecoach* (1939), and two non-Westerns for which he received Academy Awards, *The Informer* (1935) and *The Grapes of Wrath* (1940).

Forster, Edward Morgan (1879-1970) English novelist whose books explore human relationships with delicacy and intelligence, upholding the individual creative imagination as the most important quality of humanity. *Howard's End* (1910) examines with fine irony the limitations of the English sensibility, *A Passage to India* (1924) is an account of the social, moral and political difficulties of British rule in India.

Forster, Georg (1754-94) German explorer, scientist, writer and politician who pioneered the scientific travel book. He emigrated to England in 1766, and accompanied his clergyman-scientist father Johann Reinhold Forster on COOK's second world voyage (1772). Both recorded their experiences, and Georg's *A Voyage Round the World* (1777), brilliantly combined science with good writing, setting a new fashion in travel books and influenced leading German writers and scientists from GOETHE to HUMBOLDT.

Foster, Stephen Collins (1826-64) American writer of now traditional songs such as *Swanee River, My Old Kentucky Home* and *Camptown Races,* which were based mainly on the life of the Negro in the southern United States. Virtually self-taught, Foster wrote more than 175 songs before his death from alcoholism.

Foucault, Léon (1819-68) French physicist known for his researches on light and on precessional motion and who determined the velocity of light in various media. Suspending a swinging pendulum from the dome of a church, he found that the plane in which the pendulum swings twists gradually round in a clockwise direction. This proves that the Earth must turn in the opposite direction. He also invented the gyroscope (1852) and the Foucault prism (1857).

Fouché, Joseph (1763-1820) French revolutionary politician and chief of a secret political police and intelligence system. Though at first a supporter of ROBESPIERRE (1792-3) and the Terror, he changed sides and helped to bring down his master (1794) when Robespierre tried to establish his 'Cult of the Supreme Being'. As Minister of Police (1799) under the Directory, Fouché proved himself so useful that NAPOLEON retained him, with intermissions, in the same office. He survived the Restoration, maintaining contacts with METTERNICH and LOUIS XVIII, and became ambassador in Dresden.

Fouquet, Jean (c. 1420-c. 1481) French painter, whose self-portrait is the first work of its kind that is not part of a larger picture. His most characteristic works, such as the portrait of *Estienne Chevalier with St Stephen* (*c.* 1450), combine Flemish realism in the depiction of surfaces with an Italian preoccupation with classical architecture and the weight and solidity of the human figure.

Fourier, Jean Baptiste (1768-1830) French mathematician and physicist, best known for the Fourier Series, by which complex functions can be represented in terms of certain trigonometrical series. His most important work is *Analytical Theory of Heat* (1822), a mathematical study of heat transfer in which he developed the theory of the Fourier Series.

Fournier, Pierre (1712-68) French engraver and typefounder who was the first typographer to devise the points system for measuring and naming sizes of type. His main work was the *Typographic Manual* (1764).

Fox, Charles James (1749-1806) English liberal statesman and orator, champion of democratic government. Entering Parliament as a Tory (1768), he soon disputed the extent of royal authority and, proclaiming the sovereignty of the people, led Whig opposition to George's III's Tory government. He supported the American colonists against Lord NORTH's repression, and after the American War of Independence, tried, as Britain's first Foreign Secretary (1782), unsuccessfully, to achieve Britain's unconditional recognition of American independence. Later he supported the French Revolution, opposing war with France as aiding despotism. He secured Parliament's pledge to end the slave trade (1806) and urged full freedom for dissenters and Roman Catholics.

An opponent of the hidebound establishment of his day. Charles James Fox was a popular subject for lampoons

Fox, George (1624-91) English religious reformer who (*c.* 1648) founded the Society of Friends, commonly called the Quakers. Fox preached that God and the Bible could directly guide man's actions, opposed formalized religion and was often imprisoned for interrupting church services. He gained support in Britain, northern Europe, America and the West Indies, and his followers included William PENN. The monthly meeting begun by Fox became an enduring religious movement. The name Quaker reputedly comes from his telling a hostile judge to 'tremble at the word of the Lord'.

Foxe, John (1516-87) English martyrologist, a Protestant who went into exile to avoid MARY I's persecution, returning in ELIZABETH I's reign to complete his monumental *Actes and Monuments of these latter and perilous Dayes,* commonly called *Foxe's Book of Martyrs.* A graphic description of religious persecutions from WYCLIFFE to CRANMER, the book aroused bitter hostility in England to Roman Catholicism, yet Foxe was a tolerant man and opposed the execution of Jesuits in 1581.

Fragonard, Jean Honoré (1732-1806) French Rococo artist, in the tradition of BOUCHER, who developed considerable ability as a landscape artist. His 'Fantasy Portraits' (late 1760s) display an energy of brushwork reminiscent of RUBENS.

France, Anatole (1844-1924) French poet, novelist, critic and moralist. He was the author of highly successful novels *Le Crime de Sylvestre Bonnard* (1881), *Le Livre de mon ami* (1885) and *Thaïs* (1893), and of the *Histoire contemporaine* (1896-1901) – four satirical studies of French social and political life, with many allusions to the DREYFUS case. Perhaps his best novel was *Les Dieux on soif* (1912), a story of fanaticism during the French Revolution. France was awarded a Nobel Prize in 1921.

Francis I (1494-1547) King of France (1515-47) who imported Italian Renaissance culture. He built splendid châteaux at Fontainebleau, Chambord and elsewhere, commissioning leading Italian sculptors and painters, including Benvenuto CELLINI and LEONARDO DA VINCI, to design and decorate his palaces and organize royal entertainments. Primarily to further Renaissance humanist studies, Francis founded the Collège de France (1530), where lecturers taught the classics, mathematics and medicine in a progressive spirit contrasting with the conservatism of the Sorbonne. Protestant aspirations of his support for the Reformation were dashed, and after 1534 he reverted to orthodox Catholicism. Francis strengthened royal power by centralizing the financial administration, largely to pay for four costly wars fought over Italy with the Emperor CHARLES V, who had outdone Francis by winning election as Holy Roman Emperor. In the first war Francis was taken prisoner and had to concede Burgundy to gain his freedom. After losing Italy in the second war he gained some successes which gave him Savoy and Piedmont. Francis finally conquered the Imperial forces in 1544.

Francis de Sales (1567-1622) French saint whose gentle example and goodness won back for the Roman Catholic church thousands of followers of CALVIN. His first mission was to the Chablais area, where for four years he worked, often in danger of his life, applying his rule that whoever preaches with love preaches effectively. Consecrated Bishop of Geneva, the city of Calvin's Presbyterian government, he set about reforming the dioceses while continuing to preach. In 1610 he founded the Order of the Visitation, with Jane de Chantal. He was canonized in 1665 and declared a Doctor of the Church in 1877. His best-known work is the *Introduction to the Devout Life* (1608).

Francis Joseph I (1830-1916) Emperor of Austria (1848-1916) and King of Hungary from 1867. After succeeding his uncle, FERDINAND I, who abdicated in 1848, he spent the first years of his reign dealing with revolts in various parts of his Empire. Subsequently, he waged a disastrous war against his former ally, Prussia (1866), but afterwards abjured intervention in the affairs of other nations. He survived a succession of family tragedies (among them the assassination of his wife and the suicide of his son) in a long and eventful reign of almost 68 years. Francis Joseph was always prepared for expansion in the Balkans – a cause of the First World War. The spark that ignited Europe was the assassination at Sarajevo of his nephew and heir, Francis Ferdinand in June 1914.

Francis, St, of Assisi (c. 1182-1226) Italian founder of the Franciscan Order of friars, based on JESUS CHRIST's teachings on the principles of poverty and charity.

Francis Xavier (1506-52) Spanish missionary saint, the evangelist of the East Indies and Japan. With St IGNATIUS OF LOYOLA he was one of the founders of the Society of Jesus, and went to the Far East as a Jesuit, where he worked for seven years in Goa, southern India and Ceylon, combating European ill-treatment of the natives, but winning converts only among the Untouchables. In 1549 he was sent to Japan and as representative of the King of Portugal was allowed to teach Christianity in Kyoto and Yamaguchi. After two years he left his Japanese mission to his native convert colleagues, revisited Goa, and in 1552 set out for China, which was closed to foreigners. He was secretly set ashore on the island of Shangchuan where he died. His body was taken back to Goa and enshrined there.

Franck, César Auguste (1822-90) Belgian organist and composer who lived in Paris, earning his living as a church organist and later becoming organ professor at the Paris Conservatoire. While his fame as an improvisor on the organ was well known, much of his music was little heard or understood during his lifetime. After his death, works such as the *Symphonic Variations* for piano and orchestra, and his Symphony, Violin and Piano Sonata and String Quartet came to be widely admired for their warm romanticism.

Franco, Francisco (1892-1975) Dictator of Spain, who overthrew the Republican government in an armed rebellion and the bloody civil war that followed it. Disliking the Socialist and anti-clerical policies of the Azaña government, he used his position as army Chief of Staff to launch a military attack on it, employing both white and Moorish troops from Spanish Morocco. He received substantial Italian and German aid furnished by MUSSOLINI and HITLER. In a three-year civil war, in which the government was helped by an International Brigade of volunteers, he eventually gained control of the countryside and finally captured Madrid (March, 1939). His success in maintaining Spanish neutrality during the Second World War, the elimination by force of all opposition, and a measure of economic improvement (largely due to US rents for military bases in Spain) reduced to some extent a widespread reluctance to his rule. In 1947, Franco intimated that Spain would again become a monarchy after his death and in 1969 designated Juan Carlos heir to the throne. Franco resigned as Prime Minister in 1973 but remained head of state until his death.

Frankland, Sir Edward (1825-99) English chemist who originated the theory of valence. After preparing the first organic compounds containing metal atoms, he speculated why the atoms linked together in the way they did and eventually suggested that all atoms have a certain fixed capacity to combine with other atoms – the theory of valence.

Franklin, Benjamin (1706-90) American statesman and scientist, one of the pioneers of electricity. A fierce supporter of America's struggle for independence, he also played an important part in the drafting of the Declaration of Independence (1776) and the United States Constitution (1787). His most famous electrical experiment was the proof, in 1752, that lightning is an electrical phenomenon. He flew a kite in a violent thunderstorm and a spark leaped from the key he had fastened to the kite's string. Charge from the electrified air had travelled down the thread and discharged through the key. On the basis of this experiment, Franklin designed the first lightning conductor. (The next two men to try the experiment died when lightning struck their kites.)

Franklin, Sir John (1786-1847) English commander of an ill-fated expedition to explore the Canadian Arctic region for the 'North West Passage'. In May 1845, the ships *Erebus* and *Terror* left London for Greenland, which they reached, and continued north. Neither crew was seen alive again. For the next 10 years, 40 expeditions tried to discover what had happened to the Franklin expedition, and as a result of the searches the North West Passage was found and traversed.

Fraser, John Malcolm (born 1930) Australian Prime Minister (1975-83). He entered Liberal Party politics after attending Oxford University, was elected to the House of Representatives in 1955, and held several posts, serving as Minister of the Army, Education and Science, and Defence, before becoming Prime Minister. His attempts to solve Australia's economic problems were unsuccessful, and his party lost the 1983 election.

Frazer, Sir James (1854-1941) Scottish anthropologist, classical scholar and student of primitive magic and religion. His major work was *The Golden Bough*, a study of sacral kingship and animism.

Frederick I (c. 1122-90) King of Germany (1152-90), Holy Roman Emperor (1152-90), King of Italy (1155-90), called 'Barbarossa' (Red Beard), who coined the term 'Holy Roman Empire'. He restored order in Germany by appeasing the nobles, then spent 30 years trying to subdue the cities of northern Italy, with some success, before the Lombard League defeated him in 1176. In 1184 Frederick arranged a marriage that gave his son, Henry, southern Italy and Sicily, surrounding the popes (at odds with the emperors since Emperor Henry IV) by imperial territories.

Frederick I (1657-1713) First King in Prussia (1701-13). He became Elector of Brandenburg as Frederick III (1688) and greatly enhanced his state's prestige by crowning himself 'King in Prussia' (not 'of Prussia' since West Prussia remained Polish). The title of king had been Frederick's chief aim and he achieved it by the sanction of the Emperor Leopold I, to whom he promised (and later gave) military aid during the War of the Spanish Succession (1702-14). He was known as a patron of scholarship.

Frederick II (1194-1250) King of Sicily (1198-1250), King of Germany (1212-50), and Holy Roman Emperor (1215-50), a brilliant lawmaker, administrator, warrior, multilingual diplomat and patron of the arts and sciences. He founded Naples University (1224) and then made Salerno Europe's leading medical school, and financed translations of major Greek and Arabic works. He also sponsored a veterinary handbook and wrote a book on falconry remarkable for its scientific observation. As Holy Roman Emperor he continued the power struggle with the popes, fought emergent German and Italian towns, and became King of Jerusalem (1227) by capturing the city in a crusade.

Frederick II (1712-86) King of Prussia (1740-86), called 'Frederick the Great', who made Prussia Austria's rival for the leadership of Germany. Rebelling against the rigid, uncultured militarism of his father, FREDERICK WILLIAM I, Frederick wrote poetry, published treatises on political philosophy, rejected Christianity, corresponded with French writers, and gained the admiration of VOLTAIRE for preaching rule by enlightened despotism. Determined to maintain the power and prestige of Prussia, Frederick maintained a strong economy by encouraging agriculture and industry, and increasing the army. Austria and Prussia regarded themselves as rivals for the mastery of Europe and a struggle between them became inevitable. Frederick reversed his father's pro-Hapsburg policy and seized Austrian-held Silesia in 1740, thus antagonizing MARIA TERESA, and helping to provoke the War of the Austrian Succession (1740-8) and the Seven Years' War (1756-63) in which Frederick's enlarged Prussian army fended off Austrian, then French, Austrian and Russian forces. He not only retained Silesia, but took part of Poland (1772).

Frederick William (1620-88) Elector of Brandenburg (1640-88), called 'the Great Elector', who laid the foundation of Prussian power. He became ruler during the 30 Years' War and immediately started to repair the damage the war had brought to his small state. By the Peace of Westphalia, which ended the 30 Years' War, he acquired new territories. His army enabled him to force Poland to cede Brandenburg the Duchy of Prussia (East Prussia) in 1657 and to defeat Charles XI's powerful Swedish forces at Fehrbellin (1675). By clever manipulation of his allegiance he utilized his position between Poland and Sweden to secure from each recognition as independent Duke of Prussia. Outside Brandenburg-Prussia, he generally supported the Hapsburgs, the Empire and Protestant causes, and his strong army made his support sought after. He founded the Prussian navy and promoted colonization of West Africa.

Frederick William I (1688-1740) King of Prussia (1713-40) who founded its characteristic, rigidly organized military and administrative systems. Ruling severely as an absolute monarch, Frederick William created a powerfully centralized government, in every department of which he scrutinized operations and had the final power of decision. He doubled his standing army to 80,000 men (recruiting a grenadier regiment of tall men – the 'Potsdam Giants' Guard'), and seized much of Swedish Pomerania.

Frege, Gottlob (1848-1925) German philosopher and mathematician who invented a new logical notation, developed modern mathematical logic and, like RUSSELL and WHITEHEAD, sought to derive mathematics from logic, based on the notion of a formal system, with axioms and rules.

Fresnel, Augustine Jean (1788-1827) French physicist who developed the theory that light is a transverse wave motion. In the 1800s, he worked, at first with Dominique Arago, on a mathematical formulation of the wave theory of light – that light waves oscillate perpendicularly to their direction of travel – confirming his theory by developing the first successful theory of diffraction. A special type of condensing lens is named after him.

Freud, Sigmund (1856-1939) Austrian psychiatrist and founder of psychoanalysis. At the heart of his work was the belief that a complex of forgotten or deliberately buried impressions underlies all abnormal mental states. A cure, he said, could often be effected by revealing these hidden impressions, and he replaced hypnosis by making the patient talk by free association of ideas. The technique remains the basis of psychoanalytical treatment today. Freud stated that children are not, as was supposed, unaffected by their sexuality until puberty, and frequently suffer from a desire to possess the parent of the opposite sex, based upon rivalry with the same sex parent – the Oedipus complex. Eventually he concluded that arrested infantile mental processes lay at the root of all serious personality disturbances in the adult. Freud saw four stages in the development of what he called the *libido* (which is often equated with sex, but which has a wider and more general significance). These are the oral stage, from birth, when the mouth is the organ of pleasure; the anal stage, beginning towards the end of the first year, the third (phallic) stage and the fourth (genital) stage, beginning at puberty. Failure of the libido to develop smoothly through these phases led, according to Freud, to aberrations of character or sexual perversion.

Friedman, Milton (born 1912) American economist who is an important and influential member of the Chicago school of economics, supporting monetary policy as the best means of controlling the economy. His works include *A Theory of the Consumption Function* (1957), *Capitalism and Freedom* (1962), *A Monetary History of the United States 1867-1960* (1963), written with Anna Schwartz and a key book in monetary economics, *Free to Choose* (1980), written with Rose Friedman, and *Bright Promises, Dismal Performance* (1983). He was awarded the 1976 Nobel Prize in Economics.

Friedrich, Caspar David (1774-1840) German Romantic landscape painter, who, like many Romantics, held pantheistic beliefs in the divinity of nature, and expressed its moods with great conviction and sensitivity. A favourite pictorial device of his was the setting of a single figure with his back to the spectator in a landscape whose distant horizons and aerial perspective are suggestive of the infinite.

Frisch, Max (born 1911) Swiss author who, after working as a journalist and architect, devoted himself exclusively to writing novels and plays. His first plays, *Santa Cruz* and *Now Sing Again,* were completed in 1944-5, but the play which brought him wide recognition was *The Fire Raisers* (1958), originally produced as a radio play. Other works include *Stiller* (1954), a satirical novel about the Swiss way of life, *Triptych* (1981), a modern morality play, and *Bluebeard* (1983).

Frobisher, Sir Martin (c. 1535-94) English explorer who made pioneering attempts to find and sail through the North West Passage. In 1576, Frobisher sailed around the south tip of Friesland (now Greenland) looking for a short cut to the East and entered what is now known as Frobisher Bay. On his trip he met 'tawny coloured human beings wearing seal-skins' and found they used small seal-skin boats called 'kayaks'. Frobisher later served under DRAKE, and against the Armada. He befriended the Eskimos with displays of folk-dancing.

Froebel, Friedrich (1782-1852) German educator, who is particularly associated with the development of the 'kindergarten'. In 1840 he established the first of many at Blankenburg, and in 1849 he founded a training institution for kindergarten teachers. After his death, Froebel's influence continued to grow, fostered by his publications, in particular *The Education of Man* (1826), and the activities of his disciples. Believing, like ROUSSEAU and Pestalozzi, that children should be able to grow up naturally, unfettered by superfluous adult constraints, Froebel valued highly play encouraged by a stimulating environment, believing that, through such free activity, the child would develop his thoughts and feelings in a spontaneous and genuine manner.

Froissart, Jean (c. 1337-c. 1400) French medieval chronicler and poet whose *Chroniques,* detailing events of the years 1325-1400 in Western Europe – and in particular the 100 Years' War – form a lively tapestry of 14th-century feudal life.

Fromm, Erich (1900-80) German-born American psychoanalyst who adapted the theories of FREUD to allow for the special social and cultural demands on the individual in different societies. Fromm's concern with the problems facing man today is reflected in *Escape from Freedom* (1941), which analyses the roots of Nazism and the history and character of Western civilization.

Frost, Robert (1874-1963) American poet whose work is based on traditional forms, and is rooted in the land that he farmed. His rhythms are regular, his diction is colloquial and his characters are poor, labouring realists. He combines exact and beautiful descriptions of nature with humour and shrewd observation.

Fry, Elizabeth (1780-1845) British social worker and prison reformer. The daughter of John Gurney, a rich Quaker banker, she was herself a leading Quaker and a notable preacher. She married Joseph Fry (a London merchant) in 1800. She agitated for more humane treatment of women prisoners and of convicts sentenced to transportation to New South Wales, and later became active in other fields of reform, notably in raising the standards, skill, training and status of hospital nurses, and improvement in the facilities for women's education. Her fame extended far beyond Britain, and in 1838 she was requested by King Louis-Philippe of France to inspect and report on French prisons. This led to penal reforms in France.

Fuchs, Sir Vivian Ernest (born 1908) British geologist and explorer, leader of the first overland crossing of Antarctica (1957-8). His 12-man team covered the 2158 miles from Shackleton Station on the Weddell Sea to Scott Station on the Ross Sea in 99 days. They met Edmund HILLARY's team from Scott Station at the South Pole base then followed the line of supply dumps laid by Hillary.

Fugger, Jakob (15th cent.) German founder of a banking and merchant firm which, at its height, loaned money to popes and emperors, monopolized the silver and copper trades, and had a network of trading posts from the Baltic to the Mediterranean. Fugger's son Jakob II built the Fuggerei, 52 low-rent houses for poor Catholics near Augsburg, which still survives. The Fuggers also provided stocks of goods for maritime explorers like Magellan, to barter when they reached their destination.

Fujiwara Michinaga (966-1027) One of the great figures of Japanese history, who brought the power of the Fujiwara clan (858-1184) to its zenith. As Regent (998-1027) he proved an adroit statesman, retaining power by marrying five of his daughters to successive emperors. Fujiwara spent much money on decorating palaces, encouraging the arts and building Buddhist shrines. His rule witnessed a classical period of Japanese literature.

Fuller, Richard Buckminster (1895-1983) American architect and engineer who believed that only technology can solve modern world problems. He invented several revolutionary designs, the best known being the geodesic dome, a spherical structure composed of light, strong, triangular parts. He also wrote unorthodox books, such as *Operating Manual for Spaceship Earth* (1969), *Earth Inc.* (1973) and *Grunch of Giants* (1983).

Fulton, Robert (1765-1815) Irish-American inventor who, after early training as an artist, devoted his life to engineering and built the first commercially practical steamboat. In 1786, he went to England where he studied methods of improved canal construction and navigation. Fulton then journeyed to France, where he drew up plans for a submarine. His *Nautilus* was launched in 1800, but although it behaved well, Fulton could not arouse official interest in it. He had more success in the United States when, in 1807, his *Clermont* steam paddleboat started commercial trips from New York to Albany. He followed this with 17 other steamboats, a ferry, a torpedo boat which rammed enemy vessels with torpedoes mounted on a long boom, and, in 1815, a steam frigate, unfinished when he died.

Fürtwangler, Wilhelm (1886-1954) German conductor and an outstanding interpreter of the German classics, particularly of WAGNER and BEETHOVEN. Much criticized for having stood by Germany during the HITLER régime, he had nevertheless worked to protect Jewish colleagues, and was cleared by a de-Nazification tribunal in 1946.

G

Gable, Clark (1901-60) American film actor whose impudent, virile magnetism made him a screen idol for 30 years. His films included *Red Dust* (1932), *It Happened One Night* (1934), *Gone With the Wind* (1940), and *The Misfits* (1960).

Gabo, Naum (1890-1977) Russian sculptor and chief exponent of the Constructivist movement. His series of sculptures (e.g. *Head of Woman, c.* 1917-20) were mostly Cubist constructions in sheet steel or sheet steel and celluloid. In 1920, Gabo drew up the famous 'Realist Manifesto', which outlined the fundamental principles of Constructivism. That year Gabo made his first kinetic sculpture, a steel blade, circumscribing volume in space, which was set in motion by a motor. Later he adopted a style based on curved surfaces built up of slender tubes and plastic threads, as in the 85-ft-high *Construction* (1954-7).

Gabrieli, Giovanni (1557-1612) Italian Renaissance composer who was the first major musician to use polychoral effects and instrumental accompaniments. He succeeded his uncle Andrea Gabrieli, another major figure, as the chief organist at St Mark's, Venice (1585).

Gaddafi, Colonel Muamma (born 1942) Libyan political and military leader who formed the Free Officers Movement, which overthrew King Idris in 1969. He became Chairman of the Revolutionary Command Council, and Commander-in-Chief of the Libyan armed forces. He has attempted to stamp out colonialism, driving foreigners out of Libya, and has encouraged an Islamic religious revival. Unpredictable in his actions, he has supported violent revolutions abroad, while persecuting Libyan dissidents.

Gaddi, Taddeo (c. 1300-66) Florentine painter and worker in mosaic and marble, whose importance lies in his transmission of GIOTTO's style. He was probably Giotto's pupil and inherited his sober style of religious narrative painting. His best-known work is the *Life of the Virgin* cycle (*c.* 1332-8) in the Baroncelli chapel, Florence.

Gagarin, Yuri Alekseyevich (1934-68) Russian air force test pilot and cosmonaut. Gagarin became the first man in space on 12 April 1961. His spacecraft, Vostok 1, completed a single orbit of the Earth in 89.1 minutes, travelling at a maximum velocity of 17,400 mph at an altitude of 187.7 miles.

Gainsborough, Thomas (1727-88) English artist, who rivalled REYNOLDS as the most sought-after portrait painter in England. *Mr and Mrs Andrews* (1748) combines 'that branch of painting which they will pay for' (i.e. portraiture) with his own natural inclination for landscape. The discovery of RUBENS's landscapes led to a more grandiose style and a deeper palette of rich browns and greens, e.g. *The Watering Place* (1777). *The Hon. Mrs Graham* (1777) marked Gainsborough's entry into the London arena to compete with Reynolds, who, though he warned his students against Gainsborough's unlearned approach, later admitted the brilliance of his technique.

Gaitskell, Hugh Todd Naylor (1906-63) English leader of the Labour Party, who died with the Premiership almost within his grasp. He was a disciple of CRIPPS, whom he succeeded as Chancellor of the Exchequer in 1950. His introduction of National Health Service charges in that year led to the resignations of BEVAN and Harold WILSON and a long-standing feud with the left wing of the Labour Party. Gaitskell's authority grew rapidly, however, and in 1955 he defeated Bevan in the election for the leadership of the Party, consolidating his position with attacks on EDEN's Suez policy the following year. He is perhaps best remembered for his vow to 'fight and fight and fight again' to reverse a narrow Party Conference vote for unilateral disarmament in 1960, a promise which he fulfilled in 1961. He attempted the modernization of the Party, particularly with regard to modifying the doctrine of the total nationalization of the means of production, proposing the 'shareholder state' as an alternative.

Galbraith, John Kenneth (born 1908) American economist whose works have made him well known to the general public. Five of his best known works are *American Capitalism: The Concept of Countervailing Power* (1952), *The Affluent Society* (1958), *The New Industrial State* (1967), *The Nature of Mass Poverty* (1979) and *The Voice of the Poor* (1983). In general, he takes the position that many accepted theories about consumption are outmoded. An early supporter of and adviser to John F. KENNEDY, he was ambassador to India (1961-3). His autobiography *A Life in Our Times* was published in 1981.

Galen (c. 131-200) Greek physician whose anatomical works formed the basis for medical teaching for more than a millennium. An indefatigable dissector of animals and an accurate observer and describer of what he found, his experiments in physiology resulted in numerous discoveries. His works remained the ultimate medical authority until VESALIUS.

Galileo, Galilei (1564-1642) Italian astronomer, physicist and mathematician, who established the scientific method of testing theories by rigorous and extensive experimentation, one of the first men to use a telescope for astronomy, and discoverer of the principles of motion stated later in NEWTON's first two laws. Galileo was the first man to perceive that mathematics and physics were parts of one and the same area of knowledge. In his astronomical work he greatly improved the telescope and promoted the cosmological theory of COPERNICUS. Galileo's lucid and elegant exposition of his views in his *Letters on the Sunspots* (1613) caused a wide and radical movement of opinion away from the Ptolemaic theory. When, in 1616, some scholars and the Church had the Copernican theory denounced as blasphemous, Galileo wrote the *Dialogue of the Two Great World Systems,* which was hailed throughout Europe as a literary and philosophical masterpiece. Galileo was convicted of heresy in 1633 and forced to recant his views.

Gall, Franz (1758-1828) German physiologist who discovered the difference between the grey (active) and white (connective) matter in the brain, and who pointed out the localization of brain function. He is also remembered as the founder of the now discredited science of phrenology, which relates the shape and bumps of the skull to character.

Gallup, George (1901-84) American public opinion statistician, the first to conduct polls based on scientific sampling methods. The founder and Director of the American Institute of Public Opinion (1935) and its British equivalent (1936), Gallup's 1936 national poll was the only one to forecast correctly ROOSEVELT's re-election.

Galsworthy, John (1867-1933) English novelist and dramatist, best known for *The Forsyte Saga,* a trilogy that studied social change and middle-class acquisitiveness. It began with *The Man of Property* (1906) and ended with *To Let* (1921), and achieved great popularity, both in book form and as a television serial. He wrote two further trilogies about the Forsytes and a number of plays on moral issues. In 1932 Galsworthy was awarded the Nobel Prize for Literature.

Galton, Sir Francis (1822-1911) British geneticist, the founder of eugenics, the science concerned with producing finer types of human being by carefully controlled breeding. He also devised a method of identifying fingerprints.

Gama, Vasco da (c. 1469-1524) Portuguese navigator, commander of the first fleet to sail from Europe to Asia. He left Lisbon in July 1497, with four vessels, the *St Gabriel,* the *St Raphael,* the *Berrio* and a store ship. The fleet reached St Helena Bay, near modern Capetown, in November, and by Christmas Day had rounded the southern tip of Africa and sighted Natal. At Malindi, he found a Muslim pilot who conducted his ships across the Arabian Sea to Calicut (modern Kozhikode), which they reached on 21 May 1498. Although it reached its destination, da Gama's expedition was not entirely successful. Many of his men died of scurvy, and da Gama obtained few of the spices he had hoped for because his trading goods were too shoddy. Da Gama made a second voyage to Calicut in 1502 and returned home with shiploads of riches. He was made Viceroy of India in 1524.

Gandhi, Indira (1917-84) Indian stateswoman and one of the first women to become a Prime Minister. The daughter of Jawaharlal NEHRU, she joined the Congress Party in 1938. She was elected President of the Indian National Congress in 1959. When her father died in 1963 his successor, SHASTRI, appointed her to his government. Following Shastri's death in 1966, she became Prime Minister. In 1975 she was found guilty of breaking the electoral rules in the 1971 elections. She refused to resign, invoked emergency powers and in the 1977 elections her party was defeated. In spite of local support, in 1978 she was expelled from parliament and briefly imprisoned, before making a political comeback. In 1980 her party was victorious, and she was Prime Minister again. In 1984 she was assassinated by Sikh extremists, and her son, Rajid Gandhi was elected her successor.

Gandhi, Mohandas Karamchand (1869-1948) The principal creator of India's independence and most notable exponent of 'passive resistance' as a political and social revolutionary tactic. Gandhi, later known as the Mahatma (saint), was educated in London and called to the Bar in Bombay. After practising there as a barrister, he went to South Africa and persuaded its Indian population to offer passive resistance to the Transvaal government's discrimination against Indians. By 1914 he had won assurances from SMUTS of just treatment for Indian South Africans. He returned to India to lead the Indian National Congress, which was demanding *Swarj* – home rule for India. Gandhi deprecated and discouraged terrorist methods, and used instead passive resistance, boycott of British goods, development of village industries and hunger strikes. As a result, he was imprisoned four times. By 1940, Gandhi's aim had become complete independence for India, which was granted by ATLEE's Labour government after the Second World War (1947). His agreement to the partition of India and Pakistan was bitterly resented by Hindu extremists, one of whom assassinated him on 30 Jan. 1948. The spiritual content of Gandhi's political action should not obscure his considerable talents as an administrator and communicator of his views. His sponsorship of struggling and oppressed peoples made an international impact, and his campaign in India led to a moral reappraisal of British imperialism.

Garbo, Greta (born 1905) Swedish film actress whose real name is Greta Gustafsson. She became famous for her aura of mystery and ledendary romantic beauty. Her silent films include *Torrent* (1926) and *Flesh and the Devil* (1927), but her greatest successes were the sound films *Anna Christie* (1930), *Grand Hotel* (1932), *Queen Christina* (1933), *Anna Karenina* (1935), *Camille* (1936) and the comedy *Ninotchka* (1939). She retired in 1941, and since then has shunned publicity.

Garfield, James Abram (1831-81) American President, who was assassinated after only four months in office. He was a self-made man and strongly antagonistic towards slavery. During the Republican search for a presidential candidate in 1880 – in which 28 ballots had been held without success – the need for a compromise candidate was acknowledged, and Garfield, known to be a hard worker and fine speaker, was declared the Party's candidate on the 36th ballot. In office he showed himself tactless, and his support of civil service reform antagonized both his opponents and a powerful section within his own party. He gave preferential treatment to members of the radical wing of the republican Party, and was shot and mortally wounded by a disappointed office-seeker.

Garibaldi, Giuseppe (1807-82) Italian patriot, who, with CAVOUR, helped to achieve the unification of Italy. A supporter of MAZZINI's Young Italy Movement, he was forced to take refuge in South America (1834), where, during the war between Uruguay and Argentina, he commmanded the troops defending Montevideo (1843). After returning to Italy in 1848 he commanded the defence of the Roman Republic against the French (1849), but was again driven into exile. Later he led guerillas against the Austrians in the region of the Italian lakes (1859). A year later he sailed from Genoa with his 'Thousand Redshirts' and eventually conquered Naples and Sicily, thus forming the nucleus of a united Italy. He then marched northwards and joined forces with Cavour at the Volturno. His conquests, united with those of the Piedmontese, largely achieved the united Italy he had dreamed of. He made two unsuccessful attempts to capture Rome (1862 and 1867) and in 1870 led a volunteer force in the Franco-Prussian War. Garibaldi was the supreme example of the romantic patriot-leader and was greeted with enormous enthusiasm when he visited England in 1864.

Garland, Judy (1922-69) American singer and film actress who gained popularity in the Andy Hardy films and *The Wizard of Oz* (1939). Her other films included *Meet Me in St Louis* (1944), *Easter Parade* (1948) and *A Star is Born* (1954). Her later life was marked by great personal unhappiness, but she made a successful comeback on the international concert circuit, breaking box office records in the 1960s.

Garnerin, André Jacques (1769-1823) Early French aeronaut who, in 1797, was the first man to make a parachute descent in public, jumping over 2000 feet from a balloon. The first man to parachute from an aircraft was Albert Berry at St Louis, Missouri, in 1912.

Garnier, Jean Louis Charles (1825-98) French architect whose Opéra in Paris illustrates the final stage of the evolution of the Baroque in the 19th century, while, at the same time, remaining light and unlaboured. The stage is placed like a jewel in its setting and great emphasis is placed on the richness of the auditorium and foyer.

Garrick, David (1717-79) English actor and theatre manager, who was one of the outstanding men of the theatre of the 18th century. He originated the easy, natural style of acting and made London's Drury Lane Theatre the European centre of dramatic art. His first acting success was as Richard III (1741) and he played all the leading tragic roles of SHAKESPEARE, JONSON and the restoration dramatists. As manager of Drury Lane, from 1747, he pioneered the use of naturalistic backdrops and concealed lighting.

Garrison, William Lloyd (1805-79) American abolitionist, who exerted great influence on the anti-slavery movement. A pacifist, he fought for the anti-slavery cause solely by moral means, his contribution being publicly recognized by LINCOLN. In 1831, he founded the *Liberator* in Boston, which held considerable sway until Garrison closed it down in 1865, after it published the amendment to the constitution abolishing slavery in the United States. He was often the object of mob violence and subject to extreme personal danger.

Gaskell, Mrs Elizabeth (1810-65) English novelist who was brought up in Knutsford, a small northern town, whose way of life is described in her pastoral novels, such as *Cranford* (1853). Having married a Unitarian minister in Manchester, she was also able to give a first-hand picture of the hardships of industrial workers, in novels like *Mary Barton* (1848). She also wrote an important biography, *The Life of Charlotte Brontë* (1857).

Gatling, Richard John (1818-1903) American inventor who perfected a rapid-fire machine gun which fired 1200 shots per minute. The gun, adopted for the US army, was put to use in the later stages of the American Civil War and was in use until the end of the century. As a boy, Gatling helped his father to devise a machine for planting cotton seeds, and also invented a screw propeller for steamboats.

Gaudi, Antoni (1852-1926) Spanish architect, who was one of the most brilliantly inventive of the exponents of Art Nouveau. He worked largely in Barcelona, which contains his enormous, unfinished cathedral La Sagrada Familia and a number of houses. His originality lay in his use of bizarre form and structure, and the brilliant collage of appliqué materials that ornament the surface of his forms.

Gauguin, Paul (1848-1903) French Post-Impressionist painter, whose art was both a development of and a reaction to Impressionism. In 1883, he abandoned a career as a stockbroker to devote himself to painting, and learnt a great deal from PISSARRO and CÉZANNE. Becoming disenchanted with European society, he went to the tropics in 1887, visiting Panama and Martinique. In 1888, in Brittany, he painted the *Vision after the Sermon* in a new style which rejected impressionist naturalism. Synthetism, as this style was called, was a means of trying to express the essence of emotion through the technique of painting, and may be said to have contributed to the development of abstract art. Gauguin visited Tahiti between 1891 and 1893, and returned there in 1895, living in native communities whose life and beliefs he made the subject of his paintings.

Gauss, Karl Friedrich (1777-1855) German mathematician, astronomer, and physicist. He contributed widely to various aspects of pure and applied mathematics: the study of elliptic functions, prime number theory, topology and

Gauguin's studio: a rebel in art, he said of his work 'It does not stink of models, techniques or of pretended rules'.

differential geometry. He also worked in theoretical astronomy, mechanics, electricity and magnetism, optics, statistics and other subjects. Much of his most important work in mathematics was completed before he was 20, and his discoveries in number theory were published in *Disquisitiones Arithmeticae* (1801).

Gautama Buddha (c. 563-c. 483 BC) Indian-born founder of Buddhism (Gautama was his family name, Buddha means 'the enlightened'). Many details of his life story are now held to be legendary, but the outline appears to be that of a well-born, married man, disenchanted and confused about life's meaning in the face of senility, disease and death, who went away in his thirtieth year to seek understanding. He tried the traditional Hindu paths of wisdom, then asceticism, and finding himself despairingly beneath a bodhi tree, vowed not to stir until the mystery of suffering and existence was yielded to him. There he was enlightened with the Four Noble Truths, the basis of Buddhism – that all existence means suffering; suffering follows from desire; suffering ends when desire is extinguished; and to achieve this end one must follow the Eightfold Path. The Buddha gathered a community (Sangha) of monks who, with him, travelled widely to enable others to find enlightenment. They rejected the caste system, and were agnostic about a Creator. The religion founded by Gautama Buddha now has about 70 million adherents.

Gautier, Théophile (1811-72) French novelist, journalist and a major Parnassian poet, who helped to transform the Romantic tradition of the early 19th century into the aestheticism and naturalism of later decades. *Emaux et Camées* (1852), his best-known collection of poetry, is a volume of lyrics, each perfectly chiselled, a monument to Gautier's cult of beauty and purity of form. His famous poem 'L'Art', which claimed that art is the most important thing in life (*'l'art pour l'art'*: art for art's sake) became the keystone for the Parnassian poets.

Gay, John (1685-1732) English dramatist, who wrote *The Beggar's Opera* (1728), his only memorable work, which later became the basis of BRECHT's *Threepenny Opera*. His sequel, *Polly*, was politically offensive to the authorities and not produced until 1777. Gay wrote the libretto for HANDEL's *Acis and Galatea*.

Gay-Lussac, Joseph (1778-1850) French chemist who formulated the law of combined volumes, which showed that gases combined with each other in proportions by volume that can be expressed as small whole numbers (for example, two parts of hydrogen combine with one of oxygen to form water). The law was subsequently used by Jöns BERZELIUS to calculate accurate atomic weights.

Geiger, Hans (1882-1945) German physicist, inventor of the Geiger counter for detecting atomic particles. An assistant of RUTHERFORD, he developed the counter in 1913. A high voltage is applied to a chamber full of gas. The entry of an atomic particle causes an avalanche of ionization and clicking sounds in the headphones indicate the presence and level of radioactivity.

Geijer, Erik Gustaf (1783-1847) Swedish Romantic lyric poet and historian, whose lectures on Scandinavian history paved the way for Swedish Romanticism. His Gothic poems 'The Vikings' and 'The Yeoman Farmer' (1811) and his monumental histories *Annals of the Kingdom of Sweden* (1825) and the unfinished *The History of the Swedes* (1832-6) are considered his best works. He edited the first definitive edition of Swedish folksongs, *Swedish Ballads* (1814-16).

Gemayel, Amin (born 1942) President of the Lebanon since 1982, when his brother Bachir, the President elect, was killed in a bomb explosion. A moderate in the Christian Phalangist Party, he has made tireless efforts to stabilize the delicate balance of power between the Christians and Muslims through compromise and conciliation.

Genet, Jean (born 1910) French dramatist, novelist and chronicler of the underworld. The hardships of his childhood quickly led him into delinquency and crime. It is in his books such as *Our Lady of the Flowers* (1944) and *Thief's Journal* (1949) that he records his experiences of Europe's bars, brothels and prisons. His plays, among the best known of which are *The Maids* (1947) and *The Balcony* (1956), are concerned with an equivocal world of illusions, masks and mirrors.

Genghis Khan (c. 1167-1227) Mongol chief, one of the great conquerors in world history. He inherited a Mongol tribal chiefdom at 13, conquered nearby tribes, and renamed himself Genghis Khan (Very Mighty King). Embarking on a career of world conquest, he welded Central Asia's independent Mongol and Altaic nomads into a 250,000-strong well-drilled, well-armed, fighting machine. From his capital, Karakorum, in northeast Asia, Genghis Khan struck east south and west. He seized northern China (1211-15) and Korea (1218), then (1218-22) ravaged what are now Russian Turkestan, West Pakistan, Iran and southern Russia, razing towns and killing the people, until his empire spanned 4000 miles.

Gentile da Fabriano (c. 1370-1427) Italian artist whose work reveals the decorative characteristics of the international Gothic style. The *Adoration of the Magi* (c. 1422) is typical of his work, with fragile figures and schematic natural forms painted in an archaic manner.

George (4th cent.) Patron saint of England since 1349. He is said to have slain a dragon, but nothing factual is known about him, though attempts to prove that he is a myth are offset by references to him in 6th-century texts.

George IV (1762-1830) Regent (1811-20) and King of Great Britain (1820-30). He was the eldest son of George III, with whom he was on bad terms, partly on account of his friendship with FOX, SHERIDAN and the Whigs, and partly due to his extravagance and moral laxity. On becoming Regent due to his father's indisposition, he supported the existing Tory ministry of PERCEVAL, despite his earlier attachment to the Whigs, who thereafter upheld the cause of his estranged wife Caroline of Brunswick. On his accession, George attempted to divorce Caroline but was unsuccessful and attracted much public hostility by his conduct towards her. His acceptance of more liberally-minded ministers and of reform policies was given with a reluctance which did nothing to arrest the decline in the prestige of the monarchy. But although he was temperamentally difficult, he avoided direct confrontation with his ministers, unlike his father, and brother, WILLIAM IV. He was a notable patron of the arts, commissioning the portrait painter Sir Thomas Lawrence, and the building projects of Regent Street and Regent's Park (1812-13) to the designs of John NASH.

George V (1865-1936) King of Great Britain and Emperor of India (1910-36). He succeeded his father, EDWARD VII. His reign was a difficult one which had to contend with the First World War and, at home, an increasingly democratic and socialist age, marked by industrial unrest, economic depression and the constitutional problems of Ireland. During the war he opposed extreme anti-German feeling but identified himself more closely with the country by adopting the family name of Windsor (1917). When he intervened in politics (as in the case of the Parliament Bill of 1911, or the appointment of BALDWIN as Prime Minister in 1923), he did so on the suggestions of his constitutional advisers. He had a particular attachment to his Indian Empire and was the only British Emperor to visit his territories.

George VI (1895-1952) King of Great Britain (1936-52) and Emperor of India (1936-47). In the First World War he was mentioned in dispatches at the battle of Jutland, but ill-health brought his naval career to an end. His strength of character was shown in his fight against poor health and a noticeable stammer, both of which he conquered. He succeeded to the throne on the abdication of his brother EDWARD VIII in 1936, and less than three years later Britain was at war. The King visited the major theatres of war and endeared himself to his countrymen by staying at Buckingham Palace throughout the worst of the Blitz and broadcasting to the nation. In 1947 he toured South Africa with the Royal Family. His last great public occasion was the opening of the Festival of Britain in 1951.

Gerard, John (1545-c. 1607) English gardener, apothecary and superintendent of Lord BURGHLEY's gardens, who had his own physic garden in Holborn, London. In 1596 he published a catalogue of the plants grown there, including American species such as the tomato and African marigold. His *Herball, or Generall Historie of Plantes* (1597) listed native British plants and about 100 trees and shrubs introduced from abroad.

Gerhardt, Charles (1816-56) French chemist who developed a means of classifying organic compounds, called the theory of types. In collaboration with August Laurent, he suggested that organic compounds could be classified by their relationship to four basic 'types': ammonia, hydrogen, hydrogen chloride and water.

Géricault Théodore (1791-1824) French artist, best known for his boldly colourful sporting scenes and paintings with social themes. Géricault, unlike his contemporaries, painted directly on to the canvas, a technique which, in combination with his eye for detail, lends a dramatic realism to the compositions. Particularly noteworthy are his equestrian scenes and the celebrated work *Raft of the Medusa* (1819), based on a controversial shipwreck of the day.

Geronimo (1829-1909) Chiricahua Apache chief, who led one of the last serious Indian revolts against white supremacy in North America. His surrender in 1886 ended the history of Indian stands against the white man.

Gershwin, George 1898-1937) American composer and pianist who extended jazz into a concert idiom with his opera *Porgy and Bess*. This original material incorporated the spirit of jazz and negro blues. *Rhapsody in Blue* (1924), written to a commission from Paul Whiteman, was his first serious composition. Later Gershwin made his own orchestrations in such works as the *Piano Concerto* and the suite, *An American in Paris*.

Gesell, Arnold (1880-1961) American psychologist, known as the father of child psychology. His work emphasizes the constitutional aspect and cyclical nature of mental development in the child. He based his researches for the most part on the simple, accurate observation of children's behaviour (often using film cameras and two-way mirrors), and was able to establish norms, both in the ages at which specific developments occur, and in their order. His many books on the subject have helped to make child psychology popular among laymen.

Gesner, Konrad von (1516-65) Swiss physician, whose encyclopedic work, *A Catalogue of Animals* (1551-8), is considered by many to have been the starting point of modern zoology. A purely descriptive work, it reflects von Gesner's non-analytical approach to biology.

Getty, Jean Paul (1892-1976) US businessman and art collector. Reputedly one of history's richest men, he was principal owner of the Getty Oil Company.

Ghazali, Abu Mohammed al- (1058-1111) Influential Islamic mystic and theologian whose chief book, *The Revival of the Religious Sciences,* sets out, often in antagonistic terms, the religious heritage of Islam in a synthesis of orthodox dogma with Sufi mysticism. He also attacked the rationalist approach to theology in *The Incoherence of the Philosophers,* asserting that the religious life represented a higher form of understanding than that achievable by reason. In spite of AVERRÖES's counter-attack, this denigration of Arabic philosophy led to its decline.

Ghiberti, Lorenzo (1378-1455) Florentine sculptor, much of whose career was spent on the ornamentation of reliefs for the doors of the Baptistry of Florence Cathedral. Ghiberti was engaged in many other activities and had a large workshop of assistants in which many famous Florentine painters and sculptors were trained.

Ghirlandaio, Domenico (1449-94) Florentine painter, in whose workshop MICHELANGELO spent three years as an apprentice. Important frescoes by him are in Florence (Sta Maria Novella and Sta Trinita); he also worked in the Sistine Chapel, Rome. The religious themes of his frescoes are offset by bourgeois Italian settings and details, and his scenes sometimes contain portraits of contemporary Florentines.

Giacometti, Alberto (1901-66) 'Space is hollowed to build up an object and, in its turn, the object creates space,' said Giacometti, Swiss sculptor and draughtsman. Between 1925 and 1930, he created objects largely from memory, giving sculptural expression to a world of dreams. His figures, often individually placed, or arranged in small groups, form a spatial texture derived from their visual relationships, as in *Project for a City Square,* (1932). To stress their fragility, he mounted his figures on a heavy base, as in *Female Figure* (1946-7).

Gibbons, Christopher see GIBBONS, Orlando

Gibbons, Edward see GIBBONS, Orlando

Gibbons, Ellis see GIBBONS, Orlando

Gibbons, Grinling (1648-1720) English sculptor, outstanding representative of the English decorative style of the Late Stuart Period (*c.* 1668 onwards) mainly through his wood carvings at Windsor, Hampton Court, Middlesex, and St Paul's, London.

Gibbons, John Heysham (1903-73) American surgeon, who developed the first artificial heart-lung machine, which was used in May 1953. This, and later developments, although not yet practical replacements for the heart, have been used widely during surgery. With the restoration of normal heart function and circulation, the patient's life expectancy is often comparable to that of a person with a normal heart.

Gibbons, Orlando (1583-1625) English composer of Anglican church music. Gibbons, organist of Westminster Abbey, was probably the finest keyboard player of his day, whose church music includes some 40 anthems and a single set of highly distinguished madrigals. Gibbons's brothers Edward and Ellis were also composers and a few of their works survive. His son, Christopher, was organist at Westminster Abbey and private organist to CHARLES II.

Gibbs, James (1682-1754) Scottish architect, who designed St Martin-in-the-Fields and St Mary-le-Strand. The Radcliffe Camera at Oxford, one of his best-known buildings, reveals his debt to Christopher WREN.

Gibbs, Josiah Willard (1839-1903) American physicist, who founded chemical thermodynamics. Having studied the work on thermodynamics by Nicolas CARNOT, James JOULE and Lord KELVIN, Gibbs applied their approaches to chemical reactions. In the 1870s he identified the quantities, such as free energy and chemical potential, that underlie all chemical reactions, and worked out the mathematical basis of what was to become modern chemical thermodynamics.

Gide, André (1869-1951) French novelist and literary critic renowned for his meditative *Journals,* covering the years 1889-1949. In his work, Gide is perpetually torn between the puritan and the pagan in himself, the Christian and the admirer of NIETZSCHE, whose influence is apparent in Gide's defiant exhortation to his readers to assert their personal freedom in *Les Nourritures Terrestres* (1897). Among his other well-known works are *L'Immortaliste* (1902), *La Porte Etroite* (1909), the farcical tale *Les Caves du Vatican* (1914), in which the hero commits murder, Gide's most famous example of the motiveless act *(l'acte gratuit),* and *Les Faux-Monnayeurs* (1926), an experiment in the art of fiction and an important landmark in the development of the French novel. Gide was an editor of *Nouvelle Revue française,* and won a Nobel Prize for Literature in 1947.

Gielgud, Sir John (born 1904) English actor and director, considered the greatest Hamlet of his generation. He has played most major English classical roles.

Giffard, Henri (1825-82) French aeronautical engineer, who in 1852 made the first powered flight in an airship. It was fitted with a three horse-power steam engine driving a three-bladed propeller. The machine paved the way for the rigid, powered airships of the late 19th century. In 1859, Giffard invented an apparatus to inject feed water into steam engine boilers, which prevented them running out of steam when not in motion.

Gilbert, Sir Humphrey (1539-83) English soldier and navigator who claimed England's first colony in North America, in Newfoundland. A half-brother of Sir Walter RALEIGH, Gilbert was granted a charter in 1578 to explore and colonize North America. His first expedition failed, but he eventually equipped another five ships, and reached Newfoundland (1583), where he claimed an area for ELIZABETH I, but did not found a permanent colony. He explored to the south, then sailed for England, but was drowned in a storm off the Azores.

Gilbert, William (1544-1603) English physician whose treatise *De magnete* (1600) is a model of scientific method. By studying the behaviour of freely suspended magnetic needles near magnetized iron spheres, he saw that the Earth behaves like a huge magnet whose poles do not quite coincide with its geographical ones. He also introduced the word electricity, from the Greek *electron,* meaning amber, a substance that becomes 'electrified' when rubbed.

Gilbert, Sir William Schwenck (1836-1911) English humorous poet and librettist who collaborated with Sir Arthur SULLIVAN on an immensely successful series of 14 comic operas. His lyrics reveal an exuberant, often macabre humour and a talent for inventive rhymes.

Giles, Carl (born 1916) English cartoonist whose work, which has appeared in the *Sunday Express* and *Daily Express* since 1942, exhibits his feeling for linear perspective.

Giles, Ernest (1835-97) English-born Australian explorer who crossed the deserts of southern and Western Australia. In the course of four expeditions (1872-6), he explored and named the Gibson Desert, and made a formidable round trip of about 3000 miles from Beltana along the 30th parallel to Perth in five months. He returned approximately along the 25th parallel and south to Adelaide.

Gill, Eric (1882-1940) English sculptor and typographer, who designed the widely used Gill Sans-Serif, Perpetua and Joanna typefaces. His engravings for the Golden Cockerel Press, notably the type and design for *The Four Gospels* (1931), brought him international fame.

Gillette, King Camp (1855-1932) American inventor who, in 1895, devised the modern safety razor which had throw-away blades and a toothed guard, allowing the cutting edge to pass over the uneven surface to be shaved.

Gillray, James (1757-1815) English political and social caricaturist of the reign of George III and the Regency, whose savage caricatures had an enormous vogue and a considerable influence on public opinion.

Ginsberg, Allen (born 1926) American poet regarded as a leading figure of the Beat Movement. He voiced the spirit of protest prevalent among the youth of the 1950s and 1960s, especially in *Howl and Other Poems* (1956), a cry of lamentation for the sickness of urban America. His poems have been politically motivated, attacking authoritarianism in such collections as *Reality Sandwiches* (1963) and *Planet News* (1969).

Giordano, Luca (1632-1705) Italian painter, a pupil of RIBERA. He travelled widely in Italy and his work successively reflects the styles of CARAVAGGIO, PIETRO DA CORTONA and the Venetian painters. In 1692 he went to Spain, where he painted the ceilings in the Escoriál.

Giorgione (c. 1476-1510) Italian artist of the Venetian Renaissance, and pupil of Giovanni BELLINI, whose influence is found in Giorgione's first important religious work, the *Castelfranco Madonna* (1504). Only a few paintings can be definitely attributed to him, one of the most famous of which is the *Tempest.* This painting is historically important as it is the earliest picture in which the mood of a landscape is captured, and also because it is a small painting intended for a private collection rather than for a church. Giorgione's technique of 'trembling' brush strokes of fine

Cave painting, Lascaux, France *c.*15,000-10,000 BC

Egyptian glazed faience tiles *c.*1198-1166 BC

Romanesque fresco by Giotto *c.*1296-1304

Late Gothic triptych: 1428

Adoration of the Magi by Bottic

Rape of the Daughters of Leucippus by Rubens *c.*1615

Across countless centuries, Man has celebrated the world around him, his gods and his beliefs, in his art. Some of these pictures—the early examples— are by anonymous craftsmen; others were painted by masters whose names have come down the centuries with their works —and who are mentioned in *Who Did What*. The talents of the long-vanished cave- man and those of modern painters such as Cézanne and Picasso have a tangible link—a concern with the immediate facts of life, the animals with whom prehistoric man lived in harmony, the tablecloth and fruit which inspired Cézanne. Between them lie the arts of old Egypt, of Byzantium and Rome, of the giants of the Renaissance, eras in which inspiration was drawn from religion and its deities and the god-like representation of rulers

The Fifer by Manet 1866

Pompeiian wall painting *c.*AD 65-70

Byzantine mosaic: The *Baptism of Christ* 5th cent.

c.1477

David with Goliath's Head by Caravaggio *c.*1606

John the Baptist by Leonardo da Vinci *c.*1506

Pigeon with Baby Peas by Picasso 1912

Apples and Oranges by Cézanne *c.*1895-1900

disconnected lines and dots makes the entire image on the canvas appear to vibrate and focuses the attention of the onlooker on the relationship between individual objects as affected by colour and light. Giorgione's influence was extensive and his work with colour and light influenced TITIAN and the entire tradition of Venetian painting.

Giotto (c. 1266-1337) Florentine artist, who was the first painter whose works exhibit a concern for both naturalism and emotional content, the major preoccupations of artists until recent times. His first important work was the fresco cycle of the *Legend of St Francis* in the Upper Church at Assisi (*c.* 1300), a series of murals which gave visual form to the humanity of the saint. His best-preserved and most characteristic works are, however, the scenes from the lives of Sts Joachim and Anne and the Virgin and the *Life and Passion of Christ* in the Arena Chapel, Padua (*c.* 1305). These important frescoes reveal his rejection of the flat stylized forms of the Byzantine tradition in favour of figures of solidity and weight whose relationship to each other contributes to a sense of space and have an unprecedented dramatic power. The emotionally charged content of frescoes such as the *Lamentation* is achieved with an economy and directness which was later admired by MASACCIO and MICHELANGELO.

Giovanni da Fiesole, Fra see ANGELICO, Fra

Giraudoux, Jean (1882-1944) French dramatist who wrote *Siegfried* (1928), *Amphytrion '38* (1929), *The Trojan War Will Not Take Place* (1935) and other plays. His success owed much to his collaboration with the director, Louis Jouvet, which began with *Siegfried. The Madwomen of Chaillot* was successfully produced in London and New York. *Tiger at the Gates, Duel of Angels* and *Judith* were translated by Christopher Fry.

Giscard d'Estaing, Valéry see ESTAING, Valéry Giscard d'

Gislebertus (12th cent.) French Romanesque sculptor. The great imagination shown in his work, ranging from the tender to the powerful, and from small vignettes to the great tympanum relief of the *Last Judgement* (*c.* 1135), Autun Cathedral, inspired generations of carvers.

Gissing, George (1857-1903) English novelist whose work gives a grim, realistic picture of industrial poverty and despair. In his numerous novels he was influenced by DICKENS's technique. His principal work, *New Grub Street* (1891), portrays the jealousies and intrigues of the London literary world and the difficulty of artistic integrity. Gissing suffered from extreme poverty and an unhappy marriage, and in *The Private Papers of Henry Rycroft* (1903) portrayed a man in similar circumstances.

Gladstone, William Ewart (1809-98) The greatest British reforming statesman of the 19th century. First elected an MP in 1832, he was appointed President of the Board of Trade by PEEL in 1843, but after Peel's defeat in 1846 he was kept out of office until 1852 by his belief in free trade. As Chancellor of the Exchequer (1852-5 and 1858-66), he began a series of reforms by cutting tariffs and government expenditure. He became Leader of the Liberal Party in 1866 and Prime Minister in 1868. His first administration (1868-74) reformed the legal system, education and the army, disestablished the Church of Ireland and passed the Irish Land Act, and established the secret ballot at elections. During his second ministry (1880-5) his government carried the Third Reform Act of 1884, but was discredited by GORDON's death and Britain's defeats in the first Boer War (1881). Gladstone's third ministry (1886) fell when the Liberal Party split over his proposals for Irish Home Rule, which were opposed by CHAMBERLAIN and his followers. His fourth ministry (1892-4) was preoccupied with a further unsuccessful attempt to procure Home Rule. Like his chief opponent DISRAELI, Gladstone was a great orator. His political career was founded upon strong religious principles.

Glenn, John Herschel (born 1921) American experimental military test pilot, the first American astronaut in the Mercury capsule, Friendship 7, to orbit the Earth (20 Feb. 1962). This he did three times in just under five hours, covering a distance of 81,000 miles at an altitude of 160 miles. He was elected to the US Senate from Ohio in 1972.

Glidden, Joseph Farwell (1813-1906) American farmer who, in 1873, devised a reliable machine for the manufacture of barbed wire in quantity. Barbed wire fencing played an important part in the ranching of the American West and became used increasingly in military defence and during the First World War. Entanglements stretched from Switzerland to the English Channel.

Glinka, Mikhail (1804-57) Russian composer of *Russlan and Ludmilla* (1842), which, based on a PUSHKIN fairy-tale, had a sense of colour and fantasy that made it the first Russian musical work to be recognized outside his country. He travelled in Italy and Germany to study European musical traditions, and his first opera, *A Life for the Tsar* (1836), while incorporating Russian folk elements, owed a great deal to Italian operatic models.

Gluck, Christoph von (1714-87) German composer who reformed opera by insisting, in the preface to his work *Alcestis* (1767), that opera return to one of its basic principles – the subordination of the music to the drama. He wrote many operas to Italian and French librettos, the most famous of which was *Orpheus and Eurydice* (1762).

Gnaeus Pompeius Magnus see POMPEY

Godard, Jean-Luc (born 1930) French film director, at first associated with other directors, such as Truffaut, Chabrol and Resnais in the Nouvelle Vague of 1959-60 and has since become one of the most influential and controversial figures in contemporary cinema.

Goddard, Robert Hutchings (1882-1945) American physicist and pioneer of rocketry. The history of rockets as fireworks and in war dates back to the 13th century, but all early devices used solid, gunpowder-like fuel. In 1926,

The year after Gagarin first circled the Earth, John Glenn put America on terms with the Russians in a three-orbit flight

Goddard launched his revolutionary rocket on liquid fuels, the power on which modern rocketry is based. Goddard later pioneered the use of liquefied gases as propellants, rocket steering by the combination of gyroscopes and movable vanes in the exhaust gases, and instrument-carrying rockets. He also patented the multi-stage rocket.

Godunov, Alexander (born 1949) Russian ballet dancer who defected during the Bolshoi Ballet's tour of America (1979). He became the youngest principal dancer with the Bolshoi in 1971, and the first member to seek asylum in the West. A virtuoso dancer with great dramatic ability, he joined the classically biased American Ballet Theatre.

Godunov, Boris Fedorovich (c. 1552-1605) Tsar of Russia (1598-1605). Godunov founded many towns to civilize the eastern regions, recovered lands lost to Sweden and encouraged cultural and trading contacts with western Europe. In his domestic policy, Godunov favoured the middle classes at the expense of the old nobility and peasants, and his binding of peasants to the life-long service of one landowner rigidly entrenched serfdom.

Goebbels, Joseph (1897-1945) German politician and Nazi propagandist. As one of HITLER's closest followers, he was put in charge of the National Socialist Party's propaganda in 1929, and was Minister for Propaganda and National Enlightenment from 1933 to 1945. His skill in arousing anti-Semitism and in exploiting the public's basest sentiments made Goebbels one of the most dangerous men ever to hold political office. When, in 1945, it became clear that Germany had lost the War, he shot his wife and children, then committed suicide.

Goering, Hermann (1893-1946) German Nazi leader and creator of the Luftwaffe. During the First World War he served with distinction as a pilot in the famous Richthofen squadron. Goering was one of HITLER's earliest associates and helped to foster Nazi party contacts with industrialists and politicians before Hitler achieved power in 1933. He laid the basis of the police forces later controlled by HIMMLER and authorized the detention camps for political, religious and racial suspects. He was chairman of Germany's four-year rearmament plan (1936). Following the early German victories in the Second World War, which were due largely to the Luftwaffe, he was made *Reichsmarschall* (1940). He remained important in the Nazi hierarchy until at least 1941, but thereafter the failure of the Luftwaffe to maintain its ascendancy in the air and Goering's own indolence reduced his prestige with Hitler. Towards the end of the war, as Hitler's successor-designate he attempted to negotiate an armistice with the Allies. As a result, and due largely to the influence of Bormann, he was accused of treason and defeatism. At Nuremburg, in 1946, he was tried and sentenced to death but poisoned himself.

Goes, Hugo van der (c. 1440-82) Flemish painter whose style, as seen in the central Adoration panel of the famous *Portinari Altarpiece* (*c.* 1476), reveals the painstaking realism of Flemish painting enhanced by a marked emotional intensity.

Goethe, Johann Wolfgang von (1749-1832) German poet, novelist, dramatist, critic, politician, scientist, painter and philosopher, who regarded as his province the entire range of human knowledge, and excelled in many fields. His central philosophical principle was the concept of organic growth, which emerged in his biological and zoological work and in his imaginative writings. His supreme dramatic achievement, *Faust,* completed in the last years of his life, is a representation of man's unceasing search for breadth and depth of experience. His outstanding novels are *Die Leiden des Jungen Werthers* (1774), which Goethe based upon the emotions of his characters, rather than on a rational, 18th-century sytem of values, and *Wilhelm Meister* (1812), which was based closely on events in his own life. Goethe also wrote treatises on botany and optics and was a pioneer of the theory of evolution. A journey to Italy (1786) gave him the inspiration for *Römische Elegien,* translated by W. H. AUDEN and E. Mayer, and the enthusiasm to express dramatically his humanistic ideals in *Iphigenie auf Tauris* (1787). At the same time he completed *Egmont,* an historical drama which expanded Goethe's fundamental belief in the external forces which motivate men's actions, a concept which found its ultimate and most compelling expression in *Faust.*

Gogh, Vincent van (1853-90) 'I want to say something comforting, as music is comforting. I want to paint men and women with something of the eternal.' So wrote van Gogh, son of a Dutch pastor whose extremely popular work is unique in its powerful rhythmic drawing and expressive colour. He began to paint in 1880, after an unsuccessful period as an evangelist. His early pictures, before he went to Paris in 1886, are of peasants and the land they worked, e.g. *Potato Eaters* (1885), a picture of a peasant family's meal-time. In Paris, van Gogh met SEURAT, GAUGIN and PISSARRO. The impact of Impressionism upon him was immediate: his palette brightened, he became technically more versatile. In 1888 he moved to Arles in Provence, and there, in a period of insanity after a quarrel with Gauguin, he cut off his own ear. Two years later, in July 1890, he committed suicide. It was during these two years, however, that van Gogh painted his best-known works, a series of portraits and landscapes that now, in reproduction, enjoy a huge popularity. Van Gogh's collected letters are highly informative about his life and are also a moving human document.

Gogol, Nikolai Vasilievich (1809-52) Russian novelist and dramatist, author of *The Government Inspector* (1836), a satirical drama about bureaucracy, and *Dead Souls* (1842), a novel about an adventurer, the purchaser of the souls of serfs who died after the last census but who exist in law until the next, thus achieving for himself a 'prosperous' status. *The Overcoat* (1842), another of Gogol's most celebrated works, is the story of a poorly paid clerk in a government office, and is based on his own experiences. From his Ukrainian Cossack background, Gogol wrote many stories and sketches of Ukrainian life, collected in *Evenings on a Farm near Dikanka* (1831), which includes some *Cossack Tales* (enlarged and rewritten in 1842). After 1836 Gogol spent many years travelling, during which period he wrote *Selected Passages from Correspondence with Friends* (1847), a collection of essays in defence of the Tsarist régime and its institutions which provoked much criticism in Russia. Seeking comfort in religion he embarked on a pilgrimage to Palestine in 1848 but returned in the grip of a religious fanaticism, and later destroyed some of his manuscripts.

Golding, William (born 1911) English novelist whose books examine the primitive urges of man. *The Lord of the Flies* (1954) is a disturbing picture of children marooned on an island, producing 'evil as a bee produces honey'. His second novel, *The Inheritors* (1955), is an imaginative work concerning the extermination of Neanderthal man by *Homo Sapiens*. Later novels are *The Spire* (1964), *The Pyramid* (1967), *Darkness Visible* (1979) and *Rites of Passage* (1980). He won a Nobel Prize for Literature (1983).

Goldmark, Sir Peter Carl (1906-1977) Hungarian-born engineer who developed a colour television system (1940) and the long-playing gramophone record (1948). The microgroove record, playing at 33⅓ rpm and with 250 grooves to the inch, was made possible only by the development of suitable plastics.

Goldoni, Carlo (1707-93) Italian dramatist whose work led to written parts replacing the fixed characters and improvisation by actors of the Commedia dell'Arte. He wrote more than 200 plays in Italian, French or Venetian dialect, many of them realistic comedies, mildly anti-aristocratic, reflecting contemporary life in Venice. Only a few of them are still performed today, notably *La Locandiera* (1753), which was one of Eleonara DUSE's favourite parts.

Goldsmith, Oliver (c. 1728-74) Irish author, best known for *The Vicar of Wakefield* (1766), one of the first novels to make a popular blend of sentiment, domesticity and middle-class morality. His poetry is classical, 'The Deserted Village' (1770) showing a moral concern about the effects of the Industrial Revolution. His most famous play, *She Stoops to Conquer* (1773), was a success, and is still revived. Always in dire need, Goldsmith did much hack work for booksellers and journals, and tried, unsuccessfully, throughout his life, to set up as a physician. He was a member of JOHNSON's literary circle.

Goldwyn, Samuel (1882-1974) American film producer who was for many years one of the most influential and powerful men in Hollywood. His Goldwyn Pictures Corporation was one of the companies amalgamated to form M-G-M in 1924. He became famous as the discoverer of Greta GARBO and for his insistence on producing family entertainment films, including *The Best Years of Our Lives* – which won him an Academy Award in 1947 – *Guys and Dolls* (1955) and *Porgy and Bess* (1959).

Goncourt, Edmond Louis Antoine de (1822-96) and Jules Alfred Huot de (1830-70) French novelists, historians and dramatists, authors of the famous *Journal,* an invaluable record of contemporary life. Begun in 1851, it was continued by Edmond after his brother's death, and provided a series of fascinating glimpses of French society and observations on leading artists and writers of the day, particularly FLAUBERT, ZOLA, DAUDET, TURGENEV and their circle. The Goncourt brothers produced some moving and original novels, including studies of psychiatric disorders, such as *Germinie Lacerteux* (1865) and *Madame Gervaisais* (1869).

Gongo Musa (c. 1307-c. 1332) Sudanese *mansa* (emperor) of Mali who, by inheritance and conquest, ruled over most of Africa southwest of the Sahara. A Muslim like his Sudanese predecessors, he made a pilgrimage to Mecca, debasing Egypt's coinage with the huge quantity of gold brought back by his splendid retinue. The effect of his personality led to the spread of Islamic culture to West Africa and to the making of the first European map of West Africa (1375).

Góngora y Argote, Luis de (1561-1627) Spanish poet, who has had an appreciable influence on contemporary Spanish poetry. His works are written in two styles, some consisting of short poems, romances, *letrillas* and sonnets. His other style was *gongorismo,* or *culteranismo,* a more obscure style, full of wordplay, dislocated syntax and mythological allusion, as in *The Fable of Polifemo and Galeta* (1612-13). For three centuries his name was synonymous with obscurity and pedantry. He is now considered one of Spain's most important poets.

Goodman, Benny (born 1909) US musician and bandleader whose playing of both Jazz and Classical clarinet earned him worldwide fame.

Goodyear, Charles (1800-60) American inventor who developed vulcanized rubber. From about 1830 he started experimenting on methods to improve the properties of natural rubber and in 1844 patented the process of forming vulcanized rubber by heating rubber-sulphur mixtures at high temperatures. Concurrently, Charles Macintosh and Thomas Hancock were working on the same problem in Britain, where they took out key patents two months before Goodyear.

Gordon, Charles George (1833-85) English general, famous for his ten-month defence of Khartoum. He served in the Crimean War (1854), then entered the employment of the Chinese Manchu government (1860-5). His explorations, and his quelling of the Taiping rebellion (1864), earned him the nickname of 'Chinese Gordon'. From China he went to Egypt (1874) and became governor of the Sudan (1877-80), where he attempted to suppress slave-trading. After some time in South Africa he was sent to the Sudan again in 1884, to rescue Egyptian garrisons cut off by the forces of the Mahdi (the Muslim 'Messiah', who roused Sudan in revolt against Egyptian rule in 1882). He was besieged in Khartoum, and after ten months of resistance, was killed shortly before a relief force arrived. Gordon's character was complex. He was both a mystic and a man of action, with a marked sense of his own destiny. In England he was noted for his practical evangelical Christianity and was a hero of the Victorian public.

Gordon, Lord George (1751-93) Protestant extremist of Scottish descent who inspired the Gordon Riots in London. In 1780, he organized and led a march of Protestants to Parliament, petitioning for the repeal of the Catholic Relief Act, which freed Catholics from certain legal disadvantages. Reinforced by other disaffected groups, the Protestants began a riot which ravaged London for six days. Gordon was acquitted of treason but later imprisoned for libelling MARIE ANTOINETTE. He died in jail, converted to Judaism.

Gorky, Maxim (1868-1936) Russian novelist and dramatist, whose best-known books are the autobiographical *Childhood, In the World* and *My Universities,* studies of life in pre-revolutionary Russia. His popularity, particularly with the Russian working class, stemmed mainly from his realistic, boisterous short stories, portraying tramps and social outcasts. His famous play, *The Lower Depths,* was popular more for its political content than its dramatic quality. He was arrested twice for his revolutionary views.

Gottwald, Klement (1896-1953) Leader of the Communist *coup d'état* in Czechoslovakia. After spending the war years in Moscow, he returned to Czechoslovakia in 1945 and the following year became Prime Minister of a coalition government, democratically appointed by BENEŠ. Through the gradual infiltration of Communists into the organs of government, particularly the police, Gottwald ruled within the constitution for almost two years, until in February 1948 he gained complete control in a bloodless *coup de'état*, and Czechoslovakia followed in the path of Hungary, Bulgaria and Rumania. A firm supporter of the Moscow line, he became the dictator of a state constructed on the Stalinist model.

Goudy, Frederic (1865-1947) American printer and typographer, who founded the Village Press in Park Ridge, Illinois (1905). He designed all his own type, some of which is still used today, particularly Goudy Old Style.

Gould, Glenn (1932-82) Canadian pianist and composer who, as a child prodigy, was a soloist with the Toronto Symphony Orchestra at the age of 14. He was famous for his interpretations of the Romantic composers and J. S. BACH. His first string quartet was premiered in 1956. Later he concentrated on recordings, particularly of the works of Bach and BEETHOVEN.

Gould, Jay (1836-92) American financier, speculator and railway tycoon. Having acquired capital from a leather tanning business he became notorious for the promotion, sale and manipulation of railway company stock. Particularly dubious were his dealings against Cornelius VANDERBILT in connection with the Erie Railroad (1867-72). In 1869 he and his associates tried to corner the gold market and in the 1870s he juggled for control of the Union, Kansas, Denver, Central and Missouri Pacific railroads. By 1890 he owned half the railway mileage in the southwest of the US. He owned the *New York World* (1879-83) and controlled the Western Union Telegraph Co. His will disclosed a personal fortune of $77 million, but it was believed that the much larger real total had been concealed and was probably tied up in trusts for his six children.

Gorky wandered Russia, searching for work. He educated himself as he went along, and became a writer

Gounod Charles-François (1818-93) French composer and conductor remembered today for his opera *Faust* (1857), based on Part I of GOETHE's masterpiece, and for his *Ave Maria,* a 'meditation' on the first prelude of J. S. BACH's *Well-Tempered Clavier*. A pupil of Halévy, he won the Prix de Rome and wrote many church compositions. Gounod completed 13 other operas, and during a period in England (1870-5) was first conductor of the Royal Choral Society.

Gowon, Yakubu (born 1934) Nigerian soldier-politician, and Head of State, who crushed the Biafran secessionist revolt of 1967-70. As a member of the Angas tribe, Gowon was born a Christian. His education was completed at Sandhurst Military Academy in England, and in 1957 he was commissioned into the Nigerian army. While serving with a UN Force in the Congo during the war of 1960-1, he became a strong opponent of secession by member regions of African federal republics. In 1966, the government of Sir Abubaka Tafawa Balewa was overthrown in a coup which resulted in the establishment of a military government under General Ironsi. In July 1966 Ironsi (an Ibo) was himself deposed and murdered in an anti-Ibo counter-revolution. Gowon was appointed Supreme Commander of the military forces and head of the federal military government which was then set up.

Goya y Lucientes, Francisco José de (1746-1828) Spanish artist, whose portraiture combines Neoclassical control with realistic perception and a romantic feeling for form and colour, e.g. *The Maja Nude* and *The Maja Clothed.* He was court painter for 53 years and though political expediency played its part at times in the commissions he accepted, he never flattered his sitters, nor, like the Neo-classicists, idealized them, e.g. *The Portrait of Charles III in Hunting Dress* and that of *Josefa Bayeau.* Nevertheless the distinction in style and subject-matter between his commissioned and his non-commissioned works reveal the depth of Goya's own convictions. When the subject is war, e.g. *The Disasters of War* (1810-13), painted after the French invasion, realism and imaginative creation meet to expose the full horror to his audience. In 1792 Goya fell seriously ill; *The Flaggellants,* a group of 12 small paintings which concentrate on the terror of suffering; and the drawings for the 80 etchings, *Los Caprichos* (caricatures that savagely disclose the abuses in Church, Court and State), were the results of this period of illness and depression.

Goyen, Jan van (1596-1656) Dutch topographical painter, whose panoramic views of the Dutch countryside are characterized by their low horizons and effects of spaciousness, enhanced by features such as distant sailing boats, windmills or tiny figures.

Grace, William Gilbert (1848-1915) English cricketer who was the foremost influence on modern batting and bowling techniques. He scored nearly 55,000 runs and took nearly 2900 wickets in first-class cricket in a playing career of more than 50 years. He was also a medical practitioner.

The demon doctor, W. G. Grace remains the greatest legend in cricket

Graham, Martha (born 1894) American dancer and choreographer and one of the most influential figures in modern dance. She rejected classical Russian ballet and stressed bodily movements as expressions of states of mind, synchronizing breathing, movement, muscular co-ordination and balance in ways which permitted new fluid forms of dancing barefoot. Working with American composers, such as Aaron COPLAND, she wove more than 100 ballets around social, psychological and literary themes.

Graham, William Franklin ('Billy') (born 1918) US evangelist who is estimated to have been heard by more than 60 million people. He was the confidant of several presidents, including TRUMAN, EISENHOWER, KENNEDY, JOHNSON and NIXON.

Grahame, Kenneth (1859-1932) Scottish writer of children's stories. His chief work, *The Wind in the Willows* (1908), was dramatized by A. A. MILNE as *Toad of Toad Hall.*

Grainger, Percy Aldridge (1882-1961) Australian-born composer and pianist who wrote the perennial *Country Gardens,* based on a morris tune. The success of this and its companion pieces has tended to obscure his work in folk music. In 1912, Grainger recorded *Brigg Fair,* upon which DELIUS based his orchestral work. Grainger lived in America from 1915 and became a US citizen. In later life he was occupied with experimental composition.

Granados, Enrique (1867-1916) Spanish conductor, pianist and composer whose best-known work is the opera *Goyescas.*

Grandier, Urbain (1590-1634) French parish priest, notorious for his love-affairs, who was falsely charged with bewitching a convent of nuns at Loudun in France. Although the nuns co-operated with his accusers by pretending to go into convulsions and hysterics, the charge failed. Accused a second time, Grandier, who had provoked the enmity of Cardinal RICHELIEU, was tried for witchcraft, tortured and burned at the stake.

Grant, Ulysses Simpson (1822-85) US President who, as Commander of the Union army during the American Civil War, defeated the forces of the Confederacy under LEE. Grant fought in the Mexican War (1846-8), retired, then re-enlisted when the Civil War started and was appointed Major-General (1862). After receiving Lee's surrender at Appomattox (April 1865) he served for two years as Secretary for War and was then elected President, in which office he served two terms (1869-77).

Grass, Günter (born 1927) German novelist, poet and dramatist, whose famous novel *The Tin Drum* (1959) is a grotesque survey of modern Germany, from the Third Reich to the 'economic miracle'. Other novels include *Cat and Mouse* (1961) and *Dog Years* (1963). Grass has also written poems and short plays, in the manner of BECKETT, which embody his preoccupation with the 'absurd'. More recent novels are *Local Anaesthetic* (1969), *The Flounder* (1977) and *The Meeting at Telgte* (1979).

Grassman, Hermann (1809-77) German mathematician, who discovered the calculus of extension, a kind of algebra of geometry, in which geometrical entities are represented by symbols, a notion going back to LEIBNIZ. From this work, later German mathematicians developed vector calculus, which was later widely used in various branches of pure and applied mathematics.

Grattan, Henry (1746-1820) Irish statesman, champion of Irish independence and religious reform. Trained as a barrister, he entered the Irish Parliament, where his oratory helped to end Great Britain's veto over Irish legislation (1782). He demanded reforms to benefit Irish Catholics and peasants, but could not stop the Act of Union (1800), which helped Ireland's Protestant minority government to keep control over the Catholic majority. He continued the fight for Catholic emancipation after the Union.

Graves, Robert (born 1895) English poet and novelist who pursues an interest in myth and religion. His early verse reflects the effect of his service in the First World War. The poetry of his middle period, between the wars, avoids emotion, while the later poetry returns more to natural feelings. The prose works, *I Claudius* (1934) and *Claudius the God,* are imaginative recreations of the Roman mind. Reminiscences and social history in *Goodbye to All That* (1929) and *The Long Weekend* (1940) are graphically descriptive of the English society of the 1920s and 1930s. Other works are *The White Goddess* (1947), *The Crowning Privilege* (1955) and *They Hanged My Saintly Billy* (1980).

Gray, Thomas (1716-71) English scholar and poet, most widely known for his 'Elegy Written in a Country Churchyard' (1750), a melancholy reflection on life and death, which achieved great popularity. Gray twice refused the Poet Laureateship.

Greco, El (1541-1614) Cretan-born artist, with a highly individual style, characterized by asymmetry of composition, acid colours, elongated figures and ecstatic expressions and gestures. He is believed to have trained under TITIAN, and lived, from 1577 until the end of his life, in Toledo, where he received two major commissions for altarpieces (S Domingo el Antiguo and the Cathedral), but his highly original style was not always acceptable to the Church. His best-known work, *The Burial of Count Orgaz* (1586), was commissioned to commemorate the burial of a benefactor. The occasion was depicted by El Greco in dazzling colours as a contemporary event, and it embodied the reception of Count Orgaz into heaven. This part of the picture is painted in an entirely different style, in which the colours, figures and relationships of scale are anti-naturalistic. El Greco's religious works must be seen against the background of the Inquisition in Spain and particularly the *Spiritual Exercises* of St IGNATIUS. In his final years he painted the famous *View of Toledo*.

Greeley, Horace (1811-1872) American journalist whose editorial policies helped to rouse northern popular opinion against slavery. His liberal views gained him the editorship of the *Jeffersonian* (1838) and the *Log Cabin* in the presidential campaign (1840). In 1841, he founded and edited the New York *Tribune,* where his progressive Whig ideals of socio-economic reform and his powerful anti-slavery editorials were highly influential. He helped to organize the Republican Party (1854-5), and supported Abraham LINCOLN in his presidential campaign (1860). Greeley fruitlessly sought office, broke with the Republican Party and finally became the unsuccessful presidential candidate for the dissenting Liberal Republicans in 1872.

Greene, Graham (born 1904) English writer, author of *The Power and the Glory* (1940) and *The Heart of the Matter* (1948) which, like most of his major novels, portray a sad world of guilt and remorse. Greene was converted to Catholicism, and religion is a constant theme in his novels. His prose has a powerful atmosphere of misery and defeat, even in his 'entertainments', his literary thrillers, spy stories and historical fiction: *Stamboul Train* (1932), *Brighton Rock* (1938), *Ministry of Fear* (1943) and *The Third Man* (1950). In his later work, Greene abandoned explicitly religious themes, and adopted a 'softer line' on the question of morality, achieving a compromise between the serious novels and the 'entertainments'. More recent novels include *The Human Factor* (1978), *Ways of Escape* (1981) and *Monsignor Quixote* (1982). His autobiography, *A Sort of Life,* was published in 1971.

Gregory, Lady Augusta (1852-1932) Irish dramatist, who helped to establish the Irish Literary Theatre (1898-9), and the Irish National Theatre Society (1902). She wrote two full-length plays, *The Pot of Broth* and *Cathleen ni Houlihan* (1902) in collaboration with W. B. YEATS, and some one-act plays and comedies, among them *The Workhouse Ward* (1908). Her work pioneered the revival of drama in Ireland at the turn of the century.

Gregory, Sir Augustus Charles (1819-1905) British-born explorer who crossed northern Australia from near the site of Darwin eastwards to the Pacific near Brisbane (1855), and sought traces of LEICHHARDT in a transcontinental journey down the Barcoo River through east-central Australia to Adelaide (1857).

Gregory the Great, Saint (c. 540-604) Roman magistrate turned monk who, as Pope Gregory I, made the papacy a power to be reckoned with. Last of the Church fathers (after saints AUGUSTINE, Ambrose, JEROME), he strengthened Church administration, discipline and authority by proclaiming the pope head of all Christian

The main protagonists in the American Civil War, 1861-5. Grant became President of the US, Lee a hero in defeat. The intervening maps show the diminishing of Confederate territory in the conflict between North and South.

churches. He reserved the Church's right to try and punish clerical offenders, enforced celibacy of the clergy, reformed the management of Church estates and sent Benedictine monks (notably St Augustine of Canterbury) to evangelize England, Italy and North Africa. His successors' claims to absolute power derive from Gregory's successes.

Gregory Nazianzus (329-389) Greek saint, one of the four great Greek Doctors of the Church. His preaching on the doctrine of the trinity earned him fame and ensured the final rejection of Arianism by a general council in 381. But, consecrated Bishop of Constantinople, he could not face the political difficulties and retired to finish his life in contemplation.

Gresham, Sir Thomas (c. 1519-79) English merchant and royal financial agent. He worked largely in Antwerp as a private financier, and as financial agent to the English crown (1552), raising and repaying loans and organizing gold shipments to England. He established the Royal Exchange in London as a bankers' meeting house. Gresham was ahead of his time in proposing (unsuccessfully) a national equalization fund to stabilize the exchange rate of the pound sterling, which had dropped since HENRY VIII debased the coinage. He expounded what much later became known as Gresham's law, stating that money of greater intrinsic value is hoarded while that of equal monetary but lesser intrinsic value is circulated.

Greuze, Jean (1725-1805) French painter, best remembered for his lachrymose, half-draped maidens. His most important works are generally considered to be his narrative pictures, inspired by ROUSSEAU, displaying the simple virtues of the poor, e.g. *The Paralytic Tended by his Children* (1763), which extolled the Neo-classical concern with morally elevating themes.

Grey, Charles, 2nd Earl (1764-1845) English Whig politician and Prime Minister whose ministry carried the 1832 Reform Bill through Parliament. Grey had long advocated parliamentary reform, and after forming a ministry in 1830, at the reluctant request of WILLIAM IV, the government produced a Parliamentary Reform Bill (1831). This was defeated and Parliament was dissolved, but the Whigs returned to power even more intent on reform. The House of Lords rejected a similar Bill the same year, and drastically amended a third in 1832. Grey resigned but WELLINGTON was unable to form a ministry, and Grey returned to power with an undertaking by William IV to create a sufficient number of peers to enable the Bill to pass through the Lords. The threat of this alone was sufficient to get it passed. In numerical terms the franchise was not greatly enlarged but the Act marked a distinct departure from the character of politics in the pre-Reform era. Grey's ministry also carried the abolishment of slavery in the colonies (1833). Disagreement within the government over Irish policy led to Grey's retirement in 1834.

Grey, Sir Edward (1862-1933) English politician, who influenced Britain's decision to enter the First World War. He was Liberal MP for Berwick from 1885 to 1916. As Foreign Secretary (1905-16), he concluded the Anglo-Russian Entente of 1907 and was an advocate of the talks that took place between the British, French, Belgian and Russian general staffs in the period 1906-14. Despite his pacifism and belief in international arbitration, he was aware of the German threat. Although unwilling to declare war, he persuaded Parliament that Britain was bound to go to Belgium's aid when Germany invaded that country. He brought Italy into the war on the side of the Allies by the secret Treaty of London (1915), and by his awareness of the sensitivity of the US on the blockade issue, helped to secure her as an ally in 1917.

Grey, Lady Jane (1537-54) Queen of England for nine days (in 1553). Her father-in-law, the powerful Duke of Northumberland, had persuaded Edward VI to name her his heir. Northumberland was, however, unsuccessful in resisting MARY I's claim to the throne, and Jane was at first imprisoned, and later executed after the failure of WYATT's rising against Mary.

Grieg, Edvard Hagerup (1843-1907) Norwegian composer, who, at IBSEN's request, wrote the incidental music to *Peer Gynt*, first performed in 1876. At a time when Norway was seeking its national identity and independence from Sweden, Grieg's originality and lyric gifts were inspired by Norway's folk music. His *Piano Concerto in A Minor* is one of the most popular piano concertos ever written. On his return to Norway after studying in Leipzig his style became conspicuously 'nationalist'. His best-known music after the Piano Concerto is the *Lyric Pieces* for piano and the *Holberg Suite* (1884) for strings.

Edvard Grieg remains one of the most popular light classical composers

Grierson, John (1898-1972) Scottish pioneer of the British documentary film movement, a key figure in the international development of realist cinema and director of *Drifters* (1929). Grierson gave documentary its name and the classic definition: 'the creative treatment of reality'. In 1938, he established the National Film Board of Canada.

Grieve, Christopher see MACDIARMID, Hugh

Griffith, David Wark (1875-1948) American director of films who revolutionized the entire language of movies. His two great silent works are *The Birth of a Nation* (1914) and *Intolerance* (1916). The first film, dealing with the Ku-Klux Klan, roused storms of controversy, but the huge cast, the great battle scenes and the sheer scale of the picture made it a triumphant box office success. *Intolerance*, intercutting a modern melodrama, the fall of Babylon, the story of Christ and the Huguenot massacre, bewildered its audiences and was a commercial disaster. Griffith's work declined after the early 1930s.

Grijalva, Juan de (c. 1489-1527) Spanish leader of an expedition along the Mexican coast from Yucatán to modern Vera Cruz, where he received gifts sent by MONTEZUMA.

Grillparzer, Franz (1791-1872) Austrian writer, whose works combined elements of Classicism and Romanticism. His plays, which give a fine insight into the delicate and subtle feelings of the characters, are mainly concerned with individuals and their attempts to escape the role prescribed to them by divine law, nature or society. His best-known works include *Sappho* (1818), in which the heroine is torn between fulfilling her artistic calling and living life to the full, the trilogy entitled *The Golden Fleece* (1821), a tragedy based on the story of Jason and Medea, and the patriotic *King Ottocar, his Rise and Fall* (1825).

Grimaldi, Joseph (1779-1837) Anglo-Italian clown, who, as a singer, dancer, mime, actor and acrobat was a great attraction in Covent Garden harlequinades (1806-23). He created the archetypal clown known as Joey.

Son of a pantaloon player and an actress, Grimaldi grew up in a world of tumblers, tightrope walkers and buffoons

Grimm, Jacob (1785-1863) and **Wilhelm (1786-1859)** German philologists and mythologists most widely known for their collection known as *Grimm's Fairy Tales* (1812-15). Jacob's most important contribution to philology was *German Grammar* (1819-37), which included Grimm's Law, which first laid down the principle that language development is governed by regular phonetic laws and the correspondence of certain consonants within the Indo-Germanic languages. Jacob's other works include *German Legends* (1835), which traces the entire course of Teutonic myths and superstitions, and *Legal Antiquities* (1828), a study of Teutonic laws. Wilhelm collaborated with him on the *Fairy Tales,* on *German Legends* (1816-18), and on the only volume of the projected *German Lexicon* (1854) and on many editions of early literature. He also published his own translations and studies.

Nightmarish but enchanting, the stories of the brothers Grimm remain popular with children

Grimmelshausen, Jacob von (c. 1625-76) German novelist who wrote *The Adventurous Simplicissimus* (1669), a long, picaresque story of the life and adventures of Simplicissimus. The humour and sympathetic understanding with which this expresses the Christian pessimism of the age reveal Grimmelshausen's love of life and his humanity. In his boyhood he was carried off by soldiers to fight in the 30 Years' War and fought on both sides before being converted to Catholicism in 1646.

Gris, Juan (1887-1927) Spanish Cubist painter who lived and worked in France. He developed a form of Cubism characterized by a stringently controlled composition and the inclusion of still-life motifs.

Grivas, George (1898-1974) Cypriot military leader and politician at the forefront of the struggle for *Enosis,* the union of Cyprus and Greece. Although Grivas's military efforts against the British were instrumental in the formation of the Republic of Cyprus (1960), a rift developed between Grivas and MAKARIOS concerning *Enosis*, and Grivas returned to guerilla strategy.

Grock (1880-1959) Stage name of Adrien Wettach, Swiss clown who achieved fame as the greatest of his kind since GRIMALDI.

Gromyko, Andrei Andreevich (born 1909) Russian, Foreign Minister of the Soviet Union, who has represented his country at nearly all the important meetings with the West since 1945. An economist, he joined the Foreign Ministry at the outbreak of the Second World War and was made head of the American section. Later, he was sent to Washington as Counsellor at the Soviet Embassy and became Ambassador to the US in 1943. He was Soviet representative at the United Nations (1946-9), where he made extensive use of the veto, deputy Foreign Minister (1949-52), Ambassador to Britain (1952-3) and Foreign Minister in 1957, in succession to Shepilov. Although, in the earlier stages of his career, he pursued relentlessly the 'Cold War' against the West, his recent pronouncements have been in line with Russia's policy of coexistence. He attended talks early in 1985 with the American Secretary of State, George Shultz, to try and prevent the nuclear arms race in outer space. He has received the Order of Lenin four times.

Groot, Huigh de see GROTIUS, Hugo

Gropius, Walter (1883-1969) German pioneer of 20th-century architecture and design who founded the famous school of arts and crafts known as the Bauhaus (1919). Gropius studied under BEHRENS and his early works show that he was already turning his attention to industrial architecture, which demanded solutions in form, structure and materials which broke away from tradition. The Fagus factory at Alfeld and his pavilion for the Cologne Werkbund Exhibition of 1914 were also directly allied to the demands of industrialization. The Bauhaus embodied his idea that the arts should be subservient to and united in an architectural whole, with emphasis on the teaching crafts and on research into new materials. HITLER closed the Bauhaus in 1932 and Gropius fled first to England and then to America, where his works include Harvard Graduate Centre.

Grossmith, George (1847-1912) English humorist who, with his brother Weedon, contributed sketches of Victorian middle-class life to *Punch.* They were published as *The Diary of a Nobody* (1892).

Grotefend, Georg Friedrich (1775-1853) German classical scholar who pioneered the decipherment of the cuneiform (wedge-shaped) script, first copied at Persepolis in Iran in 1802, deducing correctly that the inscriptions were in three languages.

Grotius, Hugo (1583-1645) Dutch lawyer, who wrote *On the Law of War and Peace,* a treatise on international law based on the view that natural law is a dictate of right reason, independent of any religion, and that even God cannot make good what is evil.

Grove, Sir George (1820-1900) British civil engineer and musical scholar who founded and edited *Grove's Dictionary of Music and Musicians* (4 vols., 1879-99). Expanded and updated regularly, it remains a standard international work of reference. Among other varied activities, Grove built lighthouses in the West Indies and became the first director of the Royal College of Music, London.

Grünewald, Mathäus (c. 1475-1528) German painter, whose most famous painting is an altarpiece, the *Isenheim Altar,* completed *c.* 1515 and now in Colmar. The most striking part is a large crucified Christ, sombre in colour (unlike the other panels) and which is obsessed with physical pain.

Guardi, Francesco (1712-93) Italian artist, one of the major 18th-century painters of Venetian views. He collaborated with his brother Gian Antonio in painting religious pictures, but by the 1760s he was working almost exclusively on views of Venice. He could not command CANALETTO's high prices, but today Guardi's vivacity of touch, flickering light effects and poetic atmosphere are often preferred to his rival's precision.

Guarini, Giovanni Battista (1538-1612) Italian pastoral playwright and author of the elaborate Arcadian drama *The Faithful Shepherd* (1590), which gained extensive popularity throughout Europe for 200 years.

Guericke, Otto von (1602-86) German physicist who first proved the existence of a vacuum. This he demonstrated in 1650 when he removed water from a barrel with a pump. His later, successful evacuation of air from metal spheres resulted in a number of dramatic demonstrations.

Guevara, Ernesto (1928-67) Argentine-born Communist revolutionary, known universally as Che, whose theory and practice of guerilla warfare made him a hero among young left-wing revolutionaries. After being associated with revolutionary movements throughout Latin America, he joined CASTRO in Mexico (1956) and worked with him until the coup which brought Castro to power in Cuba (1958). Thereafter he served in Castro's administration, trained the militia which defeated KENNEDY's 'Bay of Pigs' adventure (a US-supported attempt to overthrow the Castro régime by Cuban exiles in 1961) and published a treatise on guerilla warfare. In 1966 he left Cuba to organize a revolution in Bolivia against the régime of President Barrientos. In October 1967 he was caught and shot by Bolivian government forces.

Guillotin, Joseph Ignace (1738-1814) French doctor and revolutionary who, in 1789, proposed the adoption of a beheading machine for administering capital punishment. His main arguments were that decapitation should not only be the privilege of the nobility, but be available to all candidates for capital punishment and, moreover, it should be as swift and as painless as possible. Similar machines had been used in medieval Europe. Guillotin's proposal was adopted in 1791 and the first machines, German-made, were used the following year. Soon they became known as *guillotines.* But the excesses of the French revolution tainted their use, and they were never widely adopted outside the French-speaking world.

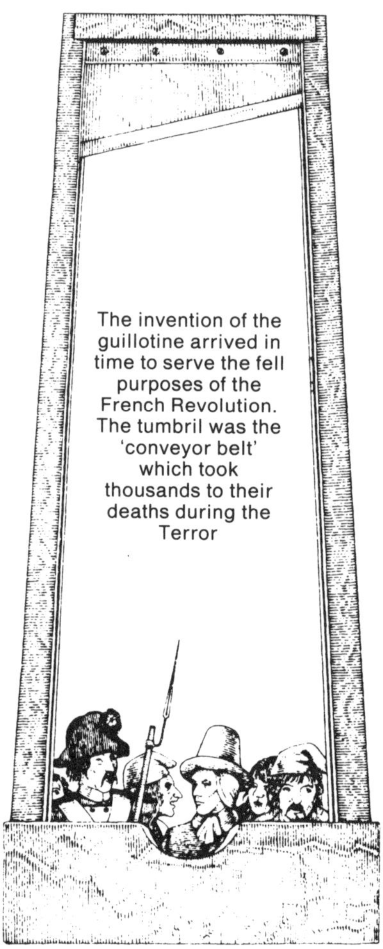

The invention of the guillotine arrived in time to serve the fell purposes of the French Revolution. The tumbril was the 'conveyor belt' which took thousands to their deaths during the Terror

Guiscard, Robert (c. 1015-85) Norman adventurer who founded Norman power in Italy and Sicily after joining his brothers, who had won most of Apulia. In a series of conquests, he drove the Byzantines out of southern Italy and began the Norman invasion of Muslim Sicily, which was completed by his brother, ROGER I of Sicily, so founding the Italo-Sicilian kingdom of Naples.

Gulbenkian, Calouste (1896-1955) Turkish-born financier and oil magnate, who founded the Iraq Petroleum Company. After admitting British, French and American participation in the company, Gulbenkian retained the share which earned him the international name of 'Mr Five Per Cent'. He left art treasures and a 70-million dollar fortune to the Gulbenkian Foundation.

Gull, Sir Willian (1816-90) British physician whose work on cretinism led him to identify myxoedema (a disease marked by thick, cold skin and thin hair), and to isolate thyroid deficiency as its cause. He also did important research on paralysis, cholera and abscess of the brain.

Gustavus I (1496-1560) King of Sweden (1523-60), who freed Sweden from Danish control and founded the Vasa dynasty (1521-1720). In opposition to Christian II of Denmark's suppression of Swedish nationalists, Gustavus led a popular revolt which ended Danish rule in Sweden and left Gustavus the elected king of an independent state. To strengthen Sweden he ended the Hanseatic monopoly of Baltic trade, made Lutheranism the state religion (subject to royal authority), promoted trade, farming and mining and quelled opposition to his ideas.

Gustavus II Adolphus (1594-1632) King of Sweden (1611-32) who made his country a military power. Determined to make Protestant Sweden secure, he fought Denmark (1611-13) and won back lands in southern Sweden, fought Russia (1613-17) and excluded her from the Baltic, and fought Poland (1621-9), achieving recognition from her as King of Sweden and winning the Vistula delta in the last two years of his life. Gustavus Adolphus intervened in the 30 Years' War, principally to ensure that the Holy Roman Emperor did not take the Baltic seaports and become a danger to Sweden, but also to aid Protestant Germany against the Catholic armies of the Holy Roman Empire. He brilliantly defeated the Hapsburg generals, Tilly at Breitenfeld and Walltenstein at Lützen, but he died from wounds received there. Sweden's domination over the Baltic survived until PETER I of Russia defeated CHARLES XII.

Gutenberg, Johannes (1398-1468) German goldsmith, traditionally credited with the invention of printing from movable type. The process had its origins in techniques used for making playing cards and mass-produced woodblock prints. Others in Europe experimented with movable-type printing at about the same time as Gutenberg, but the first large printing house to use movable type was that of Gutenberg and his partner, Johann Fust, at Mainz. In 1448 they had cast enough type to set and print a whole Bible. In 1456 there was a printing of the Bible thought to be Gutenberg's work.

Gwynn, Nell (1650-87) British actress, who became CHARLES II's mistress. Her beauty and wit took her from being an orange-seller at Drury Lane Theatre on to the stage.

H

Hachette, Louis (1800-64) French bookseller and publisher whose textbooks and editions of the classics raised the standard of French educational publishing. He first published in 1833, when the creation of primary schools produced a demand for textbooks. He also produced dictionaries, scholarly editions of the classics, a cheap railway library and guide books. In 1855 he founded the weekly *Le Journal Pour Tous.* Today the Hachette group controls major French newspapers, book publishers and booksellers.

Hadley, George (1685-1768) British meteorologist, who formulated the currently accepted theory of trade winds. He showed that to understand the movement of the trades the Earth's rotation must be taken into account and that the different speeds of rotation (fastest at the equator and relatively slower at distances) govern the circulation of these winds.

Hadrian (76-138) Roman Emperor (117-138) under whom the empire enjoyed a golden age. Hadrian succeeded his cousin TRAJAN, whom he had served in Rome's provinces, and his first act was to abandon Trajan's untenable Parthian conquests and make the Euphrates the empire's eastern boundary. Hadrian strictly supervised the provincial governors, but set the provinces on an equal footing with Rome. In Palestine he put down a Jewish rebellion led by Simon Barchocheba and during his government in Britain, ordered the building of the 73-mile Hadrian's Wall to keep the troublesome Picts and Scots out of England. At home, Hadrian carried out numerous reforms, reorganizing the civil service, law, the financial administration and the tax system. He erected many fine public buildings and founded several cities.

Hadrian IV see ADRIAN IV

Haeckel, Ernst (1834-1919) German biologist, who contended that an organism's embryological stages reflect its evolutionary history. His work leading up to the formulation of this (in fact erroneous) 'biogenetic law' was the starting-point for much late 19th-century research into evolution and embryology. Haeckel was also the first man to recognize the importance of sexual selection in the evolutionary process.

Hahn, Otto (1879-1968) German chemist who discovered nuclea fission. In the mid-1930s, with Lise MEITNER, he bombarded uranium with neutrons, and saw that an extremely radioactive substance was formed in the uranium. In 1938 he suggested that it was a radioactive form of barium, an element far lighter than uranium, formed by the splitting of uranium atoms, each into two roughly equal parts.

Hahnemann, Samuel (1755-1843) German physician, the founder of homeopathy. This is a system of curing the sick by administering minute traces of the drugs which, in healthy people, would produce the symptoms of the disease involved. His observation that insoluble substances could be dissolved by prolonged rubbing in water, heralded an understanding of colloids (a solution of particles too fine to settle but too coarse to pass through a membrane that will pass pure liquids).

Haig, Douglas, 1st Earl (1861-1928) Scottish-born soldier, Commander-in-Chief of the British army in the First World War. Haig, who distinguished himself as a cavalry officer in the second Boer War (1899-1902), commanded the 1st Army Corps of the British Expeditionary Force in 1914, fighting at Mons, on the Meuse, and at Ypres. He succeeded Sir John French as Commander-in-Chief, Western Front, in 1915, but had neither imagination nor great talent, and was distrustful of innovations in warfare. The casualties suffered by Haig's armies led to antagonism between him and LLOYD GEORGE over strategy of attrition warfare, but his prestige in the higher ranks of the army enabled him to retain his command even after his severe defeat by the Germans in March 1918. By securing the appointment of FOCH as Supreme Comander of the Allied armies in France he made a major contribution to victory.

Haldane, John Burdon (1892-1964) British biologist, who tried to link the sciences with Marxist philosophy, especially with regard to the theory of evolution.

Haldane, Richard Burdon, 1st Viscount (1856-1928) English lawyer, philosopher and liberal statesman, who was forced out of public life by the popular press for his alleged pro-German leanings early in the First World War (1915). He was educated in Germany and became an authority on German philosophy. As War Secretary (1905-12) under CAMPBELL-BANNERMAN and ASQUITH he created the General Staff (1906), the Territorial Army (1907) and Officers' Training Corps in public schools.

Haile Selassie (1892-1975) Emperor of Ethiopia. He succeeded the Empress Zauditu in 1930 and introduced a new and more liberal constitution a year later. In 1936, after MUSSOLINI had invaded Ethiopia, he was forced to leave the country and took refuge in England. Subequently he rallied Ethiopian patriots in Kenya and the Sudan and, in June 1941, he was reinstated in Addis Ababa after Ethiopia's liberation by British forces. He was deposed by a military coup (1974).

Hale, George Ellery (1868-1938) American astronomer, responsible for the founding of the Yerkes and the Mount Palomar Observatories.

The Hale 200 in reflector telescope at Palomar can be directed to any point in the sky. The observer's cage allows photographs to be taken at prime focus; there is a Cassegrain arrangement, and in the Coudé system light is reflected to a fixed position outside the telescope, avoiding the constant moving of any heavy equipment used. The telescope, was not completed until after Hale's death

1 Primary mirror
2 Observer's cage
3 Cassegrain focus
4 Coudé focus
5 Southern end of the polar axis
6 Coudé and Cassegrain secondary mirror
7 Right ascension drive
8 Declination axis
9 Dome shutter (opening 30 ft)
10 Dome (137 ft diameter)
11 Primary focus (54 ft)
12 Northern pillar
13 Southern pillar
14 Control panel

In 1889 he invented an instrument called a spectroheliograph for studying the Sun, and in 1908 discovered the existence of magnetic fields in sunspots, which led (1919) to his discovery of the periodic reversal in the polarizing of their magnetic fields.

Hale, Sir Matthew (1609-76) English jurist whose *History of the Pleas of the Crown* (1685) was an influential work on English criminal law. He played a prominent part in the trials of political offenders during the Civil War and under the Commonwealth, when he achieved a great reputation for moderation and fairness. CHARLES II appointed him Chief Justice of the Court of King's Bench (1671). His *Analysis of the Law* was the essential precursor of BLACKSTONE's *Commentaries*.

Hales, Stephen (1677-1761) English clergyman, botanist and chemist who, by inserting glass tubes into the veins and arteries of live horses, was the first man to measure the pressure and velocity of blood. His *Haemastaticks* (1733) is a classic of cardiac medicine. His experiments in plant physiology included measurements of the rate of plant growth and an explanation of the mechanism of transpiration.

Halifax, 1st Earl of see MONTAGU, Charles

Halifax, Edward, First Earl of (1881-1959) English statesman who, with Neville CHAMBERLAIN, was responsible for the Munich agreement of 1938. As Lord President of the Council (1935) with responsibility for foreign affairs, he held an appointment partly designed to enable the Prime Minister, Chamberlain, to counter the policy of his Foreign Secretary, EDEN, who disagreed with the appeasement of HITLER and MUSSOLINI. When Eden resigned (1938), Halifax took his place, carrying out Chamberlain's policy of appeasement, though he advocated a stronger line towards Germany from March 1939 onwards. He retained the same office after the Second World War broke out, but seven months after CHURCHILL became Prime Minister, Halifax was sent to Washington as Ambassador (January 1941), a post he retained until 1946.

Hall, Charles Francis (1821-71) American explorer who made three Arctic expeditions between 1860 and 1871. The first two were in search of traces of Sir John FRANKLIN's vanished party; on the first, Hall, single-handed, landed in and studied Frobisher Bay; on the second, helped by Eskimos, he explored King William Land and discovered the fate of some of Franklin's party. On his third expedition, Hall failed in a government-backed attempt to reach the North Pole, but had already sailed farther north than any other explorer.

Hall, Charles Martin (1863-1914) American chemist, who, in 1886, developed an electrolytic process for manufacturing aluminium. The French metallurgist Paul Louis Toussaint Héroult had independently also devised a similar method in the same year. The Hall-Héroult process founded the modern aluminium industry. Its wide uses have had significant results, particularly in such applications as aircraft manufacture, where the lightness of the alloy is important.

Hall, Sir James (1761-1832) British geochemist who discovered that when rocks are heated until they melt they form crystals if allowed to cool sufficiently slowly.

Hall, James (1811-98) American geologist and palaeontologist who contributed greatly to the understanding of the geology of many parts of the USA. Hall became state geologist of New York and did much field-work. His most important publication was a 13-volume monograph on the palaeontology of New York.

Hall, Marshall (1790-1857) British physician and physiologist, who carried out important work on the nervous system and saw that reflex actions occur even when the nerve cord to the brain is severed. He concluded that the nerve cord must be made up of sections that not only interact to produce co-ordinated movements, but also operate as autonomous reflex systems. His name is given to a type of artificial respiration.

Haller, Albrecht von (1708-77) Swiss physiologist, anatomist, botanist, encyclopedist, historian of medicine and poet. His account of a technique he devised for injecting blood vessels with dyes so as to make their course clear was so accurate and comprehensive that it became the basis for later cardiovascular anatomy. His were the first research works to realize the importance of the nerves in carrying sensations to the brain, and commands to the muscles from the brain. He also made pioneer studies on the digestive juices, blood clotting, the growth of bone and the mechanism of breathing.

Halley, Edmond (1656-1742) English astronomer, after whom Halley's Comet is named. While still a schoolboy, Halley became a skilled astronomer. In 1676 he went to St Helena to catalogue the stars of the southern hemisphere, and while there he observed the transit of Mercury across the Sun (1677). On his return Halley became friendly with NEWTON, and it was his discussions with Halley that encouraged Newton to write his *Principia,* which Halley financed and saw through the press. In 1721 Halley became Astronomer Royal in succession to FLAMSTEED. Close study of comets led him to the correct belief that the comet of 1682 was the same heavenly body as the comets of 1456, 1531 and 1607, and accurately predicted that it would reappear in 1758.

Hals, Frans (c. 1580-1666) One of the greatest of all Dutch portrait painters. His portraits were official studies of civic dignitaries, of the para-military groups which were formed during the Dutch wars against Spain, or less formal portraits of cavalier or bourgeois types, of which the most famous is the *Laughing Cavalier* (1624). They give an impression of remarkable spontaneity, though their liveliness also depends to some extent upon brush-strokes which appear to have been applied with great speed – although in fact the opposite is true. Hals's muted colours became more sombre in his late works.

Hamilton, Alexander (c. 1757-1804) US lawyer and statesman, who advocated a strong central government rather than loose confederation of states. In the War of Independence he raised and organized artillery regiments in New York, and from 1777 to 1781 was Washington's secretary and aide-de-camp. He drafted the report which resulted in the calling of the Constitutional Convention at Philadelphia in 1787 and in a series of essays, later published as the *Federalist* (1787-8), he advocated a strong central government. His principal opponents were JEFFERSON and Aaron Burr, who were provoked by his appointment as Secretary to the Treasury (1789-95), and by his policies of a federal tax system and the Federal Bank. His long quarrel with Burr led to a duel in which Burr mortally wounded him.

Hammarskjöld, Dag Hjalmar Agne Carl (1905-61) Swedish political economist, second Secretary-General of the United Nations (1953-61) and posthumous winner of the Nobel Peace Prize. As Secretary-General of the UN, he believed that the smaller nations had greater need of UN protection than the large, and so, unlike his predecessor, Trygve LIE, avoided involvement in great power disputes as far as possible. It was his personal integrity, however, which guaranteed the acceptance of the UN Emergency Force in Sinai and Gaza after the Suez crisis of 1956, and of UN observers in Lebanon in 1958. UN forces were also sent to the Congo when Katanga seceded in 1960, and while flying to see TSHOMBE he was killed in a plane crash at Ndola, Zambia.

Hammurabi (c. 1955-1913 BC) Babylonian lawgiver. He unified and pacified Babylonia and provided it with a written code of laws which is often regarded as the first major legislative work of the forerunners of western civilization.

Due again in 1986, Halley's comet was recorded in the Bayeux Tapestry

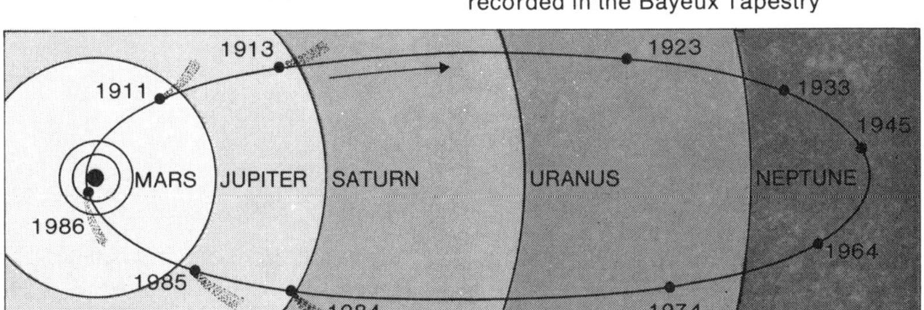

Hampden, John (1594-1643) English leader of parliamentary opposition to CHARLES I. In 1636, the king demanded that all counties make peace-time payments of ship-money, which had formerly been levied only on coastal counties in time of war, to finance the fleet. Hampden refused to pay on the grounds that the new tax was not authorized by Parliament and was therefore illegal. Charles narrowly won the consequent legal action (1637) but lost face in doing so. The incident helped to provoke the Civil War, in which Hampden died fighting for the Parliamentarians.

Hamsun, Knut (1859-1952) Norwegian novelist, dramatist and poet, who was the most considerable literary figure in Norway after IBSEN. He was chiefly concerned to show the corruption of the individual through contact with society and explored this idea in a series of ironic novels depicting the wanderings of a rootless man at grips with hunger, physical labour and danger. The best known of these is *The Growth of the Soil* (1917), in which the wanderer comes to rest. But *Pan* (1894) and *Children of the Age* (1913) are of greater literary merit.

Handel, George Friederich (1685-1759) German-born (naturalized British) composer and master of 18th-century oratorio. A four-year stay in Italy during his early twenties had a lasting effect on his style, which might be described as Italianate Baroque. An orchestral violinist, he also became a virtuoso harpsichordist and organist. Handel composed easily and quickly, but was not averse to using another's material without acknowledgement. His music has a vivid immediacy and a power to attract and had a considerable and long-lasting influence upon music in Britain. In 1732 he wrote *Esther,* the first English biblical oratorio. Of the series of oratorios which followed, the most outstanding was *The Messiah.* He also wrote Italian operas for the London stage. His anthem *Zadok the Priest* was written for the coronation of George II (1727). Handel's orchestral band suites, the *Fireworks Music* and the *Water Music,* were written for state or royal occasions.

Hannibal (247-183 BC) Carthaginian general and statesman who came near to overthrowing Rome.

Dedicated to defeating Carthage's great rival, the 26-year-old Hannibal became Carthaginian Commander-in-Chief in Spain, where he began the Second Punic War (219 BC) by seizing pro-Roman Saguntum. In the following year he marched on Italy itself, leading 40,000 troops and 38 war elephants across the Pyrenees, southern France and the Alpine passes into Italy. Hannibal lost most of his elephants and perhaps one-quarter of his men in the early autumn snow and from tribal attacks, but gained the psychological advantage over the astonished Romans. Inside Italy, Rome's troops outnumbered his, but he won (216 BC) the battles of Ticino, Trebia, Lake Trasimene and Cannae. Under Hannibal's brilliant leadership, and helped by local dissidents, the Carthaginians ravaged Italy for 15 years but did not attempt to take fortified Rome. Hannibal was forced to leave Italy in 203 BC to defend Carthaginian North Africa against SCIPIO's invasion and was defeated decisively at Zama (202 BC). After some years in civil administration, he was exiled from Carthage and finally committed suicide to avoid falling into the hands of the Romans.

Hanno (5th cent. BC) Carthaginian navigator who made the first well-documented voyage round the West African coast. Leading 30,000 Carthaginian settlers in 60 multi-oared vessels, he sailed west from the Strait of Gibraltar (*c.* 480 BC); founded towns in what is now Morocco; reached Gambia, and probably Sierra Leone and Cameroon.

Hansard, Thomas (1776-1833) English printer of the offical daily record of British parliamentary debates, originated by William COBBETT in 1803. He took over publication of the debates from Cobbett in 1809 and in 1823 established the Paternoster Row Press. *Hansard* is still the name given to the official report of debates in Parliament.

Han Yü (768-824) Chinese essayist, who is famous for the part he played in reviving the classical prose style. An active government official for most of his life, his profound belief in Confucianism is expounded in his writings attacking the influences of Taoism and Buddhism. His essays were esteemed as models of prose till the end of the empire.

Hardie, James Kier (1856-1915) Scottish politician and Labour leader. In his twenties he organized miners' trade unions in Scotland, and in 1888 founded the Scottish Parliamentary Labour Party. Five years later he was elected Independent Socialist MP for West Ham (London) and the same year founded the Independent Labour Party (1893). For 15 years, from 1900, Hardie was MP for Merthyr Tydfil and became leader of the Parliamentary Labour Party (1906). A temperance reformer, pacifist and Nonconformist, he opposed Britain's entry into the First World War.

Harding, Warren Gamaliel (1865-1923) US President, who was responsible for America's isolationism between the two World Wars. As a Republican senator, Harding opposed Woodrow WILSON's attempts to give the US an international role through the League of Nations. Chosen by a lobby of influential businessmen as a pliable candidate for the Presidency, Harding was elected in 1920 on a 'return to normalcy' ticket. His administration (1921-3) was chiefly remarkable for political dishonesty on a vast scale and the gaoling for corruption of his Secretary of the Interior, Fall. Daugherty, the Attorney-General, was also implicated. Responsibility for the loss of prestige to the office of President rested as much on the Republican party and the nation as on Harding, whose mediocre talents were ill-suited to is office.

Hardy, Thomas (1840-1928) English poet and novelist whose creation of vivid, often humorous, characters, forced to live in a world of bleak, indifferent fate, won immense popularity. Almost all Hardy's work is set in Wessex, the central counties of the south coast of England, particularly Dorset, the region of Hardy's home. His characters are mainly country people, bound up with the land which governs their lives. Hardy divided his works into three categories: novels of character and environment, which include *Far from the Madding Crowd* (1874), *The Mayor of Casterbridge* (1886) and *Tess of the D'Urbervilles* (1891); romances and fantasies, including *The Trumpet-Major* (1880); and novels of ingenuity. He also published a trilogy of plays, *The Dynasts* (1904-8), and seven volumes of verse.

The works of Hardy, chronicler of Wessex, are enjoying a new popularity

Hargreaves, James (c. 1720-78) English weaver and textile engineer. Kay's shuttle had increased the speed of weaving, which was controlled by the production of spinning yarn, and Hargreaves's invention, the spinning jenny (1764), then speeded up the production of spinning yarn. It initially took eight, and in later models up to 120 spindles, though, as the drawing was done still by hand, the yarn produced was coarse and non-uniform. It was CROMPTON's mule which eventually was capable of providing the yarn required, and this invention embodied the principal features of Hargreaves's spinning jenny.

Harness, Henry Drury (1804-83) British engineer and cartographer who helped to pioneer statistical mapping techniques. In 1837, he published maps of Ireland, designed to show regional differences in population and traffic; they were among the first quantitative maps based on censuses.

Harold II (c. 1022-66) Last King of Anglo-Saxon England. He was the son of Godwin, Earl of Wessex, and after King EDWARD THE CONFESSOR, the most powerful man in the kingdom. When Edward died in 1066, Harold became King, but he was killed by an arrow in the same year at the Battle of Hastings.

Harold III Haardraade (1015-66) Warrior king of Norway (1047-66) whose invasion of England in 1066 made possible the unopposed landing in Sussex of WILLIAM. Haardraade fled to Russia in his youth, to become the best known of the Varangians (Russian and Scandinavian warriors serving the Byzantine emperors). He returned to Norway in 1046 and became king in the following year. He invaded England (1066) but died in the Battle of Stamford Bridge. His conqueror, HAROLD II, learned of the Norman landing two days after the battle.

Harper, James (1795-1869) American publisher, the founder of Harper and Brothers. Apprenticed to a printer in New York City, he set up a printing business with his brother John in 1817, and turned to publishing, in which they gained a high reputation.

Harris, Benjamin (1673-1716) English journalist and publisher of the first newspaper printed in America. He worked as a journalist in London until 1686, and then emigrated to America, where he opened a bookshop in Boston. In 1690 he issued *Publick Occurrences Both Foreign and Domestick.* He returned to London in 1695 and published the newspaper *London Post* from 1699 until 1706.

Harris, Roy (1898-1979) American composer of whose work the *Third Symphony* and *Piano Quintet* are best known. He has extended his country's traditional music into a modern idiom. Harris, with his roots in American folk music and hymnody, was largely self-taught until studying with Nadia BOULANGER in Paris.

Harrison, Benjamin (1833-1901) Twenty-third President of the US (1889-93). The grandson of William HARRISON, and a fervent opponent of slavery, he served through most of the Civil War, distinguishing himself in SHERMAN's Atlanta Campaign. In the presidential campaign of 1889, he defeated CLEVELAND, thus achieving a victory for protection over free trade, signified by the passage in 1890 of MCKINLEY's Tariff Bill.

Harrison, James (1816-93) Scottish-born Australian journalist and inventor of the first refrigerating plant used for a manufacturing process (1851). Harrison was the first to recognize the potential of meat export to the economy of Australia, which initiated the exportation of canned meat. A meat-freezing plant was first set up in 1861 by a fellow Australian, Thomas Sutcliffe Mort. First Harrison (1873) and then Mort (1876), attempted to ship frozen meat to England, but failed owing to plant breakdown at sea. By 1877, however, frozen mutton was shipped successfully from Buenos Aires to Le Havre, so establishing the frozen meat trade.

Harrison, John (1693-1776) English horologist, who invented (1735) the first chronometer which was accurate enough for use in long distance oceanic navigation. In 1726 he invented the constant-length pendulum, made of a 'gridiron' of brass and iron, so arranged that the thermal expansions of the metals counteracted each other. His chronometer, which lost less than two minutes on a return voyage to Jamaica, won an Admiralty prize of £20,000 for a timepiece accurate enough to allow longitude to be determined to within 30 miles.

Harrison, William Henry (1773-1841) Ninth President of the US, who held office for only one month. His father, Benjamin Harrison, was one of the signatories of the Declaration of Independence, and he himself became governor of the Indiana Territory 1801-13. As commander of the troops in the northwest, he inflicted several defeats on the British forces in the war of 1812-14. In 1840 he was chosen as Whig candidate for the Presidency and was elected overwhelmingly. He died of pneumonia a month after his inauguration.

Harsha (c. 590-647) Emperor of Northern India, whose reign (622-47) marked a transitional period between ancient and medieval India. The basis of Harsha's power was the union of the Punjab and Uttar Pradesh. He expanded his territory to bring most of northern India from Malwa to the Gulf of Bengal under his sway, but failed to conquer the Deccan. He revived literature and the arts, and was himself a writer of ability. He is better known than most Indian kings because of a biography of his early life, the *Harshacarita.* His decentralized empire broke up after his death.

Hartmann von Aue (12th-13th cents.) German poet, who was one of the masters of the courtly epic. His free versions of CHRÉTIEN DE TROYES's *Erec* and *Iwein* introduced the Arthurian legends into German literature. He also wrote love lyrics and two didactic poems, *Gregorius* and *Poor Henry,* flowing religious narratives preaching the ideals of restraint and moderation.

Harun-al-Rashid (c. 764-809) Abbasside caliph (786-809) who ruled, in a golden age of Islam, all southwest Asia and North Africa. He encouraged the free interchange of goods and ideas among Arabs and non-Arabs, and reportedly had contacts with CHARLEMAGNE and with China. Music, art and learning flourished under Harun, and his capital, Baghdad, became the cultural centre of the Islamic world. His reign was disturbed by many rebellions and what are now Morocco and Tunisia broke away, beginning the political disintegration of the Islamic Empire.

Harvard, John (1607-38) English clergyman who gave his name to America's oldest university. A graduate of Cambridge University, England, he emigrated to Charlestown, Massachusetts, in 1637 as a Puritan minister. He died the following year, bequeathing his 260 books and £780 (half his estate) to the then unestablished college proposed in 1636 for Newetowne (renamed Cambridge in 1638).

Harvey, William (1578-1657) English physician who discovered the process by which blood circulates in the body. Until Harvey's time all anatomists thought that there were two blood systems in the body and that the blood flowed to and from the heart through each. Harvey published his epoch-making discovery that the blood flows from the heart in the arterial system, through the tissues, and then back towards the heart in the venous system in *The Movement of the Heart* (1628). *Of the Animal Species* (1651) summed up his important work on embryology.

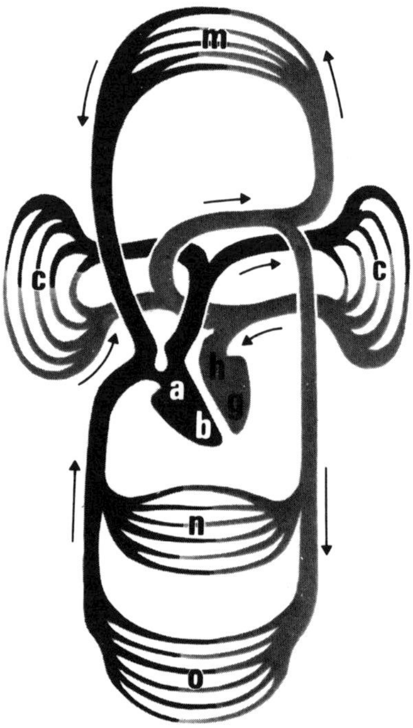

William Harvey first showed how the heart pumps blood around the body. The diagram below follows the blood as it is pumped from the left auricle *h* and ventricle *g* through the head and arms *m*, lungs *c*, trunk *n* and legs *o*. The blood then returns to the right auricle of the heart *a*

Hasan, Ali Shah (1800-81) Persian religious leader and first holder of the hereditary title Aga Khan: spiritual head of the Nizari Ismaili sect of Shi'ite Muslims, who claim direct descent from MOHAMMED's daughter Fatima. His title was confirmed by the British administration in India when the Aga fled there after leading an unsuccessful revolt. Today most Nizaris live in India, Pakistan and Africa.

Hastings, Warren (1732-1818) English colonial administrator, first Governor-General of India, who began his career as a clerk in Calcutta, with the East India Company (1750). He became a member of its Calcutta administrative council (1761) but resigned in protest against the corruption of his colleagues and returned to England (1766). Hastings rejoined the Company in 1768, became Governor of Fort William in Bengal in 1772 and Governor-General of India in 1773. After the British Government took over the running of India, numerous disputes arose between Parliament's representatives and the Company, and India became a political issue when he retired in 1785. He was impeached for corruption by political enemies, but won acquittal in a seven-year trial which left him penniless.

Haushofer, Karl (1869-1946) German general and political geographer whose theories of geopolitics helped to shape HITLER's strategy. Influenced by Ratzel, KJELLÉN and MACKINDER, he saw political states as biological units striving to dominate land masses, the control of which was crucial for their survival. He stressed the implied natural right of a dynamic, thrusting Germany to seize *lebensraum* (living space) at the expense of others, to grasp the whole of Eurasia, and hence to dominate the so-called oceanic countries. He committed suicide during Allied investigations into war criminal activities.

Haussmann, Baron Georges (1809-91) French lawyer, civil servant and architect who was responsible for the design of modern central Paris. Haussmann was commissioned by NAPOLEON III to draw up plans for improving the city. His long, straight boulevards, intersecting each other at ronds-points, were designed for the huge state processions which celebrated the visits of foreign royalty, or the opening of international exhibitions. The Franco-Prussian War, which was followed by the setting up of the Republic, ended the Baron's plans. One of the famous *grands boulevards* in Paris is named in his honour.

Haüy, Abbé René (1743-1822) French priest and mineralogist, who showed that crystals are built up of units, so founding the science of crystallography. Accidentally dropping a crystal of calcite, Haüy noticed that it broke along certain definite planes and that the smaller fragments were identical with the parent crystal.

Hawke, Robert (born 1929) Australian Prime Minister since 1983 and President of the Labour Party since 1973. He was appointed research officer of the Australian Council of Trade Unions in 1958, and became its president in 1970. Elected to Parliament for the first time in 1980, in 1983 he led the Labour Party to victory in the national elections, defeating Malcolm Fraser. He was re-elected in 1984, but with a much reduced majority.

Hawke, Edward, 1st Baron (1705-81) British admiral and pioneer of the naval blockade. He gained his reputation by defeating a French squadron protecting a convoy for the West Indies (1747), and during the Seven Year's War (1755-63) blockaded Brest, delaying a French supply convoy for French troops in Canada. He crushed a retaliatory French attempt to invade England by destroying their invasion fleet in the Battle of Quiberon Bay (1759).

Hawking, Stephen William (born 1942) English physicist and Lucasian Professor of Mathematics at Cambridge. He is primarily interested in gravity, and best-known for his calculations of the physics of the hypothetical apertures in the fabric of space-time known as black holes. Hampered by a severe neuromuscular disorder since 1963, Hawking has nevertheless been acclaimed as the most brilliant theoretical physicist since EINSTEIN.

Hawkins, Sir John (1532-95) English admiral, designer of the Elizabethan navy. Hawkins rebuilt, rearmed and modernized ELIZABETH's outdated fleet and by doing so, and by leading a naval squadron, helped to defeat PHILIP II's Spanish Armada (1588). Hawkins, who pioneered England's part in the Africa-America slave trade, died while raiding the Spanish West Indies with his cousin, DRAKE.

Hawksmoor, Nicholas (1661-1736) English architect destined in his lifetime to take second place to WREN and VANBRUGH, Hawksmoor nevertheless produced some of the most original early 18th-century architecture. As a young man he assisted Wren in his work on Greenwich Hospital, and Vanbrugh at Castle Howard and Blenheim Palace. Hawksmoor's own works range between a grave Roman style, inspired by BRAMANTE, and capricious Gothicism.

Hawthorne, Nathaniel (1804-64) American short-story writer and novelist who is famous for *The Scarlet Letter* (1850) and *The House of the Seven Gables* (1851). His background was strongly Puritan, but although his chief works revolve around the themes of sin and retribution, suffering and compensation, his morality was not bound by convention – in *The Scarlet Letter,* Hester Prynne, the mother of an illegitimate child, is worthier of respect than her husband, who degrades himself in persecution of her lover.

Haydn, Franz Joseph (1732-1809) Austrian composer known as 'father of the symphony'. He took as his starting point the symphonies of C. P. E. BACH and from them evolved the classical form of a set of contrasting orchestral movements that were musically interrelated and balanced. Similarly, he evolved the classical form of the string quartet. Haydn was largely self-taught in composition and reached maturity slowly. In 1761 he entered the service of the Austro-Hungarian Esterhazy family and was able to compose and direct his compositions with an orchestra and choir always at his disposal. He wrote 104 symphonies, many of them known by popular nicknames such as *The Farewell* (45), *The Surprise* (94), *The Clock* (101), *The Drum-roll* (103) and *The London* (104). He wrote also over 80 string quartets and 20 operas, as well as the major oratorios of his later years, *The Creation* (1798) and *The Seasons* (1801). Haydn also wrote the national anthem of Imperial Austria, *The Emperor's Hymn,* later to be used in Germany as the tune to *Deutschland Uber Alles*. He visited England, where he enjoyed great popularity and received a musical doctorate from Oxford University. His brother, Michael, was also a gifted composer and, with MOZART's father, wrote the *Toy Symphony,* for long ascribed to Joseph.

Hayes, Rutherford Birchard (1822-93) Nineteenth President of the US (1877-81), elected on the contested returns of four states. He was twice Governor of Ohio, and his nomination as Republican presidential candidate in 1876 was followed by a close election. The result hinged on the disputed votes of four states, and a congressional commission of eight Republicans and seven Democrats eventually decided in Hayes's favour by a majority of popular votes. His opponent, Tilden, gained a majority of popular votes. Under his Presidency the US recovered much of the commercial prosperity it had lost in the crash of 1873, and his policy of conciliation towards the southern states, though arousing opposition within his Party, was of benefit to the country as a whole.

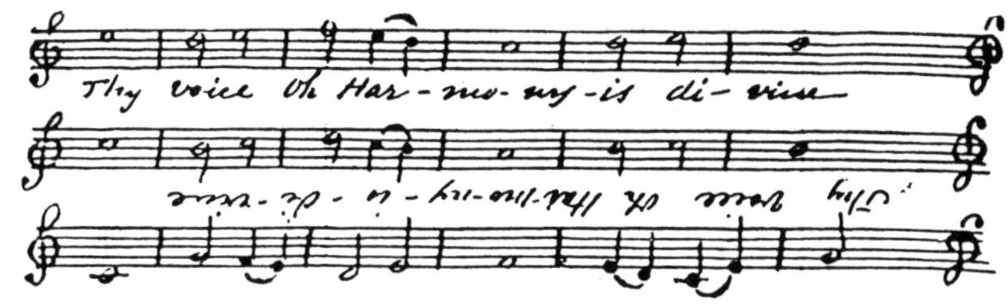

Typical of Haydn's happy approach to music, 'Thy voice, oh Harmony, is divine' can be played either forward or backward

Hazlitt, William (1778-1830) English essayist who was one of the central figures of English Romantic literature. His essays in criticism, principally the *Characters of Shakespeare's Plays* (1817-18) and *Lectures on the English Poets* (1818-19) are personal and clearly argued. His miscellaneous essays appeared in several collections, and he wrote frequently, propounding liberal arguments, in the *Edinburgh Review*.

Heaney, Seamus (born 1939) Irish poet who has written several volumes of poetry including *Eleven Poems* (1965), *Death of a Naturalist* (1966), *Door to the Dark* (1969), *North* (1975), for which he won the W. H. Smith Prize, and *Field Work* (1979).

Hearst, William Randolph (1863-1951) American newspaper publisher who expanded sensational journalism on lines begun by Joseph PULITZER, and built up a chain of 25 big dailies, starting with the *New York Journal* (1895). Hearst filled this paper with sensational reports on crime and scandal and with jingoistic foreign news reports, capped by banner headlines, and matched by lurid pictures. His organization was served by his International News Service (from 1909), and complemented by magazines like *Harper's Bazaar*. He was a member of the US House of Representatives (1903-7) and stood unsuccessfully for the mayoralty of New York City and for the governorship of New York.

Heath, Edward Richard George (born 1916) British Conservative politician. After war service, a short time in the Civil Service, and as news editor of *The Church Times* (1948-9), he was elected MP for Bexley (1950). After becoming assistant whip in 1951, he was appointed chief whip in 1955, Minister of Labour in 1959, Lord Privy Seal in 1960 and President of the Board of Trade and Secretary of State for Industry in 1963. From 1961 to 1963 he conducted Britain's initial and unsuccessful negotiations to join the European Economic Community (Common Market). In 1965, he was elected Conservative Party leader and led the Opposition until 1970. As Prime Minister he took Britain into the EEC but his industrial relations policy resulted in Labour being returned to power in 1974 and his losing the party leadership the following year. In 1977 he became a member of the Independent Commission of International Development Issues.

Heaviside, Oliver (1850-1925) English physicist who predicted the existence of a conducting layer of ions in the upper atmosphere which made long-distance radio communication possible. This layer was independently suggested by KENNELLY. Heaviside created powerful but unorthodox mathematical methods which he applied to many other electromagnetic problems; he used them to show that long telephone lines must be 'loaded' with artificial inductance at intervals to avoid serious distortion.

Hebra, Ferdinand von (1816-80) Austrian physician, whose pioneer microscope studies of ringworm, eczema and scabies showed that many skin disorders were diseases in their own right. Until his time doctors had believed skin diseases to be symptoms of disorders elsewhere in the body. He founded one of Europe's earliest and most important clinics for the teatment of skin diseases in Vienna.

Hegel, Georg Wilhelm Friedrich (1770-1831) German philosopher, the most influential thinker of the Idealist movement. Hegel derived his famous dialectical method from studying the history of Greek philosophy and saw the universe as a single system developing in time, in which the whole gives each part its own full meaning. The idea, in Hegel's terms, is like a prayer, recited first by a young child, hardly aware of what the words mean; and then once again when the child has grown into an old man who has seen life, and has come to grasp the deeper significance of the words.

Heidegger, Martin (1889-1976) German philosopher and influence on contemporary Existentialism, whose analyses of Being and Time (from a standpoint which accepts the equal reality of the mental and the physical), seek to reveal man's place in his world in the way he actually deals with it throughout his life.

Heine, Heinrich (1797-1856) German lyric poet and satirist whose reputation was established with the first two volumes of his *Pictures of Travel* (1826) and *Book of Songs* (1827). Many of these poems were set to music, notably by SCHUMANN in the song cycle *Poet's Love*. In 1831, fired by the ideals of the July Revolution, Heine went to Paris, where he remained for the rest of his life, and where he wrote *Remarks on the History of Religion and Philosophy in Germany* (1835) and *Conditions in France* (1832), intending to make the two nations familiar with each other's way of life and intellectual achievements. In Paris, too, he produced *Germany, A Winter's Tale* (1844) and *Atta Troll* (1841-6), two satirical mock-epics which reinforced his reputation.

Heinz, Henry John (1844-1919) American food manufacturer whose company, using such advertising slogans as '57 Varieties', pioneered the universal use of prepared, canned and bottled foodstuffs.

Heisenberg, Werner (1901-76) German physicist who developed the matrix mechanical version of modern quantum theory. His name is particularly linked with the uncertainty principle, according to which certain pairs of variables describing motion (such as velocity and position or energy and time) cannot be simultaneously measured with complete accuracy, because the measuring process itself interferes with the quantity to be measured. In 1932 he won the Nobel Prize for Physics.

Helmholtz, Herman Ludwig Ferdinand von (1821-94) German scientist who is best known for his statement of the first law of thermodynamics – that is, that energy can be converted from one form to another but cannot be created or destroyed. He studied acoustics and optics, making discoveries about hearing, harmony and colour vision and inventing the ophthalmoscope.

Helvetius, Claude (1715-71) French philosopher who held that all mental activity could be reduced to physical sensation. Men, he said, act from self-interest, based on an assessment of pleasure gained and pain avoided. He also argued, against ROUSSEAU, that education is effective provided only that men chose to acquire it, for by nature they are all equally intelligent.

Hemingway, Ernest (1899-1961) American novelist whose famous books, *A Farewell to Arms* (1929) and *For Whom the Bell Tolls* (1940), are about the personal dangers of war – the individual physical and emotional losses. His other novels deal principally with disillusioned characters who attempt to give meaning to their lives by a vigorous code of action. An ambulance driver in the First World War, Hemingway was a war correspondent during the Second World War.

Henry II (1133-89) First Plantagenet King of England (1154-89), ruler of territories stretching from northern Scotland to southern France. His French possessions came through his father, Geoffrey of Anjou, his wife, ELEANOR OF AQUITAINE, and his son, Geoffrey of Britanny. He inherited England through his mother, Matilda, wrenched northern England from Scotland's Malcolm IV (1157); subdued Wales (1158-65); conquered southeast Ireland by 1171; and gained recognition as Scotland's overlord (1174). Henry's territorial expansion was at first supported by his chancellor, BECKET, but when Becket became Archbishop of Canterbury the two quarrelled over clerical privilege. Henry's reign was of great importance for constitutional and legal developments, including the birth of Common Law.

Henry V (1387-1422) Lancastrian King of England (1413-22), and master of France. To restore English prestige he tried to acquire France, first by diplomacy, then by war, financed largely by parliamentary taxation. Henry set out to dominate the English Channel, and turn the towns of Normandy into English strongholds maintained by local taxes. His plan succeeded; after winning at Agincourt (1415), Henry conquered Normandy (1417-19), reached Paris (1419), and forced on the French the Treaty of Troyes (1420), which made Henry Regent of France and heir to the French throne. He died before acceding, but his son, Henry VI, became, for a time, King of France as well as of England.

Henry the Navigator (1394-1460) Portuguese prince who founded systematic sea exploration and paved the way for Europe's great age of discovery. Henry made exploration of the African coast his life's work, and founded an observatory and school of navigation at Sagres in Portugal, where he assembled cartographers, instrument-makers, astronomers, and pilots to train explorers and coordinate the results of their voyages.

Henry VI (1421-71) King of England, son of Henry V, who succeeded to the throne in his infancy, and whose reign culminated in the Wars of the Roses.

Henry VII (1457-1509) King of England (1485-1509) and first Tudor monarch. Henry was crowned after the death of RICHARD III at Bosworth Field (1485). Henry, Lancastrian claimant to the throne during the Wars of the Roses, ended hostilities and united the rival houses by marrying Elizabeth of York, heiress of EDWARD IV. He scotched two attempts, by Lambert Simnel and Perkin Warbeck, to usurp his throne and, to curb the power of the nobles to make civil war, established the Star Chamber and abolished private armies. Henry amassed a large fortune, at first to protect himself against conspiracies, later to gain prestige for England as the paymaster of Europe. He was a patron of the Renaissance, supported exploration by encouraging the CABOT family and, by marrying his daughter Margaret to James IV of Scotland, eventually brought about the union of England and Scotland (1603).

Henry VIII (1491-1547) King of England (1509-47), who, by making the Church of England independent of Rome, began the English Reformation. Henry was totally unscrupulous in bending to his own ends the constitutional forms which had by then become strongly centralized, and employed a number of able statesmen, among them Cardinal WOLSEY, Sir Thomas MORE, Archbishop Thomas CRANMER and Thomas CROMWELL. One of their tasks was to make or dissolve Henry's six largely unfruitful marriages (1) CATHERINE OF ARAGON, a marriage which ended in divorce after the birth of a daughter (later MARY I) and caused the dispute between Henry and the pope which ended with the establishment of an independent Church of England; (2) ANNE BOLEYN, who also bore a daughter (later ELIZABETH I) and was beheaded; (3) JANE SEYMOUR, who died after giving birth to the future heir, Edward VI; (4) ANNE OF CLEVES who was divorced; (5) CATHERINE HOWARD, beheaded; and (6) CATHERINE PARR, who outlived him. Henry's break with Rome made him head of the ecclesiastical as well as the secular arm of state, but he allowed few Protestant innovations. Strengthened by the absolute supremacy that this gave him, Henry dissolved the monasteries (seizing their treasures and land), strengthened central government, and built a strong navy.

Headstrong and volatile, Henry VIII remains the best-known of English kings. His popular fame rests more on his profligate use of marriage vows rather than the fundamental change in church-state relations by which the English Reformation was brought about

Henry IV (1553-1610) King of France (1589-1610), first of the Bourbons, who sacrificed his personal (Calvinist) religion in the national interest and became one of France's greatest kings. As King of Navarre (1572-89), he fought the War of the Three Henrys (1585-7) to enforce recognition that he was Henry III's rightful heir, and finally, at Coutras, defeated the Catholics under Henry III and the Duke de Guise, Henry I of Lorraine. After inheriting Henry III's throne, he spent nine years fighting Spain and the Holy League to make good his claim to rule, and embraced Catholicism (1593) to heal the wounds of religious strife. The Edict of Nantes (1598) granted toleration to, and political equality for, Protestants. His foreign policy sought to counterbalance the power of the Hapsburgs by alliances with Germany, Sweden and Switzerland, and he aided the Dutch against Spain. Henry was assassinated by a Catholic extremist, François Ravaillac, who believed he was preparing war against the pope.

Henry, O. (1862-1910) Pseudonym of William Sydney Porter, prolific and successful American author of humorous and sentimental short stories. His ironic surprise endings were particularly effective, as in the famous story, *Gift of the Magi*.

Henry, Patrick (1736-99) American lawyer and orator who, with James Otis and Samuel ADAMS, roused colonists against British rule. As a member of Virginia's legislature (1765), Henry urged the right of colonies to legislate for themselves, condemning the Stamp Act which was intended to finance British troops in America. Henry worked to arm Virginians for the American War of Independence (1775-83) and was Governor of Virginia (1776-9, 1784-6). He supported WASHINGTON during the war but afterwards opposed the proposed federal constitution.

Henze, Hans Werner (born 1926) German composer who has moved away from serialism to seek a new expression of humanism and social commitment. He wrote *Ode to the West Wind,* based on SHELLEY's poem, for cello and orchestra and the opera *Elegy for Young Lovers* (1961). More recently he composed the opera-cantata *The Raft of the Medusa,* after the painting by DELACROIX, and the song-cycle *El Cimarron* for baritone with flute, guitar and percussion accompaniment, based on the autobiography of a rebel Cuban slave.

Hepworth, Dame Barbara (1903-1975) English sculptor whose work pays particular attention to subtleties of texture and surface movement, as in *Large and Small Forms* (1945), carved in Cornish elm. Her later work, not dissimilar to that of Henry MOORE, shows a concern with geometric construction and the achievement of a tighter structure through the pierced form.

Heraclitus (6th-5th cent. BC) Greek philosopher, the first to recognize the central role of 'logos', a word with a range of meanings: *word*; *explanation*; *account*; *proposition*. Aware of the connection between opposites ('the way up and the way down are one and the same') and seeing change as the pervasive principle, he likened the world to an eternal fire, in which part is set alight and part extinguished according to set 'measures'; there is constant change while the flame itself is unchanged.

Herbert, George (1593-1633) English churchman and metaphysical poet. 'Herbert speaks to God', a clergyman said, 'like one that really believeth a God, and whose business in the world is most with God'. His religious verse is quiet and simple: *The Temple* (1633) contains about 160 poems on sacred subjects, many of them in irregular forms, some, such as 'The Altar', shaped like physical objects.

Herder, Johann (1744-1803) German philosopher and Lutheran theologian who was chiefly influential as the theoretician of the *Sturm und Drang* (Storm and Stress) movement, a movement away from sterile, foreign forms and establishing a new, national German literature inspired by SHAKESPEARE. He edited and contributed two important essays to the book which is regarded as the movement's manifesto, *On German Style and Art* (1773). His chief philosophical work is *Outlines of a Philosophy of the History of Man* (1784-91), an essay on humanism and historical evolution that anticipated HEGEL.

Hereward (11th cent) Called Hereward the Wake, Anglo-Saxon landowner who led the last English resistance to WILLIAM I's Norman invasion. Hereward led Anglo-Saxon rebels who, with some Danish raiders, sacked Peterborough Abbey (1070). When the Danes withdrew, Hereward was forced to retreat to the fens round Ely. There he led Anglo-Saxon resistance to William's onslaught in 1071, but was driven into hiding as an outlaw, and died in obscurity.

Herod the Great (c. 73-4 BC) King of Judaea, appointed by ANTONIUS and OCTAVIAN. With Roman help, Herod made Judaea a powerful state, enlarging its territory, embellishing provincial cities, building great fortresses, including Masada, and lavishly rebuilding the Temple at Jerusalem. He is remembered most for his atrocities, notably the massacre of all male children in Bethlehem under the age of two, among whom he feared a claimant to his throne, JESUS.

Herodotus (c. 484-424 BC) Greek writer whose *History* described (within its major theme of the Greco-Persian struggle) the rise of Persia under CYRUS and DARIUS I, the development of the Greek city-states and Egypt, Babylon and other parts of the Greco-Asian world in the mid-5th century. Insatiably curious, he was over-credulous of tall stories, but could apply sound critical criteria and is justly called the Father of History.

Herrick, Robert (1591-1674) English poet and clergyman, whose most famous work is the collection *Hesperides* (1648). He wrote lyrical verses of love and country matters in a great variety of metrical forms. Herrick was one of the 'sons' (disciples) of Ben JONSON.

Herschel, Sir William (1738-1822) Hanover-born British astronomer, who discovered the planet Uranus (1781) and carried out extensive systematic observations of the stars. His major results, given in papers to the Royal Society from 1770 onwards, concerned the variable star Mira Ceti, the mountains of the Moon and the rotation of the planets and their several known satellites. He was the first to discover white spots on the surface of Mars, which he concluded were deposits of polar snow. By means of more powerful telescopes he observed and described double stars, measuring their relative distances over a number of years and discovered that many were true binaries revolving around each other. He also attempted to determine the relative distances of the stars from our own Sun, and compiled extensive catalogues of the results. Herschel was at first a musician, and made a successful career as an organist and a music teacher before devoting all his time to astronomy. Following his discovery of Uranus he became private astronomer to George III.

Hertz, Heinrich Rudolph (1857-94) German physicist who discovered radio waves. Hertz conducted a series of experiments and demonstrated the existence of electro-magnetic (radio) waves. He found their velocity to be the same as that of light and showed that they can also be focused and reflected. This confirmed MAXWELL's theory.

Hertzog, James Barry Munnick (1866-1942) Advocate of South African independence and champion of Afrikaner nationalism. He was a general in the second Boer War (1899-1902) and in 1913 founded the Nationalist Party in opposition to BOTHA, its main policy being to achieve South Africa's independence from Britain, whom he refused to support during the First World War. He was Prime Minister from 1924 to 1939 (from 1933 in coalition with SMUTS), during which time Afrikaans replaced Dutch as the official language and the racial segregation laws of 1936 were passed. Because of his continued opposition to involvement in 'Britain's wars', he was forced from office (1939) when Parliament approved Smuts's motion in favour of South Africa's participation in the Second World War. He was the true founder of Boer Nationalism and Afrikaner culture, and MALAN and VERWOERD were his spiritual successors.

Herzl, Theodor (1860-1904) Father of modern Zionism, and an advocate of Jewish political autonomy. The outbursts of anti-Semitism in the late 19th century led him to publish his pamphlet *The Jewish State,* in which he argued that Jews had only two alternatives; either assimilation by intermarriage, or a separate national state. The latter course was his answer to the problem, and though his reasons were political and economic, not religious, the first Zionist Congress held at Basel in 1897 resolved to secure for the Jewish people a legally assured home in Palestine. Herzl negotiated for a Jewish homeland with the Sultan of Turkey, the Pope, and the British, French,

German and Russian governments. He accepted a British offer of land in east Africa, but this was rejected by the 1903 Zionist Congress, and when Herzl died in 1904 the territorial question was still unresolved.

Hess, Walter Richard Rudolf (born 1894) German politician, HITLER's deputy, who flew to Britain during the Second World War in order to present his own peace proposals. After the Munich *putsch* (1923) he was imprisoned with Hitler, and *Mein Kampf* was probably written by him at Hitler's dictation. In 1934 he was appointed deputy leader of the party and in 1939 Hitler's successor-designate after GOERING. Just before Germany's invasion of Russia in 1941, Hess flew on his own initiative to Scotland with compromise peace proposals for CHURCHILL. He was put in gaol, underwent psychiatric treatment, and in 1945 was sentenced to life imprisonment at Nuremberg. By 1966 he was the only remaining inmate of Berlin's Spandau prison.

Hesse, Hermann (1877-1962) German novelist and poet, whose main preoccupation is the tension between the material and the spiritual in man. This idea is given clear expression in *Steppenwolf* (1927), the story of a lonely and withdrawn artist with a split personality. In 1911 Hesse settled in Switzerland, where he wrote most of his major works, including *The Glass Bead Game* (1943), considered by some to be his greatest work. It is the story of a man who seeks self-fulfilment through an aesthetic game which develops into a form of worship. Hesse was awarded the Nobel Prize for Literature in 1946.

Heyerdahl, Thor (born 1914) Norwegian ethnologist whose 'drift voyages' in primitive craft showed how ancient people may have crossed the oceans. With five companions, Heyerdahl drifted on the single-sailed balsa raft, *Kon-Tiki*, 4300 miles across the Pacific from Peru to Polynesia (1947) in an attempt to prove that the Polynesians came from South America and not, as most ethnologists believed, from southeast Asia. Pursuing his theory, Heyerdahl led archaeological expeditions to the Galapagos Islands (1953) and to Bolivia, Peru and Colombia (1954). In 1970, Heyerdahl sailed from Africa to America in the papyrus boat *Ra II*, based on Egyptian and American Indian designs, demonstrating that the ancient Egyptians could have crossed the Atlantic in similar craft, thousands of years earlier. He has written numerous books, including *Tigris Expedition* (1981) about his journey from Qurna, Iraq, to Djibouti in a reed boat (1977-8).

Hiawatha (16th cent.) Red Indian chief remembered as the founder of an Indian league. In 1570, he reputedly tried to end tribal strife by organizing the Cayuga, Mohawk, Oneida, Onondaga and Seneca tribes into the Five Nations (Iroquois), a union which became the most effective Amerindian grouping in North America. LONGFELLOW's fictional hero, Hiawatha, was not connected with the real Iroquois statesman.

Hildebrandt, Lucas von (1668-1745) Italian-born architect who became, with FISCHER VON ERLACH, the leading exponent of Baroque architecture in Austria. He trained in Rome and his style was influenced by both GUARINI and BORROMINI. His work consists of magnificent palaces and churches in and near Vienna, notably the Upper Belvedere, built for Prince Eugen.

Hillary, Sir Edmund Percival (born 1919) New Zealand mountaineer who, in May 1953, with the Sherpa, TENZING NORGAY, was first to climb Mount Everest. They were members of Sir John Hunt's British Everest expedition, the eighth attempt on the mountain. Hillary, who was knighted for the

Hillary's feat in conquering Everest with Tenzing Norgay in 1953, ended 50 years of glorious endeavour and failure

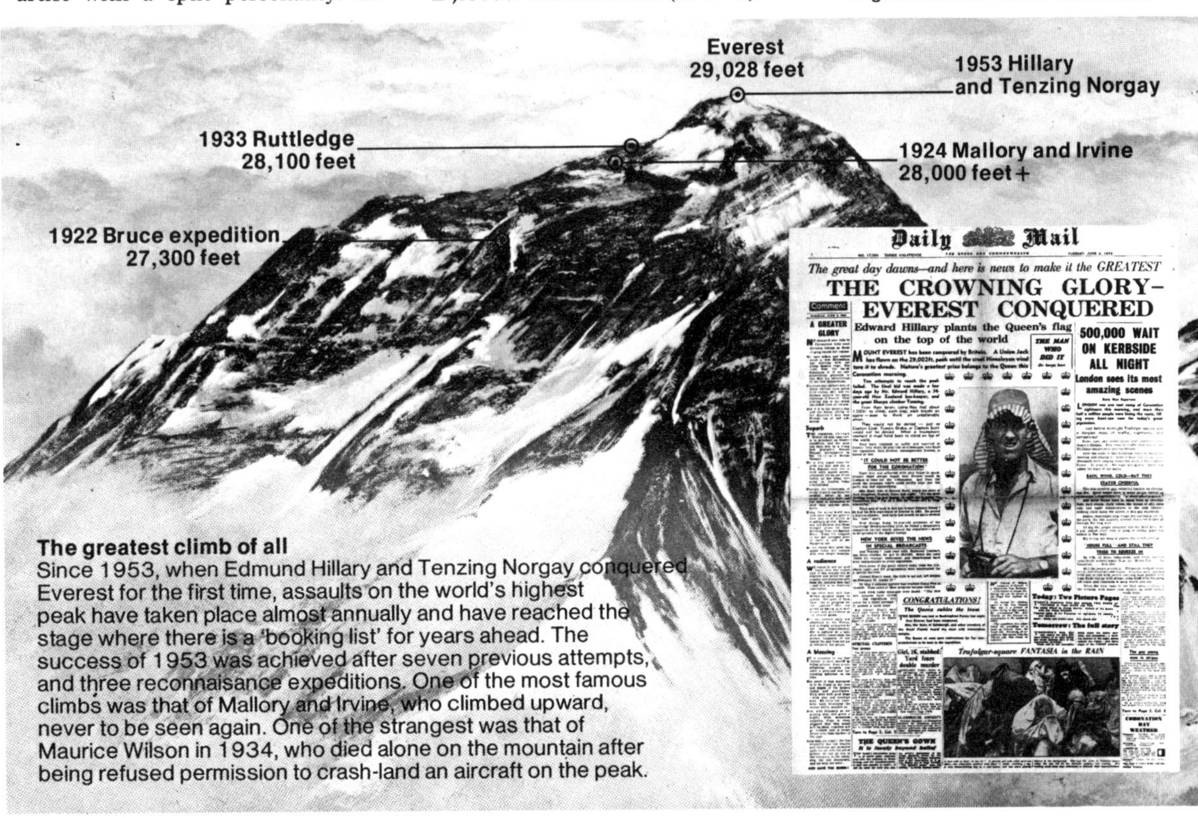

The greatest climb of all
Since 1953, when Edmund Hillary and Tenzing Norgay conquered Everest for the first time, assaults on the world's highest peak have taken place almost annually and have reached the stage where there is a 'booking list' for years ahead. The success of 1953 was achieved after seven previous attempts, and three reconnaisance expeditions. One of the most famous climbs was that of Mallory and Irvine, who climbed upward, never to be seen again. One of the strangest was that of Maurice Wilson in 1934, who died alone on the mountain after being refused permission to crash-land an aircraft on the peak.

achievement was later a member of the New Zealand expedition (1957-8) which reached the South Pole from Scott Station at McMurdo Sound, the first overland journey to the South Pole since SCOTT.

Hillel (1st cent. BC-1st cent. AD) Jewish rabbi and theologian descended from the family of DAVID, whose reinterpretation of the Bible introduced a new tone of tolerance. His sayings in some ways anticipate the attitude of JESUS and prepared the way for the later acceptance of Christian teaching.

Hillyarde, Nicholas (c. 1547-1619) English miniature painter, whose work is characterized by a languorous quality which probably derives from French painting. His work is typified by *The Young Man among Roses* (*c.* 1588), probably intended as a lover's gift and much less formal than HOLBEIN's miniatures. Hillyarde, like most early miniaturists, made little attempt to model his forms, preferring a surface pattern painted with exquisite delicacy.

Himmler, Heinrich (1900-45) German politician, creator and chief of the Gestapo, the Nazi secret police. In 1927 he became deputy-leader of HITLER's Storm Troopers (SS) and in 1929 was appointed their leader. In 1936 he assumed control of all German police forces, then, on the outbreak of war, became chief of Reich Administration and in 1943 Minister of the Interior. He was infamous for the number and horror of his atrocities and was feared even by his colleagues. On the defeat of Germany he went into hiding but was found and arrested by the British, and committed suicide.

Hindemith, Paul (1895-1963) German composer of symphonies, operas and chamber music. His early, dissonant music was replaced in the 1930s by a mellower style which informs his symphony *Mathis the Painter* (based on his score for the opera of the same name), the lyrical ballet suite *Noblissima visione* and *Symphonic Metamorphoses*. Hindemith, who was banned by the Nazis, settled in America six years before the Second World War.

Hipparchus (2nd cent. BC) Greek astronomer and mathematician, who was one of the most accurate observers of stars in ancient times and who discovered the precession of the equinoxes. His star catalogue listed over 850 stars, giving position and apparent brightness to six magnitudes.

Hippocrates (c. 460-377 BC) Greek physician, called the 'Father of Medicine'. The many writings attributed to him stress accurate observation and reject superstitions about diseases. His extensive descriptions are the bases of classical medicine, and the 'Hippocratic Oath' is the essential expression of medical ethics.

Hirohito (born 1901) Emperor of Japan. In 1921 he became the first member of the Imperial family to leave Japan when he visited Europe on a goodwill tour. He acceded in 1926 and has ruled Japan during times of internal conflict and overseas aggression, although it is probable that he genuinely desired not to enter the Second World War, and encouraged Japan's surrender in 1945. Now ruling under a modified constitution, he has attempted to break away from the traditional isolation of the Japanese Imperial Family and has made several visits abroad, including one to Britain in

Relative strengths of European powers and the US, 1939. Hitler's Germany dominated on land, with 1.5m soldiers and, in the air, with 4,500 aircraft

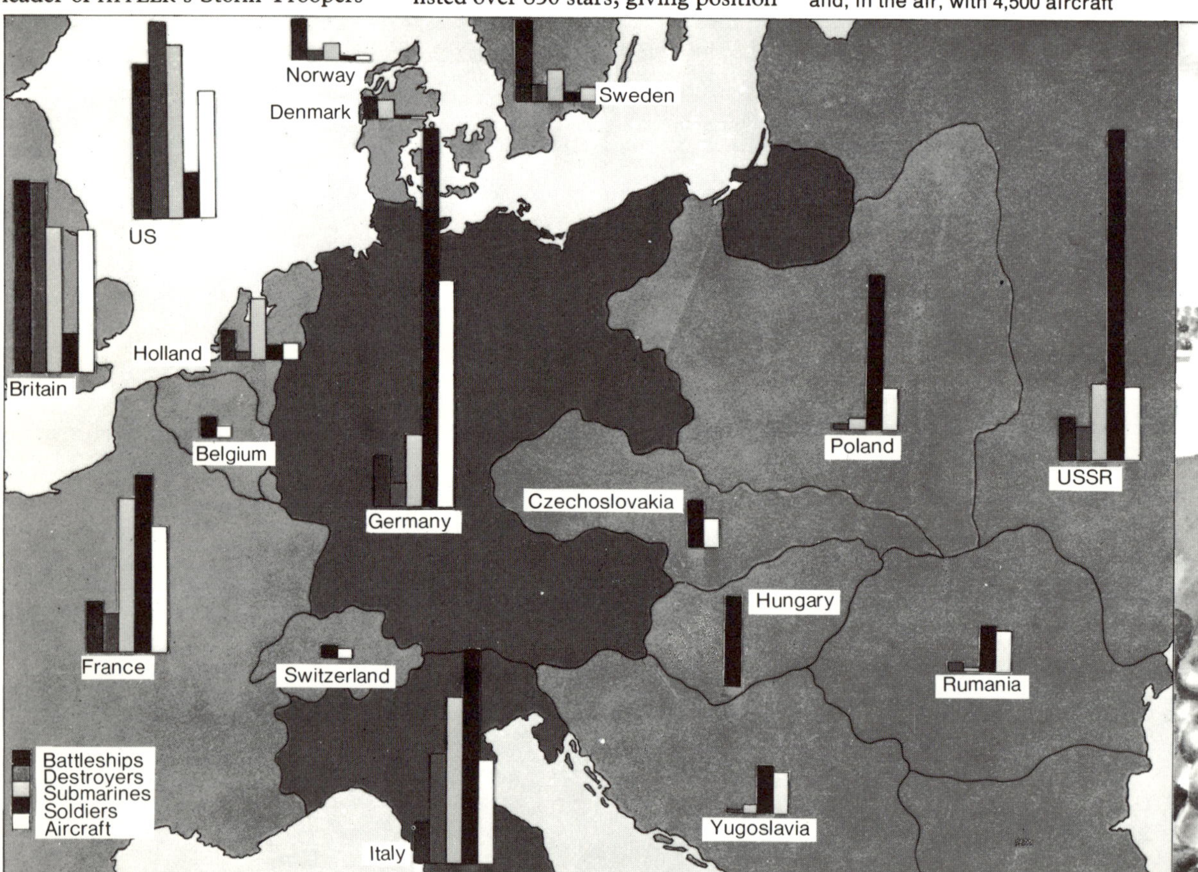

1972. He is interested in marine biology and has written a number of learned works on the subject.

Hitchcock, Sir Alfred (1899-1980) English film director and master of the thriller, who once said 'I can't bear suspense'. In 1940, Hitchcock went to Hollywood, where his work lost some of its English character, though he still retained his particular brand of humour, creating suspense by his mastery of cinematographic techniques. Hitchcock manipulates ordinary situations to heighten their fear and menace, and tension is built up by his giving to the audience rather than the protagonists as many facts as possible as early as possible. Milestones in his repertoire include *The Lady Vanishes* (1939), *North by Northwest* (1959), *Psycho* (1960), *The Birds* (1963) and *Frenzy* (1972). He was knighted in 1980.

Hitler, Adolf (1889-1945) Austrian-born demagogue and Führer of the German Third Reich, whose policies plunged Europe into the Second World War. He died by his own hand in the flames of Berlin as the conflict drew to its close. At the end of the First World War, in which he served in the German army, he joined the insignificant

Hitchcock, the master of suspense. His famous film *The Birds* is the epitome of his special talent. Hitchcock himself always appears, fleetingly, in his films.

National Socialist Workers Party, which he transformed and enlarged by his talent as a rabble-rousing orator, and in 1923 he tried, unsuccessfully, to overthrow the Bavarian government in a *putsch* at Munich. For this he was imprisoned and while in jail wrote *Mein Kampf*, in which he expounded his political and social theories. The great depression of the late twenties brought him millions of recruits from people disillusioned with other parties, frightened by inflation, workless and hungry. It also won him the support of business interests, fearful of Communism. By 1930 the Nazi Party was the second largest political organization in Germany, having achieved much of its success by offering the Germans a scapegoat for all their sufferings – the Jewish people, who were to die in their millions by 1945, at the hands of the Nazis. In 1933 President Hindenburg made Hitler Chancellor, and, by contriving the burning down of the Reichstag and blaming it on the Communists, Hitler was able to establish a dictatorship, having eliminated his main rival, Ernst Röhm. Hitler then set about rearming Germany. In a series of increasingly aggressive acts, phased to coincide with the progressive remilitarization of Germany, he embarked on the gradual conquest of Europe by sending troops into the demilitarized Rhineland (1936), forming an alliance with MUSSOLINI (formally concluded 1939) and sending his troops into Austria and Czechoslovakia (1938). By invading Poland (Sept. 1939) he precipitated the Second World War.

Hobbema, Meindert (1638-1709) Dutch landscape painter, a pupil of RUISDAEL, whose works, although less romantic, are similar to his teacher's in their detailed realism. His best-known painting is the *Avenue at Middleharnis* (1688), in which an avenue of trees leads the eye across a wide, flat landscape, but his most typical paintings are of watermills in wooded settings.

Hobbes, Thomas (1588-1679) English political theorist, lifelong controversialist and philosopher, often called the father of modern analytical philosophy. His principal work *Leviathan* (1651) argued that sovereignty is vested in a ruler when the people agree to limit their freedom in return for protection. Hobbes paved the way for Spinoza, LOCKE, HUME, ROUSSEAU and BENTHAM to develop concepts of human co-operation, as opposed to ruling authority, as the basis for social order.

Ho Chi-minh (1890-1969) Vietnamese revolutionary politician, who organized and led resistance first to French colonialism and then to the US in Vietnam. He was founder and first President of the Democratic Republic of Vietnam (North Vietnam) from 1954 to 1969. He began his political career in Paris, where he preached revolution to Vietnamese. He was trained as a Communist agitator in Moscow (1923-5), then went to Canton, and with Mikhail BORODIN helped to organize the South East Asian Comintern. In the Second World War he organized and led the Viet-minh Communist-Nationalist alliance against the Japanese forces, and in 1945 his partisan army, after receiving the Japanese surrender, turned its attention to the Anglo-French-Nationalist Chinese army of occupation. The uneasy compromise between the Viet-minh and France soon broke down. Ho was in effective control of the North only, the South having been controlled by the anti-Communist Bao-Dai, backed first by France and, when France withdrew, by the US. Ho's attempts to gain control of all Vietnam led to US intervention and the war between the North and South.

Hockney, David (born 1937) English artist who made his name during the Pop Art movement with witty, often deliberately naive paintings, such as *Flight into Italy-Swiss Landscape* (1962). In the late 1960s and 1970s he developed a more realistic, classical style, typical of which are his portrait of Celia Birtwell and Ossie Clark (1970) and *A Bigger Splash* (1967). His graphic work, executed with an economical but powerful sense of line, includes many fine portraits and his series of etchings, *A Rake's Progress* (1961-3). In 1978 he designed the set for *The Magic Flute* at Glyndebourne.

Hodgkin, Thomas (1798-1866) British pathologist. Following his work on the diseases of the lymph glands, the name Hodgkin's disease was given to lymphadenoma.

Hoffa, James Riddle (1913-77) American labour leader whose controversial leadership of the International Brotherhood of Teamsters was cut short by a criminal conviction, largely through the efforts of the then Attorney-General Robert F. KENNEDY. Hoffa's sentence was commuted in 1971 by President NIXON.

Hoffman, Ernst (1776-1822) German writer, composer, music critic and illustrator of the German Romantic period, author of *The Legacy* (1817), a short story; *The Golden Pot* (1813), an allegorical fairy tale; and *The Devil's Elixirs* (1812-16), his only novel. Hoffman's talent for inventing bizarre and grotesque adventures in an exploration of the relationship between the natural and the supernatural influenced other 19th-century writers such as BALZAC, POE and SCOTT, and inspired OFFENBACH to write his famous opera, *The Tales of Hoffmann*. He wrote an essay on MOZART's *Don Giovanni*, and *The Relationship between Artist and Society* (1819-21).

Hoffmann, Josef (1870-1956) Austrian architect connected with the Art Nouveau movement. Hoffmann studied under Otto Wagner in Austria and brought new clarity and restraint to continental Art Nouveau. In his major work, the Palais Stoclet in Brussels (1905-11), he uses rich materials in a rectilinear pattern which contrast sharply with the building's elaborate frieze, designed by Gustav KLIMT.

Hoffnung, Gerard (1925-59) British humorous artist and musician, known for his fanciful drawings of musical subjects. His work, which was somewhat Teutonic in character, shows a robust and eccentric sense of humour, though there was a profoundly serious side to his nature. His comic concerts, given at the Albert Hall, revealed his love of the absurd and an extensive knowledge of serious music.

Hofmann, Hans (1880-1966) German-born American Abstract expressionist painter. His influence on American art was considerable.

Hogarth, William (1697-1764) English artist, famous through the enormous and lasting popularity of his engravings. Wishing to be judged as a moralist as well as an artist, he painted what he called 'modern moral subjects' in a number of pictorial cycles, subsequently engraved, the first of which was the *Harlot's Progress* (1731-2). Though he twice visited Paris, Hogarth was an extreme chauvinist and refusd to recognize his debt to foreign masters. In his aesthetic treatise, *The Analysis of Beauty* (1753), he attacked the connoisseurs, the concept of ideal beauty, and the vogue for collecting Italian works at the expense of English ones. Nevertheless in *Sigismunda* (1759) he attempted, without much success, to outdo the Bolognese painters. He also made attempts at historical painting, recognizing that the practice of this genre had been an important element in the success of his father-in-law, the painter, Sir James Thornhill.

Holbein, Hans the Younger (c. 1497-1543) One of the most important German artists of the 16th century and court painter to HENRY VIII. He was trained by his father, also a painter, and from 1515 worked in Basel, where he painted portraits, received civic commissions and executed decorations for house façades, now known only through drawings. His reputation was enhanced by illustrations for LUTHER's Bible and two series of woodcuts on a medieval theme: the *Dance of Death* (1523-4) and the *Alphabet of Death* (1524). In 1523 he painted three portraits of the humanist ERASMUS and when, in 1526, the Reformation crisis forced Holbein to leave Basel, Erasmus gave him a letter of introduction to Sir Thomas MORE. One of the first commissions he obtained after arriving in England was a portrait group of More's family, of which only sketches and copies remain. By 1528, More was in disfavour and Holbein began painting portraits of German merchants in London. These pictures are characterized by an amazing virtuosity, best seen in the *Ambassadors* (1533), which led to his royal appointment.

Holiday, Billie (1915-59) American blues and jazz singer who sang in nightclubs in the 1930s and later with the bands of Count BASIE and Artie Shaw. Her memorable renditions of *My Man*, *Mean to Me* and *God Bless the Child* have a legendary status in the history of American popular and jazz music.

Holland, John Philip (1840-1914) Irish-born American inventor who developed the modern submarine. He devised the scheme of using electric motors for power under water and internal combustion engines on the surface and also introduced the method of submergence by water ballast. These systems were used in the *Holland*, the first modern submarine, purchased by the American Government in 1900.

Holly, Buddy (1936-59) American singer and songwriter who, with his group the Crickets, had a phenomenal success with such records as *That'll be the Day*, *Oh Boy* and *Peggy Sue*, all released in 1957. He pioneered double-tracking and the standard rock-group four-man line-up. He was killed in an air crash.

Holmes, Oliver Wendell (1809-94) American author and academic, best known for *The Autocrat of the Breakfast-Table* (1858) and *The Professor at the Breakfast-Table* (1860), humorous philosophical discourses. He was a central figure in the cultural life of New England, and Professor of Anatomy at Harvard (1847-82).

Holmes, Oliver Wendell (1841-1935) American judge. Appointed to the Supreme Court (1902-32) by Theodore ROOSEVELT, he urged restraint in the use of judicial power, and maintained that law is not void merely because it seems to judges to be excessive, inappropriate, or based on a morality with which they disagree; latitude must be allowed for different views. Holmes stated in *The Common Law* (1881) that law is based not on logic but on experience, and his constant re-evaluation of legal concepts in the light of social change, although arousing fierce opposition, led to the abandonment of obsolete doctrines.

Holst, Gustav Theodore (1874-1934) English composer who wrote the orchestral suite, *The Planets* (1914-16). Holst, formerly an organist and music teacher, associated closely with VAUGHAN WILLIAMS and, like him, was deeply influenced by English folk music. Holst also possessed a strong, original musical personality. He wrote equally effectively for brass band or school orchestra but moved always towards an increasing austerity of vision, as in his fine tone poem, *Egdon Heath* (based on the landscape description in HARDY's *Return of the Native*). Holst's other works include *The Hymn of Jesus* and a comic opera, *The Perfect Fool*.

Homer (8th cent. BC) Greek legendary author of the *Iliad* and the *Odyssey*. Though the authorship of the poems was not doubted in antiquity, modern research has shown that they represent the culmination of several centuries of orally transmitted poetry about the war of the Greeks against Troy. The *Iliad* is concerned with the episode in the Trojan War of the wrath of Achilles; the *Odyssey* deals with Odysseus's return from Troy, after 10 years of wandering, to his native Ithaca and his wife Penelope. The two works had far-reaching effects on Greek and Latin literature and their expression of the heroic ideal formed the basis of ancient education.

Homer, Winslow (1836-1910) American painter, who began as a journalistic illustrator. His later seascapes, for which he is now best known, show virtuoso technique, and are often dramatic in content.

Honegger, Arthur (1892-1955) Swiss composer who sought to express the conflicts of humanity in his music. In a highly individual style, he wrote five symphonies depicting the struggle between beauty and evil, peace and war, and the stage cantatas *King David* and *Joan of Arc at the Stake* (text by Paul Claudel). He also wrote a symphonic movement *Pacific 231*, depicting a steam locomotive.

Honnecourt, Villard de (13th cent.) French architect, none of whose buildings survive, but whose handbook, filled with sketches of architectural plans and details seen on his travels and with his own designs, still exists. Containing contemporary records of the cathedrals of Laon, Reims, Lausanne and Chartres, both from his designs and his sculptural drawings it is clear that he was one of the foremost architects and masons of that period.

Hooch, Pieter de (1629-c. 1684) Dutch genre painter, whose typical interiors, usually with two or three figures engaged in domestic chores, and interest in the fall of light recall VERMEER, though his work tends towards more 'photographic' realism.

Hooft, Pieter (1581-1647) Dutch poet, historian and playwright whose 20-volume *Dutch History* (1642-54) based on the work of TACITUS was a monument to his lifelong dedication to the ennoblement of the Dutch language. The most brilliant Renaissance figure in Dutch literature between 1607 and 1610, he wrote a series of Petrarchan sonnets, some tragedies based on SENECA, the pastoral play *Grandida* (1605) and the comedy *Warenar* (1616).

Hooke, Robert (1635-1703) English physicist who discovered a fundamental law describing the elasticity of springs. In 1678 he formulated what is now called Hooke's law, which states that stress is proportional to strain.

Hooker, Sir William Jackson (1785-1865) British botanist, horticulturist and the first Director of the Royal Botanic Gardens, Kew (1840), which he made the finest botanic gardens in the world. He commissioned plant collectors to bring home new species, redesigned and extended the gardens, greatly increased the collection of hardy as well as tropical plants and initiated a series of botanical studies from British colonies overseas. Earlier in his career he made botanical expeditions to various parts of Britain, Iceland (1809) and France, Switzerland and northern Italy (1814). At his Suffolk home he built up a herbarium which became known to botanists throughout the world and was eventually bought for the nation.

Hoover, Herbert Clark (1874-1964) Republican, 31st President of the US (1929-33), in office during the Great Depression. He succeeded COOLIDGE as President in 1929, and his encouragement of big business led to a handful of companies, including Standard Oil, J. Pierpoint Morgan, and the US Steel Corporation, controlling a large proportion of the country's wealth. The Wall Street crash in October 1929 indicated the failure of this policy, however, and the subsequent depression revealed Hoover's lack of political acumen. Believing the setback to be temporary, and declaring at the height of the collapse that 'the fundamental business of the country ... is on a sound and prosperous basis,' he opposed direct government aid to the unemployed and became one of the most hated men in the country. In the 1932 presidential election he was decisively beaten by F. D. ROOSEVELT, whereupon he retired.

Hoover, John Edgar (1895-1972) American Director of the United States Federal Bureau of Investigation (FBI). In 1924, he took over the directorship of the Bureau of Investigation and began to reorganize this somewhat discredited agency. Later, Congress expanded the Bureau's powers and it became the Federal Bureau of Investigation. Hoover led the FBI for 48 years.

Hopkins, Gerard Manley (1844-89) English poet, who was a great technical innovator and a potent influence on the development of 20th-century English verse. Hopkins was a Jesuit and felt that publication of his poems would be contrary to his duty. He sent most of them to friends such as Robert BRIDGES, his executor, but the boldness of his verse experiments caused Bridges to delay publication of *Poems* until 1918. His language is condensed and uses the accentual pattern of Old English verse, seeking to capture the inward peace of Christian faith, and yet expressing tormenting doubts, as in the later 'terrible' sonnets.

Hopper, Edward (1882-1967) American painter who was a pupil of Robert Henri and greatly influenced by the Ashcan School. He often placed lonely figures in his realistic, carefully drawn settings; many of them of New York City and New England.

Horace (65-8 BC) Roman lyric poet and satirist. A master of form and metre, he has been the supreme interpreter of Augustan culture to succeeding generations, and his popularity is undiminished today. His *Epodes* and *Satires*, written in a racy style, portray a variety of scene and character in contemporary life. The earlier *Epodes* are bitter in mood, but in the *Satires* and the later *Epistles* Horace's writing became more sympathetic. His sane philosophy and his gentle humour, coupled with skilful story-telling, show a depth of insight into life in general and his own in particular. The three books of lyric *Odes* which were published in 23 BC, and a fourth after 13 BC, range in subject matter from wine and women to patriotism and national purpose.

Horney, Karen (1885-1952) American psychoanalyst of German origin. Dissatisfied with the anti-feminism of much Freudian doctrine, she put forward the idea that many of the personality traits which FREUD thought of as universal were culturally and socially determined. She stressed the importance of early training, but suggested that later experiences could also influence character.

Hotspur see PERCY, Sir Henry

Houdini, Harry (1874-1926) American escapologist and illusionist, who accepted seemingly impossible challenges. He extricated himself from ropes, chains and handcuffs and from prison cells and even escaped from a strait jacket while hanging upside down. His name imitates that of the French magician, Houdin. His real name was Ehrich Weiss.

Greatest of all escapers, Harry Houdini prepares to perform one of his seemingly impossible stunts

Houdon, Jean-Antoine (1741-1828) French portrait sculptor who won renown with his classical-style statue of *St Bruno* (1764). Among his best-known busts are those of DIDEROT (1771), GLUCK (1775), Benjamin FRANKLIN and VOLTAIRE (1778) and WASHINGTON (1785). They illustrate his skill in capturing characteristic traits of gesture and expression.

Housman, Alfred Edward (1859-1936) English classical scholar and lyric poet, author of delicate, melancholy poems, often about rural tragedies. He is best known for the poem 'A Shropshire Lad' (1896).

Houssay, Bernado see CORI, Charles

Houston, Samuel (1793-1863) American soldier and statesman, who helped join Texas to the United States. The first President of the Republic of Texas (1836-8 and 1841-4), he achieved union with the United States (1845), then served Texas as senator (1846-59) and Governor (1859-61). The biggest industrial city in the southwestern US is named after him.

Howard, Catherine see HENRY VIII

Howard, Charles, 2nd Baron of Effingham (1536-1624) English admiral who defeated the Spanish Armada (1588). As Lord High Admiral on board the *Ark Royal,* he led DRAKE and HAWKINS to their victory over the Spanish fleet and saved England from threatened invasion. Howard of Effingham commanded both the army and the navy in 1598 and 1599 when there were further invasion threats, and, with ESSEX, captured Cadiz (1596). The following year he was created 1st Earl of Nottingham.

Howard, John (c. 1726-90) English prison reformer who first put forward the view that prisoners might be reformed by such methods as solitary confinement, regular work and religious instruction. Appalled to find that some gaolers existed on fees from prisoners, who, on discharge, had to pay for their release, Howard spent his life touring the prisons and hospitals of England, Ireland and the Continent, campaigning against brutal treatment of the inmates. His findings, compiled in *The State of the Prisons* (1777), had much influence.

Hrolf see ROLLO

Hsieh Ho (late 5th cent.) Chinese painter and art critic, author of the *Six Canons of Painting*. These rules, still fundamental to students of Chinese painting, summarize the principles formed in previous centuries.

Hsüan Tsung (685-762) Chinese Emperor (713-56) of the T'ang dynasty, whose reign marked a cultural zenith in Chinese history. He founded the Hanlin Academy of Letters (725) to compile histories, draft decrees and perform other literary work. He established schools throughout the empire, and attracted poets and men of the arts to the royal court. Sculpture, painting, true porcelain work and woodblock printing on paper all flourished. His reign ended when a rebellion forced him to abdicate.

Hsüan, T'ung see PU-YI, Henry

Hubble, Edwin Powell (1889-1953) American astronomer, who discovered that galaxies exist outside our own, all apparently receding at a speed that depends on their distance. In 1923 Hubble identified peripheral stars in the Andromeda galaxy and proved that its spiral nebulae are distant and separate from our own Milky Way Galaxy. By 1929 Hubble had proved that the more distant a galaxy is from us, the faster it seems to be receding.

Hudson, Henry (17th cent.) English mariner and explorer of Arctic and subarctic waters who vanished after being cast adrift by mutineers. His name is commemorated in the Hudson River and Hudson Bay, which he explored in his search for the North West Passage.

Huggins, Sir William (1824-1910) English astronomer, who pioneered the use of spectroscopic photography for investigating the chemical composition of stars. While investigating Sirius in 1868 he discovered a shift in its light towards the red end of the spectrum ('the red shift'), which enabled him to determine its velocity and that of other stars.

Hughes, David Edward (1831-1900) Anglo-American inventor of the teleprinter, which he patented in 1855. He later set out the basic principles of the 'loose contact', which underlies the various forms of microphone, such as the telephone and hearing aids.

Hughes, Howard (1905-76) American aircraft manufacturer, filmmaker and head of the $2 billion Hughes Enterprises. A keen amateur pilot, in 1935 he set a world record airspeed of 352 mph, and won the 1938 round-the-world flight record. His later years were spent in almost total seclusion.

Hughes, Langston (1902-67) American author, who was one of the first negroes to win a literary reputation and to express the negro view of America. He is admired for his poems – 'The Weary Blues' (1926) attracted readers by its attempt to introduce the rhythms of jazz and folk music into poetry. Since that time, he helped create a

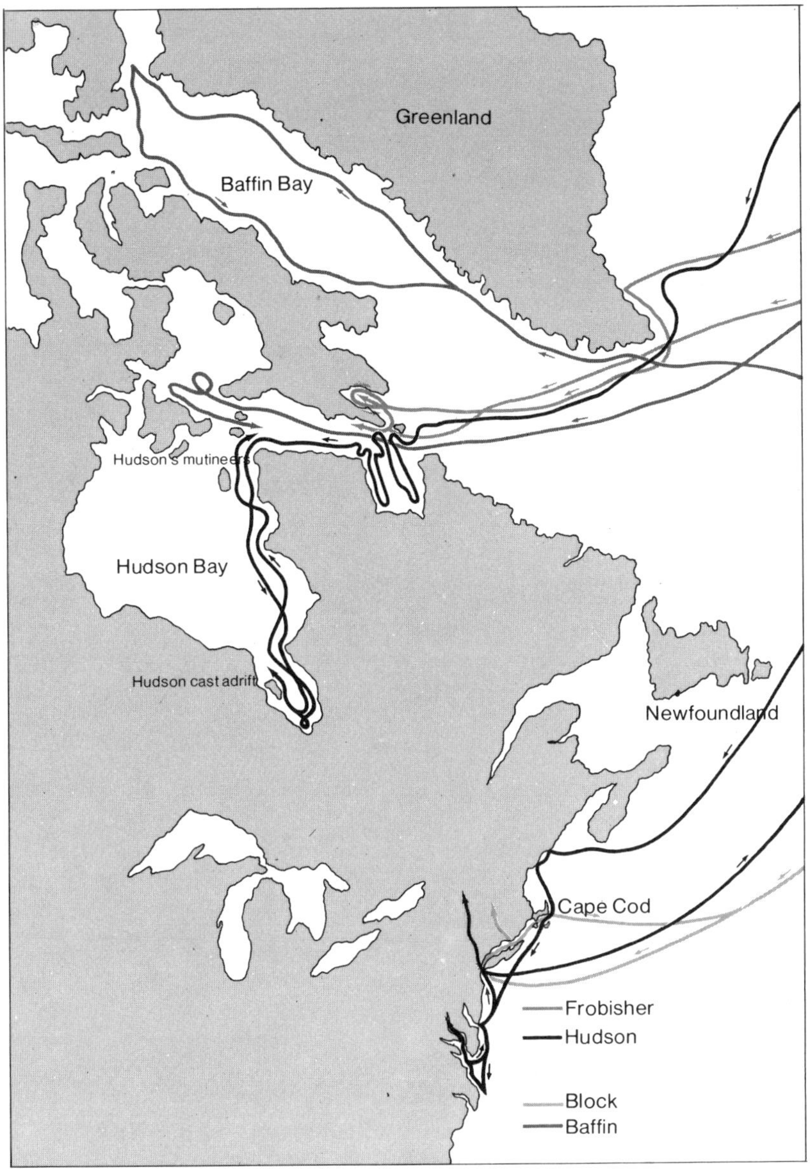

The search for a route to Cathay by a North West Passage around the Americas led to a series of fruitless attempts between 1576 and 1615

body of negro American writing, producing ballads, plays, stories and two autobiographical works, *The Big Sea* (1940) and *I Wonder as I Wander* (1956).

Hughes, Richard (1900-76) English novelist and writer of stories for children. After travels in America and the Caribbean, he wrote *A High Wind in Jamaica* (1929), a study of amiable pirates and malevolent children.

Hughes, Ted (born 1930) English poet, whose poems convey vividly the existence of natural objects, plants, animals and birds, alongside industrial and urban life. His language and imaginative perception celebrate their survival, while the human beings in his poems struggle to live. Typical collections are *The Hawk in the Rain* (1957), *Lupercal* (1960), *Crow* (1970) and *River* (1983), while he has also written verse and tales for children. In 1984 he became Poet Laureate. He was married to Sylvia PLATH.

Hugo, Victor Marie (1802-85) French author and the leading apostle of Romanticism. Hugo, a prolific writer, revolutionized poetry and the historical novel, which he developed with *Notre Dame de Paris* (1831) and in his social drama *Les Misérables* (1862) about the victims of society. Hugo had shown his passion for liberty, as well as his skill in handling technical innovations, in *Odes et Ballades* (1828) and *Orientales* (1829) and had shattered convention with his dramas *Cromwell* (1827), *Hernani* (1830) and *Ruy Blas* (1838). The 'Préface de Cromwell', setting out his dramatic precepts, came to be regarded as a manifesto of the new Romantic movement. In 1841, Hugo was elected to the French Academy, created a peer of France and began an active political life. As a result of vigorous opposition to NAPOLEON III's *coup d'état* in 1851, Hugo was obliged to live in exile in the Channel Islands, a period which prompted his scathing satirical poems *Les Châtiments* (1853). Napoleon's overthrow in 1870 facilitated his return and subsequent election to the National Assembly. A national hero and a popular symbol of humanitarian and democratic ideals, he was buried in the Pantheon in Paris.

Hui-Tsung (1028-1135) Last Emperor of the Northern Sung dynasty in China and patron of a brilliant academy of painters. A poet, calligrapher and painter of talent, Hui-Tsung continued his role as arbiter of taste until the sack of his capital by Tatars in 1126. He died in captivity in Manchuria, but the style which he encouraged had a lasting effect on the art of the East.

Hull, Clark (1884-1952) American psychologist whose reinforcement theory of learning states that learning occurs in view of anticipated rewards and dies away when these are not forthcoming. Habits are the bonds that link stimulus and response, but they acquire force only from some drive, i.e. an unfulfilled need. Hull also made a lifelong study of aptitude tests and their validity. His findings in both fields have served to reconcile and integrate the work of PAVLOV, Thorndike, TOLMAN, WATSON and others.

Humboldt, Baron Alexander von (1769-1859) German botanist and explorer whose South American journeys helped to broaden the bases of modern geography. After years of travelling in Europe, Hum-

Exiled for 20 years, Victor Hugo (right) was given a hero's funeral when he died boldt and the French botanist, Aimé Bonpland, set out on a scientific exploration of South America (1799-1804). They discovered the Casiquiare, a curious natural canal linking the Amazon and Orinoco rivers; visited Cuba and Mexico; followed the Andes from Colombia to Peru (reaching the then record altitude of 18,893 ft on Mount Chimborazo) and studied the cold Pacific stream, rich in marine life, now called the Humboldt Current. Humboldt was the first scientist to grasp relationships between certain natural phenomena, correlating rise in altitude with fall in temperature, noting that some volcanoes are aligned (hence structurally linked), and discovering connections between plant distribution and environment. He thus virtually founded modern physical geology, biogeography and ecology. Humboldt presented his new, integrated view of the universe in his most important publication, the five-volume *Kosmos* (1845-62). His work was a significant influence on DARWIN and WALLACE. Humboldt established the use of isotherms.

Hume, David (1711-76) Scottish philosopher, essayist and historian. As a philosopher, his empiricist approach went a step further than that of BERKELEY, who had denied LOCKE's assertion that there are materal objects, while retaining the concept of the mind as that which has ideas. Hume denied the existence of mind as well, and allowed merely impressions and ideas (corresponding roughly with Locke's ideas of sensation and ideas of reflection respectively). Hume argued that the only justifiable attitude is scepticism. Hume's ethical theory is based on his observing men to have moral sentiments that are motivated on broadly utilitarian lines, not just self-seeking (as with HOBBES) but for the good of the whole, an approach that greatly influenced BENTHAM and J. S. MILL. Some of his views on economics may have influenced Adam SMITH.

Hung Wu see CHU YÜAN-CHANG

Hunt, Leigh (1784-1859) English journalist, essayist and poet, whose editorship of numerous periodicals brought the work of the Romantic poets such as KEATS and SHELLEY to the public. During a period in Italy, with BYRON, he produced *The Liberal* magazine (1822), which contained some of Byron's works. Hunt was a prolific essayist on an extensive range of literary topics. His main poetic work was 'The Story of Rimini' (1816).

Hunt, William Holman (1827-1910) English artist, a member of the Pre-Raphaelite movement, which included MILLAIS and ROSSETTI. Hunt alone remained faithful to the moral and technical aims of the Brotherhood, as in *The Awakening Conscience* (1853) and *The Scapegoat* (1855).

Hunter, John (1728-93) British physiologist and surgeon, who founded surgical pathology. His *Natural History of Human Teeth* (1771-8) influenced the development of scientific dentistry. Hunter studied a wide range of subjects, including gun-shot wounds, the constitution of the blood, embryology, venereal disease and the nature of inflammation. Most of his life was devoted to the study of comparative anatomy.

Husayn, Mirza (15th-16th cents.) Timurid ruler of Khorasan (northeast Persia), soldier, poet, bibliophile and patron of the arts. He attracted the most talented men of the period to his court at Herat, including the poet Jami, the historian Khwandamir, and the painter Bihzad. His reign marked the end of Timurid power in Persia, but the high literary and artistic standards he set were to have a lasting influence on Persian cultural history.

Husein ibn-Ali (1856-1931) King of the Hejaz, an ally of T. E. LAWRENCE, and great-grandfather of HUSSEIN of Jordan. At first a supporter of Germany and Turkey in the First World War, he was persuaded by Lawrence to support the Allies, and in 1916 he proclaimed the independence of Arabia from Turkish rule. His army captured Yanbu, the port of Medina, in July 1916, and by the end of the year he was formally recognized as King of Hejaz, part of Saudi Arabia. Internal unrest and invasion by IBN-SAUD forced his abdication in 1924.

Huss, Jan (c. 1369-1415) Bohemian theologian and religious reformer, whose criticism of the malpractices of the Catholic Church directly inspired LUTHER a century later. His followers, the Hussites, who supported all Wycliffe's teachings, believed in freedom of speech, poverty of the clergy, and the punishment of notorious sinners and they campaigned for the expropriation of all church property. They were denounced as heretics for administering Holy Communion to the laity, and in 1415 Huss was burned at the stake in Constance. His martyrdom paved the way for the Reformation.

Hussein ibn-Talal (born 1935) King of Jordan. His rule began in 1952 and throughout his reign he has tried to follow a policy of compromise between friendship with the West and Arab nationalism, both within and outside Jordan. His expulsion of Sir John Glubb, commandant of the Arab Legion, in 1956, and the abrogation of Jordan's treaty with Britain was in response to Arab criticism, but he was opposed to the formation of the belligerent United Arab Republic and, in order to counteract it, established the short-lived Arab Federation with FAISAL II of Iraq. He is, however, an Arab nationalist himself, though moderate in his views, and has remained largely unreconciled to the creation of Israel. In the Arab war with Israel in 1967 Hussein was forced to take part on behalf of his Palestinian subjects but lost almost half of his territory. Nevertheless, his policy was not considered sufficiently extreme by Palestinian guerillas in Jordan, and he was faced with civil war in 1970, when they openly flouted his authority. The revolt was crushed, but Hussein lost the support of Egypt and the other Arab states as a result, and at the 1974 Arab summit meeting he was forced to relinquish Jordan's claim to west bank Jordan to the Palestinian Liberation Organization. Always under the pressure of extreme nationalism, he remains a key figure in the search for peace in the Middle East.

Husserl, Edmund (1859-1938) German philosopher and founder of phenomenology, a conceptual study of what is involved generally in outward appearances.

Hutton, James (1726-97) British geologist, who showed that in interpreting geological phenomena, the present is the key to the past. This came to be called the 'principle of uniformaterianism'. Hutton observed that geological features are produced as a result of slow change and not by a series of catastrophes. He also opposed one of the most influential of his colleagues, WERNER, denouncing the Wernerian doctrine of Neptunism (the belief that all the rocks of the Earth were originally precipitated from a solution in water). Hutton maintained that certain rocks had once been in a molten state and cooled down. This Plutonist school of thought is now known to be correct.

Huxley, Aldous (1894-1963) English novelist, whose reputation rests on clever, witty novels giving a sardonic view of English intellectual life in the 1920s. After early successes like *Crome Yellow* (1921) and *Antic Hay* (1923) he grew more pessimistic and bitterly satirical in *Point Counter Point* (1928) and the prophetic *Brave New World* (1932).

Huxley, Sir Julian Sorrell (1887-1975) British biologist and evolutionist who has drawn the social and political implications of biology to public attention in books such as *Evolution: The Modern Synthesis*. His work has been notable for its interpretation of modern biological thinking in terms comprehensive to the layman. Sir Julian was the first Director-General of Unesco.

Huxley, Thomas H. (1825-95) English biologist, who suggested that evolutionary changes need not be gradual, as DARWIN thought, but might be step-like, foreshadowing the more correct view that genetic change is due to mutation. A mutation is a sudden change in the gene structure of germ plasm, the result of physico-chemical causes.

Hu Yaobang (born 1915) General Secretary of the Chinese Communist Party since 1978. A protégé of DENG XIAOPING, he controls the *de facto* seat of power. In 1978 he became a member of the Politburo and head of the party's propaganda and organization departments. In 1981 he was made Chairman of the Central Committee.

Huygens, Christian (1629-95) Dutch astronomer, physicist and mathematician, who discovered the nature of Saturn's rings and propounded the wave theory of light. In 1655 Huygens developed a new method of polishing telescope lenses and discovered markings on Mars and on Titan, Saturn's brightest satellite, and the ring of Saturn.

Hyatt, John Wesley (1837-1920) American inventor, who in 1868 produced a cheap substitute for ivory for billiard balls. This material, which he called celluloid, was the first synthetic plastic. Although later utilized particularly for photographic films, its greatest drawback was its inflammability and consequent danger.

Hyde, Edward, 1st Earl of Clarendon (1609-74) English royalist and Restoration statesman, who helped to stabilize the monarchy after the Restoration. As an MP, Clarendon had sided with CHARLES I against Parliament's extreme reformers, believing that their demands would damage Church and State. He backed his decision with forceful arguments that won much support for Charles in the ensuing Civil War. Afterwards he was CHARLES II's chief adviser.

I

ibn-Batuta (1304-68) Moroccan traveller famous for his descriptive accounts of Mohammedan society of the Middle East and North Africa in the 14th century. He began his extensive travels when he was 22, visiting Egypt, Palestine, Mecca, Iraq and Persia. Later his travels took him to Asia Minor, Russia and, possibly, Siberia.

ibn-Hazm (994-1064) Leading Moorish scholar who is best known for two major works, a study of comparative religion and a work on romantic love, *The Dove's Necklace*.

ibn-Khaldun (1332-1406) Leading Arab historian. He held various official posts in North Africa and Spain, but his fame rests on one book, a general history of the Muslim dynasties and, more specifically, the *Muqaddima*, the introduction to this work, in which he theorized on the nature, significance and methodology of history. It was described by Arnold TOYNBEE as 'the greatest work of its kind that has ever yet been created by any mind in any time or place'.

ibn-Saud (1880-1953) Creator of the kingdom of Saudi Arabia. During the First World War, he refused to join the Arab revolt organized by T. E. LAWRENCE because the Allies had recognized Hussein of Hejaz as king of the Arabs. He went to war against Hussein (1919) and by 1925 had defeated him and his allies and seized Mecca, Medina and Jeddah. He was proclaimed King of Hejaz and Nejd (1926), and recognized as king by a series of treaties with the great powers, completed in 1932, when he renamed his kingdom Saudi Arabia. He made his country economically viable by negotiating concessions with American oil companies. During the Second World War, he remained neutral, though he maintained friendly relations with Britain. After the war, American finance and technical aid supported a large-scale programme of irrigation schemes and public works. A founder member of the Arab League (1945) he took Saudi Arabia into the United Nations.

ibn-Tashfin, Yusuf (11th cent.) Berber chieftain, one of the founders of the Almoravid Empire of northwest Africa and Spain. He and his cousin ABU-BAKR conquered Morocco, and ibn-Tashfin became its sole ruler in 1071, taking the title of amir. With Abu-Bakr, he founded Marrakesh (*c.* 1069). When Alfonso VI of Castile attacked Muslim Spain, ibn-Tashfin intervened, defeating him at Zallaga in 1086. He deposed (1090-1) the rulers of Granada and Seville and thus established an Afro-Spanish Empire in which African and Andalusian cultures gradually blended.

Ibsen, Henrik (1828-1906) Norwegian dramatist who was one of the founders of naturalistic theatre. His first play, *Catalina*, a romantic drama, was produced when he was 22. It was a failure, but won him a position as literary assistant (*dramaturg*) at the Bergen theatre, and then in Oslo. He was, meanwhile, writing prose and verse plays. As a result of the publication of his verse-drama *Brand* he was granted a state pension to enable him to write. This ponderous work about a Protestant parson's relations with God and man foreshadowed the feeling, but not the literary tact, of his later, more important plays. Next came *Peer Gynt* (1867). After two verse dramas he turned to the realistic, small-town drama for which he is best known. These were written at the peak of his powers: *Pillars of Society* (1875-7), *A Doll's House* (1878-9), *Ghosts* (1881), *An Enemy of the People* (1882), *The Wild Duck* (1884), *Rosmersholm* (1886) and *Hedda Gabler* (1890). All these plays are on the levels of the manifest and the symbolic. In *Ghosts*, venereal disease is the symbol of spiritual corruption in family life, and in *The Wild Duck* the crippled bird symbolizes the social and moral crippling of the heroine. The symbolism is less well controlled in *The Lady from the Sea* (1888), *The Master Builder* (1892) and *Little Eyolf* (1894). In *John Gabriel Borkman* (1896) and *When the Dead Awaken* (1899) Ibsen returned to the overt symbolism of *Brand*.

Ictinus (5th cent. BC) Greek architect who achieved an immortal reputation for his masterpiece, the Parthenon, which he designed with Callicrates. Until the fall of his patron, PERICLES, he enjoyed a leading position in Athens. He is believed to have designed the Doric temple of Apollo Eupicurius at Bassae, in which all three Greek Orders of Architecture – Doric, Ionic and Corinthian – were introduced.

An eternal masterpiece of architecture, Ictinus's Parthenon in Athens

Idrisi, al- (1100-66) Arabian geographer, cartographer and poet whose geography digest revealed the world as known to Muslim travellers. He studied widely in Muslim Mediterranean states, then settled in Sicily where he spent 15 years working for ROGER II to produce the *Book of Roger*. This was an ambitious compendium of world geography based partly on writings by PTOLEMY and the Spaniard Orosius, but chiefly on works by the Arabs al-Masudi and ibn-Hawqal and on Muslim travellers' tales. It abounded in geographical and mathematical errors, but contained a valuable account of Sicily.

Ignatius of Loyola, St (1491-1556) Spanish founder of the Society of Jesus or Jesuit Order. Devoted to the papal service, this order came into being when Ignatius, with six other students, including Francis XAVIER, took an oath to become a missionary to the Muslims in Palestine. The seven would-be missionaries found however that war made the journey to Palestine impossible, and offered their services to Pope Paul III. He had them ordained and later formed them into an order. Ignatius remained in Rome to direct its activities and by the year of his death there were 1000 active Jesuits in the known world. He was canonized in 1622.

Ingres, Jean (1780-1867) French artist, and the foremost exponent of Classicism in 19th-century French painting. His training included a period in the studio of DAVID, the leading Neo-classicist in art. But Ingres's preoccupation with order and clarity was complemented by an innate sensuality, apparent in his rendering of silks, velvets, lace and gold braid in his portraits, and the languorous rhythms of his nudes (e.g. *Grande Odalisque*). His art was based on the distillation, by constant repetition of his own work and imitation of others, of a formal language which grew increasingly idealized and abstracted.

Ionesco, Eugène (born 1912) Rumanian dramatist, who was the initiator and remains the leader of the Theatre of the Absurd. His aim is to shock audiences by exposing the nihilism of the Universe and man's vulnerability and isolation. His best-known works include the one-act plays *The Bald Prima Donna* (1948), *Jacques, or Obedience* (1950), *The Lesson* (1951), *The Future is in Eggs* (1951) and *The Chairs* (1951). *Amédie, or How to Get Rid of It* (1953), was the first of a series of three-act plays, which include a cycle: *The Killer* (1957), *Rhinoceros* (1958) and *Exit the King* (1961). Other plays include *Jeux de Massacre* (1970), *Macbett* (1972) and *Voyages Chez les Morts ou Thème et Variations* (1980).

Ipatieff, Vladimir Nikolaievich (1867-1952) Russian-American chemist, whose studies of high temperature catalytic reactions were fundamental to the petro-chemical industry. From 1930 he worked for an American oil company on the improvement of the octane rating of automobile fuel.

Ireland, John Nicholson (1879-1962) English composer for the piano, among the foremost of his generation. He also wrote (for orchestra) *The Forgotten Rite* (1913) and *A London Overture* (1936).

Irving, Sir Henry (1838-1905) English actor-manager, who made his name overnight in a melodrama, *The Bells,* in 1871. Manager of the Lyceum from 1878, he had a run of Shakespearean successes with Ellen TERRY as his leading lady. He was the first actor to be knighted.

Irving, Washington (1783-1859) American author, best known for his collection of essays, *The Sketch-Book* (1820), which includes the story of Rip van Winkle. He travelled widely, and many of his works, particularly on Spain and England, stem from his voyages. He also wrote a detailed *Life of George Washington* (1855-9).

Isabella I (1451-1504) Queen of Castile (1474-1504) and Aragon (1469-1504), whose marriage to FERDINAND II of Aragon (1469) united Spain's two most powerful kingdoms. Ruling jointly with her husband (who became Ferdinand V of Castile in 1474), she helped to strengthen royal rule and national prestige, promoted culture, and financed COLUMBUS's venture (1492). Her devout Catholicism made her work to reform national morality, and to introduce the Inquisition into Spain, forcing Jews and Muslims to embrace Christianity or emigrate.

Isaiah (c. 8th cent. BC) Hebrew Old Testament prophet who worked in Jerusalem and made easy contact with its rulers. The book of the Bible bearing his name is now thought to comprise at least two distinct works, the first containing material derived from the prophet himself. The second half of 'Book of Isaiah', chapters 40-66, is widely held to be the work of a man prophesying the end of the exile of the Jews to Babylon in the 6th century, and is called *Deutero Isaiah*. The characteristic themes of the man Isaiah, the holiness of God and his demand for holy living, are found throughout the whole book.

Isherwood, Christopher (born 1904) English playwright and novelist, whose tales of Berlin before the Second World War, particularly *Goodbye to Berlin* (1939), are evocative of the period. The novel was made into a play, a film and the musical *Cabaret*. During the 1930s, he collaborated with AUDEN on three plays and a travel book. More recently he has turned to Indian mysticism and written *A Meeting by the River* (1967), about the pressures on an Englishman who enters a Hindu monastery, and *My Guru and His Disciple* (1981).

Ismail I (1486-1524) Shah of Persia (1500-24) who founded the Safawid dynasty. In the confusion of power struggles following the end of unified rule of Persia by the Mongols, Ismail launched an onslaught on his Sunnite neighbours. He brought all Persia under his rule and enlarged it by conquests including that of the Uzbegs (1510). Despite losses to Turkey's Sunnite Sultan Selim I, he established the Persian state, which reached its zenith under Abbas I.

Ismail Pasha (1830-95) Khedive of Egypt whose heavy borrowing to finance schemes for internal reform led to the sale of Suez Canal shares to Britain in 1875. In 1876 further financial difficulties led to joint Anglo-French financial control over Egypt and in 1878 British and French ministers were included in the Egyptian government. His new government was dismissed after only six months and Britain and France advised him to abdicate, which he refused to do. Dismissed by the Sultan of Turkey in 1879, he retired to Constantinople.

Ito, Hirobumi (1838-1909) Japanese statesman who helped to transform Japan into a modern, westernized, industrial power. Between 1894 and 1901 he was four times Prime Minister of Japan. His main achievements were the calling of the first Japanese parliament (1890), the establishment – with the help of Admiral Togo – of the Japanese navy and the introduction of modern fiscal and bureaucratic systems. He fell from favour through opposing the Russo-Japanese war, and was sent to Korea as Governor. He was assassinated by a Korean nationalist in China.

Ivan III Vasilievich (1440-1505) Grand Duke of Muscovy (1462-1505), better known as 'Ivan the Great', the first real ruler of Russia. Ivan enlarged Muscovy by force, marriage and purchase. He conquered Novgorod (1478), absorbing all northern Russia between Lapland and the Urals, and took the lesser principalities of Yaroslavl (1463), Rostov (1474) and Tver (1485), and part of Lithuania (1503). He refused to continue tribute payments to the Tatars and ended for ever their hold on Russia. Ivan refused to share his gains with his brothers and destroyed their semi-independent principalities by changing the Russian inheritance system, so that when these princes died their estates passed to the grand duke instead of being divided among their heirs. By this means, Ivan forged a united Russian Empire, whose first (self-styled) emperor was his grandson IVAN IV.

Ivan IV Vasilievich (1530-84) First tsar, or emperor, of Russia (1533-84, crowned in 1547). Ivan's ruthless and often murderous pursuit of national and personal aggrandisement earned him the name by which he is best known – 'Ivan the Terrible'. Orphaned as the child prince of Muscovy, Ivan grew up under the regency of hereditary nobles, the boyars, for whom he conceived a deep loathing. A tsar, his purpose was to strengthen royal rule at the expense of the hereditary dukes and boyars. His armies pressed east and south to wrest Kazan and Astrakhan from the Tatars, setting Russia astride the Volga with an outlet on the Caspian. He was less successful in the west, where he was defeated by the Swedes and the Poles and driven back from the Baltic. On the death of his wife, Ivan seems to have become unbalanced, subjecting his kingdom to a reign of terror, including systematic massacres in Novgorod. Four years before his death he struck and killed his favourite son in a fit of rage.

Centuries of Tatar presence in Russia came to an end during the violent reign of Ivan the Terrible. He went out of his mind in later life

Ives, Charles (1874-1954) American composer, son of an organist and bandmaster, who was the first 'original' in US music. From about 1900-20 he wrote a wide range of songs, instrumental and orchestral works while pursuing a successful business career, and much of his work anticipated European composers in experimental techniques. He also made full use of childhood memories: two 4th July bands marching against each other in *Three Places in New England* and revivalist hymns at a camp meeting in *Violin Sonata No. 4*. Ives worked in isolation, his ideas misunderstood, his music unheard. It was only after a performance of *Piano Sonata No. 2 ('Concord')* in 1938 that he was recognized as one of the founding fathers of America's music.

Ives, Frederick Eugene (1856-1937) American inventor of the half-tone printing system, in which the tones of a picture are reproduced as small dots of varying sizes. He also invented a similar process for gravure printing in which the ink is carried, not by raised dots, but by minute pits etched into a metal plate. Among his other inventions are the photochromoscope, a device for optically reproducing objects in natural colour, and a binocular microscope. His son, Herbert Eugene, played an important part in developing television and a wire-photo system.

Iyeyasu (1542-1616) Founder of the Japanese Tokugawa shogunate (1603-1867), named after his family. As a prominent general, he helped Nobunaga and Hideyoshi to unify Japan, and became its effective leader by defeating rivals in the Battle of Sekigahara (1600). Ruling, with the puppet emeror's approval, until 1616 (as official Shogun 1603-5), he made Yedo (Tokyo) the new political, economic, and cultural capital of Japan.

J

Jabir, ibn-Haijan (c. 721-815) Arabian alchemist credited with the first preparation of the poison arsenic (arsenious oxide). He was a prolific and influential writer on chemistry.

Jackson, Andrew (1767-1845) First Democratic President of the US. A veteran of the American War of Independence, Jackson was elected a senator in 1797, but a difference with JEFFERSON led to his temporary retirement from political life. He became a national hero when, in 1815, he drove off a British attack on New Orleans. In 1818 he led a force which occupied Florida and later became its first governor (1821-3). He was elected seventh President of the US in 1828 and was re-elected in 1832 with a landslide victory as the nominee of the newly-styled Democratic Party.

Jackson, Jesse (born 1941) American civil rights leader and politician who, in the 1984 presidential election, was a candidate for the Democratic nomination, which was won by Walter Mondale. Jackson was ordained a Baptist minister in 1968, and worked with Martin Luther King, Jnr, running Operation Breadbasket, the economic organ of the Southern Christian Leadership Conference. He broke with SCLC in 1971, forming the Chicago-based Operation PUSH, a black economic organization, and has continued to work for civil rights worldwide.

Jackson, Thomas Jonathan (1824-63) American Confederate general, known as 'Stonewall' Jackson. During the American Civil War, after leading a successful campaign in the Shenandoah Valley, he joined LEE in the seven-day defence of Richmond and became Lee's most trusted subordinate. While in the Maryland campaign, he captured over 12,000 Federal troops at Harper's Ferry (Sept. 1862). The Confederate success at Chancellorsville (May 1863) was largely the result of Jackson's skill, but while returning from a reconnaissance after the battle, he was accidentally shot by his own men and died.

Jacquard, Joseph Marie (1752-1834) French silk weaver who (1801-8) perfected a loom which could weave patterns automatically. As this dispensed with guidance by hand, it aroused bitter hostility from many silk weavers, fearing for their livelihood. However, its advantages soon began to be accepted, and by 1812, 11,000 were in use in France. The looms were controlled by punched cards, which were the forerunners of those used in modern data storage systems.

Jagger, Mick (born 1943) English popular singer and songwriter who is lead vocalist with The Rolling Stones, one of the longest lasting and most successful pop groups. The Rolling Stones are renowned for their energy, rebelliousness and aggressive music, much of which has been written by Mick Jagger and Keith Richard and influenced by rhythm and blues. Among Jagger's best known songs are *It's All Over Now* (1964), *Satisfaction* (1965), *Jumping Jack Flash* (1968) and *Brown Sugar* (1971). He has also acted in a number of films, such as *Ned Kelly* (1969), *Performance* (1970) and *Gimme Shelter* (1972).

Jahangir (1569-1627) Mogul emperor of India and patron of the arts. During his reign, Indian miniature painting reached its peak of refinement as a result of the personal interest he took in the work of his artists.

James I (1208-76) King of Aragon (1213-76), called 'el Conquistador' (the Conqueror). James founded a Barcelona-based Aragonese Empire in the Mediterranean after inheriting the powerful northeastern Spanish state established by Ramón Berenguer IV. He enlarged it by conquering the Balearic Islands and Valencia, establishing an empire based on Catalonian seamanship and Jewish finance.

The music masters—Bach, Haydn, Mozart, Beethoven and others whose stories appear in *Who Did What*—were circumscribed, or given greater scope, by the musical instruments at their disposal. On this page are shown instruments which, through the ages and in many countries, have provided music for solo performance, or as accompaniments to the human voice, or as units of an orchestra

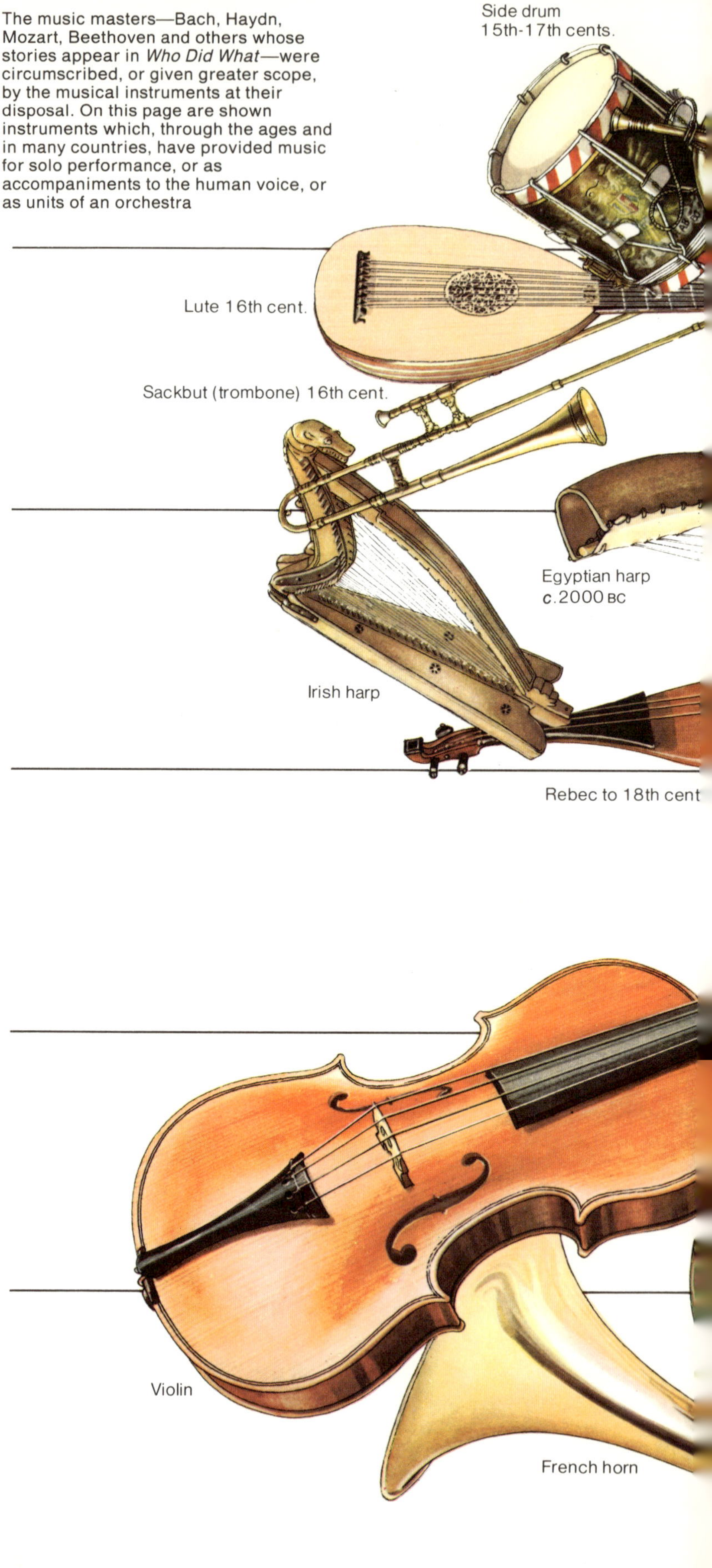

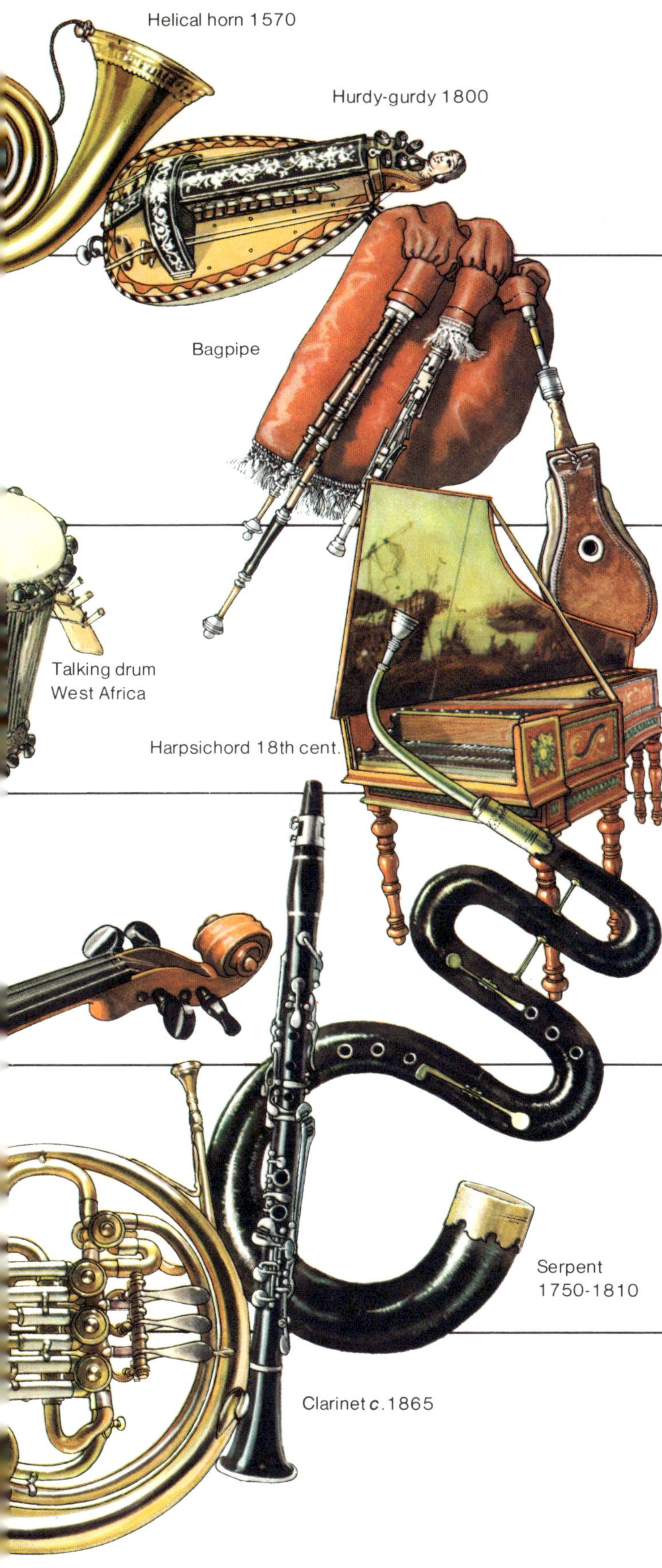

Johann Sebastian Bach
(1685-1750)

Franz Joseph Haydn
(1732-1809)

Wolfgang Amadeus
Mozart
(1756-91)

Ludwig van
Beethoven
(1770-1827)

Richard Wagner
(1813-83)

Edvard Grieg
(1843-1907)

James I (1556-1625) King of England (VI of Scotland). Although a believer in witchcraft, James was one of England's most learned monarchs, the author and sponsor of many books, including the Authorized Version of the Bible (1611). His partiality towards favourites and heavy-handed relationship with parliament made him unpopular and laid the foundation of the dispute which cost CHARLES I his head.

James, Henry (1843-1916) American novelist, who wrote subtle, complex novels which frequently examined American characters and their innocence, testing them against the established culture of Europe. James left America in 1875 and *Roderick Hudson* (1876) and *The Portrait of a Lady* (1881) pursued this theme. In *What Maisie Knew* (1897), a story of passion seen through the eyes of a child, and in the ghost story *The Turn of the Screw* (1898), his prose grew more subtle and complex, leading to the tortuous puzzles and delicate psychology of *The Wings of the Dove* (1902) and *The Golden Bowl* (1904). James wrote numerous other novels and short stories.

James, Jesse (1847-82) American outlaw who, with his brother Frank, led a gang notorious for bank and train robberies. Jesse was shot dead by an associate and Frank, who surrendered, was tried and acquitted.

James, William (1842-1910) American philosopher and psychologist who put forward the theory of pragmatism: that the criterion for the truth of a concept is its successful use in practice. His *Principles of Psychology* (1890) helped to establish psychology as a separate discipline, drawing on natural science and adopting the functionalist approach of defining mentality in terms of what it does. Along with this goes the theory that emotions are identical with bodily feelings and so subordinate to the bodily states that provoke them. This foreshadows modern behaviourism.

Janáček, Leoš (1854-1928) Czech composer who wrote some of the most strongly individual humanist operas in the modern repertoire. The best known of these are *Jenufa* (1904), *Katya Kabanova* (1921, based on OSTROVSKY's *The Storm*), *The Makropoulos Affair* (1926, from the play by Capek) and *From the House of the Dead* (1930, deried from the book by DOSTOEVSKY). Janáček matured late as a composer, but earlier studies he had made of peasant dialects deeply influenced his idiosyncratic settings of words. His other compositions include the *Glagolitic Mass,* to an ancient Slav ecclesiastical text; the Sinfonietta and the tone poem *Taras Bulba* for orchestra; two string quartets; and a song cycle, *The Diary of a Man who Disappeared*.

Jansen, Cornelius (1585-1638) French ecclesiastic who, within the Roman Catholic Church, initiated an anti-Jesuit reform movement which had much in common with Protestantism, except that Jansen rejected justification by faith and maintained the supremacy of the Roman Church. In the outcry which followed, ARNAULD and PASCAL were amongst his chief defenders. Exiled from France, Jansen lived mainly in Holland and contributed to the independent outlook of Dutch Catholicism today.

Jansky, Karl (1905-50) American radio engineer and pioneer of radio astronomy who discovered radio emission from the Milky Way. Jansky, an engineer with Bell Telephone Laboratories, was investigating the origin of 'static' when he found a new and distant source of interference originating beyond the Earth.

Janssen, Pierre Jules César (1824-1907) French pioneer of solar physics and of photography who, on 8 December 1874, made the first film recording the transit of Venus across the Sun.

Jarry, Alfred (1873-1907) French dramatist and Symbolist poet, whose work promoted the Theatre of the Absurd. His allegorical farce *Ubu Roi* (1896), a satire on bourgeois society, is generally considered his most important play. In it, the bourgeois Ubu makes himself a tyrant-king. His influence on the Theatre of the Absurd stems largely from his novel *The Deeds and Opinions of Dr Faustroll*.

Jaruzelski, General Wojciech (born 1923) Prime Minister of Poland since 1981. He had a distinguished military career, being Chief of General Staff (1965) and Minister of Defence (1968), before becoming a member of the Politburo (1971). In 1981, in an attempt to ease Poland's severe economic problems and to counteract the political influence of Solidarity, the free trade union, he declared a state of martial law. Solidarity was declared illegal, and its leaders were arrested and tried. Martial law was suspended (1982) and lifted (1983).

Jaspers, Karl (1883-1969) German Existentialist philosopher who saw, in the experience of failure, material for positive conclusions about the nature of human existence.

Jaurès, Jean (1859-1914) French socialist politician, who tried to prevent the First World War by organizing a strike of German and French workers. Co-founder, with BRIAND, of the left-wing newspaper *L'Humanité* (1904), Jaurès was one of the greatest socialist writers and orators of his time, but he was never a doctrinaire Marxist and was frequently at odds with the socialist establishment. In July 1914 he went to Brussels and called on German socialists to strike against mobilization. Back in France, he was murdered by a right-wing nationalist.

Jayawardene, Junius Richard (born 1906) President of Sri Lanka since 1978. One of the founders of the United National Party in 1946, he remained actively involved in its leadership. He became Sri Lanka's first President in 1978, and introduced a new form of government modelled on the French. He was re-elected to a six-year term in 1982.

Jeans, Sir James (1877-1946) English astronomer and physicist, and popularizer of astronomy. Though he was responsible for much original scientific work on the quantum theory, stellar radiation and the evolution of stars, Jeans was best known for books, including *The Universe Around Us* (1929) and *The Stars in their Courses* (1931), which made complex scientific theories comprehensible to laymen.

Jefferson, Thomas (1743-1826) Third US President, who drafted the Declaration of Independence (1776). Jefferson was born in Virginia and was its delegate to the Continental Congress in 1775 and 1776. After the revolution, while US Minister in Paris (1785-9), he helped to draft the Declaration of the Rights of Man and later, as Secretary of State (1789-93), resigned in protest against the federal centralization. Under ADAMS (1797-1801) he was elected Vice-President and President in 1800, serving two terms. During the first, Jefferson was responsible for the 'Louisiana Purchase' (1803) in which the US bought French colonial territory in North America. His second term of office was preoccupied with the problem of neutrality in the face of British and French wartime restrictions on trade. In retirement, he introduced English landscape gardening into America.

IN CONGRESS, JULY 4, 1776

The unanimous Declaration of the thirteen united States of America.

When in the Course of human events it becomes necessary for one people to dissolve the political bands which have connected them with another, and to assume among the powers of the earth, the separate and equal station to which the Laws of Nature and of Nature's God entitle them, a decent respect to the opinions of mankind requires that they should declare the causes which impel them to the separation. —— We hold these truths to be self-evident, that all men are created equal, that they are endowed by their Creator with certain unalienable Rights, that among these are Life, Liberty and the pursuit of Happiness. — That to secure these rights, Governments are instituted among Men, deriving their just powers from the consent of the governed, — That whenever any Form of Government becomes destructive of these ends, it is the Right of the People to alter or to abolish it, and to institute new Government, laying its foundation on such principles and organizing its powers in such form, as to them shall seem most likely to effect their Safety and Happiness. Prudence, indeed, will dictate that Governments long established should not be changed for light and transient causes; and accordingly all experience hath shewn, that mankind are more disposed to suffer, while evils are sufferable, than to right themselves by abolishing the forms to which they are accustomed. But when a long train of abuses and usurpations, pursuing invariably the same Object evinces a design to reduce them under absolute Despotism, it is their right, it is their duty, to throw off such Government, and to provide new Guards for their future security. — Such has been the patient sufferance of these Colonies; and such is now the necessity which constrains them to alter their former Systems of Government. The history of the present King of Great Britain is a history of repeated injuries and usurpations, all having in direct object the establishment of an absolute Tyranny over these States. To prove this, let Facts be submitted to a candid world. —— He has refused his Assent to Laws, the most wholesome and necessary for the public good. —— He has forbidden his Governors to pass Laws of immediate and pressing importance, unless suspended in their operation till his Assent should be obtained; and when so suspended, he has utterly neglected to attend to them. —— He has refused to pass other Laws for the accommodation of large districts of people, unless those people would relinquish the right of Representation in the Legislature, a right inestimable to them and formidable to tyrants only. —— He has called together legislative bodies at places unusual, uncomfortable, and distant from the depository of their public Records, for the sole purpose of fatiguing them into compliance with his measures. —— He has dissolved Representative Houses repeatedly, for opposing with manly firmness his invasions on the rights of the people. —— He has refused for a long time, after such dissolutions, to cause others to be elected; whereby the Legislative powers, incapable of Annihilation, have returned to the People at large for their exercise; the State remaining in the mean time exposed to all the dangers of invasion from without, and convulsions within. —— He has endeavoured to prevent the population of these States; for that purpose obstructing the Laws for Naturalization of Foreigners; refusing to pass others to encourage their migrations hither, and raising the conditions of new Appropriations of Lands. —— He has obstructed the Administration of Justice, by refusing his Assent to Laws for establishing Judiciary powers. —— He has made Judges dependent on his Will alone, for the tenure of their offices, and the amount and payment of their salaries. —— He has erected a multitude of New Offices, and sent hither swarms of Officers to harrass our people, and eat out their substance. —— He has kept among us, in times of peace, Standing Armies without the Consent of our legislatures. —— He has affected to render the Military independent of and superior to the Civil power. —— He has combined with others to subject us to a jurisdiction foreign to our constitution, and unacknowledged by our laws; giving his Assent to their Acts of pretended Legislation: — For Quartering large bodies of armed troops among us: — For protecting them, by a mock Trial, from punishment for any Murders which they should commit on the Inhabitants of these States: — For cutting off our Trade with all parts of the world: — For imposing Taxes on us without our Consent: — For depriving us in many cases, of the benefits of Trial by Jury: — For transporting us beyond Seas to be tried for pretended offences — For abolishing the free System of English Laws in a neighbouring Province, establishing therein an Arbitrary government, and enlarging its Boundaries so as to render it at once an example and fit instrument for introducing the same absolute rule into these Colonies: — For taking away our Charters, abolishing our most valuable Laws, and altering fundamentally the Forms of our Governments: — For suspending our own Legislatures, and declaring themselves invested with power to legislate for us in all cases whatsoever. — He has abdicated Government here, by declaring us out of his Protection and waging War against us. —— He has plundered our seas, ravaged our Coasts, burnt our towns, and destroyed the lives of our people. —— He is at this time transporting large Armies of foreign Mercenaries to compleat the works of death, desolation and tyranny, already begun with circumstances of Cruelty & perfidy scarcely paralleled in the most barbarous ages, and totally unworthy the Head of a civilized nation. —— He has constrained our fellow Citizens taken Captive on the high Seas to bear Arms against their Country, to become the executioners of their friends and Brethren, or to fall themselves by their Hands. —— He has excited domestic insurrections amongst us, and has endeavoured to bring on the inhabitants of our frontiers, the merciless Indian Savages, whose known rule of warfare, is an undistinguished destruction of all ages, sexes and conditions. In every stage of these Oppressions We have Petitioned for Redress in the most humble terms: Our repeated Petitions have been answered only by repeated injury. A Prince, whose character is thus marked by every act which may define a Tyrant, is unfit to be the ruler of a free people. Nor have We been wanting in attentions to our Brittish brethren. We have warned them from time to time of attempts by their legislature to extend an unwarrantable jurisdiction over us. We have reminded them of the circumstances of our emigration and settlement here. We have appealed to their native justice and magnanimity, and we have conjured them by the ties of our common kindred to disavow these usurpations, which, would inevitably interrupt our connections and correspondence. They too have been deaf to the voice of justice and of consanguinity. We must, therefore, acquiesce in the necessity, which denounces our Separation, and hold them, as we hold the rest of mankind, Enemies in War, in Peace Friends. ——

We, therefore, the Representatives of the united States of America, in General Congress, Assembled, appealing to the Supreme Judge of the world for the rectitude of our intentions, do, in the Name, and by Authority of the good People of these Colonies, solemnly publish and declare, That these United Colonies are, and of Right ought to be Free and Independent States; that they are Absolved from all Allegiance to the British Crown, and that all political connection between them and the State of Great Britain, is and ought to be totally dissolved; and that as Free and Independent States, they have full Power to levy War, conclude Peace, contract Alliances, establish Commerce, and to do all other Acts and Things which Independent States may of right do. —— And for the support of this Declaration, with a firm reliance on the protection of divine Providence, we mutually pledge to each other our Lives, our Fortunes and our sacred Honor.

Independence – the unanimous declaration of the 13 States of America in 1776

Jeffries, John see BLANCHARD, Jean Pierre

Jenkins, Charles Francis (1867-1934) American inventor, who devised a ciné projector with intermittent motion (1895), a braking system for aeroplanes, an altimeter, the conical paper drinking cup, and a self-starter for cars. He was a television pioneer and was one of the first (1925) to transmit TV pictures, although his system was not commercially viable. He made several other inventions in the fields of radio, fascimile transmissions and television.

Jenkins, Robert (18th cent.) English mariner whose ear was cut off by a Spanish sea captain, an incident which helped to cause Anglo-Spanish hostility to flare into the War of Jenkins's ear (1739-48).

Jenner, Edward (1749-1823) English physician who developed vaccination against smallpox, a discovery which stemmed from an 'old wives' tale' that dairymaids who caught cowpox never subsequently caught smallpox. Jenner investigated the various diseases called cowpox, and, isolating a pure strain of the true disease, brought it to the peak of its infective phase. In 1796 he achieved the experiment which proved the theory correct. Jenner's method of preventing smallpox by vaccination rapidly ousted the older use of inoculation.

Jenney, William Le Baron (1832-1907) American architect, who in 1884 designed the Home Insurance Company building in Chicago. Although only ten floors tall, it had a steel-frame construction, which made it the forerunner of the modern skyscraper.

Jeremiah (c. 650-c. 585 BC) Hebrew Old Testament prophet. Jeremiah bewailed the idolatry of the people of Judah, prophesying divine punishment by the destruction of Jerusalem. But, like ISAIAH, he preached a message of eventual redemption, proclaiming a new covenant between God and his people, based on moral virtue rather than outward observance. The Judean kingdom fell in 586 and Jeremiah was forced into exile in Egypt. Scholars question the dating and authenticity of much of the Book of Jeremiah, and also the rabbinic tradition that the prophet wrote the Lamentations of Jeremiah and the Book of Kings.

Jerome (c. 340-420) Dalmatian saint, one of the four Latin Doctors of the Church, and translator of the Bible into Latin (Vulgate). Brought up as a Christian, he spent some years as a hermit in Syria, learnt Hebrew and reluctantly accepted ordination. He then went to Constantinople, where he was influenced by GREGORY NAZIANZUS. In 382, he became Secretary to Pope St Damasus in Rome. Jerome's rudeness and austerity made him unpopular and when Damasus died he settled in Bethlehem, where he taught, worked on his Bible and other writings.

Jerome, Jerome Klapka (1859-1927) English author, who was most successful with *Three Men in a Boat* (1889), a picturesque, farcical and sentimental book, set in an innocent world of sunlit, idle hours on the Thames.

Jesus Christ (died c. AD 29) Founder of the Christian faith and, to its believers, the Son of God. He was born in Bethlehem, Judea, the son of Mary, by whom, according to Christian belief, he was conceived miraculously. Mary's husband, Joseph, taught the young Jesus his trade of carpenter, but beyond that little is known of his early life. His latter days are chronicled in the Gospels. After his baptism by his cousin JOHN, he gathered together 12 disciples and set forth on his missionary work. Loved by the common people for his compassion and skill with the sick, and for his attacks on the social conditions of the time, he earned the hatred of the Pharisees and the ruling classes. Their hostility culminated in Jesus's arrest by Roman soldiers, his trial and sentence of death as a blasphemer. Little more than 30 years of age, he was crucified and died, between two convicted thieves, on Golgotha – 'the green hill, far away'. His preaching of a God of Love, not of vengeance, and his emphasis on love, humility, meekness and charity gave to the world a faith that now numbers more than 900 million adherents.

Jinnah, Mohammed Ali (1876-1948) Indian Muslim politician and Governor-General of Pakistan (1947-8). Jinnah opposed GANDHI's policy of civil disobedience and was distrustful of the Hindu element in the Congress Party. He organized the Muslim League and eventually directed its policy towards separate statehood for Indian Muslims, and opposed all schemes which tried to preserve Indian unity. His continued insistence that partition was the only way of solving the Indian problem succeeded and led to the creation of the Dominion of Pakistan in 1947. After founding a religious state, however, his policy became one of secular nationalisn and co-operation with India.

Joan of Arc (1412-31) French peasant girl who became a national heroine in the 100 Years' War with England. 'Voices' urged her to help the Dauphin (later CHARLES VII), whose kingdom was under severe English and Burgundian attack. Charles granted her wish to lead an army to free besieged Orléans, and, in armour, she spearheaded the assault which freed the city (1429). Joan fought in many battles and her inspiration turned the war in France's favour. In 1430, Joan was seized by Burgundians, sold to the English, and burned as a witch at Rouen. The Church exonerated her (1455) and she was canonized (1920).

John (1167-1216) Plantagenet King of England (1199-1216), whose reign is important in the development of the British constitution. Able, but selfish, unpopular and a poor soldier, John ultimately alienated barons, Church and people alike. His conflict with the papacy over the appointment of Langton as Archbishop caused a humiliating defeat at the hands of Innocent III, and after a further defeat of his allies, his opponents seized their chance. The Church and barons forced John to sign the Magna Carta (The Great Charter) at Runnymede, in 1215. It asserted the supremacy of the law over the king and granted rights which were eventually extended to all sections of society. The Magna Carta was to influence the democratic constitutions of Britain, and British-influenced nations, including the United States.

John, Augustus (1878-1961) British artist, who, for the first quarter of the 20th century, represented all that was most rebellious, independent and original in English art. The archetypal bohemian, he painted in a style of great virtuosity that sometimes degenerated into bravura, and was also a fine draughtsman. He often portrayed the gipsy life of the Wales that he loved. Later in life he became a fashionable portrait painter.

John of Austria (1547-78) Spanish general known as Don John, victor at the Battle of Lepanto (1571). John led the Holy League's fleet formed to protect Venetian property against the Turks, whom he defeated at Lepanto. The battle, the last major conflict between oared warships, temporarily curbed Turkish aggression in the Mediterranean. John was made Governor-General of the Spanish Netherlands to suppress the insurrection of WILLIAM THE SILENT, but was forced to issue the Perpetual Edict (1577), accepting William's terms.

John the Baptist (c. 7 BC-AD 28) Hebrew preacher who urged people to repent their sins in readiness for the coming of the Messiah, and baptized JESUS and others in the River Jordan. John's ministry ended with imprisonment and execution, reputedly for condemning the marriage of Herod Antipas to his niece Herodias.

John Chrysostom (c. 345-407) Syrian saint, one of the four great Greek Doctors of the Church. Brought up as a Christian he was intended to study law, but became a hermit and in 381 was ordained in Antioch, where his preaching made him famous. Elected Archbishop of

Constantinople in 398, his reforming zeal and uncompromising tongue earned him the enmity of the rich and the opposition of Theophilus, Archbishop of Alexandria, who called a council of Egyptian and Syrian bishops in 403 and deposed him. Chrysostom was banished by the emperor, recalled, then banished twice more, first to Armenia and three years later to Iberia, dying on the way.

John, Don see JOHN OF AUSTRIA

John of Gaddesden (1280-1361) English physician, whose *Rosa Anglica* (1330) was the first book to deal with diseases systematically according to cause, symptoms, prognosis and cure.

John Paul II (born 1920) Pope since 1978, he was born Karol Wojtyla in Wadowice, Poland. He studied literature and wrote poetry, was ordained a priest in 1946, and sent to study in Rome. He became auxiliary bishop of Krakow, Poland, in 1958 and archbishop in 1964. In 1967 he was appointed cardinal. He was elected pope in 1978, on the death of John Paul I, the first non-Italian pope in 455 years. A charismatic personality and a tireless traveller, he survived an assassination attempt in Rome in 1981, and visited Britain in 1982, the first pope to do so.

John III Sobieski (1624-96) King of Poland (1674-96), who saved Vienna from the Turks. A brilliant opportunist and self-seeking military leader, he fought against the Cossacks and Turks, fought with and against the Swedes, and plotted with and against the French. He ensured election to Poland's throne by a show of military strength. In 1683 he led Polish troops to aid Austria against the Turks and headed the cavalry charge that ended the siege of Vienna himself.

John XXIII (1881-1963) 263rd pope, during whose brief pontificate (1958-63) Vatican councils initiated a number of reforming measures, and who convened the 21st Ecumenical Council to seek unity among the various Christian denominations. Born Angelo Giuseppe Roncalli, the son of a peasant, he was ordained in 1904 and during the First World War served as a military chaplain. He later held a series of increasingly important administrative and diplomatic posts, in one of which, as Papal Nuncio in France, he championed the controversial system of worker-priests. When he became pope, he broke with tradition by leaving the Vatican to visit hospitals and prisons in Rome, and at the time of his death was held in regard and affection not only by those of his faith, but by many beyond it.

John, St (1st cent. AD) Palestine-born Christian apostle and evangelist, disputed author of the fourth Gospel of the New Testament and of the three Epistles of St John. One of the greatest creative writers of early Christian literature, his Gospel differs from the three Synoptic Gospels of MATTHEW, MARK and LUKE (to which it was intended as supplement) in both content and form. Containing few parables and stressing the supernatural aspects of JESUS's life, it attempts to justify Christianity from the historical facts connected with the life of Jesus and interprets the life of Christ in mainly allegorical terms. John was a Galilean fisherman until he was converted by JOHN THE BAPTIST.

Johnson, Amy (1903-41) English avaitor who, in 1930, became the first woman to fly solo from England to Australia. She broke other records on flights to India and Japan (1931), Cape Town (1932) and, with her husband, to the US and India (1934).

Johnson, Lyndon Baines (1908-72) US politician, who succeeded to the Presidency when John KENNEDY was assassinated in 1963. Johnson was elected for a second term in 1964 with an unprecedented popular majority, but his second term was marked by the escalation of the war in Vietnam and vastly increased American involvement. Despite a number of measures towards the 'Great Society', (civil rights, tax reduction, war on poverty) the conflict in southeast Asia so undermined his prestige that he decided not to seek renomination in 1968.

Johnson, Samuel (1709-84) English critic, essayist, lexicographer and scholar who was most widely known for his witty conversation and eccentric personality recorded by James BOSWELL, and for his *Dictionary of the English Language* (1755). The *Dictionary*, intended as the definitive record of the literary language, was distinguished mainly for its pithy definitions and liberal use of quotations to illustrate shades of meaning. The reputation for scholarship, which led to Johnson's selection (1747) to compile the *Dictionary*, was based largely on two anonymously published works, 'London' (1738), a poem imitating a satire of JUVENAL, and *Life of Savage* (1744), a masterpiece of biography. His reputation was increased by the *Rambler* essays (1750-2). Johnson was not a highly creative writer, but by his conversation and presence, honesty, panoramic knowledge and strict principles, rallied and supported literature for a quarter of a century.

Heroine of the air-conscious world of the 1930s, Amy Johnson was celebrated in a popular song

Joliot-Curie, Frédéric (1900-58) French physicist who, in collaboration with his wife Irène, discovered artificial radioactivity. In 1934, they studied the effect of bombarding aluminium with alpha particles (helium nuclei) from a naturally radioactive source and found that after the bombardment the target had become radioactive and had turned into a radioactive form of phosphorus.

Joliot-Curie, Irène (1896-1956) French physicist and daughter of Pierre and Marie CURIE. With her husband Frédéric, she continued their researches into radoactivity.

Jones, Ernest (1879-1958) British psychiatrist who introduced psychoanalysis into Britain (1910). He was instrumental in bringing the aged FREUD to safety in England after the Nazi invasion of Austria.

Jones, Inigo (1573-1652) English architect, who revolutionized the English concept of what a building should look life, translating the vigour and sophistication of Italian mannerist buildings to the streets of London with his Doric St Paul's portico, Covent Garden, his lavish banqueting house in Whitehall, and his delicately elegant Queen's Chapel at St James's Palace, London. The perfectly proportioned Queen's House, at Greenwich, stands astride a covered path with no loss of compactness or restrained elegance. Jones was also famous for his stage designs.

St Paul's, Covent Garden, by Inigo Jones has a fame far beyond London. Shaw's *Pygmalion* (the musical *My Fair Lady*) has its opening scene set in the portico

Jones, John Paul (1747-92) Scottish-born American naval hero. He commanded a British merchant ship but (*c.* 1773) fled to Virginia and added 'Jones' to his original name 'John Paul' to escape a charge for murdering a mutineer. Fighting as a ship's captain for the colonists in the American War of Independence, he raided British coasts and attacked British shipping. After the post-war abolition of the American navy, he served briefly as rear-admiral in the Russian Black Sea fleet (1788-9).

Jones, Sir William (1746-94) English jurist and Oriental linguist who first perceived that Sanskrit, Greek, and Latin must have a common source. Jones's revelation and his description of Sanskrit, the first to the western world, started the study of Indo-European languages as members of one family.

Jongkind, Johan Barthold (1819-91) Dutch artist, whose influence on Impressionism was considerable. He went from Holland to Paris in 1846 and developed a sensitive response to the nuances of light, especially in his water-colours. His oils often show an affinity with the Dutch school of the 17th century.

Jonson, Ben (c. 1572-1637) English playwright and poet, who wrote the comedies *Volpone* (1606) and *The Alchemist* (1610). Jonson was one of the central figures of the literary world of London under JAMES I, who conferred a pension on him, and for whom Jonson wrote many masques, or court entertainments for which the elaborate scenery, a theatrical innovation, was often designed by Inigo JONES. Jonson's plays were frequently performed – SHAKESPEARE was in the cast of *Every Man in his Humour* (1598). Jonson was also a considerable poet, who tried to make expression in English as clear and accurate as it was in classical languages. Around him formed a group of young poets, including HERRICK and Suckling, and his verse influenced such poets as MARVELL. His chief prose work, *Timber; or Discoveries made upon Men and Matter* (1640), is a literary miscellany which demonstrates Jonson's wide-ranging intellect and strong Neo-classical views.

Joplin, Scott (1868-1917) American composer famous for his ragtime piano music, such as *Maple Leaf Rag* (1900) and *The Entertainer* (1902). He also wrote one opera *Treemonisha* (1911). His music underwent a revival in the 1970s.

Jordaens, Jacob (1593-1678) Dutch painter of portraits, genre scenes and religious and historical subjects, who early in life assisted RUBENS.

Joseph II (1741-90) King of Germany (1764-90), Holy Roman Emperor (1765-90), who introduced revolutionary social reforms. He was dominated by his mother and co-ruler MARIA TERESA until her death (1780), but then initiated radical change in place of her policy of slow progress. His beliefs were formed by reading VOLTAIRE and the *encyclopédistes,* but his instrument was an all-powerful state for which he was the sole spokesman, unhampered by any controlling laws. His measures to allow religious toleration, end the nobles' stranglehold on local government, and to promote unity by compulsory use of the German language, were not popular: clergy and nobles opposed them and even the peasants rebelled in many of his states. When he died, the schemes typical of his 'enlightened despotism' were largely reversed by his brother, Leopold II, who succeeded him.

Joule, James Prescott (1818-89) English physicist who etablished by experiment that a given amount of mechanical work produces a definite amount of heat. Similar findings, comparing electrical and chemical effects, led him to formulate the first law of thermodynamics (the law of conservation of energy), which states that energy can be converted from one form to another but cannot be created or destroyed. A unit of energy was named after him.

Joyce, James (1882-1941) Irish novelist and one of the outstanding writers of the 20th century. He moved from the naturalistic short stories of *Dubliners* (1914) to the literary realism of *Finnegan's Wake* (1939) in an attempt to recreate an idea or feeling in the reader's mind by rendering the complexities of experience in the sound, movement, associations and derivations of words, as well as in their meaning. His best-known work, *Ulysses* (1922), marked an important stage in this development. Stephen Dedalus, one of the characters in *Ulysses,* represents Joyce himself in *A Portrait of the Artist as a Young Man* (1916), a fictional, satirical autobiography of his early years and aesthetic principles. Joyce was a talented musician, an ability revealed in his verses in *Chamber Music* (1907), often based on the rhythms of Elizabethan songs. He also wrote a play, *Exiles* (1918), in the manner of IBSEN. Joyce spent most of his life abroad, but his novels are all intricate reconstructions of Dublin, his home city.

Joyce, William (1906-46) British traitor. Before the Second World War he was a member of Sir Oswald MOSLEY's British Union of Fascists and founded (1937) the British National Socialist Party. In

August 1939, Joyce left England for Germany on a falsely-obtained British passport and throughout the war broadcast Nazi propaganda in English to Britain, which came to call him 'Lord Haw-haw', because of the affectation of his speech. He was captured near the Danish border in May 1945, tried, found guilty of treason, and hanged (1946).

Juan Carlos I (born 1938) King of Spain since 1975, the year of FRANCO's death. The grandson of Alfonso XIII, Juan Carlos was designated as heir to the throne by Franco in 1969. He has proved himself to be a forceful king, has withstood two attempted coups, and has been active in negotiations for autonomy for Catalonia and the Basque region.

Juarez, Benito (1806-72) Mexican reformer and revolutionary leader. He led the successful liberal revolution of 1855 against the régime of President Santa Anna and, as a result, became Minister of Justice (1855-7). His radical reforms – judicial, educational and anti-clerical – precipitated a violent reaction, and, during the civil war which followed (1858-60), he was declared provisional President, but was forced to abandon Mexico City to his conservative opponents. However, he reorganized his forces in Vera Cruz and led them to victory. On assuming power, he suspended payment of foreign debts. This gave NAPOLEON III of France, acting ostensibly on behalf of French capitalists, an excuse to invade Mexico and set up a puppet empire, with the Austrian Archduke MAXIMILIAN as emperor. Juarez and his forces maintained their resistance, encouraged by the promise of help from the US. When, under US pressure. Napoleon withdrew his army, Juarez took the initiative and Maximilian was caught and shot (1867) Juarez was President until his death, when he was succeeded by his lieutenant, Porfirio Diaz.

Judah ha-Nasi (c. 135-c. 220) Jewish scholar and traditional compiler of the Mishnah, the first comprehensive codification of Jewish oral law. The political and religious head of Palestinian Jewry, Rabbi Judah devoted his wealth and influence to gathering earlier rabbinic teachings into a unified and acceptable legal code. Later scholars elaborated the Mishnah, which was finally edited into the vast encyclopedias of law, learning and tradition known as the Palestinian and Babylonian Talmuds.

Julian (331-63) Roman emperor from 361 to 363. Traditionally known as 'the Apostate', his policy was to restore the pagan cults, deprive the Christian Church of its privileges and re-establish Roman prestige in the East. His writings, chiefly speeches and letters, reflect his complexity as scholar, soldier, statesman and mystic.

Jung, Carl Gustav (1875-1961) Swiss founder of analytic psychology. An early friend and disciple of FREUD, he propounded his own theory of the libido as something like 'life force'. The Jungian psyche has three levels: consciousness, the 'persona' or mask; the personal unconscious, a mirror image of the persona containing unrealized possibilities and forgotten experiences (female elements of men and vice versa, extrovert elements of introverts, etc); and the collective unconscious, which contains the whole psychological heritage of the human race. Jung classified characters as introverted or extroverted, subdividing them according to the prevailing domination of feeling, intuition, sensation or thought. He saw psychic troubles as the result of unbalanced development, and treatment consisted of putting the patient into touch with his personal and collective unconscious. An important Jungian concept is that of 'archetypes', the significance of any actual person or object depending on its resemblance to certain archetypes stored in the collective unconscious.

Justinian (483-565) Roman emperor and lawgiver. He initiated the codification of the Roman law, through a committee of ten jurists under the direction of Tribonian. They produced the *Codex* (529, and a revised version in 534), the *Institutes* (based on those of GAIUS), the *Digest* or *Pandects* (533), and supplementary volumes (*novellae*).

Juvenal (c. 50-c. 140) The greatest Roman satiric poet. In his 16 *Saturae* (100-130) he bitterly attacked contemporary stupidity while avoiding mention of living people. His vivid pictures of Rome at that time ranged from attacks on homosexuality and other vices to a diatribe against women and a great sermon on the 'follies of human ambitions'. Both amusing and cruel, his epigrams are memorable and his brilliant powers of parody, irony, innuendo and invective gave a new dimension to Roman satire. He had a profound influence in the Middle Ages and modern satirists have used him as their model.

K

Kabir see NANAK

Kádár, János (born 1912) Leader of the Communist régime in Hungary after the Russian invasion of 1956. As Minister of the Interior, he played a major part in the trial of Cardinal MINDSZENTY in 1948 and in the trial and execution of Rajk, the Hungarian Foreign Minister, in 1949 on charges of supporting the deviationist line of TITO. He was a member of NAGY's government, but during the revolution of 1956, changed sides and subsequently headed a Russian puppet government. Under Kádár's administration, Hungary has achieved a greater measure of internal freedom and material progress (through the New Economic Policy of 1968, and Five-Year Plans), but Kádár has repeatedly stressed Hungarian commitment to the Warsaw Pact.

Kafka, Franz (1883-1924) Austrian novelist, whose nightmare-like parables reflect man's search for reality and identity. Only his essays and short stories were published in his lifetime, one of the most famous of which is *Metamorphosis* (1912), an early example of Kafka's dominant theme, man's predicament in an inexplicable and unsympathetic world. His major novels, *The Trial* (1925), *The Castle* (1926) and *America* (1927), were published posthumously by his friend Max Brod.

Kamerlingh-Onnes, Heike (1853-1926) Dutch physicist, who was the first to liquefy helium and subsequently to discover the super-conductivity of metals. In the late 1880s, interested by the work of Johannes van der WAALS, he began studying gases at low temperatures. In 1908, using a liquid hydrogen cooling system, he liquefied helium and found its temperature to be just four degrees above absolute zero. He discovered that at this very low temperature certain metals, such as mercury and lead, lose all electrical resistance and become what are now known as super-conductors.

Kandinsky, Wassily (1866-1944) Russian-born artist, who became a pioneer of abstract painting. From 1896 until 1914 he lived in Munich, where, with Franz Marc, he founded (1911) the *Blaue Reiter* (Blue Rider) group, which played an influential role in the German Expressionist movement. After the

First World War he returned to Germany, where he taught at the famous Bauhaus school until it was closed by the Nazis. He then moved to Paris. At the Bauhaus he had developed a vocabulary of geometrical forms; but in Paris the organic quality of his early abstracts was revived, though now disciplined by a precise technique. Underlying all his work is the Expressionist theory, which stresses the metaphysical status of art and its expressive function.

K'ang-hsi (1654-1722) Chinese emperor (as Sheng-tsu, 1661-1177), the greatest of the Manchu dynasty. He campaigned deep in Mongolia, added three provinces in the north, made a treaty with Russia on the northern border (1689), conquered Yunnan and Formosa, and won control of Tibet. While he ruled as a conqueror, keeping the peace with strategically placed garrisons, he adopted Chinese culture, encouraging the arts and sponsoring collections of Chinese literary classics and major works of reference, notably a 5000-volume encyclopedia. He tolerated the Christians and actively encouraged the Jesuit scholar-missionaries, who brought to China their scientific skills.

Kano Eitoku (1543-90) Japanese artist, renowned for his forceful outline ink painting borrowed from the Chinese, which he combined with the native tradition of bright colour against gold or silver backgrounds. Having founded the Momoyama style of painting, his sons, Kano Mitsunobu (*c.* 1561-1608) and Kano Takanobu (1571-1618), and his adopted son, Kano Sanraku (1559-1635), continued the family tradition which lasted into the 19th century.

Kano, Jigoro (1860-1938) Japanese founder of judo. He studied the many clan techniques of ju-jitsu and combined them to create judo.

Kant, Immanuel (1724-1804) German philosopher, widely regarded as the greatest modern philosopher. A lifelong teacher at Königsberg and a prolific writer – originally on the physical sciences – his later philosophical works, such as the *Critique of Pure Reason* (1781), were so influential that he became an oracle on important questions of his day. His critical philosophy is the foundation of the subsequent history of the subject.

Karadžić, Vuk Stefanović (1787-1864) Serbian scholar and folklorist, who helped to establish Serbian as an official and literary language in place of the synthesis of Russian and liturgical Slavonic.

Karlfeldt, Eric Axel (1864-1931) Swedish lyric poet and follower of Werner von Heidenstam's Nititilist school, whose *Songs of the Wilderness and of Love* (1895) captures the spirit of his native province, Dalecarlia. His fascination with ancient folk life is expressed in *The Songs of Fridolin*, published in two volumes (1898, 1901), the story of a learned man of peasant origin who returns to the countryside of his forefathers. In 1931 Karlfeldt was posthumously awarded the Nobel Prize for Literature.

Karlstadt, Andreas von (c. 1477-1541) German Puritan reformer. An early supporter, but later an opponent, of LUTHER, he advocated clerical reforms which established the bases of German Puritanism.

Karsavina, Tamara (born 1885) Russian ballerina whose artistry helped to establish Michel Fokine's new school of expressive Russian dancing in the Western world.

Kasprowicz, Jan (1860-1926) Polish lyric poet, whose famous *Book of the Poor* (1916) is the first work to give Polish folklore poetic expression. His 'Ballad of the Sunflower' is considered one of Poland's greatest poems.

Kästner, Erich (1899-1974) German writer and satirist, best known outside Germany for his children's books, notably *Emil and The Detectives* (1929).

Kaunda, Kenneth David (born 1924) Zambian nationalist politician, the first President of the Republic of Zambia. A fervent nationalist in the years leading to his country's independence, he was Secretary-General of the North Rhodesian African National Congress. He started the break-away Zambian African Nationalist Congress in 1958, and, when it was banned, was imprisoned. On his release, he became President of the United National Independence Party (1960), Prime Minister of Northern Rhodesia in 1964 and, on independence later in the same year, President of Zambia. Although Kaunda's attitude to political change was inspired by the non-violent methods of GANDHI, he has increasingly supported the African liberation movements operating in Rhodesia and Portuguese Africa.

Kautsky, Karl (1854-1938) German Social-Democratic theorist, who denounced LENIN's concept of the 'dictatorship of the proletariat' as a betrayal of true Marxism. He was born in Prague, and was a friend of MARX. Though he supported the view that socialism could be accomplished only by violent revolution, he opposed Bolshevik authoritarianism and disassociated himself from the Russian Revolution. After settling in Vienna, he devoted himself to social-democratic writing and was influential among anti-Bolshevik socialist intellectuals.

Kawabata Yasunari (1899-1972) Japanese novelist who was awarded

A master of dead-pan slapstick, Buster Keaton was second only to Chaplin

the 1968 Nobel Prize for Literature. Kawabata was deeply influenced by the Japanese cultural tradition, and his novels, the most popular of which are *The Izu Dancer*, *The Snow County*, *A thousand Cranes* and *Sound of the Mountain*, display the latent melancholy of Heian literature. President of the Japan Pen Club, Kawabata was a prominent critic and patron of new writers such as MISHIMA Yukio. Kawabata committed suicide (1972).

Kay, John (18th cent.) English inventor of the flying shuttle (patented 1733), a weaving device for automatically moving the shuttle across the warp of a loom.

Kazantzakis, Nikos (1885-1957) Greek poet whose most widely known novel is *Zorba the Greek* (1946). His 24-volume epic poem, *The Odyssey* (1938), continues HOMER's story, embracing the whole of Kazantzakis's philosophical ideas in a tapestry of symbolism and rich imagery.

Kazinczy, Ferenc (1759-1831) Hungarian literary critic and leader (through his translations) of its language reform.

Kean, Edmund (1787-1833) British actor, who was an outstanding tragedian and a romantic theatrical personality. HAZLITT and COLERIDGE were fascinated by his tragic genius, as were the audiences by his interpretations of villainy in such roles as Iago.

Keaton, Buster (1895-1966) American screen comedian who began his career in his parents' vaudeville act. His masterpieces of silent comedy include *The Navigator* (1924), *The General* (1926) and *Steamboat Bill Junior*, in which, like CHAPLIN, Keaton played the little man who always won through, though unlike Chaplin, he never slipped into sentimentality. In 1959, he was awarded a special Oscar for his contribution to cinema.

Keats, John (1795-1821) 'Here lies one whose name was writ in water', were the words Keats wanted on his tomb. An English Romantic poet, he devoted himself to literature. Although befriended by Leigh HUNT and SHELLEY, his work gained little contemporary favour at first. His narrative poems had historical subjects: 'La Belle Dame sans Merci' (1891) is an evocation of medieval romantic mystery. In his last volume (1820), containing, among others, 'The Eve of St Agnes', 'Lamia' and 'Hyperion', he worked on the haunting theme that the transient quality of beauty can only be arrested in art, as stated in 'Ode on a Grecian Urn'. Soon after, Keats died of consumption, in Italy.

Keble, John (1792-1866) British clergyman and poet, originator of the Oxford Movement, which fought the erosion of Church authority by secular elements. The movement was launched by a Keble university sermon in which he criticized the abolition of ten Irish bishoprics. Its ideas were disseminated by John Henry NEWMAN's *Tracts for the Times*, to which Keble made nine contributions. He was also joint editor with Newman and Edward Pusey of a series of new translations of patriotic writings, for which they claimed absolute doctrinal authority. After Newman's conversion, Keble remained a loyal Anglican, but still tried to 'Romanize' Church doctrine and practice.

Kekulé von Stradonitz, Friedrich (1829-96) German chemist who discovered the ring structure of benzene. His work on chemical structures, especially in organic chemistry, led to an understanding of other compounds.

Keller, Gottfried (1819-90) Swiss poet and novelist, and Switzerland's foremost narrative writer of the Realist school. His kindly, ironic humour and sympathy for his fellow men are seen at their best in the collections of stories called *The People of Seldwyla* (Part I, 1856; Part II, 1874), ten stories set in a fictitious Swiss town. He was also a notable poet; 'The Jesuit Procession' (1843) is a satirical poem on the theme of the intrigues of bourgeois society. His other major works include *Green Henry* (1755), an autobiographical novel.

Keller, Helen Adams (1880-1968) American social worker, who overcame the loss of sight, hearing and speech, yet achieved distinction as a lecturer and scholar. Illness rendered her blind and deaf at the age of nineteen months, and later she became dumb. In Anne Sullivan, who taught her to speak within a month at the age of seven, she had a dedicated teacher, and Helen Keller's ability was such that she obtained a degree in 1904 and mastered several languages. She also lectured worldwide and worked for the relief of the handicapped.

Kelly, Gene (born 1912) American dancer and actor who was one of the first to integrate dance with drama in motion pictures.

Blind and deaf from childhood, Helen Keller was a prize scholar at 24

Sinatra, Kelly and Williams star in a popular film musical of the 1940s

Kelly, 'Ned' (1855-80) Australian bushranger, whose daring crimes and outwitting of the police made him the most celebrated criminal in Australian history. In 1880, at Glenrowan, his gang failed to derail a train-load of police reinforcements sent to capture them and a gun battle followed. Kelly survived but was later arrested, charged with murder, and hanged.

Kelly, Petra (born 1948) West German politician and founder of Die Grünen (The Green Party). Her family moved from Germany to America in the early 1960s where she worked as a student volunteer on the presidential campaigns of Robert Kennedy and Hubert Humphrey. In 1972 she worked for the EEC in Brussels and became a full-time civil servant. She founded Die Grünen in 1972 and has been a member of the West German parliament since 1983.

Kelvin, Lord William Thompson (1824-1907) Scottish physicist and inventor, who devised the absolute temperature scale and so put the second law of thermodynamics on a sound theoretical basis. In 1851 he gave a full account of thermodynamic theory, co-ordinating the findings of the previous 50 years. He drew attention to the dissipation of energy implied in the second law of thermodynamics, and this 'running down' of the universe has figured largely in scientific speculation since. Also spectacular was his work on electrical theory and its application to submarine telegraph cables. He invented many instruments for use in electrical engineering (such as the mirror galvanometer). His investigation of the oscillating discharge of condensers was the basis for the later discovery, by HERTZ, of radio waves.

Kemal, Mustapha (1881-1938) Turkish soldier-statesman, known as Kemal Ataturk, who westernized and modernized Turkey. He joined the army and the Young Turk Movement, but soon quarrelled (1908) with its leader, Enver. He fought against the Italians in Libya (1911) and in the Balkan Wars. As a divisional commander of the Turkish Forces at Gallipoli (1915) he successfully resisted the British invasion but was defeated by ALLENBY in Syria. He formed the Turkish Nationalist Party (1919) to resist Greek annexation of Smyrna (Ismir). Resistance turned into revolution, and in 1920 he set up a revolutionary government in Ankara. Within two years he had driven the Greeks from Smyrna. He abolished the caliphate (1924), set up the Turkish Republic (of which he was the first President, 1923) as a wholly secular state, banned oriental in favour of European dress, emancipated women, enforced the use of the Latin alphabet, and ruled Turkey as a dictator until his death.

Kempis, Thomas à see THOMAS À KEMPIS

Kennedy, John Fitzgerald (1917-63) First Roman Catholic US President, assassinated in Dallas, Texas, by Lee Harvey OSWALD, after less than three years in office (November 1963). Educated at Harvard, Kennedy served with distinction in the navy in the Second World War. In 1946 he was elected to the House of Representatives as a Democrat, and to the Senate, for Massachusetts, in 1952. He became President in 1961, defeating NIXON, the better-known Republican candidate. His attempt to restore a right-wing government in Cuba by backing an invasion of Cuban exiles to fight CASTRO (April 1961), was a failure. In 1962 US intelligence discovered Soviet missile sites in Cuba, and Kennedy announced that Soviet ships carrying weapons to the sites would be intercepted. The Prime Minister of the USSR, KHRUSCHEV, proposed to withdraw offensive weapons from Cuba if the US would withdraw theirs from Turkey. Kennedy refused to negotiate until work on the Cuban sites stopped, missile launchers were rendered inoperable and shipment of weapons ceased. Among important elements of Kennedy's internal policy were the Civil Rights Bill, which made discrimination against negroes and racial segregation in schools and other institutions illegal. In the international field, his promotion of the General Agreement on Tariffs and Trade, signed at Geneva by many leading industrial powers, ensured a progressive reduction of tariff barriers. In Vietnam the Kennedy administration increased support of the South Vietnamese régime, increased US aid and the number of American economic, military and political advisers, a commitment which was subsequently to involve the US to a far greater extent, under JOHNSON his successor. Kennedy brought to the presidency an attractive presence, interest in art and literature and a youthful idealism which appealed to the young.

Scene aboard a 19th-century Atlantic cable-laying ship. Its success depended largely on the work of Kelvin

Kennedy, Joseph P. (1888-1969) American financier and diplomat whose ill-starred family became one of the most celebrated and potent forces in American politics. Serving as Ambassador to the UK from 1938-40, Kennedy was instrumental in securing American support for Britain in the early stages of the Second World War. When his eldest son, Joseph Jr., was killed in the war, John KENNEDY inherited the family's political mantle and rose through the Democratic Party ranks to become President in 1961. During his tragically shortened term of office, John appointed his brother Robert (1925-68) Attorney-General and his career was equally spectacular and ended as violently. Elected senator for New York in 1964, Robert was campaigning for the Presidential nomination when assassinated by a Palestinian extremist. Edward, the youngest son, has been a Massachusetts senator since 1962.

Kennelly, Arthur Edwin (1861-1939) British-born American electrical engineer, who predicted the presence of electrically charged layers in the atmosphere. In 1902, after MARCONI's experiments with radio waves, Kennelly noticed that the waves could reach beyond the Earth's horizon. He suggested that they did this by bouncing off a layer of ions high in the atmosphere. Oliver HEAVISIDE, an English physicist, made a similar proposition and the layers are called Kennelly-Heaviside layers.

Kenneth I MacAlpine (9th cent.) First king of Scotland, who subdued the Picts and, from his capital at Dunkeld, claimed to rule all territories north of the Firth of Forth.

Kent, James (1763-1847) American jurist whose writings, notably his four-volume *Commentaries on American Law* (1826-30) had a great influence on the development of Anglo-American law. He made English common law the basis of court decisions, setting a pattern adopted by New York and other American states.

Kent, William (1684-1748) English architect who, under the sponsorship and guidance of Lord Burlington, began as a painter and turned to architecture at the age of 40. Kent became an important exponent of the English Palladian style. Among his best-known works are the Horse Guards, the Royal Mews and the Treasury Buildings, Whitehall. He also influenced the art of landscape gardening, turning against the formal patterns of the time, stressing the potential harmony between a house and its setting.

Kenyatta, Jomo (c. 1893-1978) Kenyan politician of the Kikuyu tribe, first Prime Minister of his country (1963) and President the following year. A lifelong worker for the independence of his country, Kenyatta became secretary of the Kikuyu Central Association in 1928 and as its representative visited Britain. In 1947, he began a vigorous Nationalist campaign, was accused of being implicated in the Mau Mau disturbances in the early 1950s and was sent to prison for seven years (1953). Allowed complete freedom in 1961, he took the lead in Kenya's political affairs as President of the opposition party, the Kenya African National Union. After KANU victory in the election of May 1963, Kenyatta became the first Prime Minister of self-governing Kenya. He became President of the Republic of Kenya in 1964. He has since suppressed opposition.

Kenyon, Kathleen (1906-78) British archaeologist who in the early 1950s, using LIBBY's newly developed carbon dating technique, showed Jericho (now named Ariha) in Jordan to be among the oldest walled towns in the world. Her finds proved that the twin bases of civilization, farming and town life, had begun far earlier than was hitherto supposed.

Khruschev and John F. Kennedy, who was elected to the presidency of the US in 1960, and was inaugurated in 1961. During his term of office, confrontation between the US and Khruschev's USSR over Russian missiles in Cuba came near to nuclear war

Kepler, Johannes (1571-1630) German astronomer, who discovered the elliptical orbit of the Earth around the Sun, and formulated the laws of planetary motion. Kepler's religious faith convinced him that there was a harmony in the relationships of the planets. Attempting to resolve the apparent discrepancy between the observed motion of Mars and the theoretical motion as laid down in the Copernican system, Kepler formulated his major hypothesis that the orbits of the planets are elliptical. In order to account for the irregular velocities of the planets in their orbits, he sought some fundamental law of their motion, and found the solution in the discovery that the radius from a planet to the Sun describes equal areas in equal times.

Kerensky, Alexander (1881-1970) The first and last prime minister of a democratic, parliamentary Russian government. A lawyer by profession he was elected as a Social-Democratic member of the *Duma* in 1912, becoming Minister for War following the March Revolution of 1917, and by July was Prime Minister of the Provisional Government. His policy of continuing the war had no public support and he was swept aside by the October Revolution – LENIN and TROTSKY's *coup d'état* of 7 November. Kerensky tried unsuccessfully to rally resistance to the Bolsheviks but was forced to flee abroad to France and later went to the US (in 1946), where he died.

Kerouac, Jack (1922-69) American novelist, the best-known author of the Beat generation (a romantic movement of revolt against convention and authority), defined and described in such works as *Desolation Angels* (1965).

Keynes, Lord John Maynard (1883-1946) British economist who stressed the control of economic mechanisms to achieve desirable objectives. A government adviser during the Second World War, he favoured a world bank and international currency, and was one of the chief architects of the Bretton Woods Agreements in 1944 which set up the International Monetary Fund and the World Bank. In his *The General Theory of Employment, Interest and Money* (1936), he urged the government to stimulate consumption, encourage capital goods production and invest in public works, rather than waiting for automatic forces to revive employment. He resigned the leadership of the British Treasury team at the Ver-

The astronomical watershed

Johannes Kepler (right) was the first man to prove that the Sun, and not the Earth, lay at the centre of the Solar System. He calculated that the orbit of Mars (below) was an ellipse, and that the area covered by the imaginary line from the Sun (A) to the planet moving from 1 to 2 was the same as that covered from 3 to 4.

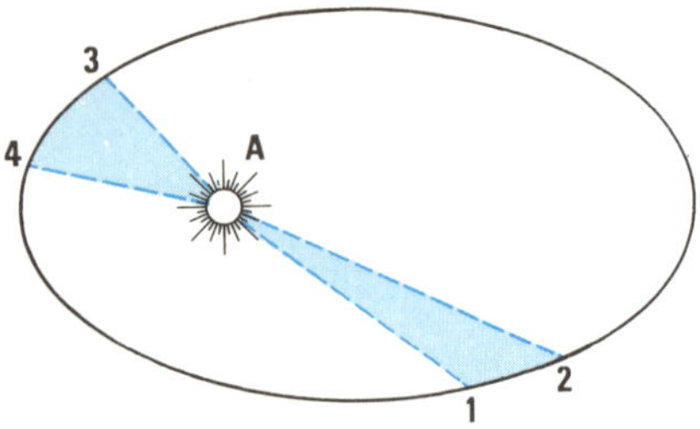

In spite of his revolutionary mathematics, Kepler was obsessed with the idea that the orbits of the planets could be constructed around geometrical solids (below). However, the years he spent fruitlessly trying to prove that the cube (1), tetrahedron (2), dodecahedron (3), icosahedron (4) and octohedron (5) contained, and were enclosed by, spheres constructed on circular planetary orbits, succeeded in throwing up, almost by chance, the proofs that denied the authority of the theory of Ptolemy, venerated for over 1300 years. In 1534, Copernicus had mapped the planets, with the Sun at the centre (right), in the correct order – Mercury (A), Venus (B), Earth (C), Mars (E), Jupiter (F) and Saturn (G), with the Moon (D) rotating about the Earth – but still believed that the orbits were perfect circles.

Sir Isaac Newton (below right), who consolidated the astronomical revolution, showed that the Moon is pulled towards the Earth by the force of gravity (bottom right), causing it to arrive at A_2 rather than at A_1, as it would if undisturbed by the Earth. The same fundamental principle proved correct Kepler's elliptical orbits.

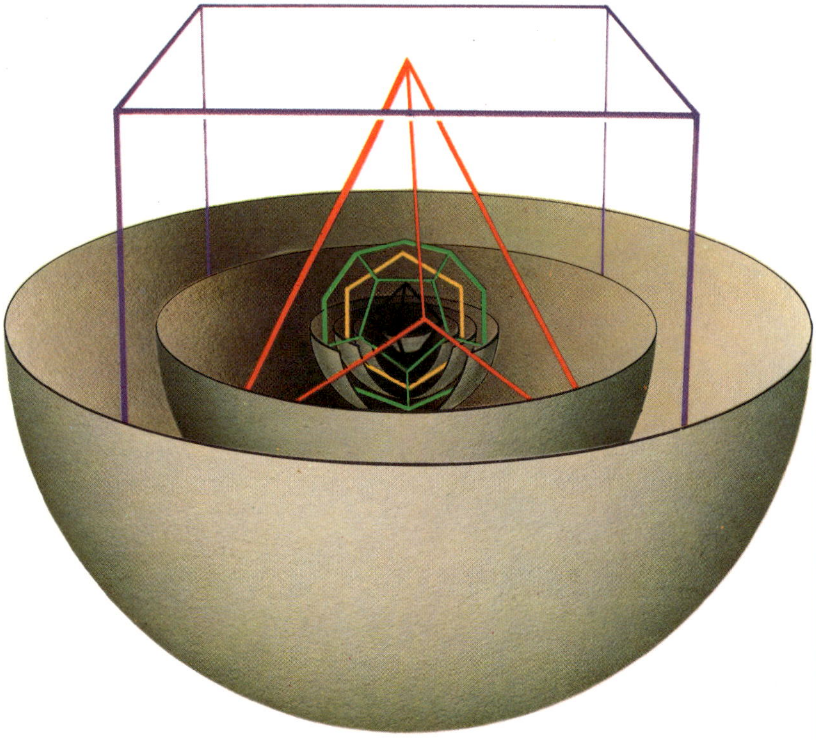

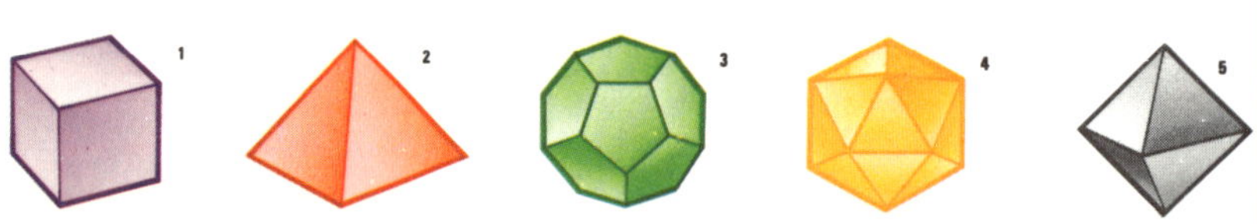

The Ptolemaic system (below)
At the centre lay the Earth. Around it moved the Moon (A), Mercury (B), Venus (C), the Sun (D), Mars (E), Jupiter (F) and Saturn (G).

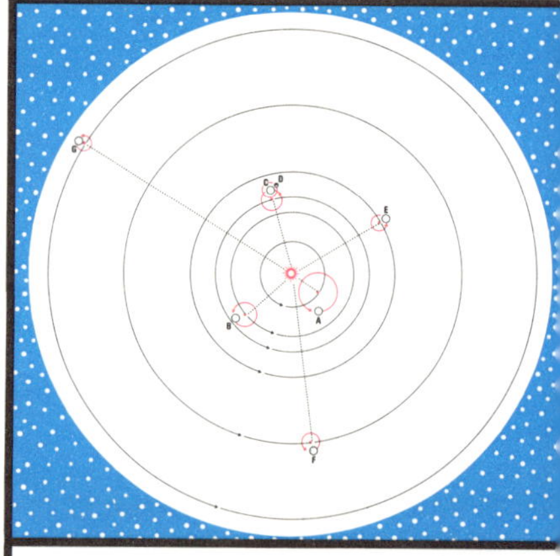

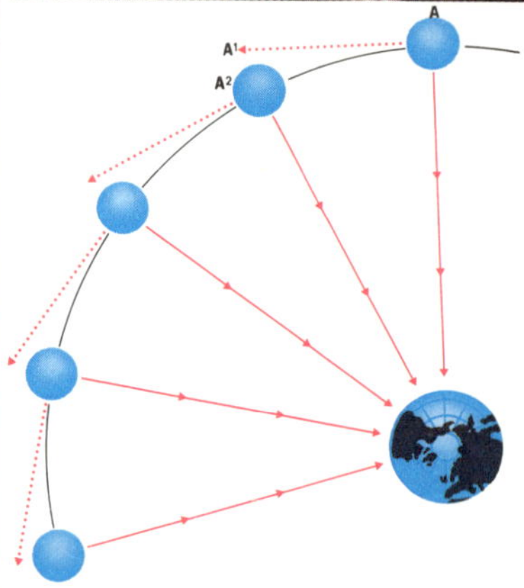

sailles negotiations (1919) to write against imposing on Germany enormous reparation payments which, he foresaw, would upset the world economy.

ibn-Khaldun (1332-1406) Leading Arab historian. He held various official posts in North Africa and Spain, but his fame rests on one book, a general history of the Muslim dynasties and, more specifically, the *Muqaddima*, the introduction to this work, in which he theorized on the nature, significance and methodology of history. It was described by Arnold TOYNBEE as 'the greatest work of its kind that has ever yet been created by any mind in any time or place'.

Khan, Mohammed Ayub (1907-74) Pakistani soldier and politician. President of Pakistan, who was deposed in 1969 by a peasant revolt. He was the first Commander-in-Chief of the Pakistani army and a bloodless military coup brought him to the presidency in 1958, when President Mirza abrogated the constitution and martial law was proclaimed. Autocratic, yet paternalistic in his rule, Ayub Khan brought a measure of economic stability to Pakistan, but lack of both industry and development funds in East Pakistan led to demands for autonomy and a revolt of the peasantry in 1969. His presidency ended as it had begun, under martial law.

Khorana, Har Gobind (born 1922) Indian-American biochemist, co-winner of the 1968 Nobel Prize for Medicine, who in 1970 manufactured the first synthetic gene. Future developments could lead not only to the treatment of diseases caused by gene deficiencies but also to the possibility of reproducing people with defined characteristics by the manipulation of genes.

Khruschev, Nikita Sergeyevich (1894-1971) Soviet politician and First Secretary, whose election to the Soviet Communist Party's leadership brought Stalinism to an end. He joined the Communist Party during the First World War, and served in the Red Army during the Civil War. A mineworker by trade, Khruschev studied engineering, meanwhile holding increasingly important political offices, until, in 1937, he was elected to the Supreme Soviet. As First Secretary of the Ukrainian Communist Party, he organised and led guerilla warfare against the Germans in the Second World War and was responsible later for the execution of a large number of Ukrainians who had collaborated with the enemy. On STALIN's death in 1953, he was elected First Secretary, and a secret session of the Party denounced Stalin's abuse of power, judicial murder of his comrades, failure to prepare for the war, and other crimes. He became Chairman of the Council of Ministers in 1958, but was dismissed from both these offices in 1964, and replaced by the triumvirate of KOSYGIN, BREZHNEV and Podgorny. There was no State acknowledgement of his death or of his achievements in office.

Khufu or **Cheops (26th cent. BC)** King of Egypt, who built the Great Pyramid, largest of the pyramids at Giza.

Kidd, William (c. 1645-1701) Scottish seaman, who, in 1696, sailed from England as a privateer officially authorized to suppress pirates, but who fraternized with Madagascar's pirates and attacked local vessels. He finally reached New England, but was seized and sent to London, where he was tried and hanged for piracy at Execution Dock on 23 May, 1701.

Kierkegaard, Sören (1813-55) Danish philosopher and theologian whose assessment of the human predicament makes him one of the sources of Existentialism. Opposed to the system building of HEGEL, Kierkegaard was impressed by the isolated and subjective life of the individual, and by the unbridgeable gap between sinful man and God. Kierkegaard saw the individual, filled with dread and overawed by the fact of being, taking refuge in a 'leap of faith' towards Christianity.

King, Billie Jean (born 1943) American lawn tennis player who won her first title at the age of 15. She was singles champion of the USA in 1967, 1971-2 and 1974; of Wimbledon in 1966-8; 1972-3 and 1975; of Australia in 1968; and of France in 1972.

King, Clarence (1842-1901) American geologist and mining engineer who laid the foundation of the geological survey of the United States. During the survey of California, he explored the Sierra Nevada and the southern Californian and Arizona deserts and led the transcontinental survey of the 40th parallel, across the Rocky Mountains.

King, Martin Luther (1929-68) American civil rights leader, whose methods of non-violent demonstration and passive resistance advanced the cause of the American negroes. A Baptist minister in Alabama, his leadership of a negro boycott of public transport (1956) resulted in a desegregation order enabling blacks to sit with whites in public vehicles. This success led him to organize and lead huge non-violent demonstrations and marches in Washington and elsewhere in support of KENNEDY's civil rights legislation. He became head of the Southern Christian Leadership and lent its weight and his personal influence to support of the National Association for the Advancement of Coloured People. He was awarded the Nobel Peace Prize in 1964 for his maintenance of non-violence in his political work. King was assassinated in Memphis, Tennessee.

King, William Lyon Mackenzie (1874-1950) Canadian statesman and Prime Minister of Canada for a total of 22 years (1921-6, 1926-30 and 1935-48). His policies for international trade and constitutional reform, and his handling of his country's part in the Second World War, raised Canada's standing in the international community.

Kingsley, Charles (1819-75) English author and clergyman, best known for his novels *Westward Ho!* (1855), *Hereward the Wake* (1866) and the children's story, *The Water Babies* (1863). An active campaigner and writer for social and national causes, his social conscience and impetuous nature brought him into controversy with Cardinal NEWMAN.

Kinsey, Alfred C. (1894-1956) American zoologist famous for his studies of human sexual behaviour. He was director of the Institute for Sex Research at Indiana State University. He is best known for his publications *Sexual Behavior in the Human Male* (1948) and *Sexual Behavior in the Human Female* (1953), each based on thousands of personal interviews.

Kipling, Rudyard (1865-1936) English author, who is famous for his record of the spirit of England's Imperial expansion in India. From *Plain Tales from the Hills* (1888) onwards, his stories of India, the sea, the jungle and many other subjects brought him popularity. His verse, as in the *Barrack-Room Ballads* (1892), is skilful, and his stories for children, including *The Jungle Book* (1894-5), display his principal quality as a storyteller.

Kircher, Athanasius (1601-80) German Jesuit polymath who helped to pioneer new map-making techniques and the magic lantern. In 1643, he made one of the first maps to show magnetic variation, and in 1665 pioneered the making of maps showing ocean currents. In 1645, he discovered how to use a powerful light, a reflector and a lens to project an image of a picture painted on a glass slide onto a screen.

Kirchhoff, Gustav Robert (1824-87) German physicist who, in the 1850s (and working with Robert BUNSEN), constructed the first spectroscope. Kirchhoff realized that every element when heated to incandescence emits its own distinctive set of spectral lines, thus enabling it to be identified. He also pointed out that the dark lines observed by Fraunhofer were due to an equally characteristic absorption, making it possible to examine the composition of the Sun and stars.

Kirkes, William (1823-64) British physician who showed that emboli (blood clots and other small solids in the bloodstream) may cause cerebral thrombosis or an acute pulmonary disorder. Priority for the discovery was disputed by VIRCHOW.

Kissinger, Henry (born 1923) German-born diplomat and consultant to four American presidents. In the 1950s, Kissinger's theories offered a moderate alternative to Secretary of State DULLES's Cold War 'brinkmanship'. As NIXON's top foreign adviser, Kissinger negotiated the settlement in Vietnam and helped build new links with China, and in 1973 he was appointed Secretary of State. He was awarded the Nobel Peace Prize (jointly with Le Duc Tho) for his role as mediator during peace talks on the war in Indochina (1973).

Kitasato, Shibasaburo see BEHRING, Emil von

Kitchener, Horatio Herbert, 1st Earl (1850-1916) Commander-in-Chief of the British army in the first half of the First World War. He served in the French army against Prussia in 1871 and in the same year was commissioned into the Royal Engineers. His first major command was as Sirdar (Commander-in-Chief) of the Egyptian army in the Sudan (1884-5). In the second Boer War (1899-1902) he was chief-of-staff to Roberts, whom he later succeeded as GOC, overcoming Boer resistance by controversial strategies which included the establishment of concentration camps. While Commander-in-Chief in India (1902-9) he assumed control of the Indian army, despite CURZON's strong opposition. From 1911-14, Kitchener ruled Egypt, as British Agent, but was recalled to Britain to become War Minister when the First World War broke out. En route to Russia for secret talks in June 1916, he drowned when HMS *Hampshire* sank.

Kjellén, Rudolf (1864-1922) Swedish political scientist who invented and explained the term geopolitics. Influenced by Friedrich RATZEL's work on political geography (which reflected DARWIN's teachings on evolution and natural selection), he declared in *The State as an Organism* (1916) that a political state is a biological organism, subject to growth and decay. Developed by HAUSHOFER in Germany and adopted by Fascist Italy and by Japan, this intellectually appealing fallacy became a pretext upon which the Axis powers justified their struggle for dominance in the Second World War.

Klaproth, Martin (1743-1817) German chemist who, recognizing that certain compounds contained hitherto unknown elements, isolated and named two of them as titanium and zirconium. A substance which he produced from pitchblende, and which he named uranium, turned out to be the oxide of that metal.

Klee, Paul (1879-1940) Swiss artist, who became a member of the *Blaue Reiter* circle in Munich before the First World War, and taught at the Bauhaus (1921-31). He was for many years in close contact with KANDINSKY. His art is remarkable not only for its small scale and its delicacy, but because Klee's creative process allowed him to achieve a new kind of harmony of formal and imaginative elements. Klee's published diaries (up to 1918) and his writings (published in English as *The Thinking Eye*) contribute to an understanding of his work.

Klemperer, Otto (1885-1973) German conductor and leading interpreter of BEETHOVEN who was, in his early days, an advocate of contemporary music associated with the works of MAHLER, SCHOENBERG, HINDEMITH and STRAVINSKY. In the 1950s Klemperer, after years of partial paralysis, emerged as a masterly exponent of Beethoven's symphonies.

Klimt, Gustav (1862-1918) Austrian painter and exponent of Art Nouveau. His work has its typical decorative emphasis, but is notable also for its symbolic iconography, usually concerned with the themes of Love or Death. Both these aspects are apparent in the mosaic frieze he designed for Josef HOFFMANN's Palais Stoclet in Brussels. He strongly influenced Schiele and the young KOKOSCHKA.

Klopstock, Friedrich Gottlieb (1724-1803) German lyric poet and dramatist, author of *The Messiah* (1748-73), a life of Christ beginning at the point when he ascends the Mount of Olives. The publication (1748) of the first three of its 20 cantos made Klopstock internationally famous. The work is written in a Neo-classical style in which Greek hexameters were used in German literature. In his odes (collected edition 1771) Klopstock used classical ode forms in verses about religion, nature and love.

Knoll, Max see RUSKA, Ernst August Friedrich

Knox, John (1505-72) Scottish writer, statesman and leader of the Scottish Reformation, a democratic religious revolution which, with English support, ended French political domination and abolished the authority of the pope, 'idolatry' and the Mass. The so-called Reformed Kirk adopted the Calvinistic *Scots Confession of Faith* and the non-episcopal Church Constitution of the *Book of Discipline*, both largely Knox's work. When Catholic MARY STUART returned as Queen in 1561, Knox and the new Church were strong enough to win political and religious supremacy.

Koch, Robert (1843-1910) German bacteriologist, and discoverer in 1882 of the tuberculosis bacillus. As well as proving that each disease is caused by a specific bacterium, and that a bacterium of one type does not change into one of another type, Koch devised techniques for the culture of bacteria, and their identification under the microscope by the use of dyes. He identified the causative organism of cholera in 1883, and introduced an inoculation against anthrax.

Kodály, Zoltan (1882-1967) Hungarian composer. Appointed a teacher of composition at Budapest Conservatory at 24, Kodály's earliest work was the collection and editing of Hungarian folk-songs, which he carried out partly in collaboration with BARTÓK. This material gave him the basis for the national idiom which is the hallmark of his style. His best-known works are the comic opera *Háry János* (1927), based on Garay's ballad of the tall stories told by a veteran of the Napoleonic Wars; the *Psalmus Hungaricus* (1923) for chorus and orchestra on an epic Old Testament theme; and a set of variations on *The Peacock* (1939), a Hungarian folk-song.

Koestler, Arthur (1905-83) Hungarian-born English author and journalist, who wrote a great number of philosophical and fictional works on the split in the Western mind between technological expertise and adherence to any non-material code of behaviour. Among his novels are *Darkness at Noon* (1940), an account of the mental and physical tyranny of a Communist prison, and *The Call Girls* (1972), a tale of international philosophic congresses. His trilogy, *The Sleepwalkers* (1959), *The Act of Creation* (1964) and *The Ghost in the Machine* (1967), forms an attempt to understand the creative and destructive tendencies of the human mind.

Koffka, Kurt (1886-1941) American psychologist of German origin who with Wertheimer and KÖHLER developed the *Gestalt* theory of psychology.

Kohl, Helmut (born 1930) West German political leader who succeeded Helmut Schmidt as Chancellor in 1982. His conservative political philosophy advocated strong support for the Western military alliance and a return to the traditional values of the West German State.

Köhler, Wolfgang (1887-1967) American psychologist of German origin who was largely responsible for developing the *Gestalt* theory of psychology, based on observable data. In the same way that a picture or a pattern is visible as colours or points are visible, so the mind can best deal with material when some pattern is perceived. In time, experiences are seen as organized events. Köhler also investigated the electrical activity which accompanies vision in the brain.

Kokoschka, Oskar (1886-1980) Austrian Expressionist painter, whose early years were spent in the Art Nouveau atmosphere of Vienna. In 1938 he settled in England, concentrating on landscapes and portraits.

Koldewey, Robert (1855-1925) German architect and archaeologist who excavated the city of Babylon. Beginning in 1899, he spent 15 years excavating and mapping the city built by NEBUCHADNEZZAR II during the 6th century BC. He identified huge palaces, massive walls, the famous hanging gardens and a ziggurat (possibly that recorded in the Bible as the Tower of Babel). Koldewey's thorough work showed that the Bible and HERODOTUS were almost certainly correct in their description of Babylon as the greatest cosmopolitan metropolis of the ancient world.

Kolff, Willem J. (born 1911) Dutch physician who, in 1944, produced the first successful clinical apparatus to take over the function of a human kidney and remove noxious waste substances from the blood.

Kornilov, Lavr Georgievich (1870-1918) Russian counter-revolutionary and leader of the Don Cossacks. Commander-in-Chief of the Russian forces in August 1917, he put forward proposals for enforcing discipline in the army. On these being rejected, he attacked the government and, after refusing to accept dismissal, marched on Petrograd with the intention of liberating the provisional government of KERENSKY from Socialist domination. Many soldiers defected, however, and Kerensky called on the Bolsheviks for support. Kornilov was defeated, but his leadership of the Don Cossacks in December 1917 marked the beginning of the Civil War. He was killed in 1918.

Kosciuszko, Tadeusz (1746-1817) Polish patriot, who provoked and led the Polish insurrection against Russian domination in 1794. He was trained as a soldier in the Prussian and French armies, and fought for the Americans in the War of Independence, for which he was given honorary US citizenship. In France, during the Revolution, he received verbal support for the Polish cause, but no practical help, though Russia and Austria were discussing a new partition of his country. He went to Warsaw, roused the people, and in April 1794, at Raclawice, overcame a Russian army sent against him. Six months later, the Russians defeated him outside Warsaw. He was captured and deported to the US, but throughout his subsequent exile in France, continued to work for Poland's independence until his death.

Kosygin, Alexei Nikolayevich (1904-80) Soviet administrator and politician, who joined the Communist Party in 1927 and became Chairman of the Council of Ministers (Prime Minister) following the dismissal of KHRUSCHEV (1964). Under his premiership Russia's foreign policy was one of peaceful co-existence with the West, but attempts to heal the breach with China were unsuccessful. He was considered mainly as an economic administrator.

Koussevitsky, Serge (1876-1951) American musician of Russian birth, conductor of the Boston Symphony Orchestra (1924-49). Koussevitsky first became known as a virtuoso double-bass player and a publisher of contemporary music in pre-Revolutionary Russia. He encouraged contemporary composers by offering commissions (Roussel and PROKOFIEV were both among the many beneficiaries). In 1942 he created the Koussevitsky Foundation in memory of his first wife, Natalie.

Kreisler, Fritz (1875-1962) Austrian violinist and the most widely known violin soloist of his day. His public success was world-wide.

Krishna Menon, Vengalil Krishnan (1896-1974) Indian barrister, diplomatist and nationalist leader. As secretary of the India League (1929-47), he was spokesman for Indian nationalism in Europe, and was India's first High Commissioner in London (1947-52). He played a leading part as an arbitrator during the Korean War (1950-3) and the Suez crisis (1956). As Defence Minister when India and China clashed in border conflicts during 1962, he resigned when the readiness and ability of the army was questioned.

Kritios (5th cent. BC) Greek sculptor whose 'Kouros', in the Acropolis Museum, marks a crucial change from the static Archaic to the organic Classical style. With his partner Nesiotes, Kritios produced a bronze group known as the 'Tyrannicides' (477 BC), depicting the slaying of the tyrant HIPPARCHOS in 514 BC by Harmodios and Aristogeiton. Copies still exist.

Kroeber, Alfred (1876-1960) American anthropologist, who examined the interrelated structure of the culture, language and religion of North American Indians. His main interest lay in the discovery of cultural patterns in, for example, changes in women's clothes, art styles and sign language. Kroeber also made important contributions to the archaeology of Mexico and Peru; his book *Anthropology* (1923) was the first textbook on the subject.

Kropotkin, Peter (1842-1921) Russian revolutionary who shares with BAKUNIN an important place in the history of anarchism. His career as a revolutionary is told in *Memoirs of a Revolutionist* (1899), but his doctrines and diagnosis of the ills of capitalist society are to be found in *Mutual Aid* (1902) and *Modern Science and Anarchism* (1912).

Kruger, Stephanus Johannes Paulus (1825-1904) Boer statesman who was also known as Oom Paul, and who started the second Boer War (1899-1902) by invading Natal and Cape Colony. At the age of 11, he made the Great Trek (1836-7) with the Boers who migrated by waggon away from British rule in the Cape to found new republics – the Orange Free State, Natal and Transvaal. His aim in the Transvaal, of which he became President in 1833, was to

Brought up on the borderland between civilization and barbarism, constantly trekking, fighting and hunting, Kruger (left) received little formal education.

keep it a simple, pastoral land. But the Witwatersrand gold strike of 1886 transformed it, despite his attempts to minimize the effects of mining by taxing the British miners heavily and refusing to give them Transvaal citizenship – acts that manifested his bitter anti-British feelings. Following the JAMESON Raid, Kruger bought German arms and invaded Natal and Cape Colony (1899). With the British successes in the second phase of the war he went to Europe (May 1900) for the help he had been led to expect from Germany. It was refused, and Kruger never returned to South Africa. He died in Switzerland.

Krupp, Alfred (1812-87) German steelmaker and armaments manufacturer who expanded his father's small iron foundry into a giant industry. He was the first steelmaker to install the BESSEMER process and was one of the leaders in the industrial development of the Ruhr valley. His son Friedrich Alfred Krupp (1854-1902) expanded into shipbuilding and the manufacture of chrome and nickel steel alloys and armour-plate. Krupp had the monopoly of German arms manufacture during the First World War. Among its products was Big Bertha, a monstrous but inaccurate train-borne gun which shelled the Paris area from a distance of 70 miles. The firm played a major role in the economic recovery of West Germany after the Second World War.

Krylov, Ivan Andreyevich (1769-1844) Russia's foremost fable writer. He translated those of LA FONTAINE, and between 1809 and 1843 published nine volumes of epigrammatic cameos attacking the self-satisfaction, pretence and arrogance of the Russian upper classes. Many of his lines have passed into the language as proverbs. TURGENEV said of him that a foreigner studying Krylov's fables would gain a clearer understanding of the Russian character than by reading treatises on the subject.

Kublai Khan (1216-94) Mongol founder of China's Yüan dynasty (1260-1368) and one of the great rulers of history. Grandson of GENGHIS KHAN, Kublai helped to subdue southern China. After his brother, Khan Mangu, died (1259), Kublai's troops acclaimed him Great Khan of the entire Mongol Empire. Kublai Khan remained in China, ending the Chinese Sung dynasty and reigned as undisputed emperor (1280-94). He founded Khanbalik (Peking) as his winter capital, restored prosperity to war-torn China, and encouraged unprecedented contacts with the West.

Kun, Béla (1886-1939) Hungarian Communist, who ruled Hungary as dictator for four months in 1919. Kun had been captured by the Russians in the First World War, had taken part in the Revolution, and was sent by the Bolsheviks to stir up revolution in his own country. After winning many converts, he overthrew Karolyi's government and seized power. Kun introduced badly needed reforms, but was discredited by atrocities committed by his followers. Military intervention by Rumania in support of the counter-revolution of Admiral Horthy brought down the Communist government and Kun fled to Russia. He reappeared in Vienna (1928), where he was imprisoned, and was later deported to Russia where he is thought to have died in the Great Purge of the 1930s.

Kurchatov, Igor Vasilevich (1903-60) Russian physicist who led the team that developed Russia's first nuclear weapon, exploded in 1949. They went on to develop the first Russian hydrogen bomb in 1952.

Kurosawa, Akira (born 1910) Japanese film director who, in *Rashomon* (1950), introduced the savage, bloodthirsty world of the Samurai warriors to Europe and America. The popularity of his genre was confirmed with *Seven Samurai* (1954), later remade by John Sturges as *The Magnificent Seven*. He has also made films in a modern idiom, notably *Living* (1952). More recent films include the two epics *Kagemusha* (1982) and *Ran* (1985).

Kutuzov, Mikhail Ilarionovich, Prince of Smolensk (1745-1813) Russian general, whose 'scorched earth' policy caused NAPOLEON's retreat from Moscow. In 1812 ALEXANDER I appointed him Commander-in-Chief of the Russian army. After the battle of Borodino (September 1812) he retreated beyond Moscow, a large part of which the Russians deliberately destroyed by fire. By laying waste the countryside as he withdrew, Kutuzov denied food to the French army. With no supplies, little shelter, and no government with which to negotiate, Napoleon was forced to retire, the French army suffering meanwhile from the winter weather and incessant Russian attacks along its flanks. Although too cautious to attack and win a convincing victory, Kutuzov's strategy resulted in the decimation of Napoleon's army of invasion. A founder of Russia's military science, he led the pursuit of the French army, and died in Silesia.

Kyd, Thomas (1558-94) English dramatist, who wrote *The Spanish Tragedy* (*c.* 1587). This revenge melodrama started a fashion for such plays and influenced SHAKESPEARE in the writing of *Titus Andronicus*, in which some critics believe that Kyd collaborated. There is also a theory that he wrote versions of *Hamlet* and *The Taming of the Shrew*, on which Shakespeare based his own plays. *The Spanish Tragedy* is Kyd's only extant play.

L

Labrouste, Henri (1801-75) French architect who popularized the use of iron in Paris. He handled the new material with great sensitivity, and the Bibliothèque St Geneviève in Paris is one of the first buildings in which iron and cast-iron were used on a large scale, in this case for the colonnades and domes.

Labrunie, Gérard see NERVAL, Gérard de

La Bruyère, Jean de (1645-96) French writer and moralist, famed for his sole work, *Les Caractères ou les moeurs de ce siècle* (1688). Written in an epigrammatic style, *Les Caractères* consists of a series of satirical portraits of contemporary characters, exposing the vices, follies and impulses of human nature.

Laclos, Pierre Choderlos de (1741-1803) French writer and soldier, whose licentious novel, *Les Liaisons dangereuses* (1782), is recognized today as one of the great works of French realism. It described, in the form of letters, the seduction of two women by an unscrupulous rake, Valmont. Though initially a *succès de scandale*, its characterization and psychological insight place it in a far higher category of fiction.

Laënnec, René (1781-1826) French physician, who invented the stethoscope to further his studies of lung disease.

Lafayette, Marie-Joseph, Marquis de (1757-1834) French aristocrat and statesman who participated in the American War of Independence, and became a revolutionary soldier and politician in France. Lafayette was commissioned into the American revolutionary army in 1777 and, together with other French aristocrats, was given command in the decisive Yorktown campaign of 1781. On his return to France the following year, he pressed for social and political reform. He was elected to the Estates General and became Vice-President of the National Assembly (1789). He helped to draft the Declaration of the Rights of Man, the American precedent for which he fully appreciated. After the defeat of the French armies by the Austrians in the autumn of 1792, Lafayette returned to Paris in an attempt to protect the monarchy of LOUIS XVI, but was impeached for his alleged military failure and fled to Austria. He was subsequently held in custody by the Prussians, but returned to France in 1799. He played no active political role during the régime of NAPOLEON and after the restoration of the Bourbons, was elected Deputy (1818) and pressed for liberal reforms, a campaign which he pursued in the early years of LOUIS PHILIPPE's rule.

La Fayette, Marie Madeleine Pioche de la Vergne (1634-93) French writer, author of *La Princesse de Clèves* (1678), a novel about a woman whose marriage is shattered by a guilty passion. It is written in a sober, classical style and with a psychological insight that anticipates STENDHAL, Jane AUSTEN and PROUST. The first perfected short novel analyzing the complexity of human emotions, it broke the tradition that love stories must be involved, unreal and very long.

La Fontaine, Jean de (1621-95) French poet, whose *Fables* published between 1668 and 1693, are among the masterpieces of French literature. La Fontaine, a meticulous craftsman, took his basic material from AESOP and the oriental fabulists, enriched and perfected it, and, mingling the animal and human worlds, satirized many aspects of French life and society. He also wrote scandalous short stories in verse, *Contes* (1664-74) (which he later repudiated), as well as plays, poems and opera libretti.

Laforgue, Jules (1860-87) French Symbolist poet, and an inventor of the free verse which revitalized European poetry by replacing lofty, 'poetic' sententiousness with the rhythms of everyday speech. The free association, puns and juxtapositions of his mocking, ironical fantasies *Les Complaintes* (1885) and *L'Imitation de Notre-Dame La Lune* (1886), can be seen as the beginnings of modern French poetry.

Lagrange, Joseph (1736-1813) French mathematician, who, at the age of 18, was appointed Professor of Geometry to the Artillery school in Turin and the following year produced a solution to an isoperimetrical problem out of which grew the calculus of variations. This solution made him one of Europe's leading mathematicians before he was 20. His writings covered partial differential equations, the theory of numbers, elliptic functions, calculus of variations and research into the propagation of sound.

La Guardia, Fiorello Henry (1882-1947) American municipal leader of Italian-Jewish origin who was Mayor of New York (1934-45). He defeated both the Democratic and the Republican official candidates when he was elected Mayor for the first time in 1934. During his term of office, he was responsible for housing and labour schemes and released New York's administration from the corrupt control of the 'bosses' and the city machine. He was an outspoken critic of HITLER's anti-Semitism. After the Second World War, he became Director of the UN's refugee relief programme.

Lamarck, Jean Baptiste de (1744-1829) French naturalist who was the first scientist to distinguish vertebrates from invertebrates. He followed the view of Buffon that species were not fixed, but that the complex developed from the simple, and put forward the idea that new organs developed as a result of new needs, while those that were little used degenerated. He also thought that characteristics acquired by an organism in its lifetime are passed on as an inheritance to its offspring, a view since disproved by modern genetics.

Lamartine, Alphonse de (1790-1869) French Romantic poet and politician. His lyrical poetry, approaching WORDSWORTH in its vision of the affinity between man, the universe and the divine, rescued French verse from the stale abstractions of classicism and strongly influenced the Romantic movement in France. Some of his best-known poems are included in *Méditations poétiques* (1820), *Harmonies poétiques et réligieuses* (1830) and *Recueillements poétiques* (1839). Lamartine was a notable orator, and became one of the popular idols of the 1848 Revolution.

Lamb, Charles (1775-1834) English writer who, with his sister Mary, wrote *Tales from Shakespeare* (1807) for children. Lamb was a friend of COLERIDGE, and the latter published some of his poems. In 1820, Lamb began contributing essays, which he signed 'Elia', to the *London Magazine*. Written in an elaborate literary style, the essays were eventually collected as *Essays of Elia* (1823-33).

Lambert, Johann Heinrich (1728-77) Swiss mathematician and scientist, who was the first to show that π is not a rational number. He made many original contributions to mathematics, physics and astronomy.

La Mettrie, Julien (1709-51) French physician, materialist philosopher and author of *L'Homme machine* (1747), a treatise whose general atheist position caused a sensation at the time. La Mettrie stated that man is a complex mechanism like a machine, and saw the soul as the thinking part of the body, which perishes with it, the only pleasures being those of the senses. La Mettrie's views influenced the utilitarian thought of Jeremy BENTHAM.

Lampedusa, Giuseppe Tomasi di (1896-1957) Italian writer and author of an outstanding novel, *The Leopard*, published posthumously in 1958. It is a long, sensual story which evokes the decadence, intrigue, corruption and violent social contrasts of 19th century Sicily at the time of GARIBALDI's invasion. Lampedusa was a wealthy prince, who travelled widely.

Lancaster, Sir Osbert (born 1908) British cartoonist, satirist and theatrical designer. He began drawing his Pocket Cartoon, featuring his best-known character, Maudie Littlehampton, in the London *Daily Express* in 1939. He also worked for the *Architectural Review*, and has produced a number of illustrated books satirizing town-planning and development, among them *Draynefleet Revealed*, tracing the plunder of an historic town.

Land, Edwin Herbert (born 1909) American inventor who, in 1937, produced a material known as 'polaroid' which has been used in polarimeters, safety glass and particularly in spectacles to reduce reflected sun-glare. Land's most ingenious and important later invention was the Polaroid camera (1947). This produces a positive print in less than a minute without a negative having to be removed separately from the camera. A colour system was later developed for the camera, and it has become a valuable aid to both the professional and amateur photographer.

Landa, Diego de (16th cent.) Spanish prelate who made possible extensive decipherment of Maya hieroglyphs. He went to Central America as a Franciscan friar, and became the first bishop of Yucatan. He destroyed every pagan Maya manuscript he found, but wrote *Account of the Facts of Yucatan*, an account of Maya life and history. This included an explanation of native numerals and day and month signs, making possible the decipherment of Maya hieroglyphs.

Landau, Lev Davidovitch (1908-68) Russian physicist whose many contributions included the basic theories describing ferromagnetism and liquid helium. In the 1930s he calculated the way in which the atoms in small regions (called domains) of a substance like iron line up in a magnetic field, creating the strong effect known as ferromagnetism. In the 1940s and 1950s he created the theory that underlies the strange ('superfluid') behaviour of liquid helium.

Landor, Walter Savage (1775-1864) English author, whose principal work was *Imaginary Conversations* (1824-48), a series of dialogues between historical characters, which were largely a vehicle for Landor's own views.

Landsteiner, Karl (1868-1943) Austrian pathologist who distinguished four different blood types, later labelled A, B, AB and O, and paved the way for scientific blood transfusion. He showed that blood of some groups is incompatible with that of others and that, if incompatible bloods are mixed, they will form clot-like lumps. His findings explained why some transfusions of blood in the past had been beneficial, whilst others had been fatal.

Lane, Sir Allen (1902-70) British pioneer of paperback publishing. Apprenticed at the Bodley Head, London, he became managing director and left the company in 1936 to found Penguin Books Ltd under whose imprint he published paperback editions of modern novels and later a wider range of literature at about two US cents each. Though booksellers were wary at first, other publishers soon followed suit, so revolutionizing book publishing.

Lang, Fritz (1890-1976) Austrian film director whose early career in Germany included two masterpieces, *M* (1932), starring Peter Lorre as a psychopathic killer, and *Metropolis* (1926), a fantasy of the future. His later Hollywood films (post 1934) are remarkable for their superb photographic composition, but the images of chaos beneath normality – whether in the dreamed violence of Edward G. Robinson in *Woman in the Window* (1944) or the actual violence of *The Big Heat* (1953) – lift the films to a new, higher level.

Lange, Carl (1834-1900) Danish physician and psychologist who (independently of William JAMES) propounded the theory that the emotions we feel result from bodily reactions rather than their cause.

Langevin, Paul (1872-1946) French physicist, renowned for his work with Chilowski (from 1915), in the development of a method, using the reflection of ultrasonic waves, to detect the range and distance of submerged objects. The impetus for this device stemmed from the need to detect submarines in the First World War, which ended before it was operational, but it was widely used during the Second World War. The system, now known as Sonar, is used extensively in oceanography and in commercial fishing for the detection of fish shoals. Langevin also studied secondary X-rays, relativity theory, magnetism and Brownian movement.

Langland, William (c. 1332-c. 1400) English poet, who probably wrote *The Vision of Piers the Plowman* (three versions, 1362, 1377, 1392), an allegorical poem in Middle English alliterative verse. The poem mixes allegory, theology, homely morality and bitter satire against the conditions of the time.

Langley, Samuel Pierpont (1834-1906) American astronomer who demonstrated the feasibility of mechanical flight. In 1881 he invented the bolometer, an instrument for accurately measuring minute quantities of heat, with which he studied the red region of the solar spectrum. He was appointed Secretary of the Smithsonian Institute in Washington (1887) and during the following decade became interested in the possibility of heavier-than-air flying machines. His steam-powered model aircraft accomplished the most successful flights of their time (1896).

Langmuir, Irving (1881-1957) American chemist who found a way of extending the life of incandescent electric lamps. In early lamps, the glass bulb enclosed a vacuum and a tungsten wire filament. Langmuir's research showed that if, instead of a vacuum, a bulb enclosed an inert gas such as nitrogen or argon, the filament lasted far longer.

Lansbury, George (1859-1940) British Labour Party politician and pacifist. Lansbury acquired experience of municipal politics among the poor in the East End of London and became an MP in 1910. He was a pacifist during the First World War, edited the socialist *Daily Herald* (1919-23), was a member of the 1929-31 Labour government, but refused to have anything to do with the MACDONALD-BALDWIN coalition (National) government of 1931. Lansbury became Leader of the Labour Party (1931-5) largely because he was the one Labour politician of Cabinet rank to keep his seat in the 1931 General Election. His devout Christian view of socialism, however, alienated his tougher colleagues, including BEVIN, and he was forced to resign the leadership. His peace-seeking visit to HITLER in 1937 failed.

Lanston, Tolbert (1844-1913) American inventor of the Monotype typesetting machine. This was the first mechanical means of casting and setting type in lines, and was controlled by coded programme tape. Its introduction revolutionized the printing industry, and in 1885 the first patents for the Monotype machine were granted. Lanston spent the following years perfecting it before introducing it commercially in 1897.

Lao-tzu (c. 604-531 BC) Chinese philosopher and founder of Taoism (named from *Tao*, 'the way'). His philosophy was that to live harmoniously with the supreme universal power, man must relinquish the struggle for wealth and live for others, but follow his own inclinations as his best ethical guide. Taoism degenerated into a religion of superstition, magic and hedonism.

Larkin, Philip (born 1922) English poet and novelist, whose verse is concerned with the problems and puzzles of personal affairs. In 'The Less Deceived' (1955) and 'The Whitsun Wedding' (1964) he developed a plain, reflective style, influenced by HARDY. He has written two novels, *Jill* (1964) and *A Girl in Winter* (1947), the former recapturing his own youthful experience at Oxford, and has edited the anthology *English Poetry of the Twentieth Century* (1973).

La Rochefoucauld, Duc François de (1613-80) French moralist and writer of maxims. His fame rests upon his *Réflexions ou sentences et maximes morales*, known as the *Maximes* (1665), a collection of 500 laconic, often finely constructed sentences analysing human conduct and aspirations.

Larousse, Pierre (1817-75) French lexicographer who compiled the 15-volume *Universal Dictionary of the 19th Century* (1866-76). This work was designed more for popular use than the scholarly earlier dictionaries and is a combination of lexicon and encyclopedia. A model for many later works, it defines common words, and contains many biographical entries, articles on history, geography and other subjects.

La Salle, St Jean Baptiste de (1651-1719) French founder of the teaching order of Christian Brothers which spread in Europe and America during the 19th century. He was canonized in 1900.

La Salle, Robert Cavelier de (1643-87) French explorer of much of the Mississippi River. He made the first complete voyage downstream to its mouth and also recorded the earliest description of the Niagara Falls (1678). In 1681, La Salle sailed down the Illinois River to the main stream of the Mississippi then on to the Gulf of Mexico. On his last journey he sailed from France to the Mississippi delta and landed in what is now Texas. During an overland march to find the Mississippi he was killed by members of his party and they, in turn, were killed by Comanche warriors.

Latimer, Hugh (c. 1485-1555) English Protestant reformer and martyr. With Thomas CROMWELL and CRANMER, he supported and advised HENRY VIII in the dispute with Rome, and his preaching as Bishop of Worcester (1535-9) did much to publicize Protestant doctrine. With Cranmer and RIDLEY, Latimer was condemned as a heretic in MARY I's reign, and was burned at the stake with Ridley.

La Tour, Georges de (1593-1652) French painter of religious and genre subjects, whose work is characterized chiefly by chiaroscuro, or contrasts between light and shade, popular among CARAVAGGIO's followers. La Tour's religious pictures, such as *St Sebastian Tended by St Irene* (*c.* 1650), are remarkable for the monumental scale of their figures, the simplification of forms, and the stillness which pervades even the most harrowing scenes – a quality due mainly to the subtle effects of light cast in predominantly dark interiors by a candle or torch. His paintings are relatively rare, and until the 20th century his reputation was modest.

Laud, William (1573-1645) English, Archbishop of Canterbury (1633-45) who supported CHARLES I and STRAFFORD against the Puritans. He demanded religious uniformity based on the views of the High Anglican Church, and used prerogative courts such as the Star Chamber to subdue dissidents with severe punishments. His actions, together with Charles's concept of absolutism, antagonized both the Presbyterian Scots and the Puritan Parliament, who impeached and imprisoned Laud (1641), condemned him to death, and had him beheaded (1645).

Lauda, Nikki (born 1949) Austrian racing driver, many times world champion of the Formula 1 circuit. He started Formula 1 racing driving in 1971 and won his first world championship in 1975. In 1977 he was awarded the Victoria Sporting Club's International Award for Valour following his recovery from a near fatal crash in the 1976 German Grand Prix. He retired in 1979 but returned to racing two years later to win both the American and British Grand Prix.

Laurel, Stanley (1890-1965) English comedian who with Oliver Hardy, an American, formed the cinema's greatest double act, whose popularity was at its height in the 1920s and 1930s. The long-suffering Hardy and the helpfully inept Laurel starred in films such as *Putting Pants on Philip* (1926), and in 1932 they won an Oscar in the Short Subjects category for *The Music Box*. In 1960, Stan Laurel was awarded a special Oscar 'for his creative pioneering in the field of cinema comedy'.

Laurier, Sir Wilfred (1841-1919) First French Canadian to become Prime Minister of Canada, an office he held from 1896 to 1911. He was responsible for giving Britain preferential tariffs, for sending Canadian troops to the South African War (1899-1903) and for trying to improve trade relations with the US, which resulted in his defeat.

Laval, Carl Gustav Patrik de (1845-1913) Swedish inventor, whose two most important contributions were a centrifugal cream separator (1877), which was soon adopted by large dairies worldwide, and the solution of major turbine problems with his 'windmill' device (1887) for small engines.

Laval, Pierre (1883-1945) French politician and leading collaborator with the Germans during the Second World War. He started in politics as a Socialist (1903) but lacked sincere convictions. Twice Prime Minister of France during the 1930s, he was forced to resign

(1936) through public indignation over his appeasement of MUSSOLINI. He supported PÉTAIN and was effective chief minister of Vichy France (1942-4), though he was careful to avoid military commitments to the Nazis. When he realized that the Allies were going to win the Second World War, he tried to rehabilitate himself by calling a National Assembly, but was arrested by the Germans. In 1945, he took refuge in Spain, but returned to France to face charges of treason. He was convicted and shot.

Lavoisier, Antoine Laurent (1743-94) French chemist who laid the foundations of modern chemical thought. His series of brilliant experiments in the 1770s demolished the prevailing phlogiston theory of combustion and established the basis of modern ideas. He showed that combustion is the combining of a substance with air (actually oxygen) and, with remarkable insight, linked it to the energy processes that generate heat within living organisms. Later, he showed that the air is made up mainly of two gases: oxygen and what he called azote (later named nitrogen). In the late 1780s, Lavoisier worked out the first logical system for naming chemical compounds and so founded the language of modern chemistry. He was guillotined during the French Revolution.

Law, John (1671-1729) Scottish financier who devised the disastrous 'Mississippi Scheme'. Law produced a scheme to enrich nations by substituting bank-notes for gold and silver coin, and France, impoverished by LOUIS XIV's wars, welcomed the scheme. Law opened France's first bank (1716), then founded the Louisiana Company to develop the French-held Mississippi Valley. The bank-note issues succeeded initially, but over-issue and misuse of them for speculative purchases of Louisiana stock led clients to demand gold for their notes. Unable to pay, the bank closed (1720), bankrupting thousands and forcing Law – then France's Director-General of Finance – into exile and obscurity.

Lawes, Sir John (1814-1900) British agriculturalist who founded the synthetic fertilizer industry by making superphosphate.

Lawrence, David Herbert (1855-1930) English poet and author, regarded by E. M. FORSTER as 'the greatest imaginative novelist of our generation'. Lawrence combined detailed realism and social criticism with a lyrical, symbolic representation of man's condition, as shown in his first major work, the loosely autobiographical *Sons and Lovers* (1913) and again *The Rainbow* (1915) and its companion *Women in Love* (1920). *The Rainbow* was at first suppressed for obscenity, and *Lady Chatterley's Lover* (1928) was banned in England until 1960. He also wrote short stories, verse and criticism.

Lawrence, Ernest Orlando (1901-58) American physicist who invented the cyclotron, the nuclear accelerator which traps nuclear particles in a large magnetic field, in which they follow circular orbits. Twice in each orbit they are accelerated by a small electric field. After a large number of orbits the particles have high energies and are deflected out of the machine for use in nuclear experiments.

Lawrence, Thomas Edward (1888-1935) British soldier and writer known as 'Lawrence of Arabia', leader of the Arab revolt against the Turks in the First World War. A knowledge of the Arabs, acquired during archaeological research in the Middle East, led to his being sent (1916), with the rank of colonel, to Jedda to help HUSSEIN, who was trying to induce the Arabs to revolt against their Turkish masters. Lawrence organized and led raids on the Damascus-Medina railway, captured various key-points, and in 1917-18 fought his way through Palestine to Damascus on the right of ALLENBY's advance. He returned to Oxford (1919) as a Fellow of All Souls' and wrote an account of the revolt, *The Seven Pillars of Wisdom* (1926). He attended the Paris Peace Conference in Arab dress, and was disgusted by what he regarded as a betrayal of the Arabs by the terms of the peace treaties, and withdrew from public life. After changing his name to Ross, he joined the RAF as an aircraftsman. When his disguise was penetrated, he changed his name again, to T. E. Shaw. He was killed in a motorcycle accident.

Layard, Sir Austen Henry (1817-94) British archaeologist, whose spectacular Assyrian finds encouraged the search for lost civilizations in the Middle East. Between 1845 and 1851, he excavated at Nimrod and Kiyunjik (Nineveh) in Iraq, and discovered the remains of magnificent palaces of the Assyrian kings.

Leakey, Louis (1903-72) British anthropologist and palaeontologist whose finds added a million years to the history of man. In Olduvai Gorge, Tanzania, between 1960 and 1963, he found fossil bones and crude stone tools in a volcanic ash shown by potassium-argon dating to be 1,780,000 years old. Leakey reconstructed this tool maker, named *Homo habilis* (handy man), as a man-like animal four feet tall. *Homo habilis*, apparently the first known tool maker and so the first true man, predates the Java man found by Eugène DUBOIS, and may have been a direct ancestor of modern man.

Lear, Edward (1812-88) English painter, poet and fantasist, who wrote *The Book of Nonsense* (1846), verses in limerick form. Their slightly melancholy tone appears more strongly in 'The Owl and the Pussycat' and 'The Dong with the Luminous Nose'.

Lebon, Phillipe (1769-1804) French pioneer of gas illumination, who from 1791 investigated methods for the production of inflammable gas from wood, which he then patented (1799). He also made notable contributions to the theory of gas lighting and foresaw most of the uses to which gas was to be put in the 19th century.

Leboyer, Frédérick (born 1918) French obstetrician whose unorthodox procedures for delivering babies aroused international interest. Leboyer was influenced by the birth trauma theories of psychoanalysis and by the teachings of Eastern religions. In 1974 he published his theories in *Birth Without Violence*, which recommends making the transition from the womb to the world as gentle as possible.

Le Brun, Charles (1619-90) French painter responsible for many of the artistic achievements of the reign of LOUIS XIV. Under the patronage of COLBERT, he became controller of most French decorative manufactures and, personally, the decorator of parts of the Palace of Versailles.

Le Carré, John (born 1931) Pseudonym of the British writer of spy stories, David John Moore Cornwell. After teaching at Eton College, Le Carré entered the foreign office where he worked from 1959-64. His first book was published in 1961 and his reputation was established by the *The Spy Who Came in from the Cold*, which won him the Somerset Maugham Award in 1963. Other titles are *Tinker, Tailor, Soldier, Spy* (1974) and *The Little Drummer Girl* (1982).

Le Châtelier, Henri Louis (1850-1936) French chemist and formulator (1888) of the law of chemical reaction known as Le Châtelier's principle. It states that if in any chemical system in equilibrium one of the factors in the equilibrium (such as temperature or pressure) changes, the system readjusts itself to minimize the change.

Leclanché, Georges (1839-82) French engineer, who, in 1867, invented an electrolytic cell which could provide an intermittent electric supply, as required. Millions of the familiar dry cells developed from this have been, and still are, used throughout the world.

Leconte de Lisle, Charles Marie (1818-94) French poet and leader of the Parnassians, a group of poets whose aim was to replace the subjective and sentimental effusions of the Romantics with a more impersonal approach. His best-known publications are *Poèmes antiques* (1852) and *Poèmes barbares* (1862). Inspired by the classical writers and attaching greater importance to craftsmanship than his Romantic predecessors, Leconte de Lisle wrote in a disciplined, formally perfect and restrained style. The pessimism of his work is relieved by exotic descriptions (some inspired by Réunion, the tropical island of his birth) and he is particularly renowned for his portraits of wild animals, e.g. 'Les Eléphants'; 'Le Rêve du Jaguar'.

Le Corbusier (1887-1965) Swiss architect who practised in France and was one of the pioneers of modern architecture. With GROPIUS and MIES VAN DER ROHE he was one of the chief influences on mid-20th century architecture. He studied under Auguste PERRET, the pioneer in reinforced concrete, and Peter BEHRENS, and designed furniture (as for the Pavillon de L'Esprit Nouveau at the Paris Exhibition of Decorative Art of 1925), and his activities eventually extended to town-planning and urban development. He conceived the cities of tomorrow as places where skyscrapers would rise up as mighty slabs of concrete, leaving the surrounding areas free for recreational parks and gardens. For Le Corbusier, a tradition of classicism comparable with that of the Parthenon could be found in the functional architecture of a Citröen car or an American grain elevator. His concept of the individual house, which he said should be a 'machine for living in', was of a structure (often lifted off the ground on stilts) that remained quite distinct from its natural settings; examples include his houses at Garches and Poissy. Public buildings designed by him include a store in Moscow and the Pavillon Suisse at the Cité Universitaire in Paris. Of his later works, the Unité d'Habitation at Marseilles, a reinforced concrete apartment block, is conceived as a total community.

Le Douanier see ROUSSEAU, Henri

Ledoux, Claude-Nicolas (1736-1806) French architect of considerable originality whose projects for buildings based upon geometrical solids have gained him a reputation as one of the most imaginative and romantic 18th-century designers. An early influential work was the Neo-classical Pavillon de Louveciennes, built for Madame DU BARRY, in which the interior decoration and furnishings were all in this style. In 1773 he was made Academician and Architecte du Roi. His gift for stark, impressive silhouettes found expression in his public buildings, e.g. the theatre at Besançon and the toll houses of Paris.

Lee, Ann (1736-84) British mystic, leader of the Shakers, or Shaking Quakers, a revivalist group that originated in France in 1688 and developed in England as a form of Quakerism, the name arising from their agitated ritual dancing.

Lee, Bruce (1940-73) Chinese-American actor and practitioner of martial arts. He moved from Hollywood to Hong Kong and became an international sensation in such Kung Fu films as *Fist of Fury* (1972) and *Enter the Dragon* (1973). His karate skills and ferocious snarl made him a cult hero and popularized Eastern martial arts in the West.

Lee, Laurie (born 1914) English poet of pastoral and lyrical verse. Most of his poetry is quiet and intimate; his images often odd and striking. His volumes include *The Sun My Monument* (1944), *My Many-Coated Man* (1955) and *Poems* (1960). *Cider with Rosie* (1959) and *As I Walked Out One Midsummer Morning* (1969) are romantic autobiographies.

Lee, Robert E. (1807-70) American general, Commander-in-Chief of the Confederate armies in the Civil War. Lee began his career as an engineer officer, and fought in the Mexican War (1846). On the outbreak of Civil War (1861), LINCOLN offered him a command, but his sympathies were Southern and he took command of the Confederate Army of North Virginia. He won a number of battles in 1863, but while advancing to invade Northern territory across the Potomac river, was defeated by Meade at Gettysburg. His subsequent defeat by GRANT at Appomattox in 1865 ended the war.

Lee, William (16th-17th cent.) English clergyman, who in 1589 invented the first knitting machine. The device consisted of a stocking knitting frame with an array of fixed hooks on which loops or stitches were lifted over the wool by a series of movable hooks.

Leech, John (1817-64) British humorous artist, whose pictorial satires on the rough designs for murals in the Houses of Parliament gave rise to the use of the word 'cartoon' to describe a comic drawing. He was among those who illustrated DICKENS's *Christmas Books* (1845) and also illustrated Surtees's *Mr Sponge's Sporting Tour* (1853) and à Beckett's *The Comic History of England* (1847). In 1841 he joined the staff of *Punch*, where he stayed until his death, producing more than 4000 drawings.

Léger, Fernand (1881-1955) French Cubist artist, a friend of PICASSO and BRAQUE. After the First World War, he incorporated mechanical and human forms into his paintings, which reflected his belief that painting's function was essentially that of mural decoration. His proletarian sympathies are apparent in the *Leisures* series of his later years.

Leibniz, Gottfried (1646-1716) German philosopher, mathematician, historian and physicist. His main contribution to mathematics was the invention of differential calculus, although his claim to be the first to do so was disputed by NEWTON. In Leibniz's extensive philosophic work, he saw the world made up of a hierarchy of simple, self-contained and mutually mirroring units (monads), with the universe as an organic whole, its logical organization reflected in its greatest and smallest parts. He also sought to establish a universal and perfectly logical language, in which true propositions are at once seen as such, and false ones seen as absurd.

Leicester, 1st Earl of see DUDLEY, Robert

Leichhardt, Friedrich Wilhelm Ludwig (1813-48) German explorer who made one crossing of

Australia, and disappeared on a second. After landing at Sydney (1842), he walked alone 600 miles north to Moreton Bay, Brisbane, then led a seven-man expedition some 2000 miles north-west across the continent to Port Essington near Darwin. Leichhardt vanished on the Cogoon River while leading a nine-man party in an attempted east-west crossing from Moreton Bay to Perth.

Lely, Sir Peter (1618-80) German-born Dutch artist, who was important in the development of English portraiture between van DYCK and GAINSBOROUGH. He arrived in England from Holland in the mid-1640s and by 1661 had become principal painter to CHARLES II. He was immensely productive throughout the Commonwealth and Restoration periods, and much of his work emulates the refinement of van Dyck's portraits.

Lemercier, Jacques (1585-1654) French architect best known today as the designer of the town of Richelieu, built for Cardinal RICHELIEU in 1631. Lemercier, who was influenced by the Italian mannerist style, was also patronized by Louis XIII. In Paris existing buildings by him include part of the Louvre Pavillon de l'Horloge, The Sorbonne and the dome of the Val-de-Grâce Church.

Le Nain, Louis (c. 1593-1648) French genre painter of the 17th century. The peasants in his rural scenes are notable for their contemplative dignity. His brothers, Antoine and Mathieu, were also painters and worked in similar vein.

Lenin, Vladimir Ilyich (1870-1924) Architect and leader of the Bolshevik revolution which created the USSR. Lenin became a revolutionary at 16 when his elder brother was hanged for involvement in a plot to assassinate the Tsar. He left Russia in 1900, living first in Germany, then Brussels, Paris and London, writing pamphlets developing Marxism, and editing *Iskra* (Spark), the Russian Social Democrat newspaper-in-exile. He emerged as left-wing leader of the Party when, at its congress in London in 1903, a vote on the composition of the paper's editorial board gave his group a majority (*bolsheviki*, members of the majority). In the revolution of 1905, Lenin returned to St Petersburg, but was again forced into exile, where he continued to prepare for the revolution. He returned to Russia following the March Revolution of 1917; attempting to take it over, he was forced to take refuge in Finland in July, but returned in October, organized the Bolshevik *coup d'état* and seized power from the KERENSKY administration. He set up, as government, the council of People's Commissars, nationalized the banks and the means of production, distribution and exchange, redistributed the land to the peasants and withdrew Russia from the war by signing the treaty of Brest-Litovsk. Meanwhile there was civil war, in which TROTSKY emerged as creator of the Red Army, on half a dozen fronts, and the strain of this fighting, combined with socialization of the whole country, caused the economy to collapse (1920). To restore it, the New Economic Policy – allowing a limited measure of capitalist enterprise – was introduced, to be abolished later by STALIN. Wounded in an attempt on his life by an anti-Bolshevik 'Social Revolutionary' in 1923, Lenin's health broke down and he died early the following year.

Lennon, John Ono (1940-80) British songwriter, musician and cultural hero. Founder guitarist and singer with The Beatles, which became the most successful rock group of the 1960s. With Paul McCartney he wrote *Help!*, *Revolution*, etc., and appeared in all the Beatles' films. After the Beatles disbanded, Lennon worked with his second wife, Yoko Ono, on a series of campaigning compositions including *Imagine* and *Give Peace a Chance*. He was assassinated in New York City in 1980, an event that triggered international mourning.

Lenz, Heinrich Friedrich Emil (1804-65) Russian physicist who formulated a law giving the direction of an induced electric current. In 1834 he summarized ideas on electrical induction in what is now called Lenz's law, which states that the direction of a current induced in a circuit by moving it in a magnetic field produces an effect tending to oppose the circuit's motion.

León, Luis de (1527-91) Spanish humanist, author and lyric poet, whose chief prose works are *Christ's Names* (1583-5), a treatise on the different names given to CHRIST in the scriptures, and *The Perfect Wife* (1583). His lyric poems celebrate the wonder of the universe. An Augustinian friar and professor of theology at Salamanca, he translated the Psalms, Proverbs, Job and the Song of Songs into Spanish, and was imprisoned by the Inquisition.

Leonardo da Vinci (1452-1519) Greatest figure of the Italian Renaissance. His significance as an artist lies in his scientific analysis of natural phenomena and the preparatory studies for his paintings, throughout which he rejects the traditional schematic depiction of matter such as rocks or the texture of clothing or drapery. This objective approach is found in the two versions of *Madonna of the Rocks*. Leonardo made further advances in multi-figure compositions based on geometrical principles: the central figures of *Adoration of the Kings* (1481) form a pyramidal group within a space constructed according to a mathematical perspective. He also broke away from the traditional portrait: the *Mona Lisa* (*c.* 1500-4) is an example of the half-length portrait in which the hands are exploited to complement the

facial expression. Leonardo's most historically influential work, in High Renaissance style, is the *Last Supper* (*c.* 1497), a mural in the Sta Maria delle Grazie monastery, which was the first painting to examine systematically the attitudes and gestures of the subjects, and to analyse the psychological relationships between them. The *Battle of Anghiari* (*c.* 1503-5) is another important, though incomplete, work. As a scientist, his achievements are equally considerable, though his influence is limited since the bulk of his notebooks and drawings were not published until the 19th century. Written, with exceptions, in the last 30 years of his life, they reveal his true nature – that of a scientist who trusts nothing. His art reflects the empirical basis of his thought and his studies of nature can be seen as a fusion of imagination and science based upon observation and experiment.

Leonidas I (5th cent. BC) King of Sparta who was killed with all his 300 men in an attempt to hold the pass of Thermopylae against XERXES I's Persian army.

Leopardi, Giacomo (1798-1837) Italian lyric poet and scholar. An invalid almost from childhood, his studies convinced him that it was man's destiny to be unhappy. The best of his poems appear in *Centi* (1831), which includes 'All' Italia', the patriotic ode which first brought Leopardi to public notice. For feeling, musicality and simple diction, it is one of the finest books of poetry in Italian literature. Leopardi also wrote a commentary on PETRARCH's *Book of Lyrics* and several important philosophical works, notably the prose dialogues, *Philosophical Studies* (1924).

Leopold III (born 1901) King of the Belgians (1934-51) whose reign was marred by tragedy when his queen, Astrid, was killed in an automobile crash in 1935. Leopold was taken prisoner during the German invasion of 1940 and never ruled again. Shortly after his return to Belgium in 1950, he abdicated in favour of his son, Prince Baudouin.

Lepsius, Karl Richard (1810-84) German archaeologist who put Egyptology on a scientific basis. Spurning the tomb-robber methods of predecessors such as Belzoni, Lepsius made extensive drawings and plans of his discoveries on his major expedition (1842-5) and published his findings in the 12-volume *Monuments of Egypt and Ethiopia* (1849-59).

Lermontov, Mikhail Yurevich (1814-41) Russian Romantic poet, dramatist and author of the novel *A Hero of our Times* (1840). His *Masquerade* (1835) is one of the masterpieces of the Russian theatre. Lermontov achieved poetic fame with 'Death of a Poet', a poem which castigated court society for its ill-treatment of PUSHKIN. For this, Lermontov was banished to the Caucasus but later pardoned. He was a major influence on Russian writers, including TOLSTOY and CHEKHOV. He was killed in a duel.

Lescot, Pierre (c. 1510-78) French architect whose work reflects the change of style brought about by the Italian Renaissance. Lescot's work can best be appreciated today in the wings he built for the Louvre, with the sculptor GOUJON.

Lesseps, Vicomte Ferdinand Marie de (1805-94) French diplomat and promoter of the Suez Canal. He first had the idea of a canal to link the Red Sea and the Mediterranean in 1832, but he did not gain the initial concession until 1854. Digging began in 1859, using 30,000 Egyptian forced labourers, who, for political reasons, were withdrawn in 1863. The work was finished with mechanical equipment from Europe. The canal was opened by the Empress Eugénie in November 1869. In 1879, de Lesseps headed a French company which began work on the Panama Canal, which he had to abandon nine years later, owing to political and financial troubles.

De Lesseps's Suez Canal toward the end of the 19th century. In the foreground is one of the dredgers constantly in use to keep sufficient depth of water beneath the keels of the larger ships. The steamer retains the masts and yards of the sailing ship era

Lessing, Doris (born 1919) English novelist, whose work concentrates on the difference in attitude of two generations, and on social and political reform. Much of her writing is set in Africa, where she was brought up. Her series of novels with Martha Quest as the heroine (1952-8) is strongly autobiographical. *In Pursuit of the English* (1960) describes her early days in London, and *The Golden Notebook* (1962) examines her central themes in a number of variations.

Lessing, Gotthold Ephraim (1729-81) German playwright and dramatic theorist. His first success was a naturalistic tragedy of middle-class life, *Miss Sarah Sampson*, but his real quality emerged in comedy of intrigue, *Minna von Barnheim* (1767). While *dramaturg* (literary reader-manager) of the Hamburg Theatre, he wrote 'Dramatic Theory of Hamburg', a study which draws heavily on ARISTOTLE.

Le Vau, Louis (1612-70) French architect who trained in Paris as a master mason. He became a successful architect and head of the vast body of artisans who produced monuments for LOUIS XIV. He was also responsible for the Château of Vaux-le-Vicomte, the sumptuousness of which may have led to the downfall of its owner, Fouquet, and also for the king's château at Versailles. His gift for grandiloquence was encouraged by Louis XIV.

Le Verrier, Urbain (1811-77) French astronomer, joint discoverer (with John Couch ADAMS) of the planet Neptune. Like Adams, he realized that anomalies in the orbit of Uranus could be due only to the gravitational influence of a hitherto undiscovered planet, but he was luckier than Adams in that notice was taken of his theory, which was proved correct by the Berlin Observatory in 1846.

Levi, Carlo (1902-75) Italian novelist and painter who exposed the plight of southern Italy in his deeply moving *Christ Stopped at Eboli* (1945), a portrayal of the misery of the peasants of Gagliano, He returned to a similar theme in two later novels, *Words are Stones* (1955) and *The Linden Trees* (1959). He served in Italy's Senate 1963-72.

Levi-Civita, Tullio (1873-1941) Italian mathematician, who, with his one-time teacher RICCI, developed absolute differential calculus (tensor analysis), which has many applications in relativity and general unified field theory.

Lévi-Strauss, Claude (born 1908) Belgian anthropologist who in his best-known book, *A World on the Wane* (1955), explains his view that, ideally, an ethnologist should only analyse the differences between himself and the people he is studying; he should not condemn or try to change them. His writings include *Elementary Structure of Kinship* (1949), a study of human kinship practices, *Totemism Today* (1962), a study of preliterate classification systems, *The Savage Mind* (1962), which contains an attack on SARTRE's existentialist view of history and progress, and *Le Cru et Le Cruit* (1964), in which Lévi-Strauss discusses the significance of cooking and the things people eat. He is now an established leader in European structuralist thought.

Lewin, Kurt (1890-1947) American social psychologist of German origin who applied the *Gestalt* theories of KÖHLER to the study of groups. He devised numerous ingenious experiments to test and measure various kinds of group activity, making studies of authority, social influence, frustration and regression, memory in real-life situations and motivation to complete or substitute tasks. Lewin's descriptions are in terms of field theory, i.e. a system of pressures operating on personality in a perceived life-space and provide an insight into group behaviour and how it may be modified.

Lewis, John Llewellyn (1880-1969) American labour leader who helped found the AFL-CIO, presided over the stormy attempts to unionize the automobile and steel industries, and headed the United Mine Workers Union for 40 years (1920-60). Lewis's controversial calling of miners' strikes during the Second World War was largely responsible for the passage of the Taft-Hartley Act (1947) curtailing union power.

Lewis, Meriwether (1774-1809) American explorer who, with William CLARK, commanded the expedition that first crossed America from St Louis to the Pacific (1804-6). The expedition sought to find out whether the Gulf of Mexico and the Pacific were linked by river systems, and if they were not, to pioneer a route across the Rockies. The expedition left St Louis, probed up the Mississippi, made the first exploration of the Missouri (discovered by Marquette and Joliet) from its headwaters to its confluence with the Mississippi, struck west across the Rocky Mountains, then followed the Snake and Columbia Rivers to the Pacific.

Lewis, Percy Wyndham (1884-1957) American-born English painter, novelist and critic, who was a founder of Vorticism, a cultural movement that believed in hard, clear images and sharply defined patterns. His own writing is vigorous, as in the ironic novel *The Apes of God* (1930), an attack on cultural life in the 1920s. His major work, a trilogy, *The Human Age* (1928-55), depicts humanity outside heaven, awaiting the final examination.

Lewis, Sinclair (1885-1951) American novelist, who wrote satirical novels about the banality and complacency of small-town life. His first novel, *Main Street* (1920), was a great success. *Babbitt* (1922) attacked the stupidities of the city businessman, and *Elmer Gantry* (1927) exposed the world of religious hucksters. He was the first American author to win a Nobel Prize (1930).

Leyden, Lucas van (1494-1533) Netherlandish graphic artist who is best known for his numerous wood and copper-plate engravings, of which the first were produced when he was only 13. Many of his prints, which are mainly of religious subjects, are influenced by DÜRER, but his larger engravings are original and characterized by extremely precise draughtsmanship.

Libby, Willard Frank (1908-80) American chemist whose method of radio-carbon dating enables archaeologists to assess the age of plant and animal remains up to 70,000 years old. In 1947, he discovered it is possible to determine the age of these remains by measuring the amount of 'decay' that has taken place in the carbon-14 – a radioactive form of carbon atom present in all organic matter. A scientist can, therefore, measure the radioactive emissions of a processed organic specimen with a Geiger counter, and determine its approximate age. This procedure has proved invaluable for dating archaeological remains, most famously in the case of the Dead Sea Scrolls, for which work Libby was awarded the Nobel Prize for Chemistry (1960).

Li Ch'eng (10th cent.) Chinese landscape painter of the late Five Dynasties period, whose desolate snow and mountain scenes were forerunners of the 'Monumental' style of the Sung period.

Lichtenstein, Roy (born 1923) American Pop artist who makes use of the cartoon and comic strip to which he gives new and critical emphasis through subtle alterations of perspective and context.

Lie, Trygve Halvdan (1896-1968) Norwegian, the first Secretary General of the United Nations (1946-53), who established the executive, rather than the administrative role for himself and his successors in office. As Foreign Minister of the exiled Norwegian government (1941-6), he was instrumental in saving the Norwegian fleet for the Allies. His most important achievement at the UN was to establish the guide-lines and the authority of the Secretary-General's position from 1946-53. During a period of Soviet boycott of the UN, it was Lie who recommended, in 1950, that a UN force should be sent to support South Korea, with the result that Russia began to recognize the significance of the UN. Russian hostility to his actions caused Lie to resign.

Liebknecht, Karl (1871-1919) German social democratic revolutionary, who was murdered with Rosa LUXEMBURG. As a member of the Reichstag from 1912-16, he was an outspoken opponent of militarism, and was imprisoned for two years during the First World War. After the armistice, he and Rosa Luxemburg started what was known as the Spartacist Revolution in January 1919. Both were arrested and murdered.

Lilburne, John (c.1615-57) English republican agitator and champion of democratic rights. He was whipped, pilloried and imprisoned (1637-40) for preaching and publishing pamphlets against CHARLES I's autocratic rule, and fought Charles's Royalists as a lieutenant-colonel in the Parliamentarian army. He resigned (1645) to help lead the Levellers, a radical movement so-called because (according to their critics) they sought to 'level' men's estates. Opposing CROMWELL's government as being too aristocratic, Lilburne urged democracy based on manhood suffrage, and law reform. He was repeatedly imprisoned and once banished.

Lilienthal, Otto (1848-96) German pioneer of heavier-than-air flight. From 1881 Lilienthal made more than a thousand flights in gliders of his own design. He showed the importance of having a curved aerofoil wing shape and of rising air currents for soaring. Lilienthal experimented with a biplane (1895) and with a small motor to flap the wings (1896).

Lincoln, Abraham (1809-65) American President who led the Union (North) to victory over the Confederate states in the Civil War (1861-5). Born into a poor, illiterate family, he began working life as a storekeeper and postmaster in Illinois while studying law. Called to the Bar in 1836, he soon made his name. He ran for the state legislature and served four terms and was Representative for Illinois in Congress (1847-9). He attained national fame in 1854 when he attacked the Kansas-Nebraska Act because it denied Congress the right to interfere in the slavery dispute in the new states. He joined the Republican Party and ran for the Senate against Douglas in 1858, losing the election but gaining enormously in stature during seven great debates with Douglas, in which he declared his anti-slavery position although without adopting extreme Abolitionism. He won the Republican nomination as presidential candidate in 1860 and then the election, as a result of splits in the Democratic Party. His known position on slavery led to the immediate secession of seven slavery states, including South Carolina where, against his Cabinet's advice, Lincoln insisted on maintaining and provisioning the garrison of Fort Sumter, thus precipitating the Civil War. In his words, the war was '. . . to save the Union, and not to save or destroy slavery', but he would not countenance punitive treatment of the South, calling for a conciliation 'with malice towards none, with charity for all'. He was murdered by an actor, John Wilkes BOOTH, at Ford's Theatre on 14 April 1865. A careful conservative, Lincoln's integrity was his strength and his monument, and his oratory was considered to be very skilled.

Lindbergh, Charles (1902-74) American aviator, the first to fly the Atlantic solo (May 1927), eight years after the first non-stop crossing by ALCOCK and Brown. The kidnap and murder of his two-year-old son in 1932 was a celebrated crime of the decade and led directly to new, anti-kidnapping legislation.

Linde, Carl von (1842-1934) German engineer who invented the first continuous process for liquefying gases. Using the JOULE-THOMSON effect, in which an expanding gas cools because of the attraction between its molecules, he was able to produce liquid air, nitrogen and oxygen in commercial quantities.

Lindemann, Ferdinand von (1852-1939) German mathematician, who proved that π is a transcendental number – that is, not the root of any equation with rational coefficients. This shows that the ancient problem of squaring the circle with a compass and ruler cannot be solved.

Lin Piao (1908-71) Chinese Communist soldier-politician, who died in a mysterious air crash after his implication in a plot to oust Chairman MAO. With CHOU EN-LAI, Lin fought against the Kuomintang (Chinese Nationalist Party) of CHIANG KAI-SHEK during the civil war of the 1930s and was with Mao Tse-tung in the Long March from Kiangsi to Shensi (1934-5). After the end of the Second World War he played a major role in defeating Chiang Kai-shek in the renewed civil war (1946-8) and later commanded the Chinese 'volunteers' in the Korean War (1950-3). He was

Lincoln's election in 1860 split the young republic into two camps and brought a fratricidal war between North and South

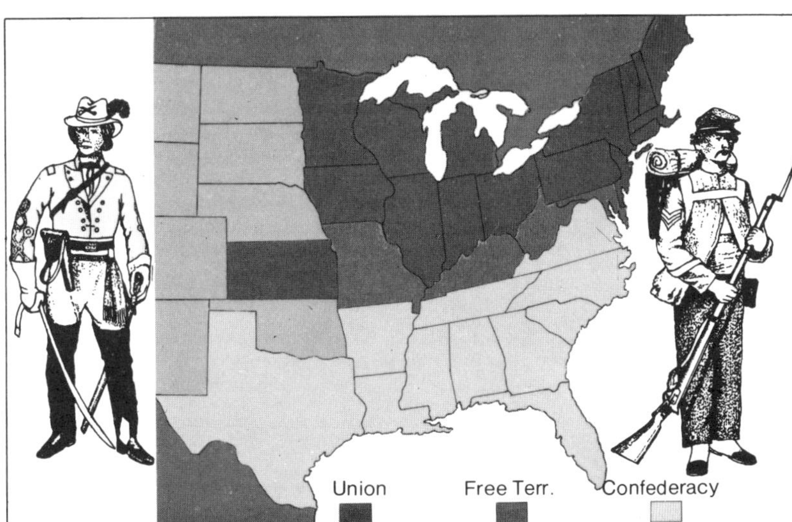

made Deputy Premier in 1954. In the following year he was admitted to the Politburo and awarded the rank of marshal. As Minister of Defence (1959) He re-established discipline in the Red Army through a programme of political indoctrination in which the *Quotations from Chairman Mao* was introduced as an army handbook. The height of Lin's power was probably reached at the ninth party congress in 1969 when he was designated as Mao's successor. It was later stated by foreign correspondents (and confirmed by the Chinese hierarchy) that Lin had died in an air crash whilst trying to escape after the detection of a plot to remove Mao.

Lipchitz, Jacques (1891-1973) Lithuanian-born sculptor whose early work was influenced by Cubism. Shedding all exterior influences by 1925, he sought a lighter sculptural form and introducing emotional values, as in *The Couple* (1928-30). Later he became involved in the surrealists' world of the subconscious (*Figures*, 1926-30). In 1941 he went to America, and developed a mature style in which he dwells on the mysteries of regeneration (*Blossoming*, 1941-2).

Li Po (701-62) Greatest (with TU FU) of Chinese poets. Sometime court poet to HSUAN TSUNG, he became involved in a revolt and was banished, only to be pardoned before he reached his place of exile. Li Po was romantic and irresponsible, and had a zest for life that is reflected in his poetry. His verse followed no rules – his poems were of all lengths, covering every subject, from moving descriptions of the countryside to bacchic celebrations. Above all, his language was plain, simple and vigorous. It is said he was drowned while drunkenly attempting to embrace the moon's reflection.

Lippi, Fra Filippo (c. 1406-69) Florentine painter and monk, best known for his completion of MASACCIO's Brancacci Chapel frescoes. He also painted altarpieces and fresco cycles at Prato Cathedral.

Li Shih Min see I'AI TSUNG

Lister, Lord Joseph (1827-1912) English surgeon and pioneer of antiseptic surgery after hearing of PASTEUR's work on putrefaction and of the disinfectant power of carbolic acid. His success was both immediate and dramatic and alerted surgeons to the importance of working in conditions as germ-free as possible. Lister's antisepsis was replaced by asepsis, which included the sterile instruments, filtered air and sterilized cap, gown and gloves of the modern operating theatre.

Liszt, Franz (1811-86) Hungarian composer and pianist of humble origins who is best known for his *Hungarian Rhapsodies*, but who also invented the tone poem. As an 11-year-old virtuoso pianist, Liszt was acclaimed by BEETHOVEN and, during his youth, was lionized throughout Europe, his flamboyant personality fascinating audiences. Liszt never married, but had a family by the Countess d'Agoult, one of his daughters being Cosima (wife to BÜLOW, then to WAGNER). The unstinting generosity he showed to fellow artists became a legend. In 1865 Liszt took minor orders as an abbé, but he was never able to settle and in his later years periods of hard work were punctuated by restless travelling. His tone poems include *Mazeppa* (1851, based on BYRON and HUGO) and HAMLET (1858); his symphonies, the *Dante Symphony* (1855-6) and the *Faust Symphony* (1857).

Litvinov, Maxim (1876-1951) Soviet statesman, who initiated the policy of co-existence of Communism and capitalism. Having lived and married in London while exiled as a revolutionary, Litvinov became Soviet Russia's first representative in Britain during the Revolution (1917-18). From 1926 onwards, he controlled Soviet foreign policy, and was officially appointed Foreign Commissar in 1930, his policy being one of conciliation of the Western powers, strong support for the League of Nations (1934-8) and resistance to the Nazis. He was dismissed when STALIN decided to appease HITLER in May 1939.

Liverpool, Robert Banks Jenkinson, Second Earl of (1770-1828) British Prime Minister in succession to the assassinated PERCEVAL (1812). Lord Liverpool remained in office until 1827, a period as prime minister exceeded only by WALPOLE and PITT.

Livingstone, David (1813-73) Scottish missionary in central Africa who explored the course of the Zambesi and the sources of the Nile. He spent some 30 years mapping 30,000 square miles of Africa south of the Equator, and his published books and journals did much to open equatorial heartlands to European missionaries and explorers, and to raise opinion against slave-trading. From 1844 on, Livingstone made many journeys, crossing the Kalahari Desert, discovering the Victoria Falls and the Zambesi. In 1858, in charge of a government expedition for exploring eastern and central Africa, Livingstone explored the Zambesi River system, and discovered Lake Nyasa. He made a last expedition to Africa, for the Royal Geographical Society, to explore the watershed between Lakes Nyasa and Tanganyika, and the sources of the Nile. He pushed from Lake Nyasa to Lake Tanganyika over unexplored country, discovering Lakes Mweru and Bangweulu, and saw the Lualaba, which he believed to be the head river of the Nile. He returned, ill, to Ujiji on Lake Tanganyika, where he was found by Henry STANLEY, with whom he later explored the northern part of Lake Tanganyika. After Stanley left, he made another search for the source of the Nile, but died during the trip.

Livy (59 BC-AD 17) Roman historian whose monumental *History from the Founding of the City* filled 142 books, 35 of which survive, covering the years down to 293 BC and from 218 to 187. Drawing on official annals and on the work of previous writers, especially Polybius, Livy traced, with patriotic zeal which sometimes confused legend with fact, the rise of the Romans to power in Italy, their conquest of HANNIBAL's Carthage and their mastery of the Eastern Mediterranean.

Li Yüan (565-635) Chinese emperor known as Kao Tsu (High Progenitor), who founded the T'ang dynasty (618-907). He began as a government official under the Sui régime, skilled in handling peasant risings and Turkish barbarian incursions into Shansi. In 617, urged on by an ambitious son, he himself rebelled, with Turkish help, and seized the key Chinese city of Ch'ang-an. Under Li Yüan and his dynamic son Li Shihmin – called T'AI TSUNG (Grand Ancestor) – the T'ang dynasty began to rank with Liu Pang's former Han dynasty as a golden era in Chinese culture.

Llewelyn ab Gruffydd (13th cent.) Prince of North Wales (from 1246) and champion of Welsh independence. He was forced at first into northwest Wales by Henry III, but by 1257 had regained much lost territory, securing in 1258 the allegiance of other Welsh princes and proclaiming himself Prince of Wales. Llewelyn was able to master all Wales while Henry's forces were engaged in the Barons' War, and was recognized as its overlord by the Treaty of Shrewsbury (1265).

When Llewelyn refused to recognize EDWARD I's overlordship (1276), Edward attacked and defeated him. Llewelyn was killed in a skirmish during another revolt, his death ending Welsh independence.

Llewelyn ab Iorwerth (1173-1240) Welsh prince of Gwynedd (North Wales) called Llewelyn the Great. He was born in exile but returned to defeat his uncle David I and claim his throne. He married the illegitimate daughter of England's king JOHN and for a time was aided by him in wars against South Wales, but in 1211 John seized all his lands. Llewelyn regained them the following year and took Shrewsbury (1215), forcing John's recognition of his rights in Magna Carta. The later years of Llewelyn's reign were comparatively peaceful.

Lloyd George, David, First Earl of Dwyfor (1863-1945) British statesman and Prime Minister. After practising as a solicitor, he was elected Liberal MP for Caernarvon (1890), representing it until his death. He first held office in 1905 as President of the Board of Trade, and became, in 1908, Chancellor of the Exchequer, in which year he put through the Old Age Pensions Act. The National Health Insurance Act followed three years later. As Chancellor (from 1908-15) his budget of 1909, which provided for super-tax and land value duties, was rejected by the Lords. The ensuing animosity between the Liberal government and the Upper House led to the Parliament Act of 1911, which curtailed the powers of the latter. As Minister for Munitions in 1915, he combined with the Conservatives in the coalition war cabinet, overthrew ASQUITH and succeeded him as Prime Minister (1916) retaining the office until 1922. Both his war leadership and his role at the Paris Peace Conference (1919) were decisive, and his government came to terms with the Irish, led by Michael Collins, in creating the Irish Free State. But eventually his coalition government fell, the Conservative element becoming alarmed at his aggressive attitude towards KEMAL over the Turkish threat (more apparent than real) to the Allied occupation force covering Istanbul. Out of office, the 'Welsh Wizard' as he was known became isolated, rejected by Liberals and Tories. He never again held office.

Lloyd Webber, Andrew (born 1948) British composer and producer of hit musicals such as *Evita* (1976) and *Cats* (1981).

Locke, John (1632-1704) English philosopher whose theory of knowledge greatly influenced the development of the British empiricist tradition. In *Essay Concerning Human Understanding* (1690), he discounted philosophical speculation as a source of knowledge, stating that this must proceed from experience, as in scientific method. The philosopher's task was to examine the scope and nature of understanding. Above all a philosopher of common sense, Locke argued against absolutism in politics, his covert target being the Stuart monarchy, but his insistence on tolerance excluded Catholicism. He distrusted religious and political fanaticism (or enthusiasm, as it was called), seeing political power as sanctioned by social contract.

Lockyer, Sir Joseph Norman (1836-1920) British astronomer who discovered the element helium. Lockyer was a pioneer in the study of the Sun's spectrum. In 1868 he developed a technique for examining prominences at the edge of the Sun, and attributed a portion of the spectrum to a new element which he named helium, 40 years before helium was discovered on Earth.

Loeb, Jacques (1859-1924) American biologist of German origin who performed experimental work on the chemical processes of living organisms and showed that both plants and simple animals respond in a similar fashion to such stimuli as light and gravity.

Lombroso, Cesare (1836-1909) Italian criminologist, who combined the evolutionary ideas of DARWIN with the pseudo-science of phrenology. He believed that criminals are distinguished from non-criminals by certain peculiarities; that criminals are biological throwbacks to earlier stages of evolution or are degenerates who have ceased to evolve progressively. Although now discredited, his theories encouraged the more humane treatment of criminals by presenting them as 'patients'.

Lomonosov, Mikhail (1711-65) Russian poet, grammarian and scientist, called the founder of Russian literature because he reformed the Russian language to produce a workable literary language. In his *Russian Grammar* and *Rhetoric*, he worked out a compromise between Church Slavonic, with its complicated syntax, and contemporary spoken Russian. Throughout his career he wrote verse, which influenced later Russian poetry. He was appointed Professor of Chemistry at St Petersburg, and became a secretary of state, in 1764.

Longfellow, Henry Wadsworth (1807-82) American poet and scholar, best known for 'Hiawatha' (1855), a long poem of American Indian life. Longfellow was a prolific poet, and wrote many volumes of Romantic verse, as well as essays, philosophical discourses and translations. He was Professor of Modern Languages at Harvard University, and in 1842 he visited London as the guest of DICKENS.

Longinus (1st cent. AD) Greek author to whom the work *On the Sublime* is ascribed. It analyses the sublime in literature, which is traced by Longinus to five sources. The author was a discerning critic, at times refreshingly outspoken, and gifted at expressing and transmitting his own enthusiasm.

Loos, Adolf (1870-1933) Austrian architect of outstanding ability in the early years of 20th-century architecture. His American Bar in Vienna employed rich materials, but he stringently refused to employ any applied decoration. His Steiner House has a façade that appears almost bleak. In 1908 he published a lecture entitled *Ornament and Crime*. His appeal to the younger generation lay in his reduction of the decorative forms of a building to a minimum so that structure and form could be seen to be related.

Lopez de Ayala, Pedro (1332-1407) Spanish statesman, poet and historian, whose chronicles of the kings ruling Castile from 1350 to 1396 are the liveliest and psychologically the most perceptive histories written in medieval Castile. His translations of LIVY, BOETHIUS and BOCCACCIO make him the first Castilian humanist, but his translations of St Gregory are equally important and strongly influence his verse, notably the *Palace Poetry*, which discussed major religious, moral and political problems.

Lorca, Frederico Garcia (1898-1936) Spanish poet and dramatist, best known for his poetic works *Gypsy Songs* (1928 and 1935), based on the gypsies of Andalusia, and for his poignant collection of verse *Poet in New York* (1929), on the theme of his vision of death in modern life. *Blood Wedding* (1933) and *Yerma* (1934), both gypsy plays, and *The House of Bernarda Alba* (1936), his last play, are the most outstanding of his dramatic works. At the height of his career, he was shot by Nationalists in the Spanish Civil War and buried in an unmarked grave.

Lorentz, Hendrick Antoon (1853-1928) Dutch physicist whose theories on the behaviour of swiftly moving electrons anticipated much of EINSTEIN's theory of special relativity. Lorentz was responsible for much of the modern electron theory of the interaction between matter and electromagnetic waves. In this field his work on the effect of magnetism on spectral lines won him the Nobel Prize in 1902. One persistent difficulty of the electron theory was the experiment of MICHELSON and Morley, which had shown that motion through the ether was undetectable. Lorentz adapted a suggestion of Fitzgerald that fast-moving bodies might contract slightly in their direction of motion and developed it in 1903 into the general 'Lorentz transformation', describing the behaviour of bodies in relativity theory.

Lorenz, Konrad (born 1903) Austrian psychologist. His most arresting experiments, demonstrating the process of memory imprinting in animals, show that some young creatures, deprived at birth of normal mother figures, will adopt whatever they see first (even a stone decoy) as a parent figure, and come to see themselves as members of the substitute parent's species for the rest of their lives, even seeking mates from within that species in preference to their own. He was awarded a Nobel Prize in 1973 for his work on animal behaviour.

Lorenzetti, Ambrogio (c. 1300-c. 1348) Sienese artist, whose most famous works are the allegorical frescoes of *Good and Bad Government* in the Palazzo Pubblico, Siena (1338-40). They depict good government in the town and country and show Siena and its environs in delightful detail. They were the first Italian paintings since Roman times in which landscape formed an integral part of the theme.

Lorenzo Monaco (c. 1370-c. 1422) Sienese manuscript illuminator and painter of altarpieces, who was also a monk at the monastery of Sta Maria Degli Angli in Florence. His larger, colourful, decorative works owe much to his illuminatory talent.

Losey, Joseph (1909-84) American film director who worked mostly in Britain. For a time he worked on small productions, turning banal science fiction tales such as *The Damned* (1962) into superb cinema. Critical success came with *The Servant* (1963), followed by *Accident* (1967), after which he was recognized as one of the cinema's great stylists.

Loti, Pierre (1850-1923) French author, whose romantic novels and travel books capture the atmosphere of faraway lands, especially the Middle and Far Eastern countries which he visited as an officer in the French navy. Among his best-known books are *My Brother Yves* (1883), *Iceland Fisherman* (1886), *Madame Chrysanthème* (1887) and *Disenchanted* (1906).

Lotto, Lorenzo (c. 1480-1556) Italian painter of religious subjects, frescoes, altarpieces and portraits. His paintings reflect a departure from the mainstream of Venetian art. He was, nevertheless, inevitably influenced by TITIAN, as in the Carmine altarpiece *St Nicholas of Bari* (1529), though he retained his own fluidity of style and, in his use of colour, broke away from Titian's golden tones to a striking boldness.

Louis IX (1214-70) Crusader king of France (1226-70). Famed for chivalry, piety and justice, he arbitrated among Europe's discordant rulers, and championed Christendom in crusades against Egypt (1248-54), during which he was held captive in Syria for four years, and against Tunis (1270), where he died from plague. Before crusading, Louis suppressed the only rebellion of his reign (1242) by defeating the nobles and Henry III of England, who assisted them. After the Egyptian crusade he maintained peace at home, enabling French trade and culture to blossom, especially in Paris, which was made a hub of Christian philosophy.

Louis XI (1423-83) King of France (1463-83), an absolute monarch who strengthened the crown by restoring centralized royal power and ruling by decree. Louis overcame the League of Public Weal (an alliance of nobles against him) by arms, treaties, intrigue, and the timely deaths of some of its most dangerous members. He defeated in battle and killed his principal rival, Charles the Bold, so gaining Burgundy. He also acquired Anjou, Var, Maine, and Provence when the powerful Anjou family became extinct. Wily, avaricious and superstitious Louis was, none the less, one of the ablest of French kings.

Louis XIV (1638-1715) King of France for 72 years, longest-reigning European monarch, an ambitious and despotic ruler who brought immense splendour to the throne and France, but at a high price. He inherited a state strengthened and centralized by RICHELIEU and MAZARIN, and, from 1661, ran it himself through able ministers such as COLBERT. Reputedly declaring 'l'état c'est moi' ('I am the state'), Louis wielded absolute power. To assure religious and political conformity, Louis, a Catholic, persecuted Huguenots and banned 'progressive' books (by DESCARTES and others). With all the powerful nobles under his aegis at Versailles, Europe's showpiece of Baroque art and architecture, Louis was able to avoid any possible threats. As patron of RACINE, MOLIÈRE, LE BRUN and others, Louis helped to raise French arts to new heights. His ambition to make France militarily supreme over the Hapsburg domains of Spain and the Empire involved France in four major wars. His armies were brilliantly directed by LOUVOIS, TURENNE and VAUBAN, but defeats by MARLBOROUGH and Prince Eugène at Blenheim, Oudenarde and Malplaquet eclipsed France's former gains, prestige and wealth.

Louis XV (1710-74) King of France (1715-74), whose chaotic and capricious reign roused in its later stages a popular hatred which culminated in the French Revolution. After the regency of the Duke of Orleans, the ministry of the incapable Duke of Bourbon, and the death of Fleury, Louis managed the administration himself. A pleasure-loving man of little ability, he let court favourites and mistresses (notably the Comtesse DU BARRY and the Marquise DE POMPADOUR) influence the administration and rob the treasury. As a result of the Seven Years' War (1756-63) he lost Canada and India, and with them the prestige which had made France supreme in Europe.

Louis XVI (1754-93) King of France (1774-92) who tried to redress the social injustices that had made the monarchy hated, and which abroad had aided the republican American colonists against Britain. Louis came to be influenced by his extravagant queen, MARIE ANTOINETTE, and the aristocracy, who blocked reforms intended to end widespread poverty in France. The ensuing social unrest and financial difficulties forced Louis to call the States General (1789), its first summons for 175 years, but demands by the commoners led directly to the French Revolution. Louis was seized and guillotined.

Louis XVIII (1755-1824) Bourbon king of France, and brother of LOUIS XVI, who ascended the throne after the defeat of NAPOLEON. He escaped from France in 1791, going first to Brunswick and then to England, where he remained until Napoleon's defeat in 1814. At a meeting in Ghent in 1814 he conceded to TALLEYRAND a guarantee for the principal reforms accomplished by the Revolution, in return for the throne. He fled to Ghent following Napoleon's escape from Elba but returned to France after Waterloo. As king, he tried to enforce his pledge, but was unable to stand up to a reactionary parliament and the ultra-royalist influence of his brother CHARLES X.

Louis II de Bourbon, Prince de Condé (1621-86) French general, called 'le Grand Condé' for his many victories. When only 21 he defeated Spanish troops at Rocroi (1643), France's greatest victory for a century. Campaigning deep into Germany (1643-66), often with TURENNE, he won many battles against the empire, including those at Dunkirk (1646) and Lens (1648). Opposing MAZARIN's régime, he sided with Spain against France (1651), continuing his victories until defeated by an Anglo-French army at Dunkirk (1658). The following year a Franco-Spanish peace treaty allowed him to return home to Chantilly, which he made a centre of culture.

Louis Philippe (1773-1850) King of France (1830-48), who was brought to power by the Bourgoisie as a reaction to the rule of the Bourbons. He was a liberal for much of his reign, supporting constitutional restraint on the monarchy and becoming known as the 'Citizen King'. He fell from power in the February revolution of 1848, when the Republic was proclaimed.

Louis, Joe (1914-81) American heavyweight boxer who became the longest-reigning world champion of any division (1937-49).

Louvois, Marquis de (1641-91) French war minister (from 1666) who, with TURENNE and VAUBAN, built up French military might for LOUIS XIV. Louvois reorganized and modernized the French army, improved soldiering conditions and planned a number of major victories achieved by the armies of Louis XIV between 1672 and 1678.

Lovecraft, Howard Phillips (1890-1937) American author of much supernatural fiction, including the *Haunter in the Dark* and *The Case of Charles Dexter Ward*, dealing with 'the cult of Cthulu', the supposed secret worship of the 'Elder Gods'. Lovecraft's theories are part of the ideology of the San Francisco-based Church of Satan.

Lovelace, Richard (1618-c. 1657) English courtier and lyric poet, who, with Suckling, is the best-known Cavalier poet. A follower of CHARLES I, Lovelace was imprisoned and impoverished in the Civil Wars, and wrote many of his polished, slightly cynical lyrics in prison. In 1649 he published *Lucasta*, containing his best poems.

Loveless, George (1797-1874) English farm-labourer and leader of the 'Tolpuddle Martyrs'. In 1834 Loveless and five other farm labourers of Tolpuddle, Dorset, formed a trade union to better the pay and conditions of farm workers. All five were prosecuted under an Act against administering oaths that was never intended for such use, and were convicted by a jury of farmer employers. They were condemned to seven years' transportation to New South Wales. Public indignation forced a bitterly anti-trade union Whig government to pardon and release them in 1836. Loveless returned to England but with four of his fellow 'martyrs' later emigrated to Canada.

Lovell, Sir Bernard (born 1913) English astronomer, originator and Director of the Jodrell Bank Experimental Station. Its 250-ft diameter radio telescope was completed in 1957, and remained the world's largest fully steerable radio 'dish' until 1971. Although famous for tracking lunar and space probes, the Jodrell Bank radio telescope is mostly used for basic researches into the nature of the Universe.

Lowell, Amy (1874-1925) American poet, one of the leaders of the 'imagist' movement, which Ezra POUND, a former moving spirit, retitled 'the Amygists'. She wrote neat, concentrated verse in *Sword Blades and Poppy Seed* (1914), then became more expansive in a vast, ornate biography, *John Keats* (1925).

Lowell, James (1819-91) American poet, critic, editor and diplomat, whose writings increased the reputation of American literature amongst the European literary establishment. Lowell attempted to found a literary magazine, *The Pioneer*, but achieved little success. He wrote romantic poetry and literary criticism, such as *The Vision of Sir Launfal* (1848) and *A Fable for Critics* (1848), and gained a reputation as a satirist after the publication of the *Biglow Papers* (1848), social and political lampoons. In 1855 he became Professor of Modern Languages at Harvard and was the first editor of the *Atlantic Monthly*, and, from 1864, of the *North American Review*. He was appointed United States Ambassador to Madrid in 1877, and to London in 1880.

Lowell, Percival (1855-1916) American astronomer, who instituted the search for the planet Pluto. Lowell set up his own observatory at Flagstaff, Arizona, where he installed a 24-inch refractor to observe the planet Mars. With this instrument he charted numerous 'canals' which he thought existed on the surface of Mars, and expounded his theory of Martian habitation in *Mars and its Canals* (1906). Lowell spent a decade computing the position of the 'Planet X' he believed must lie beyond Neptune. His final figures were published in 1915, but he died 14 years before Clyde TOMBAUGH discovered Pluto.

Lowry, Malcolm (1909-57) English writer, who drew from his experience in foreign lands and his own struggle with drink the powerful material of his novel *Under the Volcano* (1947). The stories in *Hear Us, O Lord from Heaven Thy Dwelling Place* (1961) were published posthumously.

Lowry, Thomas (1874-1936) English chemist remembered for his experiments on optical activity. Jean Biot and Louis PASTEUR had established that the polarization of light passing through what they called 'optically active' substances depended on their chemical structure. Lowry confirmed (early 1900s) that optical activity depended on the wavelength of the light.

Loyola, Saint Ignatius (c. 1495-1556) Basque founder of the Order of Jesuits. A soldier who underwent conversion after being wounded. He attracted a large following and established his militant missionary Order in 1534.

Lubbe, Marinus van der (1910-34) Dutchman who was accused of setting fire to the Reichstag. Six days before the election of 1933, the Reichstag in Berlin was burnt down. The Nazis immediately accused the Communists of causing the fire, and a case was fabricated against van der Lubbe, who was of low intelligence. At his trial, Georgi Dimitrov, later Premier of Bulgaria, accused GOERING of starting the fire for the political purpose of providing an excuse to persecute left-wing groups. Although the evidence against van der Lubbe was inconclusive, he was executed immediately after the trial. HITLER later used the fire as a pretext for disqualifying the 81 Communist Deputies in the Reichstag.

Luce, Henry (1898-1967) American founder of the international best-selling magazines, *Time*, *Fortune* and *Life*. In 1923, Luce co-founded *Time*, a weekly news magazine which built a three million circulation by idiosyncratically written, brightly presented news and comment. Luce's later successes included the luxury monthly business magazine *Fortune* (1930) and the pictorial weekly magazine *Life* (1936), which developed worldwide sales of over seven millions. By the mid-1950s, Luce's Time-Life Inc. had become one of the biggest of all private publishing concerns.

Luciano, Charles 'Lucky' (1897-1962) American racketeer who controlled New York prostitution, narcotics and 'numbers' during the 1920s and 1930s. Luciano was deported to his native Sicily in 1946, and died there, of natural causes.

Lucius Tarquinius Superbus (ruled 534-510 BC) Last of Rome's seven legendary kings, whose despotic rule ended with his being driven into exile and Rome becoming a republic.

Lucretius (c. 96-55 BC) Roman poet, author of the didactic poem 'On the Nature of Things', which gave a full account of the doctrines of EPICURUS and his school.

Lukács, György (1885-1971) Hungarian philosopher and literary critic, who was an outstanding figure in the history of Marxist thought. His most famous work was *History and Class Consciousness* (1923), which, under pressure from the Comintern, he renounced, but then republished 45 years later. His aesthetic theory is best expressed in *The Specific Nature of the Aesthetic* (1963). The finest exponent of Marxist literary criticism, he had an encyclopaedic knowledge of world literature, relating it to its historical and social context. Lukács never accepted the political dogmas of Soviet Communism, and frequently conflicted with the authorities during the 1940s and 1950s. He was Commissar for Culture in Béla KUN's Communist government (1919) and was appointed Minister for Culture in the government of Imre NAGY after the Hungarian revolt of 1956. Expelled to Rumania, he was allowed to return to Hungary in 1957 and was readmitted to the Communist Party ten years later.

Luke (1st cent. AD) Turkish-born Christian saint, apostle and evangelist, author of the third Gospel of the New Testament and of Acts of the Apostles, which together constitute the earliest history of the Christian Church. The most literary of the New Testament writers, his Gospel is the last of the three Synoptic Gospels and the only one to give an account of the Ascension. Based on eye-witness accounts and documents, it is thought to have been written in the last two decades of the 1st century. By tradition a physician, Luke is the patron saint of doctors and artists. He accompanied PAUL on his second journey.

Lully, Jean-Baptiste (1632-87) French composer at the court of LOUIS XIV. Lully, an innovatory composer, collaborated with MOLIÈRE in writing incidental music to *Le Bourgeois Gentilhomme*, among other plays. By 1684 he had secured a total monopoly of French opera. He also wrote church music and pastorals.

Lumière, Auguste Marie Louis (1862-1954) Frenchman who, with his brother Louis Jean (1864-1948), pioneered the cinema as a form of entertainment. They developed a satisfactory camera and projector and were the first to make and show films to the general public. Inspired by EDISON's kinetoscope and the hand-painted productions (forerunners of animated films) of Paris's *Theatre Optique*, they devised a claw mechanism to pull the film a fixed distance past the projector (and camera) lens while the light was cut off by a shutter. Their choice of 16 frames (pictures) per second remained the standard filming and projection rate through all the years of silent films.

Luther, Martin (1483-1546) German reformer, theologian and writer whose lifelong struggle against established Church doctrine permanently changed the face of Christianity. A monk and professor, Luther's insights emerged at a time of decadence in the Church, with indulgences peddled to raise papal income. His nailing of the 95 Theses to the door of Castle Church in Wittenburg (1517) precipitated the schism with the Church that led to his condemnation by the pope three years later. By this time Luther's religious reforms had won widespread public support, an approval that could even weather his unpopular stand during the Peasants' Revolt and his doctrinal break with ERASMUS. His many achievements include translating the Bible from the original tongues into contemporary German, and composing forceful tracts, hymns and catechisms. Luther's commentaries on books of the Bible place him highly among biblical scholars.

Luthuli, Albert John (1898-1967) South African nationalist leader and Zulu chieftain whose non-violent methods to oppose racism in his country won him the Nobel Peace Prize (1960). Having held various offices in Church and Mission movements, in 1952 he was elected Natal leader of the African National Congress and as such took part in a passive resistance campaign as a result of which the South African government deprived him of his chieftainship. In 1956 he was charged with treason, but the charges were withdrawn for lack of evidence. In 1959 he was banished to his farm under the Riotous Assembly Act. Following the police massacre of passively demonstrating Africans at Sharpeville (1960), Luthuli challenged the government's persecution of blacks by publicly burning the pass which all people of his race have to carry. He was fined, arrested, but released when the African National Congress was banned by the government.

Lutyens, Sir Edwin Landseer (1869-1944) English architect well known for his designs of large-scale buildings, notably the splendid and formally designed Viceroy's House at New Delhi, India. His feeling for the dramatic is illustrated by Lindisfarne Castle on the exposed island in the North Sea off England, and his more informal style by the country houses at Tigbourne Court and Godalming. His architecture, which varied in style from gentle arts and crafts to Neo-classicism, was usually vigorous and sympathetic to its setting, although often at variance with the ideas of his more advanced contemporaries.

Luxemburg, Rosa (1870-1919) German socialist revolutionary and joint founder, with LIEBKNECHT, of the Spartacus League. She took part in the Russian revolution of 1905 and during the First World War was imprisoned, afterwards becoming one of Europe's leading militant revolutionaries. She was seized by German officers in 1919 for her part in the Spartacist uprising in Berlin, and was murdered while awaiting trial.

Lyell, Sir Charles (1797-1875) British geologist, whose most famous work is his book *Principles of Geology*. His field work was mainly with the younger rocks, to which he gave the names (now universally accepted, with some additions and modifications), Eocene, Miocene and Pliocene to mark their geological ages. Lyell's *Principles of Geology* publicized HUTTON's theories of Uniformitarianism and Vulcanism. He was a friend of Charles DARWIN and one of the first converts to the new ideas on evolution.

Lysias (c. 456-c. 380 BC) Greek orator, recognized as a master of pure Attic Greek. His main activity was writing speeches for clients to deliver in the law-courts and most of the surviving speeches are of this kind. Of particular historical interest is the speech *Against Eratosthenes*, an indictment of one of the 30 tyrants accused by Lysias of murdering his brother Polemar-

The cave in use
This cave is modelled upon European examples of about 25,000 years ago, the time when cave paintings appear to have become widespread

A bone cave *above and below*
Since Charles Lyell's discovery in 1833 of flint implements buried in very old geological strata, almost all our knowledge of early man has come from digging. From about 100,000 years ago caves provided man with a ready-made refuge; many of these caves still exist. Although often buried under later strata, and changed by subsequent developments, it is still possible with experience to read the message contained within them

Cave art Most of the best-preserved cave paintings are found in almost inaccessible places. They usually show hunting scenes, and their power, colour and dynamic energy can be startling

Petrification Here, a large fall of rock from the cave roof preceded the gradual growth of pendulous stalactites and upright stalagmites, caused by the slow seepage through the limestone roof of water containing dissolved minerals

River level In general, the lowest geological sediments are the oldest, but this is not always the case. In this hypothetical cave the earliest of all the deposits is a river terrace A above the cave on the hillside, indicating that the whole cave was originally submerged. At about this period insoluble limestone residue was settling on the cave floor at B. As the river cut its valley its level fell to C, leaving silt bed D. Continued deepening of the valley brought the river to its present level, leaving the cave dry and eroding the thick layer of silt at the mouth of the cave

The bear cult Carefully prepared arrangements of animal bone fragments, such as in this store compartment filled with bear skulls, are evidence of early man's hunting superstitions. Men could hardly have chosen a more dangerous opponent

A rock fall A massive collapse of the cave roof left a gaping open shaft which became gradually filled in with new layers of flowstone, earth and rock debris, and sediment

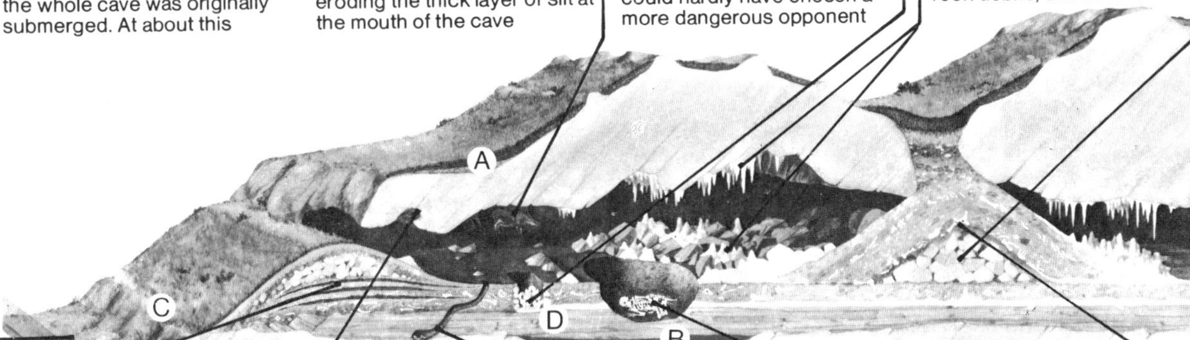

An obstructed mouth Early man sheltering in the cave mouth lit fires whose ashes gradually accumulated in three main layers. Later the cave was abandoned by man and the mouth became blocked by rock debris

A burrow in the cave Here a small animal burrowed into the cave floor, throwing up fossil bones—to die when it reached the end of its burrow

A buzzard's nest Just inside the lip of the cave mouth a bird of prey built its nest. Small rodent bones lie scattered beneath it

Human burial Early men buried their own kind in many different ways. This skeleton shows evidence of careful burial in a sleeping posture

Animal remains The cave is littered to a depth of more than a foot (0.3 m) with the debris of carnivores and the remains of animals which fell in through the hole above chus. Eloquently written, it clearly depicts the reign of terror they established over Athens.

M

MacArthur, Douglas (1880-1964) American general, Supreme Commander of occupation forces in Japan after the Second World War. As commanding general of the American armed forces in the Far East in 1941, he was forced to evacuate the Philippines when YAMASHITA captured Bataan and Corregidor in 1942. His use of combined operations and his development of the 'leap-frogging' strategy led eventually to the recapture from the Japanese of many pacific islands by 1945. After the atomic bomb attacks on Hiroshima and Nagasaki, and the Japanese surrender, MacArthur became supreme commander of the occupation forces in Japan, where for six years he exercised almost unlimited authority, demilitarizing the country and introducing sweeping reforms, among them HIROHITO's renunciation of the Mikado's traditional divinity, and a new constitution. From Japan, MacArthur directed the United Nations forces at the outbreak of the war in Korea (1950-51), and with the entry of Communist Chinese troops in North Korea, demanded forces with which to attack Chinese territory. They were refused by President TRUMAN; MacArthur appealed directly to the American people, and was dismissed by the President to emphasize the limited purpose of US involvement in Korea in support of United Nations action. In 1952, he failed in an attempt to be nominated for the presidency.

Macaulay, Baron Thomas (1800-59) British historian and statesman, who wrote a popular history of England, his (unfinished) *History of England from the Accession of James II* (1848-61), which examined the significance of the English Revolution. At one time Secretary of War, Macaulay contributed frequently to the *Edinburgh Review* and was author of the popular *Lays of Ancient Rome*. A scholar of extensive memory and mastery of detail, his critical writings often included savage reviews of the work of others. In practical politics, he contributed towards the structure of the Civil Service.

Macbeth (11th cent.) King of Scotland (1040-57) and hero of SHAKESPEARE's play *Macbeth*. Hereditary ruler of Moray and Ross, Macbeth murdered (1040) Duncan, King of Scotland, and seized the throne. Backed by northern Scotland, he fought off southern Scottish efforts to unseat him until he was killed by Duncan's son Malcolm, who then became King Malcolm III.

MacDiarmid, Hugh (1892-1978) Pen-name of Christopher Grieve, the Scottish poet, a leader of the 20th-century revival of Scottish poetry. MacDiarmid encouraged Scots poets to use 'Lallans', a language which includes English, Scottish dialect and the literary tongue of medieval poets.

Macdonald, Flora (1722-90) Scottish Jacobite supporter who helped Prince Charles Edward STUART to escape from the Hebridean island of Benbecula, where he had taken refuge after his defeat at Culloden (1746). Betrayed later by a talkative boatman, Flora was imprisoned in London until 1747.

MacDonald, James Ramsay (1866-1937) First Labour Party Prime Minister of Britain. He became an MP in 1906 and Leader of the Independent Labour Party (1911-14), but his pacifism resulted in political eclipse during the First World War. In 1922, he made a comeback as MP for Aberavon and was elected Leader of the Labour Party chiefly by the Scottish element. In 1924 the General Election gave no Party a clear majority, but the Labour Party accepted the chance to form a minority government and MacDonald became Prime Minister and Foreign Secretary. In the General Election nine months later (November 1924) right-wing sections of the press exploited the 'ZINOVIEV letter', contrived to suggest that the Labour Party was taking orders from the Russian Bolsheviks and the Labour Party was defeated. In 1929, it was returned to power and MacDonald again became Prime Minister. Within two years, financial crisis led to the formation of a Conservative-dominated coalition government. MacDonald was reluctant to abandon his position and continued as PM until 1935.

Macgregor, Robert (1671-1734) Scottish Highland clan chief known as Rob Roy (Red Robert) because of his red beard, and subject of Sir Walter SCOTT's novel *Rob Roy*. Outlawed for debts incurred in cattle dealing, he fled to the hills and lived by robbing his creditor the Duke of Montrose, and by forcing farmers to pay him. Popular legend idealized Rob Roy's crimes as robbing the rich to pay the poor.

Machiavelli, Niccolo (1469-1527) Italian writer and political theorist, whose name has become synonymous with political despotism. A professional diplomat, he expressed in *The Prince* (1513) concepts of statecraft whereby the welfare of the state is the aim to which all rulers should strive, whatever the moral consequences of their actions.

Mackenzie, Sir Alexander (c. 1755-1820) Scottish-born Canadian explorer, thought to have been the first person to cross the full breadth of North America. After several years in the fur trade Mackenzie embarked on his first voyage (1789). Travelling up to the Great Slave Lake, he continued north along the river now named after him for nearly 1000 miles, finally reaching the Arctic Ocean. Three years later, Mackenzie set out with a party of English, French, and Indian settlers in hopes of finding the Pacific. The expedition headed west along the Peace River and travelled some 500 miles to its source. Despite an accident in which they lost most of their provisions, Mackenzie's party managed to traverse the rugged Coast Range and ride down the Bella Coola River. In July 1793 Mackenzie reached the Pacific coast near Cape Menzies.

Mackenzie, Sir Compton (1883-1972) Scottish author, who, amongst numerous works, produced *Sinister Street* (1913-14), a long, detailed study of a student's development into maturity. He came to notice with *Carnival* (1912), a story of theatrical life. His best known works include the farcical novels *The Monarch of the Glen* (1941) and *Whisky Galore* (1947).

Mackintosh, Charles Rennie (1868-1928) Scottish architect who established a style of architectural Art Nouveau that was restrained and individual. Mackintosh's major works are in Glasgow, and of these his Glasgow School of Art is the most important. The houses he designed reveal a controlled rhythm, but also show a debt to traditional Scottish baronial architecture.

Maclean, Donald (born 1913) English spy for the Russians, who in 1951 fled to the Soviet Union with Guy Burgess after being secretly warned by PHILBY that the Foreign Office was investigating him.

Macleod, J. J. R. see BANTING, Sir Frederick

MacMahon, Patrice (1808-93) French soldier, of Irish descent, who became President of France, having made his name in the Crimean War by commanding the forces which captured the Malakoff Fort in 1855 and by defeating the Austrians at Magenta (1859) in the Franco-Piedmontese war against Austria. He was appointed Governor-General of Algeria in 1864. He returned to France in 1870 and fought in the Franco-Prussian war, but was beaten and captured by the Prussians. On his release he commanded the troops which suppressed the Commune (1871), and was rewarded by being elected President of the Third Republic (1873) by a royalist Assembly. He tried to use his position to restore the monarchy, but failed despite election rigging, and in 1879 he resigned. He was made Duke of Magenta in 1850.

Macmillan, Harold (born 1894) British Conservative politician, who became Prime Minister when Anthony EDEN resigned following the Suez crisis (1956). In turn Minister of Housing, Minister of Defence and Foreign Secretary during the early 1950s, Macmillan was Chancellor of the Exchequer at the time of Eden's resignation. He worked hard to repair Anglo-US relations strained by the Suez crisis, but thc closer links he established, culminating in the Nassau agreement (by which Britain gained Polaris equipment), antagonized DE GAULLE and the French. British attempts to join the Common Market were prejudiced, then vetoed by De Gaulle. Macmillan resigned in 1963 to be succeeded by DOUGLAS-HOME.

MacNeice, Louis (1907-63) Irish poet, who was noted for the wry irony of his comments on 20th-century society. Though connected in the 1930s with AUDEN and SPENDER, his verse was less political than theirs. In his several volumes of verse, the most memorable poems are the sombre ones about the tragedy and sadness of modern life. MacNeice was also known as a broadcaster.

Madero, Francisco Idalecio (1873-1913) Mexican politician and leader of the revolution against DIAZ. While opposition candidate in the presidential elections of 1910, he accused Diaz of irregularities in government, was arrested but escaped to the USA, where he issued a call for the Mexicans to revolt. He returned to Mexico during ZAPATA's revolution and, on the resignation of Diaz in 1911, became Provisional President, having won popular support through his liberal proclamations. He was elected President in November 1911 by a large majority, but found his proposed land reforms impeded by the old Diaz congress. To counter this obstruction, he appointed members of his family to various government posts. In 1913, while Zapata was still waging war in the south, a revolution broke out in Mexico City. The army deserted Madero and he was overthrown.

Madison, James (1751-1836) Fourth American President (1809-17), who was chiefly responsible with JEFFERSON for drafting the terms of the US Constitution. A Virginian, he represented the state in the Continental Congress (1780-3) and the Constitutional Convention (1787). He was Jefferson's Secretary of State (1801-9) in which office he was involved in the Louisiana Purchase (1803) and the rights of neutral states during the Napoleonic wars. He succeeded Jefferson as President. In 1812 he was re-elected, but his second term of office was marred by the Anglo-American war (1812-14), in which his leadership proved ineffective.

Madrid Hurtado, Miguel de la (born 1934) Mexican politician and President since 1982. He formulated Mexico's global development plan and then, as candidate of the Institutional Revolutionary Party, was elected President, succeeding Lopez Portillo.

Magellan, Ferdinand (c. 1480-1521) Portuguese explorer who led – for Spain – the first expedition to circumnavigate the earth, but was killed before completion of the voyage. Magellan won the backing of CHARLES V of Spain to seek a western route to the Spice Islands (The Moluccas) and set out from Spain in September 1519 with five small vessels – *Trinidad* (his flagship), *San Antonio*, *Concepción*, *Vittoria* and *Santiago*. Four ships reached the channel, now called the Magellan Strait, in October, but during the tortuous passage through it, the *San Antonio* deserted and returned to Spain. *Trinidad*, *Concepción* and *Vittoria* reached the ocean, which Magellan named the Pacific, in late November and began the long north-westerly crossing. After 98 days they discovered Samar in the Philippines, and shortly afterwards went on to Cebu, where Magellan joined in a local dispute. He and several leaders of the fleet were killed. The survivors escaped with two ships to the Spice Islands. Only the *Vittoria*, commanded by Sebastian del CANO, completed the circumnavigation of the globe.

Magritte, René (1898-1967) Belgian Surrealist painter, whose art is unlike that of other pioneers of the movement. He did not rely on automatic or unconscious techniques, but on the unexpected juxtaposition of recognizable images, painted with careful precision but placed in unlikely situations. By these means, and by contrasts of scale, he emphasized unrealized poetic aspects of

Magritte's spectral forms hover mistily over some deserted coastline

such images, he himself regarding his painting as an instrument of knowledge.

Mahavira (c. 6th cent. BC) Indian founder of Jainism, an offshoot of Hinduism. Jainism, fundamentally atheistic, rejects the authority of the *Vedas* and modifies the Hindu doctrine of transmigration by asserting that saintliness will achieve immortality immediately after death. The ethical code is high, based on the need to show kindness to all forms of life. The teaching is set out in the *Augas,* sacred books finally compiled in the 5th century AD. Jains believe that Mahavira is the last of 24 saints or prophets who, after achieving enlightened perfection, preached the faith to the world.

Mahler, Gustav (1860-1911) Austrian composer, the last major symphonist in the 19th-century tradition and one of the key figures in the development of 20th-century music. Mahler studied under BRUCKNER, and became one of the leading conductors of his day (chief conductor of the Vienna State Opera, 1897). He saw this work as a means to an end which would enable him to devote time to composition. His outstanding orchestral song cycles include *Songs of a Wayfarer* (1883), and *Songs on the Death of Children* (1902), and in them, as in his nine symphonies, he extended his personal vision and sense of harmony to their limits. By the time he wrote his last major works he was seriously ill, and eloquently communicated his sense of approaching death in his Ninth Symphony, and the song cycle *The Song of the Earth* (1911). In his vast Eighth Symphony, *The Symphony of a Thousand* (1910), Mahler wrote the first completely choral symphony.

Mahler was a bridge between 19th and 20th century music

Mailer, Norman (born 1923) American novelist whose energetic, self-centred fiction is complemented by his notorious public escapades. His most acclaimed work, *The Naked and the Dead* (1948), scrutinizes American society within the framework of a war novel, while his later writing, most notably *The Armies of the Night* (1968), is semi-journalistic in style.

Maillol, Aristide (1861-1944) French sculptor who began life as a tapestry designer and painter and took to sculpture only at the age of 40. His work was almost exclusively concerned with the female nude and after his visit to Greece in 1908 his work lost its early Romantic flavour, reminiscent of RODIN, and became more restrained in its air of classical sensitivity. Maillol's figures, apparently quietly posed but with a restrained power, have a simplicity which helps forge the link between the romantic ideal of Rodin and the fully three-dimensional forms of modern sculpture.

Maiman, Theodore Harold (born 1927) American physicist who, in 1960, was the first to generate a laser beam, an intense, narrow beam of light. Current applications of lasers include high-speed cutting of materials, precision measurement and delicate welding (including reattachment of the retina in the human eye) and as a guidance system for missiles.

Maimonides (1135-1204) Spanish-born Jewish religious writer and philosopher, known also as 'Rambam', author of *Mishne* (1180), a famous exposition of Jewish law. His *Guide of the Perplexed* (1190), a study of the Jewish religion in which he adopted methods of Aristotelian philosophy, had a profound influence upon Jews and Christians and was highly controversial for 200 years. He wrote on logic, mathematics and medicine.

Maine, Sir Henry (1822-88) English jurist and historian who pioneered the study of comparative law. In his book, *Ancient Law* (1861), he explained legal ideas and their development by tracing changes in Roman, Indian and East and West European legal systems. It established the historical study of comparative jurisprudence, shaped political theory and influenced anthropology by posing new theories on the nature of primitive law. Maine was responsible for the codification of Indian law (1863-9), and became the first Professor of Comparative Jurisprudence at Oxford (1869).

Makarios III, Archbishop (1913-1977) Ethnarch of the Orthodox Church in Cyprus and President of Cyprus. As Archbishop of Cyprus from 1950, he became deeply involved in politics as leader of the *Enosis* (Union with Greece) movement. The ambiguity of his attitude to the violent tactics of the *Enosis* militants appeared to implicate him in the terrorists' campaign, and he was deported in 1956 to the Seychelles Islands by the British Governor of Cyprus. After the settlement which followed the terrorism of 1955-9 he was released and was elected President of the Republic of Cyprus. In 1974 he was overthrown and fled to Europe but, after the Turkish invasion of the island, he took part in emergency meetings of the UN Security Council and returned to resume his presidential duties over the unoccupied part of the island.

Malamud, Bernard (born 1914) American novelist whose fiction principally deals with love, suffering, and the Jewish experience. Malamud's scope is wide, ranging from *The Natural* (1952), a mythopoetic blend of baseball lore and the Grail legend, to *The Fixer* (1966), a story of Jewish tribulations in Tsarist Russia.

Malan, Daniel François (1874-1959) Afrikaaner nationalist and prime mover of South Africa's apartheid policy. He began his career as a minister of the Dutch Reformed Church and retained a Calvinistic, crusading spirit in politics as leader of the extreme Nationalist opposition to SMUTS and HERTZOG. He was opposed to South Africa's participation in the Second World War, and in 1942 proposed that the country should withdraw from the war and separate from the British crown. His premiership (1948-54) saw the inception of republicanism and apartheid as official government policy, the Group Areas Act being the first of many aimed at dividing the country into white, black and coloured districts.

Malenkov, Georgi (born 1902) Soviet soldier and politician, the only Chairman of the USSR Council of Ministers (Prime Minister) to resign voluntarily. He was a member of STALIN's War Cabinet in the Second World War and succeeded him as Chairman when Stalin died (1953). He resigned less than two years later, pleading insufficient experience and admitting responsibility for the failure of Soviet agricultural policy. He was succeeded by BULGANIN. In July 1957, he was accused with MOLOTOV and Kaganovitch of setting up an 'anti-party' group and was dismissed from the government, the party Praesidium and the Central Committee. He was demoted to the management of a hydroelectric plant in Kazakhstan until his retirement in 1963.

Malinowski, Bronislaw (1884-1942) Austrian-born social anthropologist, who revolutionized social anthropology by living for extended periods with the societies he studied, thus providing a method of research which freed the discipline from its early reliance on travellers' tales. Malinowski aimed at establishing 'a science of culture', and the four years he spent in New Guinea and the Trobriand Islands provided him with the material for thorough analysis of his assumption that a culture is an integrated whole.

Mallarmé, Stéphane (1842-98) French poet, disciple of BAUDELAIRE, and originator of the Symbolist movement, to whose members poetry was a means of reaching beyond the everyday world to a higher reality – 'To paint, not the thing, but the effect which it produces', to suggest with words the very essence of things, was a task to which he devoted his life. Mallarmé is best known for the poem *L'Après-midi d'un faune* (set to music by DEBUSSY), the verse drama *Hérodiade* and his most ambitious work, *Un Coup de dés*, in which he experimented with typography and the possibility of random sentence and word order on the page. After 1884, the famous Tuesday gatherings at Mallarmé's Paris apartment were frequented by many leading contemporary writers.

Malory, Sir Thomas (15th cent.) English author who wrote *Le Morte D'Arthur* (1470), a prose adaptation of the French Arthurian romances. The book deals with the rise and fall of the Round Table, Arthur's court, and the search for the Holy Grail, the vessel supposed to have been used by CHRIST at the Last Supper.

Malpighi, Marcello (1628-94) Italian physiologist and microscopist who showed how blood reaches the tissues through tiny vessels (capillaries) that are too small to be seen with the naked eye. HARVEY had inferred that there must be capillaries, but had never seen them; Malpighi – the first man to use the microscope to study the fine structure of plant and animal tissues – was able to pinpoint and explain the network of tiny veins he could see on the lung surface. He extended the use of the microscope into many fields, including the study of gland cells and of the brain, and also ventured into the field of embryology.

Malraux, André (1901-76) French novelist, critic and politician. His novels of action reflect his dangerous way of life: as a Communist during the Chinese revolution in *The Conquerors* (1928); *Man's Estate* (1933), set in Shanghai, 1927; as an anti-Fascist and pilot in the Republican air force during the Spanish Civil War, *Days of Hope* (1938) and as a French Resistance fighter during the Second World War, *Les Noyers de l'Altenburg* (1948). After the war, he became an art critic and wrote the monumental *Psychologie de l'Art* (1947-50). Later, during the Fifth Republic, Malraux was appointed France's Minister for Cultural Affairs.

Malthus, Thomas Robert (1766-1834) English economist and demographer whose pessimistic *An Essay on the Principle of Population* (1798) argued that population increases geometrically to absorb resources which increase arithmetically, so that the masses remain at subsistence level. Numbers were checked by natural disasters, or by such deliberate acts as birth control, abortion and infanticide. As an explanation of poverty, the theory was appealing, but with increases in the standard of living and the failure of the 'checks', Malthus introduced a 'moral restraint', entailing late marriages and sexual abstinence. His theory discounted the ability of men to develop new resources for the more affluent societies, but its relevance to under-developed areas and his pioneering of demographic studies remain lasting legacies.

Mandela, Nelson Rolihlala (born 1918) Black South African lawyer who campaigned against the racialist policies of the South African government. As leader of the militant faction of the African National Congress (ANC), Mandela was sentenced to life imprisonment in 1964 for plotting to overthrow the government. His wife, Winnie, has continued his campaign since.

Manet, Edouard (1832-83) French Impressionist painter, whose *Déjeuner sur l'Herbe* (1863) and *Olympia* (1865) scandalized the official art world by their alleged indecency and their repudiation of the academic history-painting that was then fashionable. He was an artistic rebel and his early works are characterized by broad, fluid brushwork and a direct, rational treatment of his subject in which tonal contrasts are emphasized. After 1870, he painted in lighter, softer colours, bringing him closer to the Impressionists, though he refused to exhibit with them and still hankered for the official recognition of the academic salons. His compositional gifts and feeling for colour were of the highest order and are apparent in such paintings as *The Balcony* (1869) and *The Bar at the Folies Bergères* (1882).

Mann, Thomas (1875-1955) German novelist, author of *The Magic Mountain* (1927), an ironical analysis of contemporary civilization. *Buddenbrooks* (1901), his first important novel, and *Death in Venice* (1911), a novella, both introduce the themes with which he was concerned in many of his writings: the conflict between art and life, and the depiction of early 20th-century German society. In 1933 Mann left Germany and later settled in the United States where he became naturalized. *Doctor Faustus* (1947), the story of the life and downfall of a demonic composer, written in exile, reflects his feelings about Nazi Germany. *The Confessions of Felix Krull, Confidence Man* (1954) is a novel of Mann's old age and one of Germany's great comic novels. Its underlying theme is the author's fear that his own search for art might turn out to be a confidence trick. Mann was awarded the Nobel Prize for Literature in 1929 and the Goethe Prize in 1949.

Mannerheim, Baron Carl Gustaf Emil von (1867-1951) Finnish soldier-statesman of Swedish descent, who secured Finland's independence from Russia. Whilst Finland was a Russian Province he served in the Russian Imperial army, and in the Russo-Japanese war (1904-5). In 1918 he recaptured Helsinki from the Bolsheviks, who had seized it, and as Chief of State of an independent Finnish government (1919-20), commanded a Finnish army against the Russians, obtaining recognition of his country's sovereign status by the Soviet government. He was made a Marshal and President of the Defence Council. He returned to active service when the USSR invaded Finland in 1939. Following his country's defeat, he sought an alliance with Nazi Germany and took Finland into the war against the USSR in 1941.

Mannheim, Karl (1893-1947) German sociologist who pioneered the sociology of knowledge by studying the relationship between the ways people live and the intellectual life of their society, and highlighted in *Ideology and Utopia* (1940) the major problem of the age – the finding of a workable solution to social life between the extremes of a planless democracy and the totalitarian society. Mannheim took as an established fact that society is organized into various classes, and argued from this that the individual was bound to have a different perspective of knowledge according to his class.

Mansart, François (1598-1666) French architect whose masterpiece is Maisons Lafitte, a country house outside Paris, part of which was demolished as soon as it was built because of Mansart's insistence on perfection. His un-theatrical, elegant style epitomizes the ideals of the rich bourgeoisie, for whom he worked, in contrast to the flamboyant style favoured by the Court.

Mansart, Jules Hardouin (1646-1708) French architect, grand-nephew to François MANSART, whose best-remembered work is probably the Galerie des Glaces, Versailles, which he built in collaboration with Lebrun; it is a masterpiece totally in sympathy with his role as court architect to LOUIS XIV, and it was at Versailles that much of his work was executed.

Mansfield, Katherine (1888-1923) New Zealand short-story writer, whose delicate, impressionistic stories, in the manner of CHEKHOV, describe emotions and sensations rather than narrate events. Among her principal stories were *Bliss* (1920), *The Garden Party* (1922), *The Dove's Nest* (1923) and *Something Childish* (1924). She died of tuberculosis.

Mansur Ustad (16th-17th cents.) Court painter to JAHANGIR, Mogul Emperor of India. His earliest work appeared in manuscripts of the previous reign, but his particular talent for sympathetic and accomplished depictions of wildlife caused him to specialize in this field for his nature-loving patron. It is thought that his flower paintings, influenced by imported European herbals, were the inspiration for the decoration found on the Taj Mahal.

Mantegna, Andrea (c. 1431-1506) Italian Renaissance artist, whose paintings are noted for their illusions of realistic depth. This is seen in his *Scenes from the Life of Saint James* in the Eremitani Church, Padua, only part of which survived the Second World War. Mantegna left Padua in 1460 to become Court Painter to the Gonzagas at Mantua, for whom he decorated the Camera degli Sposi (1474).

Manutius, Aldus (1450-1515) Italian author and printer, who was the first to design and use italic type. The new italic first appeared on an illustration of *Letters of St Catherine of Siena* (1500), and the first italic book, the works of VIRGIL, appeared in 1501. He was a tutor to the princes of Carpi, and from them received money with which to establish his press in Venice, in 1490.

Manzoni, Alessandro Francesco (1785-1873) Italian novelist and poet, the leading figure in the Italian romantic school. He wrote the famous novel, *The Betrothed* (1825-7), in which irony, strong characterization and psychological penetration feature in a story of two star-crossed lovers in 17th-century Milan, which is not without reference to 19th-century Italy. The form of language used was to be fundamental to the emergence of a uniform, modern Italian.

Mao Tse-Tung (1893-1976) Chinese Communist leader and head of state. Chairman of the People's Republic of China (1949-59) and Chairman of the Chinese Communist Party (CCP) until his death, he was the most influential person in modern Chinese history. After fighting against the Manchu dynasty (1911) he became a Marxist in 1919, devoting himself after 1923 to full-time revolutionary activity. Following the split between CHIANG KAI-SHEK's *Kuomintang* and the CCP, Mao established his dominance over the CCP during the Long March of 1934-6. Between 1936 and 1949 he acquired a reputation as a theorist, adapting Marxism to the particular needs of the Chinese. Becoming Chairman in 1949, Mao developed heavy industry and emphasized the need for rapid collectivization. In 1956 he attempted to draw on China's intellectual strength by encouraging ideological debate and in the late 1950s stressed the need for decentralization and people's communes stemming from the development of labour-intensive industries. His feeling that Chinese society was becoming more elitist led to the Cultural Revolution (1966-9), but he gradually retired from administrative politics in the early 1970s.

Marat, Jean Paul (1743-93) French revolutionary leader. He assimilated his radical politics from WILKES in England, practised medicine in Paris but in 1789, abandoned it for revolutionary journalism, calling for a dictatorship of the people in his newspaper *L'Ami du peuple*. In September 1792, as a member of the Vigilance Committee, he was responsible for the massacre of aristocrats and other suspected enemies of the Revolution imprisoned in Paris. He attached himself to the Jacobins and, with ROBESPIERRE and DANTON, attacked the more moderate Girondin party who were in a majority in the Convention in 1792 and the early part of 1793. He was assassinated, in his bath, by Charlotte CORDAY.

Marconi, Guglielmo (1874-1937) Italian inventor who developed commercial wireless telegraphy. He began radio experiments in 1894 and within four years, the first commercial wireless message and also the first news transmissions were made when the results of the Kingstown (now Dun Laoghaire) Regatta were transmitted to a Dublin newspaper. He carried out the first international (England-France) (1899) and intercontinental (Poldhee, Cornwall, to Newfoundland, 1901) transmissions. Marconi's invention, together with the development of radio valves, saw the birth of modern radio. In 1909, Marconi shared the Nobel Prize in Physics and in later years experimented with shortwaves for military applications and long-distance wireless communication.

Marcos, Ferdinand Edralin (born 1917) Filipino politician who served as a congressman from 1949 with the Liberal party, moved to the Nationalist party in 1964 and was elected President in 1965. He became the first President of the Philippines to serve a second term when he was re-elected in 1969. In 1971, after increased student unrest and guerrilla activity, he declared martial law and in 1973 established a new authoritarian constitution. Martial law was lifted in 1981, the year Marcos was re-elected.

Marcuse, Herbert (1898-1979) American sociological writer who was best known for his critique of modern western society in *One Dimensional Man* (1965). He claimed that the so-called 'free' institutions and 'democratic' processes were used to limit freedom and disguise exploitation. Within this totalitarianism, only those 'outside the productive process', minorities such as students, unemployed and coloured people, would have the revolutionary energy to change society.

Marey, Etienne-Jules (1830-1904) French physiologist, and inventor of the ciné camera, which used a ribbon of light-sensitive paper moving intermittently behind the camera lens. In 1888, Marey showed his first scientific films to the Académie des Sciences. It was the beginning of cinematography. He was also the first to use high-speed (1890) and time-lapse techniques respectively to slow down and speed up motion.

Marconi, in a 'Spy' cartoon. His experiments with radio were fundamental to the rapid expansion of radio telegraphy in the 20th century

Margaret of Denmark (1353-1412) Danish-born queen, who, for a time, united all Scandinavia. The deaths of her father (WALDEMAR IV of Denmark, 1376) and husband (Haakon VI of Norway, 1380) made Olaf, her son, the nominal King of Denmark, then of Norway. But it was Margaret who actually ruled, as regent, until Olaf died, then as undisputed queen. She became Queen of Sweden (1389) on the invitation of the Swedish nobles, whose king, Albert of Mecklenburg, she had helped to depose. The Union of Kalmar (1397) officially united the three kingdoms and made Margaret's grand-nephew, Eric of Pomerania, nominally their king while Margaret retained effective control. The union did not prosper, and collapsed by the 1430s.

Maria Theresa (1717-80) Archduchess of Austria, Queen of Hungary and Bohemia (1717-80) and, for 40 years, effective ruler of the Holy Roman Empire. She was made heir to the Empire by the Pragmatic Sanction of her father, the Emperor CHARLES VI, the last male Hapsburg heir. When, on his death (1740), Bavaria, France, Prussia and Spain tried to parcel her lands in the War of the Austrian Succession (1740-8), Maria Theresa rallied Hungary to her aid. She lost Silesia to Prussia, and later saw Austria humbled by the Seven Years' War (1756-63), but, with Prussia and Russia, she gained part of Poland (1772).

Marie Antoinette (1755-93) Queen of France (1774-92), daughter of MARIA THERESA, whose marriage to the Dauphin (afterwards LOUIS XVI) in 1770 was a pledge for the new Franco-Austrian alliance. Her political influence before 1789 has been much exaggerated, but her youthful irresponsibility and extravagance cost her popularity. Between 1789 and 1792 her influence was considerable and she was rightly identified with court resistance to the Revolution. Her support for foreign intervention in France helped to cause the downfall of the monarchy (September 1792) and her own execution.

Marini, Marino (1901-66) Italian sculptor, best known for his bronze figures of horses and nude riders, e.g. *Horse and Rider* (1949-50).

Mark, St (1st cent. AD) Cyprus-born Christian, apostle and evangelist, author of the second Gospel of the New Testament. The first of the three Synoptic Gospels to be written, it provided much of the material for those of MATTHEW and LUKE. The Egyptian Church claims Mark as its founder. His gospel presents an accurate picture of the life and ministry of CHRIST, told for the first time as a continuous narrative, so that Mark can be said to have created the gospel form. Its core is the Passion of Christ. Mark accompanied PAUL and Barnabas on their first missionary journey.

Marlborough, 1st Duke of see CHURCHILL, John

Marley, Bob (1945-81) Jamaican reggae musician whose immensely popular songs spread the teachings of Rastafarianism throughout the world. In 1964, Marley formed a group known as The Wailers. After signing up with a London-based record label, The Wailers gathered a large cult following in Europe, Africa and the Caribbean. By the mid-1970s Marley was a national hero and in 1976 an attempt was made on his life. He was awarded the International Peace Medal by the UN in 1978.

Marlowe, Christopher (1564-93) English dramatist, who wrote *Edward II* and *The Jew of Malta* and who first successfully used blank verse in English. In all his writings he was concerned with the problem of power and its effects. His first success – and possibly his first play – was an historical spectacle, *Tamburlaine the Great* (1587), a masterpiece of rhetorical poetry. The *Tragical History of Dr Faustus* is the first treatment in English and in verse of what was to become an archetypal theme of European drama. *Edward II*, a subtle study of power and homosexual love, is the first historical play of its kind in English theatre. *The Jew of Malta* is melodrama informed with cruel comedy. As a poet, Marlowe is best represented by his lyric 'The Passionate Shepherd' and by the unfinished 'Hero and Leander'. It is believed that he acted as a spy for Queen ELIZABETH.

Marquez, Gabriel Garcia (born 1928) Columbian writer most famous for his novel *One Hundred Years of Solitude* (1967), which has become one of the most popular books ever in the Spanish-speaking world. His other works include *The Autumn of the Patriarch* (1976) and *A Death Foretold* (1983). In 1978 he formed Habeas, a human rights organization. He fled to Mexico in 1981 and in 1982 he was awarded the Nobel Prize in Literature.

Marshall, Alfred (1842-1924) British economist of considerable influence who defined economics as 'the study of man in the ordinary business of life'. Marshall developed, in his *Principles of Economics*, a partial equilibrium analysis to demonstrate the importance of time in determining price, value and demand, relating the classical cost of production theory to that of JEVON's marginal utility.

Marshall, George Catlett (1880-1959) Director of the American war effort, who originated the Marshall Aid Plan. He was appointed Chief of Staff in 1939, and was responsible for the direction of American strategy throughout the Second World War and for US co-operation with the Allied armies. As TRUMAN's Secretary of State (1947-9), he evolved the Marshall Plan by which American money played a huge part in the post-war reconstruction of Europe. He won the Nobel Peace Prize in 1953.

Marshall, Thurgood (born 1908) American judge. He was chief counsel for the National Association for the Advancement of Coloured People (1938-61), when his argument against racial segregation in schools in the historic *Brown v Board of Education of Topeka* case led to Earl WARREN's Supreme Court ruling of 1954 that racial segregation in public schools was unconstitutional. He was the first black to be an Associate Justice of the Supreme Court (1967).

Marti, José (1853-95) Cuban national hero, revolutionary and poet, who led the struggle for independence from Spain, and was killed in the rising. His poetry is patriotic or lyric, his style modernistic and exotic, as in *Little Ishmael* (1882) and *Free Verse* (1913). His prose works revolutionized and enlivened Spanish prose style.

Martial (1st cent.) Spanish-born Roman epigrammatist, author of books of mottoes, *Xenia* and *Apophoreta*, and of 12 books of epigrams. His work is marked by his intense interest in his fellow human beings, which he expresses with keen observation and cutting realism. Many of his epigrams, usually in elegiac couplets in imitation of CATULLUS and OVID, mirror the life of his day. A satirist at heart, with strains of obsequiousness and gross obscenity, Martial was nevertheless a writer of great versatility.

Martin, Archer John Porter (born 1910) English biochemist, who, with Richard Laurence Millington Synge, in 1944 developed paper chromatography. Their discovery showed how complex mixtures such as protein molecules could be separated into their constituents (amino acids), which had been impractical by ordinary chemical methods. Martin and Synge jointly received the 1952 Nobel Prize for Chemistry for their invention of a technique which has made possible important biochemical discoveries.

Martin, Frank (1890-1974) Swiss composer whose works include the *Petite Symphonie Concertante* (1945) for harpsichord, harp, piano and double string orchestra, and the oratorio *Golgotha* (1948). He used a modified form of note-row technique by incorporating it into a conventional harmonic setting.

Martini, Simone (c. 1284-1344) Sienese painter who was, after GIOTTO, the most important Italian painter of his time. His early work is in DUCCIO's manner, but he became increasingly attracted to the courtly style of French Gothic art. His works are characterized by graceful, curvilinear outlines and a lyrical mood. He spent his later years at Avignon, where he is supposed to have painted a portrait of PETRARCH's 'platonic love', Laura.

Martinu, Bohuslav (1890-1959) Prolific Czechoslovak composer who began his professional life as a violinist. The style he adopted was Neo-classical, as shown by his *Concerto Grosso* (1938), and he did not attempt a symphony until he lived in America during the Second World War. The six symphonies that he wrote between 1942 and 1953 were among his best work, but the standard of his output was uneven.

Marvell, Andrew (1621-78) English poet and politician who is best remembered for his early verse 'To his Coy Mistress' and 'The Garden', which show the influence of DONNE. In 1657, Marvell became assistant to MILTON at the Latin Secretaryship to the Council of the Commonwealth and was later MP for Hull. He wrote several poems in praise of CROMWELL and, later, powerful satires, such as the *Last Instructions to a Painter* (1667), on CHARLES II's policies.

Marx, 'Groucho' (1895-1977) American vaudeville comedian and humorist, who, with his brothers Harpo and Chico, formed one of the most famous theatre and cinema comedy acts. The team, which originally included two other brothers, Zeppo and Gummo, achieved a huge success with a fast, wild and disruptive approach to comedy, and no institution was safe from their attacks.

Marx, Karl (1818-83) German philosopher and theorist of socialism, author of the revolutionary pamphlet *The Communist Manifesto* (1848), which he wrote with ENGELS shortly before the revolutions of 1848, and of *Das Kapital* (1867). The official doctrine of the Soviet Union is based on his ideas. Marx's theory, much influenced by Hegelian philosophy, turns the latter upside down and makes matter rather than spirit the primary stuff of the world. His social and political influence on the 20th century has been immense.

Mary I, Tudor (1516-58) Queen of England and Ireland (1553-8). The daughter of HENRY VIII and CATHERINE OF ARAGON, she was nicknamed 'Bloody Mary' for the brutality of the attempts to crush Protestantism during her reign. She succeeded her half-brother, Edward VI, after Lady Jane GREY's brief reign. Having reversed Edward's Protestant reforms, she married the Catholic PHILIP II of Spain and began a purge of those opposed to Catholicism, in which some 300 'heretics' were killed, including such leading churchmen as Thomas CRANMER, Hugh LATIMER and Nicholas RIDLEY. During Mary's reign, France seized Calais, England's last enclave on the mainland of Europe.

Mary Stuart, Queen of Scots (1542-87) Successor to her father James V as ruler of Scotland (1542-67), Queen of France (1559-60) as wife of Francis II, and next in line to the English throne after ELIZABETH I. Mary was brought up in France and widowed at 18. She returned to govern Scotland, which had become mainly Protestant, in 1661, and, as a convinced Catholic, tried to end Protestant persecution of those of her faith. She thus made powerful enemies, including Elizabeth I, John KNOX, and leading Scottish nobles. She married the Catholic Lord Darnley, but refused to secure the throne to him in his own right on the advice of her secretary, Rizzio. Darnley murdered Rizzio, and was himself mur-

Four of the Marx brothers—Groucho, Chico, Harpo and Zeppo—in one of their early Hollywood classics

dered, almost certainly by the 4th Earl of Bothwell, whom Mary then married. The marriage provoked revolt among the nobles and Mary was imprisoned and forced to abdicate (1567) in favour of her (and Darnley's) son James VI (JAMES I of England). She escaped to England, where Elizabeth had her imprisoned for 18 years, then beheaded.

Masaccio (1401-28) Florentine painter, who inherited and developed GIOTTO's realism and narrative power. Among his works is the fresco of the Trinity in Sta Maria Novella, Florence (1425-8), a work of monumental grandeur, revealing an unprecedented ability to use perspective for illusionistic effect. His best-known frescoes, such as *The Tribute Money*, are in the Brancacci Chapel of Sta Maria del Carmine, Florence (*c.* 1425-8), and contain figures of heroic proportions, whose dramatic gestures are in strong contrast to the more decorative style of painting then current in Florence. MICHELANGELO's early work reflects his study of these paintings.

Masaryk, Jan see MASARYK, Tomáš

Masaryk, Tomáš (1850-1937) Czechoslovak philosopher-statesman who created Czechoslovakia as a sovereign state. Masaryk, a professor of philosophy, sat in the Austrian parliament representing the Young Czech Party (1891-3) and the Czech Realist Party (1907-14), but he never thought of himself as representing only the Czechs; he was respected by Croats, Serbs and Slovenes as well. He fled to London at the outbreak of the First World War to preside over the Czech National Council, working to persuade Allied politicians and journalists to aid in the establishing of a Czechoslovak nation state. He went to Russia in 1917 to organize the Czech prisoners of war into a fighting Legion, and thence by way of Siberia to the US. There he won support for his cause from President WILSON when he received recognition in September 1918 as an Allied chief-of-state. He returned to Europe as President-elect and was in office until 1935, when he resigned for health reasons. His son Jan Masaryk, Czech Foreign Secretary when the Communists seized power in 1948, died in mysterious circumstances after a fall from a window.

Masefield, John (1878-1967) English poet and novelist, notable for fluent, narrative verse and vigorous prose, who became Poet Laureate in 1930. He is best known for his verse on the sea and the English countryside, although 'The Everlasting Mercy' (1911) shows an intimate knowledge of the harsh side of country life.

Maskelyne, Nevil (1732-1811) English astronomer, whose observations revolutionized navigation. A journey in 1761 to St Helena, where he was sent to observe the transit of Venus, aroused his interest in navigation. On the voyages out and back he used lunar distances to calculate longitude at sea, and on his return published *The British Mariner's Guide* (1763).

Mason, Charles (1730-87) English astronomer who, with the surveyor Jeremiah Dixon (1733-79), was engaged by the proprietors of Maryland and Pennsylvania to survey the boundary line between the two states, which was in dispute. The line, which became known as the Mason-Dixon line, was drawn along latitude 39°43′3″N and marked by milestones. It later came to represent a division between the slave states and free states of the US, and remains an arbitrary line dividing north from south.

Massenet, Jules Emile Frédéric (1842-1912) French composer of 25 operas, including *Manon* (1884) and *Thaïs* (1894). A number of his orchestral compositions are still performed and his *Don Quichote* (1910) was popularized by Chaliapin's singing of the title role. He also composed overtures, a piano concerto, incidental music to plays and many songs.

Massys, Quentin (c. 1464-1530) Flemish painter who was one of the first northern artists to visit Italy. The architectural details in his work are classical and his figures often recall those of LEONARDO. He produced religious pictures (the landscape backgrounds of which were sometimes possibly painted by Patenier), portraits (which influenced HOLBEIN) and genre studies.

Masters, Edgar Lee (1868-1950) American poet, who, like SANDBURG, spoke with the new, distinctive voice of the American mid-West. His major work is the *Spoon River Anthology* (1915).

Masters, William Howell (born 1915) American physician who, with his colleague (and later, wife) Virginia E. Johnson, made a pioneering physiological study of human sexual function, published in *Human Sexual Response* (1966). Masters and Johnson later applied their knowledge to the treatment of sexually dysfunctional couples and published *Human Sexual Inadequacy* (1970). *Commitment* (1975) and *Homosexuality in Perspective* (1979) are the products of later studies.

Mata Hari (1876-1917) Dutch courtesan and double agent shot by the French as a spy in the First

The Ocean Cradle

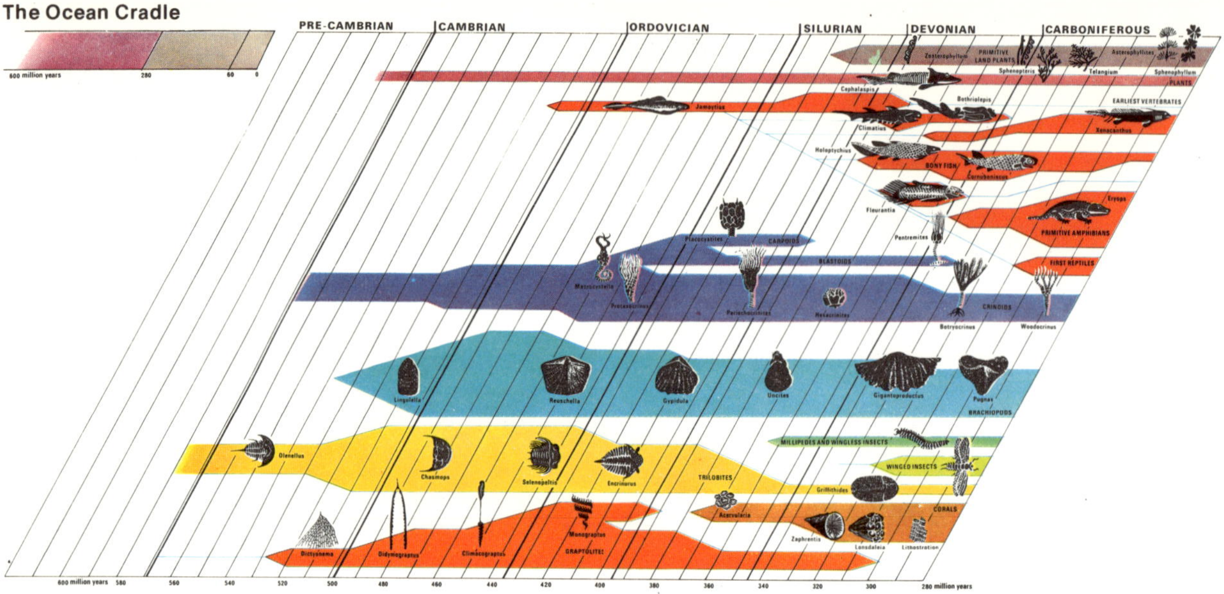

Advance to the Land

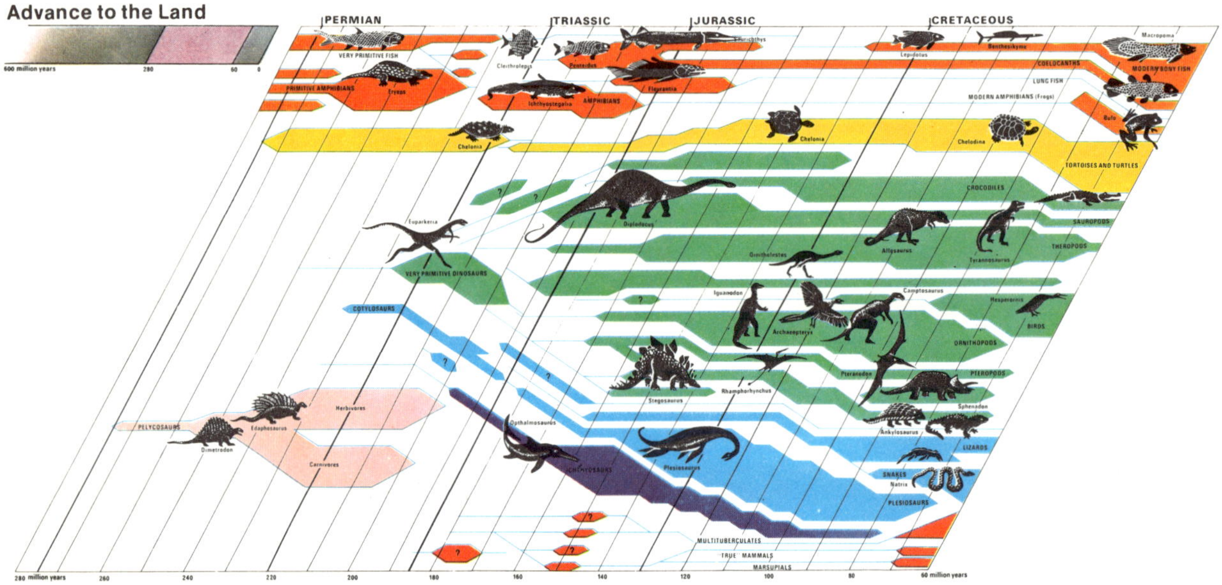

The Age of Mammals

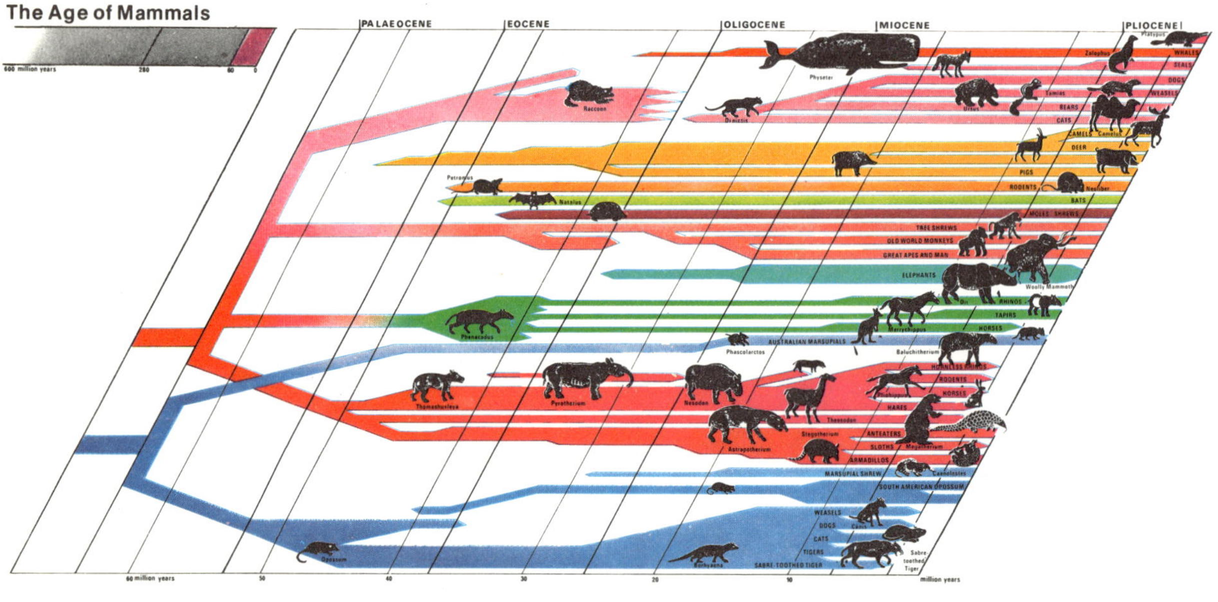

World War. Born Gertrud Zelle, she was the wife of a Dutch colonial officer named MacLeod, with whom she lived in Java until 1901. She deserted him and travelled to Europe, calling herself Mata Hari and claiming to be a former temple dancer of Javanese birth. She became a well-known demi-mondaine in Paris, distributing her favours freely while in the pay of both French and German intelligence services.

Successful courtesan, unsuccessful spy, Mata Hari was shot by a firing squad

Mather, Cotton (1663-1728) American author and Puritan minister. Mather wrote numerous books on diabolical possession and witchcraft and did much to create the hysterical atmosphere which led to the Salem witchcraft persecution of 1692, in which many innocent people unjustly perished.

Matisse, Henri (1869-1954) French artist, who asserted that colour in art should parallel light in nature. His use of complementary colours, working together in harmony, anticipated the work of the Futurists. Matisse began by studying and copying the works of the old masters and the Impressionists in the Louvre. He soon progressed from the obvious influence of BONNARD and VUILLARD, as seen in the painting *Dinner Table* (1897), and continued logically to the study of Neo-Impressionism and the works of GAUGUIN and CÉZANNE, after which he developed his own theories on the function of light and colour. In 1906, Matisse exhibited his first masterpiece, the large figurative work *Joy of Life*, and it was from this point on that colour took a leading place in his art. Matisse was regarded as the leader of the 'Fauves', an informal group of painters whose common technique of distortion and bright colour caused their work to be hung together, first in 1905.

These charts trace the story of evolution from the emergence of marine life in Pre-Cambrian times (600m years ago) to the Age of Mammals, the Pliocene era (10m years ago). Coloured bands outline the history of the main species. The Ordovician period (500m years ago) marks the appearance of vertebrates; by Silurian times (450m years ago) marine flora began to invade land and in the Devonian era (350m years ago) air-breathing creatures evolved. The Jurassic Period (c. 100m years ago) was the age of giant reptiles, lasting until the Palaeocene era (60m years ago) when mammals gained ascendancy. Leakey's *homo habilis* lived 1,780,000 years ago, but modern man is only 10,000 years old.

For further information, see the entry on Louis Leakey on page 150.

Matsuo Bashoh (1644-94) The most popular of all Japanese poets, Bashoh is notable for having brought the art of *haiku* writing to near perfection. Strongly influenced by Zen Buddhism, he rejuvenated the *haiku*, turning it into a medium capable of expressing profound thoughts and feelings, though he retained a lightness of style. From about 1680, he began to live as a recluse and to travel, at which time he began his great creative period, which produced his best-known work, *The Narrow Road of Oku*, in which the *haiku* are set in a prose narration.

Matteotti, Giacomo (1885-1924) Italian socialist deputy whose denunciation of Fascist atrocities led to his murder. Matteotti, revolted by MUSSOLINI's brutality towards his opponents, denounced Fascism in a book entitled *The Fascisti Exposed* and organized the opposition United Socialist Party. His murder (June 1924) led to widespread criticism of Mussolini's régime both abroad and in Italy, where a parliamentary crisis ensued when many non-Fascist members refused to attend the sessions. This weakened the Fascists for a time, but finally their secession served to consolidate Mussolini's position.

Matthew, St (1st cent. AD) Palestine-born Christian apostle and evangelist, author of the first Gospel of the New Testament. Based partly on the Gospel According to St Mark, it is the second of the three Synoptic Gospels and stresses the message and teachings of CHRIST. Presented in the form of ecclesiastical instructions, it has become the manual of conduct and discipline for the Church. Matthew was born Levi, a tax-collector for Herod the Tetrarch. He is thought to have been martyred 15 years after Christ was crucified.

Matthews, Sir Stanley (born 1915) English footballer, who made 56 international appearances. He played at club level till over 50 and is the only footballer to have been knighted for his services as a player.

Matthias Corvinus (1440-90) King of Hungary (1458-90), which he made the most powerful country in central Europe. A statesman, soldier and scholar, Matthias used lesser nobles to break the power of dissident rebellious lords, reformed laws, enriched the treasury by taxation and built a large standing army, the envy of Europe. It enabled him to repel his rival, the Emperor Frederick III, and to take Bohemia, Lusatia, Moravia, Silesia and Lower Austria.

Maugham, Somerset (1874-1965) English author of anti-romantic novels, short stories and plays, whose chief works include *Of Human Bondage* (1915) and *Cakes and Ale* (1930), a sardonic study of a literary man. His plays, the best known being *East of Suez* (1923), are still popular.

Maupassant, Guy de (1850-93) French novelist and author of some of the world's best-known short stories, notably *Boule de Suif* (1880) which made him immediately famous. Having learned his craft under FLAUBERT's guidance, Maupassant produced more than 300 *contes*, many of which (e.g. *Miss Harriet*) were masterpieces of their kind. He also wrote six novels, notably *Une Vie* (1883), *Bel-Ami* (1885) and *Pierre et Jean* (1888). His realistic and ironic tales, often set in his native Normandy, are told with great economy of style. As his health deteriorated, he developed an obsession with the macabre and the supernatural and later stories, like *Le Horla*, reflect these strange hallucinations. Disease and insanity ended his career.

Maupertius, Pierre de (1698-1759) French mathematician and astronomer, who is best known for his 'principle of least action', and for proving (1736) NEWTON's contention that the Earth is a sphere flattened at the poles. While at the Academy of Sciences in Berlin (1741-53), he developed his theory that all natural processes go on in such a way that a dynamic function called 'action' is a minimum.

Mauriac, François Charles (1885-1970) French Catholic novelist and author of poems, plays, biographies and literary criticism. His major novels, such as *A Kiss for the Leper* (1922), *Génétrix* (1923), *Thérèse Desqueyroux* (1927) and *The Knot of Vipers* (1932), are concerned with religious themes, particularly the problems of grace and redemption. These tense psychological dramas, smouldering behind the respectable façade of his native Bordeaux, established Mauriac as one of the masters of modern French prose. He was awarded a Nobel Prize in 1952.

Maurice of Nassau (1567-1625) Prince of Orange, who, after the assassination of his father, WILLIAM THE SILENT, successfully consolidated the position of the United Provinces. As Captain-General of the Dutch forces, he first checked Parma's advance, then (1590-1606) regained earlier losses. Maurice was one of the great military innovators of the age, adopting scientific methods of siege warfare, founding a school of engineers at Leyden, introducing the battalion of 550 men, and ensuring regular payment of troops. Though he did not favour an attack on the southern provinces, he only reluctantly accepted the Truce of 1609 with Spain. With the merchants of Amsterdam, Maurice shared an interest in Dutch expeditions to Brazil and the Far East.

Maurois, André (1885-1967) French biographer, novelist, essayist and critic, renowned for his studies of the English, including biographies of SHELLEY (*Ariel*, 1923), DISRAELI (1927) and Lord BYRON (1930). His ironical novels, *Les Silences de Colonel Bramble* (1918) and *Les Discours du Docteur O'Grady* (1922), amiable burlesques of the English character, were inspired by his experiences as an interpreter with the British Army during the First World War. His numerous publications include historical works on England (1937) and the US (1947). He was elected to the Académie Française in 1938.

Maxim, Sir Hiram Stevens (1840-1916) American-born engineer, whose most famous of many inventions, after he went to England (1881), was the first fully automatic machine gun (1883). This was an advance over GATLING's gun in that it used each bullet's recoil energy to eject the spent cartridge, insert the next round and fire it. The Maxim/Vickers gun was adopted by the British Army in 1889 and later used by every major power.

Maximilian (1832-67) Archduke of Austria and Emperor of Mexico. The younger brother of Emperor Francis Joseph, he was Governor of the Hapsburg imperial province of Lombardy-Venetia, which was 'liberated' by French and Piedmontese armies (1859). In 1863, NAPOLEON III, who was seeking to establish a 'Catholic Empire' under his domination, induced Maximilian to accept the crown of Mexico. Maximilian and his wife, Carlota, took their role seriously and adopted the last prince of the line of Montezuma as their heir, but when United States pressure forced Napoleon to withdraw his armies (1867), Maximilian was left at the mercy of the Mexican Republican forces under JUAREZ. Carlota went to Europe to beg for help, but was unsuccessful. Meanwhile Juarez's forces captured Maximilian, who was shot (June 1867).

Maximilian I (1459-1519) King of Germany (1486-1519) and Holy Roman Emperor (1493-1519), who began the growth of the dynastic empire of the Hapsburgs. His son Philip became Philip I of Spain, whose sons, CHARLES V and FERDINAND I, were the Holy Roman Emperors under whom the Hapsburg family reached its peak of imperial power. Maximilian gave little attention to governing his lands, except to raise money, and devoted himself to unrealistic plans and warfare for personal aggrandizement, which won him the title 'the Last of the Knights'.

Maxwell, James Clerk (1831-79) Scottish scientist and leading 19th-century theoretical physicist who worked out the complete electromagnetic theory of light based upon the ideas of FARADAY. His *Treatise on Electricity and Magnetism* (1873) is a landmark in the history of science. Like Faraday, Maxwell was opposed to the idea of action at a distance and adopted the notion of an all-pervading ether (originally introduced by HUYGENS in his wave theory of light) as the carrier of electromagnetic waves. Noticing that the speed of electric current in wires is roughly the same as that of light in empty space, he suggested that light is an electromagnetic vibration, a result later confirmed experimentally by HERTZ. The ether doctrine led to difficulties and became suspect after the work of MICHELSON and Morley, who failed to detect an effect predicted by the theory. Maxwell contributed also to other fields: colour sensation, Saturn's rings and, arising from this, the kinetic theory of gases.

Mayakovsky, Vladimir (1893-1930) Russian dramatist and poet, the first notable Soviet Communist playwright. *Mystery-Bouffe*, the first post-Revolutionary play, produced in Moscow in 1918, is a high-spirited drama about Communism spreading all over the world. *The Bed Bug* (1929) is a satire showing a bourgeois and a bed bug as anachronisms in a Communist world. *The Bath House* (1930) satirizes the persistence of bourgeois behaviour in Soviet society.

Maybach, Wilhelm (1847-1929) German engineer, who associated with DAIMLER in the manufacture of high-speed internal combustion engines. Maybach was associated with the early development of motor-cycles and four-wheeled cars and was responsible for several important technical innovations, notably the float-feed carburettor (1893). Maybach designed the first Mercedes car (1901). In 1907, he left the Company to set up a factory to manufacture engines for ZEPPELIN's airships.

Mayer, Louis B. (1885-1957) American film producer and founder of Metro Pictures Corp. and Louis B. Mayer Pictures Corp., which merged with Goldwyn Co. to become Metro-Goldwyn-Mayer in 1924. MGM studios developed the star system and discovered such film stars as Cary Grant, Greta Garbo and Rudolf Valentino.

Mayo, William James (1861-1939) American surgeon who, with his brother Charles MAYO (1865-1939) and his father William MAYO (1819-1911), both of them also surgeons, founded the Mayo Clinic at St Mary's Hospital, Rochester, Minnesota. William Mayo was a gastric surgeon specializing in cancer and gallstones, while his brother performed many operations for goitre.

Mazarin, Jules (1602-61) Italian-born French cardinal and statesman, one of the ministers who made LOUIS XIV all-powerful, and France a major European power. After several years as a papal diplomat, Mazarin entered the service of RICHELIEU, became a naturalized French citizen in 1639, a cardinal in 1641 and succeeded Richelieu as chief minister of France in 1642. His prime interest was foreign affairs, in which he continued Richelieu's policies, persisting successfully with the 30 Years' War. He sought to humiliate the Hapsburgs in Austria and Spain and made counterbalancing alliances with their enemies. Exiled for a time as a result of his domestic policies, Mazarin recovered his position and thereafter curbed the nobles' surviving feudal rights, continued to destroy their castles, and built the crown into the undisputed ruling instrument of France.

Mazzini, Giuseppe (1805-72) Italian patriot and revolutionary. In his twenties, he joined the Carbonari, a political secret society formed in 1815 to unite Italy as a republic. In 1831 he formed the 'Young Italy' movement and, becoming the apostle of international brotherhood, expanded it into a 'Young Europe' movement. In the revolutionary atmosphere of 1848, Mazzini's forces liberated Milan and set up a Roman republic, whose military force was commanded by GARIBALDI. As a fervent republican, Mazzini did not approve of the Kingdom of Italy created by CAVOUR and Garibaldi under the Piedmontese crown, and spent his later years in exile, though he sometimes visited Italy secretly.

Mazzola, Francesco see PARMIGIANINO

McAdam, John Loudon (1756-1836) Scottish inventor who gave his name to the surfacing of roads with granite or other durable stone, broken small enough to make a hard, smooth, water-resistant surface suitable for traffic. By the end of the 19th century, most of Europe's main roads were built according to his methods, while the word 'macadamize' is still used to describe aspects of road construction. McAdam, who spent several years in the US, was appointed Surveyor-General of London Metropolitan roads in 1827.

McCarthy, Joseph (1909-57) American senator who, from 1950-4, acquired world-wide notoriety by promoting anti-Communist 'witch-hunts'. In public sessions of Senate sub-committees he made accusations which were frequently quite without substance. He was protected from retaliatory legal action, however, by claiming Congressional privilege. His conduct eventually became so scandalous, he even began making personal attacks on Presidents EISENHOWER and TRUMAN and involved the ruin of so many careers, that in 1954 the Democrat-controlled Senate passed a vote of censure on him for bringing their House into dishonour and disrepute.

McCarthy, Mary (born 1912) American author most famous for her novels *Charmed Lives* (1955), *The Group* (1963) and *Cannibals and Missionaries* (1980). She also worked for many years as a drama critic and wrote non-fiction including *Venice Observed* (1956), *Memories of a Catholic Girlhood* (1957) and *Ideas and the Novel* (1980).

McClintock, Barbara (born 1902) American geneticist and winner of the Nobel Prize for Medicine. McClintock started her work in the field of genetics in the 1930s and became President of the Genetics Society of America in 1944. After WATSON and CRICK's discovery of DNA, McClintock's theories of genetic transposition were accepted (having been ignored for the previous two decades) and she was lauded as a visionary. The value of her work was fully recognized in 1983 when she won a Nobel Prize.

McCormack, John (1884-1948) Irish tenor whose 'golden voice' brought him great success and made him a popular legend. Like CARUSO, he lives on through the gramophone. He became an American citizen in 1917 and was raised to the papal peerage 11 years later.

McCormick, Cyrus Hall (1809-1884) American agricultural engineer who patented a harvester (1833) after others had been only moderately successful. The commercial exploitation of McCormick's machines was caused by labour shortages during the American Civil War and the resulting need for mechanization. By product improvement and better marketing than his rivals, McCormick's firm emerged as the principal American manufacturer. His twine binder and side-rake revolutionized harvesting.

McCullers, Carson (1917-67) American novelist, who presents a world of violence, pain and grief, many of its inhabitants isolated, outcast and suffering from physical or psychological disability. *The Heart is a Lonely Hunter* (1940) explores the situation of a lonely deaf-mute; *Member of the Wedding* (1946) portrays the emotional problems of a maturing adolescent; *The Ballad of the Sad Café* (1951), a collection of stories, provides an introduction to her fictional world, based on a reality of ugliness and conflict.

McEnroe, John Patrick Jnr (born 1959) An American professional tennis player since 1978, McEnroe has won many championships and is an aggressive competitor, known for losing his temper on court.

McGregor, William (1847-1911) British founder of the Association Football League. In 1888, his proposal that leading football clubs should combine to form a league and play one another in a sequence of home and away matches in an annual championship was accepted. By the addition of more clubs and the formation of first, second and third league divisions, the Football League became the biggest and most influential of all such bodies.

McKinley, William (1843-1901) American President, assassinated during his second term of office, who expanded US territory by annexing Havana, the Philippines, Puerto Rico and Guam following the Spanish-American War of 1898. He began his career as a lawyer and in the Civil War served in the Union Army. As a Republican Congressman, he advocated a high tariff policy and was elected President in 1896 as a result of a campaign managed for him by major business interests. In office, he raised US tariffs to the highest level. He was hustled into the Spanish-American war by a popular campaign (a mixture of expansionism and a real resentment of Spanish repression in Cuba). Public indignation reached its peak with the sinking of the US battleship *Maine* in Havana harbour (February 1898). In 1900, he was elected President for a second term but was assassinated by an anarchist a year later.

McLuhan, (Herbert) Marshall (1911-80) Canadian educator who virtually established a new academic field with his theories about the impact of the media on our perceptions. His works include *Understanding Media* (1964) and *The Medium is the Message* (1967). He served as director (1963-1980) of the Centre for Culture and Technology at the University of Toronto.

McMillan, Edwin Mattison (born 1907) American physicist who discovered the first transuranium elements (1940). During his study of the nuclear fission of uranium he detected the presence of a radioactive element heavier than uranium. McMillan called it neptunium, and later he discovered another, heavier element, which he named plutonium. In 1951 he shared the Nobel Prize for Chemistry with Glenn Seaborg. While working with E. O. Lawrance on the cyclotron he developed the synchrocyclotron for which he was awarded a share in the 1963 Atoms for Peace prize.

McNamara, Robert Strange (born 1916) American Secretary of Defence during the escalation of the Vietnam war. The first man outside the Ford family to become president of the Ford Motor Company, he was appointed Secretary of Defence by KENNEDY in 1961, a post he retained for seven years. McNamara subjected the Pentagon to increased cost-effectiveness, streamlined its administration and brought a semblance of unity to the various defence arms. He resigned in 1968 to become President of the World Bank, a position he held until 1981.

Mead, Margaret (1901-78) American anthropologist, who specialized in studying the relationship between personality and culture. Her first field-work resulted in *Coming of Age in Samoa* (1928), which showed that young Samoans, reared in a different family structure, do not suffer the adolescent disturbances which Western civilization regards as 'natural'. Later work in New Guinea and Bali increased her interest in the effect of child-rearing practices on adolescent and sexual behaviour, and in *Sex and Temperament in Three Primitive Societies* (1935) significant differences in these contrasted societies are shown to correlate with differences in temperament. Among her later works were *Male and Female* (1949), *Childhood in Contemporary Societies* (1955) and *Culture and Commitment* (1970). From 1926 to 1969, she served as curator of Ethnology at the American Museum of Natural History.

Medici, Catherine de (1519-89) Queen of France from 1547 and its virtual ruler from 1560-74, who, to keep her family in power, provoked continual religious wars and was responsible for the St Bartholomew's Day Massacre of Huguenots (1572). She played no part in politics until her husband, HENRY II, died. During the reigns of her three sons, Francis II (1559), Charles IX (1560-74) and Henry III (1574-89), she favoured Catholics and Protestants in turn to prevent the leading families of either faction presenting a threat to royal power.

Medici, Cosimo de (1389-1464) Florentine banker, Renaissance patron, and founder of a dynasty which ruled Tuscany until 1737. Cosimo seized power in 1434 and was virtual ruler of the State for 30 years, though he retained republican forms of government and was content to be called 'pater patriae'. He helped to make Florence the leader of Renaissance Italy in the arts and learning and was patron of men like ALBERTI, BRUNELLESCHI, GHIBERTI and DONATELLO. He sponsored the first public library in Florence, founded the Platonic Academy for the encouragement of Greek studies, and collected codices and books. The source of Cosimo's great wealth was the Medici bank, which handled the papal finances.

Medici, Lorenzo de (1449-92) Virtual dictator of Florence, known as 'The Magnificent', he wielded absolute, tyrannical power through a puppet council. Planning to unite Rome and Florence, Lorenzo schooled the future Medici popes, Leo X and CLEMENT VII, and kept peace among rival Italian states by clever diplomacy. Under Lorenzo, Florentines of all classes shared in a prosperity, based on a progressive approach to trade and industry, unrivalled in western Europe. He financed Renaissance arts and was himself a fine poet.

Mège-Mouriès, Hippolyte (1817-80) French chemist and inventor who developed an economic method for the production of an acceptable substitute for butter. It became known as margarine on account of its pearly texture (from the Latin, 'margita', a pearl). Margarine was soon manufactured widely, although it was banned for a long time by large scale butter producers. Later manufacturers substituted cheaper vegetable oils for the costly animal fats.

Mehemet Ali (1769-1849) Founder of the dynasty which ruled Egypt from 1841-1952. An Albanian, he became a soldier for the Ottoman Empire fighting against the French in Egypt in 1799. In 1805, he was made Governor of Egypt by the Turks, and then given independent authority. For helping Turkey in the Greek War of Independence (1824-7), he was made governor of Crete, but his ambitions were still not satisfied and in 1832 he attacked the Turkish Empire, and annexed Syria and Adana. Following the war of 1839-41 he was forced by the major European powers, and Britain in particular, to abandon these territories but was compensated by recognition as hereditary ruler of Egypt. A council of regency governed Egypt during the last two years of his life when he became mentally deranged.

Meikle, Andrew (1719-1811) Scottish agricultural engineer and developer, in 1786, of the first successful threshing machine, embodying the basic principle of the modern thresher, by which the grain was removed by rubbing the corn between a rotating drum and a concave metal sheet.

Meir, Golda (1898-1978) Russian-born Prime Minister of Israel. Having grown up in America, she settled in Palestine in 1921, and increasingly devoted herself to the Jewish community there, becoming a founder member of the Mapai (Labour) Party, and later playing a prominent part in the struggle to establish a Jewish state. Having been Minister of Labour for seven years (1949-56) and Foreign Minister for ten (1956-66), she became Prime Minister in 1969, on the death of ESHKOL. She resigned in 1974 after criticisrn over lack of preparedness at the outbreak of the 1973 Arab-Israeli war. She continued to play a significant role in politics until her death.

Meitner, Lise (1878-1968) Austro-Swedish physicist who worked closely with Otto HAHN in the discovery of nuclear fission. In the 1930s, Hahn and Meitner studied the effect of bombarding uranium with neutrons and established that uranium nuclei were splitting up into the nuclei of lighter elements.

Melbourne, William Lamb, 2nd Viscount (1779-1848) English statesman and mentor of Queen VICTORIA during her early years on the throne. At first a Whig MP, he lost his seat (1812) because of his support for Catholic emancipation. He became a follower of CANNING and served under him as Secretary for Ireland (1827), a post which he continued to hold under Goderich and WELLINGTON. His loyalty to Canningite principles forced him to resign in 1828 and, after refusing overtures to rejoin the Wellington ministry, he reverted to the Whigs and took office as Home Secretary under GREY in 1830. He incurred severe criticism for his uncompromising attitude towards agricultural unrest in southern England and was Prime Minister for a brief period in 1834 during the episode of the Tolpuddle martyrs. He was again Prime Minister from 1835-41, during which time he became the close and trusted adviser of Victoria after her accession in 1837, and was virtually her private secretary until her marriage to the Prince Consort in 1840.

Melville, Herman (1819-91) American poet and novelist, who wrote the huge symbolic novel

Moby Dick (1851). In seas and ships, far from the parochial subjects of American writing to this date, Melville discovered a metaphor for the strangeness and intractability of life. He spent his early years on whalers and warships and used the experience to write, producing seven works in six years. *Billy Budd* was later used by BRITTEN as the subject of an opera.

Memling, Hans (c. 1430-94) German-born painter who is one of the best-known artists of the early Netherlandish school. His religious paintings are notable for their atmosphere of calm devotion and the precise reproduction of precious materials, though they add little to the inspiration taken from his master, Rogier van der WEYDEN.

Menander (c. 342-291 BC) Greek dramatist, the outstanding writer in the New Comedy form, whose works formed the basis of the Roman comedies of PLAUTUS and Terence and stand as forerunners of all European comedy. Recent discoveries have produced one almost complete play, the *Dyscolus*, and large parts of three others, *Samia*, *Aspis* and *Sicyonius*. Considerable sections also survive of *Epitrepontes* and *Perikeiromene*, which were reconstructed by Sir Gilbert Murray.

Mencken, Henry Louis (1880-1956) American editor and satirist whose caustic wit made him a national figure. Editor and writer for four Baltimore newspapers, Mencken was known for his investigations of American linguistics. In *Prejudices* (1919-27) he coined characteristic maxims like, 'It is a sin to believe evil of others, but it is seldom a mistake.'

Mendel, Gregor (1822-84) Austrian monk of the Augustinian order, who discovered the fundamental principle of heredity which initiated the rise of modern genetics. By crossing certain varieties of garden peas he recognized that various characteristics depend on certain basic units (now called genes) that exist in either dominant or recessive form.

Mendeleyev, Dmitri (1834-1907) Russian chemist who devised the periodic table of chemical elements. By arranging the elements in order of increasing atomic weight, he was able to explain certain chemical similarities and to predict the properties of hitherto unknown elements from the gaps in the table. The table also suggested errors in some of the accepted values of atomic weights, and this too was confirmed by experiments. The periodic law put the whole of chemistry on a new rational basis.

Mendelsohn, Erich (1887-1953) German architect. An exponent of Expressionist architecture, Mendelsohn developed a sculptural feeling for fluid forms in such early works as the Einstein Tower at Neubabelsberg near Berlin of 1919-21. He later rejected this sculptural plasticity to produce buildings in a more direct line of descent from the industrialist architects BEHRENS and Poelzig. In the 1930s he settled in England but later moved on to work in Israel and the United States of America.

Mendelssohn Bartholdy, Felix (1809-47) German Romantic classical composer. A musical child prodigy, Mendelssohn was 17 when he wrote his *Midsummer Night's Dream* overture (the rest of the incidental music, which includes the 'Wedding March', was written later). During his relatively short creative life, he also composed the *Hebrides* overture and the *Scottish Symphony*, the *Italian Symphony* and the oratorio *Elijah*, first performed in Birmingham, England (1846), and for long a favourite with choral societies. The qualities of 'prettiness' in Mendelssohn's music led to his fashionable devaluation in the 20th century, but in pure musical terms his *String Quartet in F Minor* is probably the only one from the 19th century to rank with BEETHOVEN'S quartets. Mendelssohn was also a notable conductor and head of the Leipzig Conservatory. We are in his debt for the rediscovery of the music of Johann Sebastian BACH after nearly a century of neglect.

Mendoza, Pedro de (c. 1487-1537) Spanish soldier and explorer who founded Buenos Aires (1536), which later had to be abandoned because of disease, starvation and Indian attacks. He also founded Asunción, in Paraguay.

Menotti, Gian-Carlo (born 1911) American operatic composer and librettist of *The Medium* (1946), *The Telephone* (1947), *The Consul* (1950) and (for television) *Amahl and the Night Visitors* (1951). *The Consul* in particular, a contemporary fable of bureaucracy and totalitarianism, has caught the public imagination.

Menuhin, Yehudi (born 1916) American violinist and conductor who, as a child prodigy, gave his first concert at the age of seven. Regarded as one of America's leading musicians, he has toured the world, organized festivals and recorded extensively.

Menzies, Sir Robert (1894-1978) Prime Minister of Australia for 19 years in all. He entered the Victorian parliament in 1928. He was Prime Minister during the early years of the Second World War and also held the portfolios for trade and customs, treasury, munitions, co-ordination and defence. From 1943-9 he was the leader of the opposition and from 1949-66 again Prime Minister, until he retired from active politics.

Mercator, Gerhardus (1512-94) Flemish cartographer who developed the first modern type of map projection. He worked as cartographer to the Emperor CHARLES V and as cosmographer to the Duke of Jülich and Cleves (from 1559). In 1569 he produced the first nautical chart to use the Mercator projection (of which he was not the inventor). By showing lines of longitude (meridians) and latitude (parallels) as parallel lines intersecting at right angles, the projection allows seamen to draw a compass course on the chart as a straight line, and meteorologists to show true wind directions. The projection's main disadvantage is its magnification of polar areas. Mercator also popularized the name *atlas* for a bound collection of maps, by prefacing such a collection with an illustration of the Titan Atlas supporting a globe.

Gerhardus Mercator
first of the modern mapmakers

Meredith, George (1828-1909) English novelist and poet, a detached observer, who wrote with elegance and irony on human conflicts. His early *Shaving of Shagpat* (1856) was a fantasy in the manner of PEACOCK, his father-in-law. His later novels, leading up to *The Egoist* (1879), deal with social and moral conflicts set in ordinary surroundings. His poetry complements his fiction: *Modern Love* (1862), based on his first marriage, takes a bleak view of human relations. He worked for magazines, and was a friend of SWINBURNE and ROSSETTI.

Mergenthaler, Ottmar (1854-99) German-born American inventor of the first Linotype setting machine. In 1884 he patented his machine for setting solid lines of type, now used by many newspapers. The next year the machine was improved by a device which automatically justified the type, i.e. it ranged to a regular margin at both ends of the lines.

Mérimée, Prosper (1803-70) French author, and master of the novella, or long short-story; also a novelist, dramatist, essayist, historian and archaeologist. He is now remembered chiefly as the author of *Carmen* (1845), the source of BIZET's opera, and other fine stories, including *Mattéo Falcone* and *La Vénus d'Ille*. Objectivity, realism, exotic themes, an ironic humour and a terse style are characteristic of his writing. His translations from the works of PUSHKIN, GOGOL and TURGENEV first introduced Russian literature to France.

Mesmer, Franz (1734-1815) Austrian physician who claimed to be able to heal the sick by 'animal magnetism', later known as *mesmerism*. At his public demonstrations, many patients fell into hypnotic trances and convulsions. In 1784, a commission of scientists denounced Mesmer as a charlatan, and mesmerism fell into disrepute until its respectability as a form of treatment for nervous disorders was established by the English physician, James Braid.

Messerschmitt, Willi (1898-1978) German aircraft designer and industrialist, who produced many Luftwaffe aircraft (including the Me 262, the first jet aircraft to enter military service) during the Second World War. In the 1950s he helped revive the Lufthansa airline.

Messiaen, Olivier (born 1908) French composer and organist and a strongly individual voice in modern French music. Organist at the Church of La Trinité, Paris, since 1931, Messiaen's Catholicism has made his music sacred in the broadest sense, incorporating elements such as Hindu rhythm and birdsong to make a mystic's vision of creation. His works include the seven *Visions of the Amen* (1943) for two pianos, and the *Turangalila Symphony* (1948), with its vast orchestra and scoring for exotic percussion. He ranks with WEBERN as an influence on such younger European composers as BOULEZ and STOCKHAUSEN.

Messier, Charles-Joseph (1730-1817) French astronomer, who discovered 21 comets and gave his name to the 'Messier numbers' by which nebulae are identified. Nicknamed the 'comet ferret' by LOUIS XV, he observed the return of HALLEY's Comet in 1758. In 1771 he published his first catalogue of nebulae to aid his search for comets, giving them the numbers by which many are still known today.

Metsu, Gabriel (c. 1630-67) Dutch painter of genre scenes and interiors whose early religious work was influenced by STEEN and REMBRANDT. His lively depiction of outdoor scenes of the market-place and tavern and his ability to capture an expression reflects the work of his contemporary Frans HALS.

Metternich, Klemens (1773-1859) Austrian statesman, who presided over the Congress of Vienna and gave his name to the diplomatic system which controlled inter-European relations for 30 years. He became Austria's Foreign Minister in 1809 and Chancellor in 1821, positions which he held until driven into exile in the European revolutions of 1848. His aim was to maintain aristocratic government in Europe, to keep the rising radical middle-class from acquiring political power, and to keep the peace by adjusting differences at periodical congresses of the powers.

Meyer, Viktor (1848-97) German chemist who devised a method of measuring the density (mass per unit volume) of gases and vapours. His method is still widely used.

Meyerhold, Vsevolod (1874-c. 1940) Russian actor-director, who was the first great experimentalist of early Soviet theatre. He was a member of the Moscow Art Theatre (1898), toured Russia with his own Society of the New Drama, ran STANISLAVSKY's experimental theatre studio, introduced Gordon CRAIG's ideas to Russia while directing Vera Komisarjevskaya's company and directed at the Imperial Theatre. After the Revolution, he staged some *avant-garde* productions of MAYAKOVSKY's works.

Michael (1596-1645) First Romanov Tsar of Russia (1613-45). He was dominated for years by his patriot father Patriarch Philaret, who continued GODUNOV's measures to end national chaos by stopping tax-paying peasants leaving the land to become nomadic robbers, and introducing proportional taxation for formerly privileged classes.

Michelangelo, Buonarroti (1475-1564) Italian painter, architect, sculptor and poet and one of the most important figures of the Renaissance. His most famous work is the ceiling of the Sistine Chapel in the Vatican (1508-12), consisting mainly of a series of scenes from the Act of Creation to the Drunkenness of Noah, divided by painted architecture and flanked by nude youths with, below, prophets and sybils. Together with RAPHAEL's tapestry designs for the Sistine Chapel the ceiling's exaltation of the beauty of the human figure in motion has probably had more influence than any other work of art. In 1536 Michelangelo began his epic *Last Judgement* on the altar wall of the Sistine Chapel and later he painted the *Conversion of Saul* and the *Crucifixion of Peter* in the adjoining Capella Paolina (1542-50). His sculpture includes the *Fight between the Lapiths and Centaurs*, *Bacchus* (1496), *Pieta* (1498) and the famous *David* (1504).

Michelson, Albert Abraham (1852-1931) American physicist, of German extraction, who is mainly remembered for his work on the velocity of light. Using his interferometer (invented in 1881), he and Edward W. Morley showed in 1887 that the speed of light in a vacuum is the same in all inertial reference systems (co-ordinate systems moving at constant velocity relative to each other). It had been held since the days of HUYGENS that light travels through a stationary substance filling the whole of space (the so-called *ether*), but Michelson and Morley's experiments proved that there was no such thing. This led directly to the development of the special relativity theory by LORENTZ and EINSTEIN. In 1907 Michelson became the first American to win a Nobel Prize for Physics.

Michelin, André (1853-1931) French industrialist, who, with his brother Edouard, was the first to manufacture rubber tyres (1895).

Michelozzo Di Bartolommeo (1396-1472) Italian sculptor and architect, who was a contemporary and acquaintance of many early Renaissance artists in Florence, and who worked as a sculptor under both GHIBERTI and DONATELLO. He built an imposing and massive palace for the Medici in Florence (Palazzo Medici Riccardi) which influenced the style of many Italian Renaissance palaces. His ecclesiastical architecture shows great inventiveness and sensitivity and a devout respect for the classical past.

Middleton Murry, Katherine see MANSFIELD, Katherine

Mies, van der Rohe, Ludwig (1886-1969) German architect and designer of skyscrapers who, like LE CORBUSIER, studied under BEHRENS and subsequently became one of the most influential pioneers of modern 20th-century architecture. The glass-walled skyscrapers he designed after the First World War were the forerunners of buildings that have now become a predominant feature of city life, and preoccupied him in later years. The influence of the Dutch group known as De Stijl (literally 'The Style') in the 1920s, coupled with a use of rich materials and unadorned surfaces, was first seen in his German Pavilion for the Barcelona Exhibition of 1929, and subsequently in the Tugendhat House at Brno in Czechoslovakia. At about this time he was appointed director of the Bauhaus by the absent GROPIUS and he remained in this position until the school was closed (1933) by the Nazis. Shortly before the Second World War Mies moved to Chicago, where he designed the entire campus of the Illinois Institute of Technology, work in which he was involved for many years. Later office block projects in the United States included the Seagram building in New York, whilst his domestic architecture was exemplified by the translucent Farnsworth House in Illinois.

Milhaud, Darius (1892-1974) French composer who has synthesized the folk-music of his native Provence with that of Brazil. Milhaud, despite years of illness, is among the most prolific modern composers. His ballet *La Création du Monde* (1923) was the first work to make genuine creative use of jazz in a symphonic score. He collaborated with CLAUDEL on operas such as *Christopher Columbus* (1930). He was for a time a member of 'Les Six'. He also composed concertos, chamber music and religious pieces.

Mill, John Stuart (1806-73) British philosopher and economist, author of *Principles of Political Economy* (1848), one of the most important 19th-century economic texts. A liberal and originally a disciple of BENTHAM, he pursued the Utilitarian doctrine of 'greatest happiness' as an end to be achieved through legislation.

Millais, Sir John (1829-96) English painter, who co-founded with HUNT and ROSSETTI the Pre-Raphaelite Brotherhood (1848). He was a child prodigy, and his early Pre-Raphaelite pictures, e.g. *Christ in the House of His Parents* (1850), combine technical virtuosity with edifying subject matter. Later works, however, pandered increasingly to the Victorian taste for sentiment which, though held in check in *The Blind Girl* (1856) by his pictorial flair, is clearly apparent in portraits of children, one of which, *Bubbles* (1886), achieved fame as a soap advertisement.

Millay, Edna St Vincent (1892-1950) American poet, who was popular in the 1920s. Her mastery of the sonnet form can be seen in 'The Harp Weaver and Other Poems' (1923) and 'Collected Sonnets' (1941).

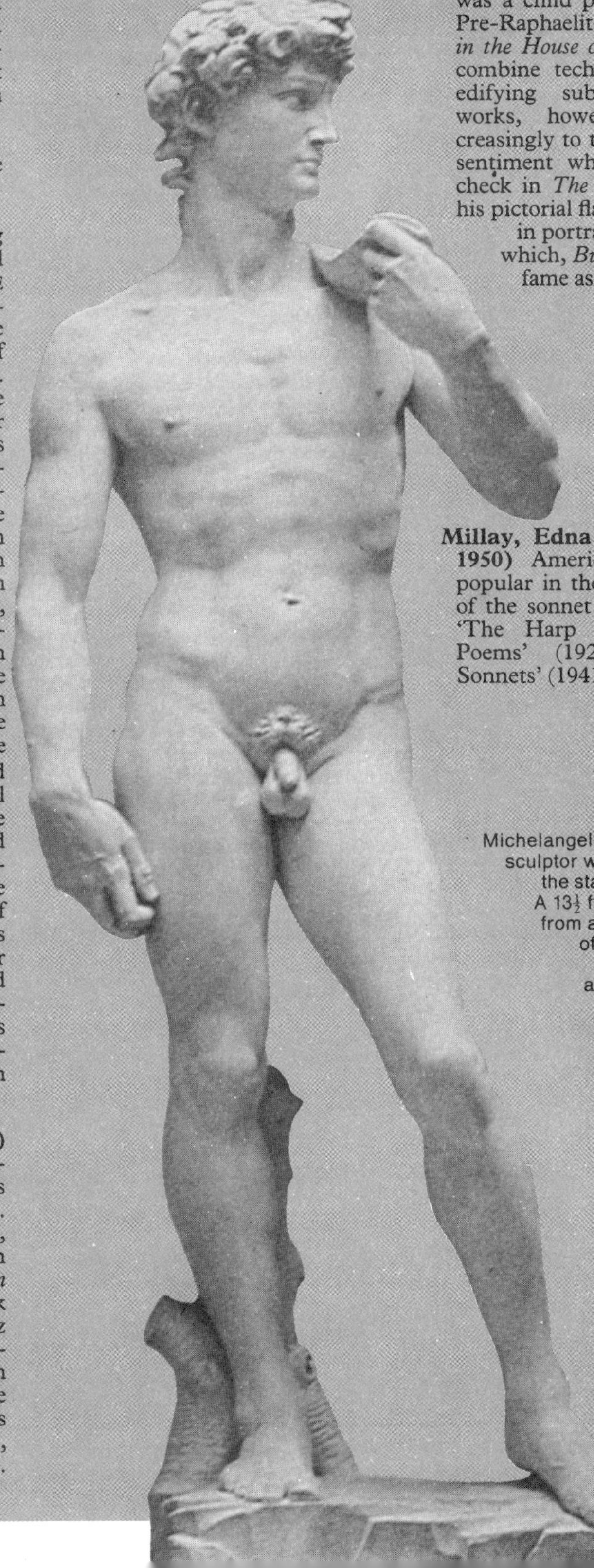

Michelangelo was already a famous sculptor when, aged 26, he began the statue of the young David. A 13½ ft colossus it was carved from a single, imperfect block of marble, its outstanding vitality the result of the artist's painstaking study of the human body

Miller, Arthur (born 1915) American dramatist, author of *Death of a Salesman* (1948). His first success was *All My Sons* (1947), a denunciation of war-profiteering. *The Crucible* (1953), ostensibly about 17th-century witch-hunting in Salem, exposed the American Senator MCCARTHY's anti-Communist 'witch-hunt' of the 1950s. In *A View from the Bridge* (1955) his characters are forced to face the truth about themselves, a theme developed in Miller's later plays. More recent plays include *The Price* (1968) and *The American Clock* (1980). He also wrote the screenplay for the film *The Misfits* (1961).

Miller, Henry (1891-1980) American writer of energetic, Rabelaisian novels such as *Tropic of Cancer* (1934). Like much of Miller's fiction, *Cancer* is written in the first person, a semi-autobiographical novel based upon his life in Paris as a struggling artist. A prolific writer, Miller's notoriety arose from his uninhibited use of sexual anecdotes in his novels; his use of obscene words was revolutionary in the 1930s and his work was banned in the United States until 1961. *Tropic of Capricorn* (1939) is a complementary volume about his early life, thoughts and adventures in New York. Between 1945 and 1960 he produced an ambitious trilogy *The Rosy Crucifixion (Sexus* (1945), *Plexus* (1949) and *Nexus* (1960)). His last published book was written in admiration of D. H. Lawrence, *The World of Lawrence* (1980).

Miller, Stanley (1930-73) American biochemist who first synthesized amino acids, a basic constituent of living matter, in the laboratory. He used his discovery to demonstrate that the atmosphere and oceans of Earth before life evolved were very different in composition from today.

Millikan, Robert Andrews (1868-1953) American physicist who determined the charge on the electron. In the early 1900s, he studied the effect of an electric field on charged droplets of oil falling freely under gravity. By 1912, he had discovered that the charge on the droplets was always a whole multiple of a certain basic quantity of charge; this, he realized, was the charge on an individual electron.

Milne, Alan Alexander (1882-1956) English essayist and children's writer, who created the world of Pooh Bear in *Winnie-the-Pooh* (1926) and *The House at Pooh Corner* (1928), tales about his son's toy animals, which became nursery classics. He also wrote verses for children and adapted Kenneth GRAHAME's *Wind in the Willows* as *Toad of Toad Hall* (1930), a play even more popular than his successful *Mr Pim Passes By* (1919).

Milton, John (1608-74) English poet who, in his writing, was a learned artist who united the classical inheritance of the Renaissance with his own Christian faith. His genius appeared early: the ode 'On the Morning of Christ's Nativity' (1629) is lyrical and rich in language. As contemporary conflicts of religion and politics grew more serious, Milton's poems became more sombre; the light delicacy of 'L'Allegro' and 'Il Penseroso' (1632) turned into the gravity of 'Lycidas' (1637). In his later years he wrote *Paradise Lost* (1667), a Christian epic to justify God's ways to man, and *Paradise Regained* and *Samson Agonistes* (1671), showing the triumph of faith over pain and trial, all written with a consummate control of rhythm, in a rich and lofty language. He was also a writer of voluminous prose, and often, as in *Areopagitica* (1644), in defence of freedom of the press, he achieved a grand, powerful rhetoric. During the Commonwealth, he was Cromwell's Latin secretary, but at the Restoration he retired, blind and in disgrace, and wrote his greatest poems.

Mingus, Charles (1922-79) American jazz bass player, bandleader and composer. He played in the bands of Charlie Parker, Stan Getz and others in the 1950s before forming his own band in New York. He was a highly innovative musician and wrote an autobiography, *Beneath the Underdog* (1971).

Minuit, Peter (c. 1580-1638) Dutch colonist who bought Manhattan Island from local American Indians and founded the Dutch colonial capital, New Amsterdam (now New York City).

Mirabeau, Honoré Gabriel Riqueti, Comte de (1749-91) French politician and orator, a powerful force in the National Assembly during the first two years of the French Revolution when he fought for the establishment of a constitutional monarchy based on the English pattern. He constantly urged that the monarchy should accept a new role at the head of the revolutionary movement, the expression of popular sentiment (rather than the interests of the *ancien regime*), while retaining real powers. Mistrusted, by LOUIS XVI and his queen MARIE ANTOINETTE, for his revolutionary convictions, and by his colleagues in the National Assembly for his ambitions and abilities, he failed to achieve his vision, but succeeded in influencing the constitution.

Miró, Joán (1893-1983) Spanish Surrealist artist, who evolved a highly personal style involving amoebic shapes in pure bright colours, often with punning and quizzical titles. He went to Paris in 1919 and from 1923 was one of the foremost, yet individual Surrealists.

Mishima Yukio (1925-1970) Japanese novelist. Mishima published his first work at 19 and by 1946 was a protégé of KAWABATA YASUNARI. His work covers a variety of themes, often displaying an obsession with the physical, written in an elaborate style with a penchant for the psychological. His best works include *Temple of the Golden Pavilion*, *Confessions of a Mask* and the posthumously published *The Sea of Fertility*. Despair over the decay of traditional Japanese values led to his ritual *seppuku* (harakiri) suicide in 1970.

Mistral, Gabriela (1889-1957) Chilean poet, who was the first Spanish-American writer to be awarded a Nobel Prize for Literature (1945). She was internationally recognized as a teacher, and collaborated in Mexico's educational reform programme in 1922. She was successively Chilean Consul and Cultural Attaché in Mexico, Brazil and the United States.

Mitchell, Reginald Joseph (1895-1937) English aircraft designer, who joined Supermarine Aviation in 1916 and four years later became their chief designer. He designed a wide range of aircraft from large flying-boats to a brilliant series of small racing sea-planes, which won the Schneider Trophy on several occasions between 1922-31. From the latter evolved his last and most famous aircraft, the Spitfire. It first flew in March 1936, and was operational in June 1938. Over 22,000 Spitfires were built, serving in many capacities during the Second World War, but they are remembered particularly for their contributions to the victory of the Allies in the Battle of Britain (1940) and defence of Malta (1942).

Mithridates VI (c. 132-63 BC) King of Pontus (*c.* 121-63 BC), and formidable rival to Rome's power in Asia Minor, who fought three wars against the Romans and massacred some 80,000 Roman citizens. In the first war (88-84 BC) he was defeated by SULLA; in the second (83-81 BC) he drove out the Roman invaders; and in the third (74-64 BC) he was defeated by POMPEY, fled to the Crimea, and committed suicide.

Mittelholzer, Edgar (1909-65) West Indian poet and novelist whose work captures the mixed racial and cultural traditions of the West Indies. His books include *A Morning at the Office* (1950) and the Guianese colonial trilogy, *Children of Kaywana* (1952), *The Harrowing of Hubertus* (1954) and *Kaywana Blood* (1958).

Mitterrand, François (Maurice) (born 1916) President of France since 1981, he has held many government posts since 1944, including Minister of Justice and Minister of the Interior. In 1946 he ran for parliament and was elected to the National Assembly. From 1959 to 1961 he served as a senator and in 1964 stood for President but was defeated by DE GAULLE. In 1974 he ran as the Socialist candidate and was narrowly defeated by Giscard d'ESTAING. He became the first left-wing President when he ran against d'Estaing in 1981.

Modigliani, Amedeo (1884-1920) Italian painter and creator of a highly personal portrait idiom in which the sitters and their features were attenuated, yet retained a remarkable degree of individuality. After training in Italy Modigliani went to Paris in 1906, where he worked as a sculptor, influenced by BRANCUSI and African art. He returned to painting in 1914, when he produced his finest art.

Mohammed (570-632) Arab prophet and founder of Islam, the world religion which now commands the allegiance of 450-500 million people. Born at Mecca, Islam's holy city, he was a rich merchant who spent years in meditation before rejecting the polytheistic beliefs of his contemporaries. Claiming inspiration from messages sent by God through the angel Gabriel, he preached belief in one God whose judgement damns the faithless and sends his Muslims ('Submissive Ones') to paradise. The simple appeal of Mohammed's message, embodied in the *Koran*, won acceptance and welded the warring tribes of Arabia into a united fighting machine. Mohammed himself acted as his empire's lawmaker, commander-in-chief, and judge; he did not set up any governmental administration, but left the conquered or converted peoples to manage their own affairs. The chief aims of the reforms he attempted were the abolition of infanticide, the granting of property rights to women, and – most important for the unity of his empire – the ending of the blood feud which held a whole tribe responsible for a murder and had led to much tribal warfare. Under Mohammed's successors the empire reached from Spain to India, but its civilizing religious role lasted far longer than its political unity, which collapsed after HARUN-AL-RASHID.

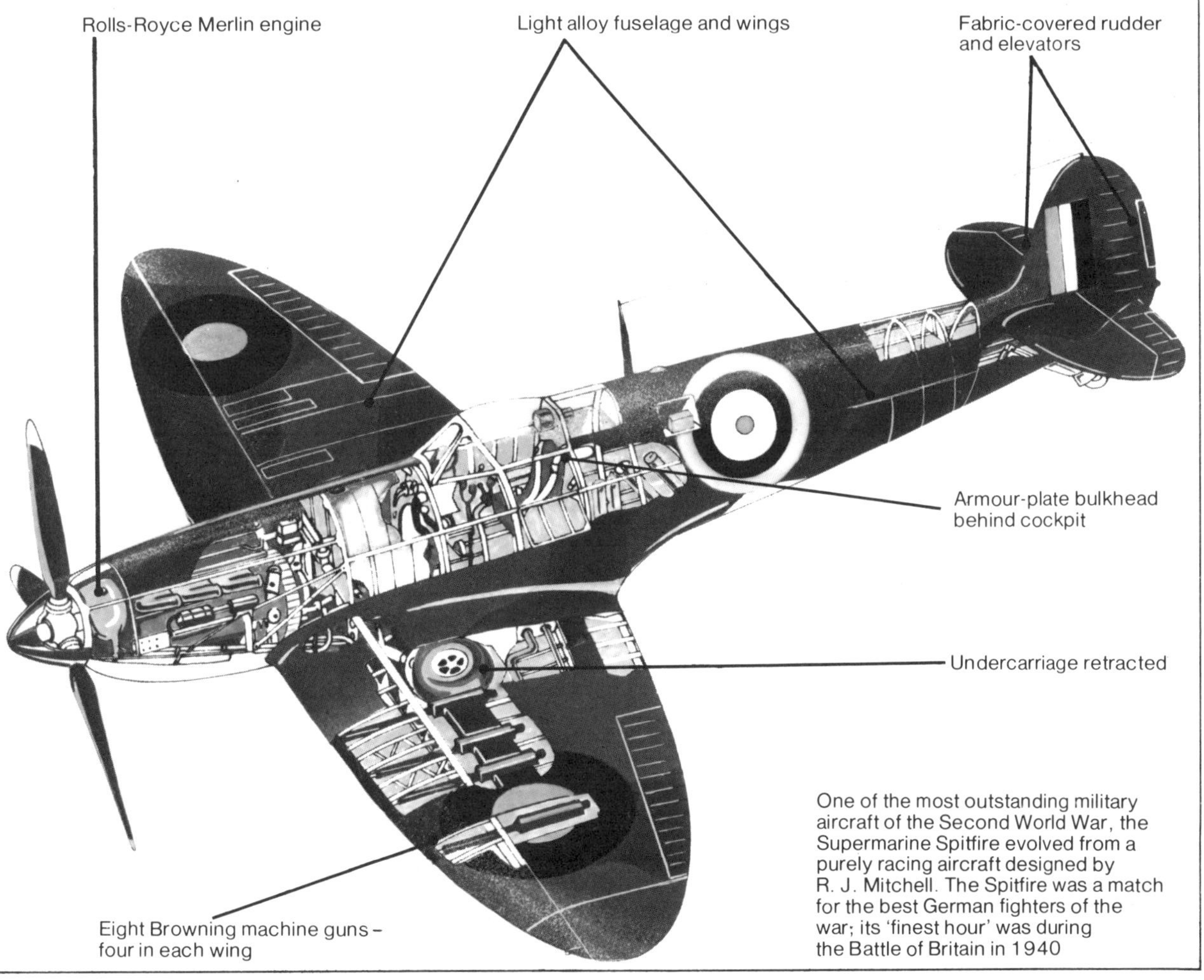

One of the most outstanding military aircraft of the Second World War, the Supermarine Spitfire evolved from a purely racing aircraft designed by R. J. Mitchell. The Spitfire was a match for the best German fighters of the war; its 'finest hour' was during the Battle of Britain in 1940

Mohammed II (1430-81) Sultan of Turkey (1451-81), called 'the Conqueror', who dealt the shrunken Byzantine empire its death blow by seizing Constantinople and Trebizond. After four months of attack (1453), Mohammed's troops swarmed through the Romanos Gate, and killed Constantine XI Palaeologus, the last Byzantine emperor, during three days of frenzied pillaging. Thereafter Constantinople became the Ottoman capital (as Istanbul). Mohammed II ended the last surviving Greek state in Asia Minor (1461), took all Serbia except for Belgrade, and conquered Bosnia, Herzegovina, Albania, Greece and the Crimea. He captured and for a time held Otranto in southern Italy.

Molière, Jean-Baptiste Poquelin (1622-73) French dramatist, the greatest writer of comedies in the French language. Among his earliest were *L'Etourdi* (1655) and *Le Dépit Amoureux* (1656), but his first great success was *Les Précieuses Ridicules* (1659), a farce satirizing the pretentious 'blue-stockings' who haunted the literary salons of the day. He later returned to the subject of women's education in two of his greatest comedies, *L'Ecole des Femmes* (1662) and *Les Femmes Savantes* (1672). Meanwhile, though his success earned him a royal pension, he also became a target for violent abuse by rivals or irate victims of his satire. His most famous and controversial play *Tartuffe*, ostensibly an attack on hypocrisy, unleashed the wrath of powerful religious interests and was twice banned before the modern, amended version was accepted in 1669. Molière had further offended the sensibilities of the devout with his *Dom Juan* (1665). As well as the hypocrite Tartuffe, other great creations of Molière's comic genius include Alceste (*Le Misanthrope*, 1666), Arpagon (*L'Avare*, 1668), M. Jourdain (*Le Bourgeois Gentilhomme*, 1670) and Argan (*Le Malade Imaginaire*, 1673). Ironically, it was during a performance of this latter play, while acting the title role, that he collapsed and died.

Molotov, Vyacheslav Mikhailovich (born 1890) Russian politician and veteran Bolshevik, who survived the STALIN era and remained in office until KHRUSCHEV's denunciation of Stalin. He was imprisoned six times and twice exiled as a Communist agitator, and was co-founder of *Pravda* (1912), with Stalin, whose second secretary he became in 1921. As Prime Minister from 1940-41 he was responsible for the two Five-Year Plans for expanding commerce and industry. In 1939, Molotov replaced LITVINOV as Foreign Minister in order to implement Stalin's peace pact with Hitler, and held the office until 1949, and again from 1953-6. Following Khruschev's denunciation of Stalin's crimes, Molotov, with MALENKOV and Kaganovich, was expelled from the Central Committee and the Praesidium, and was sent as Ambassador to the Mongolian Peoples' Republic. He became USSR representative at the International Atomic Agency in 1960. In 1964 he was expelled from the Communist party.

Monck, George, 1st Duke of Albemarle (1608-70) English general and naval commander who helped to restore the monarchy after CROMWELL's Commonwealth. He changed sides in the Civil War after supporting the king, and as a Parliamentarian fought the Dutch (1653) and became ruler of Scotland after it had been conquered (1650-1). When Cromwell died (1658), Monck changed sides again and ended the anti-royalist Rump Parliament by restoring the members expelled by PRIDE in 1648. In 1660 the enlarged Parliament invited the banished Prince Charles to return as King CHARLES II. Charles made Monck Duke of Albemarle for his smoothing of the Restoration negotiations.

Mondrian, Piet (1872-1944) Dutch pioneer of geometric abstract painting. In 1911 he went to Paris, where he became influenced by Cubism. Later, in Holland, he developed a theory of abstract painting, based on a co-ordinated system of horizontals and verticals, and in 1917 founded the De Stijl group with Theo van Doesburg. Fundamental to this was the theory of Neo-Plasticism – the use of pure abstraction to denaturalize art by eliminating representation, and suggesting three-dimensional space simply by curves and lines. His last works, the *Boogie-Woogies*, show a renewed and complex dynamism, inspired by the ambience of New York.

Monet, Claude (1840-1926) French Impressionist painter, who was at first naturalist in outlook, but showed a special sensitivity to effects of light resulting from the practice of painting out of doors. His *Impression: Sunrise*, shown at the first Impressionist exhibition (1874), gave the movement its name. Monet's work is closest to that of PISSARRO and SISLEY, but he pursued Impressionist ideas further than they, notably in several series of paintings of the same subject under different conditions, e.g. *Rouen Cathedral* (1892-4). Gradually an increasingly lyrical note entered his works, as is seen in the late paintings of *Water-lilies*.

Monge, Gaspard (1746-1818) French mathematician who invented descriptive geometry. At first the method was a military secret, but later it was published and adopted by most engineers in Europe.

Monmouth, James Scott, Duke of (1649-85) Pretender to the English throne and illegitimate son of CHARLES II. Charles made him Duke of Buccleuch and Captain-General of his forces after MONCK's death. As a popular public figure and a Protestant, Monmouth was drawn into the Rye House Plot (1683), in which radical Whigs planned to make him king by killing Charles II and his pro-Catholic heir, James. The plot failed and Monmouth fled abroad, but in 1685 he invaded Dorset to depose James, now King James II. Monmouth lost the Battle of Sedgemoor and was captured and executed. His followers were punished savagely by Judge Jeffreys.

Monroe, James (1758-1831) Fifth President of the US, who was JEFFERSON's envoy extraordinary in 1803, when he negotiated the Louisiana Purchase from France, but failed to acquire the Floridas from Spain. In 1816 he was elected President of the US and was re-elected almost unanimously four years later. The Floridas were eventually purchased in 1819, and the Missouri Compromise (1820) peacefully settled the first slavery conflict under the constitution. Monroe will always be associated with the Doctrine bearing his name, which rejected European interference in the affairs of North and South America, and remained the basis of American foreign policy for over a century.

Monroe, Marilyn (1926-62) American film star, one of Hollywood's most famous 'sex goddesses', and also a fine screen actress. She showed a great talent for comedy, as in *The Seven-Year Itch* (1955) and *Some Like It Hot* (1959). In her last film, *The Misfits* (1961), written by Arthur MILLER, she also began to show her dramatic prowess.

Montagu, Charles, 1st Earl of Halifax (1661-1715) English wit, poet, patron of literature, Whig politician and financial genius who, as a Lord of the Treasury (1692), devised ways of raising money for WILLIAM III's war with France. He started the National Debt (1693) by borrowing £1 million by life annuities, and formed the Bank of England (1694), originally as a merchant company which lent money to the government for interest and for privileges, including permission to issue bank-notes.

Montaigne, Michel Eyquen de (1533-92) French moralist and creator of the essay, a word invented by him for his written reflections, the first volumes of which were published in 1580. The *Essais*, which provide an intriguing and penetrating self-portrait of the author, are remarkable for their sincerity, lucidity, tolerance and wisdom. Written in a familiar and racy style, they influenced both French and English literature.

Montesquieu, Charles de Secondat, Baron de (1689-1755) French political philosopher, author of *Lettres Persanes* (1721), a witty satire on Parisian society, ostensibly seen through the eyes of two Persian visitors, attacking contemporary religious and political abuses. Montesquieu also published two other important works, most notable of which is his famous historical essay, *De l'Esprit des Lois* (1748), which influenced political thought in Europe and America.

Montessori, Maria (1870-1952) Italian educator who advocated 'free discipline', with children moving naturally about their tasks, and the provision of simple but stimulating teaching apparatus. She was the first woman medical graduate of Rome University, where she lectured (1900-7). Following the ideas of E. Seguin, she taught backward children to read and write – *The Montessori Method* (1912) describes how she applied similar methods to normal slum children from three to six years and *The Advanced Montessori Method* (1917) developed the material for six to ten year olds.

Marilyn Monroe, whose short life symbolized the glamour and tragedy of stardom

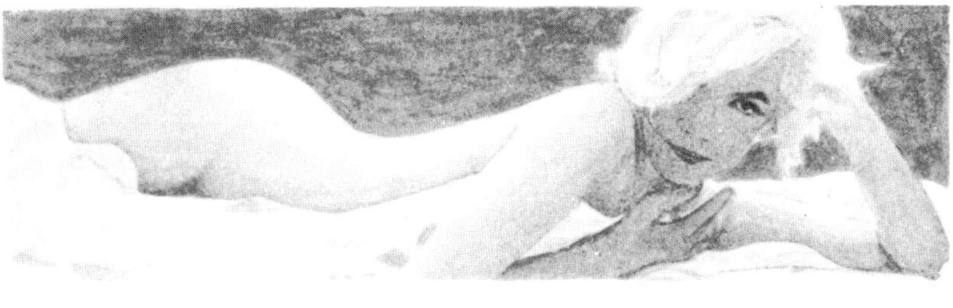

Monteverdi, Claudio (1567-1643) Italian composer of the late Renaissance. He wrote *Orpheus* (1607), one of the finest early operas, and the *Vespers* (1610), settings of the vesper psalms and motets, which were probably published as a collection to show a potential employer the range of which he was capable, and were never intended for performance as a unity. His madrigals (more than 250) show a strong sense of dramatic colour, as do his specifically religious works. Of Monteverdi's operas that survive, *The Coronation of Poppaea* (1642), on the theme of NERO's rejection of his wife for his mistress, is probably his masterpiece. Monteverdi took the post of *maestro di cappella* at St Mark's, Venice, in 1613 and remained there until he died. He became a priest in 1632.

Montezuma II (c. 1480-1520) Aztec emperor (1502-20) of Mexico at the time of the Spanish conquest. He ruled some five million people from Tenochtitlán (Mexico City), enlarging an empire that already stretched from the Pacific to the Atlantic. Unfavourable omens convinced Montezuma of impending punishment by the god Quetzalcoatl and made him try to propitiate CORTÉS, the Spanish conquistador, who imprisoned him. Montezuma was killed by his own subjects when Cortés brought him out to tell them to end their uprising against the Spaniards.

Montfort, Simon de (c. 1208-65) English statesman, 6th Earl of Leicester, who led a rebellion of barons against the autocratic rule of Henry III. His alliance of barons, knights, clergy and burgesses won the Barons' War (1263-5) and made de Montfort virtual ruler. His Parliament (1265) included (with the barons) middle-class knights and burgesses to represent shires and boroughs. De Montfort was killed at the Battle of Evesham.

Montgomery, Sir Bernard Law, First Viscount of Alamein (1887-1976) British Field-Marshal who, as Commander of British Forces in North Africa during the Second World War, defeated the legendary ROMMEL at El Alamein (October 1942) and ousted Axis forces from the continent. His success lay in careful planning, refusing to commit his forces to any action until he had sufficient supplies of men and material. He had an unusual ability to inspire men with his own confidence and to this end made a cult of his own personality. After the invasion of Normandy in 1944, his strategy of drawing the main weight of the German counter-offensive on to the British flank played a major part in the Americans' rapid advance, and he put forward a plan for a thrust to the Rhine, which might well have shortened the war, but EISENHOWER opted for a safer advance on a broad front. Montgomery's handling of the Allied armies in the Ardennes resulted in the failure of Germany's final offensive under von Rundstedt, from whom Montgomery later accepted the capitulation of the German army. He commanded British-occupied Germany (1945-6) and was Deputy Supreme Allied Commander, NATO (1951-8).

Montrose, James Graham, 1st Marquis of (1612-50) Leading Scottish royalist during the English Civil War. Deserting the Presbyterian cause, he fought for CHARLES I, winning the battles of Tippermuir, Inverlochy and Kilsyth, and seizing Aberdeen and Dundee to gain royalist supremacy in Scotland. He was defeated at Philiphaugh (1645) and fled abroad. Montrose returned to Scotland in 1650 and tried unsuccessfully to raise the clans for Prince Charles, the future CHARLES II, but was seized and executed.

Moore, George E. (1873-1958) English philosopher who, with RUSSELL, led the revolt against Idealist philosophy. His approach to analysis influenced WITTGENSTEIN and analytic philosophy at Oxford.

Moore, Henry (born 1898) English sculptor and painter of international standing. His sculpture is fairly abstract, including holes to which he gives as meaningful shape as a solid mass. The mother and child, and reclining nudes are themes central to much of his work.

Moore, Marianne (1887-1972) American poet and Pulitzer prize winner who tried to visualize 'insects, lower animals, or human beings – to wonder if they are happy and what will become of them'. The results are short, odd, colourful poems. She edited *The Dial* in New York (1925-9), and her *Collected Poems* were published in 1951.

Moraes, Dom (born 1938) Indian poet whose work brought him fame at an early age. With his first poems, *A Beginning* (1957), he became the first non-English poet to win the Hawthornden Prize. Later volumes include *John Nobody* (1965). His work is primarily concerned with racial and social issues.

Moravia, Alberto (born 1907) Pseudonym of Alberto Pincherie, Italian novelist, whose work analyses contemporary Roman society and explores the twin themes of social alienation and loveless sexuality, as in *The Woman of Rome* (1947), a sympathetic portrayal of a prostitute. His early novels were critical of Fascism and he was forced into hiding for several years. In later works he portrays working-class life, which to him is a world of boredom, indifference to cruelty, and promiscuity.

More, Sir Thomas (1478-1535) English lawyer, politician, scholar and author, who became Lord Chancellor to HENRY VIII. His best-known literary work is *Utopia* (1516), which concerns a land with an ideal form of government. More had an international reputation as a humanist scholar and was on close terms with COLET, Lily and ERASMUS. He was executed for his refusal to deny papal authority and to acquiesce in the divorce of CATHERINE of Aragon.

Moreau, Gustave (1826-98) French Symbolist painter, the teacher of MATISSE and ROUAULT. With paintings such as *Salome before Herod* (1870), Moreau both anticipated and exemplified that aspect of French Symbolism known as 'decadent', which emphasizes the morbid side of sexuality and death. The combination of Moreau's mysterious subject-matter and the enamel-like luminosity of his colours produces a bizarre effect.

Morgagni, Giovanni (1682-1771) Italian physician, founder of the science of pathology. One of the first doctors to look beyond the symptoms of disease to the inner causes and mechanisms that produce it. His *On the Sites and Causes of Diseases* (1761) contains accounts of the causes and courses of such ailments as consolidation of the lung, cirrhosis of the liver, and disease of the heart valves.

Morgan, John (1735-89) American physician, who pioneered medical education in America. He founded the school of medicine at the University of Pennsylvania.

Morgan, Thomas (1866-1945) American biologist whose work in genetics has vastly improved our understanding of the laws and mechanisms of heredity, with far-reaching consequences in medicine, animal and plant husbandry. Morgan's experiments with the fruit flies pinpointed the location of genes in the chromosomes of the cell nucleus and proved the theory of hereditary transmission. All subsequent research in genetics has been based on his pioneer work. He was awarded the Nobel Prize for Medicine in 1933.

Mörike, Eduard (1804-75) German novelist and lyric poet. His slender output of poetry, which at first passed unnoticed, was collected in *Poems* (1838), which includes 'Perigrina', 'The abandoned servant girl', and 'Agnes', lyrical works pervaded by a nostalgia for the lost happiness of youth. Mörike's educational novel, *Artist Nolten* (1832), describes the life of an artist who commits suicide and is regarded as a landmark in German Romantic fiction.

Morison, Stanley (1889-1967) English bibliographer and typographer who greatly influenced newspaper and book design. In 1923 he became typographical adviser to the Monotype Corporation and held similar positions at the Cambridge University Press and *The Times*, where he designed the Times Roman type face. He wrote the official history of *The Times* in addition to many books on typography.

Morley, Thomas (c. 1557-1603) English composer who introduced the ballet (a dance and refrain) into the English madrigal. Besides being a leading Elizabethan madrigalist, he also composed church, lute, viol and virginal music. Morley wrote a textbook, *A Plain and Easy Introduction to Practical Music* (1597), which was used for two centuries, and composed songs for SHAKESPEARE, including 'It was a Lover and His Lass' in *As You Like It*.

Morris, William (1834-96) English poet, painter, printer and designer, one of the leaders of the Pre-Raphaelite Brotherhood, who had a strong, enduring influence on English visual taste. Inspired by RUSKIN he applied himself to providing a worthy and beautiful setting to life, and with BURNE-JONES, ROSSETTI and Madox BROWN, formed a company of craftsmen and interior designers. Morris began writing poetry in the early days of the 'Brotherhood' at Oxford and in 1858 he published *The Defence of Guenevere*, which announced a new Romantic age in a rich, archaic style. As much a convinced socialist as a herald of the Gothic revival, his ideals found literary expression in political romances such as *News from Nowhere* (1891), which reveals his horror of the effects of capitalism and industrialization.

Morse, Samuel Finley Breese (1791-1872) American artist of distinction, who at the age of 40 became interested in electrical telegraphy, but was just beaten into second place for its invention by Cooke and WHEATSTONE, working independently in Britain. He introduced the use of electromagnetic relays to extend the range of transmission and also the now famous code of dots and dashes. In 1843, Congress was persuaded to finance him to set up the first experimental telegraph in the US, from Washington to Baltimore, completed in June 1844. A whole network was installed during the next decade by several competing companies, which later amalgamated into Western Union (1856).

Morton, Jelly Roll (1885-1941) American jazz pianist, band leader and composer. He started playing in New Orleans and began recording extensively in 1923. He toured America with various bands and top jazz musicians and is regarded as the first great composer and orchestrator of jazz.

Moses (late 13th cent. BC) Hebrew lawgiver whose precepts underlie Judaism and Christianity. According to the Book of Exodus in the Bible, Moses was born among Hebrew tribes enslaved in Egypt (possibly by RAMSES II), led their escape through the Sinai Desert towards Canaan, and at Mount Sinai delivered to the young Israelite nation its moral and religious basis, the Ten Commandments. The strict Mosaic law was eventually reinterpreted by JESUS.

Moses, Edwin (born 1955) American athlete who broke his own world record in the 400-metre hurdles in the 1984 Olympics. He holds the record for the greatest number of wins consecutively in any event and has made the ten fastest times ever recorded.

Mosley, Sir Oswald Ernald (1896-1980) Founder and leader of British fascism. Successively a Tory, Independent and Labour MP in the 1920s, he became a minister in the Labour Government of 1929, but resigned in 1930, complaining of the government's 'spineless apathy' in failing to combat unemployment. He founded the British Union of Fascists in 1932, which became so anti-Semitic, violent and pro-German that an Act of Parliament was passed in 1936 to suppress its para-military organizations. From 1940-3 Mosley was imprisoned under the Defence Regulations. His political life was a tragedy; in the 1920s he was regarded as one of the ablest men in Parliament and possibly a future Labour or Conservative Prime Minister. He had a brilliant mind and his economic policies were both daring and original, but his rabid anti-Semitism and Fascist sympathies eventually rendered him impotent as a political force.

Mössbauer, Rudolph Ludwig (born 1929) German physicist who showed that atoms emitting gamma-rays can sometimes do so without recoiling. Under certain conditions, atoms give out gamma-rays and recoil as they do so in the same way as a gun when it is fired. In the late 1950s, Mössbauer found that if the source of the gamma-rays is a crystalline solid, some atoms emit rays without recoiling, the recoil being taken up by the whole crystal. He explained this effect (now known as the Mössbauer effect) by showing that the overall crystal structure could take the part of the individual atom and, being far more massive, not recoil at all. Among other things the Mössbauer effect has enabled the gravitational red shift of light predicted by EINSTEIN's general theory of relativity to be measured in the laboratory.

Motherwell, Robert (born 1915) American Abstract Expressionist painter, who knew Surrealist painters, such as de KOONING and POLLOCK, in New York, and under their influence moved towards an automatic way of painting that led to Abstract Expressionism. He has written extensively on art, particularly Dadaism and the Surrealists.

Mountbatten, Louis, First Earl Mountbatten of Burma (1900-79) British naval officer and uncle of the Duke of Edinburgh, who during the Second World War was Supreme Allied Commander in South-East Asia (1943-6), and afterwards, the last Viceroy of India. A specialist in combined operations, he was responsible for the British plans for the Allied landings in North Africa in 1942, before his appointment in South-East Asia. With an army of Indian, British, Gurkha, American and Chinese troops, he drove back the Japanese and recaptured Burma. His plans for the re-conquest of Malaya were forestalled by the surrender of the Japanese in South-East Asia in 1945. In 1947 he was appointed to succeed Wavell as Viceroy of India and within five months had performed the difficult task of transferring power to India and Pakistan. Although there was animosity between the two countries, he not only retained the friendship of both, but was asked by India to become its first Governor-General (1947-8). Despite an atmosphere disturbed by the threat of violence, he was able to hand over responsibility to JINNAH and NEHRU in circumstances of comparative peace. He served as First Sea Lord and Chief of Naval Staff (1955-59). He was assassinated by an IRA bomb in 1979.

Mozart, Wolfgang Amadeus (1756-91) Austrian composer whose talents emerged at an early age. When he was six, he was a harpsichord prodigy and by 12 he had written his first opera – and had it produced. The promise which was to make him unequalled in terms of musical imagination and achievement was to be fulfilled in the course of his short creative life, but his maturity was marked by personal troubles, fickle audiences, unreliable patrons and periods of extreme poverty. Mozart wrote about 40 symphonies, important among them No. 31 (The *Paris*), No. 36 (The *Linz*), No. 38 (The *Prague*) and No. 41 (The *Jupiter*). The classical, three-movement concerto was, however, Mozart's own creation: his 21 piano concertos are the form's first and most splendidly varied monuments. He also brought operatic art to one of its highest points, first in his collaborations with Lorenzo da Ponte as librettist (*The Marriage of Figaro*, 1786, based on BEAUMARCHAIS), *Don Giovanni* (1787) and *Cosi fan Tutti* (1790), then in his humanistic masterpiece with its Masonic symbolism, *Die Zauberflöte* (*The Magic Flute*, 1791). Mozart made a distinguished contribution to chamber music with his 24 string quartets, violin sonatas and other works. His final masterpiece, a setting of the Requiem, was unfinished when he died from typhus. Mozart was buried in Vienna in a pauper's grave.

Mubarak, Lieutenant General Hosni (born 1928) Egyptian politician and President since 1981. A former pilot and flying instructor, he rose to the position of Commander of the Egyptian Air Force. He became Vice-President under SADAT from 1975 and on acceding to the Presidency, he pledged to continue Sadat's domestic and international policies.

Mugabe, Robert (born 1924) Political leader of Zimbabwe. He worked with Joshua NKOMO in the African nationalist movement and was arrested in 1962, 1963 and 1964 and was held in detention until 1974. After 1974 he went into exile in Mozambique, co-operating with Nkomo until the end of the Rhodesian war. In 1980 he was elected Prime Minister of the new Republic of Zimbabwe. He initially displayed a conciliatory attitude toward both his black and white opponents. Recently, he has discredited and imprisoned rivals such as Nkomo.

Muhlenberg, Henry Melchior (1711-87) German-born clergyman who emigrated to Pennsylvania in 1742 and founded several Lutheran churches. He is recognized as the founder of Lutheranism in the US. His three clergyman sons played a part in American political life during the War of Independence.

Muir, Edwin (1887-1959) Scottish poet, much of whose work is in the form of symbolic tales of visions and mystical events. His books include *Chorus of the Newly Dead* (1926), *The Narrow Place* (1943) and *Collected Poems* (1952). He also wrote three novels, literary criticism and an autobiography (1954). With his wife Willa, he made important translations from German literature, notably the works of KAFKA and Hermann Broch.

Müller, Paul (1899-1965) Swiss chemist who first prepared DDT. He searched for a new pesticide which, unlike those in use at the time, would be deadly for insects only, centring his work around complex chlorinated hydrocarbons. In 1939 he found what he was looking for. Its chemical name, dichlorodiphenyltrichloroethane, was abbreviated to DDT. Within a few years it was used throughout the world, especially against mosquitoes.

Müller, Johannes (1801-58) German physiologist who clarified the nature of sensory nerves. He showed that the type of response that follows stimulation of a sensory nerve depends not on the type of stimulation (heat, dampness, etc.), but on the type of sensory nerve. The optic nerve, for example, however it is stimulated, will record a flash of light.

Mulroney, Brian (born 1939) Canadian politician and Prime Minister. He was leader of the Progressive Conservative opposition to TRUDEAU's government until his surprise victory in 1984.

Munch, Edvard (1863-1944) Norwegian painter who was preoccupied with the Symbolist themes of love and death. In Paris in the early 1890s he was influenced by GAUGUIN's style, its synthetic approach to form and colour being developed by Munch as a means of expressing his own neurotic vision. He lived in Germany (1892-1908), where he influenced the Expressionist movement, especially through his mastery of woodcut and lithography.

Murasaki-Shikibu (c. 978-c. 1016) Japanese female novelist and diarist, author of what is generally recognized as the masterpiece of Japanese literature, *The Tale of Genji*, relating his adventures with women, by an allusive rather than erotic approach. Although this work contains many poems, it differs markedly from earlier works, such as Ariwara no Narihira's *The Tales of Ise*, in that it is a work of subtlety and depth in which prose and verse are equal.

Murchison, Sir Roderick (1792-1871) Scottish geologist, whose work on the rocks underlying the old red sandstone in South Wales led to the definition of the strata known as the Silurian System. He had earlier worked with LYELL on the Auvergne volcanics and with Adam Sedgwick on the structure of the Alps, and later collaborated again with Sedgwick on a study of the rocks that were to become known as the Devonian System.

Murdoch, Iris (born 1919) Irish novelist and philosopher. She took to novel writing as a hobby but soon established her reputation with books like *Under the Net* (1954) and *The Sandcastle* (1957), which combine philosophical speculations with fanciful, ironical situations. Later works include *The Red and The Green* (1965), *The Sea, The Sea* (1978) and *The Philosopher's Pupil* (1983).

Murdock, William (1754-1839) Scottish steam engineer, who invented a coal-gas process. From 1779 while working for BOULTON and WATT in Cornwall he carried out numerous investigations, including the destructive distillation of wood, peat and coal, and (1799) developed methods for storing and purifying gas.

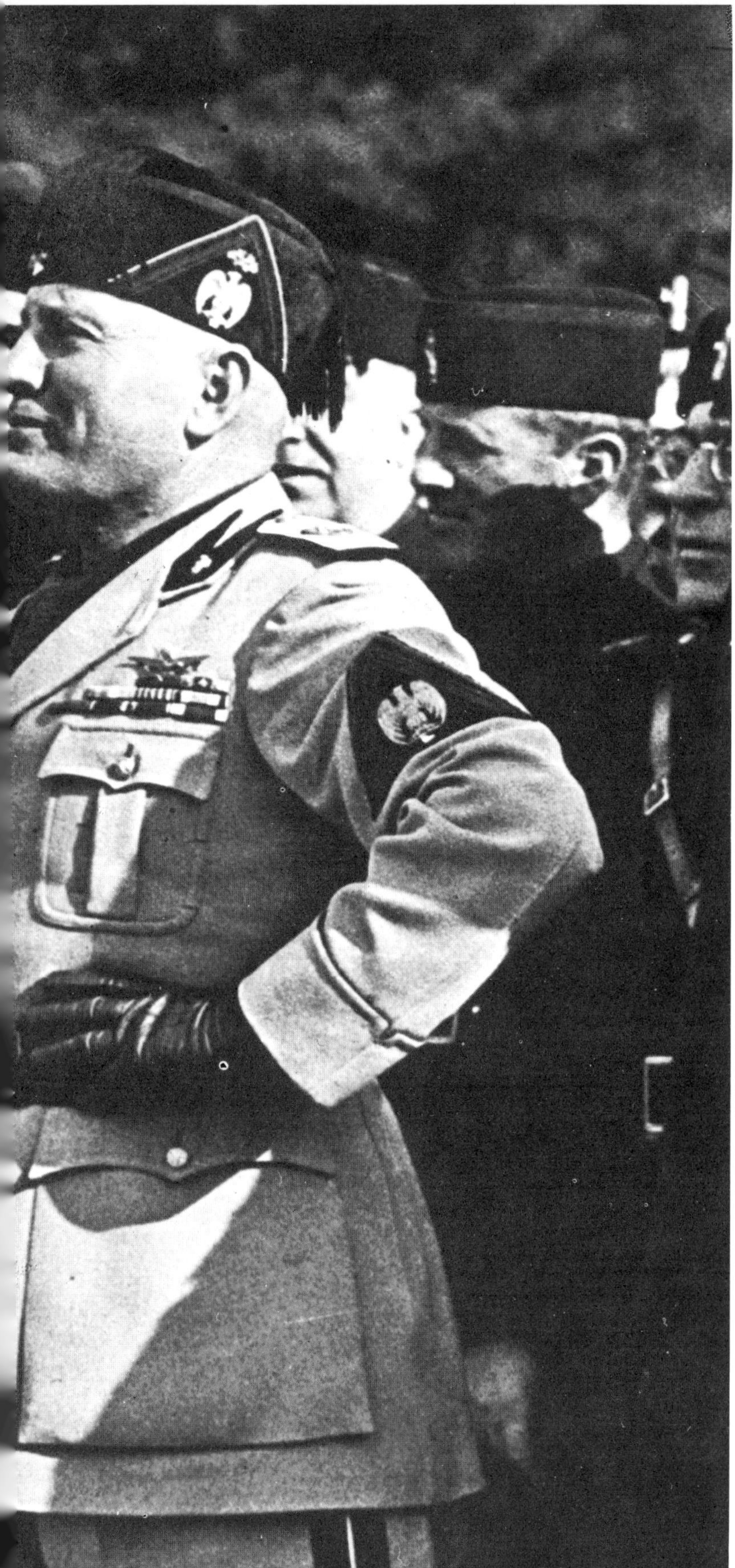

Murillo, Bartolomé (1617-82) Spanish painter of religious and genre subjects, best known for the sentimental charm of his pictures of the Virgin Mary and of beggar boys clad in picturesque rags.

Murray, Sir James (1837-1915) Scottish editor of the Oxford *New English Dictionary* (1884-1928). This monumental scholarly work listed all words current from the 12th century onward, giving for each its etymology, current pronunciation and a range of meanings, fully illustrated by quotations. Murray was appointed by the Philological Society, on whose material, including two million quotations collected from 1857, the dictionary was based.

Murray, Margaret (1863-1963) English Egyptologist, anthropologist and author who won fame with her idea that medieval witchcraft represented a survival of Stone Age religion. Her publications included *Witch Cult in Western Europe* (1921) and *Divine King in England* (1954).

Musa, Gongo see GONGO MUSA

Musschenbroek, Pieter van (1692-1761) Dutch physicist who in 1745 developed a device which could store and then release electricity from an electrostatic machine. It became known later as a Leyden jar, and was the first electric condenser (now called a capacitor).

Musset, Alfred de (1810-57) French Romantic poet, dramatist and novelist. Several of Musset's best-known works were inspired by his stormy liaison with novelist George SAND, including the novel *La Confession d'un enfant du siècle* (1836) and particularly the lyrics known collectively as *Les Nuits* (1835-7). He was also successful as a playwright with such works as *Fantasio* (1833), *Lorenzaccio* and *On ne badine pas avec l'amour* (1834).

Mussolini, Benito (1883-1945) Italian dictator, known as 'Il Duce', whose schemes for Italian aggrandizement led Italy to war in partnership with HITLER's Germany, and, ultimately, to his death at the hands of Italian partisans in 1945. A one-time Socialist, Mussolini organized 'fasci' or groups, of working men to agitate for social revolutionary change after the First World War. By 1921 these had merged into a Fascist party –

Mussolini, the pocket caesar, at his peak, with newspapers announcing his downfall

Fridtjof Nansen aboard the *Fram*

violently nationalist and anti-Communist – and the following year Mussolini led his 'March on Rome' and was invited by King Victor Emmanuel III to form a government. Mussolini assumed dictatorial powers and opponents were summarily dealt with. An aggressive foreign policy was backed by all-out militarism. When Italy invaded Abyssinia (1935), the hostility of the western democracies enabled Ciano, the Italian Foreign Minister, to bring together his master, Mussolini, and Hitler, in the 'Rome-Berlin Axis'. With support from Germany, Mussolini annexed Albania (1939), and as soon as Germany had defeated France, he entered the war in the summer of 1940. But the Italian armies were defeated in Greece, Libya and East Africa and Mussolini had repeatedly to be helped by Hitler, on whom he became completely dependent. In 1943, he was forced to resign, and was imprisoned. He was rescued by a German parachute commando (September 1943) and set up as puppet ruler of a Fascist Republic in northern Italy, under German control. When the Allies forced the Germans out of Italy, Mussolini fled to the Swiss frontier with his mistress Clara Petacci but they were caught by Italian partisans and shot.

Mussorgsky, Modest Petrovich (1839–81) Russian composer. Mussorgsky served in the army and civil service before becoming a composer whose style developed a daring, original use of harmony. He is probably best known for *Pictures from an Exhibition* for piano, and *Night on the Bare Mountain* which RIMSKY-KORSAKOV edited, but which is far more striking in Mussorgsky's rarely heard original. Rimsky-Korsakov also edited Mussorgsky's chief work, the opera *Boris Godunov*, though SHOSTAKOVICH's edition is far closer to Mussorgsky's intention. He died from alcoholism.

Mutsuhito (1852–1912) Emperor of Japan from 1867, known during his reign as 'Meiji', who broke the seven centuries' rule of the Shoguns (Feudal Lords) and initiated the Westernization of Japan. He and his Prime Minister, ITO, put an end to feudalism and Japan's isolation and set up a Western-style parliamentary and bureaucratic government. An army and a navy were raised and trained (the one on German lines, the other on British), and by aggressive expansion in Korea and Manchuria and victories over China (1894–5), and Russia (1904–5), established Japan as a world power.

Myron (5th cent. BC) Athenian sculptor of the Classical period, whose *Discus-thrower* (*c.* 440 BC) is one of the most famous pieces of all time. Originally cast in bronze, stone copies, probably Roman, are all that remain. Designed round a half-circle crossed by an S-curve, it is a convincing symbol of rapid motion, as well as a revolutionary concept for sculpture in the round.

N

Nabokov, Vladimir (1899–1977) Russian-born American novelist, poet and lepidopterist whose highly stylized fictions abound in artifice, self-parody and urbane humour. Nabokov's formal exuberance is epitomized by *Pale Fire* (1962), a curious hybrid novel in the form of a poem and its eccentric commentary. Even *Lolita* (1955) and *Ada* (1969), which explicitly treat deviant sexuality, are saturated with erudite word games and elaborate literary jokes. Nabokov considers his greatest achievement to be the discovery of a species of butterfly, which now bears his name.

Nader, Ralph (born 1934) American lawyer and 'consumer advocate' whose pressure on the US automobile industry and public opinion brought national legislation enforcing the adoption of a number of safety features in motor vehicles. Nader later turned his attention to pollution, health hazards in industry and food packaging.

Nagy, Imre (1895-1958) Leader of the Hungarian revolt against the Soviet Union in 1956. As Prime Minister (1953-5) Nagy instituted a measure of political and economic freedom, but was ousted by Rakosi, the most powerful and most hated man in Hungary. KHRUSCHEV forced Rakosi out in 1956, and Nagy became Premier once again, promising the withdrawal of Russian troops and free elections. For the first time a Communist leader tried to govern within the framework of a multi-party administration, but his efforts were foiled by the spread of the anti-Soviet revolt. Eventually, Nagy renounced the Warsaw Pact, declared Hungary's neutrality, and appealed to the United Nations for protection. Russian tanks suppressed the revolt early in November; Nagy was replaced and betrayed by KÁDÁR, a member of his government.

Naipaul, Vidiadhar Surajprasad (born 1932) Trinidad-born Indian novelist. His novels *The Mystic Masseur* (1957), *Miguel Street* (1959) and *A House for Mr Biswas* (1961) are rich comedies of Hindu life in the West Indies. *An Area of Darkness* (1964) is a sombre and powerful book about India.

Learning his lesson from ships destroyed by the crushing power of the northern ice, Nansen designed his *Fram* to survive by riding up above the pressure of the floes. It succeeded—to make an historic journey

Europe, in 1812, at the watershed of Napoleonic power. Dominated by France and the territories under its control, Europe lived for three years in the shadow of the 'little corporal' before defeat at Waterloo ended for him in exile

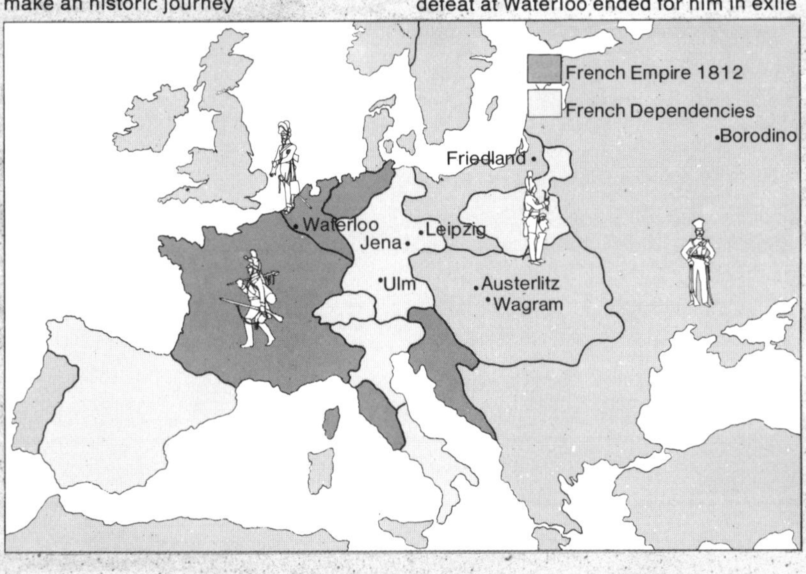

Nakasone, Yasuhiro (born 1918) Japanese politician who was elected into parliament in 1947 as a representative of the Liberal Democratic party. He held several cabinet posts and advocated economic co-operation with the US. In 1982 he became Prime Minister.

Nanak (1469-1538) Indian teacher and founder of Sikhism, a religion combining Islamic and Hindu beliefs advocating universal religious toleration and the worship of a single God. A 'sikh' or disciple of the religious teacher Kabir (*c.* 1450-1518), who held similar ideas, Nanak spread the new teaching all over India and the Middle East. Later, gurus (teachers) established a sikh centre at Amritsar and compiled the *Adi Granth*, the sacred writings. In the 17th century persecution forced the sikhs to become a militant community with special customs, including long hair and the addition of the word *singh* (lion) to their own names.

Nansen, Fridtjof (1861-1930) Norwegian explorer, zoologist, artist and statesman, who was the first man to cross Greenland (from east to west), and who tried to reach the North Pole by drifting with the ice. Off Novaya Zemlya, Nansen deliberately let the pack-ice freeze round his specially built vessel *Fram* and, using ocean currents, drifted with the ice to 85° 55′ N before abandoning it (1895). Taking to skis and dog-sleds, he reached 86° 14′ N, a record northerly latitude. Nansen became a leading Norwegian statesman, and won the Nobel Peace Prize (1922), after organizing food supplies for famine-stricken Russia and the repatriation of First World War prisoners.

Napoleon I, Bonaparte (1769-1821) French emperor and military leader of genius. Corsican-born, he became an artillery officer and achieved promotion rapidly, establishing his reputation in the Revolutionary wars in northern Italy. His marriage in 1796 to Josephine de Beauharnais helped him to political powers. In 1799 he returned from an unsuccessful campaign in Egypt to overthrow the Directory and was appointed First Consul. In 1802 he became Consul for life and was virtual dictator of France; in 1804 he crowned himself Emperor. In a series of brilliant campaigns he defeated Austria (Austerlitz, 1805) and Prussia (Jena and Auerstadt, 1806), but in the Peninsula War (1809-14) WELLINGTON's strategy drained his strength and the Continental System (1806), which entailed a commercial blockade of Britain, became unpopular with its participants, whose trade also suffered. In another campaign against Austria, Napoleon routed her army at Wagram (July 1809), and dictated peace terms in Vienna. He invaded Russia in 1812, won the battle of Borodino and reached Moscow, but was forced to retreat from the burning city which the Muscovites had deliberately fired to deny the French shelter and supplies. His Grand Army was virtually destroyed by the harsh winter during the subsequent retreat, and by Russian 'guerilla' and scorched-earth tactics. As a result of French defeats in the War of the Fourth Coalition (1813-14) the allies entered Paris at the end of March 1814. Napoleon abdicated and was granted the principality of Elba. He escaped from Elba in February 1815 and returned to France where he resumed power for the 'Hundred Days' (March-June 1815), which ended in his defeat at Waterloo (18 June 1815) and imprisonment on St Helena, where he died.

Napoleon III (1808-73) Emperor of the French from 1852-70 and creator of the Second Empire. He was the son of Louis Bonaparte (the brother of NAPOLEON I) and of Hortense Beauharnais, Napoleon's step-daughter. He was probably a member of the Carbonari secret society and led two unsuccessful risings against LOUIS-PHILIPPE's 'July Monarchy', following the second of which (1840) he was caught and imprisoned. He escaped to England and on the death of the Duke of Reichstadt (1832), the only son of Napoleon I, he became head of the Napoleonic dynasty. His family connection facilitated his election as President of the Second French Republic (1848). After a referendum in 1851 he seized dictatorial powers and in 1852 the imperial title. His successes (the Crimean War, and the subsequent Congress of Paris, 1856) gave him an international reputation, and from 1856-66 he dominated Europe. He helped Piedmont in her campaign for a united Italy, but deserted his ally (1859) when it suited him. An abortive attempt (1863-7) to set up a puppet Mexican Empire under MAXIMILIAN's rule weakened his position. He was no match for BISMARCK, who isolated him diplomatically and then provoked the Franco-Prussian War (1870) during which Napoleon was captured at Sedan after a crushing defeat. Imprisoned in Germany, he eventually died in exile in England.

The orient in an English seaside town. Nash's Brighton Pavilion was externally Indian, Chinese and Gothic inside

Narayan, Rasipuram Krishnaswami (born 1907) Indian novelist, who writes ironic, humorous fiction about the middle-classes in southern India.

Nash, John (1752-1835) English architect who developed the Regency style and also designed the fine town planning scheme for London which included Regent Street and its Quadrant. Many buildings in London bear witness to his architectural gifts, notably All Souls' Church, Langham Place, Carlton House Terrace, and the villas included in his plans for Regent's Park. Trained under a London architect, he began his career with the landscape gardener REPTON and was always ready to adapt his style to the wishes of his patron. The Brighton Pavilion, which Nash remodelled for the Prince Regent, is externally Indian in style and internally mainly Chinese and Gothic.

Nash, Ogden (1902-71) American humorous poet, who took many of the faults of bad verse – rambling, uncontrolled lines, irrelevant digressions, puns, ridiculous rhymes – and combined them into witty, satirical or fantastic works.

Nasier, Alcofribas see RABELAIS, François

Nasser, Gamal Abdul (1918-70) Egyptian soldier-politician, creator (1958) and civilian dictator of the United Arab Republic. His nationalization of the Suez Canal led to the Israeli-Franco-British attack on the Canal Zone in 1956. In 1952, his secret Free Officers Movement, with General Mohammed Neguib as its figurehead, seized power, forcing King Farouk to abdicate, making Neguib Prime Minister and President, with Nasser as his deputy. In April 1954, he accused Neguib of absolutist ambitions and assumed the Premiership and presidential powers in November of the same year when Neguib was deposed. Two years later (June 1956) Nasser was officially elected President of Egypt. Nasser's achievements included a number of important social reforms and the building of the Aswan High Dam, with Soviet aid (1964). Nasser was ousted in the Six-Day war of 1967, when Israel simultaneously defeated Egyptian, Jordanian and Syrian armies and extended her frontiers.

Nast, Thomas (1840-1902) German-born American political cartoonist, whose drawings in *Harper's Weekly* injected a new and vitriolic element into American political comment. Nast created the 'Tammany Tiger' (symbol of the corrupt Tammany Organization under 'Boss' Tweed), the 'Democratic Donkey' and the 'Republican Elephant'. His cartoons are said to have been the means of destroying Horace GREELEY's political career and hastening his death. In 1902 Nast was appointed US Consul to Ecuador, where he died.

Navratilova, Martina (born 1956) American tennis player, born in Czechoslovakia. She turned professional in 1975, the year she defected to the United States. As one of the most powerful and determined female players of all time, she has won many championships all over the world.

Nebuchadnezzar II (6th cent. BC) Chaldean King of Babylon who restored its ancient cities, perfecting the city of Babylon and its glories, the 'Hanging Gardens' and the immense ziggurat (stepped pyramid) to the god Marduk – the 'Tower of Babel'. Nebuchadnezzar defeated Necho of Egypt, drove the Egyptians out of Asia, annexed Syria, and crushed Judaea, capturing many Jews as prisoners.

Nehru, Jawalharlal (1889-1964) Indian statesman, who became the first Prime Minister of India following her independence. Nehru joined GANDHI's non-violent Nationalist Movement (1919) and was repeatedly imprisoned (1921-34) by the British for his political activities. He became general secretary of the Indian National Congress and its President (1929-30; 1936-7). He supported the British against the Axis powers in the Second World War but rejected the offer of dominion status made by the CRIPPS mission (1942). After independence (1947) he co-operated with the last viceroy, MOUNTBATTEN, in the partitioning of the subcontinent into India and Pakistan, and in the transfer of political power. As Prime Minister of India from 1947 until his death, he was a world leader of great moral stature, steadily advocating the settlement of international disputes without force, and holding a neutral position between the mutually hostile Western capitalist and Eastern Communist blocs. He committed India to industrialization and instigated the reorganization of the states on a linguistic basis.

Nelson, Horatio, Viscount Nelson (1758-1805) British admiral whose victory at the Battle of Trafalgar (1805) destroyed Franco-Spanish naval power during the Napoleonic wars. Nelson was a supreme exponent of superior fire power to annihilate the enemy. His battle plans, which left much to the initiative of his captains, depended on careful timing and surprise, the objective being to break up the opposing fleet and 'bring about a pell-mell battle'. Nelson lost the sight of his right eye in action off Corsica (1794). He was appointed commodore in 1796, Rear Admiral in 1797 and lost his right arm at Santa Cruz later that year. In 1798 he virtually annihilated a fleet of French ships near the mouth of the Nile. In 1801, he was promoted to Vice-Admiral and, in the Baltic, as second-in-command to Sir Hyde Parker, he led a crippling attack on the Danish fleet anchored off Copenhagen (2 April 1801). Following the engagement he was created a Viscount. In 1803 he was given command of the Mediterranean fleet. During the Battle of Trafalgar, 18 out of 33 enemy ships were taken or destroyed, but Nelson's fleet remained intact. Nelson himself was mortally wounded on board his flagship, *Victory*, shortly after the start of the action.

Nernst, Walter Hermann (1864-1941) German chemist who formulated the third law of thermo-dynamics (1906) and for which, with other contributions to physical chemistry, he was awarded the Nobel Prize in 1920. The law states that at the absolute zero of temperature (−273.12°C), specific heats themselves become zero. As a result, it became possible to calculate the actual values of constants that characterize chemical reactions.

Nero (AD 37-68) Roman emperor whose excesses earned him widespread hatred. Although his reign saw a number of military successes in Asia Minor, Judaea and Britain, and the formation of a Black Sea fleet, Nero preferred sport, profligacy and the arts to the tasks of government. Opponents, real and imagined, were murdered, and many of Rome's Christians were massacred as scapegoats for a fire which destroyed most of the city in AD 64. The loathing in which Nero was held, and the huge taxes levied to rebuild Rome, culminated in provincial riots, and the Senate passed the death sentence on the emperor, who subsequently committed suicide.

Neruda, Jan (1834-91) Czech radical author and critic, whose poetry ranged from the limpid lyrics of *Simple Themes* (1883) to the nationalistic visions of *Good Friday Songs* (1896). His hatred of the upper classes gave his short stories a biting realism, notably *Tales of the Little Quarter* (1878), a powerful collection of stories about the inhabitants of Prague's old quarter. After 1862, he was the drama and literary critic of the leading Prague newspaper *Národnilisty*.

Neruda, Pablo (1904-73) Penname of Neftali Richardo Reyes Basualto, Chilean poet and diplomat, author of the *Canto General* (1950), *Cantos Ceremoniales* (1962) and *Soledades*. He was awarded the Nobel Prize for Literature (1971).

Nerval, Gérard de (1808-55) French poet whose hallucinatory writings, notably *Les Chimères*, a volume of sonnets, anticipate the Symbolists and Surrealists. Nerval's works also include an account of his travels in the Near East, *Voyages en Orient* (1843-51) and a translation of *Faust*, on which BERLIOZ based his *Damnation of Faust*.

Nervi, Pier Luigi (1891-1979) Italian architect who explored the handling of the structural and engineering possibilities of concrete. A major early work was the sports stadium at Florence, and he also designed exhibition halls and hangars. Later buildings which relied on his structural knowledge are the Unesco Building in Paris, and the Pirelli Building in Milan.

Nestorius (5th cent. AD) Syrian Christian and Patriarch of Constantinople from 428 to 431. He is the author of the heresy that Mary, being human, should not be called the Mother of God. This view was condemned at the Council of Ephesus (431).

Neumann, Johann Balthasar (1687-1753) German architect and exponent of Rococo grandeur and spatial complexity. His most impressive work was in the Bishop's Residence at Wurzburg, where he redesigned the staircase. His masterpiece, the pilgrimage church of Vierzehnheiligen (1743-72), gives the finest expression to the vivacious complexities of Rococo architecture.

Neville, Richard, Earl of Warwick (1428-71) English nobleman called 'Warwick the Kingmaker'. During the Wars of the Roses, Neville first supported Richard, Duke of York against the Lancastrian Henry VI. After capturing Henry at Northampton (1460), Neville kept him as puppet king, but was himself the effective ruler. When Richard was killed at Wakefield (1460) and the Lancastrians recaptured Henry, Neville recognized Richard's son as King EDWARD IV (1461) after helping him to win the battle of Towton. Failing to manipulate Edward, he drove him away (1470) and reinstated Henry VI, by then in Yorkist hands. Edward IV returned with an army, and Neville was defeated and killed at Barnet.

Dedicated and practical nationalists, Jan Neruda and his circle aimed to create a new Czechoslovak literature

Nevski, Alexander see ALEXANDER NEVSKI

Newman, John Henry (1801-90) English theologian and a key figure in KEBLE's Oxford Movement. In 1833, while vicar of St Mary's, Oxford, Newman began producing *Tracts for the Times*, the mouthpiece of the movement. In 1841, the controversy over *Tract XC*, which argued that the 39 Articles were compatible with Roman Catholic doctrine, caused Newman to reconsider his religious position. He entered the Roman Catholic Church in 1845, and after ordination founded congregations of the Oratory in Birmingham and London. For many years he was unpopular with both Catholics and Protestants, but his *Apologia pro Vita Sua* (1864), a vindication of his spiritual quest, largely restored his reputation as an outstanding religious figure. He was made a Cardinal in 1879.

Newton, Sir Isaac (1642-1727) English mathematician and physicist, one of the greatest natural philosophers of all time, and perhaps best known for his laws of motion and gravity. In 1665-6, he discovered the binomial theorem, the basic idea of his method of fluxions (what is now called differential calculus), inverse fluxions (integral calculus), and the first ideas concerning universal gravitation. By that time, Newton had also begun his investigations on light and optics. He used a prism to split sunlight into a spectrum, so proving that white light is made up of a mixture of rays of different colours, each of which has its own refractive index. In 1668 he invented the reflecting telescope, urther investigation led him to und a sophisticated form of scular theory, which regards as a stream of tiny particles ling in straight lines. The y was criticized by HOOKE, ad adopted the wave theory of ENS. A century later the work UNG and FRESNEL overcame on's objections to the wave y, and the latter held undissway until the quantum es of the present century, are curiously reminiscent of of Newton's ideas. In 1684, on presented his theory of ation based on the inverse e law, which states that the ational force of attraction en two objects is proportional to the product of their masses and inversely proportional to the square of the distance between them. This enabled him to give a full account of the motions of heavenly bodies. In 1687 he published his masterpiece, the monumental *Philosophiae Naturalis Principia Mathematica*, one of the greatest achievements of the human mind. In the grand manner of EUCLID, the *Principia* starts with certain definitions and the famous three laws of motion: force-free motion is uniform (GALILEO's inertia principle); that accelerated motion is proportional to the impressed force; and for every action there is an equal and opposite reaction. From these, together with the inverse square law of universal gravitation, the whole science of matter in motion is derived. In particular, the new astronomical findings of COPERNICUS and KEPLER could be derived as special consequences of the laws. The approach of *Principia* has dominated science ever since, and there was no significant advance in gravitational theory until the general relativity theory of EINSTEIN.

Newton, John (1725-1807) English evangelical clergyman and author of the *Olney Hymns* (1779). Written with his friend, the poet William COWPER, they became known all over the English-speaking world. Newton's Calvinist views influenced many who took part in the Evangelical revival in the Church of England, which, like Methodism, was a reaction against an apathetic and worldly clergy.

Ney, Michel (1769-1815) French soldier in the Revolutionary and Napoleonic armies, 'the bravest of the brave', according to NAPOLEON. He first distinguished himself at the battle of Ulm (1805), and at Borodino (1812) he showed such dash and courage that Napoleon made him Prince of the Moskowa. After Napoleon's abdication, he retained his rank under LOUIS XVIII. When sent to arrest Napoleon after his return from Elba, Ney defected to his side, and fought for him at Waterloo where he commanded the Old Guard. Despite Louis XVIII's efforts to save him, he was tried and condemned for treason by the Chamber of Peers, and shot.

Nicholas I (1796-1855) Tsar of Russia (1825-55), and a reactionary successor to his brother ALEXANDER I. At the outset of his reign he suppressed the 'Decembrist Conspiracy' (1825) of army officers and nobles seeking a liberalization of government, crushed the Polish nationalist revolt (1830-1) and intervened to help Austria crush the Hungarian Revolution (1848-9). His proposals to partition the Ottoman Empire led Turkey to declare war on Russia (1853). This was one of the causes of the Crimean War, since Britain and France both decided to give Turkey active support. Alexander died as the war was drawing to a close.

Nicholas II (1868-1918) Last Tsar of Russia (1894-1917). Having been inculcated with reactionary ideas by his tutor, Pobedonstev, he was intellectually ill-suited and unprepared to rule over the disturbed state of Russia to which he succeeded on the death of his father, ALEXANDER III. Strikes, agrarian unrest, the humiliation of Russian defeat in her war with Japan (1904-5) and revolutionary propaganda, compelled him to moderate autocratic rule and call the first Russian parliament (Duma) in 1905. In addition a threat to the stability of government was presented by the influence of RASPUTIN over his wife and his heir Alexis. In 1917, after Russian defeats in the First World War, during which Nicholas had assumed personal command of the army (1915), his increasingly precarious situation compelled him to abdicate. The Imperial family was kept under house arrest until the Bolsheviks seized power in November 1917, when they were sent to Ekaterinburg (now Sverdlovsk), where they were murdered in the following year (July 1918).

Nicholson, Ben (1894-1982) British painter, and an important pioneer of abstraction, whose work is much influenced by that of MONDRIAN.

Nicklaus, Jack (William) (born 1940) American golfer who won the US Amateur title twice before turning professional in 1961. Acclaimed as the sport's greatest player, he is the leading money winner of all time in professional golf.

Nicholas II, last of the Tsars of Russia, with his generals after assuming command of his army in the First World War. Two years later he was killed by the Reds

Nielsen, Carl August (1865-1931) Danish composer whose musical career began when he was a boy bugler in the army. Later he became a notable operatic conductor in Copenhagen and turned to composition. His works include an opera, *Masquerade* (1906); a flute, a clarinet and a violin concerto; and the six symphonies by which he is best known internationally.

Niepce, Joseph Nicéphone (1765-1833) French inventor and producer of the first permanent camera photograph, using a pewter plate coated with light-sensitive asphalt. Niepce was also the inventor of photo-etching, which, together with photography, he called heliography. DAGUERRE was working concurrently on similar projects and, in 1829, they formed a partnership to perfect the process, but Niepce died four years before its completion.

Nietzsche, Friedrich (1844-1900) German philosopher and poet, author of *Thus Spake Zarathustra* (1880), the first comprehensive statement of his mature thought, whose central doctrine saw the will for power as the driving force of all human endeavour. His writings include *The Will to Power* (1888) and *The Genealogy of Morals* (1886). His influence on Existentialism, theology, psychiatry and literature has been significant.

Nightingale, Florence (1820-1910) English founder of nursing as a profession, and pioneer of hospital reform. Despite strong opposition from her family she became a nurse, and in 1854, during the Crimean War, took a party of nurses to Scutari. After the Battle of Inkerman she cared for 10,000 wounded British soldiers and found that more deaths were caused by disease and insanitary conditions than by wounds. Her fight to improve conditions and her gift for administration helped to win public support for her views. She returned to England in 1856 and with a testimonial fund of £50,000, she founded nursing colleges inside London hospitals. Her system of nursing was adopted and developed all over the world.

Nijinsky, Vaslav (1890-1950) Russian dancer and choreographer who helped to revitalize ballet outside Russia. Before he appeared in DIAGHILEV's Ballets Russes in 1909, male dancing in Western Europe had become emasculated. Nijinsky brought to the West the new Russian school of male dancing as developed by PETIPA. Insanity ended his meteoric career abruptly in 1917.

Nitze, Max (1848-1906) German urologist, who invented the cystoscope and so laid the basis of modern genito-urinary surgery.

Nixon, Richard Milhous (born 1913) Thirty-seventh President of the US. He first became known through his part in the case that led to the indictment of HISS in 1948 for perjury. He was EISENHOWER's Vice-President (1953-61), but was beaten by John KENNEDY in the presidential election of 1960. Nixon did not abandon politics, however, and in 1969 became President after one of the closest elections of the century. His withdrawal of American forces from Vietnam and limitation of US commitments to oppose external aggression (while providing economic aid to encourage Far Eastern countries to become more self-sufficient) were positive achievements. In August 1974 he became the first US president in history to resign. This followed months of investigation by a Senate Select Committee which led to his eventual admission that he had withheld knowledge of the Watergate scandal. He was succeeded in office by Gerald FORD.

Nkomo, Joshua Rhodes (born 1917) Zimbabwe politician who first became involved in black union politics and then became President of the African National Congress in 1957. In 1961 he was made President of the Zimbabwe African People's Union (ZAPU). He spent much of the 1960s in prison and was finally released in 1974, when he became a member of the African National Congress. He stood for Prime Minister when the Republic of Zimbabwe was formed in 1980 but was defeated by MUGABE.

Nkrumah, Kwame (1909-72) Ghanaian nationalist politician, and first President of the Republic of Ghana. In 1949 he founded the Convention People's Party to work against the new Gold Coast constitution, which he saw as an impediment to full independence. He was arrested for political agitation and imprisoned, but was released in 1951, when his party won the general election. He became Prime Minister of the Gold Coast in 1952 and of Ghana in 1957, and President of the Republic in 1960. Personal extravagance, reckless public spending and his authoritarian behaviour led to his deposition while he was visiting MAO TSE-TUNG in Peking in 1966. Being unable to return to Ghana, he flew to Guinea, where President Sekou-Touré made him joint head of state.

Nobel, Alfred (1833-96) Swedish explosives manufacturer, discoverer of dynamite (1867) and cordite, philanthropist and endower of Nobel Prizes. In 1886, he showed that high explosive nitroglycerine could be made safer to handle by absorbing it into an inert clay, and the result, dynamite, was the basis of his fortune. In 1875 he invented blasting gelatine and, in 1888, cordite. He also experimented with armour plate, artificial rubber and nearly 100 other patented items. The Nobel Prizes, the first of which was presented in 1901, are awarded annually for outstanding contributions to physics, chemistry, physiology and medicine, literature and peace.

Nolan, Sidney (born 1917) Influential Australian artist, whose work is characterized by oddly juxtaposed images set in boldly painted Australian landscapes.

Nordenskjöld, Nils Adolf Eric (1832-1901) Swedish mineralogist and polar explorer who found the North East Passage (1878-9). Successful early expeditions to the Arctic inspired him to try to find the long-sought North East sea passage from Europe to eastern Asia. He sailed in the steamship *Vega* from Tromsö and neared the Bering Strait before being frozen in for the winter. He continued the voyage successfully the following spring.

Norris, Frank (1870-1902) American novelist, who was one of the pioneers of naturalism in American fiction. *McTeague* (1899) shows the influence of ZOLA, mixing romance and realism. *The Octopus* (1901) and *The Pit* (1903), parts of an uncompleted trilogy on the subject of wheat, are strong indictments of the business forces that oppress the farmer. Despite Zola's influence, Norris represented the older American tradition of romantic protest.

North, Frederick, 2nd Earl of Guilford (1732-92) British Prime Minister (1770-82), better known by his courtesy title of Lord North, who, as George III's prime minister, condoned the colonial policy which provoked the American War of Independence. He promised to levy no fresh taxes on the disgruntled American colonists, but to maintain the principle of Britain's right to tax tea, provoking the Boston Tea Party, which precipitated America's struggle for independence (1775-83).

Northcliffe, Alfred Harmsworth, 1st Viscount (1865-1922) English newspaper magnate, pioneer of popular modern journalism. The 1870 Education Act encouraged him to aim at a new reading public, and in 1894, with his brother Harold (later Lord Rothermere), he bought the failing *London Evening News*. In 1896, he launched the *Daily Mail*. The secret of Northcliffe's success was that he published human interest stories and allowed his readers to see 'their own opinions and prejudices echoed in a newspaper'. By 1929 the *Mail*'s circulation was the largest in the world.

Nostradamus (1503-66) French astrologer, physician and prophet, Nostradamus was famous in his own lifetime for his alleged success in the treatment of plague and as the occult consultant of Catherine de MEDICI.

Nottingham, Heneage, 1st Earl of (1621-82) English judge who from his work in the Court of Chancery is traditionally called 'the father of modern equity'. This system of law, based on principles of justice, had since the late Middle Ages flourished in the Courts of Chancery, for which the Chancellor had special responsibility, but lacked system and organization. Nottingham maintained that cases should not be decided at the whim of a Chancellor, and his great contribution to this branch of the law was to determine and establish the principles upon which the Court would be able to act.

Nuffield, Lord (1877-1963) English industrialist who, as Henry FORD had done in America, popularized cheap motoring in Britain. He combined notable inventive powers with successful production methods and made a fortune, which he later devoted to philanthropy. As William Morris, he worked for 20 years in vehicle workshops before concentrating on cars, founding the Morris Motors Company in 1919. The firm expanded, merging with Austin (1952) to form the giant British Motor Corporation (now British Leyland).

Nureyev, Rudolf (born 1939) Russian-born dancer. In 1961 as a rising star of the Kirov Ballet he defected to the West during a visit to Paris. His partnership with Margot FONTEYN, in performances with the Royal Ballet and the Australian Ballet, have become legendary.

Nurhachi (1559-1626) Jürched tribal leader, the virtual founder of China's last imperial dynasty, the Ching or Manchu (1644-1912). As the Ming dynasty declined, Nurhachi built up Jürched power north of China proper. He united Jürched tribes, organized troops and adopted Chinese techniques to strengthen government. In 1616 he proclaimed himself Emperor, then openly attacked China. He took the Liao Basin east of Peking (1621) and ruled from Mukden (1625). His successors became undisputed rulers of all China.

Nyerere, Julius (born 1922) Tanzanian nationalist leader who became the first Prime Minister, and later President, of his country. He began his career as a schoolteacher but in 1955 decided to devote himself to nationalist politics, becoming leader of the Tanganyika African National Union, and Premier when the Union won the 1961 elections. When Tanganyika and Zanzibar jointly attained independence as Tanzania (1962), he was elected President.

O

Oates, Titus (1649-1705) English Protestant priest, who revealed the mythical Popish Plot (1678). Using knowledge gathered during spurious studies for the Catholic priesthood, Oates, with Israel Tonge, a fanatical anti-Jesuit, concocted a Jesuit plot to kill CHARLES II, place the Duke of York on the throne, burn London and massacre Protestants. When revealed, the plot terrified England and resulted in the execution of 35 probably blameless citizens. Oates was awarded a pension, but later, his perjury having been proved, he was severely flogged, successfully sued by the Duke of York for £100,000 and imprisoned.

Oberth, Hermann Julius (1894-1979) German rocket pioneer who, as early as 1923, foresaw the practicality of manned space-flight and, in 1929, described designs of suitable vehicles powered by liquid-fuelled motors and other forms of propulsion, which subsequently were developed. His research, which attracted the support of the army, eventually led to the formation of the Peenemünde research establishment in Germany and the development of the V2 missile.

Obote, Milton (born 1924) Ugandan political leader whose presidency was overthrown in 1971 by the military coup led by General Idi AMIN. Obote spent nine years in exile in Tanzania, returning to Uganda after Amin's regime had been overthrown (1979) and President Binaisa was deposed (1980). He was elected President again, on a pledge to work for national unity.

Obregon, Alvaro (1880-1928) Revolutionary and President of Mexico. In 1912 he joined MADERO in the struggle against DIAZ, and supported Carranza in the counter-revolution following Madero's death, defeating Huerta (1913-14), Zapata and VILLA in 1915. He was a man of liberal ideals and forced Carranza to agree to the restoration of land to the Indians, and later, when Carranza attempted to violate the constitution, Obregon raised a revolt which resulted in his becoming President in 1920. His administration (1920-4) was notable for its land, educational and financial reforms and the establishment of friendly relations with the USA. In 1928, Obregon was again elected President, but was assassinated before he could take office.

O'Brian, Flann see BRIAN O'NOLAN

O'Casey, Sean (1880-1964) Irish dramatist, who wrote *Juno and the Paycock* (1924). He specialized in tragi-comedies of Dublin slum life, such as *The Shadow of a Gunman* (1922), his first play. The Abbey Theatre, which had staged his other plays, turned down *The Silver Tassie* (1928), in which he shifted to Symbolism. O'Casey thereupon moved to England and for a time refused to allow his work to be performed in Ireland. The best known of his other plays are *The Plough and the Stars* (1926), about the 1916 Easter Rising, *Purple Dust* (1940) and *Red Roses for Me* (1943).

Ochs, Adolph Simon (1858-1935) American newspaper publisher who injected fresh integrity into American journalism. Buying the *New York Times* in 1896, he boosted its 9000 circulation to 466,000 before his death, publishing 'All the News That's Fit to Print' (which remains the paper's slogan), and so strengthening the high moral standards set by its first editor, Henry Jarvis Raymond (1820-69).

Octavian see AUGUSTUS

Odoacer (c. 433-93) German barbarian ruler who formally ended the Roman Empire in the West when he deposed Romulus Augustulus in 476. He was accepted as King of Italy by the eastern emperor, Zeno, and by the Roman Senate, but was killed when the Ostrogoths under THEODORIC invaded Italy.

Oersted, Hans Christian (1777-1851) Danish physicist who discovered the magnetic effect produced by an electric current (1819) after noticing that a compass needle close to a wire carrying a current swung about wildly and eventually settled at right-angles to the wire. He realized that there must be a magnetic field around the wire produced by the current. His momentous discovery was the starting point for FARADAY, AMPÈRE and other scientists.

Offa (8th cent.) King of Mercia, an English kingdom, who was the first Anglo-Saxon king to acquire a European reputation. He dominated all the kingdoms south of the River Humber and, to protect his boundary with Wales, built an immense earth-work and ditch, which still survives and is known as Offa's Dyke.

Offenbach, Jacques (1819-80) French composer of the highly successful operettas *La Belle Hélène* (1864) and *Orpheus in the Underworld* (1858), and of the opera *Tales of Hoffman* (1881), based on the works of Eta Hoffman. With their light satire and catchy tunes, Offenbach's operettas (he wrote more than 90) are important in the history of the genre.

Ogethorple, James (1696-1785) British general and philanthropist, founder of the American state of Georgia (1733). After acquiring a 21-year charter he arrived with 120 settlers to found a colony as a refuge for unemployed debtors and persecuted Protestants from Europe. Having fought off Spanish attacks, in 1752 he made over Georgia, whose population totalled 4000 colonists, to the British Crown.

Ohm, Georg Simon (1789-1854) German physicist who discovered the law describing the flow of electric current through a conductor. In the 1820s, after painstaking experiments, he found that the current flowing through a wire depends both on its length and thickness. From this he was able to define what is now called electrical resistance. By 1827 he had formulated Ohm's law, which underlies the study of current electricity. It states that the current flowing through a conductor is proportional to the voltage across it and inversely proportional to its resistance.

Oistrakh, David (1908-74) Leading Russian violin virtuoso and the first Russian musician to travel abroad and make a name in the West after the Second World War. PROKOFIEV, among other composers, wrote works especially for him. Oistrakh's son, Igor, is also a virtuoso violinist.

Olaf I, Tryggvesson (969-1000) King of Norway, who converted his country to Christianity. Olaf was converted while leading raids on the coasts of Britain and France, and employed English priests to evangelize Norway. He was eventually defeated at sea by the combined fleets of Denmark and Sweden and drowned himself.

Olbers, Heinrich (1758-1840) German astronomer, a doctor by profession, who discovered five comets (one is now called Olbers's Comet), and the minor planets Pallas and Vesta.

Olcott, Henry see BLAVATSKY, Helena

Oldenburg, Claes (born 1929) American Pop artist, inventor of soft sculpture, and, partly, of so-called happenings.

Oleg (10th cent.) Varangian (Russo-Scandinavian) leader, who consolidated the state which forms the nucleus of modern Russia. From Novgorod he captured Smolensk and Kiev, and made Kiev the capital of a Kievan-Novgorod state. He forced the Byzantine emperor Leo VI to agree to a commercial treaty, which greatly increased Russian wealth.

Olivier, Laurence, Lord (born 1907) English actor, director and theatre manager, one of the outstanding creative influences on British acting. He was director of the National Theatre from 1962-1973. Since 1974 he has appeared chiefly in films and television. His autobiography *Confessions of an Actor* was published in 1982.

Omar Khayyám (c. 1050-c. 1120) Persian astronomer and poet, known chiefly in Europe through the translation of his *Rubáiyát* by Edward FITZGERALD. He also undertook important astronomical research and supervised a calendar reform for the sultan Malik-Shah. He was one of the great mathematicians of the period.

O'Neill, Eugene (1888-1953) American dramatist whose plays, initially controversial for their use of drab, common language, combined a realism and expressionism which soon established him as a leading dramatist. He was awarded the Pulitzer Prize for his play *Beyond the Horizon* (1920), which was followed by the successful *The Emperor Jones* (1920); *All God's Chillun got Wings* (1924) which introduced the negro-white relationship; *Desire Under the Elms* (1924); *Strange Interlude* (1928), an experimental nine-act play using long asides; the trilogy *Mourning Becomes Electra* (1931) in which O'Neill recounts the Greek legend in American terms, and the comedy *Ah Wilderness* (1933). *The Iceman Cometh* was produced after 12 years silence from O'Neill. His autobiographical *A Long Day's Journey into Night* was not produced until after his death, in 1955.

O'Neill, Hugh, 2nd Earl of Tyrone (c. 1540-1616) Leader of the northern Irish in their resistance to English power in Ireland. After serving with the English, he rebelled and defeated an English force at Yellow Ford on the Blackwater River, but, even with Spanish aid, lost the crucial Battle of Kinsale (1601). He submitted to the English Crown, but later fled to Europe. JAMES I redistributed his lands in Ulster mainly among Protestant Scots and English.

O'Nolan, Brian (1911-66) Irish writer who used two pseudonyms. As Myles na Gopaleen he wrote a column for *The Irish Times* for 26 years. As Flann O'Brian he wrote anarchically funny novels, notably *At Swim Two Birds* (1931) and *The Third Policeman* (1967).

Oppenheimer, Sir Ernest (1880-1957) German-born South African mining magnate and philanthropist. In the space of 40 years, his Anglo-American Corporation of South Africa, founded in 1917, came to control 95 per cent of the world's diamond supply. He was a close friend of SMUTS and raised the Kimberley Regiment in the First World War. His benefactions include university chairs and slum-clearance schemes in Johannesburg.

Oppenheimer, Robert (1904-67) American physicist in charge of the development of the first atomic bomb. In the early 1950s, as McCarthyism raged through the United States, Oppenheimer's political motives were brought into doubt and he was declared a 'security risk'.

Orff, Carl (1895-1982) German composer whose best-known work is *Carmina Burana* (1936), a 'cantata' designed to be performed on the stage. Consisting of settings of hedonistic medieval Latin poems celebrating spring, drink and love, it shows all the characteristics of his style: constantly reiterated rhythms hammered out by a large orchestra with strong percussive support and, by consciously avoiding counterpoint, recreating some of the energy of medieval music.

Ortega y Gasset, José (1883-1955) Spanish philosopher, writer and statesman, whose most influential works are his analyses of Spain and Europe in the 1920s: *Invertebrate Spain* (1921), *The Revolt of the Masses* (1929-30) and *The Modern Theme* (1923). A humanist, he believed in individualism: 'I am I and my circumstance'.

Ortelius (1527-98) Flemish cartographer and antiquarian who produced the first known modern atlas. An engraver turned antiquarian, he began map-making after 1560 under MERCATOR's influence. In 1570 he produced *Theatre of the Lands of the Globe* – the earliest known modern collection of maps to be bound together in one volume. It comprised 53 plates totalling 70 maps produced in a standard form from the best sources available.

Orwell, George (1903-50) Pen-name of Eric Blair, English journalist, critic and novelist, who wrote

Animal Farm (1945) and *Nineteen Eighty-four* (1949), powerful political fables pointing out the dangers of bureaucratic, totalitarian government. Born in India, he left a bitter criticism of Imperial England in *Burmese Days* (1934). After a period of wandering, recalled in *Down and Out in Paris and London* (1933), he lived by writing. *Keep the Aspidistra Flying* (1936) was a document of the depression in England. In essays, from *Inside the Whale* (1940) to *England Your England* (1953), he examined the institutions and social structure of England.

Osborne, John (born 1929) English dramatist and actor, whose play *Look Back in Anger* (1956) began a revival in English drama, and introduced the term 'angry young man', personified by the leading character, Jimmy Porter. *The Entertainer* (1957), in which Laurence OLIVIER created the part of Archie Rice, was another success, and established Osborne as a leading exponent of British social drama. The musical *The World of Paul Slickey* (1959), which was a failure, was followed by the widely acclaimed *Luther* (1961). Other plays include *Inadmissible Evidence* (1964), *A Patriot for Me* (1965), *Hotel in Amsterdam* (1968) and *A Sense of Detachment* (1973).

Osman I (1259-1326) Turkish founder of the Ottoman Dynasty (*c.* 1300-1922), members of which established the Ottoman Empire, based on Asia Minor.

Ostwald, Wilhelm Friedrich (1853-1932) Russian-German chemist who established the nature of catalysis. After studying Josiah GIBBS's work on chemical thermodynamics, Ostwald suggested that catalysts are substances which can increase or decrease the rate of a chemical reaction without themselves taking part in it – a view which, in a modified form, is still held today.

Oswald, Lee Harvey (1940-63) American assassin of US President, John F. KENNEDY, on 22 Nov. 1963. He was killed by Jack Ruby, a nightclub owner, while in the custody of the Dallas police.

Otis, Elisha Graves (1811-61) American inventor of a safety device for mechanical lifts (1852), which made very tall buildings practicable. His first steam-powered passenger lift was installed in the five-storey New York store of E. G. Haughwort and Co. in 1857. The first electrically operated elevators date from 1889.

Now the commonest form of motive power for transport, the four-stroke internal combustion engine. The first of its kind was made by Otto in 1876

Otto, Nicholaus August (1832-91) German inventor, in 1876, of the four-stroke internal combustion engine. In the following decade 30,000 of his engines were sold, the forerunners of modern automobile and aeroplane power plants.

Ottokar II 'The Great' (c. 1230-78) King of Bohemia (1253-78), who made Bohemia the leading Germanic nation. He was the ruler of Moravia and Austria, which had been vastly enriched by the discovery of silver mines and enlarged by his seizure of Styria and inheritance of Carinthia and Carniola. To counterbalance Bohemia's power, the other German princes elected Rudolf of Hapsburg as emperor (1273). Ottokar, however, refused to recognize Rudolf. War ensued and he was compelled to cede all his lands except Bohemia and Moravia.

Oughtred, William (1575-1660) English mathematician who invented the slide rule. He also introduced the terms sine, cosine and tangent for the common trigonometrical ratios.

Ovett, Steve (born 1955) British athlete who won the gold medal in the 800 metre race at the 1980 Olympics. He holds the record for the greatest number of mile/1500 metre victories.

Ovid (c. 43 BC-c. AD 17) Roman poet and story teller, author of *Metamorphoses*, a collection of stories written in 15 books of hexameter verse, which have entertained and inspired artists and poets since the Middle Ages. His other works include the short, erotic elegies *Amores* (16 BC); the contrived elegiac letters of the *Heroides* and *Ars Amatoria* (*c.* 1 BC); a cynical elegiac poem in three books dealing with the *demi-monde* and presenting Love as a science, in mockery of contemporary textbooks. The disapproval caused by the work's 'immorality' was a probable cause of Ovid's banishment by AUGUSTUS in AD 8 to Tomis on the Black Sea, where he lived out his life writing verse.

Owen, Sir Richard (1804-92) British biologist, who was a pioneer in vertebrate palaeontology and in concise descriptive nomenclature. His prolific publications, including *Odontography* (1840-5), an exhaustive study of teeth, and *History of the British Fossil, Mammals and Birds* (1846), were important contributions to comparative anatomy and palaeontology.

Owen, Sir Robert (1771-1858) Welsh industrialist, who pioneered practical, cooperative socialism. After being a draper's apprentice at Stamford he borrowed capital to start his own textile workshop in Manchester. In 1800, as a result of his marriage to the daughter of David Dale, he became manager and partner in his father-in-law's textile mills at New Lanark. New Lanark became the centre not only of his business interests but also of his educational, philanthropic and propagandist activities in which he was supported by the Quaker philanthropist William Allen and the philosopher Jeremy BENTHAM. Contrary to common industrial practice, he improved the working and moral conditions of his employees.

Owen, Wilfred (1893-1918) Welsh poet, killed in action shortly before the end of the First World War, whose *Poems* (1920) portrayed, without nationalistic bias, the human suffering of war.

Owens, Jesse (1913-80) American athlete, who is famous for his performances in the 1936 Berlin Olympic Games. Owens refuted HITLER's theory of Aryan supremacy by breaking two Olympic records, equalling a third and helping smash the world record for the 400 yards relay. He became one of seven American negro athletes to win gold medals in the Games.

Jesse Owens, the US negro athlete whose achievements at the 1936 Berlin Olympics were an affront to Hitler and his beliefs in Aryan supremacy

P

Paderewski, Ignacy Jan (1860-1941) Polish virtuoso of the piano who became his country's first Prime Minister (1919-20). Internationally famous for his romantic approach, among his best-known works are his *Polish Fantasia* for piano, and the opera *Manon*.

Paganini, Niccolò (1782-1840) Leading Italian violin virtuoso of the Romantic era whose technique was such that its brilliance led to an extensive folklore about his having made a pact with the Devil. As a consequence, for five years following his death, the Church denied him burial in consecrated ground.

Paine, Thomas (1737-1809) English social and political reformer and author of *The Rights of Man*. Paine was an excise officer, but was dismissed for attempting to improve the salaries of his profession and emigrated to Pennsylvania (1774), where he wrote the pamphlet *Common Sense* (1776), in which he demanded independence for the American colonies. He fought in the War of Independence and was Secretary to the Foreign Affairs committee of the Continental Congress (1777-9). He returned to England in 1787 and published *The Rights of Man* (as a riposte to BURKE's attack on the French Revolution) which advocated the overthrow of the British monarchy and the introduction of a republican form of government. He was tried for treason *in absentia* and outlawed and fled to France. Later, he became a member of the Convention and identified himself with the Girondins, but after their fall in June 1793, he was imprisoned until the demise of ROBESPIERRE and the Jacobins (1794). In 1802 he returned to the US but found radicalism so unpopular there that he was treated as an outcast.

Palestrina, Giovanni Pierluigi da (c. 1525-94) Italian composer, regarded as one of the most important composers of sacred music. He was technically conservative, consolidating the work of precursors like DE PRES, imposing strict rules and creating absolute standards. The many masses that he composed as choirmaster at the Julian Chapel in St Peter's, Rome, are claimed ecclesiastically to be supreme examples of a liturgical style. When he died, 'Prince of Music' was inscribed on his coffin.

Palladio, Andrea (1508-80) Italian architect of the late Renaissance. Through his theoretical writings he exerted a great influence in England, Germany and Scandinavia, where a vigorous and restrained style known as Palladianism or Neo-Palladianism developed in the 18th century. His intense interest in Roman antiquity was stimulated by reading the Roman architectural scholar Vitruvius and by studying antique buildings in Rome. Most of his own work, which is in Venice and Vicenza, reveals that he was an architect of originality who could employ classical motifs to new effect. His Villa Rotunda at Vicenza has four porticos arranged symmetrically around a central hall, and other buildings by him include the churches of Il Redentore and San Giorgio Maggiore in Venice.

Palmer, Samuel (1805-81) English landscape artist, who was influenced by BLAKE in using his art to express a mystical relationship with nature. The originality of his style has the effect of focusing attention on individual objects so that their symbolic significance becomes clear to the observer.

Palmerston, Henry John Temple, 3rd Viscount (1784-1865) British statesman, notable for his vigorous and aggressive assertion of British foreign policy. He was cabinet minister for 38 of his 58 years in parliament, and Foreign Secretary almost continuously from 1830 to 1841, under GREY, and again from 1846 to 1851 under RUSSELL. As a champion of the independence of small states, he was largely responsible for the independence of Belgium in 1831, but by 1846 he had developed the high-handed imperialistic diplomacy for which he became famous – a mixture of bluff and belligerency which was the despair of both Queen VICTORIA and his colleagues, but which endeared him to the British people. The mismanagement of the Crimean War led to his becoming Prime Minister in 1855 and, partly as a result of his appointment, the war was soon brought to an end.

Pankhurst, Emmeline (1858-1928) English suffragette, whose militant actions helped to secure the franchise for women in Britain. She and her followers broke windows, chained themselves to railings in public places and even resorted to arson. After being arrested on several occasions, Mrs Pankhurst was sentenced to three years' imprisonment in 1913, though she served only one year of her sentence, during which she went on hunger strike. In the First World War, she persuaded women to do war work, which helped to reconcile masculine opinion to her cause and in 1918, women over the age of 30 received the vote. In 1928, the franchise was extended to those between the ages of 21 and 31.

Papandreou, Georgios (1888-1968) Greek politician who led a government-in-exile during World War II (1944-45). After the war he served on several Social Democratic cabinets before forming the Central Union Party in 1961. He was elected PM in 1964 but placed under house arrest after the coup of 1967.

Papin, Denis (1647-c. 1712) French mathematician and physicist. Having worked as assistant to HUYGENS, he went to England (1675) to work for BOYLE. In 1679, he showed that the boiling point of water depends on atmospheric pressure, and built the world's first pressure cooker and the steam safety valve to make the device safe.

Pappus (4th cent.) Greek geometer in Alexandria, whose *Collection*, now partly lost, is a comprehensive treatise on Greek mathematics and includes results of his own. Parts of his other works also survive.

Paracelsus (c. 1493-1541) Swiss alchemist and doctor, sometimes called the Father of Chemistry. Paracelsus ridiculed the classical theory of the four humours which dominated medieval medicine. After extensive study in the mines of the Tyrol he initiated the use of minerals such as arsenic, lead, mercury and iron, as well as tinctures and alcoholic extracts, into the chemical treatment of disease.

Paré, Ambroise (c. 1510-90) French surgeon, a pioneer of modern surgery. Haemorrhage was the greatest 16th-century surgical problem which Paré solved by using ligatures and simple dressings rather than boiling oil, as was the common practice.

Park, Mungo (1771-1806) Scottish surgeon and explorer in West Africa. Seeking a rumoured giant river, he travelled up the Gambia, crossed the upper Senegal Basin, and discovered the Niger at Segou (1795-6). Surviving fever, robbery and imprisonment, he returned to England, where his *Travels in the Interior of Africa* (1799) revolutionized knowledge of West African tribes. Park drowned in the Bussa Rapids after a 1000-mile voyage down the Niger in an attempt to trace its mouth.

Parker, Charles (1920-55) American jazz alto-saxophonist who recorded with Dizzie Gillespie in the 1940s and was one of the founders of the 'bebop' style. As one of the most widely imitated of all jazz musicians, he had enormous influence on the jazz saxophone.

Parker, Dorothy Rothschild (1893-1967) American writer and humorist who achieved literary notoriety for her acerbic poems and commentary. She once described a prominent actress as 'running the whole gamut of emotion from A to B'. She finally committed suicide.

Parkinson, James (1755-1824) English physician noted for his work on '*paralysis agitans*' (Parkinson's disease).

Parler, Peter (1330-99) German architect who designed Prague Cathedral, with its fantastic system of interlacing rib-vaults, in a style similar to that developed earlier in the west of England. Parler came from a famous family of southern German master-masons: his father, Heinrich, probably designed the chancel of Schwäbish-Gmünd, a hall church in the late Gothic style.

Parmigianino, Il (1503-40) Italian painter and etcher, whose frescoes in the Cathedral (1522) and S Giovanni Evangelista (1522-3) at Parma show the influence of CORREGGIO. Parmigianino's obsession with distorted forms is found in both the bizarre and highly artificial elongation of limbs in his Madonnas and in the early *Self-Portrait*, painted with the aid of a convex mirror.

Parnell, Charles Stewart (1846-91) Irish Home Rule leader. An Anglo-Irish Protestant, he became an MP in 1875. As leader of the Home Rule movement from 1880 he tried to further the cause by his skill as an orator, by his parliamentary tactics of disrupting House of Commons business, and by advocating protests among Irish peasants, such as the boycotting of landlords. He was arrested and imprisoned for incitement to riot (1881), but was released when GLADSTONE realized that only Parnell could pacify the Irish. Parnell supported Gladstone's Home Rule Bill of 1886 and he remained a potent influence in English and Irish politics until 1890, when he was discredited by a divorce action.

Parr, Catherine see HENRY VIII

Parry, Sir William Edward (1790-1855) British naval officer and Arctic explorer who made one of the earliest attempts to reach the North Pole. He made four unsuccessful voyages (1818, under John Ross; 1820; 1821; 1824) in search of the North West Passage from Europe to eastern Asia. In his bid to reach the North Pole (1827), he used sledge-boats over the ice from Spitzbergen to a point 82° 45′ N, for 50 years the most northerly latitude reached.

Emmeline Pankhurst's militant Women's Social and Political Union of 1903 fought press indifference to Women's Lib—but by 1910, over 500 women, Mrs Pankhurst and her daughters included, had suffered imprisonment and forced feeding

Parsons, Sir Charles Algernon (1854-1931) English developer of the steam turbine, to power generators. His first engine (1884) developed 10 h.p. at 18,000 r.p.m., and by 1900, he was building 1000 kW machines. In 1896, he built *Turbinia*, the first turbine-propelled launch, which reached the unprecedented speed of 34½ knots and created a sensation at the Spithead naval review, marking Queen VICTORIA's jubilee (1897).

Pascal, Blaise (1623-62) French philosopher, scientist, mathematician and writer whose major literary works include *Lettres Provinciales* (1656-7) and *Les Pensées* (1670). In his comparatively short life, Pascal invented a calculating machine, shared with Fermat the discovery of the theory of mathematical probability, founded the science of hydrodynamics, wrote treatises on conic sections and experimented with atmospheric pressures. In 1654, Pascal underwent a profound spiritual crisis which led him to concentrate on religious matters, rather than the physical universe. The *Lettres Provinciales* are brilliant anti-Jesuit satires in defence of Antoine ARNAULD, while the unfinished apologia for Christianity, *Les Pensées*, published posthumously and based on notes from his manuscript, is one of his most important works.

Pascoli, Giovanni (1855-1912) Italian pastoral poet whose early compositions, such as *Myricae* (1891), portray the world of nature and particularly the country life of his native Romagna. They are characterized by a considerable attention to detail and by a sense of melancholy and an awareness of death. His later *Poemi Conviviali* (1904) and *Hymns and Odes* (1906) are more preoccupied with social and moral themes.

Pasternak, Boris (1890-1960) Russian novelist and poet, who wrote *Doctor Zhivago* (1957), a vast novel which analyses the role of the intelligentsia in Russia before, during and after the Revolution, and evoking the beauty of the Russian countryside. Because the book rejected Marxism in favour of the individual it had to be smuggled out of Russia and was published in Milan. Pasternak was awarded a Nobel Prize for Literature (1958), but the Soviet authorities forced him to decline it. Eventually the Communist demand for 'socialist realism' stifled his poetic talents and he turned to the translation of foreign literature.

Pasteur, in his *Etudes sur le vin*, recorded the effect of time and oxygen on wine. Red wine A without air retains its colour; with air it fades, B; white wine without air C does not change; with air it turns brown, D

Pasteur, Louis (1822-95) French chemist, whose work, with that of Robert KOCH, led to a general acceptance of the theory that disease is caused by living organisms. He laid the groundwork for modern vaccine therapy and developed a vaccine against rabies. Pasteur's involvement with disease-causing organisms began in 1854, when he was able to prove that fermentation in sugar-beet was caused by minute living organisms. Twenty years later he was inspired by the work of Koch to study anthrax, which was at that time killing a large number of French sheep, and cholera in chickens. In the course of this work, he happened to inoculate some chickens with a culture of chicken cholera that was several weeks old, hoping that they would get the disease. But they survived, and proved immune to all subsequent inoculations of the same virus. What Pasteur had done – unknowingly – was to attenuate the virus (weaken it to such a degree that the body's natural defences could deal with it and so gain immunity). This attenuation technique is still the basis of many modern vaccines. Pasteur demonstrated its value in 1881 when, before numerous doctors and journalists, he injected 48 sheep with a virulent form of anthrax, 24 of them having been vaccinated with an attenuated anthrax culture. Only these 24 survived.

Pater, Walter (1839-94) English critic and prose writer, whose criticism and style greatly influenced 19th-century ideas on aesthetics. He became famous with *Studies in the History of the Renaissance* (1873) and *Marius the Epicurean* (1885).

Paterson, William (1658-1719) English financier who founded the Bank of England. In 1694, WILLIAM III approved his plan for a national bank formed as a joint-stock organization by merchants who raised £1,200,000 from shareholders and lent it to the king at 8 per cent interest. William granted the Bank a royal charter allowing it to issue bank notes to the value of the royal loan. Paterson thus founded what is now the United Kingdom's wholly government-owned central bank.

Paton, Alan (born 1903) South African novelist, whose books are strong and moving protests against apartheid and the treatment of Africans in his country. From his experience of politics and native life, Paton wrote the lyrical *Cry, the Beloved Country* (1948), an examination of racial relations.

Patrick (c. 389-c. 461) Romano-British saint and evangelizer of the Irish. He set up an organized church in Ireland with his episcopal see at Armagh and encouraged monastic foundations.

Patton, George Smith (1885-1945) American general, known as 'Blood and Guts'. In the First World War, he commanded an armoured brigade on the Western

Front and in the Second World War led the first American troops to fight in North Africa (1942-3). He commanded the 7th Army in the Sicilian campaign (1943) and the US 3rd Army in 1944, leading it in a sweep to Paris and beyond.

Paul (1st cent. AD) Apostle to the gentiles. Born a Jew and a Roman citizen at Tarsus (Asia Minor), into a Pharisaic family, Paul may have trained as a rabbi. His conversion to Christianity shaped the remainder of his life, driving him to preach the Gospel throughout an extensive part of gentile territory to the north of the Mediterranean until his death, which, according to tradition, was by beheading in Rome during NERO's persecution in AD 64. Paul's letters form a substantial part of the New Testament, showing him to be a vigorous man and a thinker whose statement of the Christian faith provided a framework for traditional Christian theology. In spite of severe difficulties, described by some as malaria, epilepsy or glaucoma, Paul played an important part in the growth of the Early Church, and dominated much of its later development.

Paul VI (Giovanni Batista Montini) (1897-1978) 264th Pope who, despite world-wide anxiety over the 'population explosion', reaffirmed, in his encyclical *Humanae Vitae* (1968), the Roman Catholic Church's prohibition of artificial methods of birth control. He was elected Pope in 1963. He reformed the curia by reducing the number of its departments and restricting major appointments to a period of five years instead of for life, all such appointments terminating with the death of the reigning Pope. He inaugurated in the curia a Foreign Affairs Department (the Council for Public Affairs of the Church) and authorized Mass to be said in the vernacular. He travelled extensively for world peace and ecumenism.

Pauli, Wolfgang (1900-58) Austrian physicist who discovered the exclusion principle in 1925, for which he was awarded a Nobel Prize 20 years later. The Pauli exclusion principle states that no two electrons in an atom can occupy the same quantum state at the same time. In 1931 he was the first to suggest the existence of the neutrino, a particle without charge or mass.

Pauling, Linus Carl (born 1901) American chemist and resolute opponent of nuclear weapons and the only person (other than Marie CURIE) to receive two Nobel Prizes, one for Chemistry (1954) and one for Peace (1962). He applied quantum mechanics (an approach established by Erwin Schrödinger and Paul Dirac) to the problem of how atoms and molecules enter into chemical combination with each other and (1939) he produced a full account of chemical bonding. Later he was an advocate of strong doses of vitamin C as a treatment for the common cold.

Pavarotti, Luciano (born 1935) Italian tenor who made his operatic debut in 1961. He performed with La Scala (1963-4) and toured Australia with Joan Sutherland in 1965. He is known internationally as an exceptional concert performer and has recorded over 30 albums.

Pavese, Cesare (1908-50) Italian novelist, critic and poet, author of *The Comrade* (1947) and *The Moon and the Bonfire* (1950). Pavese's novels mingle realism and symbolism with a strong sexual undercurrent highlighting his pessimistic view of the futility of a moral code, and even of life itself.

Pavlov, Ivan (1849-1936) Russian physiologist and father of behaviourist psychology. His great contribution to psychological knowledge is his theory of the 'conditioned reflex', which he took to be the basic model of mental activity. His many laboratory experiments to establish this theory included those in which the sound of a bell could be made to produce exactly the same effect on a dog as the sight and smell of food which, for instance, evokes the response of salivation. Pavlov showed that if a bell was rung when the food was presented, in time the sound alone caused salivation. The animals had thus been 'conditioned' to respond.

Pavlova, Anna (1881-1931) Russian ballerina and the first popularizer of ballet on a world-wide scale. She performed in Russia, then in 1909 became DIAGHILEV's first ballerina, gaining fame as creator of the leading roles in *The Dying Swan* and *Les Sylphides*.

Paxton, Sir Joseph (1801-65) English designer of the Crystal Palace for the Great Exhibition held in London in 1851. This enormous building made of glass, wood and iron included full-grown trees among its arcades and was a development of Paxton's previous designs for giant glasshouses at Chatsworth, Derbyshire. His use of prefabricated methods of erection on a large scale was unprecedented.

Peacock, Thomas Love (1785-1866) English critic, poet and novelist who wrote satirically of the literary, political and social fashions of the day. The satires *Headlong Hall* (1816), *Nightmare Abbey* (1818) and *Crotchet Castle* (1831) are comprised mainly of conversations at house-parties. He was a close friend of SHELLEY, 'Mr Scythrop' in *Nightmare Abbey*.

Pearson, Lester Bowles (1897-1972) Canadian Liberal statesman. As Foreign Minister from 1948 to 1957, he was Canada's spokesman at the United Nations, and was President of the General Assembly from 1952 to 1953. Russian opposition prevented his election as Secretary-General. His efforts to create a UK Emergency Force during the Suez crisis of 1956 won him the Nobel Peace Prize in 1957. He was Prime Minister of Canada from 1963 to 1968.

Peary, Robert Edwin (1856-1920) American Arctic explorer, credited with being the first man to reach the North Pole. After a four-year reconnaissance, Peary tried in 1905 to reach the Pole, and got within 200 miles of it before harsh weather forced him back. His second attempt (1908-9) proved successful and Peary finally reached the North Pole on 6 April 1909, with Matthew Henson (a negro servant) and four eskimoes. The United States Congress confirmed Peary's claim to have been first to the Pole, discrediting Frederick COOK's claim to have reached it a year earlier.

Peel, Sir Robert (1788-1850) English statesman, Prime Minister and founder of the Metropolitan Police force, known after him as 'Peelers'. In his ministry of 1841-6 the government, though committed to retain the Corn Laws, introduced a series of free trade budgets, passed measures to increase financial stability (Bank Charter Act 1844) and revised income tax (1842). As a result of the crisis caused by the Irish potato failure (1845-6), the pressure of the Anti-Corn Law League, and, perhaps, his own conviction of the inevitability of repeal, the Corn Laws were abolished. The consequent split in the Conservative party kept it out of effective office for a generation.

Pelé (born 1940) Brazilian association footballer who played his first international for Brazil in 1957. In 1969, during his 909th match, he became the world's first player to score 1000 goals in football. He retired from international competition in 1971, but later he joined the New York Cosmos in the North American Soccer League (1975-7), helping to popularize the sport in the United States.

Pellegrini, Carlo see APE

Penn, William (c. 1644-1718) English Quaker, founder of the state of Pennsylvania. Despite the later disputes that divided the colony, Penn's vision of a tolerant and humane society helped to mould American constitutional history, and his religious devotion softened hostility to Quakers in England. A life-long champion of religious toleration, Penn was persecuted for his writing and preaching, and despairing of achieving toleration in England, successfully negotiated for the new colony of Pennsylvania in 1682, seeing it as a haven in which persecuted Quakers could freely practise their religion and maintain friendly relations with their Indian neighbours.

Pepys, Samuel (1633-1703) English civil servant, who is famous for the *Diary* which he kept between 1660 and 1669. It is a vivid record of public and private London life, the court of CHARLES II and the administration of the Royal Navy.

Samuel Pepys, remembered for his diary, played a large part in the modernization of the Royal Navy

Perceval, Spencer (1762-1812) The only British Prime Minister to have been assassinated. He was Chancellor of the Exchequer under Portland (1807), and succeeded him as Prime Minister in 1809. In 1812 he was shot in the lobby of the House of Commons. His assassin, John Bellingham, was not a political opponent, but a bankrupt with a grievance against the government.

The status of Athens as the birthplace of democracy and as one of the glories of western culture owes much to Pericles, who dominated its affairs for 30 years. He was instrumental in building the Parthenon, which still looks over Athens

Percy, Sir Henry (1364-1403) English knight, known as Harry Hotspur for his fiery fighting qualities, who helped to place HENRY IV on the throne in 1399. After quarrelling with Henry, he rose in rebellion, supported by the Welshman, Owen Glyndower, but was killed at Shrewsbury.

Perelman, Sidney Joseph (1904-79) American humorist who was for a time scriptwriter for the MARX Brothers. His stories, many of them written for the *New Yorker*, appear in several collections. Their humour is based on verbal fantasy, arising out of the ironies of everyday situations.

Perez Galdos, Benito (1843-1920) Spanish novelist who has been compared, in scope, quantity and quality of work, with BALZAC, DICKENS and TOLSTOY. Beginning with *The Golden Fountain* (1870), he produced a cycle of 46 historical novels covering events in Spain between 1805 and 1875. This was followed by 30 volumes of novels dealing with contemporary Spanish life, including his most famous work, *Fortunata and Jacinta* (1886-7), a four-volume novel whose range and depth of characterization have been compared with *War and Peace*. Though concentrating on Madrid, and on the middle-classes, his attitudes developed and matured from a youthful, dogmatic belief in material progress to a more tolerant interest in all human experience.

Pergolesi, Giovanni Battista (1710-36) Italian composer who, before his early death from tuberculosis, evolved a style of exceptional charm. After his death, opportunist music publishers put out minor works under his name to exploit his popularity, hence correct attribution of his works has always been a problem: it is uncertain whether the songs STRAVINSKY used as the basis for his ballet *Pulcinella* were in fact by Pergolesi. Authenticated works, however, include several operas and a Stabat Mater.

Pericles (c. 495-429 BC) Athenian statesman, who was the dominant figure in Athens at the height of its fame and made it the intellectual centre of Greece. Pericles, who was *strategus* (general-in-command) for nearly 30 years, introduced payment for public government and jury service, and by opening government posts to all citizens, irrespective of social status, ended the privileges attached to noble birth. He made Athens artistically supreme by inviting men of genius from abroad, initiating the building of the Parthenon and other beautiful edifices, and befriending the philosophers SOPHOCLES and ANAXAGORAS, and the sculptor Phidias. At first he sought expansion by aggressive means and fought imperialist wars in Egypt, Boeotia and the Aegean Islands, but after the collapse of an Athenian army in Boeotia (447 BC), he changed his policy and began to consolidate the empire, while maintaining the naval supremacy by which Athens had attained its unprecedented commercial prosperity. Pericles died of plague whilst leading Athens in the unsuccessful Peloponnesian War against Sparta.

Perón, Juan Domingo (1895-1974) Argentinian dictator who was a member of the right-wing group of army officers who seized power in 1943. He achieved wide popularity through a programme of social reforms, and was elected President in 1946. In suppressing all opposition and trying rapidly to industrialize his country, he relied for popular support to a great extent on the personality cult of his wife, Eva, through his control of various newspapers and her much-publicized interest in social welfare. After her death (1952), however, Perón's popularity declined, and his alienation of the Church and the army led to his deposition and exile in 1955. In 1973 he once more assumed the presidency, assisted by his new wife, Isabella. He died of a heart attack in 1974 and was succeeded by his widow. She herself was deposed by a military coup.

Pérrault, Charles (1628-1703) French poet and writer of fairy tales, including *Tom Thumb*, *Red Riding Hood*, *Cinderella* and *Blue Beard*. He also wrote *Parallèles des Anciens et des Modernes* (1688-97) in which he pleaded the cause of the 'moderns' against BOILEAU.

Perrault, Claude (c. 1613-88) French architect, doctor and sculptor, who was probably largely responsible for the imposing east front of the Louvre, with its colonnade of coupled Corinthian columns. BERNINI had submitted designs for this project and LE VAU and LE BRUN were also on the design committee.

Perret, Auguste (1874-1954) French architect and early user of reinforced concrete in architecture, to whom LE CORBUSIER was once apprenticed. His early flats in the rue Franklin, Paris, were faced with Art Nouveau ceramic panels of leaves and berries, but three years later, on his Ponthieu Garage, Paris, he left the concrete structure exposed.

Pershing, John Joseph (1860-1948) Commander-in-Chief of the American forces in France in the First World War. After distinguishing himself in the Spanish-American war (1898), he was sent to the Philippines, where he succeeded in pacifying the fanatical Moros of Mindanao (1913), for which Theodore ROOSEVELT promoted him from captain to brigadier general. He was appointed Commander-in-Chief of the American Expeditionary Force to France in 1917.

Perugino, Pietro (c. 1445-1523) Italian artist of the Umbrian school, best known for his religious paintings and particularly significant because he was the master of RAPHAEL from *c.* 1500-4. Perugino's earliest surviving work is a picture of St Sebastian, which is the sole remnant of a series of frescoes that he painted in the church at Cerqueto. This painting synthesizes the highest qualities of Perugino's art and anticipates those of the High Renaissance – simplicity of composition and an uncluttered, lucid style. At the turn of the century the Perugian Guild of Bankers commissioned him to paint a cycle of frescoes in their Salo del Cambio, and it is likely that this was the period during which the young Raphael learned the basics of fresco technique. His many altarpieces are characterized by harmonious, symmetrical designs and a certain sentimentality of treatment.

Peruzzi, Baldassare (1481-1536) Italian High Renaissance architect, whose most famous building is the Villa Farnesina, Rome, which he designed and which RAPHAEL decorated. His style is often characterized by an almost flippant grace and a seemingly facile quality.

Pétain, Henri Philippe (1856-1951) Marshal of France, a hero of his country in the First World War and who died, serving a life sentence for treason, after the Second. Pétain distinguished himself in the First World War by his courageous defence of Verdun in 1916 and the following year he was appointed Commander, French Army. He was later replaced by FOCH. He was ambassador to Spain in 1939 and in 1940, when the French defences collapsed, succeeded Reynaud as Prime Minister, almost immediately signing an armistice with Germany (June). At the head of the Vichy government in unoccupied France, Pétain applied a reactionary and pro-clerical policy, but when the Germans occupied the whole of France (November 1942), he became their puppet. He was abducted to Germany by the retreating Nazis in 1944, but was arrested by the French after the war and tried for high treason. He was condemned to death, but DE GAULLE commuted the sentence to one of life imprisonment, and Pétain died in prison.

Peter I 'The Great' (1672-1725) Tsar of Russia (1682-1725), who brought Russia into Europe and transformed it from a backward country into a modern state. Peter was determined to give Russia outlets to the sea and made the study of naval and military technology the basis for a policy of forceful expansion. He made incognito visits to Austria, England, Germany and the Netherlands (1696-7), and was impressed by the West's material progress. His observations while abroad helped him to modernize the Russian army and to found a navy on Western lines. His return to Russia was precipitated by a rebellion (1698), which he suppressed. Peter then embarked on a long war (1699-1721) against Sweden, and despite a crushing defeat at Narva (1700), recovered and won the decisive battle of Poltava (1709) against CHARLES XII. Eventually, under the Treaty of Nystadt (1721), Russia acquired certain Baltic territories, which included Estonia and Livonia. By thus establishing Russia as northern Europe's leading military power, and by making his newly founded capital of St Petersburg a safe Russian outlet onto the Baltic, Peter assured the country's future as a leading European state.

Peter, St (1st cent.) Galilaean fisherman who became a leader of JESUS's disciples, their spokesman and their representative. His character is the most clearly delineated of the apostles', and his human, impetuous love of and devotion to Jesus have inspired Christians in all ages. Although little is known of his activity after Jesus's death, it is known that Peter held a leading position in the Early Church, clashed with St PAUL about the importance of the Jewish Torah (Law) for Christians, and that he appears to have travelled to Rome where, according to tradition, he was crucified upside down, possibly during NERO's persecution in AD 64. Later tradition made him the Bishop of Rome, where the Church of St Peter is said to stand upon the site of his crucifixion.

Peterson, Oscar (born 1925) Canadian jazz pianist with a formidable technique. He led his own trios from the early 1950s and was much in demand to accompany other musicians and singers, such as Ella FITZGERALD.

Petrarch (1304-74) Italian scholar and humanist, who was one of the great forerunners of the Italian Renaissance. His love poems to the unknown Laura have inspired imitators down the ages and rank among the greatest of all European love poems.

Petronius Arbiter, Gaius (1st cent.) Roman writer, author of the *Satyricon*, a picaresque novel, part verse and part prose, and extant only in fragments, but unique in Latin literature. Witty and obscene, it recounts the adventures of three disreputable young freedmen in the low haunts of Campania and Magna Graecia, and paints an unforgettable picture of the *nouveau-riche* Trimalchio, a dinner at whose house forms the subject-matter of the longest surviving part. The novel is our chief source book for 'Vulgar Latin'.

Pevsner, Antoine (1886-1962) Russian abstract sculptor and Constructivist. His abstractions were based on the pure scientific and geometric theories of aesthetics, the creation of forms being related to mathematics and physics. Pevsner worked on surfaces that enclosed, covered and separated space, as in his *Peace Column*, an abstract sculpture in bronze. With his brother, Naum GABO, he wrote (1920) the Realist Manifesto, in which were presented the fundamental concepts of Constructivism.

Pheidippides (5th cent. BC) Athenian long-distance runner who ran 140 miles in 48 hours to seek Spartan aid against Persian invaders who had landed at Marathon, and then reputedly returned to take part in the battle. This story inspired the idea of a long-distance race (from Marathon to Athens) in the first Olympiad of modern times (1896).

Philby, Harold Adrian Russell 'Kim' (born 1911) English master spy for the Russians. Recruited by them in 1933, he became a member of the British Secret Intelligence Service, and in 1944, set up the British anti-Russian counter-intelligence system, which he ran until 1946. From 1949-51 he worked closely with the American CIA in Washington and thus was able to inform Russia of almost all the West's counter-espionage operations – and to protect other Soviet agents, such as Burgess and MACLEAN, whose defection and escape he assisted in 1951. It was at this time that he came under suspicion, and was asked to leave the Foreign Service. In 1955, following a Foreign Office investigation, his reputation was rehabilitated. In 1963, however, he admitted that the allegations that had been made against him were true, and fled to Russia, where he was granted Soviet citizenship.

Philip II (1527-98) King of Spain (1556-98), whose policies permanently weakened the state that had been made powerful by FERDINAND V and Isabella I. He was the only legitimate son of the Emperor CHARLES V, and was ruler not only of Spain, but of its colonies in the New World, as well as Italy, Naples and Sicily, Milan and the Burgundian provinces of the Netherlands and Franche-Comté. Fanatically set upon championing Roman Catholicism and bolstering the power of the Spanish Hapsburgs in Europe, Philip grappled unprofitably with France (1556-9 and 1589-98); and provoked WILLIAM THE SILENT's struggle for Dutch independence, which began in 1567. After the death of England's queen, MARY I, the second of his four wives, he fought England, led by ELIZABETH I, losing the Spanish Armada (1588). With it went control of the seas, which had given Spain its immense empire in America. Though Philip successfully claimed Portugal (1580), Spain's economic decline was caused by his costly wars and inefficient government.

Philip IV 'The Fair' (1268-1314) King of France (1285-1314), who strengthened the monarchy by ending the feudal privileges of the Church. Philip's demands for taxes from the clergy caused a long dispute with Pope Boniface VIII, but Philip dominated Boniface's French successor, Clement V (who moved the Papal court to France in 1305), and founded Gallicanism (independence of the French Church). To find money for wars with England and Flanders, Philip raised levies, robbed and expelled the Jews, suppressed and despoiled the rich Order of Knights Templars, and called the first States General (1302), which he used as a means of exacting taxes from the nation.

Philip V (1683-1746) King of Spain (1700-46), first of the Spanish Bourbon dynasty (1700-1931), whose accession started a major European war. He was the grandson of LOUIS XIV of France, who contrived Philip's inheritance of the vast Spanish empire from the childless Charles II, the last Spanish Hapsburg ruler. By seemingly uniting Spain with France, Philip's accession altered the European balance of power, and provoked the War of the Spanish Succession (1701-14), which left Philip in power, but caused Spain's permanent separation from France.

Philip of Hesse (1504-67) Landgrave of Hesse (1509-67), known as 'the Magnanimous' whose activity during the Reformation decisively influenced the course of German history. After embracing Lutheranism (1524), Philip formed an alliance with Saxony which became the axis of German Protestantism. The Saxon-Hesse alliance was extended to a Protestant League (1526) and to the Schmalkaldic League (1531) to resist the Emperor CHARLES V, but, after Philip had made a bigamous marriage, widespread personal hostility forced him to submit to the emperor. Further conflict between the two caused Charles to imprison Philip in 1547. Released in 1552, he continued in vain to form a strong league of Protestant states.

Philip, Arthur (1738-1814) English naval commander, who established a penal colony (1788) in Australia at Sydney (named after the British Home Secretary of the time), and became first Governor of New South Wales.

Piaget, Jean (1896-1980) Swiss psychologist, one of the foremost researchers into the thought processes of children, whose studies on child psychology have had a vital influence on modern education policy. Piaget sees perception in the child as unstable, distorted and fraught with illusion, and the process of learning, or growing up, as a gradual advance towards an orderly organization of experience, which helps the child to adapt more comfortably to its environment.

Picard, Jean (1620-82) French astronomer who first accurately measured a degree of longitude. Working under Jean Dominique CASSINI, in 1669-70, he made the first precise measurement of an arc of the meridian when he measured a degree of longitude between Amiens and Mahoisine, north of Paris. Superseding medieval estimates of the degree, Picard's achievement – together with the triangulation surveying technique developed by Gemma Frisius – made possible the accurate mapping of the entire world.

Picasso, Pablo (1881-1973) Spanish-born artist, who was perhaps the greatest and certainly the best known of modern painters. As a boy in Spain, he possessed a remarkable technical virtuosity, and the stylistic innovations he subsequently developed must be seen in the context of this early mastery of traditional artistic means. He went to Paris in 1900, settling there in 1904. This was his 'Blue Period', so called because of the predominant colour of his canvases, which were a personal expression of the social and psychological concerns of the Symbolist movement (e.g. *La Vie*, 1903). This phase of his development was succeeded by the 'Pink Period', during which he painted the *Family of Acrobats* (1905). Then in 1907, with the large, figurative composition, *Les Demoiselles d'Avignon*, Picasso abruptly banished sentiment from his work and, with the support of BRAQUE, embarked on a series of formal researches, inspired by CÉZANNE and by African carvings. The result was Cubism, the most influential and far-reaching of all modern art movements. Picasso's individuality is evident in all but the more 'scientific' of his Cubist paintings, and from about 1915 he reintroduced a style of figurative Classicism into his work concurrent with the development of 'analytical' Cubism. In 1917 he made his first stage designs (*Parade*, in collaboration with DIAGHILEV, SATIE and COCTEAU). His later paintings (e.g. *Three Dancers*, 1925, and *Guernica*, 1937, painted in protest against FRANCO's bombing of that town during the Spanish Civil War) still owe much to Cubism, rendered highly expressive, especially in the handling of the human figure, and recalling the humanitarian motivation of his earliest work.

Piccard, Auguste (1884-1962) Swiss physicist, balloonist and deep-sea explorer. In a balloon, he reached a world record altitude of 53,153 feet in 1932 and, in a deep-sea research vessel called a bathyscaphe, he descended 10,000 feet into the Tyrrhenian Sea in 1953.

Piccard, Jacques (born 1922) Swiss oceanographic engineer who (with Don Walsh of the United States Navy) first reached the lowest-known point of the Earth's crust, 35,800 feet down, in an attempt to reach the bottom of the Challenger Deep in the Pacific's Mariana Trench.

Pickering, Edward Charles (1846-1919) American astronomer who invented the meridian photometer, a device for finding the magnitude of a star by comparison with a star of known brightness. He was responsible for the publication of a giant catalogue of the spectra of all the northern hemisphere stars.

Pierce, Franklin (1804-69) Fourteenth President of the US (1853-7), whose domestic policies caused a resumption of the conflict which led to the Civil War. In 1852, after a period of retirement from politics, he was adopted as a compromise Democratic candidate. He encouraged the building of trans-continental railroads and extended US territory by the Gadsden Land Purchase from Mexico (1853). His main achievement in foreign affairs was the opening of Japan to American trade through the expedition of Commodore Perry in 1853. He is now chiefly remembered for his approval of the Kansas-Nebraska Act, which opened up those territories for settlement, leaving the question of slavery to be resolved locally. Contrary to his inaugural promise to bury the slavery controversy, the Kansas-Nebraska Act served to raise the issue again, and his Southern sympathies alienated Northern opinion, so that under his successor, James B. Buchanan, the spectre of civil war reappeared.

Piero della Francesca (c. 1420-92) Italian artist who synthesized the Florentine interest in form with the Venetian painters' study of light and atmosphere. The scientific precision of his compositions and his eye for harmonic proportion are evident even in what is probably his earliest known work, the *Baptism of Christ*, whose pale colours, combined with the calm grandeur of the figures, lend the air of timelessness for which he is celebrated. The fresco cycle *Legend of the True Cross* (1452-*c.* 1459) in the choir of St Francesco at Arezzo, though unknown until the 19th century, is considered his greatest achievement.

Pietro da Cortona (1596-1669) Florentine architect and painter, who is particularly known for his frescoes, the most famous of which is the *Allegory of Divine Providence and Barberini Power* in the Barberini Palace, Rome.

Piggott, Lester (born 1935) British jockey who had 52 wins by the age of 15. After his champion apprenticeship, Piggott went on to become one of racing's most successful jockeys, winning 17 classics between 1954 and 1970. He is a master tactician, combining great determination with superb judgement.

Pindar (518-c. 438 BC) The most famous lyric poet of Ancient Greece. Pindar wrote all kinds of choral lyric, but the poems which survive complete are all *epicinians*, odes written to celebrate a victory in one of the great athletic festivals. His works supported moral conclusions about human virtue and the laws of the gods.

Pinkerton, Allan (1819-84) Scottish-born founder of one of the first and best known of the American detective agencies, the Pinkerton National Detective Agency. It was established in Chicago in 1850.

Pinter, Harold (born 1930) British dramatist and actor, and leading exponent of the Theatre of the Absurd. *The Birthday Party* (1957), though a commercial failure, had a critical success on the stage and subsequently on television. His first success was *The Caretaker*. He wrote a number of short plays for radio and television which were later staged. He returned to full-length plays with *The Homecoming* (1965), and has written film scripts.

Pintoricchio, Bernardino (c. 1454-1513) Italian painter of large, multi-figured frescoes, whose work developed under the influence of PERUGINO, with whom he worked as an assistant on some of the frescoes in the Sistine Chapel. The fresco cycles (1492-5) in the Borgia apartments of the Vatican and the ten scenes from the life of Pius II in Siena Cathedral Library (1503-9), are his most important works.

Pirandello, Luigi (1867-1936) Italian dramatist, who wrote *Six Characters in Search of an Author* (1921). His work has affinities with the Theatre of the Absurd. He was at one time a short-story writer and later wrote one-act plays. In 1916 came his first full-length play *Think of it, Giacomino* and *Right You Are if You Think You Are*. Apart from the world-famous *Six Characters*, his best-known plays are *Beast and Virtue*, *Man*, *Each in His Own Way*, *As You Desire Me* and *Henry IV*.

A Spaniard who turned his back on Spain, disliking its régime, Picasso ranks with the giants of art

Pisano, Nicola (c. 1225-c. 1278) Italian sculptor and architect, regarded as the last of the medieval classicists. In his first important work, the Baptistry pulpit at Pisa (1260), and in the pulpit at Siena Cathedral (1265-8) – a development of the earlier work – the classical influence is strong, in both the structure and the sculptured parts.

Pissarro, Camille (1830-1903) French Impressionist painter, whose early works were much influenced by COROT and COURBET, but by 1869 had acquired a definitive Impressionist style. His best works were done during the ensuing decade. Pissarro's example was crucial in encouraging CÉZANNE to abandon his early Romanticism. GAUGUIN too was much indebted to him, and he had the reputation of being both brilliant and sympathetic. His letters provide an anecdotal history of French painting in the second half of the 19th century.

Pitman, Sir Isaac (1813-97) English publisher, and inventor of a short-hand system of writing. The company he founded still publishes books on short-hand and commercial subjects.

Pitt, William, Earl of Chatham (1708-78) British statesman, known as 'Pitt the Elder', to distinguish him from his equally famous son, William PITT the Younger. He was called into the government to help to defeat France, Britain's greatest rival, in the Seven Years' War (1756-63). Pitt became Secretary of State (1756), and masterminded the intercontinental land and sea war. French forces in Canada and India were attacked, her communications were hamstrung by sea blockades and FREDERICK II of Prussia's continental armies were subsidized. George III, on his accession (1760), was determined to end the war, and faced with his opposition, the Cabinet refused to declare war on Spain, as Pitt wished to do, and he resigned (1761). George III's policy ended the war in 1763, but Pitt's strategy had brought the British Empire towards its zenith by assuring Britain's hold on North America and India, and annexing territories in Africa and the West Indies.

Pitt, William (1759-1806) British statesman and Prime Minister (1783-1801, 1804-6), called 'the Younger Pitt', son of William PITT the Elder. At the age of 23 he became Chancellor of the Exchequer (1782), and then, at 24, Britain's youngest Prime Minister. He increased the power of the cabinet and incidentally that of the prime minister within it. Finance was his first concern, and to reduce and fund the National Debt he floated loans, increased the tax on windows in private houses, introduced many new taxes, and organized a sinking fund. To revitalize the economy he tried to establish free trade and made a commercial treaty with France. His India Act (1784) transferred political control of the country, previously vested in the East India Company, to the crown. By formally uniting Ireland with Great Britain (1801) he established the United Kingdom. His years of office were marked by the rise of French power. After the young French republic had declared war (1793), Pitt organized and subsidized three European coalitions against France (1793, 1799, 1805). The cost of these operations undermined his financial position and forced him to raise loans, increase general taxation, impose duties on legacies and introduce income tax.

Pius IX (1792-1878) The longest reigning Pope (1846-78) who promulgated the dogmas of the Immaculate Conception (1854) and Papal Infallibility (1870). While a cardinal, he professed liberal sentiments and inspired Italian patriots, but after being elected Pope in 1846, he became progressively reactionary and during the insurrections of 1848 in Rome fled to Gaeta in the kingdom of Naples. He returned to Rome under French military protection, established the Roman Catholic hierarchy in Britain (1850) and Holland (1853), attacked all forms of social progress, and sought by new dogmas to enhance his religious authority in compensation for his loss of secular power. From the day in 1870 when Italian troops entered Rome, he regarded himself as a prisoner in the Vatican.

Pius XII (1876-1958) Pope during the Second World War, whose ambivalent attitude to the Fascist and Nazi dictatorships proved controversial. After being elected Pope (1939) he refused to condemn the seizure of Czechoslovakia, to support ROOSEVELT's appeal to HITLER to urge MUSSOLINI to desist from aggression, or to condemn the invasion and occupation of Poland. Above all, while expressing sympathy for Belgium, Holland and France when they were invaded, he refused to rebuke Germany. At no time did he condemn the Nazis' extermination of the Jews. After the war, Pius XII was influential in social and economic policies of the UN and called for disarmament.

Pizarro, Francisco (c. 1470-1541) Spanish conqueror of the Inca empire, who took part in ALMAGRO's expeditions (1524-5, 1526-7) which discovered the Peruvian civilization of the Incas. Pizarro obtained permission to conquer and govern Peru south of the Gulf of Guayaquil, and although heavily outnumbered by Inca warriors, Pizarro cowed them by killing their chief, Atahualpa (1533). He acquired great wealth in Peru and founded Lima, but fought with and killed Almagro (1538), whose followers killed Pizarro in revenge.

Planck, Max Karl Ernst Ludwig (1858-1949) German physicist, who was awarded the 1918 Nobel Prize in Physics for his discovery of the quantum theory of radiation. Planck's famous hypothesis is that energy from an oscillating particle is emitted not continuously but in discrete quanta (or 'packets' of energy). The energy for any given frequency of oscillation is h times that frequency, where h is a universal constant, later called Planck's constant. The full significance of this new idea lay in its development into modern quantum theory.

Plantin, Christophe (1514-89) French printer and typographer, whose work was characterized by its single clarity of design. A bookbinder and bookseller, he took up typography in 1555 and his books became famous for their copperplate engravings for illustrations. His most notable work was the Antwerp Polyglot Bible, an eight-volume work which attempted to standardize the texts of the Old and New Testaments. Plantin became one of Europe's outstanding printers, and a Plantin typeface is used for the main text of *Who Did What*.

Plath, Sylvia (1932-63) American poet and wife of Ted HUGHES, who, through her work, struggled with the human difficulties and torments which finally overcame her, and she committed suicide. Her best-known collection of works is *Ariel* (1965). She also wrote a novel, *The Bell Jar* (1963), and her journals, published in 1982, were awarded a Pulitzer Prize.

Plato (c. 427-347 BC) Greek philosopher in whom the great pre-Socratic strains of Greek philosophy meet: the mathematically inspired doctrines of PYTHAGORAS and his followers; the logic of Parmenides and the Eleaticism of Zeno and the theories of HERACLITUS. Plato never composed a systematic treatise of his views, believing such a treatise to be inimical to philosophy, which should be disinterested enquiry arising from the general critical examination of all knowledge. There are two phases in his work. The earlier, Socratic, stage is marked by the Pythagorean theory of Ideas or Forms. The later, Platonic, stage avoided this split between the real and the ideal, and also gave much direct advice on social matters. Throughout this development ran a theory of ethics equating the ultimate good with perfect knowledge. The *Republic*, Plato's best known work, is a discussion on the nature of justice, the citizen and the state, touching on a vast range of issues in philosophy, ethics and social sciences. Among the other dialogues, the Apology describes the trial of his friend SOCRATES, who was executed in 399 BC; the *Phaedo* records Socrates's last hours, spent in discussion with friends about immortality; the *Sophist* showed a beginning of Plato's own logical theories; the *Timaeus* presented a mathematical theory of the world and the *Laws* offered advice on practical, legal and other social problems.

Plautus (late 3rd-2nd cent. BC) Roman dramatist, highly successful in freely adapting the Greek New Comedy of Manners for Roman audiences. Unworried about realism or authenticity, he exaggerated Greek conventions and introduced Roman elements for comic effect, exploiting situations of mistaken identity or deception with great skill. Of 20 surviving plays, the *Menaechmi* was used by SHAKESPEARE for his *Comedy of Errors* and several, notably the *Captives*, *Truculentus* and *Bacchides*, are occasionally revived.

Plimsoll, Samuel (1824-98) English politician and social reformer, best remembered for his strenuous campaign to prevent shipowners from sailing undermanned, unsafe and overinsured ships. Eventually the Parliamentary Bill of 1876 gave powers of government inspection and obliged all ships to carry a mark (the Plimsoll mark) showing the waterline at maximum loading. In 1890, his publication, *Cattle-Ships*, exposed the danger and cruelty of the sea trade in cattle.

Pliny the Elder (23-79) Roman writer and author of the 37-volume *Historia Naturalis*, usually known as *Pliny's Natural History*. The most comprehensive extant work of the period, it deals with his views on cosmology, philosophy, mineralogy and the living world.

Pliny the Younger (62-113) Roman orator and writer, nephew of PLINY THE ELDER. His books of letters, polished for publication, constitute a social history, with varied pictures of cultural life under the emperor TRAJAN. An outstanding example of his descriptive style is the account of Vesuvius' eruption (AD 79), in which his uncle died. Book 10, an exchange of letters with Trajan, is of great historical interest and includes Pliny's well-known report from Bithynia of the treatment of the Christians.

Plotinus (c. 205-270) Greek philosopher, probably of Egyptian origin, and the foremost of Neo-Platonists, who saw the ultimate source of everything as the One or the Good; in contact with it, but on a lower level, is Nous or Mind, below which is the Soul. This three-fold division has influenced Christian theology of the Trinity.

Plunkett, Roy Joseph (born 1910) American chemist, who in 1938 synthesized the plastic, polytetrafluorethylene (PTFE or Teflon), whose remarkable properties include excellent electrical insulation, stability over a wide temperature range, resistance to attack by most corrosive agents and an extremely low coefficient of friction. Teflon was marketed commercially by Plunkett's company in the 1950s, and has found innumerable industrial applications, as well as providing the essential coating in domestic non-stick hardware.

Plutarch (c. AD 46-c. 120) Greek biographer whose 46 *Parallel Lives of Illustrious Greeks and Romans* remain some of the best records of eminent men of the classical world, despite some factual inaccuracy. Pairing Greek soldiers, statesmen, lawmakers, etc., with Roman counterparts, Plutarch drew comparisons between ALEXANDER THE GREAT and CAESAR, incorporating legends which Arrian (2nd century AD) omitted from his more strictly factual account.

The Plimsoll line on ships grew from a concern for the safety of mariners

Pocahontas (c. 1595-1617) American Indian princess who saved the life of John SMITH, a Virginian colonist, by shielding his head from the blows of the warriors of Chief Powhatan, Pocahontas's father. Captured by the settlers, she was converted to Christianity, married John Rolfe and voyaged to England where she died of smallpox.

Poe, Edgar Allan (1809-49) American writer of mystery stories and supernatural tales, among which was the first modern detective thriller, *The Murders in the Rue Morgue*. The outcome of his horrific tales (e.g. *The Fall of the House of Usher* and *The Pit and the Pendulum*, both of which have been filmed), many of which were written under the influence of opium, swings between death and insanity. His poem, 'The Raven' (1845), later published in book form, consolidated his success.

Polanski, Roman (born 1933) Polish film director and former actor. He made his reputation with *Repulsion* (1965). Other films include *Rosemary's Baby* (1968), *Chinatown* (1974) and *Tess of the D'Urbevilles* (1981).

Pollaiuolo, Antonio (c. 1432-98) Italian sculptor who was the first artist known to have studied anatomy by means of dissection (anticipating LEONARDO by some years), and the detailed analysis of the human anatomy under conditions of active strain. This knowledge is displayed in the painting of the *Martyrdom of St Sebastian* (*c.* 1475), and in the bronze *Hercules and Antaeus* (early 1470s). The two largest works which display Antonio's best compositional ability, as well as his mastery of the form of the human body, are the tombs of Pope Sixtus IV (1493) and of Pope Innocent VIII (*c.* 1495), the first-known tomb to display a sepulchral effigy in the form of a living man.

Pollock, Jackson (1912-56) American painter and pioneer of Abstract Expressionism. After painting in a style influenced by American Realism and the city-scapes of Joseph

Stella, he absorbed the Surrealism of MIRÓ and of Gorky, both of whom allowed the subconscious to play an important role in their painting. Pollock went further, dripping pigment over large areas of canvas to form a complex web of lines and areas of colour. This became known as 'action painting'.

Polo, Marco (c. 1254-c. 1324) Venetian merchant whose travels in Asia were probably the most extensive of medieval times. He accompanied his father Nicolo and uncle Maffeo on their second trading trek to China, reaching Peking in 1275 after travelling via Palestine, Persia, the Pamirs and the Gobi Desert. In Peking, Marco Polo entered the service of KUBLAI KHAN, who employed him on various missions in the Mongol Empire – including visits to Shansi, Shensi, Szechuan, Yunnan, the Tibetan borders and northern Burma. Kublai would not hear of the Polos returning home until, in 1292, they were allowed to take a new Mongol wife to Kublai's widowed grandnephew, the Khan of Persia. They travelled, with many delays, via Sumatra, India, Persia, Trebizond and Constantinople, eventually reaching Venice in 1295. Marco's account of his travels, *The Book of Marco Polo*, told Europeans for the first time of Oriental marvels, including asbestos, burning coal, paper money and block-printing, and gave a first glimpse of China's immense wealth, size and powerful neighbours.

Polykleitos (5th cent. BC) Greek sculptor whose *Doryphoros* (*c.* 450) illustrates his dogma that ideal beauty can be achieved by mathematics, especially in the proportion of one part of the body to another. Although famed for his bronze sculptures, the colossal statue of *Hera*, which stood in the temple near Mycenae, was probably made of ivory and gold.

Pompadour, Marquise de (1721-64) Renowned French beauty and mistress of LOUIS XV. As Jeanne Antoinette Poisson she deserted her husband to become the King's mistress, then Duchesse de Pompadour. She dominated the weak-willed Louis but had less influence on domestic and foreign policies than was once thought.

Pompey the Great (106-48 BC) Roman general and statesman, who became master of the East, and was an opponent of Julius CAESAR. He served as consul (70 BC), then, having swept the eastern Mediterranean clear of pirates (67-63 BC), assumed control of southwest Asia after defeating MITHRIDATES of Pontus (66 BC). He then seized Palestine and Syria, and penetrated as far as the Caspian and the Euphrates. With Crassus and Caesar he formed the first triumvirate (60 BC). He supported the aristocratic senate against Caesar, the popular leader, and was his last obstacle to the dictatorship. But he himself was defeated at Pharsalus (48 BC) and murdered in Egypt.

Pompidou, Georges (1911-74) French politician, who became President of France after DE GAULLE's defeat in the referendum of 1969. Pompidou fought in the Resistance movement during the Second World War and afterwards served in various government agencies. He was Prime Minister from 1962 to 1963 and, after that year's election, from 1963 to 1968, when he was dismissed by De Gaulle following the student riots and industrial unrest of that year. On De Gaulle's retirement, he stood for President and was elected at the second ballot with 58 per cent of the votes.

Ponce de León, Juan (1460-1521) Spanish explorer and apparent discoverer of Florida. Travelling with COLUMBUS, he arrived in America in 1493, and later conquered Puerto Rico (1509), where he became Governor. Under royal orders from Spain, Ponce de León once more set sail, in 1513, in a continuing search for new lands and for the legendary 'Fountain of Youth', which was said to be located on the island of Bimini. On East Sunday (in Spanish *Pascua Florida*) of that year, Ponce de León discovered the mainland and landed at a site near present-day St Augustine. He continued explorations around the peninsula and finally abandoned the search for the 'Fountain of Youth'.

One of history's most famous beauties, Antoinette, Marquise de Pompadour

Pontiac (c. 1720-69) American Ottawa Indian chief who mobilized Indian tribes against the British in North America. In 1762 (with promises of French help) he united almost all Indian tribes from the Mississippi Valley to Lake Superior in the most ambitious of all Red Indian alliances. Indians seized every major fort with the exception of Pittsburgh and Detroit in a plan to slaughter all British colonists.

Pope, Alexander (1688-1744) English poet, who was one of the foremost literary figures of the 18th century. He polished the heroic couplet, a specific metrical verse form, to an unrivalled perfection, and made it ideal for his varied subjects. His satires, 'The Rape of the Lock' (1712), a mock-heroic attack on London's fashionable society, and the 'Dunciad' (1728), a diatribe against dullness and pedantry, are outstanding for their pithy, telling criticism and their descriptions of city life. In his moral and philosophic poems – the verse 'Epistles', the *Moral Essays*, and the *Essay on Man* – the exposition is brilliant, but the thought conventional. Pope first gained public acclaim for his free translations of HOMER's *Iliad* and *Odyssey*, and became a leading member of the literary world of ADDISON, SWIFT and GAY.

Porta, Giacomo della (1541-1604) Italian architect who designed the magnificent dome of St Peter's, and façade of the Gesù, Rome.

Porter, Katherine Anne (1890-1980) American author, who often uses southern states and Mexico as a setting. She writes carefully constructed, atmospheric stories, as in *Pale Horse, Pale Rider* (1939).

Potter, Beatrix (1866-1943) English writer of children's stories. Many of her popular tales concern Peter Rabbit and other shrewd, humorous animals. Her delicate illustrations match her stories.

Poulenc, François (1899-1963) French composer and piano accompanist. Poulenc's works include the ballet *Les Biches* (1924).

Pound, Ezra (1885-1973) American poet, and one of the most influential critics and controversial writers of the century. Apart from his own writing, his principal importance was his encouragement to and battles for T. S. ELIOT and James JOYCE. He was a leading member of the Imagist and Vorticist movements, and the poems in *A Lume Spento* (1908), *Personae* (1909) and *Umbra* (1920), with their rhythms of the human voice and sharp, brilliant images, helped to continue the metric revolution begun by WHITMAN. *Hugh Selwyn Mauberley* (1920) asks poets to abandon 19th-century aesthetic pastures. Throughout his life he worked on *The Cantos* (even when declared insane and incarcerated in hospital for a time), intended as a huge, poetic, human comedy in 100 sections, reviewing world history, thought and economics.

Poussin, Nicolas (1594-1665) French artist and leading exponent of 17th-century pictorial Classicism, most of whose working life was spent in Rome. Poussin's early work was experimental and consequently crude (e.g. the series of drawings illustrating the *Metamorphoses* of OVID). For a time he followed the style of the Italian masters of the Baroque (notably DOMENICHINO), a period culminating in his large altarpiece for St Peter's, Rome, the *Martyrdom of St Erasmus* (1629). Later, under the influence of TITIAN, his work became more romantic and lyrical and by 1640, when he was summoned to Paris by LOUIS XIV and Cardinal RICHELIEU to decorate the long gallery of the Louvre, his style was modified to a more serene, geometrical design. Two years later Poussin returned to Rome where the mathematical composition of his later work and the classical themes showing the victory of virtue over vice, reason over passion, paralleled CORNEILLE's religious dramas.

Powell, Anthony (born 1905) English novelist noted for delicate, satiric social comedies about the English middle-classes. His earlier books, such as *Venusberg* (1932) and *From a View to a Death* (1933), were wittily comical. Since 1951 he has been publishing a more ambitious sequence of novels under the title *The Music of Time*.

Praetorius, Michael (1571-1621) German composer, theorist and musical historian whose *Musical Treatise* (1615-20) is one of the main sources of modern knowledge of the origins of 17th-century music. His own compositions were many and include the *Muses of Zion* (1605-10), a collection of Lutheran chorales for the Church year.

Prasad, Rajendra (1884-1963) Indian nationalist leader and first President of the Republic of India. He was a follower of GANDHI, from 1920, and was several times imprisoned for civil disobedience. He became President of the Constituent Assembly in 1946 and in 1950 first President of the Republic, an office he held for 12 years.

Presley, Elvis (1935-77) US pop singer whose first recordings in 1953 led him to dominate rock and roll until 1963. He used the three idioms of blues, country and folk music, but it was his pelvic gyrations and sexy delivery that made him a superstar.

Prévost, l'Abbé (1697-1763) Penname of Antoine Prévost d'Exiles, French novelist, journalist and historian and author of *Manon Lescaut* (1731), the story of an infatuated aristocrat's passion for a *demi-mondaine* and his final degradation.

Pride, Thomas (17th cent.) Parliamentary colonel in the English Civil War. He is remembered because of 'Pride's Purge', in which, while executing the army council's orders, he expelled or arrested some 140 Presbyterian members of parliament, the remainder, some 60 members in all, being known as the Rump Parliament. This parliament, reversing an earlier decision, ended talks with CHARLES I, who was being held prisoner, and ordered his trial, at which Pride was one of the judges.

Priestley, John Boynton (1894-1984) English author who was one of the most fertile and popular chroniclers of English life in the first half of this century. His well-known *The Good Companions* (1929) relates the adventures of a touring concert party, in a rambling book full of humour and rich characterization.

Princip, Gavrilo (c. 1893-1918) Serbian nationalist and revolutionary, who precipitated the First World War by assassinating Archduke Franz Ferdinand at Sarajevo on 28 June, 1914.

Prior, Matthew (1664-1721) English diplomat and poet, author of elegant worldly poems taking a shrewd and ironic view of love. He had a distinguished diplomatic career and prepared the Treaty of Utrecht (1713). Though he wrote long poems, such as 'Alma' and 'Solomon' (1718), Prior's reputation rests on the realistic wisdom, wit and technical experiments of poems like 'The English Padlock'.

Prokofiev, Sergei (1891-1953) Russian composer, and a leading innovator in 20th-century music. Prokofiev made his name early as a pianist and as an *enfant terrible* among composers. His style was at first marked by energetic and audacious rhythm and a melodic gift that could turn to satire. In 1918 he went to work in Europe, but in 1934 returned to the USSR. Prokofiev's works include *Peter and the Wolf*, the children's musical tale for narrator and orchestra (1936); seven symphonies (No. 1 being the *Classical*); concertos, chamber music and ballet music, including a version of *Romeo and Juliet*. He also wrote the scores for EISENSTEIN's films *Alexander Nevsky* (music that later became a patriotic cantata) and *Ivan the Terrible*.

Propertius, Sextus (c. 50-c. 15 BC) Roman poet whose four books of *Elegies* are extant, ranging in subject matter from the ecstasy of love to the fading of passion and the violence of renunciation, with its attendant melancholy and cynicism. His later work on national themes with mythological allusions, though lacking the earlier freshness of feeling, has an increased strength.

Protagoras (5th cent. BC) The first and most important of the Greek itinerant teachers called Sophists. An agnostic, he held that all knowledge is relative, based on opinion or the nature of sense perception (what is warm for one may be cold for another). This view was extended in his dictum 'a man is the measure of all things'.

Proudhon, Pierre (1809-65) French political theorist, who gave the answer 'property is theft' to the question posed by his famous essay entitled *What is Property?* (1840). He described ownership of capital as the right of *aubaine* – of exploiting the labour of others without just reward – and advocated that the ideal state should be brought about by the gradual abolition of the right of *aubaine* by progressive reductions in interest and rent. Unlike SAINT-SIMON and his followers, he mistrusted state intervention, and aimed to foster the development of the individual through associations.

Proust, Marcel (1871-1922) French author of the celebrated novel sequence *Remembrance of Things Past* (1913-17). A complex work with over 200 characters, it follows the life-span of its narrator-hero in an attempt to recapture, through art, the living past and to arrest, even if only for a moment, the passage of time. Proust's subtle exploration of the subconscious, in which a mere taste or aroma enables him to recall past experiences, makes *Remembrance of Things Past* an original work of a very high order. It has had a profound influence on the modern novel.

Ptolemy I (c. 367-283 BC) Macedonian general and founder of Egypt's Ptolemaic dynasty (which persisted until CLEOPATRA's death in 30 BC). He was one of ALEXANDER THE GREAT's generals, and after the king's death fought for lands in his recently won empire. Ptolemy seized Egypt, which he ruled (323-285 BC) first as satrap (governor), then (from 305 BC) as self-styled king. He was continually compelled to ward off attacks by Alexander's other generals, including Antigonus, who presented the greatest threat. Ptolemy built the library and museum at Alexandria and made the city the cultural capital of the Hellenistic world.

Ptolemy, Claudius (2nd cent. AD) Greek astronomer, mathematician and geographer, whose work was the basis for the study of astronomy until the Renaissance, a span of over 1200 years. Ptolemy's astronomy is contained in a work known as the *Almagest*, which dealt in detail with the motion and distance of the Sun and the Moon, their eclipses, planetary conjunctions and oppositions. Ptolemy believed in a system of solid, concentric crystalline spheres to which the planets and the fixed stars were attached. Encircling them all was the *primum mobile* ('the prime mover'), providing the energy for the motion of the Universe. Ptolemy's opinions became dogmatic articles of faith of the Christian Church, but the growing number of observations caused his system to become too elaborate. Doubts about its validity grew, until COPERNICUS was forced to conclude that it was wrong. So intense was religious feeling on the nature of the universe that GALILEO was tried for heresy for upholding the views of Copernicus.

Puccini, Giacomo (1858-1924) Italian composer whose *La Bohème* (1896), *Tosca* (1900) and *Madame Butterfly* (1904) are cornerstones of the operatic repertoire. His gift for a free-flowing melody that underlined drama and characterization made him one of the most successful composers in the genre. The harmonies he used were modern enough not to demand too much of audiences and they responded accordingly. Puccini also wrote *The Girl of the Golden West* (1910) and the unfinished *Turandot*.

Pugin, Augustus Welby Northmore (1812-52) English architect, who was one of the chief exponents of Victorian Gothic and (with BARRY) architect of the Palace of Westminster (Houses of Parliament). Pugin's architecture contained strong religious overtones and his famous book *Contrasts in Architecture* promoted his vision of what he termed the Christian architectural style and the ideals of the Gothic age. His numerous buildings include the Roman Catholic cathedral, Birmingham, St George's Cathedral, Southwark, and St Augustine's, Ramsgate.

Pulitzer, Joseph (1847-1911) Hungarian-born American newspaperman who pioneered sensational journalism and founded the Pulitzer Prizes. A journalist turned Democrat politician, he bought the *New York World* (1883) and made it the nation's biggest daily by crusading powerfully for oppressed workers and against alleged big business and government corruption, using the 'yellow-press' techniques which HEARST copied successfully. Part of Pulitzer's $2 million bequest to found Columbia University's school of journalism finances the Pulitzer cash prizes in journalism, literature and music.

Purcell, Henry (1659-95) English composer who is probably the most illustrious figure in his country's music. As a composer he absorbed the new French and Italian styles favoured at the Restoration court of CHARLES II but made of them something totally individual. He wrote many songs of great melodic beauty, as well as trio sonatas and fantasies for string groups, anthems and other church music. He composed a great deal of music for the stage, including one true opera, *Dido and Aeneas* (*c.* 1689). Some of Purcell's finest music was written for DRYDEN's extravagant stage spectacle, *King Arthur* (1691), while *The Fairy Queen* (1692) was an adaptation of SHAKESPEARE's *A Midsummer Night's Dream*. Purcell's untimely death at the age of 36 cast a shadow over the native English tradition and left a vacuum for HANDEL to exploit a few decades later. Purcell has, however, had a profound influence over such 20th-century composers, as HOLST, BRITTEN and TIPPETT.

Pushkin, Aleksandr Sergeyevich (1799-1837) Russian poet and writer. The Byronic verse-novel *Eugene Onegin* (1833), and *Boris Godunov* (1831) an historical tragic drama, provided libretti for operas by TCHAIKOVSKY and MUSSORGSKY respectively, and are considered his finest works. Pushkin was a prodigious writer; besides his verse-tales and dramas he was a master of the short story, of which *The Queen of Spades* (1834) is one of the most famous. *The Bronze Horseman*, unpublished in his lifetime, is among the best known of his epic poems and the folk poem *The Golden Cockerel* (1835) was the basis of an opera by RIMSKY-KORSAKOV.

Puvis de Chavannes, Pierre (1824-98) French mural painter, one of the few artists respected by both the academic and *avant-garde* factions in contemporary French art, belonging to no school or movement, yet strongly influencing the symbolism of GAUGUIN and the Nabis (a group which included BONNARD and VUILLARD). He painted mural decorations for public buildings all over France, among them being the *Ste Geneviève* cycle in the Panthéon, Paris. He also painted a sequence of murals for the Public Library at Boston, Massachusetts.

Pu-yi, Henry (1906-67) Last emperor of China (1908-12) and puppet emperor of Manchukuo (1934-45). He ascended the throne, his father becoming regent, in 1908, and was the last emperor of the Manchu dynasty of China under the name Hsüan T'ung. After the revolution of 1911-12 he abdicated. In 1924 (having taken the name Henry Pu-yi) he was driven from Peking, and lived under Japanese protection at Tientsin until 1932, when the Japanese appointed him head of the puppet state of Manchukuo (Manchuria), and enthroned him as the Emperor K'ang Te in 1934. He was captured by the Russians in 1945 and in 1949 handed over to MAO TSE-TUNG by whom he was set free in 1959. He became a member of the Chinese parliament in 1964.

Pym, John (1584-1643) English statesman, and leader of parliamentary opposition to JAMES I and CHARLES I. In the Short (1640) and Long (1640-60) Parliaments, Pym opposed 'papistry', monopolies and absolute royal power. He was foremost in attempts to impeach the royal favourites Buckingham, STRAFFORD and LAUD. Charles's attempt to arrest Pym hastened the Civil War, during which Pym brought about the acceptance of an excise tax and the alliance with

Scotland, and promoted the Grand Remonstrance (1641), a list of grievances against the king.

Pyrrhus (c. 318-272 BC) King of Epirus in northwestern Greece, whose name is associated with the phrase 'Pyrrhic victory'. In combat with the Romans at Heraclea (280 BC) and at Asculum (279 BC) he won, but at the cost of such enormous losses that he is said to have remarked: 'Another such victory and I shall be ruined.' He also waged war against the Carthaginians in Sicily and was defeated by the Romans at Beneventum (275 BC). He died in a skirmish at Argos.

Pythagoras (c. 582-500 BC) Greek philosopher, founder of the Pythagorean school of thought, which became a way of life for its followers. To Pythagoras, 'all things are numbers' and his mathematical work was important, reflected also in his studies of music, architecture and astronomy.

Pytheas (4th cent. BC) Greek navigator and geographer who coasted Europe's Atlantic seaboard. He sailed west from Marseille (*c.* 325 BC), passed through the Strait of Gibraltar, and explored the coasts of Portugal, Spain, France and Britain, and reached 'Thule' – perhaps the Orkneys or Norway. His account of the voyage included the first Greek description of sea ice and the first correct explanation of ocean tides, and stated – accurately – that the Pole Star is not directly over the North Pole. Only fragments of his work survive.

Q

Quercia, Jacopo della (1374-1438) Sienese sculptor to whom the tomb of Ilaria del Carretto (*c.* 1406) is attributed as his earliest known work. He participated in the competition for the Baptistry doors of San Giovanni in Florence, which was won by GHIBERTI (1401) and then from 1417-31, worked with Ghiberti and DONATELLO on reliefs for the doors of the Baptistry at Siena. Quercia's final great work was for the portals of St Petronio, Bologna, a series of reliefs of scenes from Genesis and the Nativity.

Quesada, Gonzalo Jimenez de (c. 1500-c. 1579) Spanish conquistador in South America, the most prominent of those who conquered new Granada (roughly equivalent to modern Colombia). About 20 years later, he crossed the Andes and reached the upper Orinoco.

Quételet, Adolphe (1796-1874) Belgian mathematician and scientist, who pioneered the use of statistics in the service of government and first presented the statistical concept of the 'average man' in *On Man* (1835).

Quincey, Thomas de (1785-1859) English author and critic, best known for his autobiographical *Confessions of an English Opium Eater*. After an unsteady progress by way of prostitutes, opium and Oxford, he went to the Lake District, the land of his romantic heroes, and lived by writing criticisms and essays. His critical essays were daring, typified by *On Murder Considered as One of the Fine Arts*.

Quintilian (c. 35-c. 100) Spanish-born Roman rhetorician and author of *Institutio oratoria* (*c.* 95), an account of an orator's education, the most complete in classical literature, including, in Book 10, a collection of famous critiques of Greek and Roman writers.

Quisling, Vidkun (1887-1945) Norwegian politician and Nazi collaborator. While Norway's Defence Minister (1931-3), he secretly recruited a Norwegian Nazi Party with German assistance, and on the outbreak of war went to Berlin to confer with HITLER about a Nazi takeover in Norway. After Germany occupied Norway in April 1940, Quisling became head of a puppet government (Feb. 1942-May 1945) and was in power until the country's liberation in the spring of 1945. He was tried and executed after the Allied victory.

R

Rabelais, François (c. 1494-c. 1553) French physician and humanist who became a monk and then a lay priest, and whose name added a new epithet, 'Rabelaisian' to describe a vigorous, bawdy satire, to the languages of the western world. In his satirical tales *Pantagruel* (1532) and *Gargantua* (1534), Rabelais attacked contemporary society with scatalogical humour, and in a fantastic florid style mocked pious theories on education, politics and religion. The narrative is vigorous, coarse and picturesque, reflecting the author's erudition, though anticipating MOLIÈRE in his derision of pedants and fanatics.

Rachmaninov, Sergei (1873-1943) Russian musician and the country's last important Romantic composer. Rachmaninov is said to have been the most impressive virtuoso pianist since LISZT, cultivating an often melancholy emotionalism which placed the second of his three piano concertos among the most popular works in the concert repertoire. Among his best-known works are the tone poem *The Isle of the Dead* (1907) and *Rhapsody on a Theme of Paganini* (1934). He died in America, having lived outside Russia since the Revolution.

Racine, Jean (1639-99) French poet and dramatist, the most accomplished writer of tragic verse in the French language. Unlike the super-heroes of his ageing rival, CORNEILLE, Racine's protagonists have a terrifying reality. He had a unique talent for investing simple words with intense power and significance. *La Thébaïde* (1664), his first play, and *Alexandre le Grande* (1665) were both put on by MOLIÈRE with some success. Following a quarrel with Molière, Racine's plays were staged by other companies. His first notable success, *Andromache* (1667), was one of his finest tragedies, followed by his only comedy, *Les Plaideurs* (1688). In the next ten years, he wrote six great tragedies: *Britannicus* (1669); *Bérénice* (1670) – regarded as the purest expression of the classical ideal, because of the simplicity of its plot; *Bajazet* (1672); *Mithridate* (1673); *Iphigénie* (1674) and *Phèdre* (1677). Thereafter, embittered by critics and rivals, he renounced the theatre and wrote no more plays until 1689, when, at Madame de Maintenon's request, he wrote two plays on biblical subjects, *Esther* (1689) and *Athalie* (1691 , one of his best plays).

Raffles, Sir Thomas Stamford (1781-1826) British founder of Singapore. While working for the East India Company, he persuaded Lord Minto to attempt the capture of Java. This having been accomplished (1811), Raffles was appointed its Lieutenant-Governor (1811-16) and set about reforming its administration. While Governor of Benkuilen in Sumatra (1818-23), he founded an unauthorized settlement in Singapore (1819). After being recalled to England in 1824, for disregarding government orders and taking independent steps to check the slave trade, he founded and became the first President of the London Zoological Society.

Rahman, Tunku Abdul (born 1903) Malaysian prince and politician, who became the first Malaysian Prime Minister when his country achieved its independence. Rahman, whose father was Sultan of Kedah, was elected leader of the United Malays National Organization and of the Alliance party in 1951, became Chief Minister in 1955 and Prime Minister two years later. He resigned in 1970 after race riots between Malays and Chinese.

Raleigh, Sir Walter (c. 1552-1618) English Elizabethan adventurer. After taking part in piratical expeditions against the Spaniards (1578), and overcoming rebels in Ireland (1580), he became ELIZABETH I's favourite. With her support he sent settlers to colonize North Carolina (1585), but in this, and in a later attempt to colonize Virginia, he was unsuccessful. In 1588, he was displaced as the Queen's favourite by the 2nd Earl of ESSEX. Later (1590), he was accused of atheism, then discredited for seducing one of the Queen's maids (1592). In 1595 he led an unsuccessful expedition to South America to look for gold. His exploits against Spain, at Cadiz (1596) and the Azores (1597), and against the rebellious Essex (1601), reinstated him in Elizabeth's favour, but when JAMES I came to the throne Raleigh was accused of complicity in plots against the Crown and sentenced to death. But he was only put in prison, where he wrote *History of the World*.

Ramakrishna Sri (1834-86) Indian Hindu religious teacher whose ideas, based on the ancient *Vedic* scriptures, form the basis of the Ramakrishna mission. Its impact has been considerable, not only in India but also in the West. He stressed the unity of religions, seeing them as different paths to the realization of the divine.

Rambert, Dame Marie (1888-1982) Polish-born dancer and, with de VALOIS, co-founder of modern British ballet. Influenced by Isadora DUNCAN and Jacques Dalcroze, in 1912 she helped DIAGHILEV and NIJINSKY to create a ballet to STRAVINSKY's complex rhythms for the *Rite of Spring*. In 1920, she founded the Rambert Ballet School in London on CECCHETTI's principles, establishing her Ballet Club (later the Ballet Rambert) in 1930.

Rameau, Jean Philippe (1683-1764) French composer and organist who wrote the *Treatise on Harmony* (1722), the first real attempt to categorize harmony as expression, which remains a cornerstone of musical theory. When Rameau emerged at the relatively late age of 50 as a composer, he put his theories into vivid practice, particularly in the 24 operas and ballets which led to his appointment to the court of LOUIS XV.

Ramsay, Sir William (1852-1916) Scottish chemist who discovered the so-called inert gases. With Lord RAYLEIGH, he removed from air various known gases, such as nitrogen, oxygen and carbon dioxide, leaving a gas which was chemically inert. He called it argon, from the Greek word for inactive, and found that it makes up about 1 per cent of air (1894). Later Ramsay, with his co-worker Travers, discovered small quantities of three other inert gas elements in air. They were krypton (hidden), neon (new) and xenon (stranger).

Ramses II (13th cent. BC) Egyptian pharaoh, whose buildings included the famous temples cut in the rock-face at Abu Simbel. Four statues, each 67 feet high, of the seated pharaoh guarded the great temple, which had 14 chambers, penetrating 200 feet into the cliff beside the Nile. He is thought to have been the pharaoh whose oppression of Hebrew slaves in Egypt caused MOSES to lead the Israelites out of Egypt into Canaan.

Raphael (1483-1520) Italian artist whose work most typifies the classical phase of the High Renaissance. After studying under PERUGINO, Raphael went to Florence, where both his portraits and his pictures of the Madonna and Child reflected the influence of LEONARDO's experiments in compositional arrangement. In 1508 he went to Rome, where he began work on the decoration of some of the papal apartments (The Stanze) planned by Julius II. The first of these, the Stanza della Segnatura, is the best known and contains the famous *School of Athens* fresco – a representation of philosophy which became the archetype for compositions based on the classical ideals of balance and order. The Madonnas of these years, e.g. the *Sistine Madonna*, also exhibit the idealized forms and calm dignity towards which Raphael's art was moving. Raphael made a close study of the work of MICHELANGELO, whose influence can be seen in the more dramatic style of the later Stanze, which were completed after the unveiling of the Sistine Chapel ceiling in 1512.

Rashid al-Din (c. 1247-1318) Arabic scholar-statesman in Persia, one of the foremost patrons of Persian art and learning, who compiled the major work *History of the Mongols of Persia*. Numerous scholars, artists and scribes came from all over Asia to work in the university suburb which he built outside Tabriz. It was in his book studio that the first known Persian manuscripts were produced, illustrated in a strong original style which blended Chinese and Mesopotamian influences.

Rasputin, Grigori (c. 1871-1916) Russian monk and mystic who exerted influence over Russian politics and the Court (*c.* 1911-16). His influence was based on his personal magnetism and alleged power as a healer after he had alleviated the sufferings of the haemophilic Tsarevitch, Alexei. But his drunkenness, sexual excesses and nepotism in securing the appointment of his colleagues to high office in Army, Church and State, combined with the belief that in the First World War he was a German agent, led a group of noblemen headed by Prince Yusupov, to assassinate him.

Rathenau, Walther (1867-1922) German industrialist and statesman, who devised a system of 'war-socialism' which contributed to German economic survival in the First World War. Rathenau was an engineer and economist, and head of the largest electrical combine in Europe. Under him the German Ministry of War controlled all means of production and the deployment of labour. After Germany's defeat in 1918, Rathenau founded the Democratic Party and in 1921 he became Minister of Reconstruction, and of Foreign Affairs in 1922. His internationalism, socialist sympathies and diplomatic successes, such as his financial settlements with the US and France and the Treaty of Rapallo with Russia (1922), were bitterly resented by extreme right-wing anti-Semites, by one of whom he was murdered in June 1922.

Rattigan, Sir Terence (1911-77) British dramatist, whose widely popular successes include *French Without Tears* (1936), *The Winslow Boy* (1946), *The Deep Blue Sea* (1952), *Ross* (1960) and *Goodbye Mr Chips* (1969).

Ravel, Maurice (1875-1937) French composer and a master of orchestration. He was also highly successful in exploiting harmonic colour in the piano, as in *Le Tombeau de Couperin* (1917). Ravel's works include *The Pavan for a Dead Infanta*, *Bolero*, the suite *Mother Goose* and the ballet *Daphnis and Chloë*. He also wrote the fantasy opera, *L'Enfant et les Sortilèges*, to a libretto by COLETTE, and orchestrated MUSSORGSKY's *Pictures from an Exibition*.

Ray, Satyajit (born 1921) Indian film director with a worldwide following. His trilogy of films about life in modern India, *Pather Panchali* (1954), *The Unvanquished* (1956) and *The World of Apu* (1959) is regarded as a cinema classic. Recent films include *Days and Nights in the Forest* (1971), *Distant Thunder* (1973), *The Chess Players* (1977) and *Home and the World* (1982).

Rayleigh, John, 3rd Baron (1842-1919) English physicist who opened the way to the discovery of argon, the first of the inert gases. In the 1880s Rayleigh tested William Prout's already discredited hypothesis that atomic weights are always whole multiples of the atomic weight of hydrogen. He measured the densities of gases and calculated atomic weights from them. In the course of his work he found that nitrogen obtained from a chemical compound was always slightly denser than nitrogen obtained from the air. He threw the problem open to the scientific world, and in 1894 William RAMSAY discovered that the nitrogen from air was 'diluted' by small traces of another gas which he and Rayleigh named argon.

Read, Sir Herbert (1893-1968) English scholar, poet and critic, an influential writer on culture and aesthetics. He fought in the First World War and wrote of the experience in 'Songs of Chaos' (1915) and 'Naked Warriors' (1919). His criticism of painting, literature and politics, contained in many books from *Reason and Romanticism* (1926) to *Poetry and Experience* (1966), is a modern version of Romanticism which believes in an underlying cultural order that resists the imposition of rational forms.

Reagan, Ronald Wilson (born 1911) 40th president of the United States. After graduating he worked as a radio sportscaster and newspaper sportswriter in Iowa. In 1937 he took a successful screen test and appeared in over 50 films during the following three decades. In 1947 he was elected president of the Screen Actors' Guild, serving five successive terms, until 1952, and then again from 1959-60. In 1962 he joined the Republican party and became a crusader for conservative causes and candidates. Despite his lack of political experience, he won a landslide victory over California's incumbent governor, Edmund G. Brown, in 1966. He was re-elected in 1970, serving until 1974. He ran unsuccessfully for the Republican presidential nomination in 1968 and 1976. Then he won the presidential seat in 1980 on a ticket with George Bush. In March 1981, he was wounded in an assassination attempt but made a sound recovery. He was re-elected to office in 1984 despite criticism of his economics ('Reaganomics') with reduced federal spending and expanding military defence policies.

Reith, John Charles Walsham, 1st Baron (1889-1971) First Director-General of the BBC.

Rembrandt van Ryn (1606-69) Outstanding Dutch painter, renowned for his penetrating portraits. His success in this genre began with *Anatomy Lesson of Dr Tulp* (1632) and reached its zenith with the celebrated *Night Watch* (1642). Rembrandt's best-known portraits, however, are those of individuals, and his later studies in particular demonstrate his considerable ability to probe his sitters' characters. Rembrandt was deeply religious and his fondness for biblical subjects was unusual, since there was little demand for such works and it seems likely that he often painted them without being commissioned. His marriage to Saskia van Vylenborch (who died in 1642) brought him a considerable dowry, which, with his success as a portrait painter, made him comparatively wealthy. An extravagant style of living, in particular his passion for collecting works of art, eventually created financial difficulties from which he never recovered. He was, however, assured of a steady income through the sale of his etchings, which during his lifetime were much more widely known and praised than were his paintings. The subsequent popularity of etching among artists was a direct result of Rembrandt's work, and his prints (there are about 300 different subjects) were enormously influential. Far less well known in his day were Rembrandt's drawings (nearly 2000 survive) which cover a wide range of subjects: religion, history, mythology, landscape, genre and the nude. Popular interest in Rembrandt owes much to the numerous paintings and drawings of his family (Saskia and her son Titus, and Hendrickje Stoffels, Rembrandt's mistress in his later years) but above all to the self-portraits executed at various stages of his life.

Reni, Guido (1575-1642) Italian painter who is remembered mostly for the intense pathos of his depictions of JESUS CHRIST as the Man of Sorrows, and for the bright and rhythmic *Aurora* fresco on the ceiling of the Palazza Rospigliosi, Rome (1613). The latter shows his debt to the graceful, idealizing art of RAPHAEL and, in its design and individual quotations, to antique sculpture.

Rennie, John (1761-1821) Scottish civil engineer, bridge builder and canal architect, who built the original Waterloo Bridge over the Thames (1810-17), Southwark Bridge (1815-19), London Bridge (completed by his son, John, in 1831) and many others. His canals include the Kennet and Avon, the Great Western and the Lancaster. Rennie also carried out major drainage improvements of East Anglian fens (1800), of harbours in Great Britain and abroad and several of naval dockyards. In 1804, he adopted a WATT steam engine to work the first powered bucket dredger at Hull. At Plymouth in 1811, he commenced the construction of the first breakwater on the English side of the Channel.

Renoir, Jean (1894-1979) French film director and writer, son of artist Auguste RENOIR, with whom he shared the same feeling for light and landscape and a love of nubile women, as expressed in the film classics *La Règle du Jeu* (1939) and *Le Déjeuner sur l'Herbe* (1959). In 1975 he was awarded an Oscar for his lifetime achievements.

Renoir, Pierre Auguste (1841-1919) French Impressionist painter, who developed an early admiration for the work of BOUCHER and FRAGONARD, which is reflected by his emphasis on the female nude. In 1862 he met MONET and SISLEY and through working with them, developed an impressionistic sensitivity to nuances of colour and light (e.g. *The Swing*, 1876). But Renoir was always more concerned with the human figure than any other Impressionist, except DEGAS. He designed fine sculptures, which were executed by an assistant.

Respighi, Ottorino (1879-1936) Italian composer who wrote the vivid orchestral tone poems *The Fountains of Rome* (1917) and *The Pines of Rome* (1924). In the cause of realism, the score of the latter includes a gramophone recording of a nightingale. Respighi studied with RIMSKY-KORSAKOV, and he also conducted, taught and edited early Italian music.

Retz, Gilles de (c. 1404-40) French feudal lord, distinguished soldier, and one time friend of JOAN OF ARC, who is supposed by many to be the original 'Bluebeard'. De Retz engaged in Satanic practices in the course of which he ritually murdered numerous children. He was eventually burnt at the stake.

Retz, Jean François Paul de Gondi, Cardinal de (1614-79) French ecclesiastic and politician. His *Mémoires* (first published in 1717) give a vivid firsthand account of the violent episodes of the Fronde (the two popular revolts against monarchial absolutism in 1648 and 1651-2), in which Retz played a leading role, revealing the men and events of the period.

Reuter, Paul Julius von (1816-99) German founder of one of the world's biggest news agencies. In Göttingen, he met GAUSS, then experimenting with telegraphy, and evolved the idea of a telegraphic news service. He moved to London (1851) and set up a continental cable service of stock market prices, which was later extended to general news. In 1858 *The Times* used a Reuter's report of a speech by NAPOLEON III, and the service became extensively used. As international cables were laid, Reuter's news became world-wide.

Reuther, Walter Philip (1907-70) American labour leader. An employee of the Ford Motor Co. in his twenties, he was dismissed for trying to organize a union among fellow workers. His efforts led, by 1941, to the recognition by Ford's of the Union of Automobile Workers. Reuther later became Vice-President of the combined American Federation of labour and the Congress of Industrial Organizations, and as such was one of the most powerful men in American industry, though he continued to oppose Communist infiltration of the unions. He was killed in an aeroplane crash.

Revere, Paul (1735-1818) American patriot, who rode from Boston to Lexington in two hours to warn the revolutionary leaders Adams and Hancock that British troops were about to arrest them and seize gunpowder hidden by dissident colonists. This enabled the leaders to escape and the colonists to prepare for the battles of Lexington and Concord, the first of the War of Independence, which were fought the next day (19 April 1775). Revere was immortalized in LONGFELLOW's poem *The Midnight Ride of Paul Revere*.

Reynolds, Sir Joshua (1723-92) English painter, who is one of the most important figures in British art, both for his painting and his theories. Through his painting (he was, with GAINSBOROUGH, one of the outstanding portrait painters of his day) and his ideology, propounded in discourses delivered at the Royal Academy in his capacity as its first President, Reynolds influenced taste and the practice of contemporary artists and those of subsequent generations. The foundation of the Academy (1768) and the intellectual basis on which Reynolds tried to establish a school of British painting to equal those of Italy and France, did much to improve artists' status in England.

Rhee, Syngman (1875-1965) Founder and virtual creator of South Korea. After trying unsuccessfully to bring the case of Japanese-ruled Korea to the attention of the Versailles Peace Conference, he became the head of a Korean Provisional Government in exile in 1919, and returned to Korea after the Japanese defeat in 1945. In 1948 he was elected President of South Korea, and thereafter became increasingly antagonistic to the Communist régime in the North. He was elected President for a second term in 1952. His opposition to the truce at the end of the Korean War in 1953 politically embarrassed the US but in 1956 and 1960 he was again elected President. He became increasingly authoritarian, frequently introducing martial law and resorting to intimidation. Popular indignation forced him to resign in 1960, and he went to live in Hawaii.

Rhodes, Cecil John (1853-1902) British businessman, colonial statesman and leading protagonist of imperialism in South Africa. The founder of Rhodesia. He went to Cape Colony in 1870 and quickly made a fortune from diamond mining in the Orange Free State. He used his control of the De Beers Diamond Company and his interests in the Transvaal gold mines to further his vision of British imperialism in Africa. In 1887, he founded the British South Africa Co., which received a royal charter two years later, to colonize the country north of the Transvaal, later known as Rhodesia. He entered politics and by 1890 had become Premier of Cape Colony. In 1896, he was forced to resign, because of his implication in the Jameson Raid.

Ribbentrop, Joachim von (1893-1946) Nazi diplomat. A sometime wine salesman, he joined the Nazi Party in the 1920s, and his many foreign contacts formed during his commercial travels were useful to HITLER, who in 1936 sent him as Ambassador to Britain. In 1938 he was appointed Foreign Minister and was responsible, a year later, for the Nazi-Soviet Pact which gave Hitler a free hand to wage war on western Europe. He was tried as a war criminal at Nuremburg in 1946 and subsequently hanged.

Ribera, Jusepe de (1588-1652) Spanish painter, whose paintings, which are frequently of the brutal martyrdoms or passion scenes typical of the period of the Counter-Reformation, combine a realism in the depiction of surface details with a slightly less harsh version of CARAVAGGIO's contrasts of light and shade.

Ricci, Curbastro Gregorio (1853-1925) Italian mathematician, who was the principal discoverer of the absolute differential calculus, a systematic account of tensor analysis originating from differential geometry. This work was further developed by his pupil LEVI-CIVITA.

Richard I Coeur de Lion (1157-99) King of England (1189-99), who spent less than a year of his reign in England, the rest in crusading and defending his French possessions, Normandy and Anjou. After joining Philip II of France in the Third Crusade (1189-92), he sent 8000 troops to Palestine, seized Cyprus and Acre, and fought off SALADIN before dissension forced him to return home. On the way back he was seized by Leopold of Austria (1192), but regained freedom by payment of a huge ransom raised by taxation.

Richard III (1452-85) Last Yorkist king of England (1483-5) and one of the most controversial of English rulers. Tudor propaganda depicted him as a villain, a view adhered to by SHAKESPEARE in *Richard III*, based on a suspicion of his having murdered the Princes in the Tower. Loyal to his brother EDWARD IV while he lived, Richard became regent for his young nephew Edward V in 1483, and quickly seized and executed possible opponents, especially supporters of the Queen Mother, Elizabeth Woodville. Following the liquidation of the Queen's friends, Richard seized the throne and imprisoned Edward V and his brother in the Tower, where they died in October 1483, perhaps by the King's order. Growing belief that Richard was the murderer caused his support to dwindle and helped to bring about his defeat and death at the hands of Henry Tudor (later HENRY VII) at Bosworth Field.

Richardson, Samuel (1689-1761) English novelist, who, together with DEFOE, was an important influence in the development of the novel in the first half of the 18th century. A commission to write a model letter-book gave Richardson, a printer, the form and idea of *Pamela* (1740). He followed this with *Clarissa Harlowe* (1747-8) and *Sir Charles Grandison* (1754). For the first time he made affairs of the heart, not adventure, the subject of fiction. At his best, in *Clarissa Harlowe*, he is a fine epistolary novelist with a good insight into women's psychology.

Richelieu, Duc de (1585-1642) French cardinal (1622) and statesman, who, for the greater part of Louis XIII's reign, controlled France and made royal authority absolute. From the time he became Chief Minister (1624) until his death, Richelieu dominated Louis and made the royal authority (and thereby his own) supreme, countering threats – at home – from the feudal nobles and the Huguenots, and – abroad – from the Hapsburgs of Spain and the Holy Roman Empire. Although he executed nobles who were plotting his overthrow, he showed mercy to the disarmed Huguenots and permitted them freedom of worship. To make France supreme in Europe over its Hapsburg rivals (Spain and Austria) he increased the country's influence at their expense by making alliances with German states and Sweden, capturing Rousillon from Spain, and Turin from the emperor. France was stronger than it had ever been.

Richter, Hans (1843-1916) German conductor who became the leading interpreter of WAGNER and, in Britain, a champion of ELGAR while resident conductor of the Hallé Orchestra.

Ride, Sally (born 1951) The first American woman to fly in space. Trained as a physicist, she joined the astronaut corps in 1978. She was selected to train for the space shuttle programme and acted as mission specialist and flight engineer in the 1983 shuttle flight.

Ridley, Nicholas (c. 1500-55) English Protestant reformer and martyr. As Bishop of Rochester (1547), and then of London (1549), he helped CRANMER to compile the first Book of Common Prayer and the 139 Articles of the English Protestant Church. He denounced MARY and ELIZABETH (the later queens) as illegitimate, regarding them as a danger to Protestantism, and supported Lady Jane GREY's accession When Mary I became queen, Ridley, Cranmer and LATIMER were condemned as heretics. Ridley and Latimer were burnt at the stake.

Riebeeck, Jan van (1634-77) Dutch naval surgeon and colonist, founder of Cape Town (1652). As part of the Dutch East India Company's plan for a victualling station for ships on the long voyage between the Dutch Republic and the East Indies, he built the fort which later became Cape Town.

Riefenstahl, Leni (born 1902) German actress who went on to direct the brilliant pre-war Nazi propaganda films, notably *Triumph of the Will* (1936), recording the Nuremburg rallies of 1934, and *Olympia* (1938), documenting the 1936 Olympic Games.

Riemann, Georg (1826-66) German mathematician, who was the first to formulate a general theory of multi-dimensional geometry, of which Euclidean and non-Euclidean geometries are special cases. This led directly to the later work of RICCI and LEVI-CIVITA, and to the mathematical side of the general relativity theory of EINSTEIN.

Rienzi, Cola di (1313-54) Italian notary, leader of a popular revolution which overthrew the patrician rulers of Rome (1347). Within months he alienated the masses by levying heavy taxes, and angered the pope and the Holy Roman Emperor by calling a national parliament and proposing to revive the Roman Empire. Increasing unrest caused him to abdicate and flee. Later, he returned and regained his position as tribune (1354), but was murdered during a riot.

Rilke, Rainer Maria (1875-1926) Austrian poet, widely regarded as his country's leading poet. He is the author of a number of works which typify the sentiments of the *fin-de-siècle* period, including the religious cycle, *Das Stundenbuch* (1905).

Rimbaud, Arthur (1854-91) French poet whose work had a significant influence on the development of modern poetry. He was a precocious genius and by the age of 20 had already completed his main works, *Le Bateau ivre*, *Les Illuminations* and *Une Saison en Enfer*. Ever a rebel, scornful of tradition, defiantly seeking freedom (both personal and literary), Rimbaud believed that the poet must intensify his perception by submitting himself to all kinds of experience (what he called the 'dérèglement de tous les sens') and then, without conscious control, to transmit what he perceives, a theory anticipating the Surrealists.

Rimsky-Korsakov, Nikolai (1844-1908) Russian musician and leading composer of the Nationalist school. Rimsky-Korsakov was a naval officer before making music his career and he wrote the earliest Russian symphonic poem (*Sadko*, 1867, later an opera) while on duty. In 1871 he was made a professor at the St Petersburg Conservatory. He became a notable teacher and STRAVINSKY was among his later pupils. Rimsky-Korsakov's compositions were distinguished by rich orchestration. They include the *Spanish Caprice* (1887) and the suite *Scheherazade* (1888). His best-known opera, *The Golden Cockerel*, was not performed until after his death.

Ritter, Karl (1779-1859) German founder (with HUMBOLDT) of scientific geography. He treated geography as the physiology and comparative anatomy of the Earth's surface. He rejected the old descriptive catalogue approach, and helped to give the subject system and shape by drawing attention to similarities and differences on the Earth's surface and pointing out the interconnections between its often seemingly unrelated phenomena.

Rivera, Miguel Primo de (1870-1930) Spanish general, who became dictator of Spain. When, in 1921 defeats in the Riff War in Morocco, Catalan nationalist agitation and the rapid growth of the Anarchist movement alarmed the Spanish establishment, de Rivera, with the connivance of King Alfonso XIII, seized power and dissolved parliament (1923) establishing a military directorate (1923) followed by civil dictatorship. It lasted until late 1925, when a semblance of parliamentary rule, with de Rivera as Prime Minister, was restored. He was eventually forced out of office by the king and army officers, because of growing social, industrial and intellectual unrest. He died in exile in Paris.

Robbia, Luca della (c. 1400-82) Florentine sculptor, whose first major work was the *Cantoria* for the cathedral in Florence (1431-8). Early in his career, he discovered a means of applying vitrified lead glazes to terracotta, and made a number of small half-length works of Virgins and Madonnas, being the first artist to exploit the sentimental in the motherhood theme. He built up a large business, which was carried on by his nephew, Andrea.

Robbins, Jerome (born 1918) American dancer and choreographer of some of the most popular and influential modern dance dramas and musicals, including *West Side Story*. Since 1949, he has been an associate artistic director of the New York City Ballet and has created several masterpieces which have been remounted for other companies, including a version of *L'Après-midi d'un faune* (quite different from NIJINSKY's original) and *Dances at a Gathering*, to piano pieces originally written by CHOPIN.

Robert I 'The Bruce' (1274-1329) King of Scotland (1306-29), chief architect of Scotland's independence. He filled the gap in Scottish leadership left by EDWARD I's capture of Baliol and WALLACE, and, though of Norman descent, claimed the Scottish throne and rallied the Scots against England. He was defeated by Edward I at Methven (1306), and fled to Ireland, but returned on Edward's death (1307). Gradually he won control of Scotland and in 1314 defeated Edward II's army at Bannockburn. Subsequent attacks on Scotland were warded off and in 1328 the Treaty of Northampton ended the fighting and affirmed Edward III's recognition of Scotland's independence.

Robeson, Paul (1898-1976) American negro actor and singer, famous for his performances of *Othello* and his singing of negro spirituals.

Robespierre, Maximilien de (1758-94) French Revolutionary leader. A lawyer from Arras, he was elected to the Estates General in 1789 and acquired a reputation for radicalism in the Constituent Assembly (1789-91). He was one of the founders of the Society of Friends of the Constitution (Jacobins), the most radical of the main revolutionary groups. Robespierre dominated the Committee of Public Safety (formed in the spring of 1793 after the failure of the war policy of the Girondins) and by April 1794 had overthrown his rivals, the Girondin Party, DANTON and Hébert. With his followers, he established a dictatorship from April until July 1794. Believing himself the incarnation of the people's will, he decreed the confiscation of the property of enemies of the Revolution and its distribution to the poor. Arbitrary power of arrest, condemnation and execution were given to the Revolutionary Tribunal, which Robespierre controlled, and the 'Cult of the Supreme Being' was introduced as a state religion to replace Roman Catholicism. The measures led to a *coup d'état* by moderates and Robespierre was arrested and guillotined.

Rob Roy see MACGREGOR, Robert

Rockefeller, John (1839-1937) American founder of Standard Oil, one of the world's largest petroleum companies, and of a dynasty of successful business men, administrators and public servants. After amassing a huge fortune, he engaged in planned philanthropy for the benefit of educational, cultural and medical institutions. Rockefeller began oil refining in 1863, and subsequently founded Standard Oil, which, by 1882, had a near-monopoly of the business in the US. Its dominance brought about anti-trust legislation which left Standard Oil of New Jersey the largest surviving unit. He and his son John D. Rockefeller Jnr gave away $930 million in benefactions.

Rockwell, George Lincoln (1918-67) Founder and leader of the American Nazi Party. He formed the Union of Free Enterprise National Socialists in 1959, after having organized a number of short-lived right-wing bodies throughout the 1950s; he later changed its name to the American Nazi Party. The organization subsequently underwent another change of name, becoming the National Socialist White People's Party, its efforts then being directed against negroes rather than Jews. Rockwell was shot dead in 1967.

Rodney, George Brydges 1st Baron (1719-92) English admiral in the American theatre of action in the Seven Years' War (1756-63). As Commander-in-Chief of the Leeward Islands, he subdued (1762) the French-held islands of Grenada, Martinique, St Lucia and St Vincent, and thus strengthened Great Britain's bargaining position at the time of the Treaty of Paris in 1763. He achieved victories in actions against Spanish and French fleets, and Dutch trading settlements in the West Indies, especially at the battle of the Saints (1782), which ended a French threat to the West Indies.

Rodrigo Diaz de Vivar see CID, El

Rodriguez de Fonseca, Juan (1451-1524) Spanish prelate, who founded (1511) and supervised the Council of the Indies (Spanish America), which controlled Spain's huge colonial empire. He organized its division into viceroyalties and sub-division into so-called kingdoms, each under a governor advised by a tribunal. This system was preserved until the early 1800s. Rodriguez was opposed to COLUMBUS and sent Bobadilla to displace him as Viceroy of the Indies.

Roger II (1095-1154) Norman King (1130-54) of Sicily and one of medieval Europe's most powerful and cultured monarchs. He united and enforced order in Sicily and southern Italy, which had been captured by his father Roger I and uncle Robert GUISCARD, then built up a strong fleet, which seized parts of the coasts of Tunis and Tripoli (1135-53). In 1147 he invaded Greece and threatened Constantinople (1149). Meanwhile, he organized a strong centralized government.

Rockefeller, his name a synonym for limitless wealth, founded one of the largest oil combines in the 19th century

Rolls, Charles (1877-1910) English co-founder, with Frederick Royce (1863-1933), of the car and aero-engine firm that bears their name. Royce was a superb engineer; Rolls knew the market and its needs. The first Rolls-Royce motor car, the Silver Ghost, was in production from 1906 to 1925. The firm's aero-engine division pioneered many developments, including giant jet engines and the use of carbon fibres.

Romero, Francisco (18th cent.) Spanish bullfighter and the first great professional of the sport. Fighting in Spain's oldest bullring at Ronda, he became famous as one of the *espades*, actual killers of bulls.

Rommel, Erwin Eugen Johannes (1891-1944) German general, later Field-Marshal, Commander of the Afrika Korps during the Second World War. During the invasion of France in 1940, he showed skill and resource as the head of a Panzer division. He was appointed, by HITLER, commander to the Afrika Korps in Libya, where his bold, unorthodox leadership won him the name of 'the Desert Fox'. After inflicting a number of major reverses on the British 8th Army, he was defeated at El Alamein (November 1942) by MONTGOMERY, and driven back to Tunisia. In 1944, he became commander of the anti-invasion forces in France. Following his complicity in the plot of 20 July 1944 to assassinate Hitler, he was given the choice of being court-martialled and shot, or of committing suicide. Though there is some doubt about the means of his death, it is generally assumed that he committed suicide.

Romney, George (1734-1802) Fashionable English portrait painter. Not as skilled as GAINSBOROUGH or REYNOLDS, his infatuation for Lady Hamilton resulted in the well-known pictures of her, *déshabillée*, in mythological poses.

Ronsard, Pierre de (1524-85) French Renaissance poet, regarded as the father of French lyric verse. His devotion to the Latin and Greek poets is reflected in all his work, including the *Odes* (1550), *Amours* (1552), *Hymnes* (1555) and *Sonnets pour Hélène* (1578). One of the poet's favourite themes is that beauty and joy are ephemeral and time's ravages cruel. Ronsard's principal importance was as an innovator, experimenting with forms, diversifying his style and leading the *Plèiade* poets, such as DU BELLAY, in their attempt to rejuvenate French poetry.

Röntgen, Wilhelm Conrad (1845-1923) German physicist who was awarded the first Nobel Prize for Physics in 1901 for his discovery of X-rays six years before. X-rays have been of vital practical importance, first in medicine (both to photograph bones and other body tissues and to irradiate and so treat tumours), and then in engineering for the testing of metals. They also have a great role in science itself: X-rays can be used to determine crystal structures and, since every element has a characteristic X-ray spectrum, to analyse complex mixtures of elements.

Rooke, Sir George (1650-1708) British admiral who captured Gibraltar (1704). His victory gave Britain control of the Strait of Gibraltar and prevented France's Mediterranean and Atlantic fleets from joining forces. British possession of Gibraltar dates from this time.

Roosevelt, Franklin Delano (1882-1945) American President (1933-45) who served an unprecedented third term and was elected for a fourth shortly before his death. America's leader in the years leading to the Second World War, during most of which he was a victim of polio, which he contracted in 1921, and which crippled him. In 1928, he was elected Governor of New York State and; as the Democratic presidential candidate in 1932, was returned with a majority of 12 million votes. As President, he inaugurated the 'New Deal' programme of government intervention in industry and business, to overcome the great depression, including public works on a vast scale, farm subsidies, and legislation to liberalize and control relations between capital and labour. In 1933 he recognized and exchanged diplomatic missions with the USSR and thus ended US isolationism. From 1941 he found, in the Lease-Lend Act, means to give massive support to Britain against the Nazis in the Second World War, while officially maintaining US neutrality. After the Japanese attack on Pearl Harbor (December 1941) had forced the US into the war, Roosevelt began that close co-operation with CHURCHILL, signified by periodic personal meetings, which gave cohesion to the operations of the British and American forces. He was re-elected in 1940 and 1944.

Roosevelt, Theodore (1858-1919) Twenty-sixth President of the United States. He became a national hero as the leader of 'Roosevelt's Rough Riders' in the Spanish-American War in 1898, and President on MCKINLEY's assassination in 1901. In 1905 he was elected for a second term. He campaigned against big business and began to enforce the anti-trust laws, though his supporters were disappointed that he did not do more. In foreign affairs his 'dollar diplomacy' claimed the right of the US, through its commercial interests, to intervene in Latin America, and though his mediation after the Russo-Japanese war (1904-5) won him the Nobel Peace Prize, his militaristic and threatening foreign policy betrayed his essentially pugnacious, jingoistic conception of America's role in the world. This was demonstrated when he fomented rebellion in Colombia in 1903 to facilitate the building of the Panama Canal

Rosenberg, Julius (1917-53) and **Ethel (1916-53)** American spies for the Soviet intelligence service. They were members of a transatlantic spy ring which also involved FUCHS, and obtained atomic secrets through Ethel's brother, David Greenglass, a worker at the Los Alamos nuclear research station. At their trial Greenglass gave evidence for the prosecution, and they were convicted and sentenced to death, two of the very few spies to be executed in peacetime.

Ross, Sir James Clark (1800-62) Scottish polar explorer who penetrated the Antarctic more deeply than any man before him, and located the North Magnetic Pole (1831). Later (1839-43) he led the ships *Erebus* and *Terror* in the first thrust through Antarctic pack-ice and reached 78° 9′S, which remained for 60 years the most southerly latitude reached. Ross discovered Victoria Land, the Admiralty and Prince Albert ranges, the Ross Sea, Ross Ice Shelf and Ross Island.

Rossellino, Bernardo (1409-64) Florentine sculptor and architect, best known for his tomb for Leonardo Bruno (1444-50), which was a prototype Renaissance tomb. Other works by Rossellino include a delicate terracotta *Annunciation* for the Cathedral at Pienza, which, as an architect, he designed, and a relief, the *Madonna della Misericordia*, for the façade of the church at Arezzo.

Rossetti, Christina (1830-94) English poet, who expressed a deep religious faith in simple, tender lyrics. The sister of Dante Gabriel ROSSETTI, her poetry shared with his a mysticism and a sense of colour. After *Goblin Market* (1862), the first Pre-Raphaelite literary success, her work grew more religious as seen in *New Poems* (1896).

Rossetti, Dante Gabriel (1828-82) English painter and poet who, with Holman HUNT and MILLAIS, was a founder-member of the Pre-Raphaelite Brotherhood. His first important picture, *The Girlhood of Mary Virgin* (1849), is comparable to their early works, exhibiting the same slightly gauche realism. His painting *Found* (1854) exemplifies the 'modern moral subject' with which the Pre-Raphaelites were preoccupied – in this case the 'fallen woman'.

Rossini, Gioacchino Antonio (1792-1868), leading Italian composer whose *The Barber of Seville* (1816) is arguably the world's most popular comic opera. Among his other well known operas are *The Italian Girl in Algiers* (1813), *Cinderella* (1817) and *Semiramide* (1823). He wrote no more operas after 1829 but composed his outstanding religious work, *Stabat Mater*, in 1842. His music is distinguished by a sparkling sense of melody and wit.

Rostand, Edmond (1868-1918) French verse dramatist, who wrote in a Romantic style, as in *Cyrano de Bergerac* (1898). This, his third play, was based on the life of that romantic dramatist (1620-55), who was said to have had an unusually long nose. Rostand's only other work of lasting fame is *L'Aiglon*, in which Sarah BERNHARDT created (1910) the role of NAPOLEON's son.

Rostropovich, Mtislav Leopaldovitch (born 1927) Russian cellist. As a young man, Rostropovich befriended PROKOFIEV and completed this composer's posthumous *Cello Concerto*. BRITTEN has also written for him. Rostropovich's wife is the well-known Russian soprano, Galina Vishnevskaya.

Rothko, Mark (1930-70) American painter known for his large abstract expressionistic paintings, characterized by two or three vertically arranged rectangular blocks of colour on a coloured background.

Rothschild, Meyer (1743-1812) German banker and founder of a dynasty of financiers and bankers who played a part in shaping European history. Backing the new French and German education systems, financing industry and financing or refusing to finance wars, the Rothschild bankers became wealthy enough to exercise an influence on international events. In London, they helped to introduce full political rights for practising Jews when Lionel Rothschild (1808-79) became the first Jewish member of the House of Commons in 1859 and his son, Sir Nathan Meyer, 1st Baron Rothschild (1840-1915), the first Jewish peer to sit in the House of Lords.

Rouault, Georges (1871-1958) French Expressionist painter of the school of Paris, whose colour was intense and jewel-like, with heavily outlined areas, reflecting the influence of his stained-glass work. After an apprenticeship to a stained-glass maker, he met MATISSE and MOREAU, and from 1905 was associated with the Fauve painters led by Matisse.

Rousseau, Henri (1844-1910) French 'primitive' painter, who, untutored and with naïve directness, concentrated on painting after retiring from his job as a customs officer (hence his nickname, Le Douanier). He painted Parisian landscapes, family scenes and portraits, but he is best known for a number of brightly coloured fantastic or allegorical canvases (e.g. *War*, *The Snake Charmer*, *The Dream*). These impressive pictures of visionary subjects are painted in a would-be realistic, supremely self-confident, though childlike manner and show why both PICASSO and Delaunay were among Rousseau's admirers.

Rousseau, Jean-Jacques (1712-78) French writer and philosopher born in Geneva, whose works have profoundly influenced European literary and political thought. In his first major essay *Discours sur les Arts et les Sciences* (1750), Rousseau advanced his theory of the 'noble savage' whose innate goodness is corrupted by civilization. His *Discours sur l'origine de l'inégalité parmi les hommes* (1755) is another eloquent attack on structured society. It was with the publication of his novel, *La Nouvelle Héloïse* (1761), that Rousseau emerged as the prophet of the French Romantic movement. In his next work, *Emile* (1762), Rousseau expounded his views on education, some of which have left their mark on today's schools. In 1762, Rousseau also published *Du Contrat social*, his greatest work of polemical philosophy, in which he argued that power is vested not in princes, but in the common people, and that government must be by general consent. Rousseau's bold investigation of the paradox of human society – man is born free, but everywhere is in chains – put his own freedom in jeopardy.

Rowlandson, Thomas (1756-1827) English water-colour painter and caricaturist, whose work, which is characterized by a virility of line that contrasts with the delicacy of the colouring, provides a valuable record of the manners and appearances of the Georgian era.

Rubens, Sir Peter Paul (1577-1640) Flemish painter, immensely popular throughout Europe, who sustained a prodigious and varied output. He began his career in Italy where he travelled extensively as court painter to the Duke of Mantua. In 1608 he returned to Antwerp to become court painter to the Spanish Governors of the Netherlands. His first major works on his return were the *Elevation of the Cross* (1610) and *Descent from the Cross* (1611-14) for Antwerp Cathedral, which exhibit the combination of Flemish realism and dynamic movement characteristic of his early style. Rubens was much in demand as a painter of portraits, altarpieces and, from about 1620, decorative schemes for churches and palaces. So large a number of commissions necessitated his establishing a workshop in which his sketches could be worked up by assistants. His output was vast: in addition to projects such as the *Medici* cycle painted for the Palais de Luxembourg in Paris and the ceiling of the Banqueting House in Whitehall, London, he produced hunting scenes, mythological and historical subjects, designs for triumphal processions and huge panoramic landscapes.

Rubinstein, Anton (1829-94) Russian pianist who founded the Conservatory of Music in St Petersburg and was LISZT's only serious rival.

Rudolf I of Hapsburg (1218-91) First (uncrowned) Hapsburg Holy Roman Emperor (1237-91). In the turmoil after the death of Conrad IV, the last Hohenstaufen Holy Roman Emperor (also uncrowned), Rudolf became southwestern Germany's most powerful prince. He was elected King of Germany (1273) and recognized as Emperor by Pope Gregory X, in return for a promise to end imperial aggression in Italy and to lead a new crusade. By defeating and killing his only major rival, OTTOKAR II of Bohemia, Rudolf assured that future Hapsburgs would be kings of Germany, Spain, Hungary and Bohemia, archdukes of Austria, and Holy Roman Emperors.

Ruisdael, Jacob van (c. 1628-82) Dutch landscape painter, whose work, after a relatively realistic and topographically exact early period, became increasingly romantic and for this reason influenced early 19th-century landscape painting.

Rumford, Sir Benjamin Thompson (1753-1814) American-British physicist who was the first to regard heat as a form of energy. In the 1790s, while supervising the boring of cannon barrels, he noticed that the heat generated by the drill was too great to be explained by Antoine LAVOISIER's idea that objects contain a fixed quantity of 'caloric', all or part of which can be converted into heat. Rumford suggested that as the drill bit into the metal its mechanical energy was being converted into heat.

Rupert, Prince (1619-82) German count, nephew of CHARLES I and royalist cavalry commander in the English Civil War, during which he became known as 'the Mad Cavalier', leading brave but undisciplined cavalry charges against parliamentarian troops. He fought at the battles of Edgehill, Marston Moor and Naseby, and in 1644 became royalist Commander-in-Chief. Subsequently he led a royalist fleet (defeated by BLAKE in 1650), then fought as a pirate. After the Restoration he served CHARLES II with distinction as an admiral in the second Dutch War (1664-7). He was a keen amateur scientist and developed a process of mezzotint engraving, improved gunpowder, invented a zinc-copper alloy and found a new way of boring cannon.

Rusk, David Dean (born 1909) American statesman, and an expert in Far Eastern affairs. He joined the US army in the Second World War and became Chief-of-Staff in the Far Eastern war zone. He was appointed State Department administrator in the International Security Division in 1946, and Director of the Office of UN Affairs, 1947-9. Rusk was Assistant Secretary of State with special responsibility for Far Eastern affairs (1950-2) and Secretary of State (1961-8).

Ruskin, John (1819-1900) English art critic, historian and theorist, whose writings on aesthetics and ornate prose style, greatly influenced many late-Victorian writers. In his writing, he endeavours to make beauty applicable to all walks of life, and wrote on diverse subjects such as painting and economics, literature and war.

Russell, Bertrand (1872-1970) English philosopher, mathematician, social reformer and winner of a Nobel Prize for Literature (1950).

Russell, Henry Norris (1877-1957) American astronomer who produced the diagram relating a star's luminosity and temperature. In 1913 Russell suggested that the relationship between a star's luminosity and temperature (discovered by HERTZSPRUNG) is best shown diagrammatically, and the resultant plot became known as the Hertzsprung-Russell diagram.

Russell, John 1st Earl (1792-1878) British Prime Minister, and sponsor of Parliamentary reform. In 1831 GREY entrusted to Russell the drafting and introduction of the first Reform Bill which was passed in 1832. As Home Secretary from 1835 to 1839 under MELBOURNE, Russell introduced the Municipal Reform Bill of 1835 and reduced the number of capital crimes. He supported the repeal of the Corn Laws and succeeded PEEL as Prime Minister in 1846. His Premiership (1846-52) was notable for the dominance of his foreign secretary PALMERSTON, the application of both coercion and relief to Ireland and commitment to free trade by the government. Palmerston's felicitations to NAPOLEON III on his coup in 1851, sent without Cabinet consultation, caused Russell to dismiss him from the post of Foreign Secretary. Palmerston in retaliation brought Russell's ministry down the following year. On Palmerston's death in 1865, Russell became Premier again, but his proposal of a new Reform Bill in 1866 split his Party and led to his resignation.

Rutherford, Ernest, Lord (1871-1937) New Zealand physicist, and founder of modern atomic theory. In 1910 he produced his theory of the scattering of alpha particles (helium nuclei) by atoms, which led him to picture the atom as consisting of a positively charged central nucleus surrounded by orbiting planetary electrons. It was to this model (the Rutherford atom) that BOHR in 1912 applied quantum notions and thus took the vital step towards modern quantum mechanics. Rutherford undertook a systematic study of radioactive substances and their disintegrations. This led to the idea that a substance can be made artificially radioactive by bombardment with fast alpha particles, so causing atomic disintegrations. In the early 1920s he was the first to split the atom.

Ruyter, Michel de (1607-76) Dutch admiral who, with van Tromp, made the Dutch Republic a major sea power. He fought against Spanish, English, Swedish, French and Sicilian fleets, but it was in the three Anglo-Dutch wars that he achieved his greatest success. In the first (1652-3), he helped van Tromp to out-manoeuvre the English; in the second (1665-7), he defeated MONCK's fleet off Dunkirk and made a daring raid on English shipping in the Medway; in the third (1672-4) he fought four indecisive battles, often against heavy odds, but prevented an Anglo-French invasion of the United Provinces.

S

Sachs, Julius von (1832-97) German botanist whose researches into the microchemistry of plants and especially into the mechanics of photosynthesis (the formation of organic compounds in the presence of sunlight) showed that chlorophyll acts as a catalyst in the presence of light, enabling a plant to build up more complex compounds from carbon dioxide and water.

Sadat, Anwar (1918-81) President of Egypt who was a member of the original Egyptian junta, which in 1952 seized power from Farouk and close friend and confidant of NASSER. Given important posts in the government and bureaucracy of Egypt from 1952 on, he was appointed vice-President of Egypt in 1969, and upon Nasser's death assumed power by succession. He was responsible for expelling Soviet technicians and military personnel (July 1972) and for affecting the Egyptian-Syrian alliance which culminated in the October 1973 war with Israel. In 1977 he made a historic peace mission visit to Israel and, in 1978, worked out peace terms with Israeli premier Menachim BEGIN at Camp David, Maryland. Sadat and Begin shared the 1978 Nobel Peace Prize for their efforts to end the 30-year Arab-Israeli conflict. In 1981 Sadat was assassinated by Egyptian Muslim fundamentalists.

Sade, Donatien Alphonse François, Marquis de (1740-1814) French writer, notorious for his tales of sexual perversion and cruelty, from whom the term 'sadism' is derived. His erotic novels include *Justine* (1791), *La Philosophie dans le boudoir* (1795) and *Juliette* (1798), many of them written in prison. Much in his work anticipated the writings of FREUD.

Sagan, François (born 1935) French novelist and playwright. Her novels, *Bonjour Tristesse* (1954), *Un certain sourire* (1956), *Aimez-vous Brahms?* (1959) and *Dans un mois, dans un an* (1957) are written in a spare, simple, dispassionate style, depicting a world of boredom, transient love-affairs and ephemeral happiness. A few of her popular tales have been filmed.

St-Laurent, Yves (born 1936) French fashion designer who has had a strong influence on women's dress since the 1960s. He popularized trousers for women. He also designs clothes for men.

Saint-Saëns, Charles Camille (1835-1921) French composer of *Danse Macabre* (1874) and *Carnival of the Animals* (1886) among other works.

Saint-Simon, Claude, Comte de (1760-1825) French socialist thinker, who advocated a type of meritocracy in which everyone is employed by the state according to his capacity and rewarded according to his contribution. In *New Christianity* (1825) he argued that society should strive to alleviate the lot of the poor.

Saint-Simon, Louis de Rouvroy, Duc de (1675-1755) French author and nobleman, whose outstanding *Mémoires* (written between 1728 and 1750, but published 1829-30) portray the French court during the last years of LOUIS XIV's reign. Saint-Simon's prejudiced and malicious eye makes them historically unreliable, but they are keenly observed pen-portraits of Louis's outwardly decorous court.

Sainte-Beuve, Charles-Augustin (1804-69) French poet, dramatist and critic who, after publishing several volumes of poems, devoted the rest of his career to literary criticism. His preliminary approach was biographical and his ability to dissect the life and character of a writer, combined with his shrewd, unerring aesthetic judgement, caused him to be acclaimed as a great master of literary criticism.

Saladin (1138-93) Muslim general, who put an end to the supremacy of Christian crusaders in Palestine. He was of Armenian Kurdish origin, and became vizier, then (1174) first Ayyubid sultan of Egypt. After resolving a Muslim religious schism, he organized the recapture of Syria and most of Palestine from the Christians, recovered all the kingdom of Jerusalem (founded by Godfrey of Bouillon and Baldwin I) except Tyre, and forced RICHARD I to a stalemate in the Third Crusade (1189-92). The Christians admired him for his generous treatment of prisoners, allowing Christian pilgrims free access to Jerusalem and encouraging east-west trade.

Salazar, Antonio de Oliveira (1889-1970) Portuguese politician and dictator. He was a professor of economics with right-wing Roman Catholic beliefs. He became Premier in 1932 and ruled as dictator until 1968, when he suffered a stroke. He supported the Nationalists in the Spanish Civil War but managed to keep Portugal neutral in the Second World War. He presided over Portugal's economic revival after the war but fought an unsuccessful battle to retain the Portuguese colonies in Africa.

Salinger, Jerome David (born 1919) American novelist, whose *Catcher in the Rye* (1951), the story of a teenager's weekend in 'phoney' New York, appealed to the youth of post-war America. After *Nine Stories* (1953), Salinger's novels and stories of the 1950s and 1960s have formed a continuous saga about the Glass family, the unusual, talented children of a couple who formed a Jewish-Irish stage act. *Franny and Zooey* (1961) and *Raise High the Roof-beam, Carpenters and Seymour* (1963) contain the bulk of the saga, in which Salinger writes of family relations in a middle-class home, and of childhood innocence perverted by the adult world.

Salisbury, Robert Arthur Talbot Gascoyne-Cecil, 3rd Marquess of (1830-1903) British statesman and Prime Minister. He succeeded to the leadership of the Conservative Party on the death of DISRAELI in 1881, and was three times Prime Minister; for all but a short period he was simultaneously Foreign Secretary. He was suspicious of democracy and opposed Parliamentary reform and Irish Home rule, and his later administrations were markedly imperialist in character. Though his influence in South Africa was weakened by the second Boer War (1899-1902), his handling of the Fashoda incident of 1898-9 ensured British domination of the Sudan and the Nile valley.

Salk, Jonas Edward (born 1914) American microbiologist, who developed a vaccine against poliomyelitis, which, in 1952, he successfully tested on children. By 1954 the vaccine was being produced in quantity. Subsequently, an alternative vaccine was developed which could be taken orally, and together the vaccines have greatly diminished the incidence of poliomyelitis.

Sand, George (1804-76) French novelist and feminist whose early works were unashamedly romantic and sentimental – *Indiana* (1831), *Valentine* (1832), *Lelia* (1833). Later she turned her attention from love and marriage to problems of social justice, in works such as *Consuelo* (1843) and *Le Meunier d'Angibault* (1845). Sand also wrote a number of pastoral novels and her notorious liaisons with Alfred du MUSSET and CHOPIN inspired her other writings, *Elle et lui*, *Un hiver à Majorque*.

Sandburg, Carl (1878-1967) American poet, who wrote of rural and urban life in the Middle West, giving a radically different view of America to that presented by the dominant New England tradition. His *Chicago Poems* (1916) celebrated the diversity and energy of the city. *Abraham Lincoln – The War Years* won the Pulitzer Prize (1939).

Sangallo, Antonio da (1483-1546) Italian architect, who played a significant part in the High Renaissance in Rome. He was a member of an important family of Florentine artists and his major work is the Palazzo Farnese, the most monumental of Rome's Renaissance palaces.

Sanger, Margaret Higgins (1883-1966) US social reformer who established the first birth control clinic in North America.

Sán Martín, José de (1778-1850) Argentinian revolutionary who liberated Chile and Peru from Spanish rule. After helping the newly formed Argentinian government in its War of Independence (1812-13), he was given command of the revolutionary armies operating against Spanish rule in Peru in 1814. Considering it most feasible to strike at Peru through Chile, he made an astonishing march over the Andes and defeated the Spanish army at Chacabuco, in February 1817. With the help of the former British admiral, Lord Cochrane, he afterwards formed a fleet and reorganized his army, sailing for Peru in August 1820. After six months of fruitless negotiation with the Spaniards, he entered Lima in July 1821 and accepted the title of Protector. In 1822, the rivalry of BOLÍVAR and local suspicion of Sán Martín's intentions led him to resign and leave for Europe, where he died in poverty in 1850.

Sansovino, Jacopo Tatti (1486-1570) Florentine sculptor who took the name of his master Andrea SANSOVINO. Early in the 16th century he joined BRAMANTE in Rome until its sack, and then in 1527 fled to Venice. Sansovino was responsible for several buildings in Venice, notably the Library of St Mark, the pediment of which is surmounted by many of his statues. The Scala de' Giganti contains his best works, *Mars* and *Neptune*.

Sappho (c. 7th cent. BC) Poet of Ancient Greece, a few of whose poems survive. She was the dominating figure in a group of girls bound by her forceful personality and their shared emotional sensibilities and devotion to poetry.

Sargent, John Singer (1856-1925) American portrait painter, who worked mostly in London. He was both fashionable and successful.

Sartre, Jean-Paul (1905-80) French philosopher, novelist and dramatist, leader of the Existentialist movement, who maintained that the existence of man had no predetermined purpose or 'essence', that man must assume responsibility for his own destiny and so create a meaning for his existence. Sartre's theories were first propounded in the semi-autobiographical novel *La Nausée* (1938). He also published a collection of stories, *Le Mur* (1939), and a further sequence of novels under the general title *Les Chemins de la Liberté* (1945-9). He was the author of a number of philosophical essays, including *L'Etre et le Néant* (1943) and *L'Existence est un Humanisme* (1947). Sartre was also a very talented dramatist, and as well as diffusing his theories, plays such as *Les Mouches* (1942), *Huis Clos* (1944), *La Putain respectueuse* (1946) and *Le Diable et le Bon Dieu* (1951) testify to the author's theatrical skill. In 1964 he refused the Nobel Prize for Literature.

Lord Salisbury, Prime Minister and one of a family at the heart of British politics for 300 years

Sassetta (c. 1400-1450) Sienese artist, who produced religious paintings in a Gothic style imbued with a mystic quality. A fine example of his work was the altarpiece for S Francesco, Sansepolcro (1437-44, now dismantled). Sassetta was the pseudonym of Stefano di Giovanni.

Sassoon, Siegfried (1886-1967) English poet and memoir writer, whose *Counterattack* (1918) is a bitter, satirical attack on those who prolonged the horrors of the First World War. The reminiscent *Memoirs of a Fox-hunting Man* (1928) and *Memoirs of an Infantry Officer* (1930) are accounts of social change, of the passing of a settled and privileged world into the realities of war.

Satie, Erik (1866-1925) French composer of piano pieces and one of music's eccentric prophets. As an integral part of the French *avant-garde* at the turn of the century, Satie sought to deflate both post-Wagnerian romanticism and the French musical establishment and wrote the score for COCTEAU's ballet *Parade* (1917).

Saul (11th-10th cent. BC) First king of Israel. The Israelites, threatened by the Philistines' iron weapons (their own were still of bronze), abandoned their system of government by separate tribal leaders, became united, and elected Saul as their sole leader after he had raised the siege of Jabesh.

Savonarola, Girolamo (1452-98) Italian Dominican friar and orator, who advocated the reform of the Roman Catholic Church. He was prior of St Mark's, Florence, from 1491, and in fiery sermons he condemned corruption in Church and State, claimed prophetic inspiration, and predicted that divine punishment would be visited on Italy and its immoral pope, Alexander VI. Savonarola became the leader of Florence's democratic faction, and after the death of Lorenzo de MEDICI, seized control of Florence from his successor, Pietro (1494), and tried to establish a Christian state based on the renunciation of worldly enjoyments. As a result, Alexander excommunicated him (1497). Finally he was captured by the aristocratic faction, tortured, tried for sedition and heresy, and then executed.

Sax, Adolphe (1814-94) Belgian instrument maker who invented the saxophone family of hybrid instruments, and also their brass cousins, the saxhorns.

Saxton, Christopher (c. 1542-c. 1606) English cartographer who made and recorded the earliest topographical survey of Britain.

Say, Jean Baptiste (1767-1832) French economist and businessman who stated by his 'law of markets' that supply creates its own demand. Say regarded slumps as temporary imbalances between production and consumption. He also distinguished the functions of the creative entrepreneur from those of the capitalist.

Scarlatti, Alessandro (1659-1725) Italian musician, whose works were a major influence on the development of opera. He is credited with the invention of the *aria da capo*.

Scarlatti, Domenico (1685-1757) Italian harpsichord virtuoso and composer who wrote approximately 600 one-movement harpsichord sonatas containing some of the richest music in the instrument's repertoire, at the same time contributing to the basis of future keyboard composition and the concept of the sonata form.

Scheele, Karl Wilhelm (1742-86) Swedish chemist who discovered oxygen (1771) and chlorine. Unfortunately for Scheele, his discovery was not published until 1777, by which time Joseph Priestley had also prepared the gas, later to be called oxygen, and is generally credited with the discovery. In 1774, the same year in which Priestley was experimenting with oxygen, Scheele discovered chlorine.

Schiaparelli, Giovanni Virginio (1835-1910) Italian astronomer renowned as an expert planetary observer, who discovered the association between comets and meteors.

Schinkel, Karl Friedrich (1781-1841) German architect whose public buildings in Prussia, while severely Grecian in style, are original. Many of Schinkel's works are in Berlin and include the New Guard House, The Theatre, the Old Museum and the Werdersche Kirche in the Gothic style.

Schlegel, August Wilhelm (1767-1845) German poet, critic and scholar who, with NOVALIS, Tieck, Schelling and his brother Friedrich, laid the foundations of German Romanticism with *A course of Lectures on Dramatic Art and Literature* (1809). He is chiefly known today for his translations with Tieck of SHAKESPEARE's plays, which are still in use.

Schleirmacher, Friedrich Daniel Ernst (1768-1834) Influential German Protestant theologian and philosopher, who saw religion as the expression of a dependence on something beyond the everyday world, independent of morality or knowledge. He led the movement which led to the union of the Prussian Lutheran and Reform Churches.

Schliemann, Heinrich (1822-90) German archaeologist whose spectacular excavations at Mycenae and Troy, begun in 1870, dramatically confirmed HOMER's account of life in Mycenean times and helped to inspire Sir Arthur EVANS's work in Crete.

Schmidt, Helmut (born 1918) West German political leader. Elected to the Bundestag in 1953, he became chairman of the Social Democratic Party in 1967 and Minister of Defence when the Social Democrat-Free Democrat coalition government was formed in 1969. He replaced Willie BRANDT as Chancellor in 1974 and worked toward bettering economic conditions and easing East-West tensions world-wide. He stabilized Germany's position in international politics before leaving office in 1982, when he was succeeded by Helmut Kohl.

Schoenberg, Arnold (1874-1951) Austrian composer who evolved the 'note-row', the most radical innovation in 20th-century music. Schoenberg won the early support of Richard STRAUSS and MAHLER as an exponent of 'post-Romantic music' – breaking new ground, while still influenced by WAGNER. By 1908 he had moved towards atonality, his song-cycle *Pierrot Lunaire* (1912) on 21 poems by Giraud being generally acknowledged as a cornerstone of modern music. By the early 1920s he was writing in his 12-note style – a method for imposing order on the anarchy of atonalism which he used thereafter with variable consistency. Schoenberg's other works include the impressive, though unfinished, opera *Moses and Aaron* (1957) and the moving cantata *A Survivor from Warsaw* (1947) on the Nazi persecution of the Jews, as well as concertos and many chamber works. Having been declared a 'degenerate' composer, Schoenberg was driven out of Nazi Germany and emigrated to America.

Schopenhauer, Arthur (1788-1860) German philosopher, the founder of the modern system of thought known as pessimism. An invective critic of all branches of philosophy since SOCRATES, his major contribution to philosophy was his study of the will, as expounded in *The World as Will and Idea* (1819).

Schubert, Franz Peter (1797-1828) Austrian composer who displayed a profound melodic gift and did more than any other composer to establish the German *lieder* ('songs') tradition. Schubert showed an early maturity, his first acknowledged masterpiece being a song he wrote at the age of 17. Before his early death from typhus at 31, he had written over 600 songs which explored the medium's possibilities from light lyrics to the major song-cycle of 24 poems on unrequited love, *The Winter Journey* (1827). His enormous output also included 15 string quartets, including that in D minor nicknamed *Death and the Maiden*; 21 piano sonatas and the quintet known as *The Trout*. The apparently fluent ease with which he composed in no way detracts from his standing, for as BRAHMS said, 'There is not a song of Schubert's from which one cannot learn something.' Schubert's works are now often referred to by their Deutsch (or 'D') numbers, named after the Austrian musicologist Otto Erich Deutsch, who compiled the complete catalogue (1951).

Schuman, Robert (1886-1963) Premier of France (1947-8), Foreign Minister (1948-52) and originator of the Schuman Plan (1950). This defined a policy for pooling West European coal and steel resources, and eventually took shape as the European Coal and Steel Community. From this, all subsequent progress towards European integration, including the European Economic Community, has developed. Schuman's plan was to remove national barriers to the flow of raw materials for steel products, to eliminate cartels and monopolies and to reduce the power of specific areas like the Ruhr.

Schumann, Robert (1810-56) Composer, among the leaders of Romanticism in German music. A contemporary of CHOPIN and MENDELSSOHN, Schuman set out to become a piano virtuoso, but after injuring his hand turned to composition. Among his best-known piano pieces are *Papillons* (1829-31), *Carnival* (1834-5) and *Scenes from Childhood* (1838); his contributions to the concert repertoire include a piano concerto, a cello concerto and four symphonies (the Third sub-titled *The Rhenish*), and he also wrote three string quartets. His wife, Clara Schumann, was a fine pianist and a composer of songs and piano pieces. In 1854, Schumann's mind gave way and he tried to drown himself in the Rhine. His last two years were spent in an asylum. Clara devoted the rest of her life to performing and promoting her late husband's music.

Schütz, Heinrich (1585-1672) German composer who wrote *Daphne,* the first German opera (the music is now lost), and the earliest German oratorios, including *The Seven Last Words from the Cross*. Schütz studied with GABRIELI in Venice and his music represents a synthesis of the High Renaissance Italian and the German styles of composition. His church music anticipates the Baroque style of the 18th century and the music of J. S. BACH. From 1615 until his death, he was Kapellmeister at Dresden.

Schwann, Theodor (1810-82) German physiologist who was one of the founders of the cell theory of biology according to which all living organisms are made up of cells.

Schweitzer, Albert (1875-1965) German Lutheran theologian, philosopher, musician and missionary doctor at Lambarene in French Equatorial Africa, where he built his own hospital and gave free treatment to the native population. He won a Nobel Peace Prize in 1952.

Schwitters, Kurt (1887-1948) German painter, now recognized as a leading pioneer of a major development in 20th-century art – the move away from traditional materials.

Scipio, Publius Cornelius (237-183 BC) Roman general, whose defeat of Carthage in the Second Punic War gave Rome mastery of the western Mediterranean. After reversing earlier Roman setbacks in Spain, he drove the Carthaginians out of Spain (206 BC). He invaded Carthaginian North Africa and forced HANNIBAL to abandon the invasion of Italy and defend his homeland. At the decisive battle of Zama (202 BC), which he won, Scipio abandoned the deep Roman battle phalanx and adopted Hannibal's formation of a front line concealing mobile groups.

Scopas of Paros (4th cent. BC) Greek sculptor, who assisted in the reconstruction of the Temple of Athena at Teges and in the Mausoleum of Helicarnassus (*c.* 350 BC) with Bryaxis, Leochares and Timotheus. The remains of several works from this period can be attributed to Scopas on stylistic grounds, including part of the freize from the Mausoleum depicting the Battle of the Greeks and Amazons, a marble statue of Meleager.

Scott, Sir George Gilbert (1811-78) English architect who led the English Gothic revival. Scott produced a great number of dramatic and inspired buildings – notably the red-brick Venetian-Gothic hotel for St Pancras Station, London, and the richly ornamented Albert Memorial, Kensington. He was also an active restorer of Gothic buildings and was associated with the restoration of Westminster Abbey.

Scott, Robert Falcon (1868-1912) English Antarctic explorer, leader of an ill-fated expedition to the South Pole. A naval officer, Scott had led an Antarctic expedition (1901-4) in the specially-built ship *Discovery*. He organized his own Antarctic expedition in the *Terra Nova* (1911), and, with Edward Wilson, Edgar Evans, Lawrence Oates and H. R. Bowers, set out on the expedition's final stage, intending to become the first man to reach the South Pole. Taking only one sledge of supplies, they trekked 950 miles in two and a half months to meet bitter disappointment when, on 18 Jan. 1912, they reached the South Pole and found AMUNDSEN's flag already there. Suffering from scurvy, frostbite and hunger and hampered by soft snow and unseasonable blizzards, Scott's party embarked on a grim two-month return journey that ended when the survivors Scott, Wilson and Bowers died, blizzard-bound, in their tent.

Scott, Sir Walter (1771-1832) Scottish Romantic poet and novelist, who, in such works as *Ivanhoe* (1819) and *Kenilworth* (1821), created a strong tradition of the historical novel. Scott was preeminent as a story teller. In *Waverley* (1814), *Old Mortality* (1816), *Rob Roy* (1817) and others, he created vivid stories set in detailed Scottish landscapes. His wide range of literary activities, which included contributions to the *Edinburgh Review* and the first number of the *Quarterly Review*, began with translations of German Romantic works and developed through his own collections of Scottish folksongs and ballads. His first major original work was a verse romance, *The Lay of the Last Minstrel* (1805). Scott was imbued with the traditions of an enlightened aristocracy, and bought an estate at Abbotsford. Extensive borrowing and poor business partners led to financial ruin and Scott spent his last years working prodigiously and successfully to pay off the £130,000 he owed.

Scriabin, Alexander (1872-1915) Russian composer and pianist. He is known today chiefly for two of his orchestral works: the sensuous *Poem of Ecstasy* (1908) and *Prometheus* (*Poem of Fire*) (1911). Scriabin evolved the 'mystic chord' of ascending fourths to express his personal mystical and occult beliefs.

Searle, Ronald (born 1920) English humorous artist and illustrator, who created the St Trinians series of diabolical schoolgirls. He is a prolific artist and in addition to many drawings for the press has produced book illustrations, advertisements and film credit titles.

Segovia, Andres (born 1893) Spanish guitarist responsible for the revival of the classical guitar in this century. FALLA, among others, has written for him and the soloists Julian Bream and John Williams have followed his example.

Sekou-Touré, Ahmed (born 1922) African nationalist and Marxist politician, who became first President of the Republic of Guinea when independence was declared in 1958. He has been re-elected President at every election since.

Sellers, Peter (1925-80) British actor and comedian who, together with Spike Milligan, created *The Goon Show* (1951), one of the funniest radio shows ever produced. His first major role was in the film, *I'm All Right, Jack* in 1959. But he will be best remembered for his role as the spectacularly inefficient French detective, Clouseau, in the *Pink Panther* series of films.

Seneca, Lucius (c. 54 BC-c. AD 39) Roman rhetorician, father of Seneca the Younger. A connoisseur of the art of rhetoric, Seneca drew up an anthology of rhetorical practice for his three sons: extracts from famous rhetoricians with his own pithy observations. In this work is found all that is known of Roman rhetoric in the reigns of AUGUSTUS and TIBERIUS.

Senefelder, Alois (1771-1834) Austro-Czech inventor of lithography, in which the subject matter to be printed remains effectively on the plate surface. This technique relies on the incompatibility of water and grease, so that ink from a grease base is deposited on the grease-treated printing regions and is rejected by the damp non-printing areas.

Sennacherib (705-681 BC) King of the Assyrian Empire, who waged war against the Babylonian Empire and razed its capital, Babylon, in 689 BC. Sennacherib used armies of enslaved captives to build a palace for himself at Nineveh.

Serlio, Sebastiano (1475-1554) Italian architect best known for his practical and widely read handbook *L'Architettura*, which, among other things, defined the five orders of the classical column, with base and capital. He worked in Rome under PERUZZI, in Venice and in France.

Two examples of Serlio's work can be seen today. One is at Fontainebleu

Serrão, Francisco (c. 1480-c. 1519) Portuguese adventurer who was shipwrecked in the East

Indies and became the first European to settle there. His enthusiastic letters about the islands partly inspired the voyage of his friend MAGELLAN.

Sesshu Ota (1419-1506) Japanese Zen priest generally considered to be Japan's greatest landscape painter. His Indian ink landscapes of China are more powerful and convincing than those of his contemporaries, partly due to his first-hand knowledge of the scenery gained during a visit to China (1468-9).

Sessions, Roger (born 1896) American composer and symphonist who studied with BLOCH. His eight symphonies are complex, dense constructions, based on tonality but 'modern' in effect. Other works by Sessions include a violin concerto, string quartets and choral, piano and organ music.

Seurat, Georges (1859-91) French artist famous for his 'pointillist' technique – that of using minute touches of pure colour to put the Impressionists' instinctive response to light on to a scientific basis. Seurat developed his unique style through studying various scientific and art-theoretical texts. It is to be seen at its most effective in his *Sunday Afternoon at the Island of the Grande Jatte* (1886) and in the coastal landscapes painted around Le Havre.

Sévigné, Marie de Rabutin-Chantal, Marquise de (1626-96) French socialite and friend of LOUIS XIV, whose *Lettres*, written mainly to her daughter, Comtesse de Grignan, were published posthumously from 1725 onwards. Invaluable as socio-historical documents, recounting the news and gossip of the day, the letters are written in a warm, spontaneous style, witty and yet full of compassion.

Shackleton, Sir Ernest Henry (1874-1922) English explorer, the first to attempt to cross Antarctica. After serving with SCOTT's *Discovery* expedition (1901-4), Shackleton led the *Nimrod* expedition (1907-9), which reached a point 97 miles from the South Pole. His attempt to cross Antarctica (1914-17) failed when his ship *Endurance* was crushed by ice, but he escaped, travelling 800 miles in an open boat with five companions, and finally rescued the remainder of the crew.

Shafi, Mohammed ibn Idris al- (727-820) Arab thinker and founder of the Shafite, one of four Islamic schools of law which evolved in the 8th century. Each took a slightly different view of the *Shari'a*, the sacred law.

Shakespeare, William (1564-1616) English dramatist and poet, who created the finest plays and the richest poetic and dramatic language in English literature. His plays fall into three categories: histories, comedies and tragedies. The histories form two distinct cycles, although not written consecutively. The first, the three parts of *Henry VI* and *Richard III* (1589-93), contains some of Shakespeare's earlier work and traces a sequence through the events of the War of the Roses, establishing the Tudor view of Henry Tudor's claim to the throne. The second is based upon the life of HENRY V, from his youth, in the two parts of *Henry IV* (1597-8) to his victories in France in *Henry V* (1599). The early comedies are satirical and farcical, full of verbal humour, and their central theme is the trials and joys of love, which is pursued more subtly, with greater depth of character, in such later plays as *Twelfth Night* (*c.* 1600) and *As You Like It* (*c.* 1600). The major tragedies, *Hamlet* (*c.* 1600), *Othello* (*c.* 1604), *King Lear* (*c.* 1605), *Macbeth* (*c.* 1605) and *Antony and Cleopatra* (1607) are unequalled in western literature. Their heroes are strongly individual, separate from the common run of men, with ambitions and hopes, incompatible with the circumstances around them, which end in grief. *Antony and Cleopatra* also forms part of the group of Roman plays, with *Julius Caesar* (*c.* 1599) and *Coriolanus* (*c.* 1609). Shakespeare's final plays were written for the aristocratic audience of the Blackfriars theatre, more sophisticated than the general public of the Globe. His poems include the long narratives 'Venus and Adonis' (1593) and the 'Rape of Lucrece' (1594) and the well-known sequence of sonnets. Shakespeare was a successful and immensely popular dramatist and actor in his own lifetime.

Shamir, Yitzhak (born 1915) Israeli politician and Prime Minister who was a founder member of the Stern Gang (1940-1). He was arrested by the British mandatory authorities in 1941 and exiled to Eritrea. He was given political asylum in France and returned to Israel in 1948, but retired from political activity until 1955. He held a senior Civil Service post for many years and then became a member of the Knesset in 1973. He was Speaker from 1977 to 1980 and minister of Foreign Affairs in 1980 after the resignation of Moshe DAYAN. He succeeded BEGIN as Prime Minister in 1983.

Shankara (c. 788-820) Indian philosopher and founder of the Advaita Vedanta school of philosophy, which still exercises the most profound influence on Hindu thought. The chief exponent of orthodox Hindu teaching, Shankara wrote profound, subtle commentaries on the *Upanishads*, the *Bhagavad Gita* and the *Brahma Sutra*.

Shapley, Harlow (1885-1972) American astronomer, who determined the size of the Galaxy and the Sun's position in it, and did much to popularize astronomy.

Sharp, Cecil James (1859-1924) British musician who saved the English folk-music tradition from oblivion. His life's work was the collection of over 5000 songs of the English aural tradition and he made field trips to the Appalachian Mountains in America (1916-18) to collect the English songs preserved among settlers' descendants in isolated valleys. Sharp founded the English Folk Dance Society (1911).

Shastri, Shri Lal Bahadur (1904-66) Indian statesman and Prime Minister. Influenced as a young man by GHANDI, his civil disobedience and militancy cost him a total of nine years' imprisonment. He was a leading member of the United Provinces (later Uttar Pradesh) Assembly from 1937, and succeeded NEHRU as General Secretary of the Indian National Congress. He became Minister of Transport and Railways in 1952, resigning in 1956 following a railway accident for which he felt compelled to take responsibility. He returned to his Ministry a year later, was Minister of Commerce and Industry (1958), Home Affairs (1961), and Prime Minister (1964-6).

Shaw, George Bernard (1856-1950) Irish dramatist, journalist and novelist, who was one of the leaders of a realist movement in the English theatre of the early 20th century. Throughout his career Shaw used his work to propound his views on society. In his lesser plays the dramatic quality suffers from over-insistent ideology. His first works, novels, were unsuccessful, but he achieved some renown as a drama and music critic, advocating the works of MARX, WAGNER and IBSEN, and as a socialist orator. His first play, *Widowers' Houses*

(1892), on the state of slum dwellings, had only two performances, being thought too radical for the commercial theatre, but such later works as *Arms and the Man* (1894), *Candida* (1895) and *The Devil's Disciple* (1900) gained popularity. In *Man and Superman* (1903), a well-written comedy, Shaw put forward his theory of a Life Force as the energetic impulse of man's progress. His greatest success was *Pygmalion* (1913), from which was made the musical and film *My Fair Lady*. *St Joan* (1923) is also frequently revived and *Heartbreak House* is one of Shaw's best works.

George Bernard Shaw, with members of the cast of one of his plays. A lifelong socialist, Shaw used his work to express his views on the society around him

Shaw, Percy (1890-1976) British inventor (1934) of cat's-eyes, reflectors marking lane divisions on roads. They became established during the blackout of the Second World War, as they were the only markers which reflected light in the direction from which it came.

Shaw, Richard Norman (1831-1912) English architect who designed New Scotland Yard, London. He raised the standard of taste in Victorian architecture by abandoning the over-ornamented style of many architects, and adopting simpler lines.

Shays, Daniel (c. 1747-1825) American soldier. In the depression following the American War of Independence, he led impoverished farmers protesting against their threatened imprisonment for debt. At Springfield, Mass., they clashed with the state militia (1786). These clashes, known as Shays' Rebellion, persisted until his defeat (1787).

Shelley, Mary Wollstonecraft (1797-1851) English novelist, wife of Percy Bysshe SHELLEY, who wrote, on BYRON's suggestion, *Frankenstein* (1818), a horror story which combined a Gothic atmosphere with plausible logic.

Shelley, Percy Bysshe (1792-1822) 'Poets are the unacknowledged legislators of the world,' claimed Shelley, the wildest, most ardent and most unconventional of the younger generation of English Romantic poets. After a revolutionary career at Oxford, he eloped with Mary Godwin and travelled abroad with BYRON. His longer poems, such as 'Prometheus Unbound' (1820), 'Epipsychidion' (1821) and 'Adonais' (1821), rely on grandiose symbolism for their visionary quality and unearthly atmosphere. Like Byron and KEATS, he died abroad, drowned in a storm at Spezzia.

Shephard, Sam (born 1943) Prolific American playwright and actor. His plays include *Up to Thursday* (1964), *Chicago* (1965), *Operation Sidewinder* (1970), *Suicide in B-Flat* (1976) and *True West* (1983). He wrote the script for the film *Paris, Texas* (1984) and has acted in films including *Days of Heaven* (1978) and *The Right Stuff* (1983).

Sheridan, Richard Brinsley (1751-1816) Anglo-Irish dramatist and theatre manager, whose career began with three simultaneous successes in 1775: *The Rivals, St Patrick's Day*, and a musical play, *The Duenna*. Among his other plays were *The School for Scandal* (1777), *The Critic* (1779) and *Pizarro* (1799). He became the Manager of Drury Lane Theatre (1776), rebuilt it (1794) and was financially ruined when it was burnt down (1809). After entering politics as a Whig MP (1780), he held office and took a prominent part in the impeachment of Warren HASTINGS.

Sherman, William Tecumseh (1820-91) US Civil War Unionist general. His famous offensive march through Confederate territory to the coast (Georgia campaign, 1864) left a trail of devastation and bitterness. He was Commander-in-Chief of the US army from 1869 to 1884, when he retired.

Sherrington, Sir Charles (1861-1952) English neurologist who worked out the body's motor-nerve system, introduced the concept of the synapse (a gap between connecting nerve cells across which chemicals can pass) and mapped the parts of the brain, relating them to function. He was awarded a Nobel Prize in 1932.

Shih Huang Ti (259-210 BC) First Chinese emperor (221-210 BC), who, as King of China, conquered the independent states in China and unified the country. He standardized Chinese writing and began the Great Wall, built to keep out barbarians. In 212, he decreed the burning of all historical documents.

Shivaji (1627-80) Mahratta leader and national hero, who gave the Mahrattas of India a sense of unity and purpose they had never before possessed. After several military operations against the Moguls (1659-70), he declared himself independent in 1674. He owed his military successes to a skilled infantry and cavalry, which enabled him to lay the foundations of a compact kingdom in western India, expanding to an empire in the 18th century. He organized a sound administration and tried to establish an equitable land system.

Shockley, William (born 1910) American physicist who, with Bardeen and Brattain, developed the transistor. 'Solid-state' devices – in which junctions involving materials called semiconductors act like electronic valves – had been used since the 1930s for rectification (the changing of alternating into direct current). In 1956, Shockley, Bardeen and Brattain won the Nobel Prize for Physics for their work on the development of the transistor.

Sholes, Christopher Lathan (1819-90) American inventor who, with Carlos Glidden and Samuel W. Soule, made the first prototype of the modern typewriter (1867). Encouraged by two businessmen, James Densmore and George Washington Newton Yost, Sholes eventually (1873) constructed a machine capable of rapid fingering, by the separation of the most commonly used letters as far as possible to prevent jamming. Densmore and Yost bought Sholes's patents and in 1873 persuaded the Remington Fire Arms Company to manufacture the machine. It was first marketed in 1876 and eventually, after a few years, proved a commercial success.

Sholokov, Mikhail Aleksandrovich (1905-84) Russian novelist, author of *And Quiet Flows the Don* (1934), the story of a man torn by love for two women and by his conflicting loyalties to the Cossacks and the Bolsheviks. The book describes the problems and bitterness engendered by the Revolution for those who lived through it. In 1940 he produced a sequel, *The Don Flows Home to the Sea*. While his earlier works were notable for their objectivity, Sholokov's later writings are less impartial. Between 1932 and 1960 he produced *Virgin Soil Upturned* and a second part, *Harvest on the Don*, about the collectivization campaign in the Don region. He was awarded the Stalin Prize (1941) and the Nobel Prize for Literature in 1965.

Shostakovich, Dmitri (1906-75) Russian symphonist and leading composer in his time. He wrote 15 symphonies ranging from the First, an exuberant work of his student days, to the patriotic Seventh, which celebrates the Siege of Leningrad in the Second World War, and the darker, more introspective Tenth. Shostakovich periodically encountered official disapproval. In 1936, his opera *The Lady Macbeth of Mtsensk* was denounced and withdrawn after it had angered STALIN. But Shostakovich, while admitting to certain 'errors', remained larger than the vagaries of bureaucracy and avoided compromising his status as a major artist.

Sibelius, Jean (1865-1957) Finland's leading composer and one of the master symphonists of the 20th century. Sibelius's earliest works were orchestral tone poems based on events in the lives of the heroes of the Finnish national epic, the *Kalavala*. Among these are *En Saga*, *The Swan of Tuonela* and *Finlandia*. At 32, Sibelius was granted a government annuity, enabling him to give himself entirely to composition. He wrote seven symphonies, the first in 1899 and the last in 1925. The first two showed a strong TCHAIKOVSKY influence, but thereafter the cycle developed a progressive economy of expression. In 1926 Sibelius published his last major work, the tone poem *Tapiola*, a vision of the forces of nature in the dark northern winter.

Sickert, Walter (1860-1942) German-born English artist whose style was basically Impressionistic, but which showed a marked concern for intimate subject matter that at times approached voyeurism. He studied with both WHISTLER and DEGAS and spent much time abroad, painting in Venice and Dieppe. Later he helped to form the Camden Town Group.

Sidgwick, Nevil (1873-1952) English chemist who developed the electronic theory of chemical bonding. Using Nils BOHR's idea of atomic structure, Sidgwick showed that the explanation of chemical bonding (in terms of interactions between electrons) applies also to inorganic chemistry, not merely organic chemistry as had been thought until that time.

Sidney, Sir Philip (1554-86) Aristocratic English soldier, courtier, diplomat and poet whose *Astrophel and Stella* (1580-4) was the first of the Elizabethan sonnet sequences. The prose *Arcadia* (1580-3), a chivalric romance, developed an English literary style, and his *Defence of Poesie* (*c.* 580) was the most lucid, coherent critical essay of the age, written as a reply to an abusive Puritan pamphlet.

Siemens, Sir Charles William (Karl Wilhelm) **(1823-83)** who was a member of the famous German inventive family and came to England in 1843. He is best known for an open-hearth steel-making process, utilizing his regenerative principle for the conservation of waste heat, which improved, and eventually replaced, the BESSEMER process. Other notable achievements were his design of the ship *Faraday*, which laid the transatlantic telegraph cable of 1874, and his installation of an electric tramway at Portrush, Northern Ireland (1883).

Sieyès, Emmanual Joseph (1748-1836) French Revolutionary leader and publicist, known as Abbé Sieyès. Though educated for the priesthood, Sieyès's clerical career was a mere formality, but he was moved by compassion for the poor to study social conditions and gave a clear shape to the aspirations of reformers in two pamphlets: *Essay on Privileges* (1788) and *What is the Third Estate?* (1789). During the Terror (1794) he withdrew from public life, but returned to politics as a member of the Directory in 1799, drafted the Constitution of the Consulate and helped NAPOLEON to seize power. In 1814, he took refuge in Belgium and did not return until 1830.

Signorelli, Luca (c. 1445-1523) Italian artist, and pupil of PIERO DELLA FRANCESCA, whose monumental treatment of the human form is seen in his fresco cycle illustrating the *End of the World* and the *Last Judgement* in Orvieto Cathedral (1499-1500). This shows the use of the nude figure for dramatic purposes, which was taken up by MICHELANGELO in his *Last Judgement*, painted on the wall of the Sistine Chapel.

Sikorski, Wladyslaw (1881-1943) Polish general and Prime Minister-in-exile during the Second World War. He retired to Paris (1928) after Pilsudski's *coup d'état* of 1926, and was appointed Prime Minister-in-exile (first in France, then England) when Poland fell in 1939. Realizing that the friendship with the Soviet Union was necessary for Poland's survival, he concluded an agreement with Russia in 1941, annulling the 1939 Russo-German partition of Poland and providing for the release of Polish prisoners and the formation of a Polish army in Russia. He was killed in a plane crash at Gibraltar in July 1943.

Sikorsky, Igor Ivanovich (1889-1972) Russian-born American aeronautical engineer who in 1913 built and flew the world's first multi-engined aeroplane. His many aircraft companies were merged to form United Aircraft Manufacturing Corporation for which he developed flying boats and other aircraft. Sikorsky built (1909) the first, although unsuccessful, helicopter and 30 years later, returning to this type of aircraft, developed the single-seat Sikorsky VS-300, the prototype of the modern machines.

Simenon, Georges (born 1903) Belgian-born French author of several hundred detective stories featuring Inspector Maigret of the Surêté, novels which raised the detective story to a minor art-form. He later wrote more ambitious novels, including *The Stain on the Snow* (1953). His autobiography, *Pedigree*, appeared in 1948.

Simeon (10th cent.) Bulgarian king, formerly a monk, under whom Bulgaria reached the peak of its power. Hoping to become Byzantine emperor, Simeon fought Byzantine armies five times (894-923), and though he did not achieve his aim, his capital, Preslav, rivalled Constantinople as a cultural centre.

Simon, Sir John (1816-1904) English physician, who in 1848 became London's first Medical Officer of Health. He instituted routine inspections of public and commercial premises, campaigned for the improvement of water supplies and sewage systems and began a system of quarantine and isolation for infections. He was also an advocate of compulsory immunization.

Sinatra, Frank (born 1915) American singer who became immensely popular with teenagers in the 1940s for such songs as *Night and Day*. In the 1950s he became a film actor and won an Oscar for a supporting role in *From Here to Eternity* (1953).

Sinclair, Upton Beal (1878-1968) American social reformer and novelist, who was a prolific, popular author of books exposing the limitations of capitalist society.

Singer, Isaac Bashevis (born 1904) American novelist and short story writer. He was born in Poland but emigrated to New York City in 1935. His works, written in Yiddish but translated into English, include *The Family Moskat* (1950), *The Estate* (1969), *Shosha* (1978) and *Lost in America* (1981). He won the Nobel Prize for Literature (1978).

Singer, Isaac Merit (1811-75) American inventor and manufacturer of the sewing machine, which, from the middle of the 19th century, revolutionized the manufacture of clothing and furnishings.

Sisley, Alfred (1839-99) French Impressionist painter of English descent. Confining himself almost exclusively to landscape painting, his work did not develop beyond Impressionism, as did MONET's and CÉZANNE's. Throughout his life, despite unrelieved poverty, he concentrated on sensitive and luminous interpretations of modest scenes, at different seasons. He was initially influenced by COROT and by the paintings of TURNER and CONSTABLE, which he had seen on visits to London.

Sitting Bull (1831-90) American Indian chief of the Hunkpapa Sioux. His prestige was at its height when he defeated the Seventh Cavalry under CUSTER at the battle of the Little Big Horn. During the Ghost Dance scare of 1890, he was killed resisting arrest.

Sitwell, Dame Edith (1887-1964) English poet who possessed brilliant powers of language and a humane sensibility. In 1916 she attracted attention by editing *Wheels*, an anthology of modern verse opposed to the ideals of the Georgian poets of Munro's anthologies.

Sitwell, Sir Osbert (1892-1969) English author, who wrote of himself, 'I belonged by birth, education, nature, outlook and period to the pre-war era, a proud citizen of the great free world of 1914.' His achievement in prose and verse has been a skilful re-creation of the temper and colour of those times. His best-known novel, *Before the Bombardment* (1926), is a realization of Edwardian society. He also wrote five volumes of vivid autobiography, and books of verse.

Sitwell, Sir Sacheverell (born 1897) English writer, best known for reflections on European Baroque art. His poetry, showing an affinity with the work of his sister Edith, but more traditional, draws its inspiration from the arts.

Skinner, Burrhus (born 1904) American experimental psychologist, and inventor of the Skinner Box for animal experiments. A lever, when depressed, opens a door and frees the animal, or drops a food pellet into the cage as a reward. Using this technique of conditioned learning reinforced by reward, Skinner was able to train animals to perform elaborate acts. He has since explored ways of teaching the basic skills of spelling, arithmetic, etc., to children, with the aid of specially-designed machines.

Sloane, Sir Hans (1660-1753) English physician and naturalist whose collections formed the basis of the British Museum. In 1727 he became George II's first physician, and succeeded NEWTON as President of the Royal Society. He built up and catalogued a large botanical collection, bought William Courten's unique collection of curiosities, acquired a major library, and then bequeathed his thousands of manuscripts, books and natural history specimens to the nation. The collection (with others) went on public view in London and became the nucleus of the British Museum in 1759.

Slocum, Joshua (1844-1909) American sailor who completed the first solo circumnavigation of the world. He left Newport, Rhode Island, in 1895 in the sloop *Spray* and returned in 1898, after circling the world in three years and two months. In November 1909, he set out once more, but was lost in the notorious 'Bermuda Triangle'.

Sluter, Claus (late 14th-early 15th cent.) Dutch sculptor whose importance lies in the fact that he freed sculpture from its secondary place as a part of architecture in northern Europe and, in so doing, he anticipated DONATELLO and paved the way for artists from van EYCK on. His best-known work, the *Well of Moses* (1395-1403), was carved for Philip the Bold of Normandy.

Smetana, Bedřich (1824-84) Czech composer who founded his country's musical style. He also made a name as a conductor and pianist and received encouragement from LISZT. Associated with the unsuccessful 1848 revolt against Austria-Hungary, Smetana used folk-music to evoke national feelings. *The Bartered Bride* (1886) has always been his best-known opera abroad. In 1874, while he was writing his set of six tone poems *My Country*, he went deaf and shortly afterwards his career was ended by a nervous breakdown.

Smirke, Sir Robert (1781-1867) English architect, who designed the British Museum, London, perhaps the most important of his buildings and the best example of the Greek Revival in Britain.

Smith, Adam (1723-90) British economist whose five-volume *The Wealth of Nations* (1776) laid the foundations of the classical school of economics. This work describes labour, discusses capital and the industrial development of European countries, argues for free trade and deals with the expenses of national administration. It had a profound influence on government institutions of the time.

Smith, George (1840-76) English Assyriologist whose flair for deciphering cuneiform (wedge-shaped) scripts led to discoveries which revealed the basis of many ancient Hebrew tales. In 1872 he deciphered an almost complete Assyrian account of the Flood, which closely matched that in the Bible. His discovery of other parallels with The Book of Genesis were reinforced by Sir Leonard Woolley in 1928.

Smith, Ian Douglas (born 1919) Rhodesian politician, who withdrew Rhodesia from the Commonwealth and declared 'UDI' (Unilateral Declaration of Independence) in 1965. Although he adopted a policy of apartheid in Rhodesia, a country with an overwhelmingly black population, Smith made some efforts to negotiate with black leaders in the mid-1970s. In 1976 he agreed to black majority rule in Rhodesia and stepped down in 1979 when Rhodesia became the independent Republic of Zimbabwe.

Smith, Jedediah (1798-1831) Amerian explorer, the first to make the central overland crossing of the US to the Pacific and open up the American West. Seeking fur-trade routes to the Pacific, he went by way of the Great Salt Lake and the Colorado River to San Diego (1826). He became the first to cross the Sierra Nevada and travel west to east across the Great Basin (1827) and (1827-8) made the first land exploration of Oregon and Washington. He was killed by Comanche Indians before his maps of the west were published.

Smith, John (1580-1631) English soldier and colonist, a leader of England's first permanent American colony. As one of 104 male settlers who founded Jamestown, Virginia, in 1607, he took command of the few who survived the first winter of starvation and disease, traded with Indians for maize, and organized defences against Indian attack. He explored Chesapeake Bay, the Potomac, the Rappahannock and the Chickahominy where, he claimed, POCAHONTAS saved his life. He published several works on Virginia and New England.

Smith, Joseph (1805-44) American religious leader, founder of the Church of Jesus Christ of Latter-Day Saints, generally known as Mormons. The name comes from the *Book of Mormon*, which was discovered by Smith written in Reformed Egyptian on golden plates. Smith's message, that God was coming to gather his Saints together in a New Jerusalem, gained many followers in spite of ridicule and even violence. Smith was later murdered by a mob in Illinois.

Smith, William (1769-1839) British surveyor and geologist, known as the father of English geology. His examination of the rock strata of England during the course of his work as a surveyor led him to the conclusion that each layer contains its own characteristic assemblage of fossils and that this could be used to determine the sequence and succession.

Smith, William Henry (1825-91) English founder of a bookselling chain. He developed his father's shop in the Strand, London, negotiated with the growing railway companies for rights to open station bookstalls and soon became Britain's biggest bookseller/newsagent. In 1868 he entered Parliament and had a distinguished ministerial career.

Smollett, Tobias (1721-71) Scottish novelist, who wrote in the picaresque tradition, filling his novels with incidents drawn from his own experience, especially as a ship's surgeon. His best-known novels are *Roderick Random* (1748), *Peregrine Pickle* (1751) and *Humphry Clinker* (1771), in which his blunt, vigorous style of writing is best suited to satire and caricature. Smollett wrote many miscellaneous works, including a critically respected *Complete History of England* (1757-61).

Smuts, Jan Christiaan (1870-1950) Afrikaner soldier-statesman who fought against the British in the South African War (1899-1902) and went on to become an elder statesman of the British Empire. Colonial Secretary in BOTHA's government, Smuts went to war again, on the side of his old enemies, when the First World War broke out and he defeated the German forces in South West Africa. He became a member of the Imperial War Cabinet in 1917 and, after the war, helped to draft the League of Nations Covenant. Between the wars, he was twice Prime Minister of South Africa and founded the anti-republican, anti-racialist United party in 1934. A close colleague of CHURCHILL during the Second World War, he helped to found the United Nations.

Snorri Sturluson (1179-1241) Icelandic poet, story-teller and historian, who was the most important literary figure in medieval Scandinavia. His major work, the *Edda* (*c.* 1223), a textbook for poets, includes his own poetry and his re-telling of the ancient myths, masterpieces of grace and irony. Snorri is thought also to have been the author of the *Egils Saga*. His other works include *The Orb of the World* (*c.* 1223-35), a history of the Norwegian kings down to 1177, and *The Olaf Saga*.

Socrates (c. 470-399 BC) Greek philosopher and inventor of a new method of study in terms of proposition and argument, a procedure of hypothesis and deduction which now lies at the heart of scientific method. Socrates was inspired by a divine mission to teach men their own ignorance, but the method of question and answer, by which he deflated the self-opinionated and taught those who followed him to question established assumptions, made him many enemies. He was eventually condemned to death and given hemlock to drink.

Solomon (c. 973-c. 933 BC) King of Israel, under whom it reached the height of its fame. He made allies of Tyre and Egypt and was thus free to trade profitably in the Mediterranean and southeastern Asia. He built fortified cities, sumptuous palaces, and a temple at Jerusalem. The taxes and forced labour exacted for his lavish court, harem and buildings caused discontent, which after his death split the kingdom into Israel and Judah. Solomon is credited with having written the Song of Solomon, Proverbs and Ecclesiastes.

Solon (c. 638-c. 558 BC) Athenian lawgiver, who was elected to the office of Archon in 594 BC, especially to reconcile the existing differences between the aristocratic, mercantile and popular factions. His proposals were embodied in a code, containing constitutional, economic and general reforms: his constitution provided for a limited oligarchy based on citizenship classes and a deliberative council. He passed an edict reducing the burden of debt on the poor.

Solzhenitsyn, Aleksandr Isayevich (born 1918) Russian author and poet of international reputation and outspoken critic of academic oppression in the USSR. His most famous work, *A Day in the Life of Ivan Denisovich* (1962), an account of life in a labour camp during the STALIN era, caused a sensation in the Soviet Union when it was published at the height of KHRUSCHEV's de-Stalinization campaign. Like *First Circle*, *Ivan Denisovich* was based on his own experiences of prison camps. *Cancer Ward* (1968) recalls his experiences while undergoing treatment for a stomach cancer while in exile in Kazakhstan. *August 1914* (1971), a later novel about the events leading up to the fatal battle of Tannenberg in East Prussia, is an epic work in the tradition of TOLSTOY's *War and Peace*. In 1970, Solzhenitsyn was awarded a Nobel Prize for Literature, but was refused permission to accept it by the Soviet authorities. With the publication in the West of *The Gulag Archipelago*, he was expelled from Russia in 1974.

Somers, Sir George (1554-1610) English admiral, who claimed Bermuda for JAMES I when his ship *Sea Venture* was wrecked off the Bermuda Islands (1609) on the way to Virginia with settlers. Somers took the castaways on to Jamestown, Virginia (1610), though two stayed at Bermuda and founded an English settlement. He returned to Bermuda for supplies and died there.

Sondheim, Stephen (born 1930) Celebrated American composer and lyricist who has had many Broadway and film musical successes, including *West Side Story* (1957), *Gypsy* (1959) and *A Little Night Music* (1973).

Sophocles (496-406 BC) Greek dramatist, who was one of the three great tragic poets of the period. In form, his work lies somewhere between the traditional ritual drama of AESCHYLUS and the modern, almost psychological approach of EURIPIDES. Sophocles was used as a model by ARISTOTLE, who criticized Euripides as 'decadent' in his *Poetics*. In a sense, the concept of three Unities of time, place and action, for centuries fundamental to European theatre, is derived from Sophoclean drama. Of the some 100 plays which he wrote, only seven tragedies survive: *Ajax*, *Antigone*, *Trachiniae*, *Oedipus Rex*, *Electra*, *Philoctetes*, *Oedipus at Colonnus* and some fragments (450-406 BC). A master of plot construction and the use of dramatic irony, Sophocles used three characters as well as the chorus, and, using traditional myths as his subjects, dealt in personalities, relationships and man's predicament confronted by fate.

Sorel, Georges (1847-1922) French journalist and social philosopher whose doctrine of violence, as expounded in *Reflections on Violence* (1908), is often misrepresented as one of the inspirations of Communism and Fascism. Since evolution toward socialism seemed to him impossible, Sorel advocated direct action, by means of a general strike organized by revolutionary syndicates.

Soto, Hernando de (c. 1500-42) Spanish explorer, one of the first to travel extensively in southern North America. He travelled widely in Panama, Guatemala, Yucatán and Peru, then (1539), inspired by rumours of treasure in Florida, obtained Emperor CHARLES V's commission to colonize it. He explored north to the Appalachians and west to the Arkansas River, discovered and crossed the Mississippi, surviving many attacks by hostile Indians.

Soufflot, Jacques Germain (1713-80) French architect of the Panthéon, Paris, which, although classical in style and very severe in feeling, avoids the monumental heaviness of ancient Roman architecture and has the lightness of the Gothic buildings Soufflot admired.

Sousa, John Philip (1854-1932) American bandmaster who became the acknowledged king of the American march. Sousa's intention was to write music 'for the feet instead of the head', and which would moreover make 'a man with a wooden leg step out'. In 'The Stars and Stripes Forever', 'Washington Post', 'Liberty Bell' and 'El Capitan' among many others he succeeded magnificently. In 1892, he founded the internationally famous Sousa's Band, responsible for the later high standards of American band performance. The Sousaphone, a kind of large tuba, was made for his band.

Southey, Robert (1774-1843) English author, whose poems, particularly 'Thalaba' (1801), in irregular, unrhymed form, were among the early documents of the Romantic movement. Today he is remembered for short poems like 'Bishop Hatto' and 'The Inchcape Rock'. Southey wrote a mass of miscellaneous work, the most successful of which was a *Life of Nelson* (1813). He was a friend of WORDSWORTH and brother-in-law of COLERIDGE.

Spallanzani, Lazzaro (1729-99) Italian biologist, who solved the theory of spontaneous generation. He showed that if water is boiled for long enough, no micro-organisms appear in it and deduced that if any did appear they would have to have hatched from eggs or spores already present either in the water or the air of the vessel in which the water had been boiled.

Spartacus (1st cent. BC) Thracian leader of a slave revolt which terrorized Roman Italy for two years. Two Roman armies were defeated and Rome threatened before Crassus defeated the slaves and killed Spartacus.

Spencer, Herbert (1820-1903) English philosopher whose *System of Synthetic Philosophy* (1860-93) surveyed the social and biological sciences with an underlying philosophic notion of evolution. He regarded life as a continuous process of adaptation and ethics, following his evolutionary principle.

Spencer, Sir Stanley (1891-1959) British painter of religious pictures which caused much controversy because of their earthy and recognizable settings.

Spender, Stephen (born 1909) English poet, who, with AUDEN and others, made the state of society in the 1930s the starting point for their verse. Educated at Oxford, he travelled in Germany, and worked for the Republicans in the Spanish Civil War.

Spenser, Edmund (c. 1552-99) English poet, in whose work is a rich blend of the principal elements of 16th-century English poetry. Spenser was a humanist and a classicist, learned and philosophical, and wrote in the forms the Renaissance had established – the pastoral of the 'Shepheardes Calender' (1579) in honour of Philip Sidney, the satire of 'Mother Hubbard's Tale' (1590), the sonnet-sequence *Amoretti* (1595) and the lyrical ode 'Epithalamion' (1595). But he drew from the strength of the old world also and, in the *Faerie Queene* (1590-6), joined the medieval allegory to the new romantic epic, forming a map of Christian virtue, an allegory of the State of England and a gallery of striking images.

Sperry, Elmer Ambrose (1860-1930) Prolific American inventor who is best known for the application of the gyroscope, whose properties he started to investigate in 1896. Although the invention of the gyrocompass is credited to the German Anschutz-Kaempfe (1908), the Sperry model was used in the USS *Delaware* in 1910. He introduced gyroscopic stabilizers for ships in 1931. Sperry also worked in electrochemistry, devising methods for making caustic soda from salt and recovering tin from scrap food cans. He also invented (1918) the high-intensity arc-searchlight, now standard for military and display uses.

Spielberg, Steven (born 1946) American film director of blockbuster movies. He made his debut with *Duel* (1971), a brilliant suspense film. His subsequent films have been box-office successes worldwide and include *Jaws* (1975), *Close Encounters of the Third Kind* (1977) and *Raiders of the Lost Ark* (1982).

Spode, Josiah II (1754-1827) English potter. Spode perfected the standard hybrid bone china body and was able to popularize this type of translucent china, as it met the prevailing preference for Orient-inspired porcelain. He was the foremost potter of the day, gaining a royal appointment in 1806.

Springer, Axel (born 1912) German publisher, who is one of Europe's most powerful Press magnates. His group includes a large proportion of West Germany's newspapers, including *Die Welt*, *Bild Zeitung*, *Hamburger Abendblatt*, *Berliner Zeitung* and *Berliner Morgenpost*. Springer is also the major shareholder in the Ullstein publishing house.

Ssu-ma Ch'ien (145-c. 87 BC) China's first great historian, whose vast *Historical Records* spanned some 2000 years of Chinese history from its recorded beginnings, and provided a key source for western histories of China. It included chronological tables of major events and essays on aspects of government and developments in astronomy, economics and music. It established standards of historical scholarship unmatched in the western world until recent centuries and founded a chronology and literary pattern followed in subsequent dynastic histories.

Staël, Madame de (1766-1817) French writer and literary critic whose works, particularly *De l'Allemagne* (1810) had a marked influence on the development of the Romantic movement in France. In an earlier book, *De la littérature considérée dans ses rapports avec les institutions sociales* (1800), Madame de Staël had already revealed her cosmopolitan outlook and her theories about the distinct cultures of North and South. She also wrote two sentimental novels, *Delphine* (1802) and *Corinne* (1807), the first works to introduce the idea of the liberated woman to French fiction, anticipating George SAND's work.

Stalin, Joseph (1879-1953) (real name J. Vissarionovich Dzugashvili) Russian politician who, after LENIN's death (1924) became dictator of the USSR. A member of the Social Democratic Party from 1899, after 1904, he was repeatedly exiled to Siberia for political crimes and in 1913 was imprisoned up to the 1917 February Revolution. Siding with the Bolsheviks after the party split (1903) he worked closely with Lenin, took part in the October Revolution, and became Secretary of the Central Committee of the Communist Party (1922-41). After 1924, Stalin systematically eliminated his rivals, including Trotsky, and won control over the Comintern. In the 1930s he ordered purges of the Party and Army and in 1939 he made a non-aggression pact with HITLER, but took charge of his armies after the German invasion (1941). From 1945 he extended the USSR frontiers to the surrounding satellite countries in a climate of deteriorating relations with the West. He died in uncertain circumstances, reportedly on the verge of another purge and a change in foreign policy.

Stanley, Sir Henry Morton (1841-1904) Welsh-born American journalist and explorer who traced the source of the Nile and found the lost explorer, David LIVINGSTONE. Already an experienced war correspondent, Stanley was sent by the New York *Tribune* newspaper to Africa to find Livingstone, and found him at Lake Tanganyika (1871). Stanley continued as an explorer, leading an expedition (1874-7) which traced the Nile's source, circumnavigated Lakes Victoria and Tanganyika and traced the whole course of the River Congo. He spearheaded colonization of the Congo regions for Leopold II of Belgium, and (1887-90) traced Lake Albert's source to Lake Edward and identified the Ruwenzori Range as the fabled Mountains of the Moon.

Stanley, Wendell (1904-71) American biochemist who first prepared a crystalline virus, a Nobel Prize winner (1946). Stanley's discovery that a virus is essentially a protein molecule was important, for it placed viruses on the borderline between living matter (viruses are capable of reproducing themselves) and non-living matter (they resemble enzymes in molecular structure).

Stanley, William (1858-1916) American electrical engineer who in 1885, working with WESTINGHOUSE, perfected a practical transformer for large electricity supply networks. This enabled them to carry out the first practical demonstration of an alternating current system at Great Barrington, Massachusetts, in March 1886. He also devised two-phase electric motors and generators, as well as a consumption meter in which the moving parts were suspended magnetically to avoid friction.

Starling, Ernest (1866-1927) English physiologist who discovered the laws that govern the activity of the heart and the mechanism by which lymph and other bodily fluids are secreted. He also identified a number of digestive hormones, coining the term hormone to describe these and other secretions.

Stauffenberg, Count Claus Schenk, von (1907-44) German staff officer, leader of the abortive plot against HITLER in 1944. Revolted by the Jewish pogroms of 1938 and the brutality of the SS (Sturm Schutz) on the Russian front, he was chosen by his fellow conspirators to plan and carry out the assassination of Hitler and the seizure of power from the Nazis. The deployment of troops and disarming of the SS was planned to the last detail, and on 20 July 1944, Stauffenberg attended a conference at the Wolfsschanze, Hitler's headquarters in Rastenburg. There he planted a bomb hidden in his briefcase and made good his escape. Hitler survived the explosion, and the conspirators were rounded up. Stauffenberg and about 150 alleged conspirators were executed. Some 20 others, including ROMMEL, committed suicide.

Steele, Sir Richard (1672-1729) Dublin-born playwright and essayist, whose achievement was to shape and to launch the popular literary periodical of instruction and amusement. He founded the *Tatler* in 1709, and later collaborated on the *Spectator* (1711-12) and *Guardian* (1713). Steele was more bound up in political warfare than his friend ADDISON, and his periodicals became more ardently Whig in time.

Steen, Jan (1626-79) Dutch painter of portraits and biblical scenes, who is best known for his pictures of 17th-century Dutch life and customs, such as the *Eve of St Nicholas* (*c.* 1660).

Stein, Gertrude (1874-1946) American experimental novelist who studied psychology with William JAMES, and went to live in Paris in 1903. Interested in language and psychology, spurred on by the example of modern painters like PICASSO, she began her experiments in *Three Lives* (1909); other attempts were *The Making of Americans* (1925) and *The Autobiography of Alice B. Toklas* (1933), her own career told as the life of her secretary. Her deliberately prosaic, repetitive writings are obsessed with technique.

Steinbeck, John (1902-68) American novelist, whose fiction combined picaresque description with reforming zeal. His romanticism was expressed in books like *Cup of Gold* (1929), *Tortilla Flat* (1935) and *Cannery Row* (1944). The radical, reforming theme appeared in *In Dubious Battle* (1936), *Of Mice and Men* (1937) and *The Grapes of Wrath* (1939), the latter a sombre story of the migration of sharecroppers from farms in the Mid-West to California.

Steiner, Rudolph (1861-1925) Influential Austrian educationalist. His methods, such as eurhythmy (movement to music), have had considerable impact in Europe and the US, and today there are many 'Steiner schools', noted for their success with the handicapped.

Stendhal (1783-1842) Pen-name of Henri Beyle, French author of *Le Rouge et le Noir* (1831) and *La*

Chartreuse de Parme (1839), psychologically penetrating novels describing the alienation of a central character from his environment. An army officer, he participated in NAPOLEON's disastrous 1812 campaign and after the 1830 Revolution he spent his time writing and in dilettante pursuits in Europe.

Stephen I (c. 977-1038) King of Hungary (997-1038), statesman and saint, first of the dynasty founded by Arpad. After embracing Roman Christianity, he devoted himself to defeating Hungarian chiefs who clung to paganism or Eastern Orthodoxy. He introduced Roman churchmen into Hungary and, with specially appointed nobles, they ran the land through a royal council answerable to the king. Stephen strengthened the national economy by encouraging agriculture and commerce, and organized a standing army and a system of frontier defences which helped him to withstand German and other invasions. He became the patron saint of Hungary.

Stephen Báthory (1533-86) King of Poland (1575-86), which he made supreme in eastern Europe. A powerful monarch and a gifted soldier, he routed the forces of IVAN IV at Wenden in 1578, and in 1582 forced the Tsar to cede all non-Swedish Livonia. Stephen Báthory dreamed of uniting Poland with Hungary and Muscovy in a great eastern empire at the expense of Turkey. He was a cultured man and, though a strong Roman Catholic, was tolerant of other faiths.

Stephenson, George (1781-1848) English engineer and builder of the famous *Rocket,* who became the leading figure of the new Railway Age of the early 19th century. He was appointed engineer for the construction of the Stockton and Darlington Railway (1821), which was opened four years later. In 1829, his *Rocket* (built mainly by his son Robert STEVENSON) won the famous Rainhill trials, to choose a locomotive for the new Liverpool-Manchester Railway, for which he became engineer. It was the first line to carry passengers by steam haulage, heralding the Railway Age.

Stephenson, Robert (1803-59) English mechanical and civil engineer who, in partnership with his father George STEVENSON, was a pioneer of the Railway Age. In 1827 he joined his father's firm as manager, and in 1829 was largely responsible for the design of the successful *Rocket*, the first locomotive with a multi-tubular boiler of the modern type, and later made other significant innovations in engine design. Robert Stephenson was appointed chief engineer for the London-Birmingham Railway (1831) and after surmounting considerable problems, the 112-mile-long line was opened in 1838. Robert Stevenson also designed bridges, notably the Britannia railway bridge over the Menai Straits.

Sterne, Laurence (1713-68) English novelist, whose *Life and Opinions of Tristram Shandy* (1760-7) was the most original and eccentric novel of the 18th century. It is a brilliant, wayward improvisation round the comic figures of Walter Shandy, Uncle Toby, Corporal Trim and Parson Yorick, and extended the range of the novel with a much more subjective organization of material. He also wrote *A Sentimental Journey Through France and Italy* (1768).

The works of Sterne were eccentric, sentimental – and sometimes indecent

Stevens, John (1749-1838) American lawyer, inventor and US transportation pioneer, who in order to protect his invention of a multi-tubular boiler for marine engines (1788), secured America's first patent legislation. Stevens later developed high-pressure steam engines and boilers, and in 1808 launched the *Phoenix*, the world's first sea-going steamboat, only a few days after FULTON's *Clermont*. Stevens then became interested in railways and was granted the first US charter for a railway between the Delaware and Raritan rivers (1815), founded the Cambed and Ambroy Railway Company (1830) and built and operated the first railway across New Jersey (1832).

Stevens, Wallace (1879-1955) American poet whose verse is technically accomplished and intimate poetry, unconcerned with public attitudes, rich with imagery, and often drawn from music and painting. 'Harmonium' was published in 1923, but he wrote little until he was over 50. His works include *Ideas of Order* (1935), *Notes Toward a Supreme Fiction* (1942) and *Collected Poems* (1954).

Stevenson, Adlai Ewing (1900-65) Democratic presidential candidate and champion of American liberalism, who was instrumental in the establishment of the United Nations. He was elected Governor of Illinois (1948) by a record majority and ran the State with remarkable efficiency and honesty. He was twice beaten by EISENHOWER in the presidential campaigns of 1952 and 1956. KENNEDY appointed him US Ambassador to the United Nations in 1960, a post he fulfilled with wit and humanity for over four years (1961-5).

Stevenson, Robert Louis (1850-94) Scottish author, whose individual prose style and rich invention created such novels as *Treasure Island* (1883) and many essays, fantasies, travel-books, children's tales and adventurous romances. Among them were, *An Inland Voyage* (1878), *Virginibus Puerisque* (1881) and *The New Arabian Nights* (1882). He wrote romances, usually on Scottish themes, such as *Kidnapped* (1886) and the unfinished *Weir of Hermiston* (1896); a tale of the macabre and the fantastic in *Dr Jekyll and Mr Hyde* (1886); and vivid and interesting letters. Of his poetry, *A Child's Garden of Verses* (1885) is the best known. In 1888 he left with his family for the South Seas, and died in Samoa.

Stevin, Simon (1548-1620) Dutch mathematician, civil and military engineer, who discovered the triangle of forces, a basic theorem in statics (the study of objects in equilibrium).

Stockhausen, Karlheinz (born 1928) German composer and a leader of the avant-garde in European music. Stockhausen began with serialism and moved on to become an advocate of electronic music in the 1950s.

Stoker, Bram (1847-1912) Irish novelist, who wrote *Dracula* (1897). The story of the vampire, Count Dracula, was supposedly taken from Transylvanian legend, retold by Stoker with narrative skill.

Stoppard, Tom (born 1937) British playwright whose work explores the philosophical problems of reality and communication with great wit. His reputation was established with *Rosencrantz and Guildenstern are Dead* (1966); other plays include *Jumpers* (1972) and *Night and Day* (1978).

Stowe, Harriet Beecher (1811-96) American novelist who wrote *Uncle Tom's Cabin* (1852). The novel is not only an anti-slavery tract, but also an analysis of many aspects of racialism.

Strachey, Lytton (1880-1932) English biographer and critic, who helped to debunk the grandeur of Victorian life and art. He put into practice his principles of biography which were to attack 'in unexpected places', and to send a 'revealing searchlight into obscure recesses'. *Eminent Victorians* (1918), *Queen Victoria* (1921) and *Elizabeth and Essex* (1928) were the results of this technique, which he called psychography. Strachey was a member of the Bloomsbury Group.

Stradivari, Antonio (c. 1645-1737) Italian instrument maker who brought the craft of violin making to its peak about 1700. The Stradivaris, Antonio and his sons, Francesco and Omobono, were the best known of three families of string-instrument makers at Cremona (with Amatis and the Guarneris).

Strafford, Sir Thomas Wentworth, 1st Earl of (1593-1641) English statesman, a moderate supporter of CHARLES I, who favoured the royal prerogative, but was opposed to arbitrary taxation and imprisonment. As Lord Deputy of Ireland (1633-9), he enforced his 'thorough' policy of coercing the unwilling Irish to accept English laws and increasing Protestant immigration in order to counter Catholic dissidents. In 1640 Charles I made him his chief adviser and an earl. He was impeached by Parliament, at the instigation of PYM, for abuse of fundamental English law, and was executed.

Strauss, Johann II (1825-99) The most famous member of the Viennese family of Austrian waltz composers. He wrote 'The Blue Danube' and 'Tales from the Vienna Woods', the operetta *Die Fledermaus* (1874), and more than 400 waltzes.

Strauss, Richard (1864-1949) German composer who brought the symphonic poem to its highest point of sophistication. From his earliest tone poem, *Don Juan* (1888), Strauss showed an egocentric but audacious expressiveness. The tone poems *Till Eulenspiegel* (1895), *Thus Spake Zarathustra* (1896) and *Don Quixote* (1897) followed, as did his musical 'autobiography' *A Hero's Life* (1898). Strauss's 'modernism' sometimes scandalized his contemporaries, notably in his opera *Salome* (1905), based on WILDE's play. His other operas, *Elektra* (1909), *Der Rosenkavalier* (1911) and *Ariadne on Naxos* (1912-16), with librettos by Hofmannsthal, are classics of the modern repertoire. The *Metamorphoses* (1945) for 23 solo strings is a work of his old age.

Stravinsky, Igor (1882-1971) Russian-born American composer who studied with RIMSKY-KORSAKOV, and soon attracted the attention of the impresario DIAGHILEV. The first full score he wrote for Diaghilev's Ballets-Russes in Paris was *The Firebird* (1910), which made his name. *Petrushka* (1911) followed, and *The Rite of Spring* (1913), which provoked a riot at its first performance, but which has remained a cornerstone of modern music. For the rest of his creative life Stravinsky remained a step ahead of both public and critics. He adopted Neo-classicism in the 1920s, giving it hard, monumental outlines and rhythmic subtlety, as in *Oedipus Rex* (an opera-oratorio with text by COCTEAU) or the *Symphony of Psalms* (1930). In 1939 he left for America, where he became a naturalized citizen. He had already used ragtime in, for example, his astringent chamber opera *The Soldier's Tale* (1918), and now he absorbed jazz influences, writing his *Ebony Concerto* for Woody Herman's band. In 1951, he completed the entertaining Hogarthian opera *The Rake's Progress* (with text by W. H. AUDEN).

Stresemann, Gustav (1878-1929) German statesman, who restored Germany's status in the League of Nations after the First World War. As a nationalist, convinced that Germany had a mission to dominate Europe, he believed that she must first regain the confidence of the other powers. As Chancellor (1923) and Foreign Minister (1923-9), he attempted to carry out the terms of the Treaty of Versailles. He secured the signing of the Locarno Treaties (1925), securing Germany's admission to the League of Nations as a major power (1926), negotiated a reduction in the amount of reparation payable by Germany, and persuaded the Allies to evacuate the Rhineland (Britain in 1926, France in 1930). He was awarded the Nobel Peace Prize in 1926.

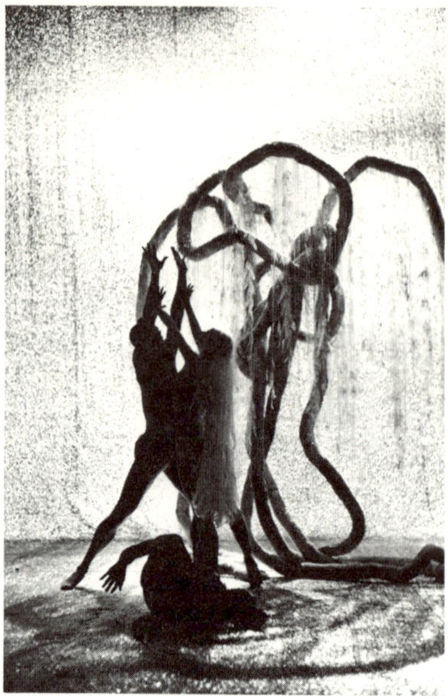

The Rite of Spring ballet, for which Stravinsky composed the score, caused an uproar when it was staged in Paris in 1913

Strindberg, August (1849-1912) Swedish dramatist who, with IBSEN, was a leading exponent of uncompromising realism. His plays were an innovation in their exposure of the battle between the sexes, notably in *The Father* (1887) and *Miss Julie* (1888). He wrote more than 50 plays, including a huge symbolic work, *To Damascus* (1898), dramas of Swedish history, and others charged with symbolism and mysticism, such as *Advent* (1898) and *Dance of Death* (1901). He helped to found the tiny Intima Teatern in Stockholm (1907), for which, in the same year, he wrote *The Storm* and *The Burnt Lot*.

Stuart, Charles Edward (1720-88) English prince, known as 'Bonnie Prince Charlie' or the 'Young Pretender'. He led the second Jacobite rebellion to oust the Hanoverian George II and re-establish Stuart rule in Scotland and England under Charles's father, James Edward Stuart (the 'Old Pretender'), son of James II. Charles landed in western Scotland from France (1745) and by sheer dash and charm rallied many highland clansmen, who, in under four months, seized Edinburgh, defeated a British army at Prestonpans and invaded England as far south as Derby before forcing their leader reluctantly to withdraw to Scotland.

The Duke of Cumberland's army shattered Charles's now ragged Jacobite force at Culloden (1746) and Charles became a fugitive. With the help of loyal supporters (notably Flora MACDONALD) he escaped to France, and lived out the remainder of his life in drunkenness and debauchery.

Stubbs, George (1724-1806) Superlative English animal painter, whose detailed observation and sense of pictorial balance distinguish him from traditional sporting painters such as Seymour and Marshall and sometimes anticipate a neoclassical interest in surface pattern and form. His opinion that nature, not art, was his tutor was endorsed by a visit to Italy, and demonstrated by his publication, after many years of detailed study, of *The Anatomy of The Horse* (1766). *Gimcrack on Newmarket Heath* and *The Grosvenor Hunt* are examples of the type of picture that won him fame among the landed gentry and aristocracy.

Sturgeon, William (1783-1850) English physicist, who devised the first electromagnet. His invention, made in 1823, consisted of a coil of insulated wire wound round a bar of soft iron; when a current flowed in the coil, the bar became a temporary magnet and could lift nine times its own weight. In 1836, he devised the moving-coil galvanometer, a current-detecting device, based on the same principle.

Sturt, Charles (1795-1869) British Army officer who explored the barren heartlands of the Australian continent. In 1828, he was appointed leader of an expedition into the interior drylands and discovered the Darling River. A year later he commanded a second expedition, which floated down the Murrumbidgee River in a whaling boat, and followed the course of the Murray River. His most ambitious expedition, in 1844, took him to the unexplored interior of the continent, north of Lake Eyre.

Suger, Abbot (c. 1081-1150) French cleric who, by drawing together architects of different regions in France, and by his own stringent and original ideas of what a building should be like, inaugurated the Gothic style in the Île de France.

Suharto (born 1921) President of Indonesia who seized office by a military coup, overthrowing SUKARNO. He succeeded as Indonesia's army commander after his predecessor was murdered in an abortive coup by the Communists in 1965, and deposed Sukarno in 1967. Suharto has pursued a fiercely anti-Communist policy ever since.

Sukarno, Ahmed (c. 1901-70) Indonesian Nationalist leader, and dictator of his country from 1949 until deposed in 1967. He first led an unsuccessful revolt against Dutch colonial government in 1926. He was arrested three times, imprisoned and once exiled to Sumatra (1940). When the Japanese drove the Dutch out of Indonesia in the Second World War, they appointed Sukarno President of the Java Central Council, and when the Japanese in turn were forced to withdraw in 1945, Sukarno declared Indonesia a republic and embarked on a four-year war with the Dutch and officially became President in 1949 when the Dutch formally ceded Indonesia. His aggressive attitude to Malaysia and his leftist leanings culminated in his implication in a Communist plot (1965) to seize power, and he was deposed in 1967 by General SUHARTO and a group of army officers. He was kept under house-arrest until his death.

Suleiman I 'The Magnificent' (c. 1496-1566) Sultan of Turkey, whose reign brought the Ottoman Empire to its peak. His troops thrust westwards into Europe (1521), took Belgrade, and – after killing Hungary's LOUIS II at Mohács (1526) – seized much of Hungary, which Suleiman ruled through John Zapolya. To retain Hungary against the claims of Ferdinand of Austria (later Emperor FERDINAND I), the Turks made several attacks on Austria which terrorized all central Europe. Possession of Hungary remained in dispute until, and after, Suleiman's death. In Asia, Suleiman ended Persian threats by seizing Georgia and Baghdad (1534). Helped by corsairs headed by Barbarossa II, he established a formidable fleet, which swept the Mediterranean Sea.

Sulla, Lucius Cornelius (138-78 BC) Roman consul, general and dictator, who reformed Roman law. Using Roman troops for the first time to suppress political rivals, he defeated Marius to become dictator (82-79 BC). His 'Cornelian laws' restored government machinery which had been crippled by wars, and rebuilt the Senate's strength at the people's expense. Antagonism to Sulla's patrician rule triggered the revolt of SPARTACUS and brought forth new, popular leaders.

Sullivan, Sir Arthur (1842-1900) British composer who collaborated with GILBERT to write the 'Savoy' operas, which have become one of Britain's national institutions.

Sullivan, Louis Henri (1856-1924) American architect, who led the so-called Chicago school of architects which, in the late 19th century, devised the massive commercial palaces of Chicago, the forerunners of skyscraper office blocks. Although he designed on an enormous scale, Sullivan's attention to decorative detail did not suffer and he retained his intense interest in the relationship of form and function. The degree of elaboration in his decoration of interiors, such as in the Chicago Auditorium, was often comparable with European Art Nouveau. He was known as the 'father of modernism' and greatly influenced Lloyd WRIGHT.

Sully, Duc de (1560-1641) French statesman, convinced Protestant and a friend of the Calvinist, Henry of Navarre (later HENRY IV). He fought for Henry in the religious civil wars and when Henry became king was appointed his finance minister (1597-1611). Sully revived France's economy and strengthened national defences, and kept internal peace by quelling religious disturbances regardless of the insurgents' faith. When Henry was assassinated, Sully was ousted.

Sun Yat-sen (1866-1925) Chinese revolutionary, who founded the Chinese Nationalist Party (Kuomintang, 1912) on the 'Three Principles' of nationalism, democracy and socialism. After revolt against the Manchu broke out in Hankow (1911), a revolutionary assembly at Nanking elected him Provisional President of the United Provinces of China. Meanwhile, the national assembly in Peking had appointed the northern general Yüan Shih-k'ai as Prime Minister (and later President). For the sake of national unity, Sun gave way to Yüan (1912), who from 1913 to 1916 used his presidency to become virtual dictator. Sun opposed this régime, but was defeated and exiled. In 1921, he returned to power as Provisional President of the South China Republic. He was deposed by the war lords, but after being restored to power at Canton in 1923, accepted Russian help to admit Communists to the Kuomintang.

Surrey, Henry Howard, Earl of (c. 1517-47) English poet who, together with Sir Thomas WYATT, adapted Italian Renaissance verse forms, especially the sonnet, to English. His translation of part of the *Aeneid* also introduced blank verse into England.

Sutherland, Graham (1903-80) British artist, who took up painting after being a railway engineer. His earliest works were landscapes and his painting has an organic feeling of growth, often based on natural forms such as roots, trees and birds. In the 1950s he began to paint portraits and turned also to religious painting. His best-known works in this vein are the *Crucifixion* for St Matthew's, Northampton, and the design for the tapestry in Coventry Cathedral.

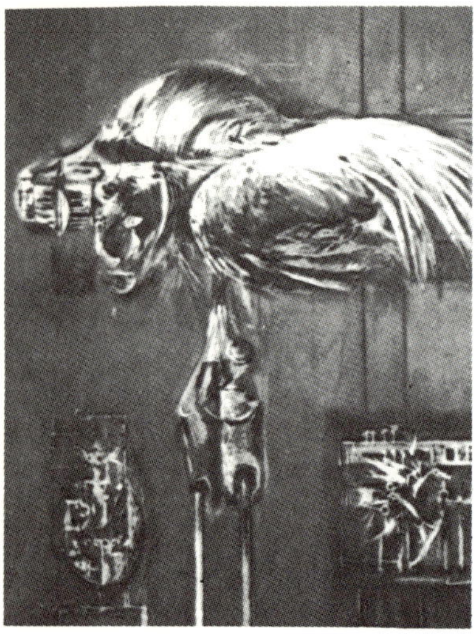

Sutherland's work draws heavily on the forms of nature

Swammerdam, Jan (1637-80) Dutch entomologist whose careful microscope studies of insect anatomy produced the first detailed descriptions of metamorphosis (change of form) in insects and of the structure of their mouth parts and compound eyes.

Swan, Sir Joseph Wilson (1828-1914) English physicist and chemist who invented several important devices and processes. For many years from 1848 he experimented (like many European and American inventors) with the production of a long-lasting electric filament lamp. In 1878, after being joined by high-vacuum specialist Charles H. Stearn, he produced a successful lamp. EDISON achieved a similar breakthrough at the same time, and just beat Swan to an English patent. The two joined to form the company of Ediswan (1883). Swan's subsequent system for making lamp filaments from nitrocellulose (1883) was adopted by CHARDONNET for making artificial silk (rayon).

Swift, Jonathan (1667-1745) Irish-born satirist, essayist, novelist and poet, the most powerful prose writer of the 18th century, who wrote *Gulliver's Travels* (1727). He became secretary to Sir William Temple, then sought a career, unsuccessfully, in the Church. He wrote many political pamphlets, and was the editor (1710-11) of the Tory *Examiner*. He formed a close association with such writers as POPE, ARBUTHNOT and GAY. Eventually, Swift returned to Ireland as Dean of St Patrick's Cathedral, Dublin, and wrote more savagely satirical pamphlets on the English administration of Ireland, in such works as *The Drapier Letters* (1724) and *A Modest Proposal* (1729).

Swinburne, Algernon Charles (1837-1909) English poet, a master of mellifluous verse with which he attempted to attack Victorian conventional morality. He was educated at Oxford, where he met ROSSETTI and the Pre-Raphaelites. Swinburne was excitable, passionate and loved to shock; the *Poems and Ballads* (1866, 1878, 1889) did shock, though their sensuality was mainly affectation.

Synge, John Millington (1871-1909) Irish dramatist, who wrote *The Playboy of the Western World* (1907), one of the masterpieces of the Irish theatre. When it was first staged at Dublin's Abbey Theatre (1907) it caused a riot. Synge wrote only six plays, but all are remarkable for their poetic interpretation of the Irish character and vernacular speech. *The Well of the Saints* (1905) and *The Tinker's Wedding* (1907) are rich with the flavour of folk-speech. He left an unfinished poetic drama, *Deirdre of the Sorrows*. Synge was director of the Abbey Theatre from 1904.

T

Tabari, al- (838-923) Arab historian, who is mainly notable for his vast history of the world, the *Annals*, from the Creation to the beginning of the 10th century, the major source book for early Arabic history. Al-Tabari was also author of one of the principal commentaries on the *Koran*.

Tacitus, Cornelius (c. 55-c. 120) Roman historian, a successful orator and politician who described the early Roman Empire after AUGUSTUS. His *Histories*, published before 110, covering the years from NERO's death (68) to DOMITIAN's (96), and his later *Annals*, covering 14-69, survive in part, revealing an essentially honest and careful writer, unable to conceal his distaste of the Imperial system.

Tagore, Sir Rabindranath (1861-1941) Indian poet, playwright and novelist. A religious and lyrical writer, Tagore revealed to the West something of the dignity, complexity and beauty of Indian culture. His life was devoted to literature, and the political and social service of his people. Although he wrote in Bengali, he translated several of his own works into English, the best known being *Gitanjali* (1912), which earned him a Nobel Prize for Literature (1913).

Taine, Hippolyte (1828-93) French historian, philosopher and critic whose theories are expounded in the Introduction to *History of English Literature* (1863) and in *On Intelligence* (1870). In accordance with his concept of criticism as a strictly objective process, Taine stresses the importance of physical, psychological and environmental factors in the study of art, literature and history, with his formula of 'la race, le milieu et le moment'.

T'ai Tsung (597-649) Principal founder of the T'ang dynasty in China, whose reign (627-49) marked the zenith of Chinese and T'ang power. After a period of chaos (618-23) T'ai Tsung reunited all China, overthrew the northern Turks in Mongolia and occupied Sinkiang. Internally he reformed the administration, established an efficient bureaucracy, and tried to prevent the formation of large estates. He endeavoured to be a model Confucian ruler, open to advice and criticism. Under his patronage there began the development of arts and literature for which the T'ang dynasty is famous.

Talbot, William Henry Fox (1800-77) English inventor who, in 1834, retired from political life and started to experiment with photography. Talbot published the first book illustrated with photographs, *The Pencil of Nature* (1844-6), pioneered flash photography of moving objects (1851), and invented photoglyphy (1852). He was also a fine mathematician, and decipherer of Assyrian cuneiform inscriptions.

Talleyrand-Périgord, Charles Maurice de (1754-1838) French statesman, who negotiated NAPO-

LEON's deposition and the restoration of the Bourbons. As Bishop of Autun, he sat in the States General of 1789, where he sided with the revolutionary party. However, he was never an extremist, and fled to the US after the execution of LOUIS XVI. Talleyrand returned during the Directory and became Foreign Minister (1797-9). He helped Napoleon seize power in 1799 and served him until 1807. Believing that Napoleon's policies would prove ruinous to France, he engaged in a secret correspondence with the Allies, notably ALEXANDER I of Russia, with whom, following the fall of Paris (1814), he negotiated the terms of Napoleon's overthrow. At a meeting with LOUIS XVIII, he secured a guarantee (the Charter of Ghent) of the main reforms accomplished by the Revolution as the price of the Bourbon restoration. At the Congress of Vienna (1814-15), he represented France and induced the Allies to deal with her not as a beaten enemy but as an equal. He helped LOUIS-PHILIPPE to attain the throne in 1830, serving him as ambassador in London until 1834.

Tamerlane (c. 1336-1405) Mongol Turkish warrior, and creator of the last great Mongol Empire. Conquering Turkestan and setting up his capital at Samarkand, he set out to restore the Mongol Empire founded by his indirect ancestor GENGHIS KHAN. His troops swept across central Asia and seized Persia, Mesopotamia and southern Russia (1380-95), and invaded northern India, sacking Delhi (1398-9). Tamerlane razed Aleppo in Syria and crushed Ottoman troops in Turkey (1401-2) before heading east to China, but died from fever on the way. His empire disintegrated, ending Mongol power in central Asia.

T'ao Ch'ien (365-427) Chinese recluse poet whose poem 'Home Again' is generally regarded as his masterpiece. T'ao Ch'ien began life as a minor official, but retired at 40 to support himself by farming. He remained poor, but it was this period which produced his finest poetry, extolling the virtues of the simple life in a complementary style which made him remarkable among contemporary Chinese poets.

Tartaglia, Niccola Fontana (c. 1500-57) Italian mathematician, who was one of the discoverers of the solution to cubic equations. The results were later published by CARDANO in a breach of confidence, and the angry dispute which followed led to Tartaglia's dismissal from his public lectureship at Brescia.

Tasman, Abel Janszoon (1603-59) Dutch navigator who discovered large parts of Australasia. Sailing from Mauritius, Tasman discovered 'Van Dieman's Land' (Tasmania) and New Zealand (1642), whose west coast he followed northward before striking northeast to Tonga and then turning west to discover the Fijis (1643). By encircling Australia (without seeing it), Tasman proved it was not part of the rumoured giant continent 'Terra Australis'. Tasman's second voyage (1644) explored the north and west coasts of Australia.

Tasso, Torquato (1544-95) Italian poet, author of *Jerusalem Delivered* (1581-4), an epic poem on the First Crusade, which elucidated the anxiety that was to overshadow Tasso's life and undermine all his subsequent work: the conflict between his lyric sensuality and his deeply held religious and moral beliefs. Unhappy about the pagan lyricism of what was essentially a religious work, he submitted the work to the Inquisition for judgement. Continuous revisions eventually transformed it into the cold, stilted *Conquest of Jerusalem* (1593). In 1573 he published the influential pastoral drama *Aminta*. The only significant work of his later years was *Re Torrismondo*, a tragedy of incest and betrayal.

Taylor, Alan John Percivale (born 1906) English historian whose prolific output has established him as one of the most widely known scholars of his generation. He has written principally on the 19th and 20th centuries and contributed major analyses in *The Course of German History* (1945) and *The Origins of the Second World War* (1961).

Taylor, Zachary (1784-1850) American general who distinguished himself in the Mexican War and became the twelfth President of the US. Taylor was elected President in 1848 and soon had to face the slavery problem. He favoured the admission of California and New Mexico to the union as an anti-slave state, but the Southern leaders violently opposed this and threatened to withdraw their support for Taylor. His contempt for the Compromise of 1850 (legislation designed to solve the dilemma of the slavery question) was undisguised, but before the measure could be passed by Congress, Taylor died.

Indian fighter and victor over Mexico's Santa Anna, Zachary Taylor was US President for only 16 months

Tchaikovsky, Pëtr Ilyich (1840-93) Russian composer. Tchaikovsky left government service at the age of 23 to study music. He reacted sharply against the Russian nationalist school of composers, and, in forming his style, looked towards western Europe. In 1877 his one attempt at marriage broke up after a few weeks. Later his work was made possible by the patronage of a wealthy widow, Nadezhda von Meck, who made him an allowance, on condition that they should never meet, although they carried on a copious correspondence. Tchaikovsky's best-known works are the fantasy overture *Romeo and Juliet* (1869-70), the concert overture *1812* (1882), which contains optional cannon in the scoring; the ballets *The Sleeping Beauty* (1890), *The Nutcracker* (1892) and *Swan Lake* (1877); the *Piano Concerto No. 1* (1875); the *Violin Concerto* (1878) and the Fourth, Fifth and Sixth

The music of Tchaikovsky – best known if by no means the greatest Russian composer – has an evergreen popularity

(*Pathétique*) Symphonies. He also wrote two major operas – *Eugene Onegin* (1879) and *The Queen of Spades* (1890), both based on PUSHKIN. Tchaikovsky died of cholera.

Teisserenc de Bort, Léon Philippe (1855-1913) French meteorologist who discovered the stratosphere. Working at first for the French Central Bureau of Meteorology and then privately (from 1896), he explored the upper atmosphere with free balloons containing recoverable instruments for measuring atmospheric temperature and pressure. By 1902, with the German, Assmann, he had found that above a certain level (ranging from five to ten miles) the atmospheric temperature stops falling with increasing altitude and remains constant, or even rises.

Telford, Thomas (1757-1834) Scottish civil engineer, who became a leading bridge, road and canal builder of the Industrial Revolution. His first major commission was the planning of the Ellesmere Canal, in Shropshire, which he began in 1793. In 1801, he received a government commission to report on the highway needs of Scotland, as a result of which he went on to build more than 900 miles of road, 1200 bridges and improve many Scottish harbours. Telford also built roads in England and Wales and his influence as a road maker was second only to that of McAdam. His other works included the Caledonian Canal (from 1804), the Menai suspension bridge, linking Anglesey with the mainland (1819-26), and the Gotha Canal in Sweden.

Teller, Edward (born 1908) Hungarian-American physicist largely responsible for the development of the hydrogen bomb. After working on the atomic bomb project at Los Alamos, New Mexico, in the 1940s, he became an enthusiastic proponent of a new and more powerful weapon, the hydrogen bomb. In the late 1970s he advocated the development of nuclear energy and the release of satellite photos to the world.

Tennyson, Alfred, Lord (1809-92) English poet, immensely popular in his lifetime, whose main achievement was his mastery of the rhythmic qualities of the English language. His subjects were mainly legendary and historical, although a principal theme in his work is the heroism of ordinary people faced with difficulties. He slowly won recognition, and in 1850 published the famous elegiac lyrics *In Memoriam*, and became Poet Laureate.

Tensing Norgay (born 1914) Nepalese mountaineer who (with Edmund HILLARY) became the first to climb Everest, the world's highest mountain.

Terborch, Gerard (1617-81) Dutch painter, best known for his elegant and harmoniously coloured genre scenes. These, like those of METSU, are usually confined to the domestic activities of the prosperous middle-classes.

Terbrugghen, Hendrick (1588-1629) Dutch artist and member of a group of Utrecht painters, who were influenced by CARAVAGGIO's pictorial innovations. After a visit to Italy, Terbrugghen adopted Caravaggio's sharp tonal contrasts and everyday realism, though he used them with less dramatic force.

Teresa of Avila (1515-82) Spanish mystic and an important reformer of the Carmelite order. Her *Life* (1562-65) describes her early mystical experiences and visions and her spiritual growth. Written in unadorned prose, it is a remarkably intimate, self-analytical document. Among her other writings are *Way to Perfection* (1565), a spiritual guide for the Avila nuns, and *The Mansions* (1588).

Teresa, Mother (born 1910) Roman Catholic missionary who tends to the homeless. sick and starving in Calcutta. She was born in Yugoslavia but began her missionary work as a teacher in India. She took her first vows in 1928 and by 1950 had established her Order of the Missionaries of Charity, which officially became a pontifical congregation in 1965. The Order's work has since expanded to Australia, Africa, South America and the Middle East. Mother Teresa won the first Pope John XXIII Peace Prize in 1971 and the Nobel Peace Prize in 1979.

Terman, Lewis (1877-1956) American psychologist who with BINET produced the first intelligence test to be put to general use. He also devised the term intelligence quotient (IQ) to describe the score achieved in a test adjusted for age so that the average person will score 100.

Terry, Dame Ellen (1847-1928) English actress, the most famous of her day and memorable as Irving's leading lady.

Tertullian (c. 160-c. 230) Carthage-born Roman ecclesiastical writer, one of the Fathers of the Church. A Christian convert, he became the chief defender of the faith and one of the greatest early Christian writers of the West.

Tesla, Nikola (1857-1943) Austro-Hungarian electrical engineer, who emigrated to the United States in 1884. There, working successively with EDISON, the Westinghouse Company and in his own laboratory, Tesla made a number of significant contributions, which made alternating current practical. These included the development of one of the earliest AC motors and generators, AC transmission systems and high-frequency AC devices.

Thackeray, William Makepeace (1811-63) English novelist, who wrote *Vanity Fair* (1847-8), one of the outstanding satirical novels of the 19th century. Thackeray was at first divided between literature and painting, but, pressed for money, took up journalism for a living. His early work – essays, stories, travel-pieces – passed without notice; in 1847 he made his mark with *The Book of Snobs* and *Vanity Fair*, and gained success as a novelist, editor and lecturer. From his lectures he published *The English Humorists of the 18th Century* (1853) and *The Four Georges: Sketches of Manners, Morals, Court and Town Life* (1860). His novels include *Pendennis* (1848-50), *Esmond* (1852) and *The Newcomes* (1853-5).

Thatcher, Margaret Hilda (born 1925) British politician and Conservative Prime Minister. She

Ellen Terry first appeared on the stage at the age of nine

entered Parliament as MP for Finchley, North London, in 1959, having formerly been a research chemist and then a barrister specializing in tax law. She held a succession of senior government and opposition posts and was Secretary of State for Education and Science 1970-4. After two successive Conservative election defeats, she succeeded Edward HEATH as leader of the Party in February 1975. In 1979 she led the Conservative Party to an election victory. As Britain's first woman Prime Minister, she used her secure majority in the House of Commons to redirect economic policy along stringent conservative lines in an effort to solve the nation's economic and social woes. In 1982 she supported Britain's decision to fight Argentina to retain the Falkland Islands. The surge of patriotic feeling which ensued helped Mrs Thatcher secure a second term in office in the 1983 election.

Themistocles (c. 527-c. 460 BC) Greek statesman who saved Athens (and Greece) from conquest by the Persians. Following the Greek victory at Marathon (490 BC), Themistocles believed that a powerful navy was essential if Athens was to survive a further Persian onslaught, and increased the Athenian navy from 120 to 300 triremes. The land defences of Greece were the joint responsibility of the Athenians and Spartans. When XERXES of Persia attacked Greece in 480 BC he was defeated in the naval battles of Artemisium and Salamis and forced to retreat. Themistocles, however, distrusted his Spartan allies and wished to break with them, but the Athenians refused to follow him in opposing Persia and Sparta simultaneously. Losing most of his power *c.* 479 BC, Themistocles was ostracized six years later.

Theocritus (c. 310-250 BC) Greek poet, originator of the pastoral idyll, who influenced VIRGIL's *Eclogues* with a group of poems which portray the timeless and romantic quality of country life in Sicily.

Theodoric the Great (c. 454-526) King of the Ostrogoths (474-526) and ruler of Italy (493-526). Commissioned by the Byzantine emperor Zeno (who sought to divide the barbarians), Theodoric attacked Italy (488-93) and killed the Herulian leader ODOACER, who had deposed the last western Roman emperor. Theodoric then ruled Italy from Ravenna and brought prosperity to the kingdom. At the end of his reign, after 30 years of peace and tolerance, Theodoric, an Arian, took savage reprisals against orthodox Roman Catholics because of Emperor JUSTINIAN's persecution of Arians.

Thiers, Louis Adolphe (1797-1877) French statesman and President of France, who negotiated the treaty that ended the Franco-Prussian War and who suppressed the Paris Commune (1871). After helping LOUIS-PHILIPPE to ascend to the French throne (1830), he became his Minister of the Interior, making himself notorious by the severity with which he suppressed working-class disturbances in Lyons and Paris. Following the Bonapartist *coup d'état* of 1851, he was exiled to the provinces. He became a deputy again in 1863, but was an opponent of NAPOLEON III's policies. After France's defeat in the Franco-Prussian War (1870), Thiers became head of the provisional government. He came to terms with BISMARCK, and in less than three years managed to raise the whole of the indemnity demanded by him through government loans, thus securing the Germans' evacuation of France. He put down the Commune by using provincial troops against Paris in May 1871 and was President of the Third Republic from 1871 to 1873.

Thomas à Kempis (1380-1471) German ecclesiastic and writer thought to be the author of *The Imitation of Christ*, the most widely read handbook of Christian devotion ever written. In simple terms it instructs the Christian on how to seek spiritual perfection by taking CHRIST as a model. Its direct call to religious devotion has appealed to Christians ever since it was first published and no book, except the Bible, has been so often reprinted in the Western World.

Thomas, Dylan (1914-53) Welsh poet, whose early verse, packed with imagery and revelling in language, formed a striking contrast with the poetry of the late 1930s. The verse of *Eighteen Poems* (1934) and *Twenty-five Poems* (1936) was a celebration of the processes of life; in his mature work, *Deaths and Entrances* (1946) and *Collected Poems* (1952), elegies and memories become part of a ritual that assures man of his triumph over death. He wrote *Under Milk Wood* (1954), a brilliant verse play for radio, the semi-autobiographical prose of *Portrait of the Artist as a Young Dog* (1940) and an unfinished novel, *Adventures in the Skin Trade* (1955).

Thompson, Daley (born 1958) British athlete and the world's greatest champion in the decathlon – the 10-event ultimate test of all-round athletic ability and endurance. He has not lost a competition since 1978 and continually improves on his own world record.

Thompson, David (1770-1857) English explorer and fur-trader who made the first reliable maps of western Canada, while working for a British fur-trading concern in western North America.

Thompson, Francis (1859-1907) English poet of ecstatic, mystical verse, whose work is strongly influenced by CRASHAW, whom Thompson greatly admired. *Poems* was published in 1893 and 1897, the former volume containing 'The Hound of Heaven', a complex ode of faith and struggle.

Thomsen, Christian (1788-1865) Danish archaeologist, who first gave shape to prehistory by dividing it into three ages. As first curator (1816-65) of the world's first ethnographical museum (in Copenhagen), he arranged the museum's prehistoric antiquities according to their composition – of stone, bronze, or iron. He believed that the huge span of prehistory could be divided into three successive technological periods: a Stone Age, a Bronze Age and an Iron Age. The first clear statement of his classification appeared in 1836.

Thomson, James (1700-48) Scottish poet who tried new subjects and other verse forms when POPE's town themes and heroic couplets were dominant. *The Seasons* (1726-30), four poems in blank verse, shows a sympathetic feeling for nature and a keen observation of the countryside. He also wrote 'Rule Britannia'.

Thomson, Sir Joseph John (1856-1940) English physicist who discovered the electron. Measuring the deflection of cathode-rays by magnetic fields, he derived the ratio of mass to charge for cathode-ray particles, about 1000 times smaller than the smallest known values for ions in solution. In this way, he discovered the first sub-atomic particle and called it *electron.* His later discovery that electromagnetic deflection of positive rays (consisting of ionized atoms) depends on their atomic weights led to the development of the mass spectrograph by Aston and others. For his work on the conduction of electricity through gases he was awarded the 1906 Nobel Prize for Physics.

Thomson, Robert William (1822-73) Scottish engineer who, in 1845, patented the pneumatic tyre, an air-filled rubber inner tube within a nonexpandable outer cover.

Thomson, Roy, 1st Baron of Fleet (born 1894) Canadian newspaper proprietor and owner of one of the world's largest publishing empires. He moved to Britain (1953) and now owns hundreds of newspapers and magazines worldwide, five publishing firms and a travel agency.

Thorndike, Dame Sybil (1882-1976) English actress, exceptionally accomplished, and famous for her portrayal of SHAW's *Saint Joan*.

Thorwaldsen, Bertel (1768-1844) Internationally famous Danish sculptor who worked mostly in Rome and became a leader of the Neo-classic movement. An antiquarian as well as an artist, he was involved in reconstruction and restoration of classical works. The *Lion of Lucerne* was the first of Thorwaldsen's many public monuments.

Thucydides (c. 471-c. 400 BC) Greek writer, considered to be the first truly critical historian. His *History* is a detailed account, based on painstaking research, of the Peloponnesian War between Athens and Sparta (431-404), breaking off unfinished in 411, to be continued by XENOPHON in his *Hellenica*. Thucydides discussed the causes of the war, explained its strategy, and, by contrasting the mercurial Athenians with the stolid Spartans and analysing the roles of such men as PERICLES and ALCIBIADES, sought to explain the defeat of Athens.

Thurber, James Grover (1894-1961) American humorous artist and author. His work is immediately recognizable by its peculiarly nebulous style. He specialized in what he defined as 'the war between men and women', in dogs and in Surrealist situations. His first drawings, which appeared in *The New Yorker* in 1930, were unlike those of anyone else, being little more than incompetent doodles.

Thutmosis III (15th cent. BC) Egyptian pharaoh, who led 20,000 troops and a fleet of warships (the world's first) to seize Palestine, Phoenicia and Syria, and subdue the Aegean islands, thus bringing Egypt's empire to its largest extent. Besides being an efficient administrator, Thutmosis built many temples and obelisks (including the 'Cleopatra's Needles', now in London and New York).

Tiberius (42 BC-AD 37) Second Roman emperor (AD 14-37), stepson of AUGUSTUS, whose policies he continued, in particular the maintenance, but not the extension, of the existing imperial frontiers. A competent soldier and administrator, Tiberius brought peace to the empire and prosperity to the provinces, but he alienated the Senate and the people of Rome by his aloof manner. After an attempt by Sejanus to seize power (AD 29), Tiberius retired to Capri.

Tiepolo, Giovanni Battista (1696-1770) Venetian Rococo artist, primarily famous for his frescoes, depicting airy historical and mythological visions, as in the Palazzo Labia. He achieved his first success in Wurzburg (1750-3), where he decorated the Grand Staircase and Kaisersaal in the Residenz. After returning to Italy, he decorated the Palazzo Valmarana at Vicenza, and in 1769 moved to Madrid, where he decorated the Royal Palace at the invitation of Charles III.

Tintoretto, Jacopo (1518-94) Venetian painter, whose work consists mainly of religious subjects. He claimed to have studied under TITIAN and is reported to have said that he wished to paint like his master and design like MICHELANGELO. His paintings, however, are highly individual: their most characteristic features are elongated figures – sometimes seen in exaggerated foreshortening – in agitated movement, sudden transitions from shadow to flickering light, and diagonally orientated compositions. His first important work, *St Mark Rescuing a Slave* (1548), his largest, the *Paradise* for the Doges' Palace and his decorations for the Scuola di S Rocco in Venice (1576-88) are generally thought to be among his best works.

Tippett, Sir Michael Kemp (born 1905) British composer whose works combined the influences of Elizabethan counterpoint and modernity, most particularly that of HINDEMITH and STRAVINSKY. Tippett has also used Negro spirituals, as in his wartime oratorio *A Child of Our Time*, and jazz, as in some of the songs in his opera *The Knot Garden*. His other works include the *Concerto for Double String Orchestra*, three symphonies and the opera *The Midsummer Marriage*.

Tirpitz, Alfred von (1849-1930) German admiral, who created the high seas fleet that waged unrestricted submarine warfare in the First World War. He began his career as a midshipman in the Prussian navy (1865), became a torpedo specialist, and embodied his ideas and reasons for a powerful German navy in a memorandum which, under Kaiser WILLIAM II's influence, was acted on in 1894. He was Secretary of State for the Imperial German navy (1897-1916) and his introduction of submarine blockades and warfare were instrumental in bringing the US into the First World War. He fled to Switzerland after the war, but returned in 1924 and became a member of the Reichstag.

Titian (c. 1487-1576) The greatest of the Venetian painters. He was probably a pupil of the brothers Gentile and Giovanni BELLINI, but the most important early influence on his work was the rich colour and poetic mood of GIORGIONE's painting. After the deaths of Giorgione and Giovanni Bellini (whom he succeeded as Painter to the Republic), Titian dominated Venetian painting. His first major work was the *Assumption* in the Friari Church, Venice (1518), which shows the influence of RAPHAEL's formal values, but places a typically Venetian emphasis on colour. Besides religious pictures Titian painted a number of mythologies (e.g. *The Bacchanal*), which were inspired by the writings of classical authors and which show the more sensuous aspect of his work. He also excelled in portraiture: the *Man with a Glove* (*c.* 1520) is typical of the elegance and, at the same time, grasp of character which he brought to the aristocratic portrait. In 1533 Titian was made court painter to the Emperor CHARLES V, of whom he painted a number of portraits, notably an equestrian picture at the Battle of Muhlberg (1548).

Tito, Marshal (1892-1980) Founder and long-serving President of Communist Yugoslavia. Croatian born, Tito served with the Bolsheviks during the Russian Civil War and on his return to Yugoslavia in 1920 became a trade union organizer and political agitator for the illegal Communist Party and was arrested and sent to prison for six years. When Germany invaded Yugoslavia in the Second World War, Tito organized the National Liberation front to resist their advance. His partisans were more effective in fighting the Germans than the royalist resistance movement of General Mihailovich, and Tito became recognized as the country's leader. In 1945, he

Titian: a self portrait. Greatest of Venetian painters, he lived into his 90s

was elected Prime Minister and Minister of Defence, and in 1953 became President of the Republic and Supreme Commander of the Armed Forces. Tito applied Marxist principles to industry, trade and the management of living accommodation.

Titus (c. AD 39-81) Roman emperor (79-81). Co-ruler with his father VESPASIAN after capturing Jerusalem (70) and sole emperor from 79, Titus showed unusual tolerance to political opponents by ending treason trials and expelling informers. In 79 he gave material aid to Pompeii when it was devastated by volcanic eruption, and to Rome when it was damaged by fire. During his reign the empire was at peace, except in Britain.

Tocqueville, Alexis, Comte de (1805-59) French historian, particularly known for his study *Democracy in America* (1835-40), an impressive analysis of a new civilization's governmental machine whose democratic principles were set before the French people for the first time. His other great work is *The Ancient régime and the Revolution* (1856), in which he sought to demonstrate that, far from being a rupture with the past, the 1789 Revolution was a logical development from the old order.

Todd, Garfield (born 1908) Rhodesian Prime Minister (1953-8) who proposed educational, electoral and wage reforms for the indigenous African population. His continued advocacy of black advancement incurred the wrath of Ian SMITH's government, which twice imprisoned Todd and his daughter, Judith. In 1976 he was the adviser to Joshua NKOMO at the Geneva conference on Rhodesia.

Tolkien, John Ronald Reuel (1892-1973) English novelist and philologist, who created an immensely popular, mythological world in *The Hobbit* (1937), relating the adventures of Bilbo Baggins and the dwarfs on their journey to recover treasure from Smaug the dragon, and its complex three-book sequel *The Lord of the Rings* (1954-5).

Tolstoy, Alexsei Nikolaevich (1882-1945) Russian novelist, poet and dramatist, author of *The Road to Calvary* (1919-41), describing his experiences in the White Army after the Revolution of 1917.

Tolstóy, Count Leo Nikolaevich (1828-1910) Russian novelist, short-story writer, dramatist and philosopher, whose greatest novels, *War and Peace* (1863-9) and *Anna Karenina* (1873-7), have become world famous. *War and Peace* is a panorama of life at every level of Russian society during the Napoleonic Wars. The longest of 19th-century novels, with over 500 characters, it is an epic in which historical, social, ethical and religious issues are explored on a scale never before attempted in fiction. *Anna Karenina* is a psychological novel in which motivation and its moral impact are analysed through the story of a morally tortured woman. Two plots and two contrasting love affairs present a dialogue on the search for faith and the meaning of life, the prevailing theme of this work, one of the world's greatest tragic novels. That he was also a powerful dramatist is evident from the tragedy *The Power of Darkness* (1886) and the satire *The Fruits of Enlightenment* (1890).

Tolstoy, Russian nobleman and author of some of the world's greatest novels

Tombaugh, Clyde William (born 1906) American astronomer, who discovered the planet Pluto. While still a student with a keen interest in astronomy, he was appointed to the Lowell Observatory in 1929 to make routine examination of photographs taken in the search for the new planet predicted by Percival LOWELL. He discovered the ninth planet of the solar system, later named Pluto, in 1930.

Torelli, Giacomo (1608-78) Italian stage designer, the greatest creative artist of the Baroque theatre and the inventor of 'wings' – narrow, obscuring flats at the side of the stage. He designed sets for the Venice Teatro Novissimo (1641-5) and, in Paris (1645-61), revitalized MOLIÈRE's theatrical mechanics at the Petit-Bourbon. His inventions and innovations made spectacular staging possible and were adopted all over Europe.

Torquemada, Tomás de (c. 1420-98) Spanish Dominican monk who organized the Spanish Inquisition. Gaining influence under ISABELLA I and FERDINAND V, and praised by popes Sixtus IV and Alexander VI, he determined ruthlessly to remove Jews and Muslims as supposed obstacles to Spain's national security and the Roman Catholic religion. Spain's first Inquisitor-General (1483), he established the Inquisition's powers to try people accused of heresy, apostasy, bigamy, witchcraft, usury, etc.; authorized the use of torture to extract confessions and regularized tribunals and their procedure.

Torres, Luis Vaez de (17th cent.) Spanish explorer and navigator. In 1605 he commanded one of three ships under the leadership of de Quirós to search for Terra Australis Incognita. After they had all reached the New Hebrides, he sailed alone on a voyage which took him through the strait between Australia and New Guinea which now bears his name. He is believed to have died at Manila in the Philippines (*c.* 1613).

Torricelli, Evangelista (1608-47) Italian physicist and mathematician – who invented the barometer. He made the fundamental discovery that a suction pump cannot lift a greater column of water than can be supported by atmospheric pressure (about 33 ft at sea level). Applying this principle to a glass tube filled with mercury, Torricelli invented the barometer, in which the height of the mercury column is a measure of the atmospheric pressure.

Toscanini, Arturo (1867-1957) Italian musician who became the most widely known conductor of his generation. He began his career as a cellist, but in 1898 became chief conductor at La Scala, Milan, where he was responsible for first performances of operas by VERDI and PUCCINI, among others. In 1928, disturbed by the rise of Fascism, he left Italy to take over the New York Philharmonic Orchestra. A prodigious musician, offset poor eyesight by a formidable memory – he never conducted with a score.

Toulouse-Lautrec, Henri de (1864-1901) French artist, whose work was much influenced by that of DEGAS. He was a master of the poster and coloured lithograph, and his ability to make a design both decorative and significant is also evident in his oil paintings. His style is characterized by a combination of plunging perspectives and flat colouring, emphasizing the picture surface. By his choice of subject, the actresses and artistes of the Montmartre cafés and dance-halls, he dispassionately records the life of the Parisian *demi-monde*.

A lithograph by Henri de Toulouse-Lautrec. The crippled son of a great French family, he was a shrewd observer of the life around him in Paris.

Toynbee, Arnold Joseph (1889-1975) English historian, who wrote world history based on a broad theory of succeeding civilizations rather than concentrating on nations or periods of rule.

Traherne, Thomas (c. 1637-74) English mystical poet and prose writer whose work is a plea for a return to a primal state of goodness and simplicity. His poetry is both exalted and stark; the Prose *Centuries of Meditations* are illuminating meditations on devotion.

Trajan (c. 53-117) Spanish-born Roman emperor (98-117). He enlarged the empire by seizing Armenia, created new provinces in Dacia, Assyria and Mesopotamia and linked Rome's northern frontiers from Britain to the Black Sea.

Travers, Ben (1886-1980) British dramatist, famous in the 1920s and 1930s for farces, such as a *A Cuckoo in the Nest*, *Rookery Nook* and *Thark*, all of which were box-office successes.

Tree, Sir Herbert Beerbohm (1853-1917) British actor-manager, who created the role of Svengali in DU MAURIER's *Trilby*. He made his debut in 1878 and went into management in 1887. His productions, mostly at the Haymarket Theatre, began with *Hamlet*, in which he played the lead.

Trevelyan, George (1876-1962) British historian, whose scholarly yet popular books on English history (*History of England*, 1926, and *English Social History*, 1942 contributed to the growth of the subject as a university discipline, stressing social and topographical importance, as well as politics and economics.

Trevithick, Richard (1771-1833) English engineer and pioneer of the steam railway locomotive. To improve the efficiency of the steam engine to cope with the increasing depth of the mines, he developed a model that used higher pressures than those of WATT, which he, and his cousin Andrew Vivian, patented in 1802 for stationary and locomotive use. Trevithick built his first steam carriage in 1801, and another in London two years later, but neither public opinion nor road surfaces were yet favourable. He then constructed a steam locomotive at the Pen-y-Darran ironworks, near Merthyr Tydfil, Wales, which 10 years before that of George STEVENSON, successfully hauled five wagons, containing 10 tons of iron and 70 men, though the track, however, proved to be inadequate.

Trevor-Roper, Hugh (born 1914) British historian who was appointed Regius Professor of modern history at Oxford University in 1957. His books include *The Last Days of Hitler* (1947), *The Gentry 1540-1640* (1953) and *A Hidden Life, the Enigma of Sir Backhouse, Bart* (1976).

Trollope, Anthony (1815-82) English novelist, author of the 'Barsetshire' novels which create in the most faithful detail the middle-class life of an English county. *The Warden* (1855) was the first Barsetshire novel, succeeded by five others, of which the best known are *Barchester Towers* (1857) and *The Last Chronicle of Barset* (1867). Equally interesting are the Palliser series, six novels on property and politics, and the famous *Autobiography* (1883).

Tromp, Maarten Harpertszoon (1597-1653) Dutch admiral who, with de RUYTER, helped to establish the young Dutch Republic as a major sea power. He won important victories against Spanish (1639), Spanish-Portuguese (1639) and English (1652) fleets. He was killed fighting English ships led by MONCK.

Trotsky, Lev Davidovich (1879-1940) Russian revolutionary, one of the founders of the USSR and organizer of the Red Army. A Ukrainian Jew, he was exiled to Siberia (1898) because of his revolutionary activities. In 1902, he escaped and came to London, where he worked with LENIN, Plekhanov and other Russian Social Democrats, but he later found his allegiance divided between Lenin and the Bolsheviks, and the Mensheviks, whose differences he tried to reconcile. He was in America when, in 1917, he received news of the March Revolution. He returned to Petrograd (later Leningrad), where he became chairman of the Petrograd Soviet. As first Soviet Commissar for Foreign Affairs (1917-18), his diplomacy and oratory gave Bolshevik Russia a breathing space by delaying the signature of the Treaty of Brest-Litovsk with Germany (signed 3 Mar. 1918). At the outbreak of the Civil War, he was made Commissar for War. He established the Red Army, and was chiefly responsible for its victories over the 'white' reactionary armies, supported by Britain, the US and Japan. Trotsky was an internationalist, who believed in 'permanent world revolution' rather than in stable, nationalist, revolution. After the death of Lenin (1924), he was manoeuvred out of office by STALIN and ZINOVIEV, and after being expelled from the Communist Party, was exiled (1929) and found asylum in Mexico, where he wrote *The Revolution Betrayed* (1937), one of the best accounts of the Revolution and its aftermath. Condemned to death *in absentio* in 1937, Trotsky was assassinated in Mexico City by an agent of Stalin. Since his death, his writings have inspired the formation of several left-wing groups.

Trudeau, Pierre Elliott (born 1919) Canadian political figure who succeeded Lester Pearson as Liberal party leader and Prime Minister in 1968. He promoted economic and diplomatic independence for Canada but lost his seat in

Buffalo Bill

Sitting Bull

Calamity Jane

General Custer

Geronimo

Legend and fact are inextricably mixed in the history of America's west. Heroes and villains came and went but have survived in a unique mythology, thanks to the movies. History is now reinstating many of the traditional 'baddies'– such as the Indians– in an heroic role, while taking a cooler look at some of the old heroes and the facts of America's unique folklore

Billy the Kid

THE KID.

REWARD.

reward to any person or per-
sons who capture William Bonny, alias
The Kid, and deliver him to any sheriff of New
Mexico. Satisfactory proofs of identity will be

LEW. WALLACE,
Governor of New Mexico.

the 1979 election. After regaining his position as Prime Minister the following year he was defeated in the 1984 election by the Progressive Conservative candidate, Brian MULRONEY.

Truffaut, François (1932-84) French film director and critic who became one of the leading lights of the French 'New Wave' cinema when his film *Four Hundred Blows* won the Cannes award in 1959. His films are distinguished by their lyrical sensitivity and intensely personal style. They include *Jules and Jim* (1959), *The Story of Adele H* (1975) and *Finally, Sunday* (1983).

Truman, Harry S. (1884-1972) Thirty-third US President who assumed office on the death of ROOSEVELT (1945). His was the awesome task of authorizing the use of the atomic bomb against Japan (Hiroshima and Nagasaki, 6 and 9 Aug. 1945), thus ending the Second World War. In 1947, he proclaimed the 'Truman Doctrine' of assistance to countries threatened by Communist expansion in the immediate post-war years. Some $400,000,000 was allocated to preserve Greece and Turkey. In 1948, he sanctioned the MARSHALL Plan to aid post-war European recovery, an offer which extended to Eastern Europe as well as to the West. Under his 'Four Point' programme of 1949, US economic, scientific and technical aid was given to under-developed countries. In 1948, he was re-elected against DEWEY in a result which confounded all predictions. At the start of his second term, his first major policy initiative was the formation of NATO in 1949. In the following year he authorized US intervention in Korea and nominated MACARTHUR as Commander-in-Chief of UN forces.

Tu Fu (712-70) With LI PO, Tu Fu is widely recognized as the greatest of Chinese poets, though his life and poetry form a complete contrast to those of the older poet, whom Tu Fu met and admired. His hard, disappointing life, in a time of national chaos and disorder, generated his moving, evocative and often tragic verse.

Tull, Jethro (1674-1741) English agriculturist, whose inventions rapidly advanced the mechanization of agriculture. He introduced the seed drill (which sowed three parallel rows of seeds simultaneously) and a horse-drawn hoe which destroyed weeds mechanically.

Turenne, Vicomte de (1611-75) French marshal who, with LOUVOIS and VAUBAN, carried out LOUIS XIV's plan to make France militarily supreme in Europe. Born in Holland, a grandson of WILLIAM THE SILENT, Turenne first fought in the Dutch War of Independence (1625-30). He left Holland to join the French army and made a reputation in successful campaigns during the Thirty Years' war. Between 1667 and 1675 he commanded the French armies in aggressive wars in the Spanish Netherlands, the Palatinate and Alsace, with a skill which impressed NAPOLEON.

Turgenev, Ivan (1818-83) One of Russia's foremost novelists, author of *Fathers and Sons* (1862) and other novels and stories which depict the life of country districts in pre-Revolutionary Russia. Turgenev, who was a friend of FLAUBERT and ZOLA, and admired by Henry JAMES, was the first Russian writer to acquire a European reputation.

Turner, Joseph Mallord William (1775-1851) English landscape painter and watercolourist, outstanding for his use of brilliant colours and delicate, luminous impressions.

Turpin, Dick (1706-39) Notorious British highwayman who was finally captured in York, charged with horse stealing and executed.

Twain, Mark (1835-1910) Pen-name of Samuel Clemens, American author, who brought the colloquial, earthy voice of the frontier West into American literature. From his time as a steamboat pilot on the Mississippi came the background for his books, *Tom Sawyer* (1876), *Life on the Mississippi* (1883) and *Huckleberry Finn* (1884).

Tyler, Wat (14th cent.) English tiler, leader of the Peasants' Revolt. In 1381 Tyler and Jack Straw led thousands of Kentish and Essex peasants, angered by the forced labour and heavy taxes following the Black Death, to London, where they were joined by others. In the rioting which followed several people were killed and buildings burned. When Richard II agreed to end serfdom and repressive labour laws, Tyler increased his demands and was killed by the Lord Mayor of London. Troops crushed the rebellion, and Richard revoked his agreements.

Tyndale, William (c. 1492-1536) English priest, translator of much of the Bible from Greek into English. He suffered ecclesiastical persecution for unorthodoxy and fled to Germany, printing his New Testament at Cologne and Worms. Tyndale's Bible translations became a basis for the Authorized Version of JAMES I and greatly influenced English prose. His Reformation teachings, which were influenced by LUTHER and ZWINGLI, helped to shape English Puritan theology. Tyndale, betrayed in Antwerp by a supposed friend, was strangled and burned there for heresy.

Tz'u Hsi (1834-1908) Dowager empress, who ruled China for 50 years. A Manchu, Tz'u Hsi, whose real name was Yehonala, began her career as a concubine of the emperor Hsien Feng (1851-61). She administered her reactionary policies with considerable statesmanship, but her extreme anti-European sentiments led her to encourage the xenophobic Boxer Rebellion against foreigners (1900) and led to foreign domination of her country.

U

Uccello, Paolo (1397-1475) Florentine painter, renowned for his experiments in perspective. In an early fresco, the equestrian monument to Sir John Hawkwood in Florence Cathedral (1436), he attempted to create the illusion of a real statue seen from below. His most famous work is the *Deluge* fresco in Sta Maria Novella (*c.* 1445), which shows the influence of ALBERTI's treatise on perspective. The combination in Uccello's work of the decorative aspects of Gothic art – brilliant colour and the use of gold – with the new science of perspective is evident in the three *Battles* (1454-7) commissioned by the MEDICI family.

Ulbricht, Walter (1893-1973) East German politician, at whose instigation the Berlin Wall was erected. During the Second World War, he was political adviser to Marshal Zhukov in Russia, and returned to Germany in 1945 to head the Socialist Unity Party, a forced merger of the Social Democratic and Communist Parties. A Stalinist to the core, with no noticeable German nationalist feeling, his policy was one of consistent sovietization of industry and agriculture. In 1953, some of his colleagues rose against him, including the secret police chief, Zaisser, but Ulbricht suppressed ruthlessly this attempt to unseat him. He survived KHRUSCHEV's denunciation of STALIN in 1956 and continued building the Berlin Wall in 1961 in an effort to halt the loss of a quarter of a million refugees to the West each year.

Unamuno, Miguel de (1864-1936) Spanish philosopher, poet, essayist and novelist, whose thought is consistently anti-rationalist but obsessed with the problems of immortality and free will. In *The Tragic Sense of Life* (1913) he argues that one should struggle to believe in God and immortality, even though it is irrational and even mistaken to do so. In novels such as *Mist* (1914) and plays like *Brother John* (1934), Unamuno studied the free will of his literary creations as a parallel to that of real men.

U Nu (born 1907) Burmese politician, and Burma's first Prime Minister after its independence. At one time imprisoned by the British as a nationalist agitator, he was released by Japanese occupation forces and made Foreign Minister (1943-44) of the puppet Burmese government. He remained in office when the Japanese withdrew, and became Speaker of the Constituent Assembly in 1947 and Prime Minister (1948-56, 1957-8 and 1960-2). He was ousted after his last period of office by an army coup, which abolished parliament and suspended the constitution. In custody from 1962-6, U Nu left Burma in 1969 to organize opposition to the military régime. He returned to Burma in 1970 to campaign against the government of General Ne Win.

Updike, John (born 1932) American novelist famous for his observations on modern American society. He joined the staff of *The New Yorker* magazine in 1955 and then left to concentrate on his own writing. His works include *The Poorhouse Fair* (1959), *Rabbit, Run* (1961), *Couples* (1968), *Marry Me* (1976), and *Rabbit is Rich* (1981) for which he won a Pulitzer Prize (1982).

Urey, Harold Clayton (1893-1981) American chemist who discovered deuterium (heavy hydrogen). In 1931, he joined the growing number of scientists searching for an isotope of hydrogen (a form distinguished from ordinary hydrogen by its higher atomic weight). Using an ingenious evaporation technique, Urey isolated a small quantity of deuterium from several litres of liquid hydrogen.

Utrillo, Maurice (1883-1955) French landscape painter whose early work resembles that of PISSARRO. His scenes of Paris, and Montmartre in particular, which have enjoyed world-wide popularity in reproduction, were mostly personal adaptations of Impressionism, though from 1910 onwards, some of his work showed a Cubist influence.

Utzon, Jørn (born 1918) Danish architect, former furniture and glassware designer, who designed Sydney's fantastical Opera House (1957-73). In 1966 he resigned after conflict over rising costs, but was awarded the Australian Institute of Architects' gold medal for 1973.

V

Valentino, Rudolph (1895-1926) Italian romantic screen actor whose success became assured after making *The Four Horsemen of the Apocalypse* in 1921. After starring in *The Sheik*, made in the same year, for five years, Valentino was the object of unsurpassed female adulation, and when he died, his funeral was an event of national importance.

Valéry, Paul Ambroise (1871-1945) French poet, critic and essayist. After experimenting with some Symbolist verse, which had echoes of MALLARMÉ, Valéry wrote two prose works, but he is chiefly remembered for the profound and subtle Symbolist poems composed in the years of his maturity – 'La Jeune Parque' (1917), 'Le Cimetière marin' (in the collection *Charmes*, 1922).

Vallejo, César (1892-1938) Peruvian poet and one of Latin America's outstanding literary figures. The Spanish Civil war inspired the poems of *España aparta di mí este cáliz*, whose main theme is death and the anguish at his inability to share the fate of his fellow men who died for their political convictions.

Valois, Dame Ninette de (born 1898) Irish-born ballerina, teacher, and, with Marie RAMBERT, co-founder of modern British ballet. A soloist for DIAGHILEV, she founded what is now the Royal Ballet and choreographed vivid dances for ballets inspired by English literature, music and painting, such as *Job*, *The Rake's Progress* and *Checkmate*. She helped create a distinctive English style of ballet.

Vanbrugh, Sir John (1664-1726) English architectural genius of the English Baroque, whose extravagant, witty and theatrical style suited the tastes of the English aristocracy, both in his dramatic works and in his architecture. After a career as soldier and playwright he was asked by the young Earl of Carlisle to design Castle Howard, a grandiose pseudo-castle set behind a series of sham fortifications. It brought him meteoric success and led to his appointment as Comptroller of the Office of Works (where he worked with WREN). It led also to his greatest architectural commission, to design Blenheim Palace, which was to be presented to MARLBOROUGH by a grateful nation after the Battle of Blenheim.

Vancouver, George (c. 1758-98) English explorer and navigator who sailed with Captain COOK on his second and third voyages. With two ships under his own command, Vancouver left Falmouth in 1791 to explore the west coast of America between latitudes 60°N and 30°N, to search for a western entrance to the North West Passage, as well as to negotiate the settlement of a dispute with the Spanish, who had seized a British outpost at Nootka Sound. He completed three seasons of work, charting the Strait of Juan de Fuca, the Puget Sound and the entire coastline to Cooks Inlet.

Van de Graaff, Robert Jemison (1901-67) American physicist who developed the high-voltage, nuclear accelerator named after him. This device, in which electric charge is carried to a hollow terminal by a continuously moving belt, was first tried out in 1931. Generators based on developments of the same basic principle are in current use in nuclear physics laboratories all over the world.

Vanderbilt, Cornelius (1794-1877) American shipping and railroad magnate, founder of the Vanderbilt fortune. By 1861, he had accumulated at least $20 million, after an enterprising career in shipping and freight. He then entered the railroad business, while continuing to exploit the nation's need for shipping and carriers during the Civil War. His methods of acquiring control of railroads resulted in a number of Congressional and other public investigations into his operations. He died worth more than $100 million.

Van der Waals, Johannes Diderik (1837-1923) Dutch physicist who formulated an equation describing the behaviour of real (as distinct from 'ideal') gases. The equation was used by KAMERLINGH ONNES in liquefying helium, and is still used as a basis for the study of gases.

Vanzetti, Bartolomeo see SACCO, Nicola

Varèse, Edgar (1885-1965) French-born American composer, who pioneered the avant-garde concept of music as pure sound. A former pupil of D'INDY and Roussel, Varèse left Europe for America in 1916, later disowning all the music he had written before that date. Typical examples of the work of his American period are *Ionisation* (1931), a complex work for 13 percussion players and two sirens, and *Density 21.5* (1936). Varèse almost abandoned composition between the late 1930s and the 1950s, when he re-emerged with some experiments in taped electronic music. He was founder and president (1921-7) of the International Composers Guild.

Varro, Marcus Terentius (116-27 BC) Roman man of letters whose *Disciplinarum libri IX*, advocating the study of seven liberal arts (grammar, dialectic, rhetoric, geometry, arithmetic, music, astronomy) influenced medieval education.

Vasari, Giorgio (1511-74) Italian Mannerist painter, and author of a celebrated history of art, *Lives of the Painters* (1550-68). The book consists of a series of biographies, beginning with that of CIMABUE and ending with those of LEONARDO da Vinci, RAPHAEL, and MICHELANGELO. Though not always reliable, it is a firsthand account of artists' personalities and techniques.

Vauban, Marquis de (1633-1707) French military engineer (the first to be appointed a Marshal of France) for LOUIS XIV. Developing fortifications on lines begun by MACHIAVELLI and LEONARDO da Vinci, he turned city walls into artillery platforms, devised defences in depth, and angled walls mathematically to cover all lines of fire. He also conducted attacks on many fortified towns, developing new artillery and mining techniques. The War of the Spanish Succession (1702-14) proved his forts far from impregnable and he lost favour.

Vaughan, Henry (c. 1621-95) Welsh metaphysical poet and physician, who, in *Silex Scintillans* (1650-5), combined the simple vocabulary of HERBERT with an imaginative mystical vision.

Vaughan Williams, Ralph (1872-1958) British composer whose roots ran deep in British folk-music and hymnody. The son of a country rector, he was a lifelong agnostic, yet edited the *English Hymnal* (1906), in which he included some of his own tunes. A notable collector of folk song, he studied with RAVEL and worked closely with HOLST, the other leading English composer of his generation. Vaughan Williams's first three symphonies (*The Sea*, *The London* and *The Pastoral*), together with such works as the *Fantasia on a Theme of Thomas Tallis*, the rhapsody for violin and orchestra, *The Lark Ascending* and the ballad opera *Hugh the Drover*, established him as a highly distinctive voice. In 1935, he wrote his violent and dissonant Fourth Symphony. In 1943 the Fifth Symphony projected an image of serenity in time of war, and in 1948, the Sixth Symphony seemed prophetic of desolation in the atomic age.

Vega, Lope de (1562-1635) The first major Spanish dramatist who ranks amongst the most prolific playwrights of all time, having written approximately 2000 plays, of which some 500 survive. He established the distinctive type of Spanish play which was to prevail for almost a century, the new three act *comedia*, an essentially popular poetic drama containing a mixture of comedy and tragedy and often centring on the theme of honour. One of his most successful historical plays, *The Sheep Well* (1614), anticipates Expressionist drama with its lively presentation of mob violence. Lope de Vega also wrote high tragedy, such as *Punishment without Vengeance*, as well as novels, pastoral romances, history and poetry. He defended his new style *comedia* in *The New Art of Writing Plays in this Age* (1609). Although ultimately limited in their range of situation and intrigue, his plays reveal his great lyrical ability and a supreme sense of stagecraft.

Velasquez, Diego (1599-1660) Spanish painter, who worked almost exclusively on portraits. His early work consists of naturalistic still-lifes with kitchen themes (*bodegones*), in which the objects portrayed are lit by strong light; he also painted some devotional pictures. In 1623 he was appointed court painter to the Spanish royal family and began work on portraits, many of which were of King PHILIP and his heir, Don Balthasar Carlos, both equestrian and full-length portraits against a plain background. During RUBENS's visit to Madrid in 1628, he obtained permission for Velasquez to visit Italy, an enterprise that resulted in his more fully appreciating Venetian painting. During a later visit to Italy (1648-51), Velasquez painted the portrait of *Pope Innocent X*, and the famous nude, the *Rokeby Venus*. His best-known work after 1651 is *Las Meniñas*, a portrait of the Infanta Margareta Teresa with her ladies-in-waiting and dwarfs, in which he included himself painting the scene. His late portraits are painted with a detachment that reveals his interest in the properties of light rather than his sitters' characters.

Venizelos, Eleutherios (1864-1936) Cretan-born Greek statesman. As Prime Minister (1910-15) he took Greece into the first Balkan War against Turkey, alongside Bulgaria, Serbia and Montenegro, and by the Treaty of Bucharest (1913) most of Macedonia was acquired for Greece. During the First World War, Venizelos set up a provisional government at Salonika, forced the abdication of the pro-German king Constantine and in 1917 took Greece into the war against Germany and her Allies. He was again in office for a short term in 1924, from 1928 to 1932 and again briefly in 1933. In 1935, he provoked a civil war in his efforts to seize power again, but was defeated and fled to Paris, where he died.

Verdi, Giuseppe (1813-1901) Italian composer, the son of an innkeeper, who brought to his country's opera the new status of music drama. Verdi's tenth opera, *Rigoletto* (1851), was the first to demonstrate fully his gift for dramatic action and characterization in music. *Il Trovatore* and *La Traviata* followed, with other works that provide opera singers with real opportunities both to sing and act. In 1871, Verdi wrote *Aïda* for the opening of the Suez Canal. In 1874 he composed his *Requiem* and proposed to write no more operas, but collaboration with the poet Boito as librettist led to his masterpieces, *Otello* (1887) and *Falstaff* (1893).

Verga, Giovanni (1840-1922) Sicilian novelist, dramatist and short-story writer, perhaps the greatest writer of fiction in Italy since MANZONI. He abandoned the style of his early sensual novels, and turned to writing about the peasants of southern Sicily. It is for the two novels of his planned realist series, *The Vanquished*, that he is most celebrated. *The House by the Medlar Tree* (1881) and *Mastro Don Gesualdo* (1889) both set out to show how underprivileged classes suffer in the wake of the progress of society. Some of his works were translated into English by D. H. LAWRENCE.

Verlaine, Paul (1844-96) French poet who was influenced at first by the Parnassian poets and later became a leader of the early Symbolists. His finest pieces are renowned for their musical quality, exquisite harmonies and suggestive power. His aesthetics are summarized in *L'art poétique* (1884) and *De la musique avant toute chose*. His wild and dissolute existence, in the course of which he fled to England and Belgium, suffering two years in gaol for wounding his friend RIMBAUD, inevitably left its mark on his work. His main collections of verse were *Poèmes saturniens* (1866), in which the Parnassian influence is apparent, *Fêtes galantes* (1869), inspired by WATTEAU's paintings, and *Sagesse* (1881), reflecting a new religious inspiration after conversion to Catholicism in prison.

Vermeer, Jan (1632-75) Dutch artist, whose few surviving pictures (about 40) have earned for him the foremost place among Dutch interior painters. His most typical paintings are of interiors with one or two figures, usually women, engaged in domestic activities, such as reading letters or making music. The difference, however, between these pictures and works by other Dutch interior painters such as METSU or de HOOCH, is that Vermeer was less concerned with anecdote or incident. His compositions (e.g. *The Lady Standing at the Virginals*, *c.* 1660), are studies in the play of light on differently textured surfaces and, above all, the arrangement of interlocking shapes, particularly rectangles, into relationships that form a two-dimensional design and create spatial depth. These paintings are, however, far from being mere geometrical exercises. They have a quality of calm and timelessness which is conveyed by Vermeer's exploitation of the qualities of light and the way it transforms the objects on which it falls. In recent times his influence is to be found in abstract geometricism of painters such as MONDRIAN.

Verne, Jules (1828-1905) French author of extremely popular science fiction stories which were strangely prophetic. His best-known works include *Journey to the Centre of the Earth* (1864), *Twenty Thousand Leagues under the Sea* (1870) and *Round the World in 80 Days* (1873).

Veronese, Paolo (c. 1528-88) Venetian painter of large, multi-figured and sensually-brilliant biblical, historical and allegorical compositions. In contrast to his contemporary, TINTORETTO, his works are balanced and orderly, but lacking in dramatic content: *Feast in the House of Levi* (1573) is typical of the way in which his themes frequently become lost in sumptuous pageantry. He was at his best in purely decorative work (e.g. the frescoes for the Villa Maser, near Vicenza, *c.* 1560).

Verwoerd, Hendrik Freusch (1910-66) Founder of the South African Republic and apostle of apartheid. Although he did much to improve housing in South African cities, he was chiefly responsible for extending apartheid legislation as Minister of Native Affairs (1950-58) under MALAN and Strijdom. This policy was further intensified when he became Prime Minister in 1958. With the Commonwealth's growing opposition to South Africa's internal policies, he declared the country a republic in 1961, a situation of which he had long been in favour, and declined to seek readmission to the Commonwealth. He was assassinated in 1966.

Vesalius, Andrea (1514-64) Belgian physician and anatomist. Vesalius broke with tradition by dissecting human corpses and by recording only what he saw instead of what the textbooks said he should see. His anatomical discoveries became the talk of Europe and students flocked to hear him. He summarized his work in *On the Fabric of the Human Body* (1543), which contradicts GALEN. Apart from his pioneer anatomical work, Vesalius is also important for being the first person to challenge ARISTOTLE's doctrine that thought and personality are in the heart; he believed that they were in the nervous system, especially the brain.

Vespasian (AD 9-79) Roman emperor (69-79) and soldier whose successes in Britain, Germany and Judaea won the support of the army, which proclaimed him emperor and defeated the armies of the rival leader Otho and the emperor Vitellius. Vespasian reorganized the Senate, the tax system, the army and the administration of the eastern provinces. He banished dissident philosophers and put down revolts, notably in Palestine. His troops thrust into Germany, and, under AGRICOLA, into Wales and Scotland.

Vespucci, Amerigo (1454-1512) Florentine explorer whose unreliable accounts of his travels show that, unlike COLUMBUS, he realized that the lands west of the Atlantic were a 'New World' and not part of Asia, and whose name was therefore given by European geographers to those lands. Vespucci made early voyages to the New World, but his claim to have discovered mainland America has long been discredited. He sailed to northern South America (1499) and (1501-2) sailed down the eastern South American coast, probably to a little beyond the Rio Grande region of Brazil (32° S), but later claimed to have reached Antarctic latitudes.

Vico, Giambattista (1668-1744) Italian philosopher, whose sociological account of man, in terms of human cultural history, broke new ground. Vico's theory of knowledge reversed the current rationalist or empiricist theories, since he held that history, being of our own making, is the field in which our knowledge if most vivid and sound, whereas the abstractions of mathematics and science are less well known to us, and can be clearly understood only by their maker, God. His view of history as being a series of cyclic developments greatly influenced later socio-political thought.

Victor Emmanuel II (1820-78) King of Sardinia-Piedmont, who became, in 1861, the first effective constitutional monarch of the kingdom of Italy. He took part in the Piedmont-Sardinia war against Austria (1848-9) and, after accession, as king of Sardinia-Piedmont, in co-operation with CAVOUR, prepared his country to take the lead in the struggle for Italian unity. To this end, he entered the Crimean War (1854-6) to gain recognition by major powers, and allied with France against Austria (1858-9) to liberate Lombardy. After the union of the northern duchies with Piedmont (1860) and the campaigns of GARIBALDI in Sicily, Victor Emmanuel became king of Italy. He took part in the Austro-Prussian war of 1866 and gained Venentia.

Victoria (1819-1901) Queen of Great Britain and Ireland from 1837, and Empress of India (1877), who gave her name to Britain's period of imperial greatness and to the architecture, art and literature of her time. She married (1840) her first cousin, ALBERT of Saxe-Coburg-Gotha, who assumed the title Prince Consort and whose influence on her was paramount. Victoria, though accepting her constitutional role in theory, was too wilful and too strong in her prejudices to refrain from interference with her ministers' policies, hampering PALMERSTON and GLADSTONE, and favouring MELBOURNE, PEEL and DISRAELI. After Albert's death (1861) she went into seclusion and consequently lost much of her popularity. But under Disraeli's influence she re-entered public life and in her later years was venerated as a matriarch.

Vignola, Giacomo da (1507-73) Italian architect, who worked mostly in Rome and introduced the oval plan into church design that was to become popular with architects of the Baroque. He designed the *Gesù*, Rome (which had a centralized plan with a dome, and a long nave necessary for processions). His palaces (Palazzo Farnese and Villa di Papa Giulio, Rome) have the rather brittle elegance of the Mannerist style.

Vigny, Alfred de (1797-1863) French Romantic poet, novelist and playwright. In *Poèmes Antiques et modernes* (1826) he affirmed the idea of the inevitable anguish and solitude to which great men are condemned (e.g. in the poem 'Moïse'). This notion, together with the conflict of the poet and society (as in the novel *Stello*, 1832, and in his best play, *Chatterton*, 1835), formed one of the dominant themes of his work. Some of Vigny's finest verse is contained in *Les Destinées* (published posthumously, 1864), poems ranging from resignation to despair and including the pinnacle of his achievement, 'La Maison du Berger'.

Villa-Lobos, Heitor (1887-1959) Brazilian, the first Latin American composer to win international standing. Villa-Lobos was a prolific composer writing in a style that drew its influences from Brazilian national folk music (Indian, Portuguese and African) with polytonality and neo-classicism. He wrote 12 symphonies, five piano concertos and a number of songs, as well as guitar and chamber music. Among his best-known works are the series of lyrical and evocative *Bachainas Brasileiras* for various combinations of instruments, which sought to introduce the spirit of BACH into a Brazilian idiom. For some years Villa-Lobos was his country's Director of Music in Education.

Villa, Pancho (1877-1923) Mexican bandit and revolutionary general. Sometime cattle stealer and bandit, he joined the revolutionary force against President Diaz in 1910, and continued his bandit-rebel activities in the north, where he became a virtual dictator during the period of ensuing political and social turmoil. In 1920, he made peace with the government, and retired to a ranch, where he lived until he was murdered in 1923.

Virgil (70-19 BC) Roman poet, author of the *Aeneid*, an epic poem telling of the wanderings of Aeneas and his fellow-survivors of the sack of Troy, until they settled in Italy as the ancestors of Rome. Virgil's intention was to celebrate the grandeur of Rome and its sense of destiny under AUGUSTUS. Earlier Virgil wrote the *Eclogues* (45-37 BC), based on THEOCRITUS's *Idylls*, with the addition of an element of Italian realism, and the *Georgics* (36-29 BC), a four-volume agricultural treatise, full of careful observation of animals and nature and written with typical Virgilian pathos and love.

Visconti, Gian Galeazzo (1351-1402) Duke of Milan (1378-1402), the most powerful member of the family that ruled Milan and much of northern Italy in the 14th and 15th centuries. He sought to rule all Italy, and by conquest, intrigue, and purchase took most of the north and centre of the country. He died of plague while attacking Florence.

Vitruvius Pollio, Marcus (1st cent. BC) Roman architect, whose *De Architectura* (though without the author's plans) is the only surviving work from antiquity on architecture and engineering. It had an enormous influence on European architects from the 12th century onwards. ALBERTI based his designs and his writings on it and it was subsequently published as a printed book first in 1486, then, with commentary and illustrations, in 1511.

Vivaldi, Antonio (c. 1676-1741) Italian composer and violinist who wrote *The Four Seasons*, a set of four 'concerto grossi' which vividly evoke the passing seasons. Vivaldi was a priest in charge of music at a girls' conservatory in Venice. He wrote over 400 concertos, mostly for strings, which had a considerable influence on J. S. BACH. Vivaldi's music was popular in his own day, but was largely forgotten until the present century rediscovered its charm and originality.

Vivar, Rodrigo Diaz de see CID, El

Vladimir I (c. 956-1015) Ukrainian-Scandinavian saint. Prince of Kiev, he was responsible for making Russia Christian. A brutal and drunken Viking until his conversion and marriage to Anne, sister of the Byzantine emperor Basil II, either his baptism or his wife civilized him. He set about imposing Christianity on his subjects through Greek missionaries, and sometimes by force, but always setting an example of mildness and charity.

Vlaminck, Maurice (1876-1958) French painter, who, with DERAIN and MATISSE, was a leading exponent of Fauvist painting between 1905 and 1907. The main source for his violent brushwork and shrill colour was the work of van GOGH, which he discovered in 1901. His most characteristic work, consisting chiefly of landscapes, was done in these early years; and it is the expression of a rumbustious personality opposed to tradition.

Vogelweide, Walther von der (c. 1170-c. 1230) Germany's greatest medievel lyric poet and author of many love poems, notably the famous 'Under the Lime Tree'. The moral and political poems of his *Sayings*, which deal with the spiritual problems of his time, are regarded as his best work.

Volta, Count Alessandro (1745-1827) Italian physicist who invented the first electric battery. In the 1780s, Galvani had found that a frog's leg, hung on a copper hook, twitched when the hook made contact with an iron plate. Volta believed that the contact of metals was generating an electric current, and not the muscle as Galvani thought. He made a 'voltaic pile' of copper and zinc discs, separated by cardboard soaked in salt solution; this was the first battery. He gave his name to the unit of electromotive force, the volt.

Voltaire, Françoise-Marie Arouet (1694-1778) France's universal literary genius, a dramatist, philosopher, poet, novelist, historian and contributor to the *Encyclopédie*. Voltaire spent his life ridiculing, with wit and irony, the vices and injustices of his time. In the best of his philosophical *contes*, such as *Zadig* (1747), *Micromégas* and, above all, in *Candide* (1759), Voltaire fused subject matter with style. In *Candide*, a vitriolic work inspired by the Lisbon earthquake and by Voltaire's earlier quarrel with FREDERICK THE GREAT of

Prussia, he ridiculed the absurdity of philosophical optimism, especially the theories of LEIBNIZ and POPE. Voltaire spent the years 1726-8 exiled in England, an experience which impressed him considerably and caused him to write his first masterpiece, the *Lettres philosophiques* of 1734, a thinly-veiled onslaught on French institutions, which has been described as 'the first bomb thrown at the *Ancien Régime*'. He also contributed articles to the monument of 18th-century rationalism and scepticism, the *Encyclopédie*. Voltaire was vehemently anti-religious and was in constant conflict with authority for attacking the tyranny of Church and State in France.

Vorster, Balthazar Johannes (1915-83) Prime Minister of South Africa. During the Second World War, Vorster was interned because of his anti-government activities, and so extreme an Afrikaner nationalist that at one time he was refused membership of the National Party. From 1961 to 1966, he was VERWOERD's Minister of Justice, and succeeded him as Prime Minister when the latter was assassinated in 1966. Although as Prime Minister he has encouraged friendly relations with black African countries such as Malawi and Botswana, he has also been responsible for laws which prescribe indefinite detention of political offenders, imprisonment without trial, and the uprooting of whole tribes in the interests of racial segregation.

Voysey, Charles (1857-1941) English domestic architect who rejected contemporary fashion for filling rooms with florid or complex objects and kept them simple and bright. His buildings, with their leaning buttresses and wide eaves, have an appearance peculiar to his style. Within the broad development of Art Nouveau, Voysey stands among the more restrained figures. There are houses by him in Hans Road and Bedford Park, London.

Vries, Hugo de (1848-1935) Dutch geneticist, whose plant-breeding experiments led him to believe that evolution proceeds in large jumps by means of mutations. Studying the American evening primrose, he showed that each separate character is passed down by means of discrete elements in the nucleus (which he called 'pangenes').

Vuillard, Edouard (1868-1940) French painter, whose early work shows affinities with that of GAUGUIN and with Japanese prints. He described himself as an 'intimiste', a term applied also to BONNARD and related to the domestic interiors which were his favourite subjects, and which were often painted in tempera, a muted medium compared with oils.

W

Wagner, Wilhelm Richard (1813-83) German composer of Romantic, monumental operas. The main influences on Wagner were BEETHOVEN, as the leading symphonist in Romantic music, and GLUCK, whose theory of opera foreshadowed Wagner's idea of 'music drama'. Wagner earned a meagre living in Paris as a music copyist, while writing his first operatic success, *The Flying Dutchman* (1843). Then, as conductor of the Dresden Opera, he turned to the Germanic myths and legends that were to be his main preoccupation, composing *Tannhäuser* (1845) and *Lohengrin* (1850). In 1848, he was implicated in the insurrection in Germany and went into exile in Switzerland, where he began work on his vast cycle of four operas, *The Ring of the Nibelung*, that took 25 years to complete. In his operas, Wagner aimed at a complete unity between all the components, wrote his own librettos and developed the *leitmotiv* – a recurring theme denoting a specific character or dramatic aspect. To secure control over every facet of production, he built the Festival Opera at Bayreuth, in Bavaria, under Ludwig II's patronage, and it was there, in 1876, that *The Ring* was first performed in its entirety: *The Rhinegold*, *The Valkyrie*, *Siegfried* and *The Twilight of the Gods*. Meanwhile, he had written *Tristan and Isolde*, a version of sublimated erotic love, and *The Mastersingers*, his one comic masterpiece. In the year before he died he completed his 'sacred music drama', *Parsifal*.

Folklore, medieval legend and Norse mythology provided the source material for the operas of Richard Wagner

Waitz, Grete (born 1953) Norwegian marathon runner who won the inaugural world championship women's marathon in 1983. She had made four world best times in this event by the age of 30.

Wajda, Andrej (born 1926) Polish film-maker and theatre director of the post-war generation. Wajda interpreted the search for national and political identity and the malaise of those of his countrymen who came to maturity in the war and post-war era, in films such as the trilogy *A Generation* (1954), *Kanal* (1956) and *Ashes and Diamonds* (1958). The trilogy marked a turning point in modern Polish cinema and established Wajda as a major international film-maker. He reinforced his reputation with *Man of Marble* (1977) and *Man of Iron* (1981), two films that finely portray the Polish situation of the late 1970s.

Waksman, Selman (1888-1973) American microbiologist of Russian origin, who won a Nobel Prize in 1952 for his work in isolating actinomycin, streptomycin, neomycin, candicidin, and other antibiotics from micro-organisms. He coined the word antibiotic.

Waldemar I 'The Great' (c. 1131-82) King of Denmark (1157-82), who brought unity to his country after a long period of civil war. Waldemar became the sole survivor of the royal line when he defeated Sweyn III in battle near Viborg (1157). With his childhood friend Absalon, Archbishop of Lund, as his able chief minister, he established law and order supported by heavy taxes. After ten years of campaigning, he defeated the Wendish pirates who had devastated Denmark's eastern coast and halted commercial progress. Waldemar seized their island stronghold (Rügen), which became the springboard for Denmark's eastward expansion under WALDEMAR II.

Waldemar II 'The Victorious' (1170-1241) King of Denmark (1202-41), who, like CANUTE, created a short-lived Danish Empire. He conquered or was recognized as overlord of territories in northwest Germany, then undertook crusades which swept through the southern Baltic lands from northern Germany to Finland, making the Baltic Sea a Danish lake. A German revolt (1223-7) ended with Waldemar's defeat at Bornhöved and the abrupt disintegration of his northern empire.

Waldemar IV Atterdag (c. 1320-75) King of Denmark (1340-75) who restored Denmark from anarchy and partition among foreign nobles. Elected king, but in fact holding only part of Jutland, Waldemar reconquered the disunited land, solved some of its economic problems by financial reforms, curbed the power of dissident nobles and churchmen, and won back much land that had been lost to Holstein, Schleswig and Sweden. By taking Visby, Waldemar incensed the mighty Hanseatic League of trading towns, which, with Norway and Sweden, forced on him the humiliating Peace of Stralsund (1370). Waldemar's daughter MARGARET began a new phase in Scandinavia's history.

Waldheim, Kurt (born 1918) Austrian diplomat, Secretary-General of the United Nations from 1972 to 1981. Early in his administration, neutral UN troops were required to maintain the cease-fire line between warring Arab and Israeli armies after the 1973 October war. He was succeeded by Peru's Javier Pérez de Cúellar.

Waldo, Peter (12th cent.) French heretic, founder of the Waldenses. A rich merchant of Lyons, Waldo renounced his wealth to become a mendicant preacher. His theme of voluntary poverty soon won disciples. Known as the 'Poor Men of Lyons', their aim was to imitate the simple life of the Apostles described in the New Testament, which Waldo had translated into Provençal. The movement was excommunicated in 1184.

Walesa, Lech (born 1943) Polish union leader. In August 1980 he organized Solidarity, an independent self-governing trade union for Polish workers. A strike committee was formed and a general strike took place. Four months later the Polish administrators signed an agreement giving the workers the right to organize freely and independently. Walesa became a symbol of the Polish workers' determination to have a greater voice in government affairs. The government outlawed Solidarity in 1981 and he was interned until late 1982 as part of the government effort to silence opposition.

Wallace, Alfred (1823-1913) British naturalist, who evolved the theory of evolution by natural selection. His views, presented jointly with those of DARWIN in 1858, clearly stated the notion of survival of the fittest in the struggle for existence (a phrase of MALTHUS), pointing out that it is the advantage of the stronger and not some effort of the will, as LAMARCK thought, that makes for survival.

Wallace, George Corley (born 1919) American politician and segregationist Governor of Alabama, elected in 1962 on a programme of opposition to integration 'in the schoolhouse doorway'. He strenuously fought a Supreme Court ruling that racial segregation in public schools was unconstitutional, but was finally forced to give way to Federal authority in 1963. In 1968 he ran as a segregationist candidate in the presidential elections and, although soundly beaten, he won five Southern states and received a larger percentage of popular votes than any third-party candidate since La Follette in 1924. An attempt to assassinate him in 1972 left him partially paralysed.

Wallace, Sir William (c. 1272-1305) Scottish patriot. He made successful attacks on the English troops who were pacifying Scotland after EDWARD I had deposed Scotland's king Baliol, and inspired the Scottish rout of Edward's army at Stirling Bridge (1297). He then pursued the retreating English to Newcastle and briefly ravaged northern England before returning north to govern Scotland. He was defeated at Falkirk by Edward I (1298), but waged war from the hills until he was caught and executed.

Wallenstein, Albrecht von (1583-1634) Austrian general who played a key role during the first half of the Thirty Years' War. With Tilly, he led the emperor FERDINAND II's imperial armies against Protestant forces, defeating Christian IV of Denmark in Saxony, forcing on him the Treaty of Lübeck (1629). Later he lost the battle of Lützen (1632), but his Swedish opponent, GUSTAVUS II ADOLPHUS, died in the fighting. After Ferdinand made him Duke of Friedland (1625), Wallenstein became over-ambitious for personal power, and began secret negotiations with Ferdinand's Protestant enemies. Ferdinand denounced him for treason, and one of Wallenstein's own officers stabbed him to death.

Waller, Fats (1904-43) American jazz and blues pianist. Early in his career he accompanied the great blues singer, Bessie Smith. He became famous making popular recordings, beginning in 1934. He composed many songs including *Honeysuckle Rose* (1929) and *Ain't Misbehavin* (1929), but owed his success as much to his happy, exuberant manner with audiences as to his musical gifts.

Wallis, Sir Barnes Neville (1887-1979) English aircraft designer. He started designing rigid airships before the First World War and was responsible for the structures of the R80, launched in 1920, and the R100, Britain's most successful airship, which first flew in 1929. Wallis designed two long-range bombers, the Wellesley (1935) and the Wellington (1938), and, during the Second World War, he devised the famous bounce bombs used by a special RAF Squadron in 1943 to breach the Möhne and Eder dams. He was responsible also for the Tallboy, armour piercing and Grand Slam (10-ton) bombs which inflicted enormous damage to Germany during the last year of the war. He worked on the variable geometry, or swing-wing, concept for supersonic aircraft (1944-56).

Walpole, Horace (1717-97) English wit, letter-writer, art historian and novelist, whose *Castle of Otranto*, a tale of mystery and horror (1764), set the fashion in England for the 'Gothic' romance. Son of Sir Robert WALPOLE, the politician, his enormous number of letters present an invaluable social history of the age, full of gossip and scandal. He collected pictures, set up a private press and printed numerous minor works, including poems by GRAY.

Walpole, Robert, 1st Earl of Orford (1676-1745) Often considered Great Britain's first true Prime Minister (1721-42), an office not officially recognized until 1905. Walpole was instrumental in developing and unifying cabinet government and shifting power from the House of Lords to the House of Commons. He became head of the Whig ministry, at first with Townshend (1721) and then alone (1730). One of his chief aims was to secure the Protestant succession and

Hanoverian dynasty by economic prosperity and by avoiding costly conflict with foreign powers, including France (then under the like-minded Fleury). Walpole's popularity began to decline with his attempts to deal with smuggling and his reluctance to fight to end Spain's exclusive claims to the New World and its searching of British vessels. He retired with the title Earl of Orford. 10 Downing Street, the official London residence of the Prime Minister, was his home, which he bequeathed to the nation.

Walras, Léon (1834-1910) French economist, author of the classic *Elements of Pure Economics* (1874-7). Using mathematical techniques, he pioneered a general equilibrium theory wherein all the individual variables of an economy are mutually interdependent.

Walter, John (1739-1812) English journalist and founder of *The Times*. He met the printer Henry Johnson, became interested in printing technology, and in 1784 purchased premises in Printing House Square. An unsuccessful printer of books, in 1785 he started a small newspaper, *The Daily Universal Register*, which, in 1788, became *The Times*. Under his son John Walter II (1776-1847) and the editorship of Thomas Barnes, *The Times* established itself as Britain's leading newspaper and daily historical record. It remains an influential newspaper.

Walton, Ernest see COCKCROFT, Sir John Douglas

Walton, Sir William Turner (1902-83) British composer who wrote *Façade* (1923) and the oratorio *Belshazzar's Feast* (1931). The first, musical parodies supporting spoken poems by Edith SITWELL, and the second, with its barbaric jazz rhythms illuminating an Old Testament text, caused some disturbance in England's conservative musical life between the wars, as did his tense First Symphony.

Wang Wei (699-759) Chinese painter, calligrapher, poet and musician of the T'ang dynasty, revered in later periods as exemplifying the artist as a man of broad culture. He held a high position in the Imperial Directorate of Music as well as a senior government post, but on the death of his wife became a Buddhist recluse devoted entirely to painting. He is considered the pioneer of monochrome landscape painting and the technique of 'broken-ink'.

Wankel, Felix (born 1902) German inventor and engineer who developed (1934-56) the first viable rotary internal combustion engine. During the Second World War, Wankel worked on the development of fighter planes, and was imprisoned by the French occupation forces. After the war, he refined his engine, which is now used in several production vehicles.

Warhol, Andy (born 1930) American painter, film-maker and cult figure. Warhol was a leader of the pop art movement of the early 1960s and the creator of many of that period's most familiar images. His style derives from his early career as a commercial illustrator. To a greater extent than any other artist, he has obliterated the dividing line between fine arts and the visual packaging of daily life. As the centre of the New York avant-garde scene, Warhol also made a number of films in which the camera was used impassively to record the everyday life of the actors.

Warren, Earl (1891-1974) American judge who presided over the Supreme Court (1953-69) at a time when its decisions led to important changes in race relations. Already known for his liberal views on civil rights, he outraged conservative Southerners by handing down in 1954 the unanimous ruling that racial segregation in public schools was illegal. In 1964 he headed the Commission enquiring into the assassination of President KENNEDY.

Warren, Robert Penn (born 1905) American poet and novelist, who explores the conflicts of the South as universal problems. His main novels are *At Heaven's Gate* (1943), about Southern capitalism; *All the King's Men* (1946), about the rise and fall of a Louisiana demagogue.

Warwick the Kingmaker see NEVILLE, Richard

Washington, George (1732-99) First American President, leader of the American colonists during the War of Independence against Britain. He served in the British army against France in the Canadian War (1755-9), but was afterwards converted to the idea of US independence and became one of its leading advocates. His principal military feat during the War of Independence was his march, with American and French forces,

A celebration in stone at Mount Rushmore, US, of Washington and other Presidents

from the Hudson to Yorktown, where he forced Lord CORNWALLIS, the British commander, to surrender (1781). The Federal Convention of 1787 at Philadelphia, having adopted the Constitution, elected Washington President of the US. He assumed office in 1789 and remained President until 1797.

Wassermann, August von (1866-1925) German bacteriologist who was the inventor of the Wassermann reaction, which remains the standard blood test for syphilis.

Waterman, Lewis Edson (1837-1901) American inventor and industrialist who, in 1884, invented the modern type of fountain pen. Self-filling pens were introduced commercially in the early 1900s.

Watson, James (born 1928) American geneticist, who, with Francis CRICK, made the first model of the DNA molecule. Watson and Crick made their discovery while working on nucleic acids, the substances in the nucleus of cells that contain inheritable material. With their colleague Maurice Wilkins they were awarded a Nobel Prize (1962). Watson later helped break the genetic code of the DNA base sequences and found the RNA (ribonucleic acid) messenger that transfers the DNA code to the cell's protein-forming structures.

Watson-Watt, Sir Robert Alexander (1892-1973) Scottish physicist who led the team which, beginning in 1935, developed the system for the radiolocation of moving aircraft. Radar stations installed around the eastern and southern approaches to Britain, from 1938, played a vital role in its defence against German air attacks during the Second World War. In peacetime, radar has developed a whole range of uses, including the location of hurricane paths.

Watt, James (1736-1819) Scottish engineer, who improved the efficiency and versatility of steam engines, which powered the Industrial Revolution. To overcome the problem of fuel wastage in each cycle of the cylinder of a Newcomen steam engine, which he was repairing, Watt proposed the introduction of a separate condenser to be kept cool; while the main cylinder could be kept hot, they needed to be connected only when the cylinder was filled with steam. Watt was granted his historic patent for 'a new method for lessening the consumption of steam and fuel in fire engines' in 1769. Six years later, he went into partnership with the Birmingham industrialist Matthew BOULTON, and together they perfected and marketed the steam engine. Watt made a number of other major contributions to the development of steam engines between 1775 and the 1790s: devising the concept of 'horse power', for the measurement of output; a double-acting engine, in which steam expanded and condensed alternately on both sides of the piston; a flying-ball governor by means of which the speed of an engine was used to control it (the first use of feed-back for self-regulation in a machine); and five ways in which the back-and-forth motion of a piston could be translated into rotary motion – to drive looms lathes, cable-drums and hoists.

Watteau, Jean-Antoine (1684-1721) French painter, originator of the *fêtes galantes*. His subject matter, epitomized by the *Departure from the Island of Cythera* (1717), emphasized the transitory quality of human happiness. His election to the French Academy was seen as a formal acknowledgement that a new era of lighthearted art to please the senses had ousted the large and formal history paintings of the age of LOUIS XIV.

Watts, George Frederic (1817-1904) English painter, best known for his allegorical paintings on themes such as *Hope*, *Destiny* and *Chaos*.

Waugh, Evelyn (1903-66) English novelist, who wrote ironic, witty novels about the English upper-classes in the mid-20th century. In the earlier books, from *Decline and Fall* (1928) to *Put Out More Flags* (1942), Waugh satirizes the foolishness of fashionable society, mixing bitter farce and sharp dialogue, creating an anarchic world. In his later works, *Brideshead Revisited* (1945) and *Sword of Honour* (1965), a rewriting of a war trilogy, his Roman Catholicism and a more tolerant humanity bring nostalgic order to the world he describes.

Webb, Matthew (1848-83) English swimmer, who in 1875 became the first man to swim the Channel.

Webb, Philip (1831-1915) English architect and an important figure in late 19th-century domestic architecture, who worked with William MORRIS to produce a style of architecture which, although it owed something to PUGIN, went a long way towards creating a kind of domestic Gothic style in red-brick.

Webb, Beatrice (1858-1943) and **Sidney (1859-1947)** English writers and social historians, members of the Fabian Society. Dedicated to socialism, they published prolifically, participated in the establishment of the London School of Economics (1895) and founded the left-wing journal *The New Statesman* (1913).

Weber, Carl Maria Freidrich Ernst von (1786-1826) German composer who established a national style in German opera and whose best-known opera is *Der Freischütz* (1821). This story of humour and magic in a German village was the first opera in the Romantic style which sought to place emphasis on the music's emotional content. Weber followed it with *Euryanthe* (1823) and *Oberon* (1826), his last opera.

Weber, Max (1864-1920) German sociologist and political economist who in the *Protestant Ethic* and the *Spirit of Capitalism* (1904-5) challenged MARX's theory that economic factors are decisive in determining the course of history. He sought to identify some of the origins of capitalism and traced the significance of religious and ethical ideas. In his *Methodology of the Social Sciences* (1922) he argued that scientific methods can be used in the study of sociology, but emphasized that the sociologist cannot be purely objective; he must attempt to put himself in the place of the people he is studying in order to understand their values and motives. Weber contributed almost more than any other scholar to comparative sociology, and, in an effort to find a basis from which comparisons can be made with other civilizations, he evolved the concept of the 'ideal type' or ideal mode of a set of social relationships.

Webern, Anton von (1883-1945) Austrian composer who was, with BERG, one of SCHOENBERG's leading disciples and of whom STRAVINSKY wrote: 'Doomed to failure in a deaf world of ignorance and indifference, he inexorably went on cutting his diamonds.' His music was written painstakingly between his occupations as a conductor at various opera houses and as a teacher of composition. From 1924 he adopted Schoenberg's note-row technique, adapting it to his own highly individual intentions. Webern's work includes a symphony as well as song settings and chamber works, including a string quartet. After surviving years of ostracism imposed by the Nazi régime, he was shot by a sentry of the occupying US army after failing to answer a challenge.

Webster, John (1580-c. 1625) English dramatist, who wrote *The Duchess of Malfi* (*c.* 1613) and *The White Devil* (1612), both of which are frequently revived. With the exception of his earliest surviving play, *Appius and Virginia* (*c.* 1609), his dramas are sombre, violent and obsessed with death, but are informed with poetry of a high order.

Wedekind, Frank (1864-1918) German dramatist who was the first to deal outspokenly with sexual themes. His *Awakening of Spring* (1891), which is concerned with adolescent sexual problems, was banned from the London stage until as recently as 1963. In both *Earth Spirit* (1895) and its sequel, *Pandora's Box* (1904), the character of Lula, a beautiful, uninhibited but soulless woman, is an incarnation of lust and the symbol of Society.

Wedgwood, Josiah (1730-95) English pottery manufacturer who introduced new processes and high standards of design into the ceramic industry.

Wegener, Alfred (1880-1930) German meteorologist, who in 1915 first propounded the theory of continental drift. He contended that evidence of past climates could not be reconciled with the fixed positions of the continents and of the north and south magnetic poles, and that the now-separate continents must at one time have formed a single large mass which later drifted apart. After decades of scepticism, evidence has now come to light to confirm the essence of his theories.

Weill, Kurt (1900-50) German composer who collaborated with BRECHT on *The Threepenny Opera* (1928) and *The Rise and Fall of the City of Mahogonny* (1930). The 'Brecht-Weill' style of song and lyric was one of the most distinctive of the inter-war years. After fleeing from the Nazis to America in 1935, Weill composed several Broadway musicals.

Weir, Peter (born 1938) Australian film director who made his name with *The Cars that Ate Paris* in 1971. Subsequent films include *Picnic at Hanging Rock* (1975), *Gallipoli* (1981) and *The Year of Living Dangerously* (1984).

Weismann, August (1834-1914) German biologist, who discovered that the germ cells that transmit the various hereditary characteristics from one generation to the next are formed by a process of division, so as to carry half the genes from each of the constituent parent germ cells. This is vital in explaining the actual genetic process and forms an important part of modern genetic theory.

Weiss, Ehrich see HOUDINI, Harry

Weizmann, Chaim (1874-1952) Jewish statesman, who became first President of Israel. He was born in Poland but emigrated to Britain, where he became a biochemist and did valuable work in the explosives department of the Admiralty during the First World War. He also became leader of the Zionist movement, whose aim was the establishment of a national home for the Jews. For this aim, he obtained the support of the British government, embodied in the BALFOUR Declaration (1917) and in the League of Nations' mandate for Palestine. As a result of these achievements, he became leader of the World Zionist Organization (1920-31), and head of the Jewish Agency for Palestine (1929-31). He was provisional President of Israel in 1948 and became the first official President in 1949.

Weller, Thomas see ENDERS, John

Wells, Orson (born 1915) American actor, director and producer, who once said, 'a film is never really good unless the camera is an eye in the hand of a poet'. His later films demonstrate the practicality of this remark. *Citizen Kane* (1942), loosely based on the life of William Randolph HEARST, was the first and most famous of the films which Wells directed, wrote and starred in, followed by the masterful *The Magnificent Ambersons* (1942) and *A Touch of Evil* (1958). He has had an equally successful acting career, notably as the black-marketeer Harry Lime in *The Third Man* (1949) and in *Chimes at Midnight* (1966), adapting SHAKESPEARE's *Henry IV* and *Henry V* for the cinema.

Actor-director Orson Wells, major influence on the art of cinema, starring here in *The Stranger*

Wellington, Arthur Wellesley, 1st Duke of (1769-1852) English soldier, who defeated NAPOLEON's armies in the Peninsular War and at Waterloo. He was commissioned in 1787, but from 1796-1805 served as both a soldier and an administrator in India. On his return to England, he became MP for Rye. In 1808, he was given command of the army that was sent to Portugal to fight the French, whom he defeated. For allowing the French to withdraw, he was recalled and court-martialled, but was exonerated. He returned to his command on the death of Sir John Moore at Corunna (1809), and in a campaign lasting from 1809 to 1814 he drove the French back to the Pyrenees and into France. He was chosen, with CASTLEREAGH, to represent Britain at the Congress of Vienna (1814-15) and brought about the final defeat of Napoleon at Waterloo (18 June 1815). He later became a member of Lord LIVERPOOL's cabinet, and attended the subsequent congresses of Aix-la-Chapelle (1818) and Verona (1822). As Prime Minister (1828-30) his obstinate opposition to parliamentary reform made him unpopular, despite his great services to the country, and on more than one occasion his house was stoned by mobs.

Wells, Herbert George (1866-1946) English novelist and social commentator, whose writings were world famous in the first decades of the 20th century. Wells was the first important writer of science fiction in English and combined scientific interest with social concern in works such as *The Time Machine* (1895), *The Invisible Man* (1897) and *The War of the Worlds* (1898). In many of his works he accurately predicted future events. His early life provided the material for his social comedies such as *Love and Mr Lewisham* (1900) and *Kipps* (1905). After 1911, his novels became social tracts, but he continued to hold an audience with his short stories, his encyclopedic *The Outline of History* (1920) and his revealing *Experiment in Autobiography* (1934).

Wenceslaus (c. 907-29) Duke of Bohemia who was canonized and became the patron saint of Czechoslovakia. He embraced the Christian faith introduced by his grandfather, Borivoy, and made it the basis for ordered civil life. This antagonized his reactionary younger brother Boleslav, whose followers killed Wenceslaus in a brawl. He was subsequently acclaimed as a Christian martyr and is remembered as 'Good King Wenceslaus' in the Christmas carol of that name.

Wentworth, Sir Thomas see STRAFFORD, 1st Earl of

Wesley, John (1703-91) English theologian and evangelist founder of Methodism. Wesley spent some time as his parson father's curate, and for a while served as a missionary to the colonists of Georgia. He extended his acquaintance with current mysticism, particularly that associated with the Moravians. In 1738 he began his lifelong work for the conversion of Britain, travelling, writing, preaching regularly and organizing his societies. A staunch Church of England man, he refused to set up a separate Church, but was pushed by hostility and the consequences of his own actions to establish a relatively independent Connexion of Societies within which a pastoral system was established.

West, Benjamin (1738-1820) American painter of historical subjects, who worked in England and succeeded Sir Joshua REYNOLDS as President of the Royal Academy in 1792.

West, Mae (1893-1980) American actress who began her career on the stage, but made her name in the cinema. In a period of sophistication, she brought a healthy vulgarity to the screen, perfecting the art of the *double entendre* in films such as *She Done Him Wrong* (1933), *I'm No Angel* (1933) and *My Little Chickadee* (1939), in which she co-starred with W. C. FIELDS. Her name became the colloquial term for an inflatable life jacket.

West, Nathanael (1903-40) Pen-name of Nathan Weinstein, American author who wrote satirically on the neuroses of modern life. His novels include *Miss Lonely Hearts* (1933) and *The Day of the Locust* (1939).

Westinghouse, George (1846-1914) American inventor and industrialist, who filed more than 400 patents during his lifetime, mainly concerning railways, the electrical industry and the utilization of natural gas. For railways he invented a device for re-railing derailed steam cars (1865), an air brake (1868) (which he made automatic in 1872 and, with it, his fortune) and pneumatic points-switching and signalling systems – which kindled his interest in electricity. From 1883 he pioneered control systems for long-distance natural-gas pipelines and for town distribution networks. In 1886 he formed the Westinghouse Electric Company and started to devise an AC power and lighting system.

Westmoreland, William C. (born 1914) American general during the escalation of the Vietnam War. In 1968, President JOHNSON transferred Westmoreland to Army Chief-of-Staff amidst disappointment at the progress of the war.

Wettbach, Adrian see GROCK

Weyden, Rogier van der (c. 1399-1464) Influential Flemish painter of religious works and some portraits. His most famous painting, which was copied several times in the 15th century, is the *Deposition* altarpiece (*c.* 1435) in which the figures are as if in low-relief sculpture – thrust to the foreground and seen against a plain gold background.

Wharton, Edith (1862-1937) American novelist, who wrote neat, competent portraits of New York and European upper-class society. *The House of Mirth* (1905) and *The Custom of the Country* (1913) are influenced by Henry JAMES. But her best story, *Ethan Frome* (1911), deals with bewilderment and pathos in Puritan New England.

Wheatstone, Sir Charles (1802-75) English physicist, who made notable contributions to acoustics and developed his own bridge method for the accurate measurement of electrical resistance. However, his most important work, from 1837, with Sir William Fothergill Cooke, was on the electric telegraph. Its main applications were for alarm systems and railway signalling. The inventors took out a joint patent for the system, which was installed the following year on the Great Western Railway.

Wheeler, Sir Mortimer (1890-1976) English archaeologist, who popularized his subject through lectures, books and television. In such books as *Rome Beyond the Imperial Frontiers* (1954) and *The Indus Civilization* (1955) he vividly proved his point that archaeology is about people, not just artefacts: interpreting archaeological finds to reconstruct the patterns of life (and death) in ancient times.

Whistler, James (1834-1903) American artist and acid wit. As a painter he sought to impose a harmony on nature rather than faithfully to transcribe her qualities, as is evident in the famous portrait of his mother (1872), whose real title is *Arrangement in Grey and Black*.

Whitaker, Joseph (1820-95) English publisher who founded *Whitaker's Almanac* (1869), the annual reference book on British politics, economics and culture. He also founded *The Bookseller* (1858), the British book trade journal.

White, Gilbert (1720-93) English clergyman, naturalist and nature-writer, whose *Natural History of Selborne* (1789) is a lucid and well-observed record, in the form of collected letters, of the countryside. This work, admired by CONSTABLE, was one of several that helped to prepare the way for the Romantic appreciation of nature.

White, Patrick (born 1912) Australian novelist. His works are long and densely detailed, often creating an oppressive atmosphere, amid which the central characters struggle to survive. His heroes, such as the visionary explorer in *Voss* (1957) or the family in *The Tree of Man* (1955), possess the pioneering fortitude that is part of the tradition of Australian society. He was awarded the Nobel Prize for Literature in 1973.

Whitefield, George (1714-70) English religious revivalist and early Methodist, famed for his preaching. He is said to have preached altogether 18,000 sermons to 10 million people, and had much influence on the revival in America (which he visited seven times) and in Wales.

Whitehead, Alfred (1861-1947) English mathematician and philosopher whose early work on mathematics and logic culminated in his joint authorship, with RUSSELL, of *Principia Mathematica* (1910-14).

Whitehead, Robert (1823-1905) English inventor of the naval torpedo. Whitehead at his works at

Fiume on the Adriatic developed a self-propelled underwater bomb, powered by compressed air (1866). By 1890 there were torpedoes capable of speeds of up to 30 knots with a half-mile range and a 200-pound warhead. The weapon's effectiveness was demonstrated by the Japanese in their attack on the Russian Fleet at Port Arthur (1904).

Witman, Walt (1819-92) American poet, who wrote with vehemence and audacity of the need for American intellectual independence, of which he became the bardic symbol. After *Leaves of Grass* (1855), his chief works were *Drum Taps* (1865), poems on the Civil War, and the prose *Democratic Vistas* (1871). His poems, on social and moral issues, are unconventionally formed; his language, said Emerson, mixed 'the *Bhagavad Gita* and the *New York Herald*'.

Whitney, Eli (1765-1825) American inventor of the cotton gin (1793). The gin removed the lint from the seeds so easily that even short-fibred cotton – the only kind that could be grown in inland America – became profitable. In 1798, he obtained a contract from the American government for 10,000 muskets, having introduced the technique of making all parts standard and interchangeable, so cutting time and costs. This was one of the early examples of mass production techniques, as later developed on a wide scale by FORD, COLT and others.

A cotton gin. Eli Whitney's invention helped cotton growing to become big business – but increased plantation slave labour

Whittier, John Greenleaf (1807-92) American poet, who won a reputation for popular poems and ballads. Coming from a Quaker family, he was a vigorous abolitionist whose obvious sincerity appeared in his anti-slavery poems in *Voices of Freedom* (1846). The popular *Snow-Bound* (1866) recalls his country childhood; his collection *In War Time* (1864) contains the well-known patriotic ballad 'Barbara Frietchie'.

Whittington, Richard (c. 1358-1423) English merchant, three times Lord Mayor of London. As a successful London mercer and husband of the heiress Alice Fitzwaryn, he became rich enough to lend money to HENRY IV and HENRY V. He left a huge sum for charity and for public works, including the rebuilding of Newgate Prison. The popular legend of Whittington as an orphan owning only a cat but rising from poverty to riches dates from a play printed in 1605.

Whymper, Edward (1840-1911) English explorer, mountaineer and artist and first man to climb the Matterhorn in Switzerland. Between 1861 and 1865, he attempted the climb six times and then, in July 1865, his seventh attempt was successful, after ascending the 'Swiss Ridge'. During the climb four men fell to their deaths, but a breaking rope saved Whymper and two guides.

Wieland, Christoph (1733-1813) German novelist and poet, author of *The History of Agathon* (1766-7), the first in a series of novels in German literature concerned with the psychological development of their heroes. His prose translations of SHAKESPEARE's plays had an important influence on the *Sturm und Drang* movement and helped to popularize Shakespeare in Germany.

Wilberforce, William (1759-1833) English philanthropist, who campaigned for the abolition of the slave trade and slavery. As an MP and a close friend of PITT, who supported his campaigns, Wilberforce devoted all his time and eloquence to denouncing the slave trade. In 1791, he introduced a Bill for its abolition, but had to fight until 1807 to get it on the Statute book. Thereafter, he devoted himself to the complete abolition of slavery in Britain and her dominions. Shortly before his death in 1833, this aim was accomplished during GREY's Whig ministry.

Wilde, Oscar (1854-1900) Irish dramatist, master of the social comedy. *Lady Windermere's Fan* (1892), an immediate success, was followed by *A Woman of No Importance* (1893) and *An Ideal Husband* (1895), which brought Wilde fame and wealth. His best-known play, *The Importance of Being Earnest* (1895), was rated the most elegant and amusing English high comedy for two centuries. A verse-drama written in French, *Salomé* (1892), was produced in France, but banned in England. In 1895 Wilde was imprisoned after being convicted of homosexual practices. In *The Ballad of Reading Gaol* he recorded his prison experiences (1898). He died in poverty and exile.

Wilder, Thornton (1897-1975) American playwright and novelist. *The Bridge of San Luis Rey* (1927), a best-selling novel which won the Pulitzer Prize, is an account of life's ironies of fate and providence, and *Ides of March* (1948) is an imaginative reconstruction of the last days of Julius CAESAR. In 1967 he published *The Eighth Day*, his first novel for almost 20 years.

Wiligelmo (11th-12th cent.) Italian Romanesque sculptor who worked in Modena Cathedral (1099-1106), where a school of sculpture appears to have been centred around him.

Wilkes, John (1727-97) English Member of Parliament and political reformer, whose attack on an autocratic speech by the king to Parliament incurred George III's anger and Wilkes's arrest under a general warrant. He was released on the grounds of parliamentary privilege and that general warrants were illegal, both grounds landmarks in British justice. Wilkes was expelled from Parliament, but after a period of exile to avoid a seditious libel action, returned and again became an MP, winning a series of elections whose validity was rejected by the House of Commons, under government pressure. An enraged public (most of whom still had no vote) supported Wilkes in a campaign for parliamentary reform, but Wilkes later abandoned his radicialism and supported the younger PITT.

Wilkie, Sir David (1785-1841) Scottish artist, whose sentimental genre painting won wide popularity.

William I (1027-87) King of England (1066-87), called William the Conqueror, who came to the throne by conquest, and substituted Norman for Anglo-Saxon rule. He was a cousin of EDWARD the Confessor, who supposedly promised him succession to the English throne. On Edward's death, William enforced this claim by landing in England and killing Edward's proclaimed successor HAROLD II in the Battle of Hastings (1066). William completed the conquest of England by 1070, ended

HEREWARD's last stand in 1071 and centralized government on feudal Norman lines, allocating big estates and high posts to leading Norman knights and churchmen to hold for the Crown. Under William, and his son Henry I, Norman rule gave England political stability and enriched it with Norman (Romanesque) architecture, and a new language, Norman-French, which eventually combined with Anglo-Saxon to produce the medieval English language.

William I 'The Silent' (1533-84) Count of Nassau, founder of the Dutch Republic. Under the emperor CHARLES V, William became Governor of the northern Netherlands provinces of Holland, Utrecht and Zeeland. Once the territory of the independent French dukes of Burgundy, the Netherlands, through marriages with the Hapsburgs, had become connected with Spain and its empire. Nationalism and Protestantism grew, intensified by the Spanish attempts to suppress them. William became a convinced supporter of both causes. When PHILIP II of Spain sent the Duke of ALVA and Spanish troops to impose Roman Catholic uniformity on the Netherlands, William led stubborn armed resistance in Holland and Zeeland, the Protestant north, and became first Statholder (1579-84) of the northern provinces. By the Union of Utrecht (1579), they were formed into one independent state, variously known as the United Provinces, the Dutch Republic and now the Netherlands. William was murdered by a Burgundian.

William I (1797-1888) King of Prussia (1861-88) and first emperor of Germany (1871-88). He was an autocrat who held extreme conservative views, and during the revolution of 1848 was briefly driven out of Prussia. After succeeding to the Prussian throne, his appointment of BISMARCK as his chief minister was momentous, for between them they forged the German Empire. William was at first unwilling to fully support Bismarck's policy of conquest, but Prussia's annexation of Schleswig-Holstein in 1864 led him to adjust his vision of Prussia's future. Prussian domination in Germany was assured by the defeat of Austria in 1866, and the German Empire was founded during the Franco-Prussian War.

William II (1859-1941) Emperor of Germany and King of Prussia (1888-1918). In 1890, two years after his accession, he dismissed BISMARCK from office in order to implement his personal policy of imperialism and industrialization. He sponsored the German challenge to British sea-power and by his 'sabre-rattling' forced the other great powers into defensive alliances. His personal responsibility for the war has probably been exaggerated, but the Allies' belief that this was so led them to refuse peace terms until the kaiser's own Officer Corps had forced him to abdicate and leave Germany (1918).

William III (1650-1702) Dutch prince of Orange, Statholder of Holland (1672-1702), King of England (1689-1702), whose policies placed a check on the vast powers of LOUIS XIV of France. When Louis XIV invaded Holland (1672), William led the resistance. He suffered defeats, but married Mary, daughter of England's future James II, with whom he opened negotiations, under threat of which Louis reached an agreement with William at Nijmegen (1678). James refused to form an alliance with William, so William turned to the English opposition and supported their disapproval of James's religious policy. After overthrowing James in the so-called Glorious Revolution (1688), William accepted invitations from the Parliaments of England and Scotland to rule the kingdoms jointly with his wife Mary, and made his throne safe by defeating James II, who had retreated to Ireland, at the Battle of the Boyne (1690). He formed two Grand Alliances against France (1689, 1701), the first leading to a war (the War of the League of Augsburg) by which William regained all his possessions taken by Louis XIV.

William IV (1765-1837) King of Great Britain and Ireland (1830-7) the third son of George III. He became king on the death of his brother, GEORGE IV, in 1830. His dislike of extreme measures led him to oppose the Reform Bill, an action by which he incurred popular dislike and which led to a political crisis with GREY, his Prime Minister. His dismissal of MELBOURNE in 1834 and the subsequent invitation to PEEL to form a ministry was the last attempt by an English sovereign to impose a minority ministry on Parliament.

William of Occam (c. 1300-c. 1349) English scholastic philosopher whose denial of the Pope's temporal power laid the foundations of the modern independence of State from Church. In logic, he held that only singular things exist, while the universals describing these qualities are merely thought. From this arose the dictum known as 'Ockham's razor', which stated that entities ought not to be needlessly multiplied.

Williams, Tennessee (1911-83) American dramatist whose plays for the stage have reached a world-wide audience through the cinema. His first Broadway success, *The Glass Menagerie* (1945), established a pattern for his later plays, with their settings in the southern States, tough heroes, shabby gentility, and confrontations between innocence and passion. These were *A Streetcar Named Desire* (1947), *Summer and Smoke* (1948), *The Rose Tattoo* (1951) and *Cat on a Hot Tin Roof* (1955). Williams also wrote some symbolic plays, such as *Camino Real* (1953), and the domestic comedy, *Period of Adjustment* (1961). More recent plays include *Suddenly Last Summer*, *Baby Doll* and *Small Craft Warnings*.

Wilson, Alexander (1714-86) Scottish astronomer and meteorologist who studied the nature of the Sun and of the Earth's atmosphere. At Glasgow University in 1749 he measured atmospheric temperatures with the help of a kite – so anticipating the use of meteorological balloons developed by Jean Pierre BLANCHARD and Gustave Hermite. In the same year he discovered the nature of the dark patches on the Sun's photosphere, now known as sunspots.

Wilson, Angus (born 1913) English author and critic, who writes subtle novels that probe, sometimes satirically, the frustrations and weaknesses of intelligent society. Among his books are *Hemlock and After* (1952), *Anglo-Saxon Attitudes* (1956) and *The Old Men at the Zoo* (1961), all lengthy novels with a Dickensian variety of characters.

Wilson, Sir James Harold (born 1916) British Labour politician and Prime Minister. He became an MP in 1945 and was appointed President of the Board of Trade in 1947, becoming the youngest Cabinet Minister (31) since PITT. In 1951, Wilson resigned with BEVAN in protests against cuts in social service spending, and he remained a Bevanite throughout the 1950s. He was elected labour leader in 1963 and was four times Prime Minister (1964-6, 1966-70, 1974 and 1974-6). He established the Open University (1970) and accelerated the growth of the comprehensive system of education. His government re-nationalized the steel industry, introduced measures for rent control and the control of prices and incomes and provided time for the passing of bills to legalize abortion and homosexual acts. In the late 1960s the crisis over Britain's balance of payments and the subsequent devaluation of the pound severely hampered his economic plans. His foreign policy was blighted by Ian SMITH and General DE GAULLE. He resigned as Prime Minister in 1976 but remained in Parliament.

Wilson, Kenneth (born 1936) American physicist who was awarded the Nobel Prize for Physics in 1982 for his development of a theory that explains the behaviour of different substances under certain conditions of temperature and pressure. After graduating, Wilson worked on quantum field theories which eventually led him to his major discovery. In 1975 he was elected to the National Academy of Sciences and in 1981 he received an honorary doctorate from Harvard University in recognition of his work.

Wilson, Richard (c. 1713-82) Welsh landscape artist, who, though he achieved little success in his lifetime, has since come to be regarded with admiration. His absorption of the idyllic calm and atmospheric light of the Roman countryside on a visit to Italy (1750-7) is evident in *Shepherds in the Campagna*.

Wilson, Thomas Woodrow (1856-1924) Twenty-eighth American President, who led the US into the First World War, and helped to found the League of Nations. He was elected President in 1913 in a campaign against Theodore ROOSEVELT and Taft. He initiated anti-Trust legislation, reformed the national banking system by the Federal Reserve Act, and sent a punitive expedition into Mexico (1916) to put down a border raid by Mexican 'generals', notably Pancho VILLA. Because of his maintenance of US neutrality for the first two years of the First World War, and as a result of his moves to restore peace by mediation, he was elected for a second term. Early in 1917, Germany resumed unrestricted submarine attacks on merchant shipping and, at the same time, tried to arrange that if this provoked Wilson to declare war, Mexico would invade the US. Revelation of these negotiations (the 'Zimmerman telegram') and the sinking of American ships brought the US into the conflict (April 1917). When he arrived in Europe for the Paris Peace Conference (1919) Wilson was hailed as a saviour, but he was bitterly disappointed by the failure of LLOYD GEORGE and CLEMENCEAU to live up to his own lofty ideals. Overwork led to his collapse in September 1919.

Winckelman, Johann Joachim (1717-68) German art historian who is often called 'the father of archaeology'. While working in Rome, he made a careful study of Greek mythology and also of Roman sculptures and ruins, becoming the first to identify styles in ancient art. His *History of the Art of Antiquity* (1764), showed that it was possible to understand ancient peoples by studying their art.

Wingfield, Walter Clopton (1833-1912) British inventor of lawn tennis. In 1874 he patented an outdoor game called Sphairistike which, in a modified form, was renamed lawn tennis. As such it was adopted by the All England Croquet Club, which organized the first Wimbledon lawn tennis championships in 1877.

Winstanley, Gerrard (1609-52) English social reformer who led and publicized the Diggers, 20 poor men who seized and cultivated common land at St George's Hill, Cobham, Surrey (1649-50). Winstanley won support for the Diggers in four more counties before mob violence and a hostile government broke up the colony (1650).

Winthrop, John (1588-1649) English Puritan lawyer, first governor of the Massachusetts Bay Colony. He sailed for America as chosen governor of more than 1000 Puritans, who reached Sale and founded settlements, including Boston. As governor almost continuously until his death, Winthrop helped to organize defence against likely English attack and became first president of the defensive union called the New England Confederation.

Wittgenstein, Ludwig (1889-1951) Austrian philosopher, one of the most influential of the 20th century. He was a colleague of Bertrand Russell and actively involved in the Vienna Circle. His work *Tractatus Logico-philosophicus* (1921) analyses the problem of language and its limits and influenced the rise of logical positivism and linguistic analysis. *Philosophical Investigations* (1953) and *Remarks on the Foundations of Mathematics* (1956) were published posthumously.

Witte, Count Sergei Yulievich (1849-1915) Finance Minister (1892-1903) and first constitutional Prime Minister of Russia (1905-6), who industrialized Russia and promoted the Trans-Siberian Railway. Despite Russia's backwardness, he forced the country into the industrial era, financing heavy industry with foreign capital (mostly French) and supporting it with foreign expertise. Witte's efforts established the foundations of modern Soviet Russia's industrial position. The Trans-Siberian Railway, begun in 1891 when he was Minister of Communications, was used in the Russo-Japanese War of 1904-5.

Wodehouse, Sir Pelham Grenville (1881-1975) English humorist, who created a remarkable and enduring fantasy world of butlers, gentle, foolish aristocrats, country houses and eccentric behaviour. His best known characters, the bumbling Bertie Wooster and his butler Jeeves are outstanding comic creations.

Wöhler, Friedrich (1800-82) German chemist who was the first to synthesize an organic chemical compound from an inorganic one. He heated ammonium cyanate and found that it turned into urea, a substance present in the urine of mammals and therefore organic in nature. This was the first of many setbacks for the then dominant theory of vitalism, which stated that organic compounds could be formed only in living things.

Wolf, Hugo (1860-1903) Austrian-born song composer who is, after SCHUBERT, the finest in the German *Lieder* tradition. Wolf's songs were written in bursts of frenzied activity. He became mentally ill and spent his last days in an asylum.

Wolfe, James (1727-59) British major-general, who added Canada to the British Empire. Fighting in North America in the Seven Years' War, he won the decisive Battle of Quebec (1759) by making a night landing from the St Lawrence River and scaling supposedly impregnable cliffs with his troops, who reached the Plains of Abraham southwest of Quebec and surprised the city's French defenders under Montcalm. Wolfe, like Montcalm, died in the battle. His victory was confirmed by the Treaty of Paris (1763), which ended France's American Empire by giving Great Britain Canada and all lands east of the Mississippi.

Wolfe, Thomas (1900-38) American novelist, who sequence of novels, from *Look Homeward, Angel* (1929), his first and best book, to *You Can't Go Home Again* (1940), follow the thinly disguised author from his Carolina home to his life and loves in New York.

Wolsey, Thomas (c. 1475-1530) English prelate, politician and chief minister to HENRY VIII of England. As Archbishop of York, cardinal and Lord Chancellor, Wolsey virtually ran both Church and State with vigorous efficiency, though with personal extravagance and pomp. He pursued an active foreign policy, endeavouring to utilize to England's advantage the rivalry between FRANCIS I of France and the emperor CHARLES V. His apparent triumphs, like the Field of the Cloth of Gold (1520), were hollow ones, and his personal ambition to be Pope merely resulted in the loss of English influence in Europe in the later 1520s. He failed in his greatest diplomatic test, the annulment of Henry VIII's marriage to Catherine of Aragon (aunt of Charles V), and his dismissal from the chancellorship followed. He died before his trial for treason.

Wonder, Stevie (born 1950) Blind American pop singer and composer. As a songwriter, his work spans the gulf between soul music and pop. His records include *Music of my Mind* (1972), *Talking Book* (1972) and *Songs in the Key of Life* (1976).

Wood, Sir Henry Joseph (1869-1944) English conductor and composer, founder, with Robert Newman, of the annual London Promenade Concerts, which he conducted until his death. He also promoted music festivals.

Wood, John (1704-54) English architect who, with his son John, re-planned the city of Bath. Their original designs in an elegant Palladian style for the building of the crescent, circus and parades draw inspiration from the buildings of ancient Rome. Wood senior built Prior Park, Bath, and his son the Assembly Rooms and Hot Baths.

Woodward, Robert Burns (1917-79) American chemist best known for his syntheses of highly complex organic compounds. Woodward began his remarkable series of syntheses by producing quinine in 1944. Subsequently, he tackled some of the most complex substances in organic chemistry; synthesizing the organic poison strychnine (1954) and the plant pigment chlorophyll (1960). His techniques enabled organic chemists to synthesize steroids and hormones.

Woolf, Virginia (1882-1941) English novelist, who was one of the foremost 20th-century experimenters with the technique and form of the novel. She was a member of the Bloomsbury Group (which included STRACHEY, KEYNES and FORSTER), amongst whom many new artistic ideas were discussed. Her novels *Jacob's Room* (1922), *Mrs Dalloway* (1925), *To the Lighthouse* (1927) and *The Waves* (1931) examine in a lyrical flow the myriad impressions of 'an ordinary mind on an ordinary day'.

Wordsworth, William (1770-1850) English poet, who believed in a new poetry of simple unadorned language, deriving its inspiration from nature and vivid experiences recalled by memory. After some unsettled years of conflicting experiences Wordsworth devoted himself to the writing of poetry. The *Lyrical Ballads* (1798), written with COLERIDGE, announced a Romantic programme to save the language and forms of poetry from formality and artifice. 'Itimations of Immortality', 'Michael' and 'The Waggoner' continue this programme with greater profundity. Wordsworth's long, autobiographical poem *The Prelude*, usually considered his masterpiece, begun in 1798, and published posthumously, contains passages of sustained intensity, particularly in Book One, about his childhood. He became Poet Laureate in 1843.

Wren, Sir Christopher (1632-1723) The most famous English Baroque architect, who was equally well known in his own day for his work in astronomy. The main basis of his style, and the mathematical genius that made his daring buildings possible, can be seen in one of his first buildings, the Sheldonian Theatre, Oxford, executed when he was already thirty, and a professor of astronomy. His most famous building, St Paul's Cathedral, London, was built to replace the medieval church destroyed in the Great Fire of 1666. It is a brilliant compromise between the Classical type of architecture, which Wren admired, and the Gothic building plan which his patrons demanded. The dome is based on MICHELANGELO's design for St Peter's, Rome, while the medieval-type flying buttresses needed for the roof are hidden behind curtain walls, covered with classical detailing that enhance the bulk of the building. Wren also built 53 churches in London, the best known being St Stephen Walbrook, and St James's, Piccadilly.

Wright, Frank Lloyd (1869-1959) American architect who, both structurally and formally, was perhaps the most brilliant American architect of his time. After training as an engineer he worked initially under SULLIVAN in Chicago. The gliding roofs and spatial plans of his early Chicago houses (the Robie House amongst them, which incorporated open plan living space) combined an aesthetic control with a wholly new dynamism and originality of detail that was to prove influential both in the United States and in Europe. Wright's interest in organic structure led to the 'mile-high' skyscraper and to the giant mushroom columns and glass tubing of the Johnson's Wax Factory at Racine, Wisconsin.

Wright, Richard (1908-60) American Negro novelist and essayist whose books contain passionate outcries against social injustice in the United States. Born on a Mississippi plantation, raised in an orphan asylum, and employed as a clerk in Memphis, Wright saw the tribulations of the poor Southern Negro at close quarters and protested angrily in *Uncle Tom's Children* (1935), *Native Son* (1940), *Black Boy* (1945), and his autobiography, *White Man, Listen!* (1957).

Wright, Wilbur (1867-1912) and **Orville (1871-1948)** American aviation pioneers and the first men to fly and control a heavier-than-air machine. They began as bicycle manufacturers in 1892 and became interested in the possibility of flight, experimenting with gliders and kites until 1903. Then in December of that year, at Kitty Hawk, North Carolina, they made their first flights, the longest being of 852 feet and lasting 59 seconds. By October 1905, they had improved the machine sufficiently to fly a full circle of 24½ miles in 38 minutes at Dayton, Ohio. Their machine was patented in May 1906. The Wright brothers popularized flying in a series of exhibitions in the US and in Europe, winning the Michelin trophy (1908) with a flight of 77 miles in two hours 20 minutes. Their 1908-9 plane designed for the US army led to the foundation of the American Wright Company to manufacture aircraft.

Wu Tao-tzu (c. 700-760) Buddhist artist of the T'ang dynasty, revered as the greatest figurative painter in

Chinese art. Highly praised in Chinese critical writings of all periods, none of his work now survives except through the medium of stone engravings and copies by later painters. He is reported to have painted 300 murals in the Loyang area, which amazed his contemporaries by their solidity and realism.

Wyatt, Sir Thomas (1503-42) English poet and diplomat. On his various embassies to Italy (1526), France (1528-32) and Spain (1537-9), Wyatt learnt the continental verse models, which he helped to establish in English. His best achievements were in lyrics, and Petrarchan sonnets. Wyatt was a lover of Anne BOLEYN.

Wyeth, Andrew (born 1917) American painter known for his meticulously detailed portraits and landscapes of rural and coastal American life. He is a member of the French Academy of Fine Arts (1977) and an honorary member of the Soviet Academy of Arts (1978).

Wykeham, William of (1324-1404) English Lord Chancellor and Bishop of Winchester, who founded establishments to help poor students and to replace trained clergy killed by the Black Death. Gaining immense wealth and political power under EDWARD II and Richard II, he founded New College, Oxford, and, to supply it with scholars, St Mary's College, Winchester – a school whose pupils are still called Wykehamists.

X

X, Malcolm (1925-65) American Black Muslim leader, born Malcolm Little. A product of the black ghetto, he joined the Black Muslim Movement and through his preaching of hatred of all white men, became second only to the Muslim leader, Elijah Muhammed. In 1964, however, while on a pilgrimage to Mecca, he became converted to Islam and opposed to the hatred and racialism of the Black Muslims. His conversion to belief in multiracial action led to his murder by Black Muslims in February 1965.

Xavier, Francis (1506-52) Navarrese Jesuit missionary and saint sometimes called the 'Apostle of the Indies'. Regarded by many as the greatest Christian missionary since the first century AD, Xavier preached in India, the Malay archipelago, Japan and China. He died in Goa.

Xenophon (c. 434-c. 354 BC) Greek historian whose writings reflected a balanced general outlook on society, rather than one of profound and specialized scholarship. His *Hellenica* was a Greek history of 411 to 362 BC. He also wrote memoirs of SOCRATES (*Apology*, *Memorabilia*, Symposium), dialogues on tyranny (*Hiero*) and estate-management (*Deconomicus*), treatises on hunting, horsemanship and the constitution of Sparta.

Xerxes I (c. 519-465 BC) King of Persia, whose failure to subdue Greece marked the end of the supremacy of the Persian Empire. In 480 BC he marched approximately 183,000 men (then the biggest army ever known) into Europe, crushed LEONIDAS's Spartans at Thermopylae, and sacked Athens, but THEMISTOCLES destroyed Xerxes's fleet at nearby Salamis. Xerxes returned to Asia Minor and the army and fleet he left in Greece were soon defeated.

Y

Yale, Elihu (1649-1721) American-born Englishman in whose honour Yale University was named. He became an official of the East India Company and was Governor of Fort St George, Madras. A noted philanthropist, in 1718 he sent a cargo of books and East India goods, which sold for £560, to the young collegiate school at Saybrook, Conn. The college took his name in appreciation of the gift.

Yamamoto, Isoroku (1884-1943) Japanese Admiral who planned the attack on Pearl Harbor. He was Chief of the Japanese First Fleet in 1939 and of the Combined Fleet in 1941, and planned the attack on Pearl Harbor in order to destroy American sea power. Though the attack was successful, it sowed the seeds of Japan's defeat: old battleships were sunk, but fuel reserves and aircraft carriers were missed, which forced the US to adopt the fast carrier strategy, by which it ultimately triumphed. Yamamoto, who was privately convinced before the outbreak of war that Japan could not defeat the US, was killed in air action when his plane was intercepted by US aircraft.

Yamashita, Tomoyuki (1885-1946) Japanese conqueror of Malaya and the Philippines in the Second World War. He was responsible for the lightning conquest of Malaya and Singapore (December 1941-February 1942). In March 1942, he was given command of the Japanese forces in the Philippines and by early May had captured Bataan and forced the Americans to surrender at Corregidor. In February 1945, however, MACARTHUR defeated him at Luzon, and a year later he was charged with the mass murder of civilians and American prisoners of war, tried and executed as a war criminal.

Yaroslav I 'The Wise' (c. 980-1054) Grand Duke of Kiev, who ruled all southern Russia, though his rule consisted mainly of receiving taxes. Yaroslav tried to strengthen his state by dynastic alliances, marrying his children into European royal families. Although he introduced an order of succession to prevent feuds, his death was soon followed by the breakdown of Russian unity.

Yeats, William Butler (1865-1939) Irish poet and dramatist who wrote a considerable amount of poetry which, for its technical control and a variety and complexity of vision, ranks him among the outstanding poets of the English language. His poetry was haunted by Irish scenery and history and his early poems, influenced by the Gaelic revival, were full of romantic nostalgia. He developed his own mystical system and his own interpretation of history, and slow changes through 'The Green Helmet' (1910), 'Responsibilities' (1914), 'The Wild Swans at Coole' (1917) and 'Michael Robartes' (1920) followed his experience of Irish independence, an obsessive and unhappy love affair, and the Irish literary movement. Yeats wanted to re-introduce verse drama into the theatre, and he directed his plays and those of other Irish writers, including SYNGE, at the newly formed Abbey Theatre in Dublin.

Yoritomo (1147-99) Shogun of Japan and founder of the Kamakura shogunate. Eliminating the rivalry of other clans. Yoritomo made the military rule of his Minamoto clan, based at Kamakura, more powerful than the imperial court at Kyoto, so starting Japan's so-called Kamakura shogunate (1185-1333). This was characterized by feudalism, Zen Buddhism, the warrior cult and the rise of the Hojo family.

Yoshida, Shigeru (1878-1967) Prime Minister of Japan, who led his country from defeat to economic prosperity. Towards the end of the Second World War, he was imprisoned by the Japanese authorities as a liberal and an advocate of peace. His views commended him, however, to MACARTHUR and, when Yoshida became Prime Minister (1946-7), the two worked closely together. He was again Premier from 1948 to 1954, and adviser in many governments after that. His ability to maintain harmonious relations with the Americans, as well as his intelligent handling of the post-war problems of a defeated nation, enabled Japan to become one of the most competitive industrial powers of the world.

Young, Thomas (1773-1829) English physicist who established the wave nature of light. He studied both NEWTON's particle theory of light and HUYGENS's wave theory, and saw that some effects (such as interference) could be predicted by the wave theory but could not occur if the particle theory were correct. In 1803, Young produced interference fringes on a screen by passing light through a pair of pin-holes in a card. Few other scientists took his work seriously, and not until Arago and FRESNEL produced a mathematical description of light waves, was Young's theory accepted.

Younghusband, Sir Francis Edward (1863-1942) English explorer and author whose Asian expeditions helped to map Central Asia and reopened Lhasa, the forbidden city of Tibet, to Europeans. He marched across the heart of Asia from Peking to Simla, India (1886-7), and later explored extensively in the Karakorum Range and the Pamirs, proving that the Karakorum Range was the watershed between Turkistan and India. Appointed British Commissioner to Tibet (1902), Younghusband led a British mission into Lhasa, and (1904) accomplished an Anglo-Tibetan treaty.

Yukawa, Hideki (1907-81) Japanese physicist who predicted the existence of the meson. In the 1930s he suggested that the powerful forces holding protons and neutrons together in the nucleus of an atom are quite different from any others known. He developed a theory picturing them as arising from a rapid back-and-forth movement between protons and neutrons of a new sub-atomic particle, later identified as a pi-meson. He won the 1949 Nobel Prize for Physics.

Z

Zeami, Motokiyo (1363-1443) Japanese dramatist and actor. The master of *Noh* drama, Zeami wrote the majority of the *Noh* plays which are performed today and, in a number of crucial essays, laid down the aesthetics of *Noh*.

Zeppelin, Graf Ferdinand von (1838-1917) German army officer who on retiring (1891) concentrated on airship design and manufacture. The first of his dirigible balloons flew in 1900 and commercial services in Germany began 10 years later. Zeppelins carried out the first air raids against civilian London and in East Anglia during the early part of the First World War.

Zermelo, Ernst (1871-1953) German mathematician, who was one of the founders of axiomatic set theory.

Zhao Ziyang (born 1919) Chinese politician and Prime Minister since 1980. He became First Secretary of Guangdong Province in 1965. Two years later he was denounced as a revisionist by fervent Red Guards and was dismissed. After CHOU EN-LAI took control in the early 1970s, Zhao Ziyang was rehabilitated and made First Secretary of Szechwan Province. His achievements there were astounding: industrial production was increased by 81 per cent and agricultural output by 25 per cent. This brought him to the attention of DENG XIAOPING, who promoted him and named him Prime Minister in 1980. Since 1980 he has extended a programme of material incentives and expansion of trade with the West.

Zia-ul-Haq, Mohammad (born 1924) President of Pakistan. After training in the Indian army he was appointed to the Command and Staff College in Quetta, Pakistan. In 1976, Prime Minister Bhutto made him Chief of Staff of the army. The following year Zia ousted Bhutto in a military coup and became President in 1978. Despite international protests he sanctioned the hanging of ex-Prime Minister Bhutto in 1979 and has frequently postponed planned elections since.

Zinoviev, Gregori (1883-1936) Russian revolutionary and founder, with LENIN and TROTSKY, of the USSR. On Lenin's death (1924), he connived with STALIN and Kamenev to ensure Trotsky's exclusion from the leadership, but later was himself tried and executed by Stalin. His name became familiar in Britain when a letter, purporting to be from him, as President of the Third International, urged British Communists to violent revolution. It was published in the press shortly before the General Election of October 1924, and probably contributed to the defeat of Ramsay MACDONALD's Labour government.

Zoffany, Johann (c. 1734-1810) German-born British artist, who painted elegant 'conversation pieces' and informal group portraits. He studied in Italy, and made his name shortly after arriving in England (1761) with the *Farmer's Return* (1762), in which the actor GARRICK, who became his patron, is depicted.

Zola, Emile (1840-1902) French novelist and journalist, author of the *Rougon Macquart* series, 70 interrelated novels documenting the life of a family under the Second Empire. *L'Assomoir* (1882), generally considered to be the model of the naturalist novel and his finest work, was followed, among other works, by *Nana* (1880), *Germinal* (1885), *La Terre* (1889) and *La Débâcle* (1893). Zola later turned to political journalism, defending DREYFUS in the celebrated article *J'Accuse*.

Zoroaster (c. 6th cent. BC) Median prophet, founder of Zoroastrianism, the religion of ancient Persia. He presented life as a struggle between the opposing forces of good and evil, equating evil with darkness and death, and goodness with light and life (personified by the angel Mithras).

Zurbarán, Francisco de (c. 1598-1664) Spanish painter, best known for the austere devotional pictures he painted for churches and monasteries. His art combines harsh tonal contrasts of CARAVAGGIO with the tactile qualities of Spanish wood sculpture. The *Martyrdom of St Serapion* (1628), in sober colours, shows the quiet, spiritual intensity of his work.

Zwingli, Huldreich *or* Ulrich (1484-1531) Swiss religious thinker and leading figure in the Swiss Reformation, though he disagreed with LUTHER on various doctrinal points. Zwingli's chief work was *Concerning True and False Religion* (1525). He was killed in an attack on Zurich by forces from cantons unsympathetic to his movement.